LOSS

During Pregnancy or in the Newborn Period

Principles of Care With Clinical Cases and Analyses

Edited by
James R. Woods, Jr., MD
Jenifer L. Esposito Woods, MBA

This book is dedicated to
Matthew John
and
Edith Rose

LOSS
During Pregnancy or in the Newborn Period
Principles of Care with
Clinical Cases and Analyses

EDITORS
James R. Woods, Jr., MD
Professor of Obstetrics & Gynecology
Director, Division of Maternal-Fetal Medicine
University of Rochester School of Medicine and Dentistry
Rochester, NY

Jenifer L. Esposito Woods, MBA
Editor and Book Coordinator
Rochester, NY

Jannetti Publications, Inc. • Pitman, NJ

Chapter Authors

Joan Arnold, PhD, RN
Associate Professor
School of Nursing
College of New Rochelle
New Rochelle, NY

David Allen Baram, MD
Associate Professor
Department of Obstetrics and Gynecology
University of Rochester
Rochester, NY

James H. Cunningham, MDiv, BBC
Director of Pastoral Care
Fairfield Health System
Cleveland, OH

John DeFrain, PhD
Professor of Family Science
Department of Family and Consumer Sciences
College of Human Resources and Family Sciences
University of Nebraska
Lincoln, NE

Judy Garza, MS
Assistant
Department of Pediatric Genetics
University of Rochester
Rochester, NY

J. Christopher Glantz, MD
Assistant Professor
Department of Obstetrics and Gynecology
University of Rochester
Rochester, NY

David Hester, MBA
Pittsford, NY

Jerald Kay, MD
Professor and Chairman
Department of Psychiatry
School of Medicine
Wright State University
Dayton, OH

Linda Closs Leoni, MS, RN
Obstetrics and Gynecology Nursing
University of Rochester
Rochester, NY

Vivian Lewis, MD
Associate Professor
Department of Obstetrics and Gynecology
University of Rochester
Rochester, NY

Mary McClain, MS, RN
Project Coordinator
Massachusetts Center for Sudden Infant Death Syndrome
Boston City Hospital
Boston, MA

Leon A. Metlay, MD
Associate Professor
Department of Pathology
University of Rochester
Rochester, NY

Richard K. Miller, PhD
Professor
Department of Obstetrics and Gynecology and Environmental Medicine
University of Rochester
Rochester, NY

Joann M. O'Leary, MS, MPH
Parent-Infant Specialist
Perinatal Center
Abbott Northwestern Hospital
Minneapolis, MN

Patricia Roles, MSW, Cert. A. Th.
Social Work Services
British Columbia Children's Hospital
Vancouver, BC, Canada

Brenda Roman, MD
Assistant Professor
Department of Psychiatry
Wright State University
Dayton, OH

Rita M. Ryan, MD
Assistant Professor
Department of Pediatrics
University of Rochester
Rochester, NY

Devereux N. Saller, Jr., MD, MS
Associate Professor
Department of Obstetrics and Gynecology, Pediatrics, and Genetics
University of Rochester
Rochester, NY

Sarah J.M. Shaeffer, PhD, RN
Assistant Professor
Department of Pediatrics
University of Maryland School of Medicine
Baltimore, MD

Heather M. Schulte, MD
Assistant Professor
Department of Psychiatry
Wright State University
Dayton, OH

Jeffrey Spike, PhD
Assistant Professor
Division of Medical Humanities
University of Rochester
Rochester, NY

Clare Thorwick, RN
Perinatal Nurse Clinician (retired)
Excelsior, MN

Ronald E. Troyer, MEd
Funeral Director
Kok Funeral Home
St Paul Park, MN

Sara Rich Wheeler, MSN, RN, CCE
Clinical Instructor
University of Illinois at Chicago
Urbana, IL

James R. Woods, Jr., MD
Professor
Department of Obstetrics and Gynecology
University of Rochester
Rochester, NY

Jenifer L. Esposito Woods, MBA
Editor and Book Coordinator
Rochester, NY

Case Commentary Contributors

Anna M. August, MD
Assistant Professor
Department of Pediatrics
Washington University School of Medicine
St. Louis, MO

Annette Baran, MSW, RSW, LCSW
Santa Monica, CA

Watson A. Bowes, Jr., MD
Professor
Department of Obstetrics and Gynecology
University of North Carolina
Chapel Hill, NC

Robert Brent, MD, PhD, DSc
Professor Emeritus
Department of Pediatrics, Radiology and Anatomy
Jefferson Medical College and AI Dupont Children's Hospital
Wilmington, DE

Micki L. Cabaniss, MD
Associate Professor
Department of Obstetrics and Gynecology
University of North Carolina
Chapel Hill, NC
and *Department of Obstetrics and Gynecology*
N. Mountain Area Health Education Center
Asheville, NC

Joanne P. Chamberlain, MS, RNC
Nurse Practitioner
Central New York Perinatal Center
State University of New York
Upstate Medical Center
Syracuse, NY

Frank A. Chervenak, MD
Professor
Department of Obstetrics and Gynecology
Cornell University Medical College
New York, NY

Nancy C. Chescheir, MD
Associate Professor
Department of Obstetrics and Gynecology
University of North Carolina
Chapel Hill, NC

Ronald A. Chez, MD
Professor
Department of Obstetrics and Gynecology
University of South Florida College of Medicine
Tampa, FL

Karen Copeland, MS, CGC
Applied Genetics
Austin, TX

M. Yusoff Dawood, MD
Professor
Department of Obstetrics and Gynecology
University of Texas at Houston
Houston, TX

Salim Daya, MD
Professor
Department of Obstetrics and Gynecology and
Clinical Epidemiology and Biostatistics
McMaster University
Hamilton, Ontario, Canada

Susan Doerr, RN
Nurse Clinician
Perinatal Clinic
Abbott Northwestern Hospital
Minneapolis, MN

Linda Ernst, PhD
Assistant Professor
Department of Family Resources
St. Olaf College
Northfield, MN

Kathleen L. Fernbach, BSN, RN, PHN
Director
Minnesota Sudden Infant Death Center
Children's Health Care
Minneapolis, MN

Reverend Thomas L. Hanson, DMin
Interim Rector
Christ Church
Pittsford, New York
Episcopal Priest
Rochester, NY

C. Lynn Keene, MD
Attending Physician
Carillon Roanoke Community Hospital
Roanoke, VA

Kenneth Kellner, MD, PhD
Professor
Department of Obstetrics and Gynecology
University of Florida
Gainesville, FL

John LaFerla, MD, MPH
St. Paul, MN

Susan Lodermeier, BS
Licensed Funeral Director
Manager
Lundberg Funeral Home
Cannon Falls, MN

Mary B. Mahowald, PhD
Maclein Center for Clinical Ethics
University of Chicago
Chicago, IL

Donald Mattison, MD, MS
Professor of Toxicology and Obstetrics and Gynecology
Dean, Graduate School of Public Health
University of Pittsburgh
Pittsburgh, PA

Laurence B. McCullough, PhD
Professor
Department of Medicine, Community Medicine and Medical Ethics
Baylor College of Medicine
Houston, TX

Jan Nealer, PhD
Assistant Professor
Marital and Family Therapy
Family and Consumer Services
University of Nebraska-Lincoln
Lincoln, NE

Geraldine J. Norris, MSN, MA, RN
Longview, TX
formerly
Deputy Chief
Early Childhood Health Branch
Maternal & Child Health Bureau
U.S. Department of Health and Human Services

Connie Nykiel, BSHA, RN
Principal
For Teen Moms Only
Frankfort, IL

Lynnda Parker, BSN, RN
Clinical Nurse Specialist
Perinatal Center
Abbott Northwestern Hospital
Minneapolis, MN

Miriam Rosenthal, MD
Associate Professor
Psychiatry and Reproductive Biology
Case Western Reserve University
Cleveland, OH

Carol L. Wagner, MD
Assistant Professor
Department of Pediatrics
Medical University of South Carolina
Charleston, SC

Sara Rich Wheeler, MSN, RN, CCE
Clinical Instructor
University of Illinois at Chicago
Urbana, IL

Table of Contents

Preface

In the practice of obstetrics, care providers are trained rigorously to perform many techniques, to learn to respond essentially instinctively to the dynamic circumstances of pregnancy, labor, and delivery. In the same way that young care providers must be able to intervene in the case of shoulder dystocia or cord prolapse, newly trained professionals must understand the principles and practical skills which are called for in the case of a patient's pregnancy loss. For the woman and her family, when their baby dies, their dreams shatter, and their anticipations fade to despair. Skilled obstetric care providers must be able to console, guide, and educate these people with the same energy, knowledge, and experience with which they can manage a normal obstetric course. Thus, all obstetric care providers require formal education and practical training in pregnancy-loss management.

Skills which care providers can apply in the case of a patient's pregnancy loss are both timeless and timely. Since the dawn of human life on our planet, pregnancy loss certainly has occurred with at least the same frequency as it now does. Earliest written records attest to the impact of pregnancy loss. Reference to miscarriage may be found in the Talmud. History notes the early pregnancy losses of both Anne Boleyn and Catherine of Aragon. Literature is replete with plots that weave into their fabric the private tragedies of stillbirth and neonatal death. Pregnancy loss indeed is a timeless fact.

Pregnancy loss is a timely topic, as well; for in our era of excellent health care, society has managed to reduce infant mortality rates, and the notion that a baby could die — during pregnancy or in the newborn period — seems unthinkable to the lay public. Within the professions of obstetric care providers, however, we know all too well that pregnancy loss is a common enough event. Yet, many are uncomfortable and awkward in managing individual cases of pregnancy loss as they occur, because of lack of training in the skills which are necessary for management of this true medical contingency. Because of, perhaps, a lapse in training, in addition to normal, human emotions which make these issues uncomfortable for care providers to confront, pregnancy-loss patients all too often, and still, may receive what they perceive as unsympathetic, indifferent responses to what truly is a major life tragedy — the death of a child.

The death of a baby initiates a series of events which are linked. We must recognize that these events are predictable and universal. Their predictability and universality — the response to pregnancy loss — provide the structure and format for principles of managing the pregnancy-loss patient. The essence of pregnancy-loss management is communication. Communication is the critical tool which care providers must be prepared to use in their work with families who have been devastated by the unexpected, usually sudden tragedy of a baby's death.

When a baby dies, we have much information to communicate to our patients. We must provide not only the important explanations of the problems which caused the baby's death and the procedures which now must be undergone, but also the introduction of sensitive special issues which now must be contemplated in the aftermath of the pregnancy loss. Families typically are at a complete loss when the unexpected has struck them. Their questions are very basic. Why did the baby die? What happens next? What should families expect? The concepts which we now need to impart to these people, who are overwhelmed, demand the utmost of our professional training. We must console these patients in their deepest anguish, being prepared to repeat fundamental facts more than once to them when they may not be receptive to our words. We must guide them through the experience, involving medical terms and procedures with which they may be utterly unfamiliar. And we must educate them about their very normal, human responses to what probably is one of the worst experiences in their lives.

Communication is the primary tool with which obstetric care providers must work, beginning with the moment when we must inform patients of the fact that a pregnancy has failed. By all accounts, the most-feared sentence in obstetrics — for care providers and patients alike — is, "I am sorry to have to tell you that we have found a terrible problem." The words which follow this statement may describe fetal anomaly, fetal demise, or major complications of pregnancy. But, in any case, the outcome now is doomed. Some complex course follows those initial words of communication between care providers and their unfortunate patients. How well do we continue to communicate with our pregnancy-loss patients from this point forward? How far do our responsibilities take us, following pregnancy termination, or stillbirth delivery, or transfer of a critically compromised neonate to the NICU?

The healing power of language is demonstrated with a simple example. After premature delivery and death of her first baby, a young woman sends a letter of courteous thanks to hospital administrators. Ironically, she identifies in her letter a member of the housekeeping staff as someone who offered her comfort as she recovered from the birth. What important "service" had this employee provided? — Simply that this person, while cleaning the patient's room, expressed genuine sadness about the patient's baby's death. Such an encounter may represent the most emotional outpouring of sympathy that the woman received during her postpartum stay.

It is understandable if many care providers would find excuses to avoid such direct communications with patients who have experienced pregnancy loss. Many of us selected obstetrics as a field because our work would involve happy, healthy patients who delivered normal babies. Care providers may never have been trained formally to manage the all-too-common pregnancy loss which destroys the patient's hopes for her baby's arrival. Daily bedside rounds do not provide adequate time to discuss such complicated issues. Many young care providers have yet in their own lives to face a crisis of such magnitude; so they have no personal experience with which to relate to this crisis in a patient's life. They may be unclear about how to provide effective therapy to pregnancy-loss couples, believing this task to be unstructured, with vague objectives and variable timelines. And, after all, isn't this the role of the family, or a therapist, or somebody else?

For those in the health care professions who continue to deny their responsibility for applying their skills to the management of pregnancy-loss patients, it is time to set the record straight. Pregnancy-loss management is an obstetric responsibility which, when performed well, demonstrates the timeless nature of the art of medicine. Pregnancy-loss management indeed possesses intrinsic structure and form. Its principles can be learned by those without prior formal training or personal experience. And, those who assert that they are too busy with daily ward rounds to discuss open-ended pregnancy-loss issues should conduct a 10-minute, by-the-clock bedside chat with a suffering patient, if only as an exercise for their own information. We believe that a simple, 10-minute effort would demonstrate to the doubtful care provider that a seemingly brief discussion actually can encompass a wide breadth of feelings and facts, useful information, and invaluable communication.

This book is the result of both sequence and consequence. Its predecessor, published in 1987, was written to provide structure to a field of obstetrics that had been ignored by mainstream obstetric practice. Many care providers offered compassionate care to their pregnancy-loss patients, but there were no guidelines. For too long, there had been no validation of the significance of this critical, too-familiar, and yet very basic aspect of obstetric care.

This present textbook examines the biologic implications and psychologic challenges of loss of a baby, during pregnancy or in the newborn period. The book is intended to complement the technical information of textbooks in obstetrics and pediatric management. Unlike our first textbook, which was descriptive in its effort to define the field, this book includes practical clinical cases with commentaries provided by outside professional practitioners. We hope that these chapters, along with clinical case analyses, will serve as a reference text for busy clinicians. Moreover, we offer this book as a tool for training young professionals in diverse fields — medicine, social work, clergy, funeral services, and others — who surely will need resources from which to draw as they inevitably encounter their future patients' or clients' pregnancy-loss experience.

Finally, this present book is the result of the tragic death of a baby boy named Matthew John Hester. Matthew's impact is responsible for the generous support of his extended family and their friends, which led first to a seminar on pregnancy-loss management on April 7, 1995, and then to the creation of this book. It is remarkable what a difference can be made by one person's existence — however brief.

James R. Woods, Jr., MD
Jenifer L. Esposito Woods, MBA
Editors

Chapter 1

Pregnancy Loss and the Grief Process

Jerald Kay
Brenda Roman
Heather M. Schulte

Despite the universality of grief, it is striking that scientific study of this process is only 50 years old. While it is true that Freud (1917) first drew attention to the ubiquity and types of loss and to the distinction between mourning and depression, it was not until Lindemann's (1944) classic study of survivors of the Coconut Grove fire that a detailed symptomatology of grief was presented to the health professions. Psychologic and physical effects of loss of a loved one, be it spouse, parent, or child, now are widely acknowledged. Yet, only very recently have the full impact and consequences of pregnancy loss become appreciated. In this chapter, the authors review normal mourning and bereavement, then examine unique aspects of those processes that relate to pregnancy loss. Also included is a discussion of potential psychopathology that may complicate bereavement after a pregnancy loss.

The response to loss has been termed "bereavement," "grief," or "mourning," largely because many disciplines have studied this same process and its consequences. In this chapter, bereavement is defined as the entire process which is precipitated by loss through death; grief, the specific subjective feelings that accompany this loss; and mourning, the process through which resolution of grief is accomplished.

Unique Aspects in Response to Pregnancy Loss

Any examination of the response to loss must acknowledge the numerous forms which grief and mourning may take. This is especially true for pregnancy loss. Given individual circumstances surrounding miscarriage and ectopic pregnancy, stillbirth, or neonatal death, any or all of the following may come into play: real (actual) loss of a person, threatened or impending

Figure 1-1.
Elements of Psychologic Pain with Pregnancy Loss

• Loss of loved one	• Damaged self-esteem
• Loss of status	• Existential loss
• Threatened loss	

loss of a person, loss of status (motherhood), damaged self-esteem, and existential loss. Existential loss associated with pregnancy loss frequently has been overlooked, but it can be summed up by the following: "When your parent dies, you have lost your past. When your child dies, you have lost your future" (Luby, 1977, p. 23).

Frequency of Pregnancy Loss

Although a number of characteristics are distinctive to pregnancy loss, infrequency is not among them. Indeed, pregnancy loss is by no means uncommon. In fact, 10 out of 100 early pregnancies end in miscarriage, and 1% to 2% of late pregnancies end in perinatal death (Cunningham, MacDonald, Leveno, Gant, & Gilstrap, 1993). Furthermore, of so-called "occult" pregnancies (those which are detectable by serum human chorionic gonadotropin [HCG] prior to missed menses), approximately 22% end with a seemingly normal period (Cunningham et al., 1993). This has implications for infertile couples and recipients of *in vitro* fertilization who may be monitored more closely. Within the field, the sheer magnitude of pregnancy loss may help to account for the prevailing attitude that such events represent only the loss of nonviable life. Until recently, obstetric and neonatal interventions have been directed exclusively to the emergency or crisis component of the event and not to its psychologic significance (see Figure 1-1). Rapid and highly visible technologic advances in the general obstetric, perinatal surgical, neonatal, and fertility areas also obscure the frequency of pregnancy loss.

Death rarely is predictable or expected at any but the final stage of the life cycle. For postneonatal loss, fortunately, numerous social institutions support the bereavement process. During gestation, death seems most remote of all. Thus, fetal or neonatal death may be the last type of loss to be accorded its due. Uniformly recognized or available social rituals have yet to be associated with pregnancy loss: "It is celebrated only in the tears of

Figure 2-1.
Psychologic Process of Becoming a Parent

- Feelings of procreativity or generativity.
- A sense of continuity through the generations.
- Responses to quickening and bodily changes.
- Fears and expectations about the coming baby.
- The impact of this exciting process on expectant parents' relationship at home.
- Changes that the baby will bring to their careers and to their lives in general.
- Attachment to real and idealized aspects of the infant.
- Self-esteem building.

women" (Friedman & Cohen, 1982). Such losses frequently are referred to as "nondeaths" (Phipps, 1981) or "nonevents" (Bowlby, 1940) of rarely named "nonpersons" (Lewis, 1976), which negates the reality of the loss. This attitude persists despite documentation of the developmental processes of expectant parenthood (Anthony & Benedek, 1970).

Motherhood as a Biopsychosocial Event

For the woman, expectant motherhood is a discrete biopsychosocial process that transforms and broadens her role to that of mother. This process is accomplished largely before delivery, through a host of important responses and reactions to pregnancy which are summarized in Figure 2-1.

The pregnant woman experiences a unique psychologic state, a turning inward, wherein she focuses significant emotional energy on herself, her baby and the baby's father, the future, and her relationship with her own mother, both past and present. Through pregnancy, a woman comes to "know" her baby intimately as a consequence of rich fantasies, fears, and dreams and to become attached both to the real experience of her baby *in utero* and her idealized image of who that child will be. Childbearing can provide a potent sense of personal contribution and value that transcends one's own life, a sense of healthy omnipotence, and an added sense of importance in a person's family and social world. These normal self-esteem building functions of childbearing are important elements of bereavement responses particular to pregnancy loss.

It also should be noted that ultrasound and amniocentesis significantly increase prenatal bonding (Fletcher & Evans, 1983). Routine and exceptional technologies are likely to enhance and accelerate all elements of adjustment, attachment, and self-esteem building during the course of pregnancy (Leon, 1992).

Expectant Fatherhood

The woman is not alone in her response to prospective parenthood. Herzog (1982) has eloquently delineated three psychologic approaches to fatherhood. His study of 103 fathers-to-be reveals that there are most-, less well-, and least-attuned groups of expectant fathers, with attunement essentially corresponding to a man's empathic intimacy with the pregnant woman. Intimately involved fathers-to-be, the "most-attuned" group, passed through characteristic stages of expectant fatherhood. These involve a getting-ready period, a time of fullness and ecstasy after conception, a refocusing on the relationship with his own father, and a reworking of his own caregiving ideas and expectations as intimacy with his partner intensifies.

Phases of Mourning

Numerous clinicians and researchers have documented characteristics of normal grief (Bowlby, 1940; Clayton, Desmarais, & Winokur, 1968; Lindemann, 1944; Parkes, 1969; Parkes & Weiss, 1983; Pollock, 1961; Raphael, 1983). A degree of uniformity is sufficient to merit the designation of mourning as a syndrome with an expected course and a resolution. Three approximate phases have been described: protest, disorganization, and reorganization. The description of these stages must be preceded by the caveats that variation among grieving individuals is considerable and that the process is more fluid than an ordering of discrete phases would seem to imply. As has happened with the misapplication of Kübler-Ross' (1969) stages of death and dying, the clinician must guard against inappropriate expectations of the patient.

Protest

Protest, the initial phase of mourning, lasts from a few hours to several days. It is marked by a desperate and frantic attempt to reinstitute the relationship with the lost person. This is likely to consist of an immediate, pervasive sense of shock, numbness (lack of emotional reaction), disbelief, and denial. In most instances, the apparent inability to grasp what has transpired is short lived. Distress soon follows, as manifested by weeping and sighing.

These immediate responses, as well as those that follow, probably emanate from childhood attachment behavior. Premature separation of a child from his mother is accompanied by crying, which is both an attempt to recover her and a protest against her loss. The child's response is striking in its similarity to adult grief. Our capacity to bond or affiliate with others is precisely what leaves us vulnerable to grief when a relationship is abruptly ended. Anger and hostility frequently are present during the initial phase of mourning. Both may be directed at physicians and nurses in the hospital setting. Or they may be toward oneself, specifically for having failed to do something to avert the loss.

Disorganization

The second phase, disorganization, introduces developing awareness of finality. Emotions become explicitly painful and are accompanied by profound sadness and deep yearning in search of the lost person. Feelings of intense loneliness, isolation, and meaninglessness predominate. Freud (1917) made an enduring distinction between these normative, although very disruptive, feelings on the one hand and pathologic grief or melancholia on the other. Only the latter involves a prominent lowering of self-esteem, which often is expressed through self-reproach. Because of the normal self-esteem building functions of pregnancy, however, Freud's distinction may not be as valid with pregnancy loss as it is for more typical reactions to loss of an adult or an older child.

Somatic expressions of grief, frequently evoked by memories or comments about the lost person, may include any or all of the features as summarized in Figure 3-1. Also prominent during the stage of disorganization is a significant withdrawal from the outside world. This withdrawal is evidenced by introversion, lack of spontaneity and warmth, and disinterest in eating and grooming.

The most characteristic feature of this phase is preoccupation with thoughts of the deceased while the mourner relives his or her relationship with the lost one. These memories are intrusive, unbidden, unwanted, and painful; they constitute, however, the necessary grief work that eventually helps the mourner to relinquish the important attachment. Denial frequently reappears in an attempt to hold on to things as they were previously. The

Figure 3-1.
Somatic Expressions of Grief

• Decreased appetite	• Choking sensations
• Difficulty in sleeping	• Sighing
• Weakness	• Lethargy
• Tightening of the throat	• Anergy
• Empty feeling in the stomach	

person's attitudes and behaviors reflect this effort, and there are wish-fulfilling dreams and daydreams wherein the deceased returns. Characteristically, there are restlessness and aimlessness during this phase. The mourner often finds it difficult to sit still or to concentrate. He or she must make an effort to function, performing chores routinely and automatically, many times without paying conscious attention.

Reorganization

In the third phase of mourning, reorganization, the bereaved person slowly reinvests interest in the world. This process varies greatly in duration from individual to individual. Painful memories become less frequent and are replaced by more positive ones. New activities are begun. New relationships are entered into, and old ones are re-established. However, there may be transitory feelings of guilt about having survived the loss and enjoying life in spite of it.

As is true in all phases of human development, a life crisis can bring on despair and regression, or it can promote growth through acquisition of new insights, attitudes, strengths, and values. This is true of successful bereavement. Traditionally, the process just described extends for at least 1 to 2 years. Bereavement nears completion as a person enjoys life again, and begins looking to the future.

Maternal Grieving and Pregnancy Loss

An understanding of the experience of expectant parenthood provides the groundwork for appreciating the intensity of the response to pregnancy loss. The richness of the psychological journey eventuating in strong attachment to the unborn baby and the identification of oneself as a parent speaks loudly against a superficial and one-dimensional biomedical view of pregnancy loss as nothing more than the loss of nonviable "products of conception." Moreover, intense grief following pregnancy loss should not be viewed suspiciously as a histrionic overreaction. Rather, it should be seen as an indication of the mature capacity for relatedness and affiliation, which ultimately are a function of a cohesive sense of self and an effective self-esteem regulation.

Regardless of the nature of a pregnancy loss, the bereavement process is both universal in many respects and uniquely varied for each individual. In particular, a woman's capacity to adapt to pregnancy loss is a function of those same factors determining her capacity to deal with uncomplicated pregnancy, namely personality structure or character, coping skills, life setting, and family constellation (Bibring, Dwyer, Huntington, & Valenstein, 1961).

Component Losses of Pregnancy Loss

Pregnancy loss has a number of important component losses. Not only are there both real and fantasized loss of a baby, but there are also significant self-esteem losses as well. These include loss of being pregnant and of the sense of oneness with the fetus, loss of anticipated motherhood, loss of the special attention and care frequently accorded a pregnant woman, and loss of prenatal medical care. In addition, there is a crucial loss of self-esteem resulting from the woman's inability to rely on her body and successfully give birth. How one perceives one's body is a fundamental constituent of a person's total identity and sense of self. A closely related phenomenon occurring in expectant parents whose pregnancy loss is associated with fetal anomalies is the lowering of self-esteem from carrying defective genes.

Disruptions in the self-esteem building functions of childbearing are particularly important because they likely affect this type of loss in a way that is distinct from other types of bereavement (Leon, 1992). Pregnancy loss turns a self-enhancing experience into a time of devastation. Features of pregnancy loss suggestive of injury to self-esteem are the profound sense of worthlessness, emptiness, shame, and failure reported by many mothers. The physical sense of needing to suckle the lost infant or hearing the baby cry can be seen as evidence of fragmentation of a parent's sense of self (Leon, 1992).

Assault on one's sense of competence or worth often leads temporarily to reactive rage, hostility, or displaced blame that might take the sting out of one's own sense of failure. In the case of pregnancy loss, this may take the form of rage against medical personnel which can be expressed in litigation.

Understanding the assault to self-esteem that can be experienced by these parents may allow providers to be particularly sensitive to parents' reactions and minimize the chance of litigation erupting from further traumatization. A requisite in addressing these needs is clear, repeated, empathic communication. Parents often need to hear information many times to make sense of what has happened. Dissatisfied parents often cite unempathic treatment, lack of follow-up for providing autopsy reports and death certificates, and inadequate explanations from caregivers as sources of their anger (Covington & Theut, 1993). For those families who enter psychologic treatment following pregnancy loss, the health care provider must accept the parents' overwhelming loss; must understand the precise meaningfulness of the loss for both partners; and must assist them in psychologically integrating the loss, especially those aspects that may be outside the awareness of the couple.

Future research efforts which attempt to identify differentiating features of this type of bereavement should explore this dimension and attempt to compare responses of bereaved parents with people suffering other types of losses, in order to develop specific effective treatment modalities (Zeanah, 1989).

Early versus Late Gestational Losses

Maternal grieving after pregnancy loss follows the typical process described earlier. There is, however, one important distinction between early pregnancy loss (miscarriage, ectopic pregnancy, or elective abortion) and stillbirth or neonatal death. In the latter instances, the mourning process can be facilitated by the presence of a body and/or pictures of the stillborn fetus or dead neonate. To mourn for a baby lost early in the pregnancy, whose existence goes unrecognized by so many, often is more complicated because there is no recognizable body to visualize. To complicate matters further, in early loss there usually is an absence of the social supports and rituals to facilitate mourning that normally accompany the death of a loved one (Costello, Gardner, & Merenstein, 1988). A stillbirth or a neonate who was alive only for a short time nevertheless can be viewed, held, and photographed; named, eulogized, and buried by his or her parents. This permits a much more concrete attachment by parents with resultant prominent memories. Manifestations of this different experience of pregnancy loss in early versus late gestation are demonstrated by more intense acute grieving and a tendency to experience a resurgence of grief during a subsequent pregnancy, either parallel to the gestational age when the loss occurred or near/at term (Goldbach, Dunn, Toedter, & Lasker, 1991; Lasker & Toedter, 1991; Theut,

Zaslow, Rabinovich, Bartko, & Morihisa, 1990). On the other hand, with early gestational loss, parents report much greater dissatisfaction with their medical care (Harmon & Graham-Cicchinelli, 1985; Goldbach et al., 1991; Theut et al., 1990). Parents cite callousness on the part of the staff who may less readily recognize the impact of the loss than a staff confronted by the death of a fully developed infant (Costello et al., 1988; Cuisinier, Kuijpers, Hoogduin, de Graauw, & Janssen, 1993).

Process of Mourning a Pregnancy Loss

The initial phase of maternal grief is marked by emotional numbness and denial. There is shock even when the loss is anticipated, as is the case in some stillbirths or neonatal deaths. This shock may be more pronounced when an unexpected death occurs at or shortly after the time of delivery. However, even when fetal death is diagnosed prior to delivery, and therefore anticipatory grieving is possible, there generally is still very strong shock and disbelief at the time of delivery (Kirkley-Best & Kellner, 1982): "Instead of the expected cry of the healthy baby within the delivery room, there is only silence" (Harmon & Graham-Cicchinelli, 1985).

Blame and Anger

An increasing acceptance of the death characterizes the second or disorganization phase of mourning. The woman more freely experiences her feelings of loss, sadness, emptiness, anger, inadequacy, blame, and jealousy. There almost always are significant feelings of guilt centered around fantasies of having either caused or contributed to the pregnancy loss in some fashion. Concerns over excessive exercise or heavy lifting, improper diet or consumption of alcohol, insufficient rest, and too-frequent sexual relations are commonplace. In cases where a woman has undergone a previous elective abortion, the authors never have failed to uncover some well-circumscribed belief linking that earlier decision somehow with the present pregnancy loss. In such instances, there is the belief that the current loss is a punishment for the abortion or is in some other "medical" way consequent to it. Blame and anger frequently accompany pregnancy loss, as a response to intense feelings of helplessness. This can be directed toward the women's partner, doctor or midwife, religion, and, of course, herself. With regard to anger at the physician, Wolff, Nielson, and Schiller (1970) reported that, of those women in their sample conceiving after a stillbirth, 50% changed obstetricians. It would be highly speculative to assume that such a change of physician indicates only unresolved anger from the pregnancy loss. However, this finding may speak to numerous insensitivities experienced by pregnancy-loss patients, and it may be reasonable for women to opt for such a change.

Envy and Jealousy

Envy and jealousy toward other pregnant women are ubiquitous following a pregnancy loss. Although these feelings generally are more intense toward relatives and friends, it is not at all uncommon for women who have experienced pregnancy loss to report envious and jealous feelings toward pregnant strangers or toward mothers they meet on the street or in social encounters. In the early months following pregnancy loss, many women avoid social situations in which they would have to interact with others who are pregnant or who recently have become mothers.

Return of Menstruation

One event which generally is perceived as helpful in the process of resolution or reorganization is the return of menstruation. The first period after pregnancy loss ushers in the hope that pregnancy can be attempted again. Also, menstruation offers women reassurance, to varying degrees, that their reproductive processes are functioning correctly. It should be noted, however, that subsequent periods are received more ambivalently, because these mark the failure to conceive and may aggravate feelings about the pregnancy loss.

The final stage of the mourning process is characterized by the diminution of feelings of self-reproach, loneliness, and emptiness. The woman, and those in her life as well, note a return to "normality." She can enter the room and handle the clothes once designated for the baby without becoming overwhelmed. Renewed interest in activities and in others is evident. She once again can be around babies and engage them without undue painful emotional consequences. For many women, however, a complete sense of acceptance or integration of the loss comes only with the subsequent delivery of a healthy baby. (See Chapter 15, "Impact of Pregnancy Loss on Subsequent Pregnancy," for discussion of this topic.)

Variations among Individuals in the Degree of Resolution

A critical clinical point about bereavement following pregnancy loss is that the degree to which resolution is achieved varies from individual to individual. The psychoanalytic literature in particular has addressed a mother's unique loss of a child in terms of discontinuity or broken connection of the generations. Such losses are understood to be more difficult to work through when compared with other more typical losses (Gorer, 1965; Videka-Sherman, 1982).

'Shadow Grief'

Peppers and Knapp (1980) allude to this characteristic of the post-mourning process through use of their term "shadow grief." Although physical sensations such as dull ache or unresponsivity can be associated with any loss of a loved one, this manifestation of grief is an especially apt way to note the tendency for painful memories and sensations to arise on anniversary dates such as the stillborn baby's due date and delivery date or the neonate's death date and/or birthday. These events are marked by tears, mild sadness, emptiness, and occasional low levels of anxiety which leave the person with a sense that something is "not quite right." Although no formal studies exist on this particular facet of bereavement with regard to pregnancy loss, the authors contend that shadow grief is very much related to the profound sense of isolation (from physicians, nurses, partners, relatives, friends, and others) experienced by women suffering pregnancy loss. Many have addressed this "conspiracy of silence" that surrounds perinatal death, wherein a mother is not encouraged to explore her feelings about her loss and is even discouraged from doing so (Lewis, 1979). She is discouraged from appropriate mourning by unempathetic comments from doctors, nurses, family, friends, and even her partner; by remarks about her presumed ability to have another child; by use of sedatives and minor tranquilizers; and by the failure of others to allow her to have contact with her baby and to be involved in funeral or burial activities (Friedman & Cohen, 1982; Gorer, 1965; Stringham, Riley, & Ross, 1982).

Unique Aspects of Pregnancy Loss

Circumstances surrounding two particular types of pregnancy loss are worthy of mention at this point because they often constitute more intense forms of shadow grief, but frequently they go unrecognized because of the conspiracy of silence. In the first, with the loss of one of a set of twins, even less support than usual appears to arise for the mother (Wilson, Fenton, Stevens, & Soule, 1982). The most frequent response by everyone, except the grieving mother, is that she should be thankful for the survival of one of the babies. The second case involves the instance in which complicated decisions about prolonging neonatal life are necessary and/or there is some debate about whether or not to intervene medically or surgically with a baby in whom there is likelihood of severe handicap. These two types of loss carry especially high risks of being associated with prolonged or complicated bereavement (LaRoche et al., 1982).

Impact of Pregnancy Loss on the Family

The bereavement process following pregnancy loss is not limited to the mother. Although not nearly as intimate or direct, the expectant father's emotional experience is analogous to his partner's during her pregnancy. Even though the expectant father is likely to have less attachment to the baby following a miscarriage than his partner, his attachment may be great in the case of neonatal death. This is especially so if he can catch up with his partner's bonding process when time permits him to interact with their newborn prior to death.

Lower level of attachment to the fetus by men has been postulated as an explanation for why men consistently demonstrate lower acute grief scores than women after pregnancy loss. Interestingly, men show much higher scores on measures of anger, aggression, and denial than do women. Also, grief scores tend to equalize between couples by 12 months following the loss (Goldbach et al., 1991). Men may demonstrate grief in a different way than do women. Also, societally defined male roles for caretaking during a crisis such as this may preclude a full expression of bereavement for men in the acute period (Costello et al., 1988). Since males express distress in a more behavioral way than women, their lack of direct emotional expression may be misconstrued as an absence of pain. If couples can understand gender influences in coping, relationship tensions regarding the perception of incongruent grieving may be reduced. It is also important to keep in mind, when measuring differential grief responses, that there is tremendous individual variability and that 22% of men actually may demonstrate greater grief responses than do their female partners (Zeanah, 1989).

Impact of Pregnancy Loss on Marital Stability

A man's calm exterior commonly is misinterpreted by his partner as an absence of feeling or response to pregnancy loss. As he begins to be in touch with his feelings of loss, the man himself may experience a strong sense of isolation, and he may feel that there is no one with whom to share his grief. He may be in conflict about sharing his loss with his partner for fear of further upsetting or depressing her. Frequently, a man may feel angry toward his partner when she, because of her own grief, fails to respond to his efforts at intervention and support. Absence of mutual support and sharing during grieving are the most significant contributions to complicated bereavement following pregnancy loss.

A Woman's Sense of Failure

The more general feelings of disappointment felt by bereaved expectant parents often obscure a nearly universal sense of failure experienced acutely by the woman. This sense of failure takes the form of having disappointed her partner because she has been unable to give birth to a healthy baby. She has failed in her attempt at loving procreation. Although many women may not be able to articulate this fear to their partners, they nevertheless are intensely worried that their partners do indeed hold such a view. These feelings are not limited to fantasy, for frequently a woman has accurately interpreted her partner's attempt to rationalize the tragic loss through blaming another — her. The degree to which committed partners can address these troublesome thoughts and fantasies will enhance their ability to assist each other in their acute grief.

It is important to recognize that not all couples who experience pregnancy loss automatically go on to an intense state of dysfunction in their relationship. In fact, the opposite may be more common. Harmon, Glicken, and Seigel (1984), in a study of 38 women grieving from neonatal loss, found that at both 3 and 9 months post loss these women reported more closeness with their partners than previously. Only 10% stated that the pregnancy loss had created difficulties for them with their partners. Nevertheless, most clinicians agree that the potential for conflict for a couple is very great after pregnancy loss.

Response of Children to Pregnancy Loss

Children in the family also react to pregnancy loss (Cain, Erickson, Fast, & Vaughan, 1964). What determines the child's response to the loss depends for the most part on two factors: his or her cognitive development and therefore capacity to understand death; and the response of his or her parents, especially the primary caregiver, to the loss. Wass and Corr (1984) point out that concepts of death develop in four stages. No specific ages can be attached to these stages, since many factors determine when a particular child will advance to the next stage.

A Child's Developing Concepts of Death

In the first stage, during infancy, a baby has no concept of death. Although babies can form internal images, these images are of things encountered in their immediate world such as people, food, or toys. The second developmental stage in the concept of death occurs in early childhood. The child's own experiences govern his or her understanding of events. Children at this stage believe that everything in the world, including tricycles and stones, is alive and that everything is manufactured for people's convenience. They believe that whatever is desired or wished for will happen, that anything is possible. They also believe that events happen for personal reasons. A bad dream may happen because a child has been bad. Three, four, and five-year olds have difficulty comprehending that death is final and that they have no control over the event.

In the third stage, during late childhood and pre-adolescence, death is understood to be an irreversible event. However, children at this stage hope to escape the process entirely themselves or at least to delay any experience with death for a very long time. They begin to find the physiology of death, dying, and decomposition a source of interest. The fourth, mature stage of understanding death is achieved in adolescence. Death finally is understood to be irreversible and inevitable. Adolescents develop personal, abstract, and theological views toward death and are aware of the meaning of the experience for others.

As does the expectant father, children have varying degrees of involvement with and attachment to the fetus or neonate. When pregnancy loss occurs, children may develop symptoms (anger, depression, aggression, phobic behavior, anxiety, sleep disturbances) because the loss actualizes for them the ambivalence with which they have regarded the expected sibling. It is one thing to feel that the forthcoming baby is a rival and intruder and appropriately to wish it dead; it is quite another and scary event to have that wish come true. Yet, in the very concrete and egocentric world of the young child, this is precisely the scenario. Some children may blame the mother for the loss of a new sister or brother, and they become resentful, especially toward the mother. This is exquisitely painful to a grieving woman.

Impact of Mother's Preoccupation with Mourning

Ultimately, what makes children vulnerable is that they are very dependent on the adults in their environment. A mother's quite normal sadness after her pregnancy loss temporarily renders her emotionally less accessible and responsive to her children. It is this perceived withdrawal that is most threatening to a child. Thus, it is advisable to call upon other familiar adults in the extended family or neighborhood to be available to children during the period of mourning.

Importantly, children need age-appropriate explanations for the loss. Their fantasies and fears should be explored with special attention to their fears of dying, losing other family members, or blaming themselves for the death. Children's responses to stress may be poorly differentiated and as such may be manifested by oppositionality, hyperactivity, behavioral disturbances, or developmental regressions. Parents should be educated to recognize these as grief equivalents or as responses to family stress and parental grief (Costello et al., 1988).

Pregnancy Loss and Psychopathology:

Bereavement as a Factor in Illness Onset

The limited literature on pregnancy loss addresses primarily two subjects: (a) complicated maternal bereavement following neonatal death, and (b) the impact of the hospital milieu and doctor-patient relationship on parental grieving. There remains significant controversy in the adult psychiatric literature as to whether or not increased physical morbidity and mortality are associated with bereavement. Clayton (1979) concluded from her prospective studies of widows and widowers that there was no appreciable increase in mortality or morbidity in the bereaved. However, others demonstrated significantly higher morbidity and mortality rates in the bereaved, and cited bereavement as a major factor in illness onset (Kaprio, Kosekenvuo, & Rita, 1987; Parkes, 1969; Rees & Lutkins, 1979).

Risks of Experiencing Prolonged Grief

Similarly, with regard to psychopathology following pregnancy loss (excluding the questionable literature on emotional responses to spontaneous abortion), Wolff et al. (1970) found that, among 40 women who lost a baby at or shortly after birth, there were no psychiatric sequelae at 3-year follow-up. Jensen and Zahourek (1972) studied 25 women who experienced neonatal death and found that, after 1 year, a significant number of them still were depressed. One third of Cullberg's (1972) neonatal loss subjects demonstrated serious mental symptoms, including psychosis, phobias, anxiety attacks, and severe depression at 1- to 2-year follow-ups. In a retrospective study by telephone interview 10 to 20 months after pregnancy loss, 23% of mothers were diagnosed as having prolonged grief reactions. Those with a surviving twin or subsequent pregnancy which began less than 5 months following the death were at higher risk of prolonged grief reactions than were those without subsequent pregnancy or with pregnancy which began more than 6 months later (Rowe et al., 1978). Harmon et al.'s (1984) neonatal loss study found that at 3 and 9-month follow-ups women described a baby's death as having a major impact on their well-being and functioning. At 3 months, approximately four-fifths, and at 9 months, approximately three quarters of their sample indicated that their lives were changed substantially directly by the loss. Nearly 75% admitted to being depressed at 9 months and attributed it again to the neonatal death. At the 9-month follow-up, approximately one half reported irritability and crying episodes. More than one third were still angry at health care professionals for their alleged role in that loss.

Abnormal Grief Reactions

Most bereaved persons are supported sufficiently by their social milieu so that bereavement is concluded successfully within a year or so. The results of a number of studies, however, suggest that alcohol abuse frequently is correlated with negative bereavement outcomes (Clayton, 1979; Parkes, 1969). One of the strongest predictors of complicated bereavement is a history of poor psychologic functioning prior to pregnancy loss. A comprehensive personal and marital history can alert health care professionals to the greater likelihood of future difficulties in mourning. In general, the woman who is psychologically vulnerable prior to pregnancy loss and who is without adequate emotional support from those around her especially deserves close follow-up after pregnancy loss. Significant factors correlated with more intense or complicated grief are summarized in Figure 4-1. The cause of the baby's death seems to have a differential impact on mourning. Maternal factors such as preeclampsia, prematurity, and placental problems are associated with greater grief than are pregnancy losses which are associated with fetal abnormalities (LaRoche et al., 1982). Perhaps maternal health problems inspire more maternal guilt than do factors that can be construed as originating from the baby.

Prolonged Grief

Complicated bereavement or abnormal grief reactions after pregnancy loss generally take one of these two forms: (a) chronic, prolonged grief, or (b) absent grief. Lasker and Toedter (1991) have identified complicated grief after perinatal loss as different not only in intensity but also in character from

Figure 4-1.
Factors Associated with Intensity of Grief

- Previous poor adjustment
- Loss of a planned pregnancy
- Not seeing the baby
- Marital problems
- Presence of a surviving twin
- Subsequent pregnancy less than 5 months after the loss

normal grief reactions. Specifically, they found more despair and difficulty coping early on and later in those women with prolonged grief responses. This feature was independent of the intensity of the initial grief response and was predicted largely by a lack of social support. The degree of acute grief intensity was predicted by length of pregnancy, marital satisfaction, and prior mental health.

Absent Grief

Lack of any apparent grief response, particularly to stillbirth and neonatal death, should raise suspicions about another form of pathologic mourning — absent grief. Although this form of abnormal grief is relatively infrequent, it is sometimes difficult to diagnose because the person reports no feelings of distress and takes great pride in carrying on with his or her life in spite of the apparent importance of the deceased. However, astute observation will reveal that there almost always is heightened irritability and tension in these people. It is common for those with absent grief reactions to present with a multiplicity of somatic complaints to their physicians or emergency rooms.

Major Depression

When does prolonged grief become a disabling depression? It is customary to define major depression as the presence of a persistent dysphoric (sad) mood or loss of interest in activities and pastimes, as well as presence of at least four of the characteristics listed in Figure 5-1. This is a critical diagnostic concern, since the presence of major depression always requires psychiatric intervention. A confounding variable can include the higher risk of a range of dysphoric responses in the normal postpartum period, from post-

Figure 5-1.
Symptoms of Major Depression (DSM-IV)

- Significant change in appetite with either weight loss or weight gain
- Sleep disturbance (insomnia or hypersomnia)
- Psychomotor agitation or retardation
- Decrease or loss of interest and pleasure in activities and sex
- Anergy and fatigue
- Feelings of worthlessness and lowered self-esteem
- Decreased ability to think and concentrate
- Paranoia or hallucinations

partum blues to depression or even psychosis. In the case of pregnancy loss and bereavement, the combination of loss, stress, and biologic changes can be difficult to sort out. It is critical that clinically significant depression not be attributed prematurely to bereavement. Pregnancy loss support teams may be especially effective in identifying clinical depression in need of treatment, since they are familiar with the range of normal responses to pregnancy loss, and they are experienced in facilitating appropriate referral.

Posttraumatic Stress Disorder

Another potential category of psychologic complications with which health care professionals should be familiar is posttraumatic stress disorder (PTSD). Diagnosis of this anxiety disorder depends on the "experiencing, witnessing, or being confronted with an event that involves actual death or serious injury or a threat to the physical integrity to self or others and which is responded to with intense fear, helplessness, or horror" (DSM IV, 1994). Persons suffering from PTSD re-experience psychologic trauma as manifested by repetitive and unwanted memories and/or dreams of the event. There may be sudden acting or feeling as if the trauma were reoccurring. After the trauma, persons with PTSD typically have a numbing of responsiveness to or reduced involvement with the world, as indicated by decreased interest in one or more significant activities, feelings of detachment or estrangement from others, and/or constricted affect (the capacity to experience only a limited number of feelings). There may be a hypervigilance or startle response,

Figure 6-1.
Symptoms of Posttraumatic Stress Disorder (DSM-IV)

Re-experiencing the Trauma
- Intrusive recollections
- Dreams or nightmares
- Flashbacks
- Physiological distress at reminders
- Physiological reactivity to reminders

Increased Arousal
- Sleep disturbance
- Irritability
- Impaired concentration
- Hypervigilance
- Exaggerated startle response

Avoidance Symptoms
- Avoiding thoughts, activities, conversations, or feelings associated with the trauma
- Amnesia for parts of the trauma
- Diminished interest in activities
- Sense of interpersonal detachment
- Restricted affect
- Sense of foreshortened future

sleep disturbance, survivor's guilt, difficulty in concentrating or remembering, avoidance of activities reminiscent of the traumatic event, and intensification of symptoms by exposure to events that either symbolize or resemble the traumatic event (see Figure 6-1).

Many of the characteristics of PTSD commonly can be observed in complicated bereavement. This is especially true when dramatic circumstances surround the pregnancy loss, as in instances of neonatal death from prematurity, when labor was induced by a traumatic psychologic or physical event such as a car accident or an assault. In such cases, mourning can be complex and protracted, with many or all of the features of PTSD. Patients with such responses can be treated readily with intensive psychotherapy, and they should be referred to a psychiatrist.

Recommendations

Recent research provides guidance in caring for families following perinatal loss. Supportive counseling by well-trained multidisciplinary grief-support teams can facilitate recovery (Forrest, Standish, & Baum, & 1982; Lake, Knuppel,

Murphy, & Johnson, 1983; Lake, Knuppel, & Angel, 1987). Such teams address initial and longer-term grief reactions, provide supportive follow-up, serve as a liaison between the family and the other health care providers, and provide family and marital support. Every effort should be made by the team to respect grieving people's decisions and allow them as much control as possible.

Specific efforts which are aimed at facilitating a rapid recovery include interventions both at the time of death and at follow-up. In the initial loss period, parents should be assisted in establishing memories (the foundation of grief work) and in participating in social rituals for the dead. Whenever possible, babies should be seen, held, dressed, named, and included in religious ceremonies applicable to birth and death. Even malformed babies can be seen and held by parents who have been prepared adequately. Memorial services can be a helpful venue for family members to say goodbye and to support one another. Some parents may not wish to participate in these activities, and their decisions should be respected. Photographs and memorabilia can be obtained by the hospital and archived for later retrieval by the parents who often may seek out these items at variable intervals after their loss.

Autopsy is a particularly sensitive issue that should be addressed with compassion in a collaborative way with parents. The purposes and procedures of an autopsy should be negotiated specifically with the parents. Special care should be taken to make results easily accessible to parents when they become available (Covington & Theut, 1993; Knowles, 1994).

Parents should be counseled on the expected course of mourning, and the father (when available) should be included actively in all aspects of the post-loss follow-up, not only as a support for the mother, but also as a mourner in his own right. After the initial loss, parents often are overwhelmed by the enormity of their loss and grieving. Information should be repeated many times and, even more helpful later on, written down. Parents find that a follow-up phone call or a scheduled visit with a member of the treatment team can be very helpful and comforting. Referral to a pregnancy-loss support group at this point may be indicated.

Parents usually want to know when they can conceive again and what the risk is of another pregnancy loss. Since parents at this time are quite sensitive to empathic failures, their input and collaboration regarding their future childbearing are essential. Evidence that parents rarely adhere to physician's recommendations about when to re-conceive may suggest that parents perceive these suggestions as paternal or, at least, as out of touch with their personal circumstances (Covington & Theut, 1993; Zeanah, 1989).

Figure 7-1.
Stresses in Technology-Assisted Pregnancies

- Long waiting lists
- High cost — generally not covered by insurance
- Fears about the invasive nature of the fertilization process
- Anxiety about the nature of sperm donation
- Fears of being harmed during laparoscopy
- Concern about embryo transfer
- Anxiety about pregnancy tests
- Onset of menses, signaling failure

Grief and Infertility

Given the dramatic increase in the availability of various technologies to assist fertility and conception, a chapter on pregnancy loss would be incomplete without discussing the psychologic impact of failed attempts at pregnancy. Since most couples have pursued various infertility treatments before reaching such options as *in-vitro* fertilization, gamete intrafallopian transfer, and ovum donation, emotional stress during these procedures may be quite intense (see Figure 7-1). Despite the relatively low pregnancy success rates, couples often have unrealistically high expectations for success. Moreover, such procedures frequently are viewed as the last hope for a biological child (Black, Walther, Chute, & Greenfeld, 1992; Greenfeld, Diamond, & DeCherney, 1988).

In general, grief reactions after failed *in-vitro* fertilizations (IVF) mirror symptoms of women suffering a pregnancy loss, including anxiety, depressive symptoms, guilty preoccupation, hostility, and irritability (Black et al., 1992; Siebel & Graves, 1980). Greenfeld et al. (1988) found the grief reaction to be greatest following a failed first attempt of *in-vitro* fertilization, although the reactions also can be intense after the last *in-vitro* fertilization attempt, if this is viewed as the very last chance for pregnancy.

Greenfeld et al. (1988) hypothesized that the various reproductive technologies inadvertently can foster and intensify a women's attachment to the expected pregnancy. They may create unrealistic expectations simply because of the technology that makes the fertilization process visually alive, in a way that generally does not occur in the vast majority of pregnancies. For example, daily ultrasounds are performed in IVF to observe the number of ovarian follicles that develop as a result of the follicular stimulation phase. Because eggs are visualized, the entire process often becomes emotionally intense. Knowing that fertilization has occurred and that embryos are developing increases a woman's hope that pregnancy is inevitable. Physical, emotional, and financial demands of such procedures also may contribute to the intensity of the failed-pregnancy loss, especially for those whose life savings have been spent on the costly procedures.

Despite psychologic investments in technology-assisted pregnancies and their knowledge of the low success rates, women maintain high rates of optimism. Black et al. (1992) found that some women were even more optimistic on a subsequent trial, reasoning that, "The first trial represented a learning experience for their physicians and that their chances would now be better" (p. 12).

In view of the intense feelings that can develop after many failed attempts at pregnancy through various technologies, clinicians should be aware of the potential for a more intense grief reaction, although transient mourning is the norm. In follow-up appointments, women should be asked about incidence of dysphoria, sleeping patterns, irritability, and feelings of guilt. Guilt and self-blame should be explored, particularly if the couple voluntarily delayed pregnancy to the latter childbearing ages of the woman, or if the infertility problem is a complication of a sexually transmitted disease. If significant emotional problems persist, counseling or therapy should be encouraged strongly. Support groups for infertile couples also may be helpful.

As might be expected, men do not experience the same emotional distress as do their partners in response to a failed attempt at pregnancy (Greenfeld et al., 1988). One might speculate that, due to the invasive nature of these procedures for women, a greater investment in the expected pregnancy results — thus leading to a more intense grief reaction.

If pregnancy is achieved, new issues can arise for the previously infertile couple, including delayed attachment and persisting doubt (Garner, 1985). Shapiro (1986) found that the initial joy which a couple experiences when a pregnancy is confirmed can be replaced by other feelings later in the pregnancy, including disbelief, denial, and problems in feeling attached to the fetus. Conflicted feelings may be even more problematic if the pregnancy is complicated. Clinicians may experience frustration and become impatient with couples who develop ambivalent feelings about achieving a long-awaited pregnancy.

We tried for so long to conceive, so when I became pregnant, I didn't take any chances. I ate very well, avoided any fumes, and ended sexual relations with my husband, fearing possible injury in some way. I know it was silly, but I never felt reassured from my obstetrician that intercourse was okay. My husband was supportive initially, but we grew apart physically and emotionally. My OB kept telling me everything would be fine after the baby was born — but it only got worse. He failed to see my postpartum depression and the marriage further deteriorated.

With the various technology-assisted pregnancies also come the possibilities of difficult decisions; for example, if multiple ova are implanted successfully, does the couple decide to pursue a selective abortion procedure, so as to give the remaining babies a greater chance of survival? Practitioners must feel comfortable discussing such issues openly and to accept ambivalent feelings that may arise between the couple. Suddenly, the successful procedure that results in a long-awaited pregnancy can become a source of pain and conflicted feelings, including anger as illustrated in the following vignette.

I was ecstatic to learn that I was pregnant — finally after five IVFs — but also terrified until my first ultrasound, because I didn't want to face a decision if I had four or more embryos implanted. I only became slightly less terrified with the knowledge that my first ultrasound brought, that I had triplets. Being a physician, I knew the increased risks of birth defects in multiple births, and I feared premature labor. I don't think my OB ever understood my fears, or my depression. He wasn't really equipped to deal with my conflicted feelings and probably couldn't understand why I was anything but ecstatic.

If a couple does pursue selective abortion, a grief reaction similar to other pregnancy losses is likely to occur.

For the previously infertile couple who gives birth to a child or children who are sick or premature, susceptibility to complicated grief reactions may be increased. Old feelings of anger and guilt may resurface, especially if the couple feels responsible for the great difficulty in conceiving (Furlong-Lind, Pruitt, & Greenfeld, 1989) due to delaying childbearing or sexually transmitted diseases. Some may find it difficult to visit the baby in the nursery or to be involved in medical decisions. Not unexpectedly, others may have great difficulty in accepting a grave prognosis, and consequently they may feel paralyzed in their attempts to make medical decisions regarding withholding treatment in terminal cases (Furlong-Lind et al., 1989). Other couples may feel so grateful to have a child, however, that they are very accepting of the situation, and they become very involved. If, however, parents view themselves as defective because of the infertility, the perception of a "defective" child may further impair self-esteem (Menning, 1977). In situations where a baby dies after several weeks in a NICU, the mourning process may be even longer and more complex for the couple who previously had been infertile.

Conclusion

It is apparent from this chapter, and indeed this entire book, that the tragedy of pregnancy loss largely goes unrecognized by significant segments of health care professions, as well as by society at large. Many grieving women and men are very much left on their own to navigate this bereavement process. The authors hope that the account in this chapter of the normal process undergone by almost all who have experienced such loss will enable professionals to be more empathic with these patients. Often, what is most poignant about events surrounding pregnancy loss is the absence of professional empathy, which unnecessarily traumatizes patients even further. Although it is true that anger and hostility are normal reactions to such a loss, it also is true that such feelings sometimes are appropriate responses to hospital staff who are insensitive to the personal meaning of these experiences for the individuals involved. The response by others in the health care environment to a traumatic episode may be equal to, if not more important than, the precise nature of the overwhelming event itself. A pregnancy-loss patient in particular is at high risk for sustaining psychic trauma. That suffering may be compounded by care providers who should be — but are not — available to provide emotional support. Care providers of all disciplines will be eminently more successful and will grow professionally when they can respond in-depth to an individual patient's or couple's plight.❏

Case Study 1-1

Lack of Care Provider Relationship

A 26-year-old nulliparous married female presented for her initial obstetric examination at approximately 11 weeks gestation. At the end of the visit, the obstetrician informed her that her fundal height was small for her dates and then scheduled her for an obstetric ultrasound. She received the ultrasound 1 week later. It was performed by a different physician, because the woman's initial obstetrician was on vacation.

During the ultrasound, the patient heard the obstetrician say something about the absence of a fetal pole. The obstetrician told the woman to continue with her usual activities, and that she would learn the results when they called her on the phone. The following week, she was called and asked to return for another ultrasound. At this second examination, the obstetrician reported that he could not detect a fetal heartbeat and would like to consult with a colleague. Next, she had blood drawn for a quantitative beta-human chorionic gonadotrophin (HCG) study, and this was repeated 2 days later.

While she was awaiting news of the findings of these procedures, the woman was frightened and confused. She continued to work and pursue her usual activities. She had many questions, but she hesitated to "bother" her doctor with a telephone call. Instead, she called a relative who was a physician, hoping to be reassured. She was unable to relay enough accurate information, however, so this relative could not make any meaningful comments about the prognosis for this pregnancy. Although the woman felt supported, she still was distraught and concerned.

One week later, the woman received a telephone call from her obstetrician, who reported that the fetus was not viable and that it was likely that she would miscarry within a few days. The obstetrician told her that she could conduct her usual work and other activities until she miscarried. The woman was overwhelmed with disbelief, sadness, and fear. She could not imagine continuing this pregnancy while she only could anticipate an inevitable pregnancy loss. She also was frightened about what kind of pain she would experience, about the unpredictable timing of the miscarriage, and about how she could cope with the event when it occurred.

Two days later, on a Saturday, she began to experience cramping and bleeding. The obstetrician who was on call told the woman that she need not be seen, but that she should come in for a suction curettage on Monday if she still was symptomatic. By early on Sunday morning, the woman found the pain to be intolerable. She went to her hospital emergency room and was admitted. When she requested pain medication, a nurse told her, "If you think this is bad, you'll never be able to handle labor." The woman underwent a suction curettage later that day, and then she was discharged home.

She was offered no follow-up supportive care, other than instructions to schedule a routine 6-week follow-up obstetric visit. She did not seek counseling services. She and her husband took a week of vacation from work, to support each other in their grief. For several months, the woman experienced dysphoria, tearfulness, nightmares, poor sleep, and repetitive thoughts about her miscarriage. She alternated between sadness and disbelief, saying things such as, "I was pregnant, and then suddenly I wasn't. It is hard to understand." Gradually, her symptoms resolved, but then they recurred transiently 6 months later, when she again became pregnant. The symptoms had resolved once more by the time the woman was 20 weeks pregnant. For the current pregnancy, she had interviewed several new obstetricians. She selected a woman who she expected would be sensitive to her concerns and would offer complete explanations to the questions which arose. This pregnancy was successful. The woman gave birth to a healthy baby. This time, she was satisfied with her care.

Commentary

This 26-year-old nulliparous woman (the case history does not say whether or not she ever had been pregnant before) learned in a very disorganized fashion that her pregnancy was not proceeding well. We are not told if this was a planned or a wanted pregnancy, although we assume that it was. The patient was frightened and confused by the mixed messages which she received from her obstetric care providers.

It is normal to experience some ambivalence early in pregnancy. This may cause considerable guilt for this woman. She may have believed that she was being punished for not eating right, or for being too active physically, or for having sex. She was seen by different care providers, and she did not have an established, good relationship with any one of them. Having a trusted physician or nurse might have been very helpful for the woman as she experienced her pregnancy loss.

Thoughtless comments also were harmful, as were discussions which occurred on the telephone. Pregnancy loss is experienced as a loss of part of one's body by the woman undergoing it. This is true for early pregnancy loss, a fact which unfortunately is disregarded for many reasons. For even the most caring of fathers, this is not the same experience. The sense of grief and mourning can persist for some time, especially if there have been other instances of unresolved grief. In this case, it would have been very helpful for the woman to have been seen around the time of the miscarriage by her primary physician, to review the situation, to be informed about the physical and psychological reactions to miscarriage, to learn about causes for the pregnancy loss, and to receive advice about a future pregnancy. It is essential to stress that such counseling is important, because the woman can become pregnant again soon. Moreover, the woman should have been contacted after the curettage procedure at the hospital, with follow-up by the medical staff who cared for her when she experienced the pregnancy loss. To dismiss her from the hospital with no other care instructions other than to wait until a 6-week checkup for counseling is unconscionable.

Grief reaction is quite normal after miscarriage. Family and health care professionals can provide necessary support. The couple, especially the woman, needs time to mourn the loss, and to understand that feelings of guilt, sadness, and anger all may be anticipated, and that these feelings can be resolved with time. The woman may feel very anxious at the start of another pregnancy, and she should be told that this is normal. There must be some time for emotional healing after a miscarriage before a couple plans a new pregnancy. The interval of time varies for each individual and couple. Pathological grief is that which persists after 6 months, and it may be expressed via a variety of physical or psychological symptoms.

Case Study 2-1

Loss Issues Related to Donor Egg Pregnancy

Mrs. B. is a 38-year-old married female. She and her husband of 8 years have tried desperately to conceive for the last 6 years. Despite extensive workups, the woman's infertility remains unexplained. Past attempts at *in-vitro* fertilization failed to stimulate enough eggs that could be retrieved. Thus, 2 years ago, Mrs. B. and her husband adopted a baby daughter, whom they adore. Mr. and Mrs. B. still longed for a biological child; so they pursued the option of donor egg. Ultimately, they were accepted into the infertility program at a local university medical center, and Mrs. B. became pregnant after two attempts.

Initially, both Mr. and Mrs. B. were thrilled to be pregnant. During the first ultrasound, however, Mrs. B. began to cry. Her husband was quite perplexed by his wife's reaction, but Mrs. B. insisted that she was fine. After that visit, Mr. B. noticed a new emotional distance between the two of them, as well as a marked reluctance to discuss the pregnancy on Mrs. B.'s part. During her next obstetric checkup, Mrs. B. became tearful again. She told the nurse, "I don't feel right. This isn't my baby." As she talked with her doctor, she even admitted that she was contemplating having an abortion, because, "I don't think I ever could bond with this child, since it's not mine." Her obstetrician referred her to a therapist, but Mrs. B. refused. Therefore, he scheduled her for a visit in 1 week, because of his concern about her level of distress.

One week later, Mrs. B. acknowledged that she was disturbed by her thoughts, and she agreed to see a therapist, because, as she said, "I can't talk with my husband about this. He's so excited about the baby." In therapy, Mrs. B. discussed her feelings about her infertility, saying, "It's me who has something wrong. I couldn't even make a viable egg." She spoke fondly of their adopted daughter, and she believed that she had no difficulty in accepting this daughter as their own child; but she felt that this new baby would be different: "It's my husband's baby, not mine. It's almost as if he had an affair." Mrs. B. explained further that, "Every time I feel the baby move, I know I should be happy. Instead, I'm just reminded that this life inside of me really isn't part of me."

As her pregnancy progressed, Mrs. B. became less depressed, although her husband noted that she continued to seem distant. The delivery was uncomplicated. When she first saw their new son, Mrs. B. cried. It was clear that she did not share her husband's joy. She had difficulty with breastfeeding and quickly switched to bottle feedings for the baby. She became more withdrawn, spending most of her time with her daughter while her husband cared for the baby. Mr. B. became increasingly frustrated with the situation, especially with his wife's reluctance to resume sexual relations with him, as well as her inability to care for her children appropriately.

In addition to the individual therapy, Mr. and Mrs. B. began marital therapy. For the first time, Mrs. B. expressed her envy toward her husband for his ability to have a biological child, and she said that she feared that he would favor his own child over their adopted child. She therefore had a feeling that she needed to protect their daughter against her fears of her husband's preferential treatment of their son.

Over time, both Mr. and Mrs. B. learned to share their feelings and concerns openly. Mrs. B. felt reassured about her role as mother to both children. She became involved with her baby, and finally she was able to bond intensely with her new son.

Commentary

Mrs. B. is a 38-year-old woman who never has been able to become pregnant, despite extensive infertility investigations and treatments. After 6 years of trying unsuccessfully to conceive, she most probably has experienced a strong sense of loss and grief at not being able to achieve a pregnancy. For Mrs. B., each menstrual period may have been a painful reminder of this failure. Her infertility was said to be unexplained, which may be even more frustrating for her, since she may have the feeling that nothing is wrong, yet conception does not occur. Since egg donation was attempted, it is likely that Mrs. B. suffered from premature ovarian failure. Her ability to love and bond with her adopted daughter suggests that Mrs. B. has the normal ability to establish relationships. The adopted child was not related biologically to either Mrs. B. or her husband. So, she may have felt that there was an equality with both gametes coming from others. One strongly suspects that the infertility issues were not resolved for Mrs. B. She may feel that her husband blames her for the infertility.

After she became pregnant with a donor egg, Mrs. B. became increasingly depressed at the thought of the fetus growing inside her who she felt was not really her baby. Usually, women start to bond with the baby prenatally, even when a donor egg was used to establish pregnancy. Many of the feelings of inadequacy and loss obviously began to surface during Mrs. B.'s pregnancy, however. She felt that her husband was able to father a child, while she could not provide genetic material even though she was able to carry a baby throughout the pregnancy.

It would be important for Mrs. B. to receive psychotherapy during her pregnancy and after the delivery, focusing first on her sense of loss. This may have been related to earlier losses in her life which were not resolved, making her feel less secure now. Second, the therapist could help with emphasizing and supporting her ability to gestate and carry a baby to term, and to care for and nurture her children. There also should be some emphasis on the marital relationship which may contain elements of competitiveness in other spheres of their lives together.

Mrs. B. suffered from postpartum depression, which occurs in 10% to 15% of women who have normal, healthy babies. She would have been much more vulnerable at this time, and appropriate treatment was indicated and appeared to be successful. This case very poignantly points out the need for good mental health care, as well as physical management, during treatments with reproductive technologies, in order to provide the best possible environment for the parents, as well as any children who thereby are brought into the world.

References

Anthony, E.J., & Benedek, T. (1970). *Parenthood. Its psychology and psychopathology.* Boston: Little, Brown & Company.

Black, R.B., Walther, V.N., Chute, D., & Greenfeld, D.A. (1992). When in-vitro fertilization fails: A prospective view. *Social Work in Health Care, 17*(3), 1-19.

Bibring, G.L., Dwyer, T.F., Huntington, D.S., & Valenstein, A.F. (1961). A study of the psychological processes in pregnancy and of the earliest mother-child relationship I and II (pp. 9-24). In *Psychoanalytic study of the child, Vol. 16.* New York: Inter University Press.

Bowlby, J. (1940). *Loss: Sadness and depression — Attachment and loss.* New York: Basic Books.

Cain, A.C., Erickson, M.E., Fast, I., & Vaughan, R.A. (1964). Children's disturbed reactions to their mother's miscarriage. *Psychosomatic Medicine, 26*(1), 58-66.

Clayton, P., Desmarais, L., & Winokur, G. (1968). A study of normal bereavement. *American Journal of Psychiatry, 125*(1), 64-74.

Clayton, P.J. (1979). The sequelae and nonsequalae of conjugal bereavement. *American Journal of Psychiatry, 136,* 1530-1534.

Costello, A., Gardner, S.L., & Merenstein, G.B. (1988). State of the art: Perinatal grief and loss. *Journal of Perinatology, 3,* 361-370.

Covington, S.N., & Theut, S.K. (1993). Reactions to perinatal loss: A qualitative analysis of the national maternal and infant health survey. *American Journal of Orthopsychiatry, 63,* 215-222.

Cuisinier, M.C., Kuijpers, J.C., Hoogduin, C.A., de Graauw, C.P., & Janssen, H.J. (1993). Miscarriage and stillbirth: Time since the loss, grief intensity and satisfaction with care. *European Journal of Obstetrics and Gynecology, 52,* 163-168.

Cullberg, J. (1972). *Psychosomatic medicine in obstetrics and gynecology* (Third International Congress). London: Basel and Karger.

Cunningham, F.G., MacDonald, P.C., Leveno, K.J., Gant, N.F., & Gilstrap III, L.C. (1993). *Williams obstetrics* (19th ed.). Norwalk, CT: Appleton and Lange.

Diagnostic and Statistical Manual of Mental Disorders. (1994). Washington, DC: American Psychiatric Association.

Fletcher, J.C., & Evans, M.I. (1983). Maternal bonding in early fetal ultrasound examinations. *New England Journal of Medicine, 308,* 392-393.

Forrest, G.C., Standish, E., & Baum, J.D. (1982). Support after perinatal death: A study of support and counselling after perinatal bereavement. *British Medical Journal, 285,* 1475-1479.

Freud, S. (1957). *Mourning and melancholia. The standard edition of the complete psychological works of Sigmund Freud* (Vol. 14). London: Hogarth Press and Institute for Psychoanalysis.

Friedman, R., & Cohen, K.A. (1982). Emotional reactions to miscarriage. In M.T. Notman & C.C. Nadelson (Eds.), *The woman patient* (Vol. 3). New York: Plenum Press, 173-187.

Furlong-Lind, R., Pruitt, R.C., & Greenfeld, D. (1989, May). Previously infertile couples and the newborn intensive care unit. *Health and Social Work*, 127-133.

Garner, C.H. (1985). Pregnancy after infertility. *Journal of Obstetric, Gynecologic, and Neonatal Nursing, 14*(Suppl.), 585-625.

Goldbach, K.R., Dunn, D.S., Toedter, L.J., & Lasker, J.N. (1991). The effects of gestational age and gender on grief after pregnancy loss. *American Journal of Orthopsychiatry, 2*, 461-467.

Gorer, G. (1965). *Death, grief, and mourning.* New York: Doubleday.

Greenfeld, D.A., Diamond, M.P., & DeCherney, A.H. (1988). Grief reactions following in-vitro fertilization treatment. *Journal of Psychosomatic Obstetrics and Gynecology, 8*, 169-174.

Harmon, R.J., Glicken, A.D., & Seigel, R.E. (1984). Neonatal loss in the intensive care nursery: Effects on maternal grieving and a program for intervention. *Journal of the American Academy of Child Psychiatry, 23*, 68-71.

Harmon, R.J., & Graham-Cicchinelli, D. (1985). Fetal and neonatal loss. In R.C. Simons (Ed.), *Understanding human behavior in health and illness* (pp. 151-157) (3rd ed.). Baltimore: Williams & Wilkins.

Herzog, J.M. (1982). Patterns of expectant fatherhood: A study of the fathers of a group of premature infants. In S.H. Cath, A.R. Gurwitz, & J.M. Ross (Eds.), *Father and child: Development and clinical perspectives* (pp. 301-314). Boston: Little, Brown & Company.

Jensen, J., & Zahourek, R. (1972): Depression in mothers who have lost a newborn. *Rocky Mountain Medical Journal, 69*, 61-63.

Kaprio, J., Kosekenvuo, M., & Rita, H. (1987). Mortality after bereavement: A prospective study of 95,647 widowed persons. *American Journal of Public Health, 77*, 283-287.

Kirkley-Best, E., & Kellner, K. (1982). The forgotten grief: A review of the psychology of stillbirth. *American Journal of Orthopsychiatry, 52*, 420-429.

Knowles, S. (1994). A passage through grief — The Western Australian rural pregnancy loss team. *British Medical Journal, 309*, 1705-1708.

Kübler-Ross, E. (1969). *On death and dying.* New York: Macmillan.

Lake, M., Knuppel, R.A., Murphy, J., & Johnson, T.M. (1983). The role of a grief support team following stillbirth. *American Journal of Obstetrics and Gynecology, 146*, 877-881.

Lake, M.F., Knuppel, R.A., & Angel, J.L. (1987). The rationale for supportive care after perinatal death. *Journal of Perinatology, 2*, 85-89.

LaRoche, C., Lalinec-Michaud, M., Engelsmann, F., Fuller, N., Copp, M., & Vasilevsky, K. (1982). Grief reactions to perinatal death: An exploratory study. *Psychosomatics, 23*, 510-518.

Lasker, J.N., & Toedter, L.J. (1991). Acute versus chronic grief: The case of pregnancy loss. *American Journal of Orthopsychiatry, 61*, 510-522.

Leon, I.G. (1992). The psychoanalytic conceptualization of perinatal loss: A multidimensional model. *American Journal of Psychiatry, 149*, 1464-1472.

Lewis, E. (1976). The management of stillbirth: Coping with an unreality. *Lancet, 2*, 619-620.

Lewis, E. (1979). Mourning by the family after a stillbirth or neonatal death. *Archives of Diseases in Childhood, 54,* 303-306.

Lindemann, E. (1944). Symptomatology and management of acute grief. *American Journal of Psychiatry, 101,* 141-149.

Luby, E. (1977). *Bereavement and grieving* (p. 23). In H.S. Schiff, *The bereaved parent.* New York: Penguin Books.

Menning, B.E. (1977). *Infertility: A guide for childless couples.* Englewood Cliffs, NJ: Prentice Hall.

Parkes, C.M. (1969). Broken heart: A statistical study of increased mortality among widowers. *British Medical Journal, 1,* 740-748.

Parkes, C.M., & Weiss, R.S. (1983). *Recovery from bereavement.* New York: Basic Books.

Peppers, L.G., & Knapp, R.J. (1980). *Motherhood and mourning: Perinatal death.* New York: Praeger Scientific.

Phipps, S. (1981). Mourning response and intervention in stillbirth: An alternative genetic counseling approach. *Social Biology, 28,* 1-13.

Pollock, G.H. (1961). Mourning and adaptation. *International Journal of Psychoanalysis, 42,* 341-361.

Raphael, B. (1983). *The anatomy of bereavement.* New York: Basic Books.

Rees, W.D., & Lutkins, S.G. (1979). Mortality of bereavement. *British Medical Journal, 4,* 13-16.

Rowe, J., Clyman, R., Green, C., Mikkelson, C., Haight, J., & Ataide, L. (1978). Follow-up of families who experience perinatal death. *Pediatrics, 62*(2), 166-170.

Shapiro, C.H. (1986). Is pregnancy after infertility a dubious joy? Social Casework, 66, 306-313.

Siebel, M., & Graves, W.C. (1980). The psychological implications of spontaneous abortion. *Journal of Reproductive Medicine, 25,* 161-165.

Stringham, J., Riley, J.H., & Ross, A. (1982). Silent birth: Mourning a stillborn baby. *Social Work, 27,* 322-327.

Theut, S.K., Zaslow, M.J., Rabinovich, B.A., Bartko, J.J., & Morihisa, J.M. (1990). Resolution of parental bereavement after a perinatal loss. Journal of the *American Academy of Child and Adolescent Psychiatry, 29,* 521-525.

Videka-Sherman, L. (1982). Coping with the death of a child: A study over time. *American Journal of Orthopsychiatry, 52,* 688-698.

Wass, H., & Corr, C. (1984). *Helping children cope with death-guidelines and resources.* Washington, DC: Hemisphere.

Wilson, A.L., Fenton, L.J., Stevens, D.C., & Soule, D.J. (1982). The death of a twin: An analysis of parental bereavement. *Pediatrics, 70,* 587-591.

Wolff, J.R., Nielson, P.E., & Schiller, P. (1970). The emotional reaction to a stillbirth. *American Journal of Obstetrics and Gynecology, 108,* 73-77.

Zeanah, C.H. (1989). Adaptation following perinatal loss: A critical review. *Journal of the American Academy of Child and Adolescent Psychiatry, 28,* 467-480.

Chapter 2

The Biology of Early Pregnancy Loss

Vivian Lewis

Clinically recognized pregnancy loss occurs in about 15% of patients, making this a fairly common event. Yet pregnancy loss is far more common than we recognize clinically, occurring in up to 40% to 50% of women (Speroff, Glass, & Kase, 1994). Estimates of first trimester pregnancy loss, based on hCG, detected in the urine in the interval between implantation and menstruation, indicate a 22% pregnancy loss rate in unrecognized pregnancies (Wilcox et al., 1988). Other data suggest that another 15% of fertilized eggs never implant (Little, 1988). These events add substantially to the recognized rate of pregnancy loss, and they are important because they point out that establishing pregnancy is more complicated than most people realize. There are many reasons for these early losses. Some are known from clinical medicine, whereas others may be suspected on the basis of investigations in the fields of genetics, cell biology, and *in vitro* fertilization (IVF).

Genetics

Chromosomal abnormalities are the most common cause of early pregnancy loss, accounting for about 70% of recognized first-trimester losses (Boue, Boue, & Lazar, 1975; Guerneri et al., 1987). Most of these have an abnormal number of chromosomes: aneuploidy (addition or deletion of one or two chromosomes) or polyploidy (additional haploid sets of chromosomes). To understand how this could occur, it is important to review the events of meiosis and fertilization. This involves reducing the chromosome complement to the haploid (23 chromosomes) during gametogenesis so that the newly formed zygote will have the full complement of chromosomes.

In females, meiosis begins *in utero*, when the supply of immature gametes, or primary oocytes, is established. Primary oocytes contain 46 chromosomes, each with a double complement of DNA, as the DNA replicates in preparation for meiosis. Early in prophase, the 23 homologous chromosome pairs align themselves closely to allow for exchange of genetic material, called crossing over. This process makes for greater genetic diversity in the population; if unequal exchanges occur or if there is an unstable region in a chromosome, however, genetically abnormal gametes will result. In oocytes, meiosis stops here until just prior to ovulation. Since the full complement of oocytes is present *in utero*, the oocyte could remain at this point for up to 45 or 50 years.

After puberty, systematic growth of a dominant ovarian follicle to the ovulatory stage is seen with each cycle. The mature follicle triggers a luteinizing hormone (LH) surge, which leads to resumption of the first meiosis, which will be rapidly completed. The nuclear membrane disappears (germinal vesicle breakdown) and there is dispersion of the chromosomes into the first polar body and the secondary oocyte, thereby completing meiosis I. Ovulation occurs about 24 hours after the start of the surge. The oocyte that is released contains 23 chromosomes, each with two chromatids; essentially diploid because the strands of DNA have not separated. The cell moves directly into meiosis II and arrests in metaphase, with the 23 chromosomes lined up on the equatorial plate and the apparent absence of the nuclear membrane. The second meiosis then resumes if sperm penetration occurs. Each chromosome separates at the centromere into two chromatids and the maternal genetic material is dispersed to the second polar body.

In males, a supply of primordial germ cells is established *in utero* and will remain dormant until puberty, when spermatogenesis will begin. By contrast with women, primordial germ cells will replicate (mitosis) and also differentiate into mature spermatozoa. This process occurs continuously until death, with each cycle requiring about 64 days. The initial mitosis takes place in about 16 days. The first meiosis, which produces secondary spermatocytes, requires about 8 days. Meiosis II takes 16 days and produces spermatids that must undergo further maturational changes, spermiogenesis, over the final 24 days.

To summarize the entire process, there are two meiotic divisions in both sexes, which involve reduction in the chromosomal number and the creation of gametes that differ from the parental genome, due to the crossing-over process. In women, the latter occurs in early life, followed by prolonged arrest and reactivation during reproductive years. In men, the process is continuous after puberty. The process of fertilization completes meiosis in the female, which is critical for the zygote to acquire a normal chromosomal complement.

Control of Meiosis

The mechanism of the prolonged arrest of meiosis in prophase I is unknown. There probably are antral proteins which are important, as well as regulatory protein kinases and purines within the oocyte and/or granulosa cells. Oocyte meiosis inhibitor (OMI) is a polypeptide that has been partially purified from porcine follicular fluid. OMI can inhibit germinal vesicle or nuclear membrane breakdown of oocytes attached to cumulus cells (Schultz, 1991). It is unclear, however, whether the inhibitory activity comes from several chemically different compounds or from different forms of the same compound, causing some to question the role of OMI (Eppig, 1991a; Schultz, 1991). Another follicular fluid protein, Müllerian-inhibiting substance (MIS), which also is responsible for regression of Müllerian duct structures, has been proposed as a meiosis inhibitor. Again, there are conflicting reports of the extent of its inhibitory activity, depending upon the method of purification (Takahashi, Koide, & Donahoe, 1986; Tsafriri, Picard, & Josso, 1988). Thus, both OMI and MIS may play a role in meiosis inhibition; however, further study is needed to clarify their importance.

Several species apparently require cAMP, generated by the cumulus cells and transferred through gap junctions, to prevent meiosis. The influx of cAMP activates a protein kinase that stimulates protein phosphorylation and maintains meiosis arrest. Purines, especially adenosine and hypoxanthine, apparently can act synergistically to inhibit meiosis, possibly through inhibition of phosphodiesterase and maintenance of increased levels of cAMP (Eppig, 1991a & b). The LH surge, which triggers meiosis I resumption, causes a loss of gap junctions between the oocyte and cumulus cells. This allows levels of cAMP to drop and meiosis to progress (Eppig, 1991a & b). Recent work with rat oocytes suggests that the cumulus granulosa communications must uncouple to allow release from the cAMP inhibition in the oocyte.

There also are data which suggest that meiosis is stimulated at certain points. Maturation promoting factor (MPF) is a complex of cyclin, regulatory kinases, phosphatases, and p39mos, a proto-oncogene product. A bioassay has been developed in which oocyte cytoplasm is removed and injected into Asterina pectinfera oocytes which are rated for nuclear envelope breakdown. Mouse oocytes apparently show peaks of MPF activity with each metaphase by this bioassay. The proposed sequence of events would be that, once the LH surge begins, the meiosis inhibition is removed, and the activity of MPF stimulates nuclear envelope breakdown (Dulcibella, 1992; Schultz, 1991). The chromosomes move to the equatorial plate, prior to extrusion of half of the material into the first polar body, resulting in formation of the secondary oocyte. Another protein, cytostatic factor, then stabilizes MPF so that the oocyte stops meiosis until fertilization occurs.

Fertilization

Entry of the sperm into the egg causes zona and cortical reactions to occur which block entry of other sperm. Meiosis then must resume. Finally, oocyte metabolism must switch over to fuel the development of the pre-embryo.

The zona pellucida (ZP) is an acellular coating over the plasma membrane of the mature oocyte. It contains several proteins that are important for normal fertilization, including the block to polyspermy (Dulcibella, 1992). In some species, one such protein, ZP3, acts as a sperm receptor that sets in motion the acrosome reaction, which involves the release of enzymes necessary to penetrate the cell surface. The acrosome then binds ZP2 and penetrates the zona. After fertilization, conformational changes in ZP2 and ZP3 no longer allow sperm binding. Cortical granules, which contain hydrolytic enzymes, develop within the oocyte cytoplasm during follicle maturation. These also act to block polyspermy by altering the ZP sperm binding sites and probably through changes in the plasma membrane. We do not know the details of this process in humans; however, it seems that both the zona and plasma membrane are important (Shabanowitz & O'Rand, 1988a & b; Shabanowitz, 1990). It is possible that the release of those enzymes creates a plasma membrane block to polyspermy, which is partial in humans. Plasma membrane components also are important, as well as the release of cytoplasmic granules, which cannot take place until the germinal vesicle breakdown stage. Data from human IVF programs suggest that fertilization can occur before this stage, but rates of polyspermy are increased (Shabanowitz & O'Rand, 1988b; Shabanowitz, 1990).

After penetration of the zona, the plasma membranes of the sperm and egg fuse. The molecular events are poorly understood. It appears, however, that there probably are specific proteins that allow for receptor ligand-like interaction. Bronson and Fusi showed that sperm penetration of the zona-free hamster oocyte could be prevented by the addition of various peptides containing the arginine-glycine-aspartine amino acid sequence, a sequence present in fibronectins, which potentially could recognize the integrin family of receptors (Boldt, 1992; Bronson & Fusi, 1990). Data also suggest that fusion sets in motion activation of a G-protein initiated sequence of protein phosphorylations that ultimately increases intracellular calcium (Boldt, 1992). Cytostatic factor, which has been important in halting the second meiosis, then is ablated by the rise of intracellular calcium which allows completion of meiosis and extrusion of the second polar body.

Since the role of these putative regulators of meiosis is as yet not well-defined, there are no known associated clinical sequelae. Malfunction of one of these proteins or purines, however, theoretically could interfere with normal meiosis and cause polyploidy. There are well-known problems with meiosis which do predispose women to pregnancy loss.

During the process of "crossing over" in the first meiosis, if uneven portions of homologous chromosomes are exchanged, an unbalanced translocation results. Nondisjunction, or unequal distribution of chromosomes, occurs frequently, especially in gametes from older patients. It can lead to aneuploidy in the gamete and subsequent embryo, and this is a common cause of early pregnancy loss. These types of chromosomal problems are usually random events. Some patients harbor balanced translocations of chromosomal material, or another abnormality such as ring chromosome or sex chromosome mosaicism, which will predispose to recurrent pregnancy loss. Only about 3% to 8% of couples with recurrent pregnancy loss have these types of karyotypic abnormalities, and their histories usually include pregnancy losses interspersed with normal pregnancies (Speroff et al., 1994).

Random spontaneous abortion is far more common than are recurrent losses. Data from karyotypic analysis of spontaneous abortuses show that about 60% to 65% are abnormal. The most frequent abnormality is autosomal trisomy, especially trisomies of chromosomes 13, 16, 18, and 21 (Boue et al., 1975; Speroff et al., 1994). Most likely, these trisomies result from nondisjunction of chromosomes during meiosis, which is more common in older women. By contrast, polyploidy is no more common in older women and accounts for about 25% of karyotypic abnormalities. This can result from abnormal fertilization either by more than one sperm or by a sperm which has not completed meiosis (Boue et al., 1975; Kaufman, 1991). Oocytes lacking in zona pellucida activity or with insufficient release of cortical granular enzymes may allow for fertilization by more than one sperm. Fertilization of immature oocytes *in vitro* is more likely to result in polyspermy. Some have attributed the use of gonadotropin therapy to release and fertilization of cytogenetically abnormal oocytes (Collins, 1991; van Blerkom, 1991).

Until there is a better understanding of the cellular events which are involved in meiosis and fertilization, little can be offered therapeutically. For many patients, the knowledge that chromosomal problems are usually random events is important in offering them hope that the next pregnancy will be normal.

Hormonal Causes of Pregnancy Loss:
Luteal Phase Defect

Ideally, a cohort of healthy ovarian follicles is recruited at the end of each menstrual cycle in which there is no conception, a process mediated principally by follicle stimulating hormone (FSH). Secretion of relatively large amounts of FSH continues into the early follicular phase and begins to decline in the mid-follicular phase, as estradiol and inhibin from an emerging dominant follicle cause feedback inhibition. Luteinizing hormone (LH) also declines during this time because of negative feedback. As the follicle reaches a critical size, it secretes large amounts of estrogen, which triggers positive feedback at the hypothalamic pituitary axis, and the gonadotropin surge begins (Speroff et al., 1994). This final release of hormones is necessary for oocyte maturation (germinal vesicle breakdown and resumption of meiosis). The estrogen which is secreted by the granulosa cells and progesterone from the corpus luteum induces histologic changes within the endometrium that are important for implantation to occur. During the follicular phase, the glands, stroma, and blood supply of the endometrium proliferate. The secretion of progesterone then induces glandular secretion and decidual stromal changes, which are maximal several days after ovulation, in the so-called window of implantation (Giudice, 1994 & 1995). In patients with luteal phase defect, the progestational effects are too brief or of insufficient amount to allow or maintain implantation.

The early work of Segar Jones described the association of poorly developed endometrium with decreased progesterone secretion and infertility (Jones, 1976). The clinical definition of such a population poses certain problems, though it is widely accepted that this is an important physiologic entity. Horta and colleagues described a group of patients with recurrent spontaneous abortions and lower progesterone levels in the luteal phase of nonconception cycles (Horta, Fernandez, Soto de Leon, & Cortes-Gallegos, 1977). However, random progesterone levels may be difficult to interpret because they vary considerably throughout the day (Fujimoto, Clifton, Cohen, & Soules, 1990). Therefore, the endometrial biopsy is more likely to give an accurate picture of the sum total effect of daily progesterone secretion (Wentz, 1980). Since out-of-phase biopsies are found in anywhere from 4% to 20% of normal ovulatory women (Li, Dockery, Rogers, & Cooke, 1990; Grunfeld et al., 1989), a repeat biopsy is usually suggested for confirmation. Disagreements arise over timing of the biopsy, whether late or midluteal biopsy is preferred. Wentz and Jones have argued for late luteal biopsy, because the cumulative effect of progesterone should be more apparent (Jones, 1976; Wentz, 1980). Recent knowledge about the importance of physiologic events that occur at the time of implantation has led some to argue for midluteal biopsy. Despite these disagreements, few would argue that the endometrial environment is critical for successful embryo implantation. The development of proper endometrial environment depends largely on events that lead up to ovulation.

The secretion of gonadotropins and steroids during the follicular phase is important in subsequent luteal function. DiZerega and co-workers produced luteal defects in the monkey model by creating cycles with low levels of gonadotropins which barely were sufficient to permit ovulation (DiZerega et al., 1981). Clinical studies of women with a short interval (<10 days) between the LH surge and menses showed that they are more likely to have poorly developed ovarian follicles before ovulation, by ultrasound, and lower circulating concentrations of FSH and estrogen (Dodson, MacNaughton, & Coutts, 1975; Geisthovel, Skubsch, Zabel, Schillinger, & Breckwoldt, 1983). Another entity associated with luteal phase defect is hyperprolactinemia, which may suppress normal gonadotropin secretion and corpus luteum function (McNatty, Sawers, & McNeilly, 1974). These studies suggest that inadequate luteal phase results from inadequate gonadotropin stimulation before ovulation.

Recent data suggest that excessive amounts of LH also can produce a tendency to miscarry, as well as luteal phase defects. Elevated LH level (>10 miu/ml) on Day 8 of a normal menstrual cycle predicted infertility and miscarriage in a group of 161 normal women who were followed prospectively for 18 months (Regan, Owen, & Jacobs, 1990). Others report that chronic elevation of LH is associated with higher rates of spontaneous abortion in women with polycystic ovaries and in women undergoing IVF (Stanger & Yovich, 1985). The mechanism of these losses may be interference with the normal progress of meiosis, or there may be endometrial dysynchrony produced by the early production of progesterone stimulated by excessive LH. Therapy should be individualized according to the specific hormonal defect.

Ovulation induction agents often can overcome inadequate gonadotropin secretion by promoting the maturation of more than one follicle, which results in an increase in the total amount of estrogen and progesterone secretion (Guzick & Zeleznik, 1990). Progesterone supplementation also has been used successfully to prevent miscarriage in several uncontrolled studies (Daya, Ward, & Burrows, 1988; Tho, Byrd, & McDonough, 1979). Patients with elevated LH levels can be treated with gonadotropin-releasing hormone agonists and gonadotropin injections. The biological mechanisms of this entity now are being investigated on a cellular level.

Endometrial Factors

In recent years, several growth factors and cytokines, induced by estrogen and progesterone, were described as important in establishing pregnancy. Growth factors are peptides or polypeptides that can activate cell division, differentiation, or growth arrest by interaction with specific membrane receptors. Numerous growth factors have been described in the human endometrium, many of which are thought to regulate endometrial proliferation and differentiation. These include epidermal growth factor, transforming growth factor, and insulin-like growth factors I and II (IGF-I and II) (Giudice, 1995). It is likely that they play a role in implantation because they are expressed cyclically in the endometrium. Colony stimulating factor (CSF-1) is present in the human endometrium in increased amounts in the mid-secretory phase, with further marked increases in early pregnancy (Giudice, 1995). Its importance for implantation is in part suggested by a mouse model (op/op) in which a null mutation for the CSF gene results in infertile mice with low rates of blastocyst implantation and decreased fetal viability (Cross, Werb, & Fisher, 1994). Treatment of these mice with CSF-1 allows them normal fertility. It is believed that the CSF in the endometrium interacts with a CSF receptor present on trophectoderm to allow attachment. Characterization of these growth factors in human endometrium is underway; at present, their exact role is unknown (Cross et al., 1994; Giudice, 1994).

Cytokines are immmunoregulatory proteins that act primarily as autocrine or paracrine regulators rather than as hormones. Leukemia inhibitory factor (LIF) is one such cytokine, and it is present in the human endometrium in a cycle-dependent manner (Cross et al., 1994; Giudice 1995). Data from a mouse model show that females who are homozygous for an LIF mutation cannot implant blastocysts. Transfer of the same blastocysts into the uteri of wild-type mice resulted in pregnancy and delivery (Stewart et al., 1992). Other data suggest that endometrial LIF may induce embryo-derived metalloproteinases, which are important in trophoblast invasion (Cross et al., 1994). LIF also can increase the synthesis of fibronectin, a cell adhesion molecule, by human trophoblasts (Nachtigall, Kliman, Feinberg, Meaddough, & Arici, 1994).

Various endometrial proteins no doubt also are involved in implantation. One of the most interesting is the integrins, a group of cell adhesion molecules (Lessey et al., 1992). Human endometria express several integrins throughout the menstrual cycle, but during the window of implantation, alpha 5 beta 3 integrins normally appear. Human trophoblasts also express these integrins, and it is thought that binding occurs as an early step in implantation (Damsky et al., 1994). Women with luteal phase defect often lack alpha 5 beta 3 integrins during the window of implantation. Lack of this protein also has been used to explain infertility in patients with mild endometriosis and patients with hydrosalpinges (Lessey et al., 1994a & b). The details of the interaction between endometrial and trophoblast integrins are unknown. It is likely that both integrin-to-integrin and also integrin-to-extracellular matrix interactions are involved (Cross et al., 1994). This cellular marker likely will prove clinically useful in our understanding and treating luteal phase defect and the resultant infertility and pregnancy loss.

Vascular Factors

The earliest development of the human placenta starts with the growth and differentiation of the trophoblast cells in the blastocyst. Soon after embryo attachment, the trophoblast cells develop into two layers that become the syncytiotrophoblast and the cytotrophoblasts. The syncytial layer is the invasive layer that develops a system of lacunae that form the basis for the uteroplacental circulation. Cytotrophoblasts extend into the syncytium forming a column which becomes the primary stem villous, about 2 weeks after conception (Genbacev White, Gavin, & Miller, 1993). During this time, syncytiotrophoblasts must invade the maternal spiral arteries, such that the embryo actually is separated from maternal circulation by a shell of trophoblast cells (Jaffe & Woods, 1993; Kurjak, Zudenigo, Predanic, & Kupesic, 1994). The intervillous space then is perfused intermittently, but may contain other fluid, during the first trimester. Failure to establish this pattern may result in abortion, growth restriction, or pre-eclampsia.

Recent advances in ultrasound technology have allowed *in vivo* assessment of early placentation. Data from color Doppler ultrasound studies of normal women show decreased resistance index in the decidual spiral arteries and the absence of blood flow in the intervillous space (Jaffe & Woods, 1993). By contrast, patients with missed abortion or spontaneous abortion fail to show this pattern (Jaffe, 1994; Kurjak et al., 1994). While our current knowledge does not allow this to be used therapeutically, it may be useful in certain diagnostic settings, particularly where there is a question of blood flow.

Anatomic Factors

Anatomic distortion of the uterus may predispose to pregnancy loss. The incidence of hysterosalpingographic abnormalities of the uterus is about 15% to 30% in series of women with recurrent pregnancy loss (Harger, Archer, Marchese, Muracca-Clemens, & Garver, 1983; Stray-Pedersen & Stray-Pedersen, 1984). Uterine myomas, the most common abnormality, potentially can disrupt the blood supply of the implantation site and create biochemical changes in the endometrium (Buttram & Reiter, 1981; Lev-Toaff et al., 1987). Submucous myomas, in particular, frequently are identified in patients with recurrent spontaneous abortions. Uncontrolled data show excellent term pregnancy rates after corrective surgery (Buttram & Reiter, 1981; Stray-Pedersen & Stray-Pedersen, 1984). Recent basic science studies have suggested a potential mechanism through which myomas might prevent proper implantation. Explants of leiomyomata secrete IGF-I and II, *in vitro*, in greater concentrations than normal myometrium (Rein, Friedman, Pandian, & Heffner, 1990). Similarly, expression of these two growth factors is increased in myomas compared with normal myometrium (Boehm et al., 1990). The clinical significance of these findings is unknown, but some mammalian pre-implantation blastocysts can bind IGF-I and II (Heyner, Smith, & Schultz, 1989; Mattson, Rosenblum, Smith, & Heyner, 1988).

Intrauterine adhesions can result from curettage, surgery, or infection. In severe cases, amenorrhea results. However, those with mild to moderate adhesions often miscarry, presumably due to poor blood supply and abnormal endometrium. The diagnosis is made by hysterosalpingogram or hysteroscopy. The latter is the preferred method of adhesiolysis (Lewis & Abramowicz, 1994).

In women with congenital Muellerian anomalies of the uterus, there is an increased tendency toward early pregnancy loss attributed to difficulties with establishing an adequate blood supply. Histologic studies of uterine septa show thin endometrial tissue with decreased vascularity. Sonographic data show higher rates of pregnancy loss if implantation occurs on the septum (Candiani, Fedele, Zamberletti, DeVirgiliis, & Carinelli, 1983; Fedele, Dorta, Brioschi, Giudici, & Candiani, 1989). Less common Müllerian anomalies such as unicornuate uterus and bicornuate uterus also appear to predispose to early pregnancy loss, though less is known of the mechanism. Resection of an intrauterine septum or possibly metroplasty should be considered in patients with a history of pregnancy losses (Lewis & Abramowicz, 1994).

Lastly, diethylstilbestrol (DES) exposure *in utero* is associated with about a two-fold relative risk of early pregnancy loss (Swan, 1992). There are characteristic anatomic uterine changes described which are more common in DES-exposed women with poor reproductive histories, such as T-shaped uterus, hypoplastic cavity, and periosteal adhesion bands. It is not known how these anatomic differences affect ability to carry a pregnancy; in animal models, however, endometrial secretory proteins can be altered for life by *in utero* exposure to DES (Maier, Newbold, & McLachlan, 1985).

Environmental Factors

The conceptus is comprised of rapidly dividing cells that are particularly sensitive to toxins or drugs. Even before conception, a variety of agents can damage germ cells during meiosis, predisposing to aneuploidy. It is impossible to review potential toxins comprehensively within the scope of this chapter. Nonetheless, some of the more common exposures from home, work, and medical therapy are discussed. (The reader is referred to Chapter 8 for an in-depth discussion of teratogenic exposures and their impact on pregnancy.)

Some of the most common exposures implicated in pregnancy loss are alcohol, tobacco, and heavy caffeine intake (Armstrong, McDonald, & Sloan, 1992; Harlap & Shiono, 1980). Much of the data are hard to interpret because of the inclusion of women with multiple exposures and the difficulty without defining exposure doses. For example, alcohol has direct cytotoxic effects, seen *in vitro*. However, the threshold dose at which this is clinically important in humans is unknown (Brent & Beckman, 1994). Miscarriage is more common in women who consume large amounts of ethanol, but this same group of women also are more likely to smoke cigarettes and have poor nutrition. Caffeine also is likely to cause abortions at an unknown threshold dose. In animal studies, doses of 60-300 mg/kg (>9 cups coffee) per day caused increased early pregnancy loss. Data in humans are conflicting, but they seem to suggest that moderate consumption of caffeine in divided doses would account for only a very small number of early pregnancy losses (Nehlig & Debry, 1994).

By contrast, cigarette smoking appears to predispose to early abortion in a dose-related manner (Walsh, 1994). Tobacco smoke contains over 4,000 chemicals, including such known toxins as nicotine, carbon monoxide, cyanide, and cadmium (Naeye, 1981; U.S. Department of Health and Human Services, 1980). Smoking probably increases the risk of abortion by 20% for every ten cigarettes smoked per day (Armstrong et al., 1992). Since smokers are more likely to drink alcohol or to ingest large amounts of caffeine, these effects may be compounded (Walsh, 1994).

Many patients are concerned about occupational exposures and their possible relationship to miscarriage. This is a very difficult area to study because of problems with defining magnitude of exposure and controlling for confounding lifestyle variables. Nonetheless, there are some agents that seem to have consistent effects. Anesthetic gas exposure during pregnancy apparently increases risk of abortion in patients who undergo surgery and for health care workers (Tannenbaum & Goldberg, 1985). Several studies of male health workers, especially in dentistry, showed increased abortion rates after paternal exposure (Guirguiss, Pelmear, Roy, & Wong, 1990; Savitz, Sonnenfeld, & Olshan, 1994). Heavy metal exposure, especially mercury and lead, may cause spontaneous abortion (Rom, 1976; Savitz et al., 1994). Studies in which urinary levels of mercury were documented among male workers showed increased rates of abortion among their partners (Alcser, Brix, Fine, Kallenbach, & Wolfe, 1989; Lindbohm et al., 1991). Similar studies of men who were exposed to lead at work seem to imply a threshold effect for this agent on spermatogenesis (Lindbohm et al., 1991). However, a large epidemiologic study of women living near a lead smelter in Yugoslavia did not show an increase in abortion over a considerable range of blood lead levels (Murphy et al., 1990).

Exposure of either sex to industrial solvents may increase the risk of miscarriage. The solvents and other chemicals which are used in rubber manufacturing and petroleum refinement increased risk of abortion in surveys of exposed workers (Lindbohm et al., 1991; Savitz et al., 1994). Tetrachloroethylene, an agent used in dry cleaning, may increase risk of abortion with maternal but not paternal exposure (Speroff et al., 1994a; McDonald et al., 1989). Video display terminals were thought to cause spontaneous abortion after reports that electromagnetic radiation could induce damage in chick embryos (Delpizzo, 1994; Ubeda, Leal, Trillo, Jimenez, &

Delgado, 1983). Most epidemiologic studies, however, have not shown an effect (Delpizzo, 1994; Schnorr et al., 1991).

Medications or other therapies that affect cell metabolism are particularly damaging to the rapidly developing conceptus. Chemotherapeutic agents, such as methotrexate, would be an obvious example. Isotretinoin (Accutane®) is a commonly used dermatologic agent that increases risk of abortion (Lammer et al., 1985). Ionizing radiation in therapeutic doses increases the risk of abortion; however, the usual exposure from diagnostic tests (<5 rads) does not (Brent & Beckman, 1994). Similarly, most radioisotopes which are used diagnostically do not increase the risk of abortion because of the very small amount of radiation that actually reaches the implantation site (Brent & Beckman, 1994).

Immune Causes

Autoimmune conditions are those in which cellular or humoral immunity is directed against the body's own antigens. A particular autoimmune condition, anticardiolipin antibody syndrome, has gained considerable attention in recent years because of its association with spontaneous abortion, pre-eclampsia, and intrauterine fetal death. This syndrome is defined by the presence of circulating antibodies to cardiolipin and/or inappropriate coagulation parameters, plus poor reproductive outcome, systemic lupus erythematosus, or spontaneous thrombosis. Affected patients have circulating antibodies to cardiolipin, a phospholipid found in beef heart. Because these antibodies often cross react with other phospholipids, such as phosphotidylserine and phosphotidylinositol, the syndrome is sometimes called the antiphospholipid antibody syndrome (Harris, 1990).

Many patients are positive for the lupus anticoagulant, so named because the property of prolonged coagulation times in certain laboratory tests first was described in patients with systemic lupus erythematosus. The lupus anticoagulant (LAC) is a circulating antibody complex which cross reacts with the phospholipids necessary for the prothrombin-activator complex, which is an important determinant of *in vitro* coagulation. The tests used to look for such activity are the activated partial thromboplastin time, the dilute Russell viper venom test, and the kaolin clotting time (Out, Bruinse, & Derkson, 1991). Although positive findings for these laboratory tests suggest an inability to develop normal clotting, paradoxically, these patients experience thrombotic episodes. LAC binds to the phospholipid component of the endothelial cells or platelets, initiating cell damage, release of thromboxane, and thrombotic episodes. This can cause decidual and placental vasculitis, and infarction. But, the presence of antibodies or LAC alone is not sufficient to predict poor pregnancy outcome.

Low levels of cardiolipin antibodies were found in 6% of 1,520 normal pregnant women (Harris & Spinatto, 1990). Therefore, clinical history is important in interpreting the laboratory data. It is important to detect any history of systemic lupus erythematosus, unexplained thrombotic episodes, or recurrent spontaneous pregnancy losses. Patients with such histories have a higher prevalence of LAC or cardiolipin antibodies, and they are more likely to have a poor outcome (Harris, 1990; Reece et al., 1990). It is likely that IgG antibodies correlate better with the clinical outcome than IgM (Harris, 1990). It also is important to be familiar with people at the laboratory where the test is analyzed. Despite international efforts at standardization, there may be considerable interlaboratory variation (Harris, 1990; Peaceman, Silver, MacGregor, & Socol, 1992).

Treatment includes prednisone, aspirin, or heparin. Recent trials have studied the use of intravenous immunoglobulin therapy. Two randomized trials compared prednisone to aspirin with or without heparin (Cowchock, Reece, Balaban, Branch, & Plouffe, 1992; Out et al., 1992). Both studies showed similar outcomes for the two types of therapy, with a significantly higher rate of serious side effects seen from the steroids. Several investigators have used intravenous gamma globulin, which may act nonspecifically to reduce antibody production (Out et al., 1991). The outcomes were satisfactory; there are no controlled or large series, however. Few data are available on the natural course of this condition. Out et al. (1991) summarized outcomes in 19 pregnancies where no treatment was given. Despite the history of multiple pregnancy losses in most patients, only three women experienced loss in the current pregnancy. Because the number of patients in Out et al.'s review was quite small, and the laboratory data were not standardized, it is wise to exercise caution.

Alloimmune Causes

Alloimmune responses are immune reactions to tissues from another individual of the same species. In pregnancy, maternal alloimmune responses include the production of antibodies to human leukocyte antigen (HLA) antigens. About 20% of primiparas and 40% of multiparous women make antibodies against paternal HLA antigens that are inherited by the fetus (Ober, 1995). In cases where the fetus and mother have the same antigens, antibodies will not be produced. One school of thought suggests that the maternal immune system must recognize the fetus as immunologically foreign by the HLA system and produce blocking antibody to enable the pregnancy to progress.

Human leukocyte antigen sharing between parents initially was proposed as a cause for lack of immune response in the form of blocking antibody. There were discrepancies on the matter of whether Class I or II HLA antigens were important (Ober, 1995). An interesting prospective study by Ober on the Hutterites, an inbred religious community, found no couples with clinically recognized recurrent spontaneous abortion and only a small (though significant) effect on family size of sharing HLA antigens. Median family size was 6.5 among those who shared HLA-DR and 9.5 among those who did not. It is not known whether this represents a direct effect of sharing HLA antigens or whether this is an indirect effect of other genes in the same region. In other mammals, there are loci on chromosome six near the HLA determinants which influence other aspects of reproduction: spermatogenesis, embryo cleavage rates, and fetal development (Ober, 1995).

Leukocyte immunization using white blood cells from the father has been proposed as a means to boost the immune response in women with recurrent pregnancy loss who lack blocking factor or antibody (Beer, Quebbeman, Ayers, & Haines, 1981). Since the initial hypothesis, there have been four randomized, controlled studies, only one of which found benefit from the therapy (Mowbray et al., 1985). A multicenter, NIH-sponsored trial currently is in progress to study this issue further.

Recent work has focused on the local regulation of the immune response, largely mediated by cytokines. The trophoblasts at the maternal-fetal interface express HLA-G nonclassical antigens. These may play a role in suppression of the natural killer T-cells found within the endometrium (Cross et al., 1994). In mice, the decidual T-cells have been characterized during early pregnancy. The cytokines produced by these cells were classified as T-helper 2 (TH-2), which promote circulating antibody response and minimize T-helper 1 (TH-1) type responses. The typical TH-1 response promotes cytotoxicity and delayed hypersensitivity (Dudley, Chen, Mitchell, Daynes, & Araneo, 1993). Peripheral blood mononuclear cells from women with recurrent spontaneous abortions produce TH-1-type cytokines in response to trophoblast antigens, which are toxic to embryos *in vitro* (Hill, Polgar, Harlow, & Anderson, 1992; Hill, Polgar, & Anderson, 1995). By contrast, mononuclear cells from normal women and men produced TH-2-type cytokines, after the same antigenic stimulus. These cytokines are found at the maternal-fetal interface in mice and may play a role in suppressing the cellular response to allow the pregnancy to implant (Hill et al., 1995). Studies such as these will be necessary to evaluate recurrent pregnancy loss completely in the future.

Infection

Numerous pathogens have been implicated in the etiology of spontaneous abortion. Establishment of causation often is difficult, especially when the infection is chronic. By contrast, there are several pathogens which cause pregnancy loss by either direct or indirect effects. Some of the microbiology and proposed mechanisms will be reviewed.

Chlamydia trachomatous causes acute and chronic infection of the endometrium, which could interfere with implantation. Acute infection causes cell death in the endometrium and other parts of the reproductive tract. It is not known whether the infection or the resultant immune response is responsible for the sequelae of this infection, and there is evidence that the immune response is modulated with time, allowing an infection to become chronic. Chlamydia infection can induce the production of TH-1-type cytokines with time, which could potentially impair embryo development (Cooper, 1995; Hill et al., 1995). It is not known whether this is the mechanism, but several investigators have observed an increased prevalence of previous pelvic inflammatory disease or circulating chlamydia antibodies among women with recurrent spontaneous abortion (Heisterberg, 1993; Stray-Pedersen & Stray-Pedersen, 1984). This has not been confirmed in all studies (Harrison et al., 1983; Plouffe et al., 1992).

Mycoplasma hominis and *Ureaplasma urealyticum* have been implicated in recurrent pregnancy loss, prematurity, and premature rupture of the membranes (Stray-Pedersen, Eng, & Reikvam, 1978). Treatment does not necessarily effect outcome (Harwick, Purcell, Iuppa, & Fekety, 1970). Recent data continue to show the controversy over the importance of Ureaplasma urealyticum in spontaneous abortion, as it was found more frequently in the abortion specimens of 63 patients with spontaneous loss than among specimens from 21 patients undergoing elective terminations (Joste, Kundsin, & Genest, 1994).

Certain primary viral infections can cause pregnancy loss. Cytomegalovirus (CMV) has been proposed as a cause of random abortion (Summers, 1994). Data from large series, however, suggest that this is rare (Stagno et al., 1982). While it is possible for CMV to be transmitted from maternal decidual tissue to the fetus in the first trimester, this does not necessarily prove causation (van Lijnschoten et al., 1994). Herpes simplex virus (HSV) is another virus which is implicated in pregnancy loss. However, recurrent HSV infection probably is not an important cause of early pregnancy loss (Summers, 1994). Infection with the human immunodeficiency virus (HIV) does not seem to increase rates of early pregnancy loss among asymptomatic women (Minkoff et al., 1990; Selwyn et al., 1989).

Conclusion

The biology of early pregnancy loss is a multifaceted problem that relates to multiple areas of physiology. The most common cause of spontaneous abortion is genetic abnormality, which usually is a random event. Implantation problems also are common and may result from hormonal abnormalities, or vascular or anatomic distortion of the intrauterine milieu. Exciting new research in immunology and growth factors likely will become critical to our understanding of early events in pregnancy.❏

Case Study 1-2

First Trimester Pregnancy Loss

F.D. is a 36-year-old woman who presented in 1994 with a history of pregnancy loss and infertility. Her only two prior pregnancies occurred in 1990 and 1991, respectively. Both pregnancies ended spontaneously at 6 to 7 weeks gestation. F.D. became depressed after her second loss, and she was fearful of attempting another pregnancy. But she changed her mind in 1992 and sought medical care from her physician in 1993. Previous workups suggested a luteal-phase defect. F.D. had regular menses every 26 days with ovulation on day 14 or 15. Serum progesterone levels were >10 ng/ml, but two late luteal-phase endometrial biopsies were 4 to 5 days out of phase. Circulating levels of prolactin and thyroid function tests were within normal limits.

A diagnosis of luteal-phase defect was made, and F.D. was treated with clomiphene citrate, eventually at a dose of 100 mg daily for 5 days, and progesterone suppositories were added during her luteal phase. A diagnostic laparoscopy showed minimal endometriosis (peritoneal surface of the posterior cul de sac), a normal-appearing uterus, and patent fallopian tubes. F.D.'s husband's semen analysis also was normal. F.D.'s past medical history was unremarkable except for cigarette smoking, about one pack per day, which the patient was advised to stop. The couple then was referred to our center for further evaluation and care.

The endometrial biopsy was repeated during a cycle in which F.D. had taken clomiphene and progesterone. A 4-day lag was noted between the pathology report and time of ovulation. Gonadotropin therapy was begun with luteal-phase progesterone supplementation, and the patient promptly conceived on the first cycle. Beta hCG levels rose starting 2 weeks after ovulation. F.D. began to bleed and cramp 1 week later and her hCG levels began to decline, however. Further evaluation for causes of pregnancy loss was carried out. Cervical cultures were negative. Serum levels of anticardiolipin antibody were slightly increased (IgG at 26 gpl; normal is <23 gpl), and the lupus anticoagulant was negative. Karyotype of both partners was normal. A hysterosalpingogram showed a slightly arcuate uterus. F.D. was started on aspirin therapy. Her circulating progesterone levels were 30 ng/ml in the luteal phase. F.D. conceived again, but she miscarried once again at about the same point (early first trimester). A hysteroscopy was performed, and F.D.'s intrauterine septum was resected.

Commentary

The problems or factors that may be associated with this patient's recurrent spontaneous miscarriages include luteal phase defects, arcuate uterus, mildly elevated circulating anticardiolipin antibody, and minimal endometriosis.

Her miscarriages occurred at 6 to 7 weeks gestation (4 to 5 weeks after ovulation), and her endometrial dating using both ovulation time and the next menstrual period support luteal phase inadequacy as a possible contributing factor to her miscarriages. However, failure to sustain gestation after the luteal phase inadequacy has been corrected with gonadotropin therapy and progesterone suggests some other etiologic factor. Nevertheless, I would consider adding human chorionic gonadotropin (hCG) in doses of 5,000 IU intramuscularly 4 days after ovulation, and monitoring her serum hCG and progesterone serially (twice a week) from around the time of anticipated missed period. A transvaginal ultrasound should be performed if the woman's hCG levels exceed 1,500 mIU/mL, to demonstrate an intrauterine gestational sac and subsequently fetal cardiac activity.

Elevated levels of anticardiolipin antibody are strongly linked with fetal loss (DeCarolis et al., 1994). Although aspirin appropriately was given and pregnancy ensued, this patient again miscarried between 6 and 7 weeks gestation. Study of her anticardiolipin antibody levels ought to be repeated while the woman is on the aspirin therapy. Further evaluation of autoimmune factors might shed some light on the prognosis of future, if not on specific, therapeutic plans. A positive test for beta 2-glycoprotein I (beta 2 GPI)-dependent anticardiolipin antibodies is a better marker of miscarriage risk than the beta 2 GPI-independent anticardiolipin antibody (Aoki et al., 1994). Her serum could be tested for anti-ganglioside-GM3 antibodies. A negative test is associated with a higher chance of a live birth (94%, compared with 46% live births if the test is positive) (Ozaki, Aoki, Aoyama, & Kunimatsu, 1995). Again for prognostic purposes, HLA typing of the mother might be of some value, since maternal HLA allogenotype DR1/Br, DR3, and DR10 have increased risk and predisposition to unexplained recurrent fetal loss (Christiansen et al., 1995). The Th1 embryotoxic factor test might be worth doing for its prognostic value if positive, rather than any proven specific therapy that can be employed currently.

Debatable, and considered experimental, most treatments of alloimmunity-associated recurrent spontaneous miscarriage have produced inconclusive, encouraging, or conflicting results. Examination of several trials leads to the conclusion that immunization of the female partner with paternal leukocytes has a small treatment effect of 8% to 10% of affected couples, but live birth rates were lower with positive anticardiolipin antibodies and also for older females (Recurrent Miscarriage Immunotherapy Trialist Group, 1994). Given the age of this particular patient and her positive anticardiolipin antibodies, she is unlikely to benefit from alloimmunization with paternal leukocytes. Limited trials with intravenous (IV) immunoglobulin (Ig) have suggested that either it is ineffective (Mueller-Eckhardt, 1994) or it may be of some value (Coulam, 1994) in preventing recurrent spontaneous abortion. Therefore, such a treatment cannot be considered for this patient. More likely to be of value is treatment with aspirin (minidose of 60 to 80 mg daily) combined with prednisolone (40 mg daily). It is preferable to start this treatment 6 to 8 weeks before initiating ovulation. The serum levels of anticardiolipin and anti-phosphatidylserine antibodies are worth repeating after 6 to 8 weeks of therapy for a decline in level. Treatment with prednisolone combined with aspirin reduced antiphospholipid antibody titers within 8 weeks and was effective in achieving successful pregnancy and preventing fetal growth restriction (Hasegawa et al., 1992). Cowchock, Reece, Balaban, Branch, and Plouffe (1992) reported that heparin (prophylactic dose) plus aspirin is preferable to prednisolone plus aspirin. Heparin compensates for activated protein C, which inactivates clotting factors Va and VIIIa; it is the increased or accelerated thrombosis or infarction of the trophoblast or placenta in early implantation and pregnancy that leads to the early and even late pregnancy losses.

Whereas hysteroscopic resection of the patient's uterine septum was appropriate, hysterosalpingogram probably should have been considered earlier, after the second or third miscarriage. Even if the arcuate or septate uterus were responsible for any of her miscarriages, this would be difficult to establish one way or the other, in the absence of sonograms to demonstrate a septal implantation site. Recent analysis of 188 congenital uterine anomalies detected in 1,200 women with reproductive losses indicated a rate of 84% for successful pregnancy maintenance after metroplasty, compared with 94.4% spontaneous first-trimester miscarriage in control groups with anomalies (Makino, Umeuchi, Nakada, Nozawa, & Iizuka, 1992). Therefore, given that the patient had four miscarriages shortly after implantation, and that hysteroscopic resection of uterine septum can be performed easily, such metroplasty could have a positive impact on future pregnancy implantation. An intravenous pyelogram also should be carried out, as renal-tract anomalies commonly are associated with Müllerian anomalies.

While the karyotypes of both partners were normal, karyotyping of the third or the fourth pregnancy should have been performed. Karyotyping for this patient should be performed, and she should be instructed to save expelled tissues if she miscarries again.

Although older reports have implicated endometriosis in increased spontaneous miscarriage, more recent analysis suggests no increase. Whereas endometriosis may have an increased association with luteal-phase defect, the latter has been and will continue to be corrected with the gonadotropin and progesterone therapy in this patient. Her minimal endometriosis is unlikely to contribute significantly to her pattern of recurrent miscarriage; so this does not warrant treatment, since pregnancy rates are the same irrespective of therapy in women with minimal endometriosis.

In summary, this patient's serum anticardiolipin antibodies study should be repeated, and her HLA allotype, serum anti-phosphatidylserine beta 2 GPI-dependent anticardiolipin, and antiganglioside-GM3 levels should be determined. An intravenous pyelogram should be performed. Aspirin (80 mg daily) and prednisolone (40 mg daily) can be initiated, and the anticardiolipin and anti-phosphatidylserine antibody levels should be repeated in 8 weeks. While the patient continues her aspirin and prednisolone therapy, ovulation induction with gonadotropins followed by hCG can be performed.

After ovulation, progesterone can be given for luteal support, and she should receive a dose of 5,000 IU hCG 4 days post-ovulation. Luteal phase serum progesterone levels should be determined. Serum hCG is determined 2 weeks after ovulation and repeated twice a week, together with serum progesterone. If the hCG titers exceed 1,500 mIU, then transvaginal sonography should be carried out to confirm an intrauterine pregnancy sac, to be followed later by a repeat ultrasound to demonstrate fetal cardiac activity. As for all women who are contemplating pregnancy, this woman should commence folic acid supplement even before she tries to get pregnant, and she should continue the supplements throughout pregnancy.
— *M. Yusoff Dawood, MD*

Case Study References

Aoki, K., Matsura, E., Sasa, H., Yagami, Y., Dudkiewicz, A.B., & Gleicher, N. (1994). Beta 2-glycoprotein I-dependent and -independent anticardiolipin antibodies in healthy pregnant women. *Human Reproduction, 9,* 1849-1851.

Christiansen, O.B., Andersen, H.H., Hojbjerre, M., Kruse, T.A., Lauritzen, S.L., & Grunnet, N. (1995). Maternal HLA Class II allogenotypes are markers for the predisposition to fetal losses in families of women with unexplained recurrent fetal loss. *European Journal of Immunogenetics, 22,* 323-334.

Coulam, C.B. (1994). Immunotherapy with intravenous immunoglobulin for treatment of recurrent pregnancy loss: American experience. *American Journal of Reproductive Immunology, 32,* 286-289.

Cowchock, F.S., Reece, A.E., Balaban, D., Branch, D.W., & Plouffe, L. (1992). Repeated fetal losses associated with antiphospholipid antibodies: A collaborative randomized trial comparing prednisolone with low-dose heparin treatment. *American Journal of Obstetrics and Gynecology, 166,* 1318-1323.

DeCarolis, S., Caruso, A., Ferrazzani, S., Carducci, B., DeSantis, L., & Mancuso, S. (1994). Poor pregnancy outcome and anticardiolipin antibodies. *Fetal Diagnosis Therapy, 9,* 296-299.

Hasegawa, I., Takakuwa, K., Goto, S., Yamada, K., Sekizuka, N., Kanazawa, K., & Tanaka, K. (1992). Effectiveness of prednisolone/aspirin therapy for recurrent aborters with antiphospholipid antibody. *Human Reproduction, 7,* 203-207.

Makino, T., Umeuchi, M., Nakada, K., Nozawa, S., & Iizuka, R. (1992). Incidence of congenital uterine anomalies in repeated reproductive wastage and prognosis for pregnancy after metroplasty. *International Journal of Fertility, 37,* 167-170.

Mueller-Eckhardt, G. (1994). Immunotherapy with intravenous immunoglobulin for prevention of recurrent pregnancy loss: European experience. *American Journal of Reproductive Immunology, 32,* 281-285.

Ozaki, Y., Aoki, K., Aoyama, T., & Kunimatsu, M. (1995). Clinical significance of anti-GM3 antibodies in recurrent pregnancy loss with elevated level of antiphospholipid antibodies. *American Journal of Reproductive Immunology, 3,* 234-242.

Recurrent Miscarriage Immunotherapy Trialist Group. (1994). Worldwide collaborative observational study and meta-analysis on allogenic leukocyte immunotherapy for recurrent spontaneous abortion. *American Journal of Reproductive Immunology, 32,* 55-72.

Case Study 2-2

Alloimmunity and Recurrent Miscarriage

J.M. was a 38-year-old G4 P1031 woman who presented in 1994 with long-standing infertility and recurrent pregnancy loss. The patient had practiced unprotected intercourse since 1981 and first consulted her physician about her infertility in 1983. J.M.'s hysterosalpingogram was normal, as was her husband's semen analysis. An intermittent short luteal phase was found on basal body temperature (BBT) charting, although her serum progesterone values and endometrial biopsy were normal. Serum prolactin, gonadotropins, and thyroid function tests also were normal. A diagnostic laparoscopy showed stage I (AFS) endometriosis, which was coagulated by laser. J.M. and her husband were treated empirically with several cycles of intrauterine insemination both with and without clomiphene citrate; but no conception occurred.

In 1987 and 1988, gonadotropin therapy with inseminations was begun. J.M. conceived, but unfortunately she suffered three early pregnancy losses. During each cycle, progesterone supplementation was used, and J.M.'s luteal phase progesterone levels ranged between 20 ng/ml and 50 ng/ml. Positive pregnancy tests were noted consistently 14 days after ovulation, and levels of hCG increased before the next 8 to 10 days before spontaneous loss. Karyotype of the couple's white blood cells was normal. There was no evidence of anticardiolipin antibodies, lupus anticoagulant, or cervical infection. J.M. was referred to a specialist in the immunology of pregnancy loss.

A battery of tests was performed to look for an alloimmune cause for J.M.'s pregnancy losses. HLA phenotyping was carried out, demonstrating that the couple shared A3 and DQw1 antigens. J.M. was negative for anti-lymphocytoxic antibodies, and her serum was without blocking activity in the mixed lymphocyte culture (MLC) test. She therefore was immunized with one unit of her husband's washed white blood cells, administered by subcutaneous, intradermal, and intravenous routes. J.M. further was treated with gonadotropins 2 weeks later, and she did conceive on that cycle. At 7 weeks gestation, transvaginal ultrasound showed three intrauterine sacs, one of which contained a viable fetus. The patient carried her pregnancy to term and had an uncomplicated delivery of a healthy baby boy.

In 1991, the couple began trying to have a second child, and again they presented to a physician in 1992 when they were unsuccessful. Repeat endometrial biopsy and semen analysis were normal. J.M. once again was treated with inseminations and, later, gonadotropins plus inseminations. Another biochemical pregnancy occurred during the second cycle of gonadotropin therapy. J.M. requested repeat lymphocyte transfusions. She was tested for antilymphocyte antibodies; these were negative, however. Repeat lymphocyte transfusion was performed.

Commentary

Recurrent early pregnancy loss can result from a variety of factors including uterine anomalies, endocrine dysfunction, chromosomal anomalies, infections, autoimmune abnormalities, and psychogenic and environmental influences (Daya, 1993). In addition, there now is increasing evidence to support an alloimmunologic mechanism for the losses, particularly those occurring in women with primary recurrent spontaneous miscarriage (RSM) (no pregnancy sustained beyond 20 weeks gestation).

Elevated levels of circulating natural killer (NK) cells, which can damage the trophoblast, have been observed in women with RSM (Clark, 1995). There is evidence to suggest that the cytotoxic action of NK cells occurs at the implantation site, where immunosuppressive activity is necessary if the resulting miscarriage is to be prevented. Several immunosuppressive mechanisms have been proposed to act at the maternal-fetal interface, to enable a successful pregnancy to occur. These mechanisms include progesterone activation of T-cells to secrete a protein that can suppress the cytolytic activity of NK cells; activation of T-cells to produce cytokines that can stimulate better growth of trophoblast; activation of T-helper cells preferentially along the Th 2 type pathway, which is protective, rather than the Th 1 pathway, which results in activation of tumor necrosis factor alpha producing cells that promote miscarriage; and activation of natural suppressor cells in the decidua to produce immunosuppressive factors (Daya, in press). These mechanisms appear to be necessary for pregnancy success, and it is likely that they are interrelated. Consequently, a failure in this alloimmune recognition process that is necessary to produce immunosuppression may be viewed as a partner-specific problem that results in pregnancy loss, and this may be immunologically modifiable.

Currently, there is no definitive method of making the diagnosis of alloimmune recognition failure, because sensitive diagnostic tests have not been developed yet. The belief that cytotoxic antipaternal, antilymphocytic antibodies (APLA) appear to be necessary for a successful outcome, however, leads one to conclude that this antibody test may be a useful discriminator.

Thus, women with RSM who have undergone complete evaluation with no obvious cause being identified and who have no detectable APLA are believed to have alloimmune recognition failure. In these women, exposure to paternal antigens via a nonuterine route should produce antibodies that can induce the appropriate protective immune responses at the materno-fetal site. Alternatively, intravenous immunoglobulin (IVIG) obtained from a large pool of donors should contain specific preformed antibodies to be an effective method of passive immunization.

Intravenous Immunoglobulin

The exact mechanism of action of IVIG in preventing miscarriage is not understood completely, but most likely it acts through its immunosuppressive properties. Recently, it was observed that the infusion of IVIG was associated with a decrease in the concentration and cytotoxic activity of NK cells within 7 days of treatment (Kwak, Kwak, Ainbinder, Ruiz, & Beer, 1996; Ruiz et al., 1996).

The first pilot study of IVIG showed promise, with an 86% success rate in women who had suffered two or more previous miscarriages (Mueller-Eckhardt, Heine, Neppert, Kunzel, & Mueller-Eckhardt, 1989). When the therapeutic effect of administering IVIG in pregnancy was evaluated in a multicentered, randomized study, however, there did not appear to be any improvement when compared with placebo (The German RSA/IVIG Group, 1994). In contrast, in another randomized study in which IVIG was commenced before pregnancy and continued every 28 days until at least 28 to 32 weeks of gestation, a significantly higher successful pregnancy rate was observed compared with placebo (Coulam, Krysa, Stern, & Bustillo, 1995). The difference in treatment protocols between the two studies may have accounted for the difference which was observed. The role of NK cell activity in miscarriage suggests that, for benefit to be derived, treatment should be commenced prior to implantation so that the cytotoxicity from NK cells can be minimized — if not eliminated. Observations that the NK cell suppressive effect of IVIG is evident 7 days after treatment is in keeping with this notion. Thus, based on the evidence that currently is available, it appears that IVIG is efficacious in women with recurrent miscarriage, provided that treatment is commenced before conception occurs and is continued every month until the end of the second trimester of pregnancy.

Leukocyte Immunization

Leukocyte immunization appears to occur by activating natural suppressor cells in the decidua and by boosting the production of cytokines produced in the Th 2 pathway. The efficacy of leukocyte immunization first was demonstrated more than 10 years ago, but since then several trials have been unable to support this observation. In part, conflicting observations can be explained on the basis of small numbers of participants and because of heterogeneity in the study samples (Clark & Daya, 1991). Recently, a worldwide collaborative study confirmed that leukocyte immunization was efficacious (The Recurrent Miscarriage Immunotherapy Trialists Group, 1994). Furthermore, by restricting analysis to the data from women with unexplained primary RSM and no evidence of APLA or autoimmune abnormalities, the likelihood of successful pregnancy was much higher (Daya, Gunby, & The Recurrent Miscarriage Immunotherapy Trialists Group, 1994). The effect of treatment is higher in women with more pregnancy losses, indicating that immunization is more efficacious in the more severe category of this disorder.

The challenge that awaits is for us to develop better diagnostic tests to identify those with alloimmune recognition failure, so that immunotherapy can provide the best chance of success. Also, long-term follow-up studies are necessary to identify whether treatment has any complications or adverse effects in the recipients or their offspring.

Psychological Impact

It is well-recognized that women who have miscarriages experience intense feelings of grief, helplessness, guilt, and anger. Acknowledging the loss that has occurred and providing support during the grieving process is essential in helping couples to cope with a miscarriage. Women mourn the loss of an unborn child in the same way that they would mourn the loss of a living child. Grieving after miscarriage is a complex process and may be difficult to resolve. Not acknowledging the seriousness of these feelings may encourage women to suppress them, with consequences that can last for a very long time.

Individualized attention and follow-up care provided by the physician are important components for a normal grieving process, and such interventions can significantly reduce the likelihood and severity of subsequent grief reactions and psychosomatic disorders. Couples should be encouraged to discuss their feelings and to ask questions. A sensitive and compassionate attitude is essential to the healing process. The first 3 months after miscarriage is the time during which the emotional impact is usually the greatest; couples should be advised not to plan on trying again for pregnancy until this period has passed. Thereafter, they should be encouraged to attempt pregnancy, because their prognosis for a successful outcome with appropriate therapy is excellent.

— *Professor Salim Daya, MD*

Case Study References

Clark, D.A. (1995). Is there an immunological cause of repeated pregnancy wastage? *Advances in Obstetrics and Gynecology, 3,* 321-342.

Clark, D.A., & Daya, S. (1991). Trials and tribulation in the treatment of recurrent spontaneous abortion. *American Journal of Reproductive Immunology, 25,* 18-24.

Coulam, C.B., Krysa, L., Stern, J.J., & Bustillo, M. (1995). Intravenous immunoglobulin for treatment of recurrent pregnancy loss. *American Journal of Reproductive Immunology, 34,* 333-337.

Daya, S. (1993). Habitual abortion. In L.J. Copeland, J. Jarrell, & J.A. McGregor (Eds.), *Textbook of gynecology* (pp.204-230). Philadelphia: W.B. Saunders Company.

Daya, S. (In press). Immunotherapy for unexplained recurrent spontaneous abortion. *Infertility Reproduction Medicine Clinical.*

Daya, S., Gunby, J., & The Recurrent Miscarriage Immunotherapy Trialists Group. (1994). The effectiveness of allogeneic leukocyte immunization in unexplained primary recurrent spontaneous abortion. *American Journal of Reproductive Immunology, 32,* 294-302.

The German RSA/IVIG Group. (1994). Intravenous immunoglobulin in the prevention of recurrent miscarriage. *British Journal of Obstetrics and Gynaecology, 101,* 1072-1077.

Kwak, J.Y.H., Kwak, F.M.Y., Ainbinder, S.W., Ruiz, A.M., & Beer, A.E. (1996). Elevated peripheral blood natural killer cells are effectively downregulated by immunoglobulin G infusion in women with recurrent spontaneous abortions. *American Journal of Reproductive Immunology, 35,* 363-369.

Mueller-Eckhardt, G., Heine, O., Neppert, J., Kunzel, W., & Mueller-Eckhardt, C. (1989). Prevention of recurrent spontaneous abortion by intravenous immunoglobulin. *Vox Sang, 51,* 122-126.

The Recurrent Miscarriage Immunotherapy Trialists Group. (1994). Worldwide collaborative observational study and meta-analysis on allogenic leukocyte immunotherapy for recurrent spontaneous abortion. *American Journal of Reproductive Immunology, 32,* 55-72.

Ruiz, J.E., Kwak, J.Y.H., Baum, L., Gilman-Sachs, A., Beaman, K.D., & Kim, Y.B. (1996). Intravenous immunoglobulin inhibits natural killer cell activity *in vivo* in women with recurrent spontaneous abortion. *American Journal of Reproductive Immunology, 35,* 370-375.

References

Alcser, K.H., Brix, K.A., Fine, L.J., Kallenbach, L.R., & Wolfe, R.A. (1989). Occupational mercury exposure and male reproductive health. *American Journal of Industrial Medicine, 15*(5), 517-529.

Armstrong, B.G., McDonald, A.D., & Sloan, M. (1992). Cigarette, alcohol, and coffee consumption and spontaneous abortion. *American Journal of Public Health, 82*(1), 85-87.

Beer, A.E., Quebbeman, J.F., Ayers, J.W., & Haines, R.F. (1981). Major histocompatibility complex antigens, maternal and paternal immune responses, and chronic habitual abortions in humans. *American Journal of Obstetrics and Gynecology, 141*(8), 987-999.

Boehm, K.D., Daimon, M., Gorodeski, I.G., Sheean, L.A., Utian, W.H., & Ilan, J. (1990). Expression of the insulin-like and platelet-derived growth factor genes in human uterine tissues. *Molecular Reproduction and Development, 27,* 93-101.

Boldt, J. (1992). Regulation of sperm-egg interaction during mammalian fertilization. Post-graduate course syllabus (Course VIII-C), American Fertility Society. In *Oocytes and embryos: Basic and clinical considerations* (pp. 43-61).

Boue J., Boue A., & Lazar P. (1975). Retrospective and prospective epidemiological studies of 1500 karyotyped spontaneous human abortions. *Teratology, 12,* 11-26.

Brent, R.L., & Beckman, D.A. (1994). The contribution of environmental teratogens to embryonic and fetal loss. (Review). *Clinical Obstetrics and Gynecology, 37*(3), 646-670.

Bronson, R.A., & Fusi, F. (1990). Evidence that an Arg-Gly-Asp adhesion sequence plays a role in mammalian fertilization. *Biology of Reproduction, 43*(6), 1019-1025.

Buttram, V.C., Jr., & Reiter, R.C. (1981). Uterine leiomyomata: Etiology, symptomatology, and management. *Fertility and Sterility, 36*(4), 433-445.

Candiani, G.B., Fedele, L., Zamberletti, D., DeVirgiliis, D., & Carinelli, S. (1983). Endometrial patterns in malformed uteri. *Acta Europaea Fertilitatis, 14*(5), 311-318.

Collins, R.L. (1991). Recent progress in gonadotropin therapy. In R.L. Collins (Ed.), *Ovulation Induction* (pp. 69-91). New York: Springer-Verlag.

Cooper, M.D. (1995). Mucosal immune response of the human female genital tract to sexually transmitted disease pathogens. In *Post-graduate course syllabus (Course IX), American Society for Reproductive Medicine* (pp 165-193).

Cowchock, F.S., Reece, E.A., Balaban, D., Branch, D.W., & Plouffe, L. (1992). Repeated fetal losses associated with antiphospholipid antibodies: A collaborative randomized trial comparing prednisone with low-dose heparin treatment. *American Journal of Obstetrics & Gynecology, 166*(5), 1318-1323.

Cross, J.C., Werb, Z., & Fisher, S.J. (1994). Implantation and the placenta: Key pieces of the development puzzle. *Science, 266,* 1508-1518.

Damsky, C.H., Librach, C., Lim, K.H., Fitzgerald, M.L., McMaster, M.T., Janatpour, M., Zhou, Y., Logan, S.K., & Fisher, S.J. (1994). Integrin switching regulates normal trophoblast invasion. *Development, 120*(12), 3657-3666.

Daya, S., Ward S., & Burrows, E. (1988). Progesterone profiles in luteal phase defect cycles and outcome of progesterone treatment in patients with recurrent spontaneous abortions. *American Journal of Obstetrics and Gynecology, 158,* 225-232.

Delpizzo, V. (1994). Epidemiological studies of work with video display terminals and adverse pregnancy outcomes (1984-1992). *American Journal of Industrial Medicine, 26,* 465-480.

DiZerega, G.S., Turner, C.K., Stouffer, R.L., Anderson, L.D., Channing, C.P., & Hodgen, G.D. (1981). Suppression of follicle-stimulating hormone-dependent folliculogenesis during the primate ovarian cycle. *Journal of Clinical Endocrinology & Metabolism, 52*(3), 451-456.

Dodson, K.S., MacNaughton, M.C., & Coutts, J.R. (1975). Infertility in women with apparently ovulatory cycle. I. Comparison of their plasma sex steroid and gonadotropin profiles with those in the normal cycle. *British Journal of Obstetrics and Gynaecology, 82*(8), 615-624.

Dudley, D.J., Chen, C., Mitchell, M.D., Daynes, R.A., & Araneo, B.A. (1993). Adaptive immune responses during murine pregnancy: Pregnancy-induced regulation of lymphotine production by activated T lymphocytes. *American Journal of Obstetrics and Gynecology, 168*(4), 1155-1163.

Dulcibella, T. (1992). *Oocyte maturation.* Post-graduate course syllabus. *American Society for Reproductive Medicine,* 21-40.

Eppig, J.J. (1991a). Mammalian oocyte development *in vivo* and *in-vitro.* In P.W. Wassarman (Ed.), *Elements of mammalian fertilization.* Vol. I (pp. 57-76). Boston: CRC Press.

Eppig, J.J. (1991b). Maintenance of meiotic arrest and the induction of oocyte maturation in mouse oocyte-granulosa cell complexes developed *in-vitro* from preantral follicles. *Biology of Reproduction, 45,* 824-830.

Fedele, L., Dorta, M., Brioschi, D., Giudici, M.N., & Candiani, G.B. (1989). Pregnancies in septate uteri: Outcome in relation to site of uterine implantation as determined by sonography. *American Journal of Roentgenology, 152*(4), 781-784.

Fujimoto, V.Y., Clifton, D.K., Cohen, N.L., & Soules, M.R. (1990). Variability of serum prolactin and progesterone levels in normal woman: The relevance of single hormone measurements in the clinical setting. *Obstetrics and Gynecology, 76*(1), 71-78.

Geisthovel, F., Skubsch, U., Zabel, G., Schillinger, H., & Breckwoldt, M. (1983). Ultrasonographic and hormonal studies in physiologic and insufficient menstrual cycles. *Fertility and Sterility, 39*(3), 277-283.

Genbacev, O., White, T.E.K., Gavin, C.E., & Miller, R.K. (1993). Human trophoblast cultures: Models for implantation and peri-implantation toxicology. *Reproductive Toxicology, 7,* 75-94.

Giudice, L.C. (1994). Growth factors and growth modulators in human uterine endometrium: Their potential relevance to reproductive medicine. *Fertility and Sterility, 61*(1), 1-17.

Giudice, L.C. (1995). A primer to cytokines and growth factors: Trophoblast/endometrial interactions. In *Post-graduate course syllabus (Course XIII), American Society for Reproductive Medicine* (pp. 13-26).

Grunfeld, L., Sandler, B., Fox, J., Boyd, C., Kaplan P., & Navot, D. (1989). Luteal phase deficiency after completely normal follicular and periovulatory phases. *Fertility and Sterility, 52,* 919-923.

Guerneri, S., Bettio, D., Simoni, G., Brambati, B., Lanzani A., & Fraccaro, M. (1987). Prevalence and distribution of chromosome abnormalities in a sample of first-trimester internal abortions. *Human Reproduction, 2*, 735-739.

Guirguis, S.S., Pelmear, P.L., Roy, M.L., & Wong, L. (1990). Health effects associated with exposure to anaesthetic gases in Ontario hospital personnel. *British Journal of Industrial Medicine, 47*(7), 490-497.

Guzick, D.S., & Zeleznik, A. (1990). Efficacy of clomiphene citrate in the treatment of luteal phase deficiency: Quantity versus quality of preovulatory follicles. *Fertility and Sterility, 54*(2), 206-210.

Harger, J.H., Archer, D.F., Marchese, S.G., Muracca-Clemens, M., & Garver, K.L. (1983). Etiology of recurrent pregnancy losses and outcome of subsequent pregnancies. *Obstetrics and Gynecology, 62*(5), 574-581.

Harlap, S., & Shiono, P.H. (1980). Alcohol, smoking, and incidence of spontaneous abortions in the first and second trimester. *The Lancet, 2*(8187), 173-176.

Harris, E.N. (1990). Maternal autoantibodies and pregnancy-I: The antiphospholipid antibody syndrome. *Balliere's Clinical Rheumatology, 4*(1), 53-68.

Harris, E.N., & Spinatto, J. (1990). Anticardiolipin screening of healthy pregnant women is not a useful predictor of outcome. *Clinical and Experimental Rheumatology, 8*, 220 (abstract).

Harrison, H.R., Alexander, E.R., Weinstein, L., Lewis, M., Nash, M., & Sim, D.A. (1983). Cervical Chlamydia trachomatis and mycoplasmal infections in pregnancy. Epidemiology and outcomes. *Journal of the American Medical Association, 250*(13), 1721-1727.

Harwick, H.J., Purcell, R.H., Iuppa, J., & Fekety, F.R. (1970). Mycoplasmahominis and abortion. *Journal of Infectious Diseases, 121*(3), 260-268.

Heisterberg, L. (1993). Factors influencing spontaneous abortion, dyspareunia, dysmenorrhea, and pelvic pain. *Obstetrics and Gynecology, 81*(4), 594-597.

Heyner, S., Smith, R.M., & Schultz, G.A. (1989). Temporally regulated expression of insulin and insulin-like growth factors and their receptors in early mammalian development. (Review) *Bioessays, 11*(6), 171-176.

Hill, J.A., Polgar, K., Harlow, B.L., & Anderson, D.J. (1992). Evidence of embryo- and trophoblast-toxic cellular immune response(s) in women with recurrent spontaneous abortion. *American Journal of Obstetrics and Gynecology, 166*(4), 1044-1052.

Hill, J.A., Polgar, K., & Anderson, D.J. (1995). T-Helper 1-type immunity to trophoblast in women with recurrent spontaneous abortion. *Journal of the American Medical Association, 273*(24), 1933-1936.

Horta, J.L., Fernandez, J.G., Soto de Leon, B., & Cortes-Gallegos, V. (1977). Direct evidence of luteal insufficiency in women with habitual abortion. *Obstetrics and Gynecology, 49*(6), 705-708.

Jaffe, R., & Woods J.R., Jr. (1993). Color Doppler imaging and *in vivo* assessment of the anatomy and physiology of the early uteroplacental circulation. *Fertility and Sterility, 60*(2), 293-297.

Jaffe, R. (1994). Color Doppler imaging and assessment of early placental circulations. In R. Jaffe, R.A. Pierson, & J.S. Abramowicz (Eds.), *Imaging in infertility and reproductive endocrinology* (pp. 345-354). Philadelphia: J.B. Lippincott.

Jones, G.S. (1976). The luteal phase defect. *Fertility and Sterility, 27*(4), 351-356.

Joste, N.E., Kundsin, R.B., & Genest, D.R. (1994). Histology and Ureaplasma ure-alyticum culture of 63 cases of first trimester abortion. *American Journal of Clinical Pathology, 102*(6), 729-732.

Kaufman, M.H. (1991). New insights into troploidy and tetraploidy, from an analysis of model systems for these conditions. *Human Reproduction, 6*(1), 8-16.

Kurjak, A., Zudenigo, D., Predanic, M., & Kupesic, S. (1994). Recent advances in the Doppler study of early fetomaternal circulation. *Journal of Perinatal Medicine, 22,* 419-439.

Lammer, E.J., Chen, D.T., Hoar, R.M., Agnish, N.D., Benke, P.J., Braun, J.T., Curry, C.J., Fernhoff, P.M., Grix, A.W., Jr., & Lott, I.T. (1985). Retinoic acid embryopathy. *New England Journal of Medicine, 313*(14), 837-841.

Lessey, B.A., Damjanovich, L., Coutifaris, C., Castelbaum, A., Albelda, S.M., & Buck, C.A. (1992). Integrin adhesion molecules in the human endometrium. Correlation with the normal and abnormal menstrual cycle. *Journal of Clinical Investigation, 90*(1), 188-95.

Lessey, B.A., Castelbaum, A.J., Sawin, S.W., Buck, C.A., Schinnar, R., Bilker, W., & Strom, B.L. (1994a). Aberrant integrin expression in the endometrium of women with endometriosis. *The Journal of Clinical Endocrinology & Metabolism, 79*(2), 643-649.

Lessey, B.A., Castelbaum, A.J., Riben, M., Howarth, J., Tureck, R., & Meyer, W.R. (1994b). Effect of hydrosalpinges on markers of uterine receptivity and success in IVF (p. S45). *Program Supplement, American Fertility Society.*

Lev-Toaff, A.S., Coleman, B.G., Arger, P.H., Mintz, M.C., Arenson, R.L., & Toaff, M.E. (1987). Leiomyomas in pregnancy: Sonographic study. *Radiology, 164*(2), 375-380.

Lewis, V., & Abramowicz, J.S. (1994). Hysterosalpingography of the abnormal pelvis. In R. Jaffe, R.A. Pierson, & J.S. Abramowicz (Eds.), *Imaging in infertility and repro-ductive endocrinology* (pp. 321-334). Philadelphia: J.B. Lippincott.

Li, T.C., Dockery, P., Rogers, A.W., & Cooke, I.D. (1990). A quantitative study of endometrial development in the luteal phase: Comparison between women with unexplained infertility and normal fertility. *British Journal of Obstetrics and Gynecology, 97*(7), 576-582.

Lindbohm, M.L., Hemminki, K., Bonhomme, M.G., Anttila, A., Rantala, K., Heikkila, P., & Rosenberg, M.J. (1991). Effects of paternal occupational exposure on spon-taneous abortion. *American Journal of Public Health, 81*(8), 1029-1033.

Little, A.B. (1988). There's many a slip 'twixt implantation and the crib (editorial). *New England Journal of Medicine, 319*(4), 241-242.

Maier, D.B., Newbold, R.R., & McLachlan, J.A. (1985). Prenatal diethylstilbestrol exposure alters murine uterine responses to prepubertal estrogen stimulation. *Endocrinology, 116,* 1878-1886.

Mattson, B.A., Rosenblum, I.Y, Smith, R.M., & Heyner, S. (1988). Autoradiographic evidence for insulin and insulin-like growth factor binding to early mouse embryos. *Diabetes, 37*(5), 585-589.

McDonald, A.D., McDonald, J.C., Armstrong, B., Cherry, N.M., Nolin, A.D., & Robert,

D. (1989) Fathers' occupation and pregnancy outcome. *British Journal of Industrial Medicine, 46*(5), 329-333.

McNatty, K.P., Sawers, R.S., & McNeilly, A.S. (1974). A possible role for prolactin in control of steroid secretion by the human Graafian follicle. *Nature, 250*(458), 653-655.

Minkoff, H.L., Henderson, C., Mendez, H., Gail, M.H., Holman, S., Willoughby, A., Goedett, J.J., Rubinstein, A., Stratton, P., Walsh, J.H., & Landesman, S.H. (1990). Pregnancy outcomes among mothers infected with human immunodeficiency virus and uninfected control subjects. *American Journal of Obstetrics and Gynecology, 163*(5), 1598-1605.

Mowbray, J.F., Gibbings, C., Liddell, H., Reginald, P.W., Underwood, J.L., & Beard, R.W. (1985). Controlled trial of treatment of recurrent spontaneous abortion by immunisation with paternal cells. *Lancet,* (8435), 941-943.

Murphy, M.J., Graziano, J.H., Popovac, D., Kline, J.K., Mehmeti, A., Factor-Litvak, P., Ahmedi, G., Shrout, P., Rajovic, B., & Nenezic, D.U. (1990). Past pregnancy outcomes among women living in the vicinity of a lead smelter in Kosovo, Yugoslavia. *American Journal of Public Health, 80*(1), 33-35.

Nachtigall, M., Kliman, H., Feinberg, R., Meaddough, E., & Arici, A. (1994). *Potential role of leukemia inhibitory factor (LIF) in human implantation* (Abstract). 41st Annual Meeting of the Society for Gynecological Investigation, Chicago, IL.

Naeye, R.L. (1981). Influence of maternal cigarette smoking during pregnancy on fetal and childhood growth. *Obstetrics and Gynecology, 57*(1), 18-21.

Nehlig, A., & Debry, G. (1994). Potential teratogenic and neurodevelopmental consequences of coffee and caffeine exposure: A review on human and animal data. *Neurotoxicology and Teratology, 16*(6),531-543.

Ober, C. (1995). Immunogenetics of recurrent pregnancy loss. In *Post-graduate course syllabus (Course IX), American Society for Reproductive Medicine* (pp. 195-203).

Out, H.J., Bruinse, H.W., Christiaens, G.C.M.L., van Vliet, M., de Groot, P.G., Nieuwenhuis, H.K., & Derksen, R.H.W.M. (1992). A prospective, controlled multicenter study on the obstetrics risks of pregnant women with antiphospholipid antibodies. *American Journal of Obstetrics and Gynecology, 167*(1), 26-32.

Out, H.J., Bruinse, H.W., & Derkson, R.H. (1991). Anti-phospholipid antibodies and pregnancy loss. *Human Reproduction, 6*(6), 889-897.

Peaceman, A.M., Silver, R.K., MacGregor, S.N., & Socol, M.L. (1992). Interlaboratory variation in antiphospholipid antibody testing. *American Journal of Obstetrics and Gynecology, 166*(6), 1780-1787.

Plouffe, L., Jr., White, E.W., Tho, S.P., Sweet, C.S., Layman, L.C., Whitman, G.F., & McDonough, P.G. (1992). Etiologic factors of recurrent abortion and subsequent reproductive performance of couples: Have we made any progress in the past 10 years? *American Journal of Obstetrics and Gynecology, 167*(2), 313-321.

Reece, E.A., Gabrielli, S., Cullen, M.T., Zheng, X., Hobbins, J.C., & Harris, E.N. (1990). Recurrent adverse pregnancy outcome and antiphospholipid antibodies. *American Journal of Obstetrics and Gynecology, 163*(1), 162-169.

Regan, L., Owen, E.J., & Jacobs, H.S. (1990). Hypersecretion of luteinizing hormone, infertility, and miscarriage. *Lancet, 336,* 1141-1144.

Rein, M.S., Friedman, A.J., Pandian, M.R., & Heffner, L.J. (1990). The secretion of insulin-like growth factors I and II by explant cultures of fibroids and myometrium from women treated with a gonadotropin-releasing hormone agonist. *Obstetrics and Gynecology, 76*(3), 388-394.

Rom, W.N. (1976). Effects of lead on the female and reproduction: A review. *Mount Sinai Journal of Medicine, 43*(5), 542-552.

Savitz, D.A., Sonnenfeld, N.L., & Olshan, A.F. (1994). Review of epidemiologic studies of paternal occupational exposure and spontaneous abortion. *American Journal of Industrial Medicine, 25*, 361-383.

Schnorr, T.M., Grajewski, B.A., Hornung, R.W., Thun, M.J., Egeland, G.M., Murray, W.E., Conover, D.L., & Halperin, W.E. (1991). Video display terminals and the risk of spontaneous abortion. *New England Journal of Medicine, 324*(11), 727-733.

Schultz, R.M. (1991). Meiotic maturation of mammalian oocytes. In P.W. Wassarman (Ed.), *Elements of mammalian fertilization.* Vol. I (pp 77-104). Boston: CRC Press.

Selwyn, P.A., Schoenbaum, E.E., Davenny, K., Robertson, V.J., Feingold, A.R., Shulman, J.F., Mayers, M.M., Klein, R.S., Friedland, G.H., & Rogers, M.F. (1989). Prospective study of human immunodeficiency virus infection and pregnancy outcomes in intravenous drug users. *Journal of the American Medical Association, 261*(9), 1289-1294.

Shabanowitz, R.B., & O'Rand, M.G. (1988a). Characterization of the human zona pellucida from fertilized and unfertilized eggs. *Journal of Reproduction and Fertility, 82*, 151-161.

Shabanowitz, R.B., & O'Rand, M.G. (1988b). Molecular changes in the human Zona Pellucida associated with fertilization and human sperm-zona interaction. *Annals New York Academy of Sciences, 541*, 621-632.

Shabanowitz, R.B. (1990). Mouse antibodies to human zona pellucida: Evidence that human ZP3 is strongly immunogenic and contains two distinct isomer chains. *Biology of Reproduction, 43*(2), 260-270.

Speroff, L., Glass R.H., & Kase, N.G. (1994). *Clinical gynecologic endocrinology and infertility.* Baltimore: Williams and Wilkins.

Stagno, S., Pass, R.F., Dworsky, M.E., Henderson, R.E., Moore, E.G., Walton, P.D., & Alford, C.A. (1982). Congenital cytomegalovirus infection: The relative importance of primary and recurrent maternal infection. *New England Journal of Medicine, 306*(16), 945-949.

Stanger, J.D., & Yovich, J.L. (1985). Reduced *in-vitro* fertilization of human oocytes from patients with raised basal luteinizing hormone levels during the follicular phase. *British Journal of Obstetrics and Gynaecology, 92*(4), 385-393.

Stewart, D.L., Kaspar, P., Bryant, L.J., Bhatt, H., Gadi, I., Kontgen, F., & Abbondanzo, S.J. (1992). Blastocyst implantation depends on maternal expression of leukemia inhibitory factor. *Nature, 359*, 76-79.

Stray-Pedersen, B., Eng, J., & Reikvam, T.M. (1978). Uterine T-mycoplasma colonization in reproductive failure. *American Journal of Obstetrics and Gynecology, 130*(3), 307-311.

Stray-Pedersen, B., & Stray-Pedersen, S. (1984). Etiologic factors and subsequent reproductive performance in 195 couples with a prior history of habitual abortion. *American Journal of Obstetrics and Gynecology, 148*(2), 140-146.

Summers, P.R. (1994). Microbiology relevant to recurrent miscarriage. *Clinical Obstetrics and Gynecology, 37*(3), 722-729.

Swan, S. (1992). Pregnancy outcomes in DES daughters. In *NIH workshop, long-term effects of exposure to Diethylstilbestrol (DES)*. Bethseda, MD: National Institutes of Health.

Takahashi, M., Koide S.S., & Donahoe, P.K. (1986). Mullerin inhibiting substance as oocyte meiosis inhibitor. *Molecular and Cellular Endocrinology, 47*(3), 225-234.

Tannenbaum, T.N., & Goldberg, R.J. (1985). Exposure to anesthetic gases and reproductive outcome. A review of the epidemiologic literature. *Journal of Occupational Medicine, 27*(9), 659-668.

Tho, P.T., Byrd, J.R., & McDonough, P.C. (1979). Etiologies and subsequent reproductive performance of 100 couples with abortions. *Fertility and Sterility, 32*, 389-395.

Tsafriri, A., Picard, J.Y., & Josso, N. (1988). Immunopurified anti-Muellerian hormone does not inhibit spontaneous resumption of meiosis *in-vitro* of rat oocytes. *Biology of Reproduction, 38*(2), 481-485.

Ubeda, A., Leal, J., Trillo, M.A., Jimenez, M.A., & Delgado, J.M. (1983). Pulse shape of magnetic fields influences chick embryogenesis. *Journal of Anatomy, 137*(Pt. 3), 513-536.

U.S. Department of Health and Human Services. (1980). *The health consequences of smoking for women: A report of the U.S. Surgeon General*. Rockville, MD: USDHHS.

van Blerkom, J. (1991). Extrinsic and intrinsic influences on human oocyte and early embryo potential. In P.W. Wassarman (Ed.), *Elements of mammalian fertilization*. Vol. II. (pp. 82-106). Boston: CRC Press.

van Lijnschoten, G., Stals, F., Evers, J.L., Bruggeman, C.A., Havenith, M.H., & Geraedts, J.P. (1994). The presence of cytomegalovirus antigens in karyotyped abortions. *American Journal of Reproductive Immunology, 32*(3), 211-220.

Walsh, R.A. (1994). Effects of maternal smoking on adverse pregnancy outcomes: Examination of the criteria of causation. *Human Biology, 66*(6), 1059-1092.

Wentz, A.C. (1980). Endometrial biopsy in the evaluation of infertility. *Fertility and Sterility, 33*(2), 121-124.

Wilcox, A.J., Weinberg, C.R., O'Connor, J.F., Baird, D.D., Schlatterer, J.P., Canfield, R.E., Armstrong, E.G., & Nisula, B.C. (1988). Incidence of early loss of pregnancy. *New England Journal of Medicine, 319*(4), 189-194.

Chapter 3

Pregnancy-Loss Counseling: The Challenge to the Obstetrician

James R. Woods, Jr.

The role of the obstetrician in pregnancy-loss counseling remains enigmatic. As noted by Patel, "Promoting life, not prolonging death, and encouraging quality — even meaning — in both, are talents exalted all too frequently in medical school" (Patel, 1993).

Some obstetricians, because of lack of training in medical school or residency, are unprepared to help their patients confront pregnancy loss. For others, the need for honest interaction, which this distressing event requires, generates feelings of uneasiness or even fear. Finally, pregnancy loss counseling may appear to be an art, with widely varying objectives and a unique, dynamic process in each case.

For parents, the tragedy of pregnancy loss is twofold. Not only has their expected baby died, but also their family has been changed forever. Preparations done in anticipation of the baby's arrival now must be undone. Any items procured for the baby must be sorted, stored, or returned; the crib, dismantled. Gifts meant for the baby must be disposed of, too. Friends or neighbors must be informed, and this draining task often becomes even more difficult when unexpected encounters occur in a grocery store or other such public place which inherently lacks privacy and intimacy. Finally, after all these necessary chores are completed, the family must live with their loneliness and sadness of knowing that they never will be able to tell their baby of their vision of his or her future. In this context, the image of "empty arms" described by women after a baby dies assumes a palpable poignancy.

I have written this chapter to achieve three goals. First, despite many recent efforts — through writing, teaching, presentations, videos, and patient input — unfortunately, it still is necessary to establish that pregnancy-loss

**Figure 1-3.
Editorial Cartoon by Jim Borgman,
The Cincinnati Enquirer.**

WE TAKE WALKS IN THE
EVENING AND SING LITTLE
SONGS TO EACH OTHER
AS THE SKY GROWS
DARK. FINALLY, MY SONG
GETS NO ANSWER, AND
I KNOW HE HAS FALLEN ASLEEP.

AS WE WALK HOME I TALK TO HIM
ABOUT MANY THINGS. BECAUSE
I AM HIS FATHER.

JIMBORGMAN'91

Reprinted with permission.

counseling is first and foremost an obstetric responsibility. Second, this discussion is intended to demonstrate that counseling after pregnancy loss can be a structured and defined process, the components of which I will detail. Third, I seek to provide a compelling argument that pregnancy-loss counseling is a skill that can be acquired as surely as can any other concrete, obstetric technique and that, when performed well, is a powerful and noble art for obstetricians to master.

Similarities Between Obstetricians and Their Patients: A Foundation for Pregnancy-Loss Counseling

To be an effective pregnancy-loss counselor, it is helpful to appreciate personal attributes which we and our patients share, because these similarities provide the foundation for pregnancy-loss counseling. The significance of our roles as parents is captured in the cartoon by Jim Borgman, published in *The Cincinnati Enquirer* one Father's Day [June 17, 1984] (see Figure 1-3). We all recognize the important role which parents play in the lives of their children. The obstetrician's understanding that this role now will be denied parents whom we are counseling following pregnancy loss provides the basis for compassion and insight which we can offer to ease a patient's grief.

As we assess our strengths in this field, it is important to recognize our own emotional needs as they relate to family structure. On a wall, mantel, or bookshelf perhaps, many of us display photographs or paintings of family members who no longer are living. Nearby, a broken pocket watch, a soiled baseball hat, or a piece of jewelry testifies to the value of mementos which tie us emotionally to our loved ones. During a visit to a cemetery where a family member has been buried, how many of us have longed to speak with that individual, to bring him or her up to date on recent successes or failures, or just to reassure the loved one, "I miss you. I want to tell you that I'm doing fine." Why do we experience these emotions and behave in these ways? I believe that these actions represent efforts to maintain a connection or bridge with those whom we love, who no longer can be part of our lives. In this context, then, why should it be surprising that a patient whose baby has died would seek anything less than this type of connection?

Images of Ultrasound

Ultrasound technology has enabled expectant parents to crystallize this view of the fetus into an image of their baby, with clarity that no other technology before it was able to achieve. Via endovaginal scanning, the sonographer projects an image of the 6-week fetus and yolk sac, characterized by an as yet undeveloped fetal body with pulsating heart. But parents who view the same ultrasound screen see nothing undeveloped about this image. Rather, they exclaim about the baby's jawline, gender, or facial features, which immediately allow them to establish a link between this baby and their family. Care providers may overhear statements such as, "He has my nose and your smile!" The sonographer knows that those observations are not derived from the image on the screen. Our patients' perspective, however, can remind us that we do not necessarily perceive the same image as do parents whose fetus we scrutinize intently for myriad possible anomalies or complications. Later in gestation, we provide videotapes and photographs of the fetus which clearly show facial contours, lips, the forehead, and the baby's body, all physical features which parents can see on the ultrasound screen. Thanks to superb technology, these images are not ill-defined. Instead, a graphic, readily identifiable image of the baby now is presented to parents. There even can be a clear view of external genitalia, enabling definitive recognition of the baby's sex. The baby becomes even more vivid for parents who are able to select an appropriate gender name prenatally. "If it's a girl, we will name her ___, and if it's a boy, we will name him ___" has been replaced by statements such as, "This baby is a girl, and her name is ___." From the moment when ultrasound confirms the baby's sex, parents narrow down their name choices and usually select a name soon, and they can fantasize more specifically about personality or gender-related characteristics attributable to the unborn daughter or son. No wonder that, when a baby dies, the parents lose what has become for them a clear sense of their child, who is regarded as a member of their family, who actually has been seen already, and who has been the source of great anticipation for weeks or months before the unfortunate outcome.

Obstacles to Communication

Many forces work against obstetricians' ability to communicate with their patients. We all engage in a "conspiracy of silence" (Lewis, 1979). Use of the term "conspiracy" serves to characterize the pattern,

> ...if you (the patient) don't talk about it (your baby's death), you won't think about it. If you don't think about it, you will forget.

This implicit attitude provides an excuse for some care providers who imagine that, if the baby's death is not discussed, then the emotional impact of this tragedy will dissipate more quickly. How ironic that this misconception represents the greatest obstacle to adequate communication between care provider and patient when a pregnancy loss occurs. This issue was even addressed in *The Wall Street Journal*, in an article, "Sometimes, Talk Is The Best Medicine" (Winslow, 1989). In this article, Ron Winslow notes that "...Poor communication between doctors and patients is the single most common cause of malpractice suits...Doctors who are arrogant or otherwise poor communicators are easy marks for malpractice lawyers." The author adds, "There are barriers to good doctor-patient interaction. Many medical schools pay only lip service to the subject, and physicians who generally earn more money spend less time with patients and probably listen less." Unfortunately, a lack of confidence in care providers by pregnancy loss patients seeking supportive care is not new. Knapp and Peppers (1979) wrote of their findings from 100 unstructured interviews with physicians and patients following fetal or infant deaths. Understandably, physicians found it difficult to change from "healer to counselor-consoler." The sad result was

Figure 2-3.
Letter Received by Dr. Woods from a Pregnancy-Loss Patient

My husband got to see her twice. I thought she was buried in a little sleeper that I planned to bring her home in. For 4 years, I thought my baby was freezing underground. My husband finally told me he had bought a coat, hat, and dress for her to be buried in. No one will talk about her. She would have been 13 years old on June 25th. I ache to hold her. I hurt so much at times I want to go to the cemetery, dig her up, and look at her even now.

that over half of these couples viewed their physicians as "insensitive, aloof, and unconcerned" (Knapp & Peppers, 1979). In a more recent study surveying support systems described by 85 women with prior losses, partners were named most frequently (41%) as having demonstrated the best supportive sympathy, followed by the women's mothers (12%), and finally health care providers (10%) (Rajan, 1994).

Unfortunately, obstetricians are not the only group guilty of subscribing to the "conspiracy of silence." Concerned family members or well-intended friends can contribute unknowingly to parents' sense of isolation and lack of sympathy following pregnancy loss. During a period in which I was caring for a young woman who had experienced a term intrauterine fetal death, I received a telephone message that read: "Aunt called and requested that no one send her anything at all to remind her about her baby." It is not surprising that, if the family actively seeks to discourage any references to the issues, and if the care provider also colludes with this approach, then parents almost certainly will be isolated and confused, and their sadness exacerbated. In fact, in Lindemann's classic studies of acute grief, increasing distance from others and loss of warmth in relationships with others were common reactions following the death of a loved one (Lindemann, 1944). In these situations, success in the process of building a relationship between care providers and parents must reside with the care provider (Knapp & Peppers, 1979).

Unfortunately, care providers in obstetrics are not viewed as skilled in the area of delivering bad news. In a conversation which I had with a young woman who was recovering after a 30-week intrauterine fetal death, the fol-

Figure 3-3.
Document Posted on the Internet by Bereaved Mother

A year ago today, my baby died. The worst part is the passage of time. It just gets further and further away from the time when my baby was with us. It's hard to remember how he felt. I'll of course never forget. Life goes on and so do his memories. He changed my life forever. Thanks for listening.

lowing dialogue occurred. The patient asked, "Are you a psychologist?" when I asked her about her reaction to her baby's death. I replied, "No, I am an obstetrician. Why do you ask?" She said, "Because you are asking me all of these questions about my feelings." Quietly pleased, I pursued this by asking, "Why does that surprise you?" The young woman responded, "Because I thought all obstetricians came in, did their thing, and went on about their business." This exchange starkly conveys time-tested lack of confidence which patients have in their physicians' ability to counsel them adequately when adverse events occur.

Sadly, when adequate counseling is not initiated at the time of the pregnancy loss, the pain and feelings of emptiness can persist indefinitely. This impact is best documented by a letter which I received several years ago, shown in Figure 2-3. What is noteworthy in this letter is that this woman experienced the death of a newborn, yet she relates emotionally to her daughter as if the daughter now were 13 years old. Moreover, she pictures activities in which her daughter now would be engaged, based on those in which her relatives' and friends' 13-year-old children participate. The sentiment of this letter also suggests that, with each passing birthday, her daughter will continue to "grow" a year older, in her mother's mind. The "teenager" will mature into a "young woman" who will continue to miss life's rites of passage that her mother had hoped her daughter would experience. Another mother expressed similar sadness many years later, saying, "My daughter is still dead. She isn't a seventh-grader this year. She will be dead every day for the rest of my life." The sense of lost relationships, which would have evolved from that child's presence, can continue through the years — even to include sadness about the grandchildren who never will be born to this lost child.

Technologies change, but human emotions remain unaltered. The need for parents to talk to willing listeners when a child has died is a powerful force. A document posted on the Internet in 1994 testifies to how this need can be transferred readily to any medium of communication, even one as impersonal as cyberspace (see Figure 3-3). The desire to retain memories literally and figuratively seems to be universal. In the concluding monologue of Woody Allen's film, *Radio Days,* the narrator speaks about the unfulfillable longing to retain links with loved ones departed by commenting, "...With the passing of each New Year's Eve, those voices grow dimmer and dimmer."

Medical Obstacles to Better Pregnancy Loss Care

Careless use of medical and obstetric terms presents a major obstacle to good communication with couples who have had a pregnancy loss. Terms such as "vanishing twin" or "incompetent cervix," and ambiguous statements such as, "We're not able to see all of the baby's spine" (implying to the sonographer that fetal position limits ultrasound visibility of the full anatomy of the baby), may be understood and repeated by the woman as meaning that her baby is developing without a spine. No wonder that obstetricians are not applauded for communication skills.

Pregnancy Loss as a Continuum

Clinical challenge: You have just been called by the sonographer or physician at the ultrasound laboratory. "Your patient has a blighted ovum." You are fully booked at the office that day. Your response?

Our improved abilities to manage patients with sudden, unexpected outcomes during the first and second trimesters of pregnancy have been enhanced significantly by two trends: (a) the increasing acceptance by obstetricians that pregnancy loss is an integral part of obstetrics, and (b) technologic refinements in ultrasound which now allow for unprecedented prenatal diagnoses.

A broader definition of pregnancy loss as a continuum involving all departures from normal fetal and newborn development has helped us to recognize that patients with a variety of perinatal outcomes grieve similarly. As a consequence, techniques learned from patients with stillbirths or miscarriages now can be extended to those whose babies are born with structural or genetic defects, and even to patients who decide to relinquish a baby for adoption (see Chapter 14, "Birthparents' Grief: Relinquishing a Baby for Adoption"). However, Worthington (1994) reminds us that, in this context, the grief process may differ among individuals. For those whose babies have died, linear grief may define that process in which the final outcome is known, the individual will adjust to the cause of the grief, and the source of the grief is no longer physically present. These individuals should progress normally through the grief experience, possibly with a period of reduced emotional stability, and finally toward resolution of grieving. In contrast, the impaired or chronically ill baby may generate cyclical grief, in which new stressors are encountered periodically as additional developments in the child's problems occur. Parents and other family members must respond and adjust to these new stressors. In this setting, the new grief event leads to emotional disruption, then to emotional healing until a new event or an additional problem provokes a new cycle of grieving. Similarly, parents who relinquish a baby for adoption may find that subsequent events in their own lives can trigger a new or a previously unresolved grief crisis.

Our expanded awareness of pregnancy loss as a continuum has alerted us to the needs of a far more diverse group of pregnancy-loss patients than previously were appreciated. Pregnancy loss should be defined as any one of the following:

- A departure from normal
- A loss of expected outcome
- A loss of living qualities
- Loss of a loved one
- Loss of a desired family unit

By expanding our definition of pregnancy loss, we recognize that the greatest significant loss is that moment when parents learn that the baby will not be normal. But, departure from normal can take many forms. Stillbirth and neonatal death are acknowledged as the most extreme examples of a loss of normalness. When a baby is born with a meningomyelocele or critical cardiac defect, early pediatric management suddenly diminishes the possibility that this baby's childhood will be normal. This departure from normal forces parents to view the future for their baby as limited, and loss of living qualities begin to erode the dreams that parents had cherished for their child. They must confront the fact that society does not tolerate the impaired, the deformed, or the handicapped. It will be in this uncaring world that their child must struggle to succeed.

The Obstetrician's Role: An Historic Perspective

With the advent of ultrasonography, a major change in professional responsibility for the management of couples experiencing a pregnancy loss has occurred. In the late 1960s and early 1970s, fetuses with unexpected outcomes such as hydrocephaly, severe growth restriction, or structural abnormalities of the heart or kidneys were delivered without prior anticipation of such defects. The obstetrician often identified hydrocephaly in advanced labor after palpating widely spaced cranial tables and a soft fluctuant anterior fontanel. Abnormalities of the face or body were realized abruptly at birth. Responsibility for management, instead of residing with the obstetrician, defaulted, perhaps naturally, to the pediatrician at delivery (Knapp & Peppers, 1979). For parents and obstetrician alike, the terrible outcome was unanticipated and confronted everyone without warning. Parents' grief reaction focused upon the outcome of care in the newborn period. In a sense, obstetricians and parents were forced into the role of passive observers in this life crisis.

In today's technically advanced health care environment, prenatal diagnosis and anticipation of outcome have become the accepted norms. By contrast with earlier times, obstetrician and patient now have been placed in the unique, complex position of active participation in predicting and making difficult decisions about managing the outcome for an abnormal or a dying fetus. In many planned, happily anticipated pregnancies, parents are thrust into the unenviable position of being fully advised as to painful information about their baby, and of being given responsibility for choosing future management direction.

Reactions of parents who chose to terminate a pregnancy due to a fetal anomaly which is incompatible with life has received little attention until recently (please refer to Chapter 9, "Termination of Pregnancy for Fetal Abnormalities," and Chapter 7, "Genetics and Pregnancy Loss"). In a recent report, grief reactions of 23 women with ultrasound diagnoses of fetal anomalies were compared with those of a group of women who were similar in demographics but who experienced spontaneous late pregnancy loss. At 2 months following delivery or termination of the pregnancy, both groups exhibited similar grief reactions and a similar incidence of major depression (Zeanah, Darley, Rosenblatt, & Saller 1993).

The Ultrasound Unit: Opportunities for Success and Failure

With the advent of the ultrasound laboratory as the common pathway through which prenatal diagnosis is made and perinatal management is determined, a need now exists to standardize an approach for patient management in this highly technical and often intimidating medical environment. This is where an unsuspecting sonographer, routinely scanning an obstetric patient, discovers absence of cardiac activity in a near-term fetus, or a blighted ovum in a woman who is hoping for a successful pregnancy following *in-vitro* fertilization. It is in this environment that a woman at 38 weeks gestation first realizes from sonographers' facial expressions or behavior that her baby has died. It also is in this setting where many questions arise and few answers are provided in any standardized manner.

What should be said first to the parents when a major fetal anomaly or intrauterine death is discovered? Who should relay this information to parents? How should counseling proceed once the diagnosis is confirmed? What are the expected reactions of parents who, in a period of only minutes, are taken with little or no warning from happily anticipating a healthy child to learning that their baby has died? How can anyone truly make such a shattering transition so quickly, even as the sonographer or attending physician explains often complicated information about the ultrasound findings?

Picture the Worst Scenario
- No fetal heart beat is detected in the office. The woman is told, "You need to go get an ultrasound." It goes without saying that ultrasound documentation of fetal viability should be accomplished that very day. Despite the logic and basic humane treatment which should dictate that this be the case, on occasion our ultrasound department still receives requests for ultrasound to be conducted "tomorrow" or "when you can find an opening," as follow-up to absent audible fetal heart tones.
- At the ultrasound site, the patient is seated in the waiting room with other pregnant women. During the actual examination, the ultrasonographer scans the patient, but says little, and then leaves quickly to call in a physician.
- The physician enters and performs the scan hurriedly, to confirm the finding reported by the sonographer, but he or she hardly speaks to the patient.
- Because of the speed with which the physician can confirm that the fetal heart has stopped beating, the ultrasound evaluation is discontinued or the machine is turned off very soon, from the patient's perspective.

Figure 4-3.
Former Surgeon General Dr. C. Everett Koop's Suggestion for Delivering Bad News

- Choose a pleasant, quiet room.

- Present the news to both parents together.

- Use words that are clear, factual, and free of cliches.

- Use lay language, if possible.

- Listen for evidence of selective hearing. If needed, have another family member present to absorb the facts.

- Touch as in holding a hand or even a hug is alright.

- Provide latitude for response comments like "Why did God do this?" These statements may be the first emotional response; they seldom require an answer or worse, an argument.

- The physician tells the patient, "I do not see a heartbeat. The results will be sent to your doctor."
- The patient hears these statements and wonders, "Is there something wrong with the machine, or is this doctor not very good, since he (or she) can't see the heartbeat? Could there be something wrong with my baby's heart? And is my baby okay?" The patient is sent home feeling frightened, confused, and possibly quite angry.

Developing Standards for Pregnancy-Loss Care

The proper approach for managing patients under these circumstances requires an appreciation for the emotional toll that a pregnancy loss will take upon the family. Combined with the medical skills with which the physician is well-equipped, this understanding enables the physician to integrate psychosocial counseling with his or her explanation to the patient of the medical facts. The concepts of care have been well-defined for decades, as illustrated by recommendations by former Surgeon General C. Everett Koop (1974) (see Figure 4-3).

When crisis threatens a family, their needs differ little from those which we would seek for ourselves. These needs include:

- To be treated with dignity
- To be given simple explanations
- To be spared innocuous small talk
- To be allowed (encouraged) to cry
- To be guided through unfamiliar issues and painful decision making
- To be comforted, not to be isolated

The following principles have been used in the perinatal ultrasound laboratory at the University of Rochester for nearly a decade, and they have proved invaluable in establishing a level of confidence between physician and patient and, we hope, helping all parties to avoid misconceptions and miscommunication.

- *Extend the time allotted for ultrasound scanning.* Even though, with available technology, a diagnosis of fetal death often can be made within seconds after the ultrasound transducer is placed on the patient's abdomen (such as if the fetal heart is not beating, or if there is overriding of the skull bones), the sonographer or physician should continue to scan while explaining to the patient, "I understand that this is very difficult for you. We need to spend several minutes to examine all of your baby's anatomy, before we draw any conclusions." In this manner, the patient is informed politely that a thorough ultrasound scan will be performed. This is helpful for the patient to understand, if a diagnosis of intrauterine fetal death or fetal anomaly is made following the examination. When a brief or cursory scan is performed, and then this is followed by a devastating diagnosis such as intrauterine fetal death, parents may be uncertain about the possibility that someone has made a mistake or that the ultrasound machine was not functioning properly. It is not uncommon, between the moment of diagnosis and finally the delivery of the severely compromised or stillborn baby, for parents to harbor unfounded hopes that the baby really may be healthy after all.

- *Acknowledge the event.* If the diagnosis is clear, most physicians struggle with the difficult, first descriptive statement. In the absence of a more appropriate first sentence, I usually say, "I am very sorry. I have to tell you that we have detected a major problem, which we need to talk about." At that point, if I am certain of the diagnosis, I will state our finding in the clearest, simplest terms possible. "I am sorry to tell that your baby has died" is difficult to say, but this statement leaves no opportunity for misunderstanding. With a diagnosis such as fetal death or hydrocephaly or some other life-threatening condition, parents seldom comprehend much more than the first few sentences. It serves no purpose to begin a lengthy, technical explanation of the finding immediately, since the initial shock of hearing the news prevents parents from understanding or being able to ask questions.

• *Show the ultrasound screen to parents, if they wish to see it.* Before parents are asked to move from the ultrasound room to meet in a conference room, they should be asked whether or not they would like to see on the screen what we have seen which has led to the diagnosis. Many parents, in fact, will request this of their own accord, even as they are weeping and expressing shock and grief. If they choose not to look at the ultrasound screen at this time, the option may be offered again later, depending on the circumstances.

• *Have someone remain with parents.* In our ultrasound suite, parents are escorted across the hallway to a private consultation office, where there is a telephone with outside phone lines. Typically, I spend a quarter of an hour or so with parents at this point, reiterating as necessary and explaining in simple terms what the findings mean. When films are available, I use them to illustrate our findings. I ask if there are any questions, but I emphasize that it is understandable and natural that, because of stress and the shock of the moment, they may not be able to articulate questions at this time.

• *Offer parents private time, with telephone access.* With a basic grasp of the situation, parents usually desire to be left to themselves for 10 to 15 minutes. This is an appropriate moment to suggest that they call on relatives or friends, to begin to reach out for their own support network. Meanwhile, I telephone the woman's care providers to relay information about our findings. If parents wish but are too overwhelmed to make personal calls themselves, I may offer to call family members to notify them about what has happened. I then return, and while sitting with parents, will ask if they have any questions. I also offer again to let them review the ultrasound images. On occasion, parents who initially refuse to look at the ultrasound screen will request to see the films or the results of real-time scanning at this point in the consultation.

• *Allow the couple to return home.* I provide instructions from the woman's own care providers which I may have obtained during our initial phone call. Typically, the message concerns an appointment for the woman to see her physician that day or the next. During this part of our discussion, I offer parents an opportunity to return to our office the next day to discuss any questions regarding the ultrasound finding and its clinical significance. In my conversations with patients' care providers, I always mention that I have offered this opportunity to the patient. This removes the burden from her obstetric care providers to address complex issues regarding the ultrasound finding and management, and it also allows them to remain involved in managing these patients.

What Do Patients Need When Bad Events Occur?

When a woman first learns about the loss of her baby, she and her family are confused about what comes next. Patients expect that their physicians' care will provide answers to the following questions:

- What does this horrific information that you have provided mean?
- How did you arrive at this terrible conclusion?
- Is my own health or life at risk?
- [Spouse:] Is my wife at risk?
- Do we know everything we need to know?
- What are my options?
- How quickly do I have to make decisions?
- In what order must these decisions be made?
- How will I respond to questions from my family?
- How will I tell my kids (relatives/friends) about what has happened?

Types of Losses

We have learned a great deal about how parents react to a wide range of pregnancy losses and about how, when a more standard approach to conveying this information is developed, our care becomes more comprehensive.

> *Clinical challenge: Your patient miscarries. You perform the curettage in the emergency department. When would you tell her to return for an appointment in your office? How much time would you book for the visit? Where would she wait before being seen? How would you open the discussion?*

For years, the impact of spontaneous abortion has been overlooked, dismissed as an insignificant, and often-seen, pregnancy loss. Because of its very frequency, obstetricians easily can become inured to the emotional nature of the event from the patient's perspective. This lack of attention should be understood in an historic context, wherein miscarriage has been acknowledged for many centuries. Records of the phenomenon of miscarriage trace back as far as the early civilizations of Rome, Africa, and India. Miscarriage is mentioned in the Talmud, and it is noted to have occurred for such women as Anne Boleyn and Catherine of Aragon (Dewhurst, 1984; Kuller, & Katz, 1994). Terms such as "blighted ovum," "vanishing twin," "passage of tissue," or "fetal wastage," while perhaps they do convey medical information from one care provider to another, often are heard by patients and perceived as insensitive statements which negate the significance of the early pregnancy for families. Many couples select names for their babies early in the first trimester of pregnancy — or even before conception has occurred. The name symbolizes a baby's personality and individuality. Because of the improved technology of transvaginal ultrasound, parents receive clear images of their baby beginning as early as 7 or 8 weeks from the woman's last menstrual period. It is understandable, therefore, why miscarriage is perceived by many couples as having the same impact as late pregnancy loss.

In some ways, loss from a miscarriage is even more complicated. Cuisinier, Kuijpers, Hoogoluin, deGraauw, and Janssen (1993) surveyed 143 women who experienced either a miscarriage (occurring before 20 weeks gestation) or a stillbirth (occurring after 20 weeks gestation), to evaluate women's responses to the loss and their perception of the care which they received. Using a modified perinatal grief scale (Potvin, Lasker, & Toedter, 1989; Toedter, 1988), these investigators found a correlation between length of gestation and intensity of grief reaction. Of note, while length of time elapsed since the loss and gestational age at the time when the loss occurred were generally the major determinants of the grief reaction, women who had experienced miscarriages were the least satisfied with their care (43%), when compared with those women whose losses occurred after more than 20 weeks of gestation (29%). Specifically, lack of understanding, impersonal attitudes, lack of information, and brevity of care were identified as specific failings of care providers.

Despite the frequency of miscarriage, because of today's insurance-constrained hospital protocols, most miscarriage patients are cared for in an emergency room; following dilatation and curettage, these women are discharged home with minimal counseling or education. From telephone interviews with 44 women who were treated in the emergency room for miscarriage, Zaccardi, Abbott, and Koziol-McLain (1993) found that 82% expressed grief about their loss and 77% reported that their daily activities had become disrupted immediately after the miscarriage occurred. The atmosphere of most emergency rooms precludes allotting time for education, or for ensuring that miscarriage patients receive time with traditional care providers such as nurses or social workers. As a consequence, the burden of follow-up defaults to the woman's obstetrician, with inconsistent results. Her regular obstetric care providers may not even be notified of the miscarriage until after the fact. This unwarranted gap in standard of care seems to occur in most communities. Continued pressure by health maintenance organizations to provide care for miscarriage patients in an outpatient setting broadens the challenge of providing supportive care and follow-up counseling to this group.

A complicating issue for sufferers of miscarriage is that parents may never learn whether the baby was a boy or a girl. This means that they cannot use the name which they have selected with any confidence that it is appropriate for the baby's sex. Additionally, there can be a more pronounced disjunction between men's and women's responses to early pregnancy loss. Because men cannot experience any early pregnancy sensations, such as nausea and breast tenderness, they have less sense of connection with the pregnancy, however much desired the pregnancy may be. Women, on the other hand, do experience the physical processes of pregnancy, and these sensations lead them to assume complete responsibility for the outcome. After a loss, many women bear considerable guilt for actions, such as having drunk a glass of wine or having had sexual intercourse, or even having lifted a heavy object or having exercised "too strenuously" early in the pregnancy. Even if such actions were undertaken with no awareness of the pregnancy at the time, women later may discern a cause-and-effect relationship between the action and the miscarriage. Most women do take blame for the miscarriage when it occurs, despite any and all reassurances that they could not have influenced the outcome of the early pregnancy.

Blighted Ovum

For most care providers, a blighted ovum represents a failed embryonic development, often associated with trisomy 16, in which the chorion and amnion develop in the absence of a fetal pole. Although discussion about this information may help parents to understand the etiology of this type of early pregnancy loss, it should be conveyed in a manner which validates for parents that the pregnancy did indeed exist — not that this was a "nonpregnancy."

Ectopic Pregnancy

Sadly, ectopic pregnancy never has been managed first and foremost as a legitimate pregnancy loss. Physicians, of course, must respond aggressively to the emergency component of ectopic pregnancy, but they should not present the facts to parents in strictly clinical fashion.

Clinical challenge: You just have completed surgery this morning on your patient with an ectopic pregnancy. During the afternoon, you visit this patient as you make rounds, and you describe the surgical results to her. What do you say, and how do you refer to her pregnancy?

Certainly, when the physician discusses with the woman the nature of ectopic pregnancy, both pre- and postoperatively, details of the surgery are important. During such discussion, however, it is important to acknowledge sadness over the woman's loss of her baby. Recognizing the otherwise unstated impact of the loss conveys the message that the surgeon did not remove only "tissue," as in other types of surgery, but by necessity was involved in the process of the pregnancy loss. This approach requires that the physician appreciate the balance that must be achieved between emphasizing the surgery's ultimately critical importance to the woman's health and communicating awareness of the emotional toll of loss of the anticipated pregnancy.

Most recently, methyltrexate has been used successfully to treat unruptured ectopic pregnancies by attacking the placental tissue, thereby ending the pregnancy and eliminating the need for abdominal surgery (Glock, Johnson, & Brusmstead, 1994; Stovall, Ling, & Gray 1991). It is unstated, in these initial studies, whether or not the topic of pregnancy loss emerges in counseling of these patients. It would seem appropriate for care providers to address this outcome as they explain ectopic pregnancy to patients. Although terminating the pregnancy is the objective of the medical treatment, this may or may not be discussed in these terms with the patient.

Fetal Structural Anomalies which Are Incompatible with Life

In many ways, types of fetal structural anomalies and conditions can be discussed collectively. When the fetus exhibits a structural anomaly such as a congenital heart lesion, dysplastic kidneys, hydrocephaly, or hypoplastic left heart, a common theme emerges. Over time, parents can adjust intellectually to the realization that a fetus with severe hydrocephaly, or a large meningomyelocele, dysplastic kidneys, or hypoplastic heart may be so severely impaired as to compromise or altogether prevent any semblance of a normal lifestyle. If the baby's condition is not lethal but requires multiple major operations, with little hope that the child will live a normal life, this loss becomes for parents a perinatal "death" in its own right. For this reason, initial diagnosis in the ultrasound suite often resonates later for parents as the most intense and most devastating moment. With time and proper counseling, they gradually will understand the ramifications of their baby's diagnosis. Even when the baby's death has not yet occurred, the greatest and deepest sense of loss still devolves from that first moment when parents learn that their baby has a significant malformation. Parents who have discussed the impact of this realization, during counseling 1 or 2 years later, still recall with vivid detail their experience in the ultrasound suite. This episode clearly has the greatest effect, because parents' recollections about the circumstances of subsequent management and counseling sessions with obstetricians and other care providers, even as they were informed with greater detail about the baby's problems, fail to equal the inital emotional response.

With improvements in ultrasound technology and with our ability to diagnosis major fetal structural abnormalities prenatally, parents find themselves in the dreadful position of needing to participate in making choices regarding management. For some people, termination seems to be the "best" step, when diagnosis of a lethal or near-lethal condition is encountered prior to 24 weeks gestation. Such conditions include anencephaly, holoprosencephaly, bilateral dysplastic kidneys, hypoplastic left heart, Trisomy 13 or 18, cystic hygroma with ascites, and renal agenesis. If they decide to terminate the pregnancy, then parents should be informed about alternative techniques, and they should be referred to physicians who are skilled in this field (see Chapter 9, "Termination of Pregnancy for Fetal Abnormalities," for discussion about this topic). On the other hand, when parents elect to continue the pregnancy, despite the finding that the baby cannot survive, then they must be reassured that their baby and they will be provided appropriate care to prevent or minimize suffering throughout the rest of the pregnancy, during delivery, and after. They will want care providers to provide their baby adequate comfort, support, and respect, although the death is certain to occur.

For parents whose baby is found later than 24 weeks to have a near-lethal or lethal condition diagnosed by ultrasound, the options become more limited. If anything, decisions become more complex. Four options which parents and care providers must consider are:

1. *Allow labor and vaginal delivery to occur unmonitored, with the understanding that cesarean section would not be indicated for fetal distress.* Patients seldom choose this option, in spite of its logic and suitability for delivery of most babies with lethal conditions. From an emotional standpoint, however, many women cannot bear the possibility that the baby could die during labor, because this would mean that they never will see the baby alive.

2. *Perform a cesarean section, with the patient's understanding that it will not change the outcome.* For many people, this approach — which only a few

years ago would have been considered heresy by medical authorities — allows them to spend irreplaceable moments or hours with the baby before he or she dies. In my experience with parents who have chosen this route and who have been counseled later, no one regrets having made this choice.

3.   *Conduct tests of fetal well-being because of the remote possibility that the diagnosis is incorrect, and perform a cesarean section immediately if fetal distress is encountered.* In our initial experiences managing pregnancies complicated by fetal renal disease, and for many conditions which are debilitating but not necessarily lethal, this approach was chosen by patients. Among those for whom neonatal death was the inevitable outcome, none has regretted having undertaken the additional procedures, if they were well-advised and if the management plan was clearly understood.

4.   *Attempt vaginal delivery with continuous fetal heart-rate monitoring, with immediate cesarean section planned as an option if fetal distress is encountered.* For many conditions such as omphalocele, gastroschisis, and various forms of dwarfism, where cesarean section has not been recommended definitively as the preferred method of delivery, this management approach has satisfied parents and has facilitated the circumstances of such outcomes.

It is clear that, with technologic support available, long-standing opinions regarding pregnancy loss must make way for newer approaches, which recognize that pregnancy loss is a broad term. "Loss" encompasses a wide range of outcomes and prenatal diagnoses, many of which are influenced by the technology of ultrasound and by our improved understanding of the psychosocial impact of these types of losses upon parents. Although ultrasound technology in many ways has redefined obstetrics, obstetricians' rapport with patients will never be displaced as the cornerstone of the best possible medical care.

Managing Labor and Delivery

For patients with intrauterine fetal death, the components of proper care during labor and delivery require that medical staff (a) recognize unique aspects of labor resulting in delivery of a dead fetus, (b) be in constant, compassionate attendance, and (c) be aware of professional resources in the hospital which are beyond the scope of obstetrics but complement obstetric care in pregnancy loss.

Unlike labor resulting in delivery of a healthy baby, labor with an intrauterine fetal death offers no reward at the end. Consequently, concerns or fears that are often part of a normal labor process ("Will I tear?" "Will I embarrass myself?") are intensified by the knowledge that the labor process will only result in delivery of a dead baby. Anesthesia for labor should be planned with two objectives: (a) to make the patient comfortable during labor, and (b) to avoid heavy sedation that hinders efforts by medical personnel to address psychologic needs of the patient during this emotionally difficult labor. Once labor is established effectively, epidural anesthesia accomplishes both objectives. The patient may labor in a generally pain-free state (although some women may choose to labor without receiving pain medication, as they had planned to do before the baby died). The alternative of analgesic-free labor may represent a personal and painful sacrifice to balance guilt felt by the woman because her baby has died.

Medical personnel can provide emotional support to the woman as her labor progresses toward delivery. Providing sips of water or juice, making a radio or television available, and welcoming the companionship of family members — even bending rules to ensure that the patient benefits from ongoing family support — help to relieve the sadness of this patient's tedious, unrewarding labor process. It is important during labor that care providers be attentive to the patient. Many women remember feeling isolated in a labor room and being left alone during labor with an intrauterine fetal death. Impressions created by this type of care are, "No one cares about me," "This is so awful that even the medical staff are repelled by my labor," or "I'm repulsive to the medical personnel because of my condition."

Unfortunately, in many cases medical personnel *do* avoid the patient, primarily because care providers may feel inadequate when they know that they cannot offer any way to improve the situation ("save the baby's life"). For some care providers, being physically removed from the patient is less threatening personally. This desire to withdraw from a patient is a natural and common response by the obstetric community. It is difficult to sit at a patient's bedside during this type of labor, not knowing what to say or how to say it. Nonetheless, it is not appropriate to shy away from a patient because of such insecurities about confronting death. The woman is not asking for much — only that medical personnel not abandon her during her crisis. Merely remaining in the room provides comfort and companionship that will be remembered by the woman and her family long after the topics of conversation are forgotten. No one should be left alone and therefore lonely during labor for a stillbirth.

Occasionally, the woman in labor may feel left out of casual conversations and informal interaction between care providers and her family. It is common for conversations to involve her partner or relatives more than the woman herself, especially if active labor is in progress. There may be no way to resolve the conflict in the patient's mind of being isolated, suffering the discomfort of labor, and forgotten while conversation goes on around her but does not include her. For those engaged in idle conversation, this may represent "safe communication" which fills the silence while it avoids the issue of the fetal death. This conflict for the patient may be discussed openly in the early part of labor, to let the woman know that such emotional conflicts may surface as her labor progresses.

Addressing Feelings of Fear

Patients who are laboring with a known intrauterine death are overwhelmed by the sense of loss surrounding the baby's death, and care providers are incapable of "fixing" this tragic outcome. Instead, care providers must focus on those emotions which *can* be mitigated as labor and delivery progress.

With seemingly nothing to look forward to following delivery (a healthy baby), the patient may lose her perspective on the normal pains of labor as a natural physiologic process. Spontaneous or oxytocin-induced labor is characterized by periodic contractions and may be tolerated better by the patient than are prostaglandin-induced contractions, which characteristically are sustained, tetanic contractions. Unmonitored labor, by itself, may raise concerns for the woman about the possibility of damage to her reproductive organs.

A second source of fear may be based on the woman's expectations about her baby's appearance at delivery. Her idea of how the baby, dead *in utero* for days or weeks, will look at delivery almost always exaggerates the degree of change in physical appearance that a fetus undergoes following death. Some patients even may imagine that a process of decay already is well underway, an image of death often depicted on television and in films. Fears about the physical appearance of the baby, if not countered by caregivers, may influence parents' desire to see or hold their baby after delivery.

Guilt

Guilt is a common human emotion reflecting people's need to understand why a tragedy has occurred. The sense of absolute responsibility for fetal death is much more likely to be assumed by the woman than by her partner. "After all," she thinks, "I was the one who carried our baby in my uterus." This sense of responsibility for the baby, experienced by most women during pregnancy, now may be translated into assumption of utter responsibility for the baby's death. She irrationally may evaluate physical activities, conflicts, sexual intercourse, arguments, or eating habits in an effort to assign blame. Although many of these "causes" involve other people, the sense of personal responsibility for the fetal death is a major obstacle for these patients.

Anger

Anger may surface as a protective shield. It is a device used to ward off feelings of guilt or personal blame which may be present, but which are too painful to acknowledge. Anger may, however, be directed at obstetric care, medical personnel, or extraneous life events whose cause-and-effect role may be perceived by the woman. A well-informed patient is less likely to exhibit anger that is unwarranted by the circumstances. For the poorly informed patient, anger — irrespective of its focus and logic — may provide temporary insulation from her more frightening feelings of guilt or fear. In this case, anger is likely to interfere with supportive efforts made by care providers during the woman's labor and delivery.

Loneliness and Isolation

A sense of loneliness reflects the woman's feelings of isolation and fear of abandonment as she confronts her baby's death. Often phrased, "Why me?", this feeling may be coupled with guilt, as the woman wonders if she has done something "wrong" and now is paying for it. People with strong religious beliefs may interpret this event from within their faith's framework. Some may fear that they have been singled out because of some wrongdoing, and that now they are being punished. Others may respond to this tragedy as but another sad event in a life filled with crises. The majority of people, however, struggle with accepting an inexplicable and devastating loss. They have a hollow sense that for some reason they are being deprived the rewards of their dreams.

Managing Delivery of a Stillborn Fetus

At delivery, care providers must balance the patient's perception of events with technical aspects of the procedure. All too often, stillborn fetuses are delivered into a pan or in the labor bed. Although these approaches may satisfy clinical standards for a stillbirth delivery, they can impart a negative and uncaring attitude to the woman, as well as to her family. It is difficult for care providers, physicians or nurses alike, to recognize how differently the woman and her family perceive the dead baby. Care providers may focus on problems with the patient's labor, concerns with bleeding, fears of uterine rupture, and postpartum infection. Under these circumstances, they may neglect to consider such mundane issues as: Was the dead fetus delivered gently? Was the baby placed in a blanket? Was he or she traumatized at delivery? Naturally, these are issues of concern during delivery of a live baby, but often they are overlooked entirely during delivery of a fetus known to be dead — overlooked, that is, by all involved persons except the family. To the mother of this baby, how the baby was handled, wrapped, and treated often are no less important now than if the baby was born alive. Perhaps these issues become even more important in the case of stillbirth, when a woman struggles with feelings of guilt and the need to "do right" for her baby, while simultaneously she worries about things that she may not have done properly during her pregnancy.

If the baby is delivered in bed, he or she immediately should be wrapped in a blanket (not just covered by one). The umbilical cord should be clamped, and then the baby should be moved to an appropriate resting site. At no time should the baby be left lying in the bed between the patient's legs while the placenta is delivered. Likewise, no baby should be delivered and placed into a pan or bucket, or deposited thoughtlessly on the delivery cart. This image may linger with parents long after their baby has been buried. Once the baby is wrapped and separated from the placenta, he or she may be presented to the mother or retained in the blanket in a nearby room until the mother is ready to see her baby. Statements such as, "You have a boy; there are no obvious abnormalities," may ease the initial tension of the moment. In a combined labor and delivery room, the patient may wish to view the delivery itself. Requests such as this are appropriate and should be granted. Watching her stillborn baby's delivery can help the woman to begin the process of bonding that eventually can lead to a more satisfactory emotional recovery.

Delivery of a stillborn baby in the delivery room carries many of the same admonitions. No woman wants to think that her beloved but dead baby was delivered into a pan. The painful image of this manner of delivery is inappropriate for a human life now extinguished. Qualities that one attributes to living people are superimposed by parents onto their dead baby. Intellectually, they realize that life cannot be restored in their baby. Still, they expect their baby to be treated with the dignity which should be accorded to all persons in death. The request that a loved yet dead baby be treated with respect and honor is simple to fulfill. To do so, delivery of the stillborn baby must be viewed through the parents' eyes. Conversation among care providers in the room should be quiet, respectful, and focused upon the patient. Care providers must remember during delivery that the patient is observing them as they handle her loved baby. Only when care providers have successfully achieved a compassionate delivery can they establish foundations for the subsequent care and counseling that are crucial for parents during the postpartum grieving period.

Showing the Stillborn Baby to Parents

Once the care provider has removed the placenta from the uterus, he or she may choose to offer the baby for parents to view in the delivery room. This "disclosure" for many couples begins the labor of mourning (Patel, 1993). An alternative approach is to move parents to a quiet labor room or to an isolated area in the recovery room where they can spend time privately with their baby. Occasionally, it is appropriate to show the baby to the father or another close relative, while the mother is being moved out of the delivery room to a quieter area. A possible advantage of presenting the baby first to the father is that he then may be able to offer additional support if the woman is fearful of seeing her baby. Subsequently, the woman should be given the identical, full explanation which was received by the father. It is unrealistic to expect the baby's father to explain as well or even at all the information which was explained to him beforehand.

The woman should be awake and alert when she sees her baby. This may require that time be allowed to elapse for any anesthetic effects to wear off, if the type of anesthetic used can affect her ability to concentrate on her baby. It is a tragedy to hear a patient later regret the fact that she was too sleepy from the delivery medication to appreciate what was said to her or that she was too uncomfortable to enjoy holding her baby.

When care providers examine the baby in the presence of parents, they should realize that all people have a tendency to shy away from the dead. It is common to see a father standing nearby but unable to reach out and touch his stillborn baby. Some parents truly do not want to see or touch their baby. For many, however, this initial negative response reflects fears and misconceptions about death. Unfortunately, a woman who declines the offer to see and hold her baby often will regret this decision weeks, months, or years afterward. Later, families may question why care providers were not more helpful in advising and working with them during this period of confusion. It is important to educate parents explicitly, so that they may take their time to become comfortable with holding their child, even if this takes several hours.

To help parents to see their stillborn baby for the first time, several techniques may be helpful for the care provider. Wrapping the baby in a colorful blanket is a gesture which endows the baby with a measure of normality. More important, parents should be warned about the potential for changes in skin color and the skin desquamation that normally occur after death. These changes in integrity and color of fetal skin occur rapidly, often within 24 hours after death, and therefore they are encountered as a matter of course during delivery of a stillborn baby. Presenting the baby wrapped in a blanket so that at first parents see only the face gives them a few moments to adjust to their baby's lifeless body before they have to confront all the physical changes which are associated with death.

When the wrapped baby is presented to parents, certain mechanical maneuvers may enhance his or her appearance. Often, a stillborn baby has accumulated fluid in the scalp, thereby giving the skull a puffy, bloated appearance. When a hand is placed behind and under the head to relieve some of the superficial pressure, the baby's face and head can be made to appear more normal. This maneuver can also be used while the baby is being photographed. Once parents have seen their baby, care providers may help them to overcome any initial hesitation to hold their baby by emphasizing the normal appearance of features of the baby's anatomy. Holding the baby's hand or counting toes and fingers, for example, gives parents a moment to adjust subconsciously to the skin's condition and other physical changes that might startle or repel them from further contact with their baby's body.

If the woman is encouraged to examine more impersonal areas of her baby's body first, she is apt to be more relaxed once the baby is more fully exposed. At first, the presence of a care provider during parents' initial examination often helps them to overcome fears of touching a dead baby. The care provider may step back, after initial physical contact is established between parents and their baby. Generally, parents will continue to touch and handle their baby curiously and naturally.

It is also important to realize that, while medical professionals may view the disfigured head or body of a stillborn baby as an unattractive sight, parents who are properly guided in the initial examination of their baby can begin to project their own perceptions of the "future child" onto their stillborn baby. Parents do not see just the remains of their baby. Unlike proud parents of a healthy newborn, who are excited about tiny fingers and feet, or even the umbilical site, parents of a stillborn look beyond the baby's appearance, yearning to gain a sense of the person whom their baby would have become.

Physicians and nurses often ask, "How long should parents hold the baby?" "Are there 'rules' which apply to this experience?" Based upon years of observations, my answers are simple. Parents alone should determine when they have spent sufficient time with their dead baby. Or, stated differently, no physician or nurse, who may feel pressure because of other clinical commitments, should influence the duration of this moment. I have never encountered anyone who abused my time or this privilege.

As to "rules," there are only those which are absolutely necessary for compliance with hospital policy. If parents wish to have their stillborn son circumcised, for example, this request should be honored. If siblings are able to be present and, indeed, to be included in the experience of holding the baby, then this decision should be a family's personal choice, not one that is influenced by preferences of care providers. Weeks or months later, when children are asked to illustrate their impressions of this experience, a common, effective therapeutic technique, they draw pictures of balloons, flying carpets, and other symbols of hope and love, not of objects or symbols which are associated with fear. Many children draw images which portray the process of death and a child's concept of the resting place of the deceased sibling.

Because of common traditions which are part of health care practice, grandparents, as well as children, usually are shut out from the grieving process. Typically, there is the presumption that these family members need only be delegated the responsibility of support for their adult children who have suffered a devastating pregnancy loss. Yet for grandparents, too, the baby's death very much engulfs them in a prolonged cycle of grief. The grandchild's brief life may well become an important element in their experience of the cycle of life, prompting them to reflect anew upon their own mortality. How ironic it is that, when the daughter whose baby has died was young herself, her parents seemed to be able to solve all of life's problems. Now, these parents, as grandparents to the stillborn baby, in no way are able to protect their own adult child from the cruel pain of grief, from the terrible loss of a child. This is one reason why grandparents should be included, not excluded, from this process. In a simple way, care providers can bring grandparents' grief into perspective, as part of the mosaic of responses to the death of a young member in their family. By directing specific inquiries about their feelings to the grandparents during discussion and counseling, care providers often find themselves as participants in a rich and productive dialogue with multiple generations of a grieving family.

Postpartum Pregnancy-Loss Management in the Hospital

After delivery of a stillborn baby, interaction with the woman in the hospital often is stilted and unsatisfactory for professional and patient alike. Faced with the awkwardness of treating the postpartum woman who has just experienced a pregnancy loss, physicians often withdraw from much contact, diminishing their role (and value) in this critical phase of care for pregnancy loss patients. Under the best conditions, physician-patient contact while women remain hospitalized following delivery is brief. When pregnancy loss has occurred, the woman's postpartum stay may be even briefer. Coupling such a short hospitalization with the natural disinclination to say much under the circumstances, physicians may lose the window of opportunity for initiating invaluable postpartum follow-up with pregnancy loss patients who most need their obstetric care provider's ongoing support.

As the relationship between patient and physician becomes awkward during hospitalization, the gap created by this strained interaction is filled by willing nurses, social workers, or chaplains. Frequently, housekeeping personnel contribute appropriate expressions of sadness about a patient's baby's death. Picture these staff members who see patients daily as they clean the room, empty trash and say, with simple compassion, "I heard your baby died; I'm so sad for you." It is no wonder that a woman who may refer later to the nursing, social work, or clergy's efforts at comforting her in the hospital often will mention by name such a housekeeping employee, but unfortunately will fail to mention the physician among this group of supportive care providers who helped her when her baby died.

Bergman (1974) described the skill required of the obstetrician as "the art of therapeutic listening, that being there physically and spiritually is more important than what is said." By offering this type of counseling, the obstetrician communicates two important types of information. First, uncompromised attention, at the patient's bedside and later in the office, conveys interest, attentiveness, and compassion. Although it is not verbalized, this message reassures the patient that she will not be abandoned to struggle alone with her baby's death. Second, the obstetrician may, over several sessions, address facts essential to the patient's understanding of and recovery from her pregnancy loss. This level of care also should be extended to patients during a subsequent pregnancy.

Care Following a Pregnancy Loss

Contact in the hospital with pregnancy-loss patients can and should follow a standardized format. The woman should be visited once in the morning and once in the afternoon while she is hospitalized. During rounds, the physician should sit at the patient's bedside, allowing eye-to-eye contact at the same level, and the physician should not be hurried or impatient. Some care providers will challenge this recommendation, saying that time on work rounds does not permit this type of counseling. I suggest that, when a patient experiences a pregnancy loss, the physician should sit with the woman for 10 minutes (by the clock). During those 10 minutes, the discussion should focus exclusively on the baby. Most physicians who have tried this report that 10 minutes is ample time, and they comment that the encounter was extremely meaningful for the patient. Some physicians express surprise at how long 10 minutes can seem and at how many ideas can be conveyed in this brief amount of time.

Naming the Baby

If the baby's name has not been discussed before delivery, it is very important after delivery to ask parents what they have named their daughter or son, and to refer to the stillborn baby by the baby's given name thereafter. This courtesy transforms an otherwise anonymous "pathology specimen" into a human being and conveys an element of respect and dignity to the stillborn baby. The name which parents choose often reflects the significance of the moment. Some families initially may think that they want to "save" a previously selected name and to use instead a family name that will memorialize the dead baby. As a consideration, parents may be advised to reconsider using the name which they originally had selected. This gesture is helpful in acknowledging this baby as a person who did exist, so that parents will not fuse a subsequent baby's identify with that of this dead child. Answers to a simple question such as, "Why did you choose that name for your son (or daughter)?" often provide insight as to the emotional significance which parents attach to this baby. This line of questioning encourages parents to speak frankly about their feelings for their baby and about how they perceive him or her in the context of their family heritage.

Obtaining Permission to Perform an Autopsy

Among the questions most frequently asked months or years after delivery of a stillborn baby are, "What went wrong?" and "Will it happen again?" Answers to these questions may be found after a carefully conducted autopsy is performed (see Chapter 11, "Value of the Perinatal Autopsy," for a full discussion). Requesting permission to conduct an autopsy immediately after delivery of a stillborn baby, however, can seem uncaring and callous. It is easy to understand why requests for this procedure often are refused by distraught parents and are not pursued by care providers.

Patients often deny autopsy requests because they do not understand the value of the results and the nature of the procedure. When asked how they visualize an autopsy, many people describe a procedure which is a disfiguring, mutilating operation. It is not surprising then that many parents, even if they appreciate the importance of the findings, will refuse to subject their baby to such a procedure.

When seeking autopsy permission, care providers must consider the timing of their request and inquire into the patient's concept of the procedure. It may be useful to address the issue of autopsy in initial discussions, following diagnosis of the intrauterine fetal death, or at least in the early phase of labor. This approach, however uncomfortable it may be for care providers, familiarizes parents with concepts that later may be reinforced after delivery. Often it is inappropriate to approach a patient with an autopsy request in the first hour or hours after delivery of her stillborn. The shock of the event may lead the woman reflexively to refuse autopsy consent, despite its predictive value. The error of approaching a woman too soon after delivery may be compounded if the care provider accepts as final her decision to forego an autopsy. Valuable information is lost forever. Later, the woman may come to understand how useful the information could have been, and she may regret not having had the autopsy performed.

The proper approach toward obtaining permission to perform an autopsy is to delay making the request until parents have had some time to begin to assimilate the impact of the event. For some people, this period may only be 1 or 2 hours; for others, up to an entire day may be required. In the meantime, the baby should be kept in the morgue. Once parents are approachable, they should be informed as to the importance of information to be gained and asked about their concept of an autopsy. Gross misconceptions often may be picked up at this stage of counseling. Even if a woman refuses an autopsy for her baby, care providers should approach her again at a later time. It is a tragedy to lose the important data which an autopsy can yield because parents were confronted with this decision too soon after delivery or they refused because of lack of understanding. When the autopsy is described as a surgical procedure that will not disfigure the baby, as a procedure that may give important information as to why the baby died, most parents readily grant permission. Reassurance that the baby may be buried and granted the respect and love that parents wish to bestow upon him or her diminishes many fears which are associated with an autopsy.

Photographs

Clinical challenge: You have just delivered your patient with a fetal death at 38 weeks. The baby is macerated, yet the parents have requested that photographs be taken. What is your response? What techniques would you apply to obtain the most natural, normal image?

Care providers must appreciate the importance of photographs of the baby. These, and a blanket or other hospital items which may be collected as mementos, represent the only permanent evidence that the child was part of this family. In some cultures, displays of mementos or pictures are valued highly. Olali (1993) reviewed 86 obituaries which were published in 11 Nigerian newspapers. These "death advertisements" may occupy as much as one-half of a newspaper page. The obituaries serve as a link between the deceased and the bereaved, and they are a method of transmitting information from one generation to the next. Most include photographs which show the individual smiling, emphasizing this culture's concept of life and death as a continuum (Olali, 1993).

Several techniques are helpful for creating a more appealing image when it is time to photograph a dead newborn. The photographer must remember that he or she views the baby's body quite differently from the way in which it is perceived by the family. One picture should be taken with the baby partially clothed, which may help to obscure malformations. Actions such as bringing the baby's arm in front of his or her chest, or placing a cap on the head, help to create a more normal appearance, especially when there are malformations. Turning the head slightly can offer a better view of the facial characteristics, including the baby's profile. Consideration should be given as to whether the baby's eyes should be open or closed. Moistening the baby's lips helps to promote a more natural appearance. In past years, the recommendation has been to take instant snapshots, probably because these can be given immediately to the family and therefore are less likely to be misplaced. More often now, parents request that a 35 mm camera be used, so that the images are of better quality than can be captured in instant photographs. Many parents request that several photographs be taken, some with the baby clothed and some with the baby completely unwrapped. The different poses relieve any anxiety that important aspects of the baby's body were hidden by the blankets, presumably to hide a "shameful" malformation. The impact of parents' possessing photographs is best illustrated for me by what happens during a pregnancy-loss counseling session when I have requested that parents show me a picture of their baby. They often will pull out one of these photographs and display it with the same pride that I feel when I show somebody a photo of my adult daughters.

For those families who decide not to have photographs taken, photographs should be taken anyway and filed away. At a later time, many families return to ask if any photos were taken after all. Such photographs have great emotional impact when, several weeks after delivery (at which time the offer to take photographs was declined), parents call the office asking whether, by chance, any photographs were taken of their baby. Affirmation that, indeed, pictures are available has on occasion stopped a conversation because of the outpouring of tears and gratitude.

The impact when pictures are not taken is shown by an excerpt from a letter which was sent to me several years ago. It read:

> Thirty six years ago, we lost our first child — stillborn. My husband and mother saw him, and how I wish they had taken a picture of that baby. It would have been so much better for me. No one knows how much I wanted to see that baby.

Postpartum Issues

Breast engorgement is a specific postpartum occurrence that must be addressed for the woman who has suffered a late-term pregnancy loss. Before the patient's discharge from the hospital, her physician should verify that the woman is aware that this natural postpartum process following delivery is likely to serve as an emotional and stressful reminder of her tragedy. Although it is customary for a nurse to instruct the maternity patient about breast management, this issue may be overlooked (or avoided) by both physician and nursing staff following a fetal or neonatal death.

Managing the Patient after Hospital Discharge

The belief that obstetricians are not or cannot be concerned with the whole patient is reinforced when a woman returns for a postpartum examination following her pregnancy loss. As a rule, this visit at 6 weeks after delivery is the first contact that she has had with her obstetrician since discharge from the hospital. During those 6 weeks, families have struggled unaided and uninstructed through the most difficult period of their recovery. What happens, most often, is that they have been grieving for their baby. At the 6-week examination, the initial exchange — in the 15 minutes usually allotted for the postpartum examination — may take place in awkward and intimidating circumstances. In many busy practices, the woman may have been asked to undress and drape for her examination before the obstetrician enters the room.

OBSTETRICIAN: Hello, Mrs.___. How are you doing today?

PATIENT [*Feeling actual or presumed pressures of the short time interval set aside for the office visit and the authoritative posture of the busy obstetrician*]: I'm fine.

OBSTETRICIAN [*Immediately focusing on medical issues*]: Have your menstrual periods resumed yet [*even though resumption of menses may serve as a painful reminder of the failed pregnancy*]? What do you want to use for contraception?

[*The patient gives brief answers to these questions. The nurse enters the room; the patient is examined; and then the obstetrician steps out while the patient dresses.*]

OBSTETRICIAN: If you have any questions [*may not even state questions about what*], I want you to be sure to ask me.

[*Patient may ask some trivial questions in response to the obstetrician's question; otherwise smiles and says little.*]

In this oversimplified scenario, obstetrician and patient have both failed to address the true issues. The patient has not expressed her sadness, concerns, questions, or fears. The obstetrician (perhaps unconsciously) has relied heavily on medical issues to use up any time allotted for discussion. He or she has managed the postpartum visit normally, in spite of the patient's abnormal outcome. No effort has been made to put the woman at ease, so that she might feel comfortable enough to discuss the painful feelings that have been dominating her life in the aftermath of her pregnancy loss. In the end, both parties avoid the real reason for the visit. This example illustrates how their mutual behavior exacerbates problems caused by unskilled or insensitive care providers following pregnancy loss:

1. PROBLEM: *No contact until 6 weeks postpartum creates a major break in continuity of care.* The need for information is well-documented in a summary of 413 responses to an open-ended questionnaire seeking information about a woman and her pregnancy (Covington & Theut, 1993). These 413 women, whose responses were abstracted from those of 18,594 women who were surveyed as part of the 1988 National Maternal and Infant Health Survey, responded because they had experienced a pregnancy loss. More than 50% wanted more information about the baby or the health care which they had received, and 20% felt that the information provided by care providers was too technical and therefore

lacked sensitivity. This group's thirst for information was suggested strongly by the observation that women who experienced a stillbirth were 3 times more likely to respond to the questionnaire than were women who delivered a healthy liveborn baby. SOLUTION: See the woman and her partner, for counseling only, in the office within 1 week after discharge from the hospital. One visit or several weekly visits may be necessary to address the couple's needs. Defer a physical examination until 6 weeks postpartum.

2. PROBLEM: *One 15 minute appointment for the first postpartum visit is inadequate to provide appropriate care after a pregnancy loss.* SOLUTION: The initial office visit in the first week postpartum should be at least 30 minutes (and perhaps as much as 1 hour) long. Discussion should be devoted entirely to reviewing medical issues about and discussing emotional reactions to the woman's pregnancy loss. These topics may need to be addressed more than once. The woman also should be given more time during her 6-week postpartum follow-up visit, so that she may have time to discuss any remaining concerns with her obstetrician.

3. PROBLEM: *Failure on the obstetrician's part to address the subject of the loss usually intimidates the woman, who interprets this as a cue that she should not mention her failed pregnancy.* SOLUTION: The obstetrician must initiate (if necessary) a discussion about what happened and must be specific and directive in his or her questions, in order to encourage good physician-patient communication.

When and How Should the First Office Visit After Discharge Be Conducted?

During the hospitalization, the physician should encourage the woman and her partner, and the extended family if desired, to meet with him or her within the first week to 10 days following the pregnancy loss. That may seem too soon to some, but a meeting within this interval is extremely important, since the entire discussion time may be consumed by a conversation solely about the family's first day after they left the hospital. Did someone dismantle the nursery while the woman was in the hospital? Have they been able to sleep through the night? Is anyone having nightmares? How have family and friends reacted? Discussion of these and many other questions (see following) easily occupies a 1-hour counseling session. Note that physicians who acknowledge the value of this type of pregnancy loss counseling should create a flexible block of time to allow for scheduling such postpartum sessions.

The argument may be made that, in a busy obstetric practice, in which pregnancy loss unfortunately occurs frequently, such counseling sessions will be necessary on a regular basis, so that committed obstetricians should factor this type of care into their schedules.

What Style of Counseling Should be Adopted?

In initial postpartum (outpatient) counseling sessions, a directive and instructional approach to patient counseling serves several purposes.

1. The overall tone of the counseling sessions is one of informing the woman about events that led up to her pregnancy loss. This instructional form of counseling fulfills important early needs of the patient to learn facts. It sets the tone for a more in-depth discussion of the emotional consequences of pregnancy loss. Many people become uneasy if, as the sole purpose of the outpatient counseling session, they feel obligated to share their emotional response to this life crisis at a time in their recovery when they probably are not yet able to engage in this type of intimacy. Counseling sessions may be offered as an opportunity for the patient to talk openly if she desires. The invitation to talk may or may not be acted upon, and care providers should respond accordingly.

2. The directive, instructional approach allows physicians to reinforce and support the concept that a patient is exhibiting an appropriate response to her crisis. The purpose of initial outpatient visits should not be to probe for deep-seated neurotic or psychotic tendencies to "blame" for the patient's response to her pregnancy loss. In most cases, parents who are seen in these sessions are normal people recovering from a terrible experience. Their method of recovery follows no guidelines or rules. They have to learn for themselves how to carry on with their lives. Physicians can contribute greatly to their recovery by providing understanding and helpful advice, which can simplify this process.

3. This approach utilizes experience and ideas gained from counseling former patients and therefore conveys the message, "You are not alone in your response." The author often uses the expression, "This may not pertain to you, but I have had other patients tell me..."

It is critical that office staff be alerted when a pregnancy loss patient is coming to the office, so that she is not forced to remain in the waiting room with pregnant women. Instead, she and her partner or family should be ushered immediately into an examination room, where they can wait in privacy, and possibly may be seen more promptly.

Figure 5-3.
Suggested Questions Which Care Providers May Ask at the First
Postpartum Visit after a Patient's Pregnancy Loss

- Did the staff at the hospital treat you well?
- How did it feel to leave the hospital and go home?
- What was the hardest part for you?
- What do you think caused your pregnancy loss?
- How did your friends act?
- How have people in your family responded to what happened?
- [If the patient and/or her husband/partner has/have returned to work] How are your co-workers responding to what happened?
- How did your child/children react?
- What did you tell your child/children?
- Do you have any questions that you want to ask me?

Several questions can be offered in the first postpartum counseling visit, which will provide a basis for further communication (see Figure 5-3). Subsequent visits allow for more comprehensive discussions of the events. They also allow several questions to be asked which might be more effective at a later time than they would be during the initial consultation (see Figure 6-3).

Exploring Potential Hostile Emotions of Patient toward Physician

When a patient's pregnancy loss occurs, many a physician's first thought is, "Did I miss something?" It is understandable why, during counseling sessions after such a loss, this may be a difficult line of questioning to broach. To bring up this sensitive topic may be personally threatening to care providers. No matter how clearly the pregnancy loss is understood, or how obviously the baby's death was no one's "fault," many patients direct great anger toward their care providers, simply because there is no other target for blame. Nevertheless, I strongly advocate the policy of bringing these issues into the discussion, to defuse a patient's anger — be it justified or unjustified — and to facilitate resolution of that anger as much as possible. Examples of frightening and painful questions that the physician would like answered are shown in Figure 7-3.

Figure 6-3.
Suggested Questions Which Care Providers May Ask at Follow-up
Pregnancy-Loss Counseling

- [Repeat any of the questions from the first visit (see Figure 3).]

- [Review the patient's perception of the cause of her pregnancy loss.]

- Since you have been home and have spoken with your family and friends, do you have new questions about your baby and what happened?

- Have you and your husband/partner been able to share your feelings about your baby's death?

- Would you like to attend a support-group meeting for people like you who have experienced a pregnancy loss? Members of the group ma have insights into their experiences and recovery that might help you.

- Do you have any questions that you want to ask me?

Unfortunately, questions like this often may elicit the admission that parents indeed feel that the physician should or could have done more to save the baby's life. Regardless of the facts of an individual case, even though a patient's expression of anger would make any care provider uncomfortable, it is better to bring these emotions out in this manner. Otherwise, it is more likely that anger will be manifested by a lawsuit sometime later.

Feelings Generated by Encounters with Others

There appear to be common, uncomfortable encounters which couples who are recovering from a pregnancy loss experience. Two general types of these encounters are discussed below.

1. *"My family and friends avoid me."* Relatives and friends represent the most important long-term support system for couples and families as they grieve for their pregnancy loss. Unfortunately, few people are at ease discussing the death of a baby, regardless of the strength of the relationship between parents and their relatives or friends. More commonly, family or friends are solicitous and attentive for the first day or couple of days after the woman returns home. Then, naturally, most outsiders become pre-

Figure 7-3.
Direct Questions Which Encourage the Pregnancy-Loss Patient
to Confront Anger

- Are you angry at me for not doing something sooner?
- Do you feel that I should have done more to identify the problem?
- Do you feel that I caused this?
- Do you think that I may have overlooked something?

Indirect Questioning Can Accomplish Similar Goals, to Explore Hostile
Emotions, Using a Neutral, Less Confrontational Approach.

- You seem angry. Can you tell me what it is caused by?
- Some couples at this point are very angry. Do you have these feelings? If so, where are they directed?
- It is understandable that you might feel angry or frustrated that more should have been done or that something should have been done earlier. Do you have these feelings?

occupied once again with their own activities and commitments shortly thereafter. Worse, some family members or friends avoid the couple altogether. Misconceptions that motivate this avoidance behavior are simply that relatives and friends may not know what to say. They also are afraid that they will "say the wrong thing." They worry that if they say something "wrong" and the woman cries, then they will have caused her to be sad. They fail to recognize that the woman often cries because someone, finally, has said, "Tell me how you feel." When family or friends stay away, the woman is apt to interpret this action as reflecting an uncaring and indifferent attitude.

2. *"I run into friends or acquaintances who are unaware of my pregnancy loss."* Unexpected encounters, where the shock of seeing the formerly pregnant woman who no longer is pregnant must be grasped, often occur in public places. For example, many women recount the dismay on both sides when they meet members of their natural childbirth classes in public. In these circumstances, the woman is unsure whether to be honest and state what happened or to ignore the other person in order to avoid an unpleasant encounter, to either protect herself or "spare" the other. On

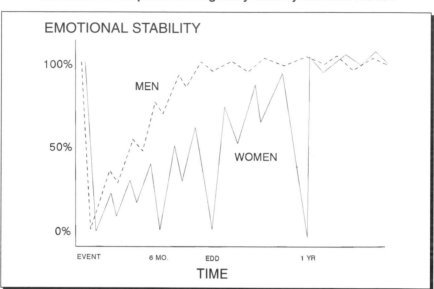

Figure 8-3.
Difference in Response to Pregnancy Loss by Men and Women

EDD = Estimated Date of Delivery

the other hand, the woman who has lost her baby may realize that her acquaintance behaves as though she has not recognized her, and there is a sense that people are avoiding her in the wake of her "bad luck."

It is not unusual for friends or relatives, especially those who themselves are pregnant, to pull away from contact with someone whose pregnancy has failed, because of the irrational urge to see that woman's tragedy as contagious.

Fortunately, most people who are recovering after a pregnancy loss will find more comfort than pain among their family, friends, and acquaintances. It is valuable to help patients recognize that some painful encounters will be branded forever in the memories of grieving parents, and to encourage them to seek support from those who prove most capable and willing to provide it to them over the long run.

Differences Between Men and Women Affect Pregnancy-Loss Counseling

It goes without saying that men and women differ in their recovery following a pregnancy loss. It is not that one approach is right while the other is wrong, only that they are different. Appreciating the differences enables pregnancy-loss counselors to direct their style of discussion to meet the needs of the couple individually and collectively. Figure 8-3 illustrates the differing recovery patterns among men and women which I have encountered during my counseling of pregnancy loss patients and their partners.

For men and women alike, there is an initial period in which the impact of the pregnancy loss places them in a synchronized phase of grief. This period may be brief, however, as the recovery patterns of the partners diverge. Men appear to recover relatively rapidly; but, in doing so, they may find themselves engaging in additional activities. Some will take on a new job, while others may take up a hobby or a new pastime to keep busy. Some men find themselves assuming or being thrust into a problem-solving role. With an increase in activity or action, men sometimes try to suppress guilt feelings about their not having spent sufficient time with their partner before or during the pregnancy loss (Carr-Gregg & Lennox, 1993). Women are much less likely to approach their grief and recovery from pregnancy loss in these ways. Women will have good and bad days; but they may experience significant regression in the grieving process at critical anniversaries, such as 6 months or 1 year after delivery, or at the estimated date of delivery.

It is important that men and women be informed that they very likely will differ in their responses to the pregnancy loss. This knowledge will provide a foundation for their mutual recovery as a couple. To evaluate differing responses of couples to pregnancy loss, Black (1991) surveyed 121 women with a questionnaire and interview, conducted at 1 to 2 months and then at 6 months after the pregnancy loss. At 1 and 6 months, 65% and 54% of women expressed their ability to talk with their partner about their feelings, while only 18% and 19%, respectively, were unable to benefit from this level of communication. Over 50% of couples at both interview points felt that they were reacting similarly to the way in which the partner was reacting. Moreover, 62% felt closer to the partner immediately after the pregnancy loss; only 7% felt more separated. At 1 month after the pregnancy loss, 19% of respondents acknowledged having sexual difficulties. While these data support the strength of a relationship following pregnancy loss, these women generally indicated that they grieved longer and more intensely than did their partners.

How Long Will They Grieve?

Answers to the question of how long it normally takes to grieve depend upon the individual, the event, the nature of family support, and how the process of grieving proceeds. Lindemann, in his evaluation of grief, believed that individuals resolved their feelings in 6 to 10 weeks (Lindemann, 1944). In the absence of pathologic grief, women who experience a pregnancy loss appear much more protracted in their normal grieving process. As noted by Jellinek (1994), the individual's prior experiences with similarly adverse circumstances undoubtedly affect the nature and duration of the grief response. Perhaps more importantly, the duration of grief depends upon the "grief work accomplished," which Lindemann believes allows the individual, over time, to become released from "bondage" to the deceased, while readjusting to a new environment and developing new relationships. If, on the other hand, someone avoids the intense distress associated with working within the grief experience, then only limited, true recovery is achieved, and the duration of grief actually is prolonged (Lindemann, 1944).

Certainly, during the first few months, intense grief following a pregnancy loss should be viewed as normal. Hunfeld (1993) reported on a series of 41 women who were evaluated first within 2 to 6 weeks following ultrasound confirmation of life-threatening anomalies and then 3 months postpartum. The level of grief had not diminished over this period of time, even though psychologic instability was less at 3 months postpartum.

In my personal experience, an interval of 6 to 18 months seems consistent with a normal period of grief. I have identified this interval as a result of hundreds of pregnancy-loss counseling sessions which I have conducted with couples in the months after suffering a pregnancy loss, and in sessions to evaluate risks which may recur during a subsequent pregnancy. During these sessions, I include questions about the baby's name and place of burial, and the parents' memories of the past event. Although a number of these consultations purportedly are requested to discuss the future pregnancy, I often find that more than half of the consultation is used eagerly by the woman or couple to recall and perhaps be reacquainted with the dead baby. Tears often are generated during these sessions, reflecting the very long grieving process which healthy couples experience, even as they focus on future events.

To emphasize the importance of the 1-year anniversary following a baby's death, I encourage physicians to instruct their receptionists to note in their calendars 1 year from the day when this event has occurred, so that the physician can telephone the patient near that critical date. Physicians frequently are impressed by the reaction that women exhibit in response to this thoughtful gesture.

Figure 9-3.
Letter Written by Father to His Stillborn Son

Dear Son:

When I kissed you and left last night, I realized there were many things that I hadn't said to you. I forgot to tell you how proud mom and I were when we first found out she was pregnant with you. Grandma and Grandpa said you would be a boy; I thought so, too. I'll never get to buy you that baseball glove I saw at the store the other day. We'll never take those camping trips when Grandpa, and I would have taught you to fish. We won't ever have time to replace the old engine on my motorcycle. I was going to repaint the bike when you were old enough to drive it.

During your mom's pregnancy, I made a lot of plans for you and me. I guess all dads do that. I'll just have to keep these dreams in my heart until we meet again.

Mom and I will love you forever.

Dad
(June 1983)

The Value of Writing about or Recording this Experience

It is important that parents be informed of the value of capturing their emotions during the early phase of the grieving process. This is the time when parents are most closely attuned to their deepest and most intimate feelings about the pregnancy loss. Writing, recording on cassette, or videotaping meaningful statements about the significance of this experience in life becomes both a cathartic activity and a priceless memento in honor of this lost child. Care providers should suggest that patients make some effort to record their feelings soon after the pregnancy loss. The need for early timing of this action is demonstrated by women who initially decide not to write down their feelings but then attempt to capture their emotions months later. In these circumstances, they commonly find that, when they try to write about the baby, the experience, and their feelings long afterwards, the emotions cannot be stated as clearly, and the impact cannot be captured as vividly, as they can be immediately after experiencing the pregnancy loss. I often suggest that people simply write a letter about the event. The style of the letter can take many forms. Some people begin to write a journal or diary, to express their thoughts each day during their time of grieving. Couples sometimes write letters to each other. Others write a separate or a joint personal letter to their baby. Often, the idea to do this can be motivated by the physician's suggestion, with an opening line such as:

"I am writing this letter to tell you about the hopes and dreams that we had for you, but now never will be able to say to you...We had a lot of plans..."

I have heard women describe writing, and crying, all through the night as they compose a letter such as this. Later on, they will reflect proudly on the importance of this effort. This letter will probably never be discarded. Additionally, it will be kept along with the blanket, photographs, and other mementos as physical proof that this experience occurred and that this baby existed. The letter shown in Figure 9-3 was shared with me by a father who wrote to his stillborn son.

Conclusion

In the end, why should care providers become involved with patients following a pregnancy loss? For some, there is the reassuring knowledge that "grief is a dynamic, individual, pervasive process but with a strong normative component" (Rodgers & Cowles, 1991). Or, as quoted by Grobstein (1978), "Mourning is the transition from grief to memory." Patel (1993) provided another answer by quoting the French physician, Edward Livingston Treudeau: "To cure sometimes, to help often, to comfort and console always." Another, and perhaps more personal answer, is expressed eloquently in a poem by Robert Browning Hamilton:

> *I walked a mile with pleasure*
> *She chattered all the way;*
> *But left me none the wiser*
> *For all she had to say*

> *I walked a mile with sorrow*
> *And ne'er a word said she;*
> *But, oh, the things I learned from her*
> *When sorrow walked with me.* (Robert Browning Hamilton)

In summary, pregnancy loss *is* an obstetric responsibility. Pregnancy loss management has a structured format, and its implementation by caring providers demonstrates that medicine remains a noble and compassionate art.❏

Case Study 1-3

Facilitating Introspection

You are called by an obstetric colleague from another group practice who seeks your advice. The patient of your colleague is a 28-year-old G2P1, Class C diabetic whose prenatal course was complicated by weight gain from 175 to 245 pounds and only modest compliance with a proposed diet from the American Diabetes Association. Although frequent attempts were made by her physician to control her plasma glucose levels by dietary and insulin adjustment, her hemoglobin A1C values remained above 8%. By serial ultrasound evaluation, the patient was known to carry a macrosomic fetus, and antepartum testing carried out from 32 weeks confirmed good fetal health.

The patient experienced spontaneous onset of labor at 38 weeks gestation and entered a normal labor pattern. A spontaneous vaginal delivery was under way. But, upon delivery of the head, the shoulders impacted. The McRoberts maneuver and suprapubic pressure were carried out along with rotation of the shoulders resulting in delivery after 7 minutes of manipulation of a depressed newborn male with Apgar scores at 1, 5, and 10 minutes of 3, 5, and 6, respectively, despite the presence and active intervention of a pediatrician. The neonatal course of the baby was stormy, complicated by detection of Bell's palsy and a fractured left clavicle.

The colleague tells you that, due to the anxiety generated by the delivery and the clinical course of the newborn, he was unable to find adequate time in the hospital to sit with the couple during the immediate postpartum period. Upon discharge, the physician claimed that it was impossible to coordinate visits to the neonatal intensive care unit with those of the parents. The physician now confides in you his inability within his busy practice to schedule a time to sit down with the parents to discuss the birth events. Further conversation reveals that the physician also is experiencing justifiable fear and anxiety that the father of the baby may threaten physical harm if such a meeting were to occur. The anger which was exhibited by the father was noted by nurses who attended the patient in her labor. They question whether the father's anger in fact was directed toward his spouse, because of her poor compliance with her diet, which may have produced the macrosomia.

Your colleague seeks your advice and also asks if you would sit in on a counseling session with the couple and the physician, to act as mediator for a potentially complex and emotional discussion.

Commentary

When there is an adverse outcome in pregnancy, there is the potential for finger pointing and a need to assign blame. There are at least three players in this particular equation. They are the physician and health care team, the patient herself, and her husband. None may be at fault, or all may have contributed to the outcome of the pregnancy. It is not my place to assign blame or to be a judge. My colleague has asked for my advice, however, and I am willing to explore his contributions or lack of them, in an attempt to facilitate his own introspection and his own ability to interact effectively with the couple.

In doing so, I would ask my colleague to enunciate what his goals and objectives are for the meeting and, also, what he thinks the couple's goals and objectives are for the meeting. I would encourage him to have as his objectives a review of the antepartum care, a review of what took place during labor and delivery, and a review of the subsequent medical course of both mother and infant.

I am reluctant to sit and moderate a session between the physician and the couple. I am concerned that my presence would disempower the role of my colleague, would suggest that a third-party mediator and witness must be present during a potential confrontation, and might appear to be a show of force against the couple. My other considerations are that I do not have a prior therapeutic relationship with the couple, and I have not obtained their permission to meet with them. I also do not know my colleague well enough to anticipate how he is going to react in general to the interaction or in specific to questions I or the couple may pose.

I am worried about my colleague's inability to find the time to meet with the couple during the postpartum hospital stay and then, subsequently, during the newborn's hospital stay. I consider it a fundamental error in his overall management of the patient's perinatal care. As a result, I believe that he now needs to play catch-up and could have trouble doing so. This apparent inaction lends itself to a number of uncomplimentary interpretations. They include lack of caring, callousness, guilt, or lack of experience in this type of patient relationship. I would caution my colleague about invoking a busy practice or time constraint as an excuse. These facts alone indicate that he set priorities and made the time for those things for which he wished to make time. Unfortunately, it too often is true that the attitude, "I don't have the time," is equated with, "I don't care." The latter can be what patients "hear." In this case, it also creates for the couple the impression that something which the physician did was amiss.

It is not clear to me to what extent my colleague believes that he was responsible for the adverse outcome of both macrosomia and shoulder dystocia with the resultant injury. Therefore, I would offer to review both the prenatal and the intrapartum medical record with him. This is an attempt to reinforce or to be critical of the care which he provided. I would explore his care in detail in order to evaluate his knowledge base of how to manage a diabetic pregnancy. This knowledge of technique would include how to manipulate the variables of caloric intake, insulin dosing, and activity to obtain and maintain euglycemia; the appropriate use of consultants such as dieticians and nurse case managers to help to motivate the patient to be an active participant in her care; and an appropriate plan for managing labor and delivery. In doing so, I am trying to ascertain if or why the patient was unable to adhere to a regimen which is designed to minimize diabetic fetopathy.

I would assess my colleague's awareness of the risk factors for shoulder dystocia, his evaluation of the labor curve as a clue to its potential, and the extent to which he was prepared to deal with it at the time of delivery. I believe that 7 minutes is a long time for a skilled obstetrician to effect delivery when there is a shoulder dystocia. Therefore, I would review the actual sequential steps which he took, and those which he knew to take once the dystocia was recognized.

After collecting all of this information, I then would offer to role play my colleague's anticipated interaction with the affected couple. First, I would assume his role with the couple while he acted their roles, and then I would take the role of the couple while he took his own actual role. This might help my colleague to clarify what he wants to say and how he wants to say it.

I can appreciate the husband's potential anger, perhaps born of powerlessness or helplessness to make things right. The possibility that he will engage in some sort of physical violence is extremely unlikely. I think that this concern reflects either the physician's sense of guilt for the outcome or rationalization to avoid further interaction with the couple.

In his actual conduct of this session, I would ask my colleague to think in terms of "win/win" — that is, the ability to recognize the truth when it is spoken and to agree with it, to acknowledge that there is sadness and disappointment when a perfect perinatal outcome is not achieved, and to help the couple to differentiate between what was preventable from what was not. I purposely would inquire about future pregnancies and take a proactive approach to preconception counseling and care for the next pregnancy. In doing so, I would be prepared to discuss the probability of a recurrent macro-somic newborn and shoulder dystocia. Finally, I would remind my colleague that it is essential that he write or dictate a complete note in the patient's medical record after this discussion has occurred.

— *Ronald A. Chez, MD*

Case Study 2-3

Diagnosis of Fetal Death, Labor and Delivery, and Post-Loss Office Visit

Your patient is a 25-year-old G1P0, whose prenatal course had been uncomplicated. Then, at 39 weeks gestation, the woman notes a sudden decrease in fetal movement. She comes to your office for her weekly scheduled appointment. She tells the nurse that her baby is not moving very much. The nurse attempts to listen to the baby's heartbeat and then calls you into the examining room. You cannot detect fetal heart tones, and intrauterine fetal demise is confirmed by ultrasound later that day. You advise induction of labor, which is undertaken the next day. After uncomplicated labor, the still-born baby girl is delivered by you. After delivery, a newly trained nurse who was attending the delivery approaches you. This was the first time that she has witnessed a stillbirth delivery, and she seeks comments from you about what fundamental issues an inexperienced care provider should remember about labor and delivery management for a patient in these circumstances.

Also following the delivery, the postpartum nurses approach you for advice as to how they can complement your efforts while your patient still is in the hospital. Moreover, you call your office to schedule an appointment for the couple within the first 2 weeks after delivery, and the office nurse asks you what preparations should be made to help alleviate the couple's distress and sense of isolation when they come for the appointment.

Commentary

Part A: Diagnosis of Fetal Death

Telling a woman that her near-term fetus is dead is one of the most dif-ficult situations that an obstetrician, family physician, or nurse-midwife faces. Everyone in the room is anxious when a woman has diminished fetal movement, as the nurse searches with the doptone. It is almost as if patient and care providers alike hold their breath while the doctor searches for a heartbeat with the ultrasound. The way that a woman is told about her fetus's death may have a lasting impact on her and her family.

The physician must inform the patient of the death of the baby in an unambiguous but gentle fashion. Almost all pregnant women who have had an ultrasound can identify the beating heart of the baby. Thus, it is helpful to show the ultrasound image to the woman and any members of the family who are with her, point out the heart and say that it is not beating. By showing her the ultrasound image, stating the problem which is demonstrated, and then telling her that her baby has died, the physician will have been as unambiguous as possible. If the woman has a supportive family member or friend with her, it is certainly ideal to share this news with her when she has a support person around. It is critical to remember, however, that you as her health care provider are also an integral part of the support provided to the patient. It is essential that the person who communicates the news of the fetal demise remain with the patient for a reasonable period of time after confirming this distressing event.

The patient's emotional reactions can vary across the spectrum of human emotions: patients can react in silence with no outward signs; they may weep quietly and express disbelief; or they may break into anguished sobbing. At some point, a patient may exhibit intense anger at her physician, in a somewhat classic "shoot the messenger" reaction. It is critical that the physician, who herself or himself is feeling sadness and anxiety about the death of the baby, not become defensive with the patient. Allow the woman to cry and to vent her sadness and anger. Accept the fact that, for the most part, this is a diffuse anger and not directed at the physician personally. Stay with the woman. It is appropriate to hold her hand, to allow her to cry on your shoulder, or even to cry with her. It is reasonable to provide a washcloth, a drink of water, and tissues for tears. Make it clear that such items are available, but do not thrust them on her. She may feel much better just weeping inconsolably. As long as the patient is not left alone, it is reasonable after a 5- or 10-minute interval to leave her with her support person or another member of the health care team. If necessary, after a short time the patient and others may be moved from the examining room into a counseling room or office for further discussion.

The series of questions that arise once confirmation of the fetal death occurs can be predicted. The most common question is, "Why did my baby die?" It is important to outline steps to determine the cause of death. It is critical to warn the family that no cause might be identified despite an extensive evaluation. High-risk factors such as hypertension, diabetes, underlying fetal anomalies, maternal substance abuse, or traumatic injury to the woman's abdomen should be sought by history and review of prenatal records. Laboratory analysis should be obtained in the first few hours after the diagnosis if the patient is able to tolerate phlebotomy. Further sonography should include Kleihauer-Betke, maternal type and screen for irregular antibodies, a toxicology screen, evaluation for fetal infections, and a careful physical examination. Detailed sonography of the fetus before delivery might reveal fetal anomalies — and, indeed, might be more revealing than a later autopsy if significant maceration has occurred. If the patient will allow it, amniocentesis prior to delivery or amniotic fluid which is obtained via an intrauterine pressure catheter at delivery carries a higher rate of cell growth than obtaining pericardium or tendon from the stillborn baby.

A frequently asked question is, "Do I need to decide immediately what I should do about labor?" In the absence of an acute obstetric event (for example, placental abruption or severe hypertension), there is no immediate maternal risk in carrying a dead fetus. Many couples will choose to return to their home, to discuss the next series of steps with other family members.

Once the patient is calm enough to leave the office, it is important to be sure that she has a safe way home. Frequently, people in this situation feel stunned and disoriented. If there is a back door through which the patient can exit the office without walking past a waiting room of obviously pregnant women, this would allow her to save some dignity and would avoid upsetting other patients. If another driver is not with the patient, it might be necessary to call someone from home or have a taxi take the patient home if she seems unable to drive a car.

An important part of the communication for the physician and the patient is for the physician to share his or her own grief and sadness with the patient. Saying, "I'm sorry that you've lost your baby..." to the patient certainly does not imply the physician's or nurse-midwife's contribution to the death of the baby but communicates your caring to her.

Another feature of the immediate interaction with the family once a fetal death has been confirmed is that of giving the woman and her family some control over management decisions. Many families in this situation describe at the moment when the diagnosis is made an immediate loss of control in their lives. While the news might stun them to the point of inability to make a decision, at least ask them whom you can call for them, and give them some choice in the immediate events that are to follow.

Part B: Labor and Delivery

The nurse's concern about being supportive of the medical goals for the delivery of the patient with a term stillbirth is a key factor in the care of a patient with a death *in utero*. The nurses in most labor and delivery units spend more one-on-one time with the patient and her family than does the attending physician. If labor and delivery rules are written such that there is a limited number of family members who are permitted to remain with the patient, it might be reasonable to ask for a relaxation of the rules if having others would be supportive for this patient. The nurse who is involved with the care of the patient should be willing to provide extra emotional support herself. The process of labor with a dead fetus can be complicated. If placental abruption is a component of the cause of death, uterine activity can be altered and more painful. Certainly a coagulopathy would alter immediate medical management. If chorioamnionitis has contributed to or resulted from the fetal demise, the woman might experience greater physical discomfort, and labor can be more complicated with an infected uterus.

Certainly, an induction rather than a spontaneous labor can take longer, and efforts should be made to provide for cervical ripening. Higher doses of Pitocin® than those which are used in standard labor management frequently are employed. Nonetheless, clear guidelines with the nursing staff for how high the Pitocin can be administered is critical. The second stage of labor can be complicated, depending on the length of time which has passed since fetal demise occurred. The head of a dead fetus is considerably softer than that of a live baby and might not provide the dilating wedge for purposes of cervical dilation. Additionally, traumatic injury to the fetal body during delivery is more likely to occur in this setting. Care should be taken, and the nurse should be advised of this, so that expulsive efforts can be supported. Pain relief is an important issue. Once fetal demise has been diagnosed, a common request from patients is to be "knocked out," so that psychically they will not have to feel any of the process. It is important to avoid sedating such a patient in excess of what is normally done for laboring patients. Such a delay in emotional involvement with the death only serves to make the process of grieving and resolution more difficult. Nursing staff members should be advised that only under unusual circumstances would it be necessary to remove the baby quickly from the delivery area without allowing time for the patient and her family to see and hold their baby. The patient should be advised during her labor process that it is usually beneficial that she see her baby. It also is important to ascertain the name that the family has planned to give to the baby, so that at the time of delivery the baby can be addressed by his or her given name. Most families appreciate an emphasis on the humanity of their baby at birth and a de-emphasis of medical components of their care at that moment. An offer to provide pastoral counseling or support by her clergy member either during labor or at the time of birth should be considered and respected.

At the time of delivery, either the physician or the nurse should take the time, within the realm of the patient's acceptance, to show the baby to the family in a quiet, dignified manner. It is useful to point out normal features of the baby. Hands and feet carry great emotional symbolism, and it is nice to count fingers and toes, similar to what is done with a living baby. Providing the family with a lock of hair or a footprint for the delivery record and a receiving blanket or identification bracelet can be important components of the family's grieving process. Additionally, photographs can be taken of the family holding their baby. These sort of gatherings of mementos are frequently within the realm of the nurse's roles with these patients.

In the past, patients who experienced a stillbirth frequently have been discharged from labor and delivery to the gynecology ward, in order to protect them from the sounds of crying babies and the sight of happy couples. For some families, this is an appropriate choice; but the woman should be given the option of having her postpartum stay on the obstetric service. It might be easier for some women to deal with acute grieving and the sight of newborns in a controlled fashion where there are health care personnel available to be supportive, rather than a week after discharge in the grocery store.

Part C: Post-Loss Office Visit

The fact that the office staff is aware of the fetal demise is a positive reflection on the communication systems in this office. Patients who are seen throughout the course of pregnancy in an obstetric practice also are seen, of course, by the front desk personnel, the nurses, the insurance coders, and others who build a relationship with patients. It is critical that these people who may be interacting with the patient be apprised of the death so they do not inadvertently ask "How is your new baby?" when the patient calls for an appointment. Some sort of communication system is important so that such embarrassing and mutually painful episodes can be avoided. If possible, in order to give full attention to the patient and her needs and to help the woman avoid a full obstetric clinic waiting room, patients who have had a poor pregnancy outcome can be scheduled at the extremes of the day. Front desk personnel can be advised to contact local newspapers and squelch hospital birth announcements that sometimes are listed routinely, so that families with a pregnancy loss are not inundated with unwelcome sales solicitations and inquiries about their baby. Additionally, front desk staffers can send a condolence card, to express the group's sympathy 1 or 2 weeks after the patient has delivered. Having all the people who know the patient sign the card might be appropriate. At the time of the follow-up visit, any laboratory test results which might be relevant to the cause of death of the baby should be shared with the patient. The chart should be flagged with the infant's name, so that office personnel and the physician can refer to the baby by his or her name. Because acutely grieving individuals may have a lower tolerance for inefficiencies and perceived slights, the office personnel should be advised to provide extraordinary treatment for these patients.

When a family has had a bad pregnancy outcome, it is important to realize that, at times a patient may choose to have any follow-up care or future pregnancy care with another provider. This is commonplace even though a woman's care was flawless and the physician or nurse-midwife did not in any way contribute to the death of the baby. This should not be taken as a personal affront; cordial, responsive, and sympathetic provision of records to, and sharing of information with, other physicians should be facilitated without hesitation.

— *Nancy C. Chescheir, MD*

References

Bergmann, A.B. (1974). Psychological aspects of sudden unexpectant death in infants and children. *Pediatric Clinics North America, 21*, 115-121.

Black, R.B. (1991). Women's voices after pregnancy loss: Couples' patterns of communication and support. *Social Work in Health Care, 16*, 19-36.

Borgman, J. (1984, June 17). Editorial cartoon. *The Cincinnati Enquirer.*

Lewis, E. (1979). Mourning by the family after stillbirth or neonatal death. *Archives of Diseases in Children, 54*, 303-306.

Carr-Gregg, M., & Lennox, N. (1993). Perinatal grief and the grief of a father. *Australian Family Physician, 22*, 1187-1189.

Covington, S.N., & Theut, K. (1993). Reactions to perinatal loss: A qualitative analysis of the national maternal and infant health survey. *American Journal of Orthopsychiatry, 63*, 215-222.

Cuisinier, M.C.J., Kuijpers, J.C., Hoogoluin, C.A.L., deGraauw, C.P.H.M., & Janssen, H.J.E.M. (1993). Miscarriage and stillbirth: Time since the loss, grief intensity and satisfaction with care. *European Journal of Obstetrics and Gynaecology and Reproductive Biology, 52*, 163-168.

Dewhurst, S.J. (1984). The alleged miscarriages of Catherine of Aragon and Anne Boleyn. *Medical History, 28*, 49-56.

Glock, J.L., Johnson, J.V., & Brumsted, J.R. (1994). Efficacy and safety of single-dose systemic methotrexate in the treatment of ectopic pregnancy. *Fertility and Sterility, 62*, 716-721.

Grobstein, R. (1978). The effect of neonatal death on the family. In O.J.Z. Sahler (Ed.), *The child and death* (p. 98). St. Louis: C.V. Mosby.

Hunfeld, J.A.M., Wiladimiroff, J.W., Passchier, J., Venema-Van Uden, M.U., Frets, P.G., & Verhage, I. (1993). Emotional reactions in women in late pregnancy (24 weeks or longer) following the ultrasound diagnosis of a severe or lethal fetal malformation. *Prenatal Diagnoses, 13*, 603-612.

Jellinek, M. (1994). Editorial. *Clinical Pediatrics, 301.*

Knapp, R.J., & Peppers, L.G. (1979). Doctor-patient relationships in fetal/infant death encounters. *Journal of Medical Education, 54*, 775-780.

Koop, C.E. (1974). The seriously ill or dying child: Supporting the patient and the family. In N. Schnaper et al. (Eds.), *Management of the dying patient and his family* (pp. 187-196). New York: MSS, Information Corporation.

Kuller, J.A., & Katz, V.L. (1994). Miscarriage: A historical perspective. *Birth, 21*, 227-228.

Lindemann, E. (1944). Symptomatology and management of acute grief. *American Journal of Psychiatry, 101*, 141-148 [Reprinted in *American Journal of Psychiatry, 151*, 6].

Olali, A.O. (1993). Management of death and grief in obituaries and in memoriam pages of Nigerian newspapers. *Psychology Reports, 73*, 835-842.

Patel, R.M. (1993). Small perfect circles. *Journal of the American Medical Association, 270*, 2618.

Potvin, L., Lasker, J., & Toedter, L.J. (1989). Measuring grief: A short version of the perinatal grief scale. *Journal of Psychology and Pathology Behavioral Assessment, 11*, 24-45.

Rajan, L. (1994). Social isolation and support in pregnancy loss. *Health Visitor, 67,* 97-101.

Rogers, B.L., & Cowles, K.V. (1991). The concept of grief: An analysis of classical and contemporary thought. *Death Studies,* 15, 443-458.

Stovall, T.G., Ling, F.G., & Gray, L.A. (1991). Single-dose methotrexate for treatment of ectopic pregnancy. *Obstetrics and Gynecology,* 77, 754-757.

Toedter, L.J., Lasker, J.N., & Alhadeff, J.M. (1988). The perinatal grief scale: Development and initial validation. *American Journal of Orthopsychiatry,* 58, 435-449.

Winslow, R. (1989, October 5). Sometimes talk is the best medicine. *The Wall Street Journal.*

Worthington, R.C. (1994, May). Models of linear and cyclical grief: Different approaches to different experiences. *Clinical Pediatrics,* 297-302.

Zaccardi, R., Abbott, J., & Koziol-McLain, J. (1993). Loss and grief reaction after spontaneous miscarriage in the emergency department. *Annals of Emergency Medicine,* 22, 799-804.

Zeanah, C., Darley, J.V., Rosenblatt, M.J., & Saller, D.N. (1993). Do women grieve after terminating pregnancies because of fetal anomalies? A controlled investigation. *Obstetrics and Gynecology,* 82, 270- 275.

Chapter 4

Loss in the Neonatal Period: Recommendations for the Pediatric Health Care Team

Rita M. Ryan

As a neonatologist, I have been involved in many cases of infant death in the newborn period. All of these losses are sad and difficult, but there are actions that we, as health care providers, can take to ease or facilitate each situation. We need to understand and learn about the grieving process and how to communicate with families during these difficult times. The skills and knowledge required to fulfill this role are generally not available in the mainstream pediatric literature, nor is this topic commonly addressed during formal training. This chapter includes discussions of reasons for death in the newborn period, the grieving process related to death of a newborn, what health care professionals can do in these difficult situations, and lastly, specific recommendations for a number of possible circumstances. With knowledge and understanding, as well as compassion, we can help parents and families as much as possible during the difficult experience of losing a newborn baby.

Death in the Newborn Period

The death of an infant in the perinatal period is not uncommon. Virtually all individuals caring for a pregnant woman or her infant will be involved in the tragic situation of a stillbirth or neonatal death. Although the U.S. infant mortality rate (deaths <1 year of age per 1,000 live births) continues to decline (Wegman, 1994), nearly 1 in 100 infants will die within the first year of life (see Figure 1-4).

The reaction of parents to the death of a baby in the neonatal period cannot be "standardized," but some general concepts exist. Although it is difficult for parents of a very premature infant who has died, it may be harder for

Figure 1-4.
Deaths at <1 year of age per 1,000 live births in the United States

1993:	8.3
1992:	8.5
1990:	9.2
1980:	12.6
1960:	26.0

(Adapted from Wegman, 1994)

the family of an older gestational age infant. As the baby approaches term, the parental expectation that the baby will be problem free increases. In addition, the shock may be greater for a parent who has a baby with unexpected problems in the delivery room or nursery, compared with an infant for whom problems were anticipated due to known congenital abnormalities or problems during the pregnancy. Lastly, the death of a critically ill infant who lives for several days allows for the possibility of some adjustment to the idea that the baby is sick, as compared with the utter lack of preparation for parents of a baby who dies immediately in the delivery room. More importantly, in the former case, as will be discussed later, there is at least some time (albeit too short) for the family to be with their baby.

Reasons for death also are somewhat different for term versus premature infants. Deaths of full-term infants usually are the result of congenital anomalies (which generally account for 50% of term deaths), infection, severe respiratory distress, or perinatal asphyxia. Perinatal asphyxia can include the added traumatic complication of a woman's giving birth to an infant who is alive, supported by mechanical ventilation, but who has suffered possible irreversible brain injury. If severe neurologic impairment is expected, a discussion of withdrawing ventilatory support may be brought up by the medical team to the parents. Premature infants also may have severe respiratory problems or may be at the borderline of viability (currently at approximately 23 to 24 weeks, with a 5% to 10% survival rate for infants who are at 23 0/7 to 23 6/7 weeks' gestation, versus a 50% survival rate at 24 0/7 to 24 6/7 weeks). Premature infants also can have brain injury, often secondary to severe intracranial hemorrhage, and, again, the possibility of withdrawing ventilatory support may be discussed with parents, making an already difficult situation more complex and stressful.

The Grieving Process
(Unique Aspects of Death of a Newborn Infant)

Several decades ago, there was an expectation that an infant might die; but this is no longer the case. With each pregnancy, parents believe that their baby will be born healthy. As infant mortality rates have declined, the medical community's appreciation for the profound grief which families, particularly mothers, experience when a baby does die has diminished. Care providers' inclination to disregard the impact of a baby's death, because of the relative infrequency of the event, conveyed the message that people were not "permitted" to grieve for their newborns. Fortunately, most modern health care teams recognize that the death of an infant is a profound loss, and that it is important and advantageous to acknowledge families' appropriate need to grieve for their babies. An outstanding book which discusses the process is **Empty Cradle, Broken Heart** (1991), by Deborah Davis, PhD, a helpful tool for parents and care providers alike.

The death of a baby is especially difficult to endure. Parents envision an entire future for their baby from the moment they know that they have conceived, and their vision builds over time. With the death of their baby in the perinatal period, parents lose an entire future. Parents also grieve for the loss of their own parenthood. Part of their vision of the future includes their role as a mother or father for that infant, and this is lost, as well. In years past, a woman often was told, "Well, you didn't know the baby," implying that it would be easier for her to lose a baby rather than someone with whom she had spent more time. In fact, the woman has invested a "lifetime" with her baby in her thoughts during her pregnancy, and the lack of real time spent with the baby alive actually makes this loss more, not less, difficult.

Also, other children cannot substitute for the one who has died. Parents still grieve for that specific baby. Groping for words of comfort to offer in these situations, outsiders (including care providers) may be tempted to say, "Maybe you can try again," or "At least you have other children at home." But, we do not say, "At least you have another parent at home," after someone's mother or father has died.

Lastly, it is critical that every attempt be made for any available family members to spend time with the baby before and after death. Health care

Figure 2-4.
Common Phases of Normal Grieving Process

• Shock, numbness, anxiety	• Depression, apathy
• Denial, yearning, preoccupation	• Resolution
• Anger, guilt, sense of failure	

(Adapted from Davis, 1991)

professionals have gotten much better at ensuring that parents spend time with their infant, but the importance of including other family members is less recognized. Parents' grief is "validated" when their own parents, siblings, children, and even close friends can be with the baby, however briefly. This is a good reason why hospitals should institute more liberal neonatal intensive care unit (NICU) visitation policies. If a baby dies after a prolonged NICU course, individuals can be more supportive to the family if they, too, have their own memories of the baby.

The Normal Grieving Process

The grief parents experience after their baby's death includes an initial period of shock, numbness, and anxiety, similar to that felt after the loss of any loved one. There also are denial, tremendous yearning for the baby, and strong preoccupation with the baby. Often, both parents experience anger, guilt, and feelings of failure, although sometimes the mother feels more guilt than the father. In the months after a neonatal death, there may be depression, apathy, and, in most cases, resolution. Resolution does not mean that the grief has vanished. Rather, it means that parents grow more able to function in their relationships and to "move on with their lives" psychologically (see Figure 2-4).

Many parents, particularly mothers, report experiences that appear unusual to them. But, in fact, the feelings are common (see Figure 3-4). It is important that health care professionals know about these common feelings, offer "anticipatory guidance," and talk about them with parents, particularly in the days, weeks, and months after a neonatal death. Parents may think that they are "going crazy." They often have vivid dreams about the baby, includ-

Figure 3-4.
Common Responses of Parents after a Baby's Death

• Feelings of "going crazy"	• Feelings of isolation, loneliness
• Dreams about the baby	• Suicidal thoughts
• "Aching arms"	• Sleep disturbances
• Sense of hearing the baby cry	• Decreased appetite

(Adapted from Davis, 1991)

ing dreams that the baby really survived, and dreams about what the baby's and their own lives would have been like. The feeling of "aching arms" is well reported; the woman aches to hold her baby. There is a physical feeling of emptiness. Feelings of isolation are common and can be compounded by friends and family who urge the woman to "get on with her life" and "get over it." Family members and friends must understand, and health care professionals can help to educate them, that this loss is every bit as difficult (if not more difficult) than any other.

Sleep disturbances, decreased appetite, and suicidal feelings, all symptoms seen in depression, can occur as part of the normal grieving process. Not every parent will experience every symptom listed in Figures 2-4 and 3-4; rather these are general guidelines to help in follow-up with parents. *Grief is different for different people.* Parents may each progress through stages and exhibit various "symptoms" over different timetables. Couples probably cannot synchronize their grieving processes, and sometimes this can be a source of interpersonal stress. There really is no systematic progression or pattern that will describe every person's response to a baby's death, because grief for each individual, by nature, is unique.

Lay literature (see later suggestions) for parents, usually provided by a social worker, may help with feelings of isolation and loneliness. Physicians and nurses can gently remind parents about the availability of books and pamphlets, especially those materials which are written by parents and/or which describe how others have coped with and ultimately survived such a tragedy. Parent support groups also can be enormously helpful to certain families.

Figure 4-4.
Factors Which May Increase Risk of Prolonged Grief Response

> • Mental health problems prior to pregnancy
>
> • Inadequate family support
>
> • Loss occurring late in pregnancy or in the neonatal period
>
> • Planned pregnancy

(Adapted from Lasker and Toedter, 1991)

What Can Health Care Providers Do?
(Identify Parents Who Are Most at Risk for Prolonged Grief Reaction.)

A good description of prolonged grief reaction is provided by Raphael (1983):

> *Months or years later, the bereaved still appears actively grief stricken, is still preoccupied with the lost person, visits the grave again and again, daily or weekly, talks, thinks, feels nothing that doesn't relate to the death and the dead, cries at the slightest reminder, and is chronically angry, perhaps guilty (p. 209).*

This type of reaction would be considered abnormal, wherein referral to a psychologist, psychiatrist, or counselor, especially a professional who is experienced in bereavement counseling, would be appropriate. Sometimes, even in the initial stages, the health care professional may sense that a woman or man is reacting differently or with greater intensity than "normal." Referral, again, should be considered and offered. Keep in mind, however, that grief is different for different people.

Lasker and Toedter (1991) identified risk factors (see Figure 4-4) that can alert health care providers to parents who may be at higher risk for developing an abnormal grief reaction, such as a prolonged grief. These include the parents' mental health prior to the pregnancy. A prior history of depression, in particular, greatly increases the risk of difficulty in resolving grief. Lack of family support, particularly soon after the loss, also is a risk factor. In general, the later in gestation that the loss occurs, especially when the pregnancy was planned, the greater the chance that a prolonged grief reaction may ensue.

Figure 5-4.
Breaking Bad News to Parents

• Genuinely unhurried attitude	• Ensure that mother is not alone to hear news.
• Private area for discussion	• Provide detailed, complete information.
• Okay to show personal feelings	• Designate person to give further information.
• Display understanding and caring.	• Follow-up with telephone contact.

Improve Immediate Interaction with Parents

When relaying disturbing information to patients, ideally, talk with them in a private area, in an unhurried fashion (see Figure 5-4). It is appropriate for care providers to show their concern and feelings, to be understanding and caring. A common mistake is to tell a mother bad news when she is alone in her hospital room. In the haste to be forthcoming, sometimes health care professionals forget that they will be leaving the woman alone when they return to their duties. Ideally, it is preferable if the baby's father, or another support person for the woman, such as her mother, a sister, or an obstetric nurse, stay for a time after the news is delivered.

If possible, relay information to both parents together. Try to overcome the common reaction of men to "protect" their partners by not allowing the mother to hear bad news about her baby. Parents appreciate an honest discussion of why their baby died. It is important to say, when appropriate, "We did everything we could to give your baby a chance, but there were so many problems stacked against him/her." Review what the problems were and what was done, in a humane manner. Give parents complete information (in appropriate language); parents do not want to feel as if the health care personnel are hiding something from them. It is important to designate a health care professional whom patients can contact for further information. Parents report that follow-up contact, especially by the health care personnel who were present at the time of the baby's death, is very helpful and appreciated (Finlay & Dallimore, 1991).

Figure 6-4.
What to Do While the Baby Is Dying

- Parents need to spend time with their baby.

- Offer repeatedly to have them hold their baby.

- Remember that privacy is very important.

- Encourage siblings, relatives, and friends to see the baby, even after death.

- Warn parents about gasping and movements.

- Reassure parents that their baby was not alone.

- Remember that mementos create memories later.

- Offer spiritual support.

Specific Actions at the Time an Infant Is Dying and Has Died

It cannot be emphasized enough: *Parents need to spend time with their dying or already dead baby* (see Figure 6-4). Reluctant parents should be coaxed. In the rare instances in which I was unable to convince a family to see a baby who has died, there was usually regret later. Fortunately, in most cases, after initial resistance, it is obvious that parents really do want to touch and hold their baby. In these cases, they later reported that they were happy and grateful to have been "pushed" a little into taking advantage of the only time that they would have with their child. This is true as well for infants with congenital anomalies (discussed later in more detail). It is helpful to offer several opportunities for time with the baby to all parents, not only to those who have refused to interact with their baby. Sometimes, after returning the baby to the caregivers, parents decide that they want to have more time with the baby, but are too intimidated to ask. Privacy is important, including privacy for the mother, father, and baby as a group. Occasionally, additional family members, whose contributions are extremely important and supportive, must be asked gently to give the parents some time alone with their baby. This issue may arise more frequently when the parents are not married and perhaps not a stable "couple;" but, again, they need a short time for themselves without having grandparents or others present.

It is also important that any additional relatives or friends who wish to see the baby be allowed to do so. As discussed earlier, all of these individuals can validate the baby's existence, his or her death, and thus, the parents' need to grieve. This is true even if the baby is already dead (for example, a death in the delivery room). These individuals (for example, grandparents) also will have their own grief. The infant's siblings, in particular, should see and hold the baby too.

Parents and family should not be rushed through this experience. They should be able to hold their baby for as long as they desire. This is an individual decision which may depend partly on the situation (for example, unexpected death at <24 hours of life vs. expected death at several weeks of age). Caregivers must not judge the time which parents spend with their infant as "too short" or "too long." As noted earlier, however, all parents should be encouraged strongly to spend some time with their baby. At a minimum, they should at least view their baby.

If a baby has not died when he or she is given to the parents to hold, it is helpful to warn parents in advance about gasping breathing and some jerking movements that might occur. This can be difficult for families: "If she can gasp, can't you save her?" "Is my baby in pain?" Talk about these possibilities ahead of time. If a baby dies in the NICU while the parents are at home, or while the woman is under anesthesia and her partner is unavailable, parents will want to know that their baby was not alone. This is an extremely common concern for parents. Reassurance that caring individuals (usually nurses) were there to hold and comfort their baby makes a difference to parents. Having these individuals eventually contact the baby's mother can be very helpful. For example, if a baby dies in the delivery room, one of the physicians should talk with the mother. Often, this is the obstetrician. Obstetric nurses continue to have contact with the woman, too. But, later that day or the next day, a visit by the pediatrician, or (especially) some of the nurses who cared for the infant during attempted resuscitation, can be extremely helpful and always is greatly appreciated. Many times nurses offer the woman mementos at that time. Specific examples of mementos are suggested later in this chapter, but note that some of the mementos must be obtained around this time (for example, a lock of hair, footprints, and photographs). These become very meaningful and precious to families, and they must not be forgotten or misplaced.

All families should be offered spiritual support from their own minister, rabbi, or a hospital chaplain. Some hospitals have bereavement teams. Baptism can be a major concern for certain families. If time permits, the fam-

Figure 7-4.
What Not to Do

- Do not leave the mother alone initially.

- Do not abandon parents immediately after informing them of their baby's death.

- Do not act "clinical," or distant.

- Do not rush parents into decisions that later may make their grieving process more difficult.

- Do not deny requests because of restrictive hospital procedures; any reasonable request should be honored.

(Adapted, in part, from Welch, 1991)

ily may wish to have their baby baptized by clergy prior to death; when time is too short, a nurse or physician can baptize the baby, if necessary. If the parents' own or the hospital's chaplain is available, and if time permits, a baptism can be an important ceremony for parents and other family members.

Autopsy requests and discussion of funeral arrangements are on the parents' minds, but these do not need to be undertaken immediately. A later, second conversation may be a more appropriate time to discuss these sensitive topics. However, some families may bring them up right away; care providers can take their cues from the mother and father. The issue of organ donation is often not relevant to many cases of neonatal death. However, in those instances in which an infant would be an eligible donor, the option of organ donation should be discussed. This may bring some small comfort to the parents. Finlay and Dallimore (1991) report that nearly 60% of patients not offered a discussion of organ donation wished that they had been.

If a situation arises that is in conflict with a specific hospital policy, flexibility is important (see Figure 7-4). An excellent example is described by a nurse (Fina, 1994). A 3-day-old baby with congenital heart disease was dying in the operating room; the mother wished to spend those last few minutes with her son and requested to go into the OR. Her request was denied. The admirable nurse involved in this case was distressed by the situation. Over the next months, she worked through appropriate channels to change the hospital's policy. She also enlisted the help of this baby's parents, and they felt good knowing that their efforts would help future families who find

Figure 8-4.
What to Do and Say

- Be simple and straightforward.
- Be comfortable showing emotions.
- Listen; touch.
- "I don't know what to say. My heart is with you."
- "I'm hurting with you."
- "I wish things could have been different for you and your baby."
- "I'm sorry."

(Adapted, in part, with permission from Welch, *Neonatal Network*, 1991.)

themselves in similar crises. The case report is moving, and the reader wonders why the rules were not stretched at the time. For parents, their brief moments with their dying or dead baby are fleeting and cannot be replaced. If necessary, nursery or labor and delivery visitation policies should be bent, and any reasonable request accommodated.

Specific Statements

In the moments before and after a newborn's death, it can be difficult to find words to say. It is okay not to say anything, but just to sit quietly with the family. It is okay to show your own feelings and to be sad — these are sad events. Be simple and honest; listen to and touch the parents. Some suggestions of appropriate comments come from Welch (1991) (see Figure 8-4). I usually say something like, "I'm so sorry — I wish it could have been different," or, "I'm sorry for your loss." Some individuals believe that a physician never should say "I'm sorry," because somehow this might be perceived as incriminating. I do not believe this; you can be sorry about something, although it is not your fault. Try to avoid statements such as those in Figure 9-4. When you think about it, no one would say, "At least you have another parent," (or "sister") to someone whose father (or sister) has just died. Remarks about the family's surviving children as a source of comfort are not appropriate; children at home do not replace the baby who just has died.

Figure 9-4.
What Not to Say

- "You always can have another baby."
- "At least you have other children."
- "You will get over this in time."

(Adapted from Welch, 1991.)

Memories

The opportunity to collect mementos, which are so helpful for creating memories in these situations, can be quite short. Therefore, it is important to be prepared in the event of a neonatal death. Almost everything associated with the baby can become a memento (see Figure 10-4). The thoughtful task of gathering items often falls to nurses who are involved with the baby's care. This is a valuable contribution which care providers can make to a bereaved family. In addition to the mementos themselves, the manner in which such items are offered to the family also can make a difference. Sensitivity and compassion go a long way. In our NICU, we often collect mementos and give them to parents in a memory box. (One bereaved family donated money to provide these boxes for other families.) Through another family's donation, we obtained a new 35 mm camera, and film is provided. Our social workers or nurses take pictures for families. Photographs of the baby probably are the most cherished mementos. Parents typically want several (not just one), and they especially appreciate photographs taken of their baby before death. Whether taken before or after death, these pictures are treasured by families, to be looked at over and over again. Some families videotape the baby. Our NICU social worker encourages families to bring in a camcorder if they have access to one.

Anything associated with the baby (including a lock of hair, a blanket that was used to wrap the baby, etc.) is an important treasure. Literally any and all items, such as those mentioned in Figure 10-4, will be cherished. "Official" documents, such as the card on which a baby's weight and height are recorded, or birth and death certificates, validate the existence and life of the baby. In one instance, a mother repeatedly requested a copy of the autopsy report. She could understand little of it, but that was not the point. She wanted to add it to her box of mementos at home and she truly needed it for closure.

Figure 10-4.
Memories

• Photographs, including ultrasound images	• Stuffed animals
• Footprints	• Time spent holding, dressing, looking at the baby
• Hair	• Autopsy report
• Clothing, hat	• Birth certificate
• Blankets	• Death certificate
• Record of baby's weight and height	• Memorials
• Baby's hospital identification bracelet	

A memorial service also can create memories, and can be important for closure and saying goodbye (see Chapters 16 & 17). There is a wide range of choices about disposition and ceremonies for the baby which parents must consider, from cremation to a graveside service to a complete funeral service. Families should be encouraged and supported to do whatever is right for them.

Autopsy

Obtaining autopsy consent is often very difficult for physicians. It creates so much anxiety, that sometimes we feel as if we have to rush right in and get the "asking" over with. Remember that most parents expect the physician to ask about an autopsy at some point. This does not have to be done immediately after the baby's death. Only under very unusual circumstances is an immediate postmortem examination crucial. Again, if parents bring it up (as some do quite easily), that is your cue. If they do not mention an autopsy themselves, give things time. Delay your request for a little while, and after you have returned to talk with the family, for a second or third time, raise the issue. Sometimes a nurse or social worker can "break the ice" by bringing up the issue.

If the parents initially refuse, it is reasonable to approach them again later. This is often a very difficult issue for parents. Explain (in appropriate, clear language) what an autopsy specifically includes, and tell parents what information may be gained. It is often useful to point out that information may be gained which could benefit existing siblings and/or be helpful to know for future pregnancies. Also, when parents refuse the request to perform an autopsy, it may help to offer a restricted autopsy, with any number of limitations possible. For example, if a baby with congenital heart disease dies, a family who is uncomfortable with consenting to a full autopsy may be willing to agree to an isolated cardiac autopsy. One pathologist suggests that even an autopsy which is limited to a small right flank incision, to obtain pieces of lung, liver, kidney, and adrenal gland, may yield helpful information. Explaining that an autopsy will not interfere with having the baby's casket open at the funeral service, or about topics such as returning organs to the baby's body, may ease the parents' decision.

In certain cultures and religious groups, an autopsy is looked upon as causing the infant's spirit harm, as an act of the devil, or contrary to God's wishes. Although autopsies should be encouraged in general, parents' wishes must be respected.

Information obtained from the autopsy should be imparted to the family in a timely fashion. Giving parents expectations about the timing of autopsy results is helpful. I usually tell them that they will receive some information in about 1 day, but that it will take another 2 months (at least) to completely process all of the information gathered during the autopsy. I usually telephone parents to explain the results of the gross autopsy preliminary report; this rapid follow-up is critical. When detailed microscopic results become available, I call parents again. Depending on their feelings, on the clinical situation, and on actual autopsy results, I will either arrange for a meeting or discuss results with parents over the telephone. The length of time until the autopsy report is "final" differs from institution to institution. Again, giving parents some realistic expectation for when the final report will be available is helpful. Lastly, I have no hesitation in granting parents' requests for a copy of their baby's autopsy report.

Specific Situations

The prior information presented is widely applicable to multiple situations involving a neonatal death. The following suggestions are presented for specific circumstances.

Stillbirth or Immediate Unexpected Death

Remember to inform the pediatrician of the pregnancy's outcome, even if he or she was not present. The pediatrician or physician who the family had intended to provide care for the baby can be a support person for the family, particularly if the parents have older children and already have established a relationship with that physician.

One other important comment about the unique circumstances surrounding a stillbirth concerns the woman's incapacity, at times, during and immediately after delivery, to see and hold her dead baby. For example, a woman may have been under general anesthesia at the time of delivery. Even regional anesthesia and/or certain medications may prevent the woman from comfortably sitting up, holding her baby, and possibly even remembering these moments clearly for hours after delivery. This is the only time that she can ever spend with her baby, her only chance to create memories. She must not be cheated out of time with her baby and her chance to create memories. It may be necessary to delay further actions until the mother spends quality time with her baby, and she may not physically be capable of this for several hours after delivery.

In the delivery room, if things are not going well, let the parents know as soon as possible. Be honest. Ask about parents' wishes for baptism; or baptize the baby, if you are not sure — this may be quite important to a given family.

Congenital Anomalies

The delivery of a baby who has congenital anomalies is a difficult situation, whether the anomalies were known antenatally or not. Sometimes, a mother or father does not want to see the baby. They are fearful about seeing "monster"-like deformities. I was involved in only one case in which a mother did not look at and hold a baby born with congenital anomalies. The mother was adamant about refusing to see her baby, who was very abnormal in appearance. This woman wanted to remember the baby the way that she had pictured her. Sometimes, a parent wants to see the baby but does not want to see the abnormalities. Often, these can be disguised initially by taking thoughtful care in wrapping the baby with a blanket. Usually, I will eventually show the parents the abnormalities. Their ideas of how the baby looks are almost always worse than reality.

Although some parents may be reluctant initially, perseverance on the part of the health care professional to encourage strongly that they spend at least a short time with their baby is worth it. Parents later regret it if they did not see and hold their baby, even when a baby had severe anomalies. They can frequently look past any abnormalities and say, for example, "He looks like his father," or "She looks like her grandmother." One obstetrician reports:

> *Although I have difficulty looking at some fetal anomalies, there has never been an anomaly at which any of my parents evidenced horror at viewing. The baby's perfect features hold sway (Chez, 1995, p. 1060).*

In one study, in which 13% of the babies were macerated, 37% had anomalies (including holoprosencephaly and conjoined twins), and 3% had both, 100% of the bereaved mothers found that "...seeing and holding the baby after death" was helpful (Sexton & Stephen, 1991).

Babies in the NICU

Most babies go home and do not die in the NICU, but we cannot always predict this with certainty. Therefore, while a newborn is in the NICU, care providers must treat this time as an opportunity to create memories. What can be done in the NICU to help families? Using the baby's correct name and gender individualizes that baby. Caregivers can talk to parents about what the baby likes or how he or she is unique. Nurses more often are able to do this since they spend more time with the babies and probably get to know their personalities better. Even if the baby is doing quite well, be particularly sensitive about the day when the woman goes home from the hospital while her baby remains hospitalized. One overriding concern for parents is that their baby will be left alone or will be lonely.

While parents are visiting, encourage them to bond physically with their baby. There truly are very few circumstances in which a parent's gentle touching or stroking is harmful to the baby. When possible, allow parents to hold their baby.

I recall caring for a baby born at 25 weeks gestation. His mother had asked but never had held her son, and he was doing quite poorly from a respiratory standpoint. He was on a ventilator, and his weight was below the minimum standard in our NICU (1,200 grams at that time) for being held. But, he was about 6 weeks of age, at much less risk for temperature instability problems, and, quite frankly, his respiratory status could not have gotten much worse by having his mother hold him. Besides, I was not sure that he would survive; so this may have been the woman's only chance to hold her baby alive. After discussing it first with the nurse who was caring for the infant (to help the staff feel comfortable when "bending" the rules), the mother was able to hold her baby. Fortunately, the baby did not decompensate acutely . The baby ultimately survived and went home. About 9 months after discharge, the parents brought their baby back to visit the NICU. The mother asked if I were available. She wanted to show me her son. The first thing she said was, "You were the one who let me hold my baby."

Parents also should be allowed and encouraged to bring in toys for their baby. These can later serve as mementos if the baby dies. Sibling's drawings on the side of the Isolette and family pictures "decorating the baby's home" are all possible. One woman suggested to me that tapes made by parents (especially of their own voices) can be soothing to a baby and also may become a memento. Parents, siblings, and other family members should be encouraged to spend as much time as possible with their baby. In recent years, many NICUs have greatly liberalized their visiting policy, including sibling visitation, to facilitate families' spending time with babies.

Early NICU Death

If things are not going well, care providers must be honest and let parents know the seriousness of the problems. Remember that the woman and even her partner may be exhausted after the labor and delivery, and the woman may be experiencing pain or medical complications. If her baby required transport from another hospital, and the baby is very sick, try to arrange for transfer of the mother as well. In my opinion, it is always appropriate medically to transfer a mother whose baby has been transferred to the NICU (unless her own condition is a contraindication). In these days of managed health care, however, financial issues sometimes appear to take precedence. But, in the case of a critically ill infant, no obstacle should prevent transfer of the mother (if she is able), to improve her ability to see her potentially dying infant. After the baby dies, that time is irretrievable. Do not give up without trying. A phone call by the neonatologist to the woman's obstetrician, family medicine physician, or nurse-midwife to detail the critical nature of the baby's condition can make a difference.

Remember that the woman should see her baby before the transfer. Prior to transport, bring the baby to the woman's room, if the baby's condition permits a brief delay for this purpose. Let the woman touch and see her baby as best she can. Often, the father or another relative can accompany the baby on the trip to the receiving NICU, while the mother typically will not. Even if you are communicating with the father in the NICU, call the mother back at the other hospital. Again, if the baby is not doing well, allow liberal visitation by other family members to validate the baby's existence. Give them time to create their own memories which can be shared with the parents later as they grieve over their baby's death.

Death in the NICU

When informing parents of a change for the worse in their baby's condition, tell the truth. If death occurs suddenly, again think about baptism, if appropriate. Parents want to be reassured that their baby was not in pain and that someone was with their baby. If death is imminent, try to keep the baby alive, if possible, until the parents arrive. Allow parents and any other family members to spend whatever time possible with their baby. Remember that any way to make the situation more private in a busy NICU should be used.

Withdrawal of Support

The ethical, medical, legal, and emotional issues involved in withdrawing life support could fill many books. As noted by Woods and Esposito (1987):

> This option should never be offered in such a manner as to suggest that the decision to withdraw life support rests with the baby's parents. Parents must not feel that they are responsible for their baby's death (p. 97).

One social worker commented to me that sometimes parents will say, "They want me to pick the day to kill my baby." She suggests that it may be helpful to present the issue of withdrawing support with the following comments: "We have done everything we can for your baby. There is nothing more we can do, so we would like to take away all the machines and let you hold your baby." Since parental permission is required, I might add, "I think we should stop. With your permission, I would like to remove Joshua's breathing tube. I really believe that stopping is the right thing to do for Joshua." This is far more preferable than stating to parents, "You have some decisions to make here." Also, this approach is helpful if the concept of "futile" treatment and the possibility of stopping support have been discussed several times *prior* to withdrawing support. Statements such as, "We may come to a point when it really won't be in Mary's best interest to continue supporting her. We're not there yet. I will let you know if I feel that we are getting to that point," can lead the way for later conversations regarding withdrawal of support.

If the decision to withdraw support is made, there are some practical ways to ease the situation. Remove as much of the equipment as possible, so that parents can hold their baby more easily. If the baby cannot survive very long without assisted ventilation, the baby can be bag-ventilated via the endotracheal tube, using oxygen from a portable tank, and still be moved to a private family room, at which time the tube can be removed when the baby is given to the parents. Wrap the baby for the parents, so that they can hold a swaddled infant. Warn parents about the possibilities of gasping and movements. I sometimes give the baby pain medication such as morphine when withdrawing support. I inform parents of this, and they generally appreciate that we are giving medication to decrease any discomfort which their baby may experience. Let parents know that sometimes it is hard to predict how long the baby will live after mechanical ventilation is withdrawn. Lastly, in instances in which a baby has been given heavy sedation or has been paralyzed with muscle relaxants, consider stopping these medications so that parents will have the chance to see their baby open his or her eyes or move on his or her own prior to death.

Postpartum

It is important to keep in mind how a mother is feeling, not only emotionally, but also physically after a stillbirth or neonatal death (Davis, 1991). Such women have all the signs of pregnancy and birth, but no baby. Postpartum depression may be compounded. Women, especially those who had planned to nurse the baby, are reminded constantly by breast engorgement and leaking that they have lost the baby. There are physical discomforts after either vaginal or cesarean section deliveries. After pregnancy loss, many women report that they are impatient for the signs of pregnancy to disappear.

Twins

When one twin dies and the other survives, parents naturally have mixed feelings (Bryan, 1991). Do not say, "At least you still have one healthy baby." It may be difficult for parents to rejoice about the surviving baby when they are grappling with the death of another baby. One note is that it is best to tell the surviving twin from earliest childhood about his or her twin's death, and to understand that such twins can have survivor's guilt throughout their lives. *A common regret later is if there are no pictures of the two babies together.* Parents who lose one twin may have more difficulty during bereavement than parents losing singleton infants (DeKleine, Cuisinier, Kollée, Bethlehem, & DeGraauw, 1995). This is a unique situation requiring special attention.

Siblings

In the immediate period following the baby's death, but more importantly in the weeks and months to follow, attention must be paid to the baby's siblings (see later suggestions for specific literature available for parents with other children). Often, siblings will blame themselves, since they "wished the baby dead," so they think that it must be their fault that the baby died. Much of the parents' attention may be focused on the dead baby, and the sibling will try to measure up to the lost baby. Children may feel that, since their brother or sister died, one of their parents, or even they themselves might die next. Some children blame their mother for the baby's death.

Siblings can develop some of the same symptoms that parents experience after a loss, such as anger, depression, aggression, phobic behaviors, anxiety, and sleep disturbances. Additionally, parents commonly become overprotective of their surviving children.

Children often feel pushed away by their parents after the death of another child in the family. Therefore, it is important to encourage parents, as soon as they are able, to spend time with each of their surviving children. It is most important that parents communicate honestly with their other children. Children may feel increased anxiety and isolation if there is no discussion about what happened or if they feel excluded. If they are old enough (older than 3 years), then they should be included in saying goodbye and in any memorial or funeral ceremonies. The author of **The Bereaved Parent** (1977), Harriet Sarnoff Schiff, reports her mistake of not allowing her 12-year-old son to view his 10-year-old brother's dead body, and not allowing her 4-year-old daughter to attend her brother's funeral.

Survival of an Abnormal Baby

When a baby is born with a congenital abnormality and/or has neurologic abnormalities, parents grieve over the loss of a "normal" baby, even though their baby has survived. This may be true even in the case of a relatively minor anomaly (for example, a cleft palate), although the grief is less significant. If a baby is born with a severe chromosomal abnormality and will likely be severely impaired, parents' grief can be just as strong as that of parents whose infant actually has died. But, in the case of a surviving abnormal infant, the guilt of somehow being responsible for the baby's condition may be compounded by guilt over grieving about a live — but imperfect — baby, and even about possible thoughts of wishing that the baby had not survived. Parents have lost many of their hopes and dreams for their baby's future. Sensitivity on the part of the short-term and long-term care providers is important for these families. It is good to initiate a cooperative, working relationship early with these parents, since it is likely that such babies will

Figure 11-4.
Role of the Pediatrician

- Go to the hospital to be with parents.
- Establish telephone contact within first day or two.
- Have parents visit in your office several weeks later.
- Report and follow up on autopsy results.
- Help parents to understand, communicate with surviving children.
- Offer counseling in general.
- Observe family for long-term resolution of their grief.
- Notify woman's obstetrician of outcome, if death occurred later.
- Include the woman's husband/partner in discussions, counseling.

require a great deal of medical care; some of the health care team may be interacting with these families on a long-term basis.

Role of the Pediatrician

The pediatrician has a valuable opportunity to support the family in the event of neonatal death (see Figure 11-4). If the pediatrician is not involved initially with the baby's death (for example, stillbirth, death in the delivery room, or if a partner was covering your service at the time of delivery or when the baby died, etc.), go in timely fashion to the hospital to be with the parents. This helps more than you can imagine. Parents often comment, "It meant so much to me that my baby's doctor came to the hospital." Parents feel comforted and genuinely cared for when such a visit is made.

Call the parents by phone sometime during the next day or two. Plan to have them come to your office several weeks later. This is an appropriate time to discuss autopsy results. Some authors recommend follow-up visits at 4 to 6 weeks, 3 to 6 months, and 1 year after a perinatal death (Kowalski, 1991). During these visits explain to parents about the nature of the grieving process, find out how they are doing, answer questions and give information you may know about their baby's death, and discuss autopsy results. Pediatricians can help parents understand how to talk with their children (the baby's grieving siblings) and what is appropriate for a given child's developmental age. An article by Trouy and Ward-Larson (1987) may be helpful to both physicians and parents.

Offer counseling to the parents. There is some controversy as to whether formal counseling is beneficial to all families (Ewton, 1993; Lilford, Stratton, Godsil, & Prasad, 1994; Schneiderman, Winders, Tallett, & Feldman, 1994). Know the names of counselors in your region who specialize in neonatal bereavement or who helped families in similar situations. Know the support groups in your community. For many grieving parents, hearing how others have coped with similar situations helps a great deal. If you are unaware about support groups or of the names of specific counselors who specialize in grief, pediatric social workers at your hospital may be a great resource.

Follow bereaved families to monitor their long-term resolution of their grief, and talk with them about their daily activities to determine if any dysfunction exists. Openly discuss marital stress that may be occurring. Ask about drug and alcohol use; there may be an increase in the use of sedatives and alcohol after a neonatal death (Vance et al., 1994). Note that some families may increase their visits to you, due to increased anxiety for their other children's well-being. Checklists are available for obstetric and pediatric nursing and medical staffs to remind them of their important roles in these situations (Ewton, 1993; Ryan, Cote-Arsenault, & Sugarman, 1991).

When a baby dies outside of the delivery room, remember to inform the individual who delivered the baby. It is horrible for an obstetrician to walk into a 3-day postpartum woman's room, or to see a patient at her 4-week follow-up checkup, not knowing that this woman has lost her baby. This includes babies who were transferred into your NICU from other hospitals. Make it your practice to inform the obstetrician and also the referring pediatrician about the unfortunate outcome of the baby's course in your institution.

Remember to include fathers. Often, attention is focused more on the woman, especially in the particularly vulnerable postpartum period. Men have just as many hopes and dreams for their baby and future parenthood as women have. Since they may be less visibly emotional, men can be ignored and left out of efforts to counsel and comfort the bereaved. Kimble (1991) reported that men's responses to neonatal death actually are qualitatively quite similar to those of women. A study of bereavement after multiple births found no difference in responses between women and men (Harrigan, Naber, Jensen, Tse, & Perez, 1993). A pamphlet edited by Nelson (1994) provides tremendously moving examples of fathers' grief. Men can feel even more isolated and alone with their grief after a baby's death, since they are expected to be strong and to support women. Men need attention and support as well.

Summary

The woman who transcribed my first draft of this manuscript was new to our Division of Neonatology when I gave her this material. I had no idea that she, like many others, had personal experience with a neonatal death. Thirteen years ago, she delivered a 25-week gestation baby who was not resuscitated. She told me that she wished some of the actions about which I had written had been performed at that time. *She never saw her baby.* She thought that she would not want to "see a baby she couldn't have." She now regrets her decision, and also she regrets that no one encouraged her to see and hold her baby. An unfortunate comment that she never has forgotten was made by a nurse, who said, "Well, at least you got a tax deduction." This secretary did go on to have two other babies, one of whom was born at 28 weeks. Both of her surviving children are normal and healthy. But, she never has forgotten her baby who died, nor the associated events.

> *Bereaved parents never forget the understanding, respect, and genuine warmth they received from caregivers, which can become as lasting and important as any other memories of their lost pregnancy or their baby's brief life (Leon, 1992 p. 373).* ❏

Acknowledgments

I would like to thank Mary Steigerwald, MSW; Ronnie Guillet, MD; Carol Wagner, MD; and Christine LeMoine, RN, NNP, for their helpful comments.

Literature for Parents

In many institutions, a social worker will have literature available for parents. In our NICU, we have a packet of information that we give to bereaved parents. If this resource is not available to you, the following information about pamphlets may be helpful. These materials are generally available at reasonable cost. Most of the pamphlets discuss grief and specifically talk about the loss of a baby; some also may address the actual memorial service.

- *Newborn Death*, by Joy and Dr. Marvin Johnson, with Chaplains James A. Cunningham and Sarah Ewing; and RNs Dale Hatcher and Carol Dannen. From Centering Corporation, 1531 North Saddle Creek Road, Omaha, NE, 68104, (402) 553-1200.
- *Planning a Precious Goodbye*, by Susan Erling, Sherokee Ilse, and Mary Jo Flynn, from Pregnancy and Infant Loss Center, 1421 East Wayzata Boulevard, #30, Wayzata, MN, 55391, (612) 473-9372.

- *The Rocking Horse is Lonely, and Other Stories of Fathers' Grief,* by James D. Nelson, also from Pregnancy and Infant Loss Center.

There are some pamphlets that address sibling grief and how children's questions can be answered.
- *Sibling Grief,* by Marcia G. Scherago, Medic Publishing Co., PO Box 89, Redmond, WA, 98073-0089, (206) 881-2883.
- *Answers to a Child's Questions About Death,* by Peter Stillman, Guideline Publications, Stamford, NY, 12167.
- *What Do You Say to a Child About Death? Unavoidable Questions That Must be Answered,* by Brenda Crowe, reprinted with permission from *Marriage and Family Living Magazine,* November 14, 1976, from N.H. SIDS Project, Bureau of Maternal and Child Health, 61 South Spring Street, Concord, NH, 03301.

For parents of twins:
- *The Death of a Twin: Miscarriage, Stillbirth, Infancy,* Parents of Multiple Births Association of Canada, Inc., 283 Seventh Avenue S., Lethbridge, Alberta, Canada, T1J 1H6, (403) 328-9165.

For information about local support groups, a hospital social worker can provide information; if not, parents can contact:
- The Compassionate Friends, P.O. Box 3696, Oak Brook, IL, 60522-3696, (312) 990-0010.
- Centering Corporation or Pregnancy and Infant Loss Center (information above).
- Your local county health department.

At Strong Memorial Hospital, University of Rochester School of Medicine and Dentistry, we also give out various readings, poems, etc. Two books which we most often suggest to parents are by Davis (1991), and Schiff (1977). Find what works for you and your patients, and then make sure that they can obtain a variety of information according to their particular needs.

Case Study 1-4

Multiple Medical Problems in an Extremely Premature Infant

Baby Boy W. was born with a birth weight of 860 grams at 26 weeks gestation. His mother was a 34-year-old woman with a prior history of a preterm birth at 24 weeks with neonatal demise at 3 days, and one living 7-year-old child who was born at term. The woman presented in active labor at an outlying hospital, and she delivered precipitously 3 hours later. The baby required ventilation and intubation, had significant respiratory distress, was stabilized, and then was transferred by helicopter to our neonatal intensive care unit (NICU).

Baby W. had significant respiratory distress syndrome (RDS), and he required maximal ventilatory support and surfactant, with little improvement. On day 2 of life, he was placed on high-frequency jet ventilation and steroids. The parents were aware that their son was critically ill and that his chance of survival was low. Because of problems with transportation, the parents did not arrive to see their son until postnatal day 3. The baby's respiratory status had improved. An ultrasound on day 3 revealed a Grade 1 intraventricular hemorrhage. Over the next 4 days, Baby W. remained stable on jet ventilation.

On day 8 of life, although he had not been fed, Baby W. developed necrotizing enterocolitis, signs of sepsis, and low-grade disseminated intravascular coagulopathy (DIC). He developed pulmonary hemorrhage, which was treated successfully with intratracheal epinephrine. Although the baby was gravely ill, he continued to be alert and responsive.

The family remained at Baby W's bedside, and they appeared to understand how ill he was. They "wanted everything done," as this was the woman's last chance (in her mind) of having a second baby. She had suffered emotionally after the loss of her other premature baby. Both parents reiterated time and time again that they did not want their son to suffer. Yet, during the first 3 weeks of Baby W's life, although the option of withdrawal of support was offered, they would not consider this, because they continued to hope that their son would recover.

The baby's course deteriorated over the next several days. He developed intestinal perforation for which a Penrose drain was placed; the pediatric surgeon did not believe that Baby W. was an appropriate candidate for surgery because of his degree of illness and instability. A follow-up ultrasound revealed periventricular leukomalacia and dilated ventricles. The parents were aware of these findings and their significance, and understandably they were distraught. They did not want to prolong their baby's suffering. On the other hand, they did not want to be the ones to make the decision to "pull the plug" and terminate Baby W's life support. When it was pointed out that their baby was dying, and that we were prolonging the inevitable and his suffering, they agreed to withdraw support. We provided comfort care, allowing the parents to hold their son as they had done many other times during Baby W's stay in the NICU, but this time they finally were able to hold him without all the wires and tubes which had been hooked up to him. He was given morphine to decrease any discomfort that he may have experienced. He died several hours later in his parents' arms.

A month after Baby W's death, the parents continued to grieve their loss. They could not afford a burial service, so the baby's body was cremated by the hospital. They expressed sadness over this, but they were happy to receive a lock of Baby W's hair, his birth card, photographs, and a book containing information from his short life. The parents expressed that they did not completely understand how "God could do this twice to us," and they were struggling to maintain their faith. While it was a very emotional and difficult struggle, the parents were relieved that Baby W's last moments had been spent in their arms.

Commentary

The case of Baby W. is a poignant example of an extremely premature infant's eventual death from multiple medical problems and the difficulties of the parents in accepting the reality while wanting to hold on to their hopes and dreams. It was the parents' wish to do everything; yet, they came to understand that there is a point when "doing everything" for a dying infant is to let the parents hold their baby without the distractions of monitors and alarms, tubes and lines, and the invasive procedures that come with intensive care medicine.

As is pointed out throughout the preceding chapter, each parent brings with him or her a unique, personal way of grieving. Baby W's parents were dealing not only with the loss of this baby but also with the loss of their other preterm infant who had died a year earlier. The woman's feelings of inadequacy, of not being able to produce a viable, healthy baby were evident. Although the father was supportive, he also had to mourn the loss of his son. What made the situation even more difficult is that the parents had been unable to see their son for the first 3 days of his life, due to transportation problems. They were kept informed of their son's status appropriately by telephone, but they did not have an opportunity to interact directly with him.

We met in person for the first time at Baby W's bedside, so that we could establish a common link. Only after we had shared that time together did I suggest moving to our conference room to discuss management issues privately with the parents. The primary nurse and the social worker were present to lend support to the parents as well. Our conversation began with an overview of how Baby W. was doing. Then, we asked an open-ended question regarding their understanding of their son's condition. This meeting established the parents' involvement early on and assured them that we were aligned in the care of their son. It is important during these first meetings to establish a positive relationship. This becomes even more essential should the baby's clinical course deteriorate, as it did in this case.

We had frequent meetings with the parents to keep them informed of their son's worsening status. When Baby W's clinical status deteriorated, we discussed limitations of care and resuscitation, as well as the possibility of withdrawing support. Once the parents could truly understand that "everything has been done that can be done to save your son, and despite all our efforts, your son is dying," then they could accept withdrawal of support and comfort care. Ultimately, this became in their minds "the right thing to do."

— *Carol L. Wagner, MD*

Case Study 2-4

Transferring Decisions in a Critically Ill Newborn

Three days after Christmas, I received a phone call at 3 am from our Level II special care nursery (SCN). The resident had just finished resuscitating a newborn who had no heart rate for the first 15 minutes. Now, the baby was intubated and ventilated and was relatively stable. Our usual course of action is to arrange for transfer to our Level III NICU about 20 minutes away; I made the necessary phone calls.

A nagging thought entered my mind: Is transfer really the right thing to do for this baby and his parents? The transport team arrived and called me with their report. The baby still had never had any spontaneous movements, the cord pH was now 6.6, and the baby had started having seizures at 1 hour of age. Although it is our routine to transfer such infants, I found myself saying to the transport resident, "If we had any shred of compassion left, we wouldn't transfer this baby." When I hung up the phone, the nagging thoughts continued. Why should I separate this baby and his mother so I can transfer the infant and have the "backup" support of a pediatric neurologist, another neonatologist, EEG, and others tell me what I already knew: Due to severe brain injury, we would be removing this baby from ventilatory support in the next few days.

At 5 am, I examined the baby and found everything as it had been reported to me. The baby was making my decision easier, unfortunately — now he was desaturating on 100% oxygen and maximal ventilatory support. I knew that it was not right to transfer this baby. He was unlikely to survive. If he did survive, he might not be able to breathe on this own, or, at best, would be severely impaired. I voiced my opinion to the nurses and physicians present. Everyone was in agreement. My greatest support came from the transport nurse who was part of our NICU transport team; she was probably the person with the most experience.

I went to talk with the parents. They were a lovely couple who had been trying to have a baby for 7 years. The woman had gestational diabetes that had been somewhat difficult to control. She had a reassuring ultrasound only a few days earlier. I again spoke with the delivering obstetrician (who was covering for the woman's vacationing obstetrician). Even in retrospect, he could find no indication of trouble *in utero*. I explained to the parents what I thought about the baby's neurologic status. I also told them that the baby was having decreased levels of oxygen on maximal support. Now, I explained, I was worried that if we did transfer the baby, then he would die before the parents could spend any time with him. I recommended that we let the baby die here in this hospital where both parents could remain with him.

Baptism was extremely important to this family, particularly baptism prior to death. After the chaplain had baptized the baby, we removed the endotracheal tube and handed the baby to his mother. He survived for 45 minutes. He had gasping breaths that were difficult for the family to witness. Many family members were there and they held the baby before and after his death. The pediatric resident who had resuscitated the baby at delivery felt very bad about having done such a "good job" of reviving him at birth. I told the resident not to feel bad, because he had given the family several precious hours with their baby which they otherwise would not have had.

When I got back to our NICU, the transport nurse was waiting for me. She told me that the decision I had made was the "most humane thing" she had seen "for a long time" and that it "restored" her "faith in the NICU."

Later that day, I learned that the woman's own obstetrician was coming back early from his vacation that day specifically to see her and the family. That restored *my* faith. And, that evening when I got home from the NICU, I celebrated my own son's 1-year birthday.

Commentary

There are several basic principles that I follow when dealing with most families of infants who are hospitalized in the NICU. These principles apply whether a baby is critically ill or relatively stable. These methods of interacting with families come from feedback from parents, reflecting families' experiences not only while their infants are in the NICU, but also months and years later, after a baby either died or went home.

I find it very important to maintain appropriate hope for a baby to have a good outcome, even when the situation looks bleak (until it is obvious that a baby will be left with major morbidity or cannot survive). And it is important to relay this hope to the family. Also, it is critical to remember that the parents' wishes and desires should strongly influence our management and that we should take responsibility for making difficult decisions for our patients. Developing a rapport with the family by showing that you care for their infant, using language with which they are familiar, and taking time with them all will help build a trusting relationship.

Situations such as the case presented are always difficult, and making these major decisions does not get easier with time and experience. What makes such decisions easier is knowing that, even though you may be unable to help the baby, you can do much to affect the parents' lifelong memories of their child. I feel that I have accomplished a great deal if I can orchestrate events so that the family leaves with the least amount of guilt and doubt, and with some pleasant memories of time spent with their baby. This often requires taking primary responsibility for decisions, even though they may be difficult to make.

When meeting a family for the first time, and at the same time having to give them devastating news about their infant, it is still possible to develop a positive relationship with them. By showing compassion and understanding and communicating your desire to give their baby the best outcome, even though that may be withdrawing support and giving him time with his parents, you can obtain some trust. Although you do not have much time to sort through a family's wishes and desires, by paying close attention to their verbal and nonverbal responses, you can gain insight into their feelings.

Maintaining hope for a child is extremely important, and parents are usually aware of this from our words and actions. When they realize that we care and are appropriately optimistic for their child, they become even more trusting of us. As a result, we can more easily take over and make the difficult choices for them. Parents find comfort in knowing that we care for their child and are not giving up prematurely. This can be conveyed clearly to them by our careful choice of words, using language that is appropriate for their understanding, being gentle with bad news, and spending time with them.

Too often, parents are told that their baby probably will not survive, and then they are asked to make major medical decisions when they do not even know what different interventions are or how they may influence their baby's course. Unless they have a medical background, and even though we may thoroughly describe the situation and what options are available and how they may benefit the baby, parents cannot really be expected to grasp the significance of all of this. This can create additional stress for parents. By taking such great responsibility out of their hands, we leave them with fewer doubts and less guilt later.

There will be times when it is obvious that the baby will not survive, or, if he does survive, that his or her prognosis will be grim. In circumstances such as this, redirecting care by helping to orchestrate the baby's death can have a great benefit. In the case presented, it would have been easiest for the doctors who were caring for the baby to transfer him, seek second opinions, get additional data, and then make a decision. Although this is what usually occurs, it probably is much more damaging for the families, especially for the woman who is still hospitalized following the baby's birth. Often, babies are delivered at community hospitals, and care providers there may not have enough experience to be comfortable making a similar decision about withdrawing support. In some instances, it may be useful to have a transport team comprising an experienced physician and nurse, who then may be able to decide if transfer is indicated.

This case was made easier by the oxygen desaturation values. When the neurologic exam still is profoundly abnormal after several hours, moreover, the chance of recovery is bleak. Some of these severely injured babies may survive if they continue to be supported, but they will not regain much neurologic function, and in many cases this is the worst outcome. Although these decisions should not be rushed, the family must be made aware of the grim prognosis and the implications of continuing support. Many families will indicate that they do not want their child to suffer or to have an existence that is profoundly handicapped. Others will express a desire to have their baby supported regardless of the outcome. I always follow the family's lead, and then I try to take over with the major decisions, once I have better insight into the family's desires.

When the decision to withdraw support is made, every attempt should be made to make the baby appear normal. Although this varies with the situation, we usually remove as much technical equipment as possible. When parents see their baby free of wires and lines and tubes, and they can hold him or her in their arms, then they are given memories that we hope will remain more strongly etched in their minds than those of the baby lying on a bed connected to machines. Frequently, we observe how parents' anxieties decrease, after their longing to hold the baby is fulfilled. Later, after the baby died or went home, parents always relate that their most meaningful memory was the first time that they held their baby. Oftentimes, parents have accepted the fact that the baby will not survive, and all that is going through their minds is that they have never held him or her.

These situations require that care providers who make the decisions have experience and expertise. This does not mean, however, that these decisions cannot be made by community pediatricians, especially if they know the family well.

— *Anna M. August, MD*

References

Bryan, E. M. (1991). Perinatal bereavement after the loss of one twin. *Journal of Perinatal Medicine, 19*(Suppl. 1), 241-245.

Chez, R. A. (1995). Acute grief and mourning: One obstetrician's experience. *Obstetrics and Gynecology, 85*(6), 1059-1061.

Davis, D.L. (1991). *Empty cradle, broken heart: Surviving the death of your baby.* Golden, Colorado: Fulcrum Publishing.

DeKleine, M., Cuisinier, M., Kollée, L., Bethlehem, G., & DeGraauw, K. (1995). Guidance after twin and singleton neonatal death. *Archives of Diseases in Childhood, 36,* F125-F126.

Ewton, D.S. (1993). A perinatal loss follow-up guide for primary care. *Nurse Practitioner, 18,* 30-36.

Fina, D.K. (1994). A chance to say goodbye. *American Journal of Nursing, 94*(5), 42-45.

Finlay, I., & Dallimore, D. (1991). Your child is dead. *British Medical Journal, 302* (6791), 1524-1525.

Harrigan, R., Naber, M.M., Jensen, K.A., Tse, A., & Perez, D. (1993). Perinatal grief: Response to the loss of an infant. *Neonatal Network, 12*(5), 25-31.

Kimble, D.L. (1991). Neonatal death: A descriptive study of fathers' experiences. *Neonatal Network, 9*(8), 45-49.

Kowalski, K. (1991). No happy ending: Pregnancy loss and bereavement. *NAACOGS Clinical Issues in Perinatal & Women's Health Nursing, 2*(3), 368-380.

Lasker, J.N., & Toedter, L.J. (1991). Acute versus chronic grief: The case of pregnancy loss. *American Journal of Orthopsychiatry, 61*(4), 510-522.

Leon, I.G. (1992). Perinatal loss: A critique of current hospital practices. *Clinical Pediatrics, 31*(6), 366-374.

Lilford, R.J., Stratton, P., Godsil, S., & Prasad, A. (1994). A randomised trial of routine versus selective counselling in perinatal bereavement from congenital disease. *British Journal of Obstetrics and Gynecology, 101,* 291-296.

Nelson, J.D. (1994.) *The rocking horse is lonely, and other stories of fathers' grief.* Wayzata, MN: Pregnancy and Infant Loss Center, Inc.

Raphael, D. (1983). *The anatomy of bereavement.* New York: Basic Books.

Ryan, P.F., Cote-Arsenault, D., & Sugarman, L.L. (1991). Facilitating care after perinatal loss: A comprehensive checklist. *Journal of Obstetrical, Gynecological, and Neonatal Nursing, 20*(5), 385-389.

Schiff, H. S. (1977). *The bereaved parent.* New York, NY: Penguin Books.

Schneiderman, G., Winders, P., Tallett, S., & Feldman, W. (1994). Do child and /or parent bereavement programs work? *Canadian Journal of Psychiatry, 39,* 215-218.

Sexton, P.R., & Stephen, S.B. (1991). Postpartum mothers' perceptions of nursing interventions for perinatal grief. *Neonatal Network, 9*(5), 47-51.

Trouy, M.B., & Ward-Larson, C. (1987). Sibling grief. *Neonatal Network, 5*(4), 35-40.

Vance, J.C., Najman, J.M., Boyle, F.M., Embleton, G., Foster, W.J., & Thearle, M.J. (1994). Alcohol and drug usage in parents soon after stillbirth, neonatal death or SID. *Journal of Paediatrics and Child Health, 30,* 269-272.

Wegman, M.E. (1994). Annual summary of vital statistics—1993. *Pediatrics, 94*(6 Pt 1), 792-803.

Welch, I.D. (1991). Miscarriage, stillbirth, or newborn death: Starting a healthy griev-ing process. *Neonatal Network, 9*(8), 53-57.

Woods, J.R., & Esposito, J.L. (1987). *Pregnancy loss: Medical therapeutics and practical considerations.* Baltimore: Williams & Wilkins.

Additional Readings

Appleton, R., Gibson, B., & Hey, E. (1993). The loss of a baby at birth: The role of the bereavement officer. *British Journal of Obstetrics & Gynecology, 100*(1), 51-54.

Bourne, S., & Lewis, S. (1991). Perinatal bereavement: A milestone and some new dan-gers. *British Medical Journal, 302,* 1167-1168.

Brost, L., & Kenney, J.W. (1992). Pregnancy after perinatal loss: Parental reactions and nursing interventions. *Journal of Obstetrical, Gynecologic, and Neonatal Nursing, 21*(6), 457-463.

Covington, S.N., & Theut, S.K. (1993). Reactions to perinatal loss: A qualitative analysis of the national maternal and infant health survey. *American Journal of Orthopsychiatry, 63*(2), 215-222.

Harper, M.B., & Wisian, N.B. (1994). Care of bereaved parents: A study of patient satis-faction. *Journal of Reproductive Medicine, 39*(2), 80-86.

Hudome, S.M., Kirby, R.S., Senner, J.W., & Cunniff, C. (1994). Contribution of genetic disorders to neonatal mortality in a regional intensive care setting. *American Journal of Perinatology, 11*(2), 100-103.

Jellinek, M.S., Catlin, E.A., Todres, I.D., & Cassem, E.H. (1992). Facing tragic decisions with parents in the neonatal intensive care unit: Clinical perspective. *Pediatrics, 89*(1), 119-122.

Lemmer, C.M. (1991). Parental perceptions of caring following perinatal bereavement. *Western Journal of Nursing Research, 13*(4), 475-493.

Thearle, M.J., & Gregory, H. (1992). Evolution of bereavement counselling in sudden infant death syndrome, neonatal death and stillbirth. *Journal of Paediatrics and Child Health, 28*(3), 204-209.

Chapter 5

Reaching Out to the Family of a SIDS Baby

Joan Arnold
Mary McClain
Sarah J. M. Shaefer

Sudden Infant Death Syndrome (SIDS) remains an unknown cause of infant mortality, yet SIDS is the leading cause of death in infants from 28 days to 1 year of age (Willinger, James, & Catz, 1991). It is a diagnosis of exclusion. SIDS is a recognized medical disorder, listed in the International Classification of Diseases, 9th Revision (ICD-9-CM, 1978). The cause or causes of SIDS remain unexplained, despite remarkable progress in refining the definition for death, identifying risk factors which increase the likelihood of occurrence, isolating potential causative mechanisms through research, and implementing a national network of services for affected families and caregivers. Classically attributed to a negative autopsy, the definition of SIDS has undergone scrutiny and has been expanded in recent years. SIDS now is recognized as the "sudden death of an infant under 1 year of age which remains unexplained after a thorough case investigation, including performance of a complete autopsy, examination of the death scene, and review of the clinical history" (Willinger et al., 1991). Key to the assignment of SIDS as the cause of a baby's death are a complete autopsy (inclusive of gross examination of the body, and microscopic and toxicologic studies), an investigation of the death scene, and recognition of the importance of a clinical history. Use of standard necropsy protocols to define SIDS has enabled independent agreement among pathologists in assigning the cause of death. The unexplained nature of these infant deaths continues to elude scientists, sounds an alert to communities to respond to the crisis, and leaves families reeling from the devastating nature of such a profound loss. The death of an infant child is a loss that is grieved by parents, family members and friends, other caregivers, and society. The whole community is affected as families and health care providers confront the reality that they are powerless to protect our most vulnerable members of society from a tragic death.

Although the incidence of SIDS appears to be on the decline nationally (Willinger, Hoffman, & Hartford, 1994), about 5,000 infants (about 1 in 1,000 live births) are reported to die from SIDS each year in the United States. Significant research is being conducted to determine the causes of SIDS. Despite approximately 30 years of investigation, we have not developed the means to predict or prevent the occurrence of SIDS for any given baby. Research has uncovered a wealth of information, however. The assumption that an apparently healthy infant dies suddenly and unexpectedly has been replaced by the assumption that a vulnerable infant, exposed to exogenous stressors during a critical developmental period (Filiano & Kinney, 1995), dies suddenly, and a thorough case investigation fails to explain the death.

Although preventing death is not possible, a campaign to reduce the risk of SIDS has been undertaken by a coalition of agencies committed to decreasing the occurrence of SIDS. Through a collaborative mass educational effort, the United States Public Health Service, American Academy of Pediatrics, SIDS Alliance, and the Association of SIDS and Infant Mortality Programs initiated the *Back to Sleep* campaign which encourages parents habitually to place healthy infants to sleep in the supine position (see Figure 1-5). This sleeping position should be evaluated case-by-case for every baby. It is important to note that parents and other caregivers, including day care workers, should consult with health care providers about their children's health status, since certain infant health conditions may preclude the supine sleep position, including gastro-esophageal reflux, and certain upper airway malformations.

There also may be other specific infants for whom the risk/benefit balance favors a prone sleeping position. The *Back to Sleep* campaign, which focuses on sleep positioning, has been coupled with recommendations for more generalized infant health promotion practices. Other guidelines recommended in the *Back to Sleep* campaign concern: (a) bedding — assuring the use of firm mattresses or other firm surfaces; avoiding fluffy blankets or comforters under the infant; contraindicating waterbeds, sheepskins, pillows, or other soft materials as sleeping surfaces; and removing soft stuffed toys and pillows from the crib; (b) temperature — avoiding overheating by regulating the room temperature; (c) smoke-free environment — creating a smoke-free zone around the infant; (d) doctor or clinic visits — assuring speedy response to illness through contact with health care providers;

Figure 1-5.
Frequently Used SIDS Literature for Parents and Professionals

---

Directory of SIDS Program Coordinators & State Title V Maternal & Child Health Directors*
Lists more than 60 professional SIDS information and counseling programs providing services to SIDS families and the community.

Infant Sleep Position and SIDS: Counseling Implications‡
Brief summary of the *Back to Sleep* campaign including background with suggested counseling guidelines for parents of newborns and child care providers and also those whose infant has died in any position.

Information Sheet: What is SIDS?*
A four-page general information sheet about SIDS and the grief of families.

Questions and Answers for Professionals on Infant Sleeping Position and SIDS†
Provides professionals with background information and recommendations for groups of infants to place on back for sleeping.

Reduce the Risk of Sudden Infant Death Syndrome (SIDS)†
Provides parents with basic SIDS information and what parents can do to decrease their infant's SIDS risk.

SIDS Research: An Analysis in Three Parts, June 1993.*

Sudden Infant Death Syndrome: Trying to Understand the Mystery*
SIDS overview that includes current theories and research, affect of SIDS on families and others, federal initiative, and frequently asked questions.

Sudden Infant Death Syndrome (SIDS) Research: A Selected Annotated Bibliography for 1991. *

---

†*Back to Sleep* Campaign
‡Association of SIDS and Infant Mortality Programs (ASIP)
*National SIDS Resource Center (can request order form with publications listed)

emphasizing the importance of well-infant care, specifically maintenance of an up-to-date immunization schedule; (e) prenatal care — underscoring the significance of early and regular prenatal care; recognizing that increased risk for SIDS is associated with maternal smoking during pregnancy; avoiding alcohol and nonprescription drugs during pregnancy; (f) breast feeding — recommending breast feeding for newborns, because breast milk contains healthful antibodies and nutrients; and (g) enjoy your baby! — expressing concern that fear of SIDS should not alter the inherent joys of having a new baby.

Clearly, monitoring maternal health and behavior during pregnancy, and maintaining prenatal health assessment for the fetus are crucial to decreasing the risk for SIDS and reducing the incidence of SIDS. These variables are not reliable in predicting SIDS. The *Back to Sleep* campaign highlights those risks. But how, when, why, or if SIDS will occur cannot be answered through these efforts to reduce risk. The National Sudden Infant Death Syndrome Resource Center lists maternal risk factors including cigarette smoking during pregnancy, maternal age less than 20 years, poor prenatal care, low weight gain, anemia, use of illegal drugs, and history of sexually transmitted disease or urinary tract infection (SIDS: Trying to Understand the Mystery, 1994). This report concludes on the basis of these risk factors, which are often subtle and may go undetected, that SIDS somehow is associated with a harmful prenatal environment.

Infants whose deaths are attributed to SIDS are believed to be those who are born with one or more conditions which precipitate their vulnerability to stresses that occur in normal neonatal life. For example, the newborn's age is considered to be a risk factor. As many as 80% of SIDS deaths occur by the age of 6 months, with the greatest number of deaths occurring between 2 and 4 months. This age is considered to encompass a critical developmental period, reflecting physiologic vulnerability to factors which contribute to the incidence of SIDS. SIDS occurs in all types of families and is reported to be largely indifferent to race or socioeconomic level. Dwyer and Ponsonby (1995) report that, although an association between lower socioeconomic status and SIDS has been documented in many studies, the independent contribution of poverty (once adjusted for such factors as maternal age, parity, bottle feeding, and cigarette smoking) still needs to be evaluated fully (Dwyer & Ponsonby, 1995). There is a 60%/40% male-to-female ratio and SIDS is more common among infants of higher birth order. Seasonally, more deaths occur in autumn and winter, in both the Northern and the Southern hemispheres. Medical factors, including cyanosis, tachycardia, respiratory distress, irritability, hypothermia, poor feeding, and tachypnea are among the risk factors which occur with statistical significance in a greater number of SIDS infants than non-SIDS cases in the neonatal nursery.

Leading hypotheses about the mechanism of death in SIDS cases include rebreathing-asphyxia associated with face-down positioning for sleep, which may be associated with increased metabolic rate as a consequence of hyperthermia and blunted arousal or ventilatory responses. This altered arousal or ventilatory response may be permanent or transient (Brooks, 1995). Brooks concludes that, although other mechanisms such as primary cardiac arrhythmias, metabolic disorders, and upper airway obstruction in infants who are not sleeping in the prone position are possible causes of death, supportive data for these hypotheses are not as strong. Always necessarily lingering in the minds of investigators is the association between SIDS and infanticide. Historically, families have been tormented because of this inevitable relationship. Some parents have been charged with the homicide of their infants. For others the cast of aspersion remains, leaving them alienated and guilt-ridden, blaming themselves for their own perceived contribution to their child's death, through an act of either omission or commission. Unable to assert the actual proportion of cases which are diagnosed as SIDS but which actually are instances of infanticide, Brooks (1995) estimates that the figure is less than 1% and recommends a complete postmortem evaluation in every case of sudden unexpected infant death (with careful, standardized, death-scene investigation by a highly sensitized individual, respectful of the feelings of the family) to address the potential for this error.

The future for extending science in the SIDS arena is promising. Epidemiologic, pathologic, physiologic, and clinical studies are drawing closer to a fuller understanding of mechanisms which are responsible for the tragic loss of so many infants. The *Back to Sleep* campaign, coupled with rigorous research efforts, may be expected to extend our knowledge about SIDS. It is hoped that this work will decrease the incidence of SIDS as well as influence infant mortality in the United States. The National Sudden Infant Death Syndrome Resource Center, U.S. Department of Health and Human Services, Public Health Service has selected annotated bibliographies available on research endeavors. Figure 2-5 summarizes current understanding about sudden infant death.

Figure 2-5.
Current Understanding about Sudden Infant Death Syndrome (SIDS)

SIDS Is:

- The major cause of death in infants from 1 month to 1 year of age, with most deaths occurring between 2 and 4 months
- Sudden and silent — the infant was seemingly healthy
- Currently, unpredictable and unpreventable
- A death that occurs quickly, often associated with sleep with no signs of suffering
- Determined only after an autopsy, an examination of the death scene, and a review of the clinical history
- Designated as a diagnosis of exclusion
- A recognized medical disorder listed in the International Classification of Diseases, 9th Revision (ICD- 9)
- An infant death that leaves unanswered questions, causing intense grief for parents and families

SIDS Is Not:

- Caused by vomiting and choking, or by minor illnesses such as colds or infections
- Caused by diphtheria, pertussis, tetanus (DPT) vaccines, or other immunizations
- Contagious
- Child abuse
- The cause of every unexpected infant death

Source: Information sheet: "What is SIDS?" (1993). National SIDS Resource Center, Vienna, VA

Finding the Infant

When an infant dies of SIDS, family members are devastated. All of those who are involved in the immediate response also are affected profoundly. In most cases, the baby is discovered by the primary caregiver — usually the parent, but sometimes a babysitter or day care provider. The infant is found lifeless and cannot be "woken up." The horror and shock of this discovery leave the parent/caregiver in an intense state of disbelief and bewilderment. Under normal circumstances, all parents somehow learn to live with the omnipresent fear that death is always lurking. In the usual course of living, that fear is suppressed and denied; otherwise, parents could be consumed with the thought. Parents are completely responsible for the care and nurture of their vulnerable infants. When something goes wrong — when anything goes wrong — parents feel an enormous sense of self-responsibility, and they accept the burden of failure willingly. But, when parents actually are confronted with the sight of their dead infant, the levels of horror, disbelief, and self-imposed guilt are unfathomable. Standing over one's dead infant is an experience that infiltrates every cell of parents' being and leaves them in a despair with which they must reckon for the rest of their lives.

Parents or caregivers may attempt resuscitation, pick up the baby and cradle him or her while weeping, or flee the scene calling for help from anyone. A multitude of reactions can ensue, since the uncontrollable nature of this discovery is impossible to comprehend. Depending on the amount of time that has elapsed between death and discovery, the baby may have blood-tinged froth exuding from the nose and mouth and bruising from the pooling of blood in dependent areas of the body (lividity). These postmortem signs unfortunately can be misdiagnosed as signs of abuse by the uninformed eye of a first responder. Unexpected outbursts from a guilt-ridden parent or caregiver sometimes lead responders to question parental involvement in the baby's death. Key to a therapeutic response to parents, and to protecting the integrity of the death scene, is education of first responders, including police officers, fire fighters, emergency medical responders, and coroners or death investigators. Professional program providers affiliated with SIDS information and counseling programs are instrumental in providing education sessions and ongoing support for first responders. Special training videos and core curricula for the education of immediate responders are available.

First responders generally attempt resuscitation even when it is clear that the baby is dead, since no one wants to abandon hope that the child could be saved. Emergency response generally is aggressive and is instituted speedily, given any possibility that the baby still could respond to life-saving measures. These actions may be continued while the baby is being transported to the local emergency department, where a new set of skilled professionals takes over and continues to institute measures to restore vital signs (McClain, 1994). Parents or caregivers usually want desperately to keep in constant sight of the baby as these efforts are pursued, hoping against all odds that someone may be able to save their child. It may be in the best interest of parents, with respect to their long-term grief response and recovery, to allow family members to witness emergency efforts. If family members are whisked away and escorted to a quiet area, they may resist, determined not be separated from the baby. Their presence in view of life saving procedures which are being carried out may be much less distressing than otherwise might be expected. At such a moment, parents are not concerned about procedures or the sight of blood which they may witness. On the contrary, it can be helpful in the long run if parents can be assured that everyone worked heroically to save the baby's life. Valiant efforts by physicians, nurses, technicians, and others who are surrounding their child, attempting to pump life into the small lifeless body, are the best form of support which parents may derive from anyone in such a situation. Some parents or caregivers, on the other hand, may prefer to pace the waiting room floor, or sit motionless, and await the outcome as news is brought to them. Individual needs of parents are evident in their behavior.

Superseding individual need to gain access to the baby or to wait for information about his or her condition is the need to vent anguish and grief naturally. If a parent is wailing in despair, it actually is best if the care provider sits close by and accepts the tears without trying to quiet them. Grief must be expressed. The emergency department becomes the initial setting in which parents must establish a release for their grief. If agitation and crying are quieted by tranquilizers, then the immediate grief reaction is blunted. Once it has been diminished or restrained, grief is altered. It may be turned inward and contorted into something which is deemed somehow to be more acceptable for outsiders. But the full and true nature of grief cannot be contained, for it will be revealed in defensive and inappropriate behaviors. Enabling the full expression of grief in the emergency department setting is the beginning of therapeutic outreach. No two people will grieve in the same way. All reactions are accepted and interpreted as a way of expressing the pain of loss.

Emergency department responders care not only for the lifeless infant but also for the grief-stricken family. A careful assessment of family interactions and documentation of statements made by family members assists in developing a clear picture about the circumstances of death. Communication is not accusatory; but, rather, it is focused on listening, to clarify the chain of events and the family's reaction to finding the lifeless baby. It is especially useful to determine who among the family members is the key informant, so that more effective communication can be established and information can be shared with the one who is in the most reliable position to retain it. Directions about autopsy, the medical investigation system, and funeral arrangements should be written, since expecting families in such circumstances to remember verbal information accurately in the midst of such a crisis is unrealistic. The name and telephone number of an emergency department contact should be given to the family, since family members may have questions hours and days after pronouncement of the baby's death. Finally, family members may need transportation to return home, since they frequently travel in an ambulance or police vehicle on the way to the hospital. Moreover, most family members would be too overwhelmed to drive safely. If the family member is alone and now must leave the emergency department without his or her baby, this person should be detained and comforted, and not left alone to wait, until a relation or friend can arrive at the emergency department and accompany the parent home. It also is helpful to ensure that the baby's clothes, blanket, or other belongings be returned to the family before they leave the hospital. Additionally, in some cases, a locket of hair or a photograph may be provided to the family, so that the family leaves the emergency department with precious mementos of their child (McClain, 1994).

The Autopsy

The infant's body is generally removed from the emergency department and transferred to a coroner or medical examiner's jurisdiction. Known for her long-standing commitment to assuring dignified and thorough autopsy in cases of sudden and unexpected infant death and for her research on pathologic findings, Valdes-Dapena (1995) believes that, above all, the autopsy is important for parents. Valdes-Dapena asserts that parents need to know why the baby died. They need to have assurance that their baby's death was "natural" and could not have been predicted or prevented. She links psychologic recovery from the loss with such knowledge. Since SIDS is not accountable for every unexplained infant death, the autopsy may reveal an unusual or genetically linked disease. Valdes-Dapena's approach is to identify differential diagnoses of sudden, unexpected death involving the following body systems and organs: cardiovascular, respiratory, gastrointestinal, pancreas, endocrine, central nervous system, and systemic disease. Finally, a post-autopsy conference is highly recommended, to help parents to understand and deal with the reality of their loss (McClain & Shaefer, 1995; Valdes-Dapena, 1995). Ideally, a post-autopsy conference is scheduled approximately 3 weeks after the baby's death. All available findings from the autopsy are reviewed. Post-autopsy conferencing is important to all families, but it is particularly critical in situations when the cause of death is signed out as "pending further study." Without closure on a final cause of death, parents

Figure 3-5.
Key Elements for a Therapeutic Response
to Families Affected by SIDS

- Empathy — to comprehend the magnitude of the family's loss on the death of their baby
- Acceptance — not rejecting or limiting
- Listening — recognizing the family's loss and ensuring that they will be respected for their ability to deal with the vastness and pervasiveness of their loss. Legitimizing their loss by talking openly about the dead child. Silence denies the child's existence and denies parents their relationship with this special person. Grief can be shared.
- Fostering strengths — maximizing family strengths and their ability to cope; fostering decision making which rebuilds self-esteem
- Maximizing existing networks of support — making the most of a family's supportive ties and connections, and fostering new avenues of support
- Facilitating effective communication among family members — assisting the family's means of self-recovery through listening, clarifying, promoting, and encouraging interchange. Support families as they learn to live with their pain and to live without their baby.

are left to wonder and doubt themselves throughout the rest of their own lives. Assignment of cause of the baby's death is essential. The assignment of SIDS as the cause of death enables parents to develop an identity as a parent of a baby whose death was attributed to SIDS and to avail themselves of support services through local and statewide SIDS centers and programs, as well as voluntary peer groups.

Support for Families

A community-wide response is indicated in order for an adequate response to be directed to families who are affected by the sudden and unexpected death of their baby. An entire community is involved and affected by this crisis and the ongoing nature of loss when a baby dies. Key elements for a therapeutic response by health care professionals are described in Figure 3-5 (Arnold & Gemma, 1994).

The core of services which must be provided to families affected by SIDS is managed and directed by local SIDS information and counseling programs. These programs or SIDS centers generally are state-wide but also may be available in specific cities or territories across the country. The best way to access a local SIDS program is through the National Sudden Infant Death Syndrome Resource Center (see Figure 4-5). These programs are situated in local or state health departments, medical examiner offices, city/county hospitals, medical centers, and universities. They provide a wide array of services including case management, direct contact with families, telephone support, facilitation of home visits to affected families for information and counseling, group support, and widespread community education to first responders, health professionals, and students in the health professions; funeral directors and chaplains; and day care providers, child welfare workers, and the public in general. The centers are linked to each other through voluntary participation in an organization called the Association of SIDS and Infant Mortality Programs (ASIP), which advocates for continued development and expansion of SIDS and bereavement services; organizes activities which promote professional growth including the development of practice standards and links among practitioners working with SIDS families; joins with maternal and child, public health, and other health care providers to serve all families affected by infant death; and finally represents professional SIDS information and counseling services at the state, national, and international level (see Figure 4-5).

Professional SIDS programs are dedicated to assuring that postmortem examinations are provided including autopsies on all cases of sudden and unexpected infant deaths; SIDS is cited as a cause of death when appropriate; parents are notified of the preliminary cause of death, preferably within a 24- to 48-hour period; counseling is provided to families bereaved by the sudden and unexpected deaths of their infants; educational programs are conducted; and epidemiologic data are collected, analyzed, and furnished related to SIDS and infant mortality.

There also are a number of voluntary peer support agencies (including the National SIDS Alliance) which provide parent-to-parent contact via telephone and parent support groups. Parent-to-parent self-help is important to parents as they struggle with their grief and with life without their child. Surviving parents serve as role models who help newly bereaved parents realize that they too can survive their baby's death. Self-help is a form of care that benefits parents as well as the ever-widening circle of family members and friends who are affected by the death of a baby. An organization named AGAST, the Alliance of Grandparents Against SIDS Tragedy, is concerned with peer support for grandparents who witness the grief experienced by their own

Figure 4-5.
SIDS Resources

Association of SIDS and Infant Mortality Programs
Center for Infant and Child Loss
630 W. Fayette Street, Room 5-684
Baltimore, MD 21201
(410) 706-5062

***Back to Sleep* Campaign**
PO Box 29111
Washington, DC 20040
(800) 505-CRIB

National SIDS Resource Center
2070 Chain Bridge Road, Suite 450
Vienna, VA 22182
(703) 821-8955 ext 249 or 474

SIDS Alliance
1314 Bedford Avenue, Suite 210
Baltimore, MD 21208
(800) 221-SIDS

AGAST
Alliance of Grandparents Against SIDS Tragedy
1915 Apollo Avenue
Tempe, AZ 85283
(800) 793-SIDS

---

children at the same time that they grieve the painful loss of a grandchild (see Figure 4-5).

Parental Grief

The nature of grief as it relates to sudden and unexpected infant death is unparalleled. A baby represents new life and hope, the antithesis of death. A baby is pure, innocent, dependent, and vulnerable. The baby is known and bonded with before birth and in anticipation through adoption. An infant cannot survive without the love, nurturance, and care of parents or caregivers. Parents know that they are responsible for this fragile and dependent life. In the back of their minds, parents always are fearful that a child can die. When a baby does die, a parent's deepest and most alarming fear is realized.

Compounding this intense emotion is the horror of finding one's baby dead. In most cases of SIDS, it is the parent who confronts the sight of his or her lifeless child and is left devastated by this image, which will play over and over again in the mind's eye. The picture of one's lifeless child and the horrifying swell of emotions that consume parents are totally devastating. Parents are plunged into a state of shock and disbelief, and somehow they now must integrate into their lives that they are the parents of a dead child. The permanence of death is impossible to realize in the crisis. The realization that this child's life has ended before it really began is hard to appreciate. Parents are shattered, changed forever by their loss. The sense of guilt, self-blame, and profound remorse that follow are indescribable. There is a deep sense of failure in one of life's most precious responsibilities, caring for and protecting an innocent, helpless child. No advice or support will take away that sense of blame at having failed to predict and prevent the baby's death.

When a baby dies, parents experience a double grief: the pain of losing their own special child and also the death of part of themselves. The young, precious child, with his or her own unique personality, is dead and never will grow to become the inquisitive toddler, young child, adolescent, or mature adult. This child never will age, to die in the natural order of life's span. This child will be a baby forever. Parents will not rejoice at this child's first step. They will not be able to walk hand-in-hand with their young child to the first day of school, or to celebrate graduation. They will not be able to witness this child's first love, this child's marriage. They will not become grandparents through this child, and they will not be able to envision the family's future generations descending down through this child's genealogy. This child's death ends this precious life and ends the progression of the family through his or her growth and development.

Parents also experience a personal death when a baby dies. When a baby dies, an inherent part of a parent's being dies also, never to be filled and not to be recovered. Parents describe this inner death as if a vital part of themselves has been severed or cut away. There is a peculiar violence in this personal death. It is as though the baby was ripped away from the parents, and they were left with a raw and aching void — an emptiness that becomes the baby's space. In time, that space becomes the parent's connection to the child. But, in the intense period of grief, that space feels like an enormous void, and a vital part of the self is missing.

The physical symptoms of intense grief are pervasive. Parents may feel an empty abdomen, a phantom sense of having been stripped of the baby. Arms may ache for wanting to hold the baby. Tears stream and feel blood-filled as one weeps one's insides out. Breasts still may be producing milk to nourish the baby. The body is emptied as grief occupies more and more of the parent and death consumes a parent's being. Parental grief is twofold; parents grieve for the child and grieve for that part of themselves that never will be returned.

Parents' instinct is to continue to parent the baby, despite his or her death. It is not uncommon for parents to experience visions of the baby, or they hear the baby cry and respond as though this were the reality, while the baby's death is just a dream. In part, parents live in a state of denial, hoping that the nightmare will come to an end, that their lives will return to the normal patterns of living, and that the baby will appear again safe in the crib or in their arms. In addition, these visual and auditory experiences are attempts by the parent to connect with the dead baby; that is, to continue to parent by responding to the imagined sight and sound of the baby. Parents are supposed to respond to the wants and needs of the baby, and in their imaginations they still can respond when the baby calls. These are wished-for chances to parent again, to soothe the baby. This is the expression of a parent's continuing to parent in the face of death — hoping against hope that this is another opportunity to prove capable of meeting the baby's needs. Thoughts of the baby in the grave are also common, particularly on a cold, rainy, or snowy day. It is not that parents imagine that the baby is buried alive, but rather that they yearn to reach out beyond the grave and death itself to protect the baby from the elements and, more importantly, from the unknown. Again, this is an attempt to carry out parenting functions, which transcends the child's death. Parental love transcends death. The connectedness between parent and child continues throughout a parent's life. Grief continues throughout parents' lives, as well.

Parental grief related to sudden infant death is profound. Parents of a dead baby have relatively few concrete and tangible memories to hold on to when the baby dies. For some parents, there may be footprints or an identification bracelet from the hospital, which were obtained when the baby was born; baby clothes or a special blanket; photographs; perhaps a lock of hair. Many parents treasure photographs of the funeral and even photographs which were taken after their baby died. Ordinary items that were the baby's become sacred possessions for parents. Some parents are left desolate when the police, emergency medical technicians, or hospital emergency department staff fail to return the sheet which the baby last slept on or the blanket in which the baby was wrapped for the final trip to the emergency room.

These items hold the baby's smell and provide a physical connection which parents need in order to remain close to their dead baby. Even blood stains on a sheet or blanket, remains of blood-tinged froth from the infant's nose or mouth, become precious connections to the dead baby. Some parents wear a piece of the infant's undershirt pinned to an undergarment to feel close to the baby. Others create shrines in their homes and light candles to memorialize their baby. Some cannot return home and cannot enter the place where the baby lived and then ceased to exist. The memories are too painful.

Manifestations of the grief of parents subsequent to sudden infant death are wide-ranging and unique. Each parent grieves in a style that is complex and profoundly personal. No two people are alike, and no two parents are alike in their grief. Vast differences in response can emerge and create a gap between the baby's mother and father. At best, there is acceptance for each other's uniqueness in the manner in which grief is expressed or contained. At worst, there is a complete dissociation and disengagement in the relationship, as grieving styles and personal needs collide and create disunity and alienation (Carroll & Shaefer, 1993-94). Striking at the heart of parental grief is the issue of blame. If parents blame each other for acts of omission (what one should have done) or accuse and question each other about the days, hours, or minutes leading up to the baby's death, then their relationship very well may be sacrificed. Doubt and mistrust take over. Grief can be isolating and alienating. A couple may feel pulled apart from each other at a time when they really need unconditional acceptance from each other.

Particular times of the day are very difficult for grieving parents, but nighttime seems to be especially painful. Alone in the darkness, parents are left with random agonizing thoughts and doubts. Images preoccupy and torment them as parents try to make sense of why the baby died. Blame is always an issue. Anger may be directed at a pediatrician or nurse, for not recognizing that something was wrong with the baby; at the police, for the possibly suspicious nature of their response; at the emergency department staff, for not saving the baby; even at the world in general, for being a place where a parent must bear the grief of a baby's death. Parents ask, "Why *me*? Why did *my* baby die? What is wrong with *me*?" Blame may be other-directed, but all avenues for blame lead back to the parents themselves. Ultimately, parents feel responsible for the baby's death. For some parents, this recognition and admission of self-blame and the feeling of being diminished as a failed parent, may be repressed. Parents may be stuck in anger, capable only of venting hostility until their grief is released and the personal tragedy has been confronted.

Parents of a dead baby often feel contaminated by death. They may elect to give their baby's clothes to a friend or relative as a symbol of their love and desire to see another enjoy the things that were chosen so carefully for their child. Such gifts, however, may be greeted by refusal, which is propelled by others' more or less conscious unwillingness to accept death into their homes. Parents may begin to feel that they are jinxed by death — that everything they touch will die and that they are incapable of raising a child because of their association with the baby's death. Some parents doubt their ability to care for their surviving children.

When a baby dies, the void is so wide and so deep that some parents seek to fill that void with another pregnancy, in hopes of diminishing their intolerable emotional pain. Pregnancy may be desired as soon as possible. Given the unpredictable and uniquely complex nature of parental grief, it is unlikely that both parents will feel the same way at the same time. The other parent may feel that the pain of grief is so intense that he or she never again will be willing to be exposed to the possibility of losing another baby. Therefore, for this parent, pregnancy is out of the question.

In some relationships sex may be avoided, since sex could result in another pregnancy and also because sex is pleasurable. Personal pleasure is shameful to experience when one's defenseless baby is dead and buried in the ground. Parents may deny themselves needed touch and intimacy and feel that they cannot give themselves pleasure when their child never will know pleasure. Survivors of sudden infant death are riddled with complex and confusing emotions. Learning to become a survivor and how to function fully again takes time, as well as willingness to express grief and to integrate loss into one's self image. Regaining one's integrity as a person and as a parent is the work of grief.

Grieving parents may feel that life is not worth living anymore and even might consider joining the baby in death. Although the risk of suicide is possible, it usually is more indicative of a feeling of hopelessness and futility which preoccupies the parent. Parents feel that it would not matter if the traffic mowed them down or if their lives were snuffed out, because life does not seem worth living anyway. The injustice of losing a baby is too much to bear. Nothing justifies a baby's death. Innocence dies when a baby dies. A baby is supposed to outlive parents and to meet or exceed parents' hopes and dreams. Often, parents with little in the way of material possessions or stature believe that their baby's new life represents a chance for the family to break out of their cycle of poverty, or that the baby will grow up to become someone whom others admire — someone who is capable of having a happier life. Parents are not supposed to bury their children, and no parent should have to bury an infant child. Small white coffins should not exist. The natural order is for the baby to grow into childhood and finally adulthood and to live beyond the parents. Parents feel failure in the ability to assure the natural order of life, and, moreover, they feel the guilt of being a survivor.

The whole family is affected by an infant's sudden death. No one is prepared or has time to prepare. The sudden, unexpected nature of SIDS leaves family members and the wider circle of friends and relatives confused. Some will question the parents' capability to parent, particularly if the mother and father are young and inexperienced. If the parents have little in the way of resources, they may be blamed for not providing for the needs of their child. If a parent is single and raising the baby alone with no others to offer supportive assistance, then she may be viewed as incapable.

SIDS introduces doubt into the minds of most people. In fact, it is not a cause for death. The cause remains unknown, which underscores the doubt. SIDS is a syndrome, an assignment about the nature of death that cannot be explained in any other way. SIDS is listed as a cause of death when every other known cause of death has been excluded. Parents, family members, friends, and the larger community may find SIDS difficult to accept as the cause of death. Each looks for a cause, the "real" cause, which may further undermine the integrity of the parent-child relationship. SIDS introduces doubt, and the worst kind of doubt is when a parent is accused of perhaps intentionally having ended the baby's life. Unspoken, but close to the surface, is recognition of how easy it would be to end a baby's life — through suffocation, shaken-baby syndrome, an unreported fall, or some other accident. Parents feel self-blame and they doubt themselves as competent parents. When others look askance or when an investigator asks too many questions or when the death scene is treated like a crime scene, then parents feel accused implicitly or explicitly. Some parents have been detained by police or forbidden to re-enter their homes until the criminal investigation concludes with the issuance of the cause of death. The damage done in these cases is impossible to take back. When parents are treated as potential murderers until negative autopsy findings vindicate them, they are marked in their communities. Their anger is difficult to convert into other forms of therapeutic grief.

The Affected Family

Each member of the family faces his or her own frailties in confronting a baby's death. Surviving siblings may feel guilty or responsible for the baby's sudden and unexpected death. Young siblings may be jealous of the new baby and feel that they have lost their prominence and proximity to the parent. A sibling may wish the baby dead. When the baby does die, the sibling may believe that these thoughts killed the baby. Although this is recognized as magical thinking and is viewed as a developmentally appropriate cognitive style, the sibling is left feeling responsible for the baby's death. Intervention must be swift and successful in preventing this kind of sibling self-blame (Mandell, McAnulty, & Reece, 1983; McClain & Shaefer, 1995; Shaefer, 1992; Siegel, 1985).

Compounding the bereavement issues for surviving siblings is the terrifying sense of vulnerability which they may experience. Death came into the family and took their baby away. Depending on the developmental stage of the sibling, death may be viewed mysteriously or may be personified as a frightening intruder. If the baby could just disappear, then surviving siblings may wonder if they too will vanish and never return to the family. Siblings fear that their parents also could be taken from them just as the baby was taken away. This fear may motivate the sibling to seek the protection of the parents and to cling to them, believing that this connection will ward off death. Parents, typically overcome by their own grief, often are unavailable to their surviving children, to help them with their responses to the sibling baby's death. Parents may not even be aware of their children's profound need for safety and security. Parents may be emotionally unable to respond and unintentionally may push the child away. Siblings' feelings may result in panic or may be transformed into symptoms that require parental intervention. The need for parental contact is so dramatic that some children will require medical intervention. Parents may feel incompetent about responding to their children's problems for fear that any parental intervention will result in death. Parents feel contaminated by death, and their surviving children feel that, without their parents to rescue them, they too will be grabbed by death and disconnected from any security which they had derived unquestioningly from their parents' love and their family's unity. The family is changed by the sudden and unexpected death of an infant. Death has fractured the family. Whatever was previously secure is now shaken. The family is in a state of disequilibrium, and a new balance is hard to achieve while each member struggles to make sense of the devastating loss which has changed the family forever.

The dead baby is a vital member of this family and always will remain a member of this family despite death. The family who is willing to integrate this loss into their identity is the family that can grieve effectively. The resulting ability of the family to move on in life depends on the ability of the members and the family as a whole to integrate the baby's death into their identity. The family continues to care for and about all of its members, living and dead. The family will find its own special way to commemorate the death of this special baby. Some families will create a memory book, others will visit the grave with regularity, still others will organize a special event or will volunteer their efforts to help others who also have faced sudden infant death. Regardless of the manner in which individuals and families honor their own dead baby, each can be connected to the baby by finding a link to the empty space which has been created by the baby's death. It is this connection to the dead child and to memories of the child that enable other family members to grieve. Grieving is the healing connection to the child that is facilitated by integrating the infant child's death into their continuing lives.

The long-term consequences of sudden infant death are unique to a given family. Some families will employ cultural beliefs and practices that sustain them and provide continuity through the generations in expressing their grief and making meaning of the baby's death. Culture will determine how and if grief is processed and the boundaries for behavior that are deemed acceptable and necessary to honor the baby and to characterize the death (Lawson, 1990; Spector, 1996). Death rituals and practices are determined by cultural affiliation, and these add multiple dimensions to expressing grief for an infant's sudden death. Religion and the particular belief system of the family likewise add the possibility of support for families. Some families may feel that a baby's death is not justifiable in any way, and this can cause a schism within themselves in relation to long-standing personal values. Some family members may feel that their belief in a higher power no longer can be sustained because their faith has failed them. This upheaval in values and beliefs is not uncommon after the sudden and shocking death of a vulnerable and pure baby. Others may find respite from their pain in their religious beliefs, and thereby they reaffirm or strengthen their religious beliefs and values. The range of expression is wide and different for each situation. Nevertheless, an infant's sudden and unexpected death does mobilize cultural, religious, and moral systems of belief in the progression of grief.

Conclusion

Sudden Infant Death Syndrome represents the sudden and unanticipated death of a young child. A baby is the future and the hope of a better life, one that reaches ahead to new horizons. When a baby dies suddenly and unexpectedly for no apparent reason, logic and emotions are turned inside out. The sudden death of a baby represents the death of innocence. Parents, surviving siblings, subsequent siblings, the ever-widening circle of relatives and friends, the multitude of caregivers and responders to this crisis, and the community at large are all affected. The death of one innocent baby challenges family life, personal and community beliefs and values, and the entire health care delivery system. Infants are not supposed to die. Sudden Infant Death Syndrome takes the lives of thousands of infants each year, leaving families devastated and communities alerted to the urgency of protecting our most vulnerable citizens.❏

Case Study 1-5

Cultural Sensitivity and Competence of Health Care Providers

Carmen Lopez is a 19-year-old Latino woman who is involved with Juan Gomez, a 22-year-old Latino male. Carmen's family strongly disapproves of her relationship with Juan, because he is a drug abuser and a dealer. When Carmen became pregnant with Juan's baby, she and her 4-year-old daughter from a previous relationship moved a hundred miles away with Juan. The Lopez family continued to disapprove of Carmen and Juan's relationship, and resentment grew between the two families. Baby Carlos was born after an uncomplicated pregnancy and delivery. Juan continued to use drugs heavily during Carmen's pregnancy, and for 3 to 4 months after Carlos's birth, at which time Juan entered a drug rehabilitation program.

Carmen went home to visit her family 2 weeks before Christmas, when Carlos was 6 months old. Juan protested her visit, and they argued before Carmen left. Juan felt that Carmen was his "wife," and that she should do what he told her to do. Nevertheless, Carmen went to visit her family.

Early one morning while she was visiting her parents, Carmen found Carlos in bed, not breathing and unresponsive. He was taken by ambulance to the local hospital. While resuscitation attempts ensued, Carmen telephoned Juan to tell him about Carlos. Juan became very angry and threatened to kill Carmen if Carlos did not recover. Resuscitation attempts failed, and Carlos was pronounced dead. The autopsy determined that Sudden Infant Death Syndrome (SIDS) was the cause of Carlos's death. After the funeral, Carmen returned with Juan to their home. She felt safe and believed that Juan no longer blamed her for Carlos's death.

Carmen and Juan met with a SIDS counselor 2 days after their baby's funeral. Carmen was deferential to Juan during the visit. She expressed guilt about Carlos's death, that she thought that she should have taken him to the doctor, and that she shouldn't have gone to visit her family. She felt guilty about disobeying her "husband's" wishes. She was angry at Juan because of his drug use, which had made him unavailable to Carlos while the baby was alive. She expressed this anger when Juan made it clear that he did not believe that Carlos had died of SIDS. Juan believed that his son had died because Carmen's mother had cast the "evil eye" on Carlos because of her hatred for Juan. Both Carmen and Juan expressed a belief in spiritism. Juan particularly was angry with Carmen and her family because it was a son who had died. The counselor was unsure of the appropriate response to such statements and said nothing.

Both parents expressed a strong desire to have another child. Carmen wanted to delay pregnancy, while Juan wanted to conceive immediately. Carmen became pregnant $2^1/2$ months after Carlos's death. She subsequently delivered a baby girl, who looked strikingly like Carlos. Juan's drug and partner abuse continued.

Juan was skeptical about the purposes of counseling visits, but he allowed the SIDS nurse to come again. He did not participate in further visits. During a follow-up counseling visit, Carmen informed the SIDS counselor that she now had the strength to leave Juan. Two weeks later, Carmen moved home without Juan's knowledge. The SIDS counselor felt that no counseling referrals were necessary.

Commentary

In the case under consideration, the parents of baby Carlos are referred to as "Latinos." This does not provide specific information necessary to understand and appreciate the cultural beliefs, values, prescriptions for rituals and rites, nor language preference of a particular individual or family. Over several centuries and even today, "Latinos" have immigrated to what is now known as the United States from different areas of the world. There are differences in each group's cultural heritage and degrees of acculturation into the dominant culture. That is, individuals from Mexico, Puerto Rico, Cuba, El Salvador, Argentina, or Spain exhibit a wide range of cultural beliefs, practices, and language preferences from slightly similar to absolutely different. Their differences in acculturation are influenced by the degrees to which they either have socialized with or have remained isolated from other cultural groups, particularly the dominant cultural group, and by the number of generations who have lived in this country. The importance of the health care provider's sensitivity to these cultural issues and respect for the practices of the patient and her family are major factors that influence the effectiveness of health services and information provided, the patient and her family's acceptance of medical diagnoses and treatment options, and the patient's compliance and satisfaction.

While death and grief are universal experiences, the physical, behavioral, and emotional consequences are embedded deeply in each person or family's cultural heritage. The death of a loved one may precipitate such strong basic human responses that the bereaved individual or family may seek security and comfort in their cultural beliefs, values, and practices; as well as in food and language preferences from the past.

Cultural competence and sensitivity require that health care providers honestly examine their own cultural heritages and attitudes, in order to understand, appreciate, and respect the culturally based patterns and the strengths of others with whom they interact therapeutically.

Family Roles

In most Latino cultures, the male in the family assumes the dominant role and makes most, if not all, decisions for the family. The woman's role is to maintain the home and to care for the children. It is critical that care providers include both parents in planning and conducting interventions for their patients. This couple's practice of their culturally influenced roles was exemplified by Carmen's move from her own family's home to one with Juan, even though Juan continued to exhibit macho characteristics — including abusive behavior towards Carmen — and he continued to be a drug user and dealer.

Following the death of Carlos, Juan's anger was precipitated by Carmen's disobeying his demand that Carmen not leave to visit with her parents without him, and from his avowed belief in spiritism (Juan attributed Carlos's death to the "evil eye" which Carmen's mother had cast, because of her dislike of Juan). Carmen's sense of guilt arose from her belief that Carlos would not have died, had she obeyed her boyfriend and remained with him during the holidays. Such cultural beliefs exemplify the complexities of providing correct information and support services to families whose cultural heritage is different from that of care providers, as well as from the dominant culture. It is no simple matter to win the trust of families from other cultural groups, so that learning can take place and problems within the family can be prevented, ameliorated, or resolved.

Latino men generally object to contraception and abortion practices. Therefore, women in this culture are subject to early and rapid repeat pregnancies, as was true in the case of Carmen and Juan. While both parents wanted another child after Carlos's death, Carmen's preference was to delay a subsequent pregnancy. Juan did not want to delay. Thus, it should have come as no surprise to learn that Carmen became pregnant again so quickly after the death of her son. It is possible that this pregnancy was the critical incident that provided Carmen with the strength to terminate her relationship with Juan and to return to her parents' home.

Strength of Kinship Within Latino Families

There are many cultural ties that bind a Latino woman to her family of origin. Parents and other close kin willingly share the care of immediate family members, as well as that of extended family members, particularly when they are stressed by domestic or financial problems. Health care providers cannot make decisions for a patient or her family, except in extreme emergencies, such as in cases in which life has been threatened and someone is eminently endangered. Care providers can listen to an individual who is contemplating making a change, help her to consider options, and refer her to resources that provide assistance to women in domestic crisis. It is not known whether or not Carmen was referred for such services.

Future Services for Carmen and Her Daughter

Once Carmen informed the SIDS counselor about her decision to leave Juan and return to her parents' home, the SIDS counselor, who had been unsure of how to respond to this family in the past, closed the case, noting that "...no counseling referrals were necessary." Three health and social-service concerns for Carmen and her daughter should be addressed, in fact:

1.   There was no discussion by the SIDS counselor about either parent's final understanding that SIDS was the cause of Carlos's death, nor about the progress which Carmen and Juan did or did not make in dealing with their

grief. There are no cultures who do not grieve the loss of a respected or loved individual. The responses and behaviors of the bereaved family members remain deeply embedded in the members' cultural heritages, even though the individuals may be undergoing acculturation. Health care providers who counseled this family failed to appreciate that grief is not expressed in the same way by everyone; that resolution does not occur in the brief period of 2 or 3 months; and that grief does not occur in isolation from other concurrent domestic problems. How this grief is dealt with now could have serious and lasting consequences for Carmen, her 4-year-old daughter, and possibly even for the unborn subsequent child. Because the care providers could not be responsive to this family's needs, it is questionable whether an accurate assessment of their grief could be made and used as the basis for determining whether or not referral for further grief counseling or for other services was needed.

2.   It is imperative that a public health nurse promptly telephone or visit Carmen to ensure that she is receiving prenatal care and to assist Carmen in finding care for herself, since she already is in the second trimester of her pregnancy. One critical issue, since her boyfriend is a drug user and dealer, is that efforts should be made to learn if Carmen is using drugs herself during this pregnancy, in order to assess potential risks to the fetus. If Carmen has no visible means of support, a referral to an appropriate social service agency to determine if Carmen is eligible for any assistance for herself and for her daughter also seems appropriate.

3.   There was no mention of the health status of Carmen's 4-year-old daughter nor the source for her health services. If arrangements for her health care have not been scheduled, then Carmen should be encouraged to seek preventive health services, including immunizations for this child. Generally, Latino families are respectful of authorities whose interests are directed toward the improved health, welfare, and safety of their family members, but Carmen may require guidance, emotional support, and financial assistance to obtain the necessary health and social services, considering her current stressful circumstances.

— *Geraldine J. Norris, MSN, MA, RN*

Case Study 2-5

Support for Teen Parent Following a SIDS Death

Sandra Smith is 16 years old and lives with her mother and her 14-year-old sister. Her mother is an executive secretary for a local insurance company. Her parents were divorced 3 years ago. She and her sister spend every other weekend with their father. Sandra's infant son Sam died of SIDS approximately 1 year ago. Since her baby's death, Sandra has not done well in her schoolwork, and her grades have dropped from Bs and Cs to Cs and Ds.

Within the past month, Sandra has reported a variety of somatic complaints and was sent to the school nurse, Ms. Malone. Ms. Malone did not find any physical basis for Sandra's complaints. After further discussion with Sandra, the nurse noted that the somatic complaints had started about 2 weeks before the anniversary of Sam's death. Ms. Malone asked Sandra if she were thinking about Sam. Sandra became tearful and stated that she did not know why he had died, and that she had tried to be a good mother.

Ms. Malone listened and reassured Sandra that she would try to find out the cause of death, and that they could meet again to discuss this. Ms. Malone called the SIDS program and learned that Sam had died of SIDS. Twelve contacts with Sandra's family were noted in the program's records, including a home visit by a community health nurse. Record notes revealed that these contacts were with Sandra's mother and grandmother. These adults expressed the hope that Sandra would put her pregnancy and her baby's death behind her. Neither the nurse nor the SIDS program contact person had spoken directly with Sandra. They were told that the SIDS information would be relayed to Sandra. Sam's father was not mentioned in the records.

Ms. Malone obtained the SIDS information and scheduled a meeting with Sandra to discuss the cause of Sam's death. She also contacted Sandra's mother to relate her concern that Sandra needed to understand why the baby had died. Sandra's mother was more than willing to assist in this process. The mother also expressed mixed feelings of sadness and relief that Sam had died. She stated that her only wish was for Sandra to continue in school and have a "normal" adolescence. Sandra's mother had not realized that her daughter's grades had declined, and she stated that this was "a bad year for everyone." Ms. Malone suggested that the first priority should be to answer all of Sandra's questions about the cause of Sam's death, and then the issue of Sandra's grades should be addressed.

Ms. Malone met with Sandra and discussed SIDS with her. Sandra appeared to be reassured and appreciative of the information. She brought a picture of Sam to show to Ms. Malone. The nurse was surprised at her own feelings of sadness about Sam's death, since she never had met the baby. She agreed with Sandra that he had been a darling baby, and she said that she was sure that Sandra had taken very good care of the baby. Ms. Malone was unsure about what follow-up Sandra needed, and she decided to stay in contact with her over the next few months. Ms. Malone discussed concerns about Sandra's poor grades and referred Sandra to the school counselor.

Commentary

The lack of bereavement services and absence of supportive care for teen parent Sandra Smith following the SIDS death of her son unfortunately are too often the norm when a young woman experiences the death of her child. This reflects the community's ambivalence toward adolescent pregnancy and parenting. Much like Sandra's mother and grandmother, health care providers and adults in the school community with whom Sandra spent so much of her time chose not to acknowledge the significance of Sam's life and the impact of his death on Sandra. Rather, their hope was that Sandra now would "get on with her life" and return to being a "normal" adolescent. As a result, 1 year later, Sandra's schoolwork quality declined dramatically, and she began to have somatic complaints, which further impaired her functioning.

Health care providers overlooked several opportunities to provide bereavement services to Sandra, and they failed to mobilize two of Sandra's greatest assets — her concerned family and her continuing involvement in school — to help this grieving young mother. First, the SIDS program should have enlisted the help of Sandra's mother and grandmother to engage Sandra in meeting directly to discuss the SIDS information and to offer supportive care to Sandra. The fact that Sandra's mother and grandmother had 12 contacts with the SIDS program indicates that there was information and help which they were receiving that should have been extended to Sandra to benefit her directly.

Second, in addition to meeting with Sandra and her family after Sam's death, the SIDS program staff could offer to meet with or send SIDS information to Sam's father and to Sandra's school (targeting the school nurse, counselor, or other school personnel whom Sandra or her family identify as being significant to Sandra). This strategy educates those most available to

Sandra on a daily basis about SIDS, sensitizes them to the bereavement issues which Sandra might be experiencing, and informs them about available resources for Sandra and themselves.

Third, Ms. Malone should conduct further assessment to identify Sandra's needs, so that an appropriate counseling referral can be made, if necessary. The referral to the school counselor at this time may be premature and too abrupt a transition to be a truly helpful resource for Sandra. Her developing relationship with Sandra may make Ms. Malone the more appropriate person to help Sandra process her experience. A decline in school performance or workplace productivity often is demonstrated after the stress of a death. Sandra may benefit from an ongoing relationship with a caring adult, who is knowledgeable about SIDS and bereavement, and who may listen to the feelings that Sandra is experiencing. The goal would be to normalize these feelings and to enable Sandra to attain a healthy resolution about what has happened to her and her son. Only then will Sandra be able to return to her previous level of functioning.

Ms. Malone is to be commended for her sensitivity to Sandra's bereavement experience and for identifying Sandra's apparent reaction to the anniversary of Sam's death. The nurse mobilized a support system for Sandra by coordinating information with the SIDS program and Sandra's mother. Ms. Malone recognized how critical it was for Sandra to know the cause of Sam's death before she could complete her grief work; and the nurse was proactive in helping to get that information to Sandra. Ms. Malone also recognized the intense blow to parental self-esteem that a baby's death delivers, and she offered positive reinforcement to Sandra by looking at the photographs of Sam with Sandra, commenting on the baby's beauty, and reassuring Sandra about the good care that this young mother had given to her son.

Additional assessment by Ms. Malone would include an exploration of Sandra's attachment to Sam, the identification of her support system, a discussion of other losses which Sandra may have experienced before or since Sam's death (such as Sandra's parents' divorce), the quality of Sandra's relationship with Sam's father, and, finally, Sandra's plans for any future pregnancies, as well as her knowledge and use of contraception. Ms. Malone not only should provide information about SIDS and other resources which were available for Sandra, but also should discuss what the grief experience might be like for Sandra. This includes addressing anniversary reactions, and Sandra's need to revisit Sam's life and death at different periods throughout the rest of her own life. In this way, Ms. Malone can help Sandra to anticipate and prepare for the variety of experiences which she might have because of Sam and his death from SIDS. Thus, she also can help Sandra to mobilize or develop an appropriate support system for herself.

Furthermore, Ms. Malone should continue to communicate with Sandra's mother, to reinforce the grief information. Also, this contact can help Sandra's mother to understand and anticipate anniversary reactions and Sandra's need to revisit this experience at subsequent milestones in her own life. By including Sandra's mother throughout the process, Ms. Malone both creates a partner in supporting Sandra and provides the support which Sandra's mother may need as a bereaved grandmother.

Finally, Ms. Malone should seek consultation with the school counselor and staff personnel at the SIDS program, to guide her in her work with Sandra. This also might lend support to Ms. Malone herself, which she may need to process her own feelings of sadness that are evoked so often when professionals come to know a baby who has died and to witness the pain of bereaved parents.

— *Kathleen L. Fernbach, BSN, RN, PHN*

References

Arnold, J.H., & Gemma, P.B. (1994). *A child dies: A portrait of family grief.* Philadelphia: The Charles Press Publishers.

Brooks, J. (1995). Overview. *Pediatric Annals, 24,* 348-349.

Carroll, R., & Shaefer, S.J.M. (1993-94). Similarities and differences in spouses coping with SIDS. *Omega, 28,* 273-284.

Dwyer, T., & Ponsonby, A.L. (1995). SIDS epidemiology and incidence. *Pediatric Annals, 24,* 350-356.

Filiano, J.J., & Kinney, H.C. (1995). Sudden Infant Death Syndrome and brainstem research. *Pediatric Annals, 24,* 379-383.

ICD-9-CM: Vol. I: International Classification of Diseases (9th rev.). (1978). Ann Arbor: MI: Commission on Professional and Hospital Activities.

Lawson, L.V. (1990). Culturally sensitive support for grieving parents. *MCN, 15,* 76-79.

Mandell, F., McAnulty, E., & Reece, R. (1983). Unexpected death of an infant sibling. *Pediatrics, 72,* 652- 657.

McClain, M. (1994). Sudden Infant Death Syndrome. In S. Kelly (Ed.), *Pediatric emergency nursing* (2nd ed.). Norwalk, CT: Appleton and Lange.

McClain, M.E., & Shaefer, S.J.M. (1995). Supporting families after sudden infant death. *Pediatric Annals, 24,* 373-378.

Shaefer, S.J.M., (1992). Adolescent pregnancy loss: A school based program. *Journal of School Nursing, 8*(2), 20-26.

SIDS: Trying to understand the mystery. (1994). Rockville, MD: Bureau of Maternal Child Health, Department of Health and Human Resources

Siegel, B. (1985). Helping children cope with death. *American Family Physician, 31,* 175-180.

Spector, R. (1996). *Cultural diversity in health and illness* (4th ed.). Stanford, CT: Appleton and Lange.

Valdes-Dapena, M. (1995). The postmortem examination. *Pediatric Annals, 24,* 365-372.

Willinger, M., Hoffman, H.J., & Hartford, R.B. (1994). Infant sleep position and risk for Sudden Infant Death Syndrome: Report of meeting held January 13 and 14, 1994, National Institutes of Health, Bethesda, MD. *Pediatrics, 93,* 814-819.

Willinger, M., James, L.S., & Catz, C. (1991). Defining the Sudden Infant Death Syndrome (SIDS): Deliberations of an expert panel convened by the National Institutes Child Health and Human Development. *Pediatric Pathology, 11,* 677-684.

Chapter 6

Technologies for Antepartum Fetal Assessment

J. Christopher Glantz

Perinatal mortality is defined as the sum of all fetal deaths at or beyond 20 weeks estimated gestational age, and all neonatal deaths through the first 28 days of life. The perinatal mortality rate (PMR) is the number of perinatal deaths per 1,000 births. Over a 20-year period between 1950 and 1970, the PMR fell from 39 to 28.9 (Cunningham, MacDonald, Gant, Leveno, & Gilstrap, 1993). During this time, perinatal mortality in cases for which a cause of death could be determined (80% of 1,435 deaths studied by Naeye) were as follows: 47% due to placental and umbilical cord complications, 17% due to intra-amniotic infection, 10% due to premature rupture of the membranes, 9% due to congenital anomalies, and 20% unknown (Naeye, 1987). In an effort to reduce PMR due to uteroplacental factors, methods for antepartum fetal surveillance were devised to detect early signs of intra-uterine hypoxia and to predict which fetuses are at risk for hypoxic damage. The goal of antepartum fetal surveillance is to enable delivery before such damage occurs. Concurrently, neonatologists worked to develop and refine expertise in caring for preterm and compromised neonates.

In the 1970s, antepartum fetal heart rate monitoring became available. Through the use of antepartum fetal heart rate monitoring, in conjunction with continued improvements in antenatal management of medical and obstetric complications and in neonatal care, the PMR declined to 17.5 per 1,000 by the end of the decade. The 1980s brought further refinement in interpreting antepartum heart rate testing, as well as increased use of ultrasound as a testing modality. By the late 1980s, the PMR fell to 13.7/1,000. As progress was made in fetal monitoring and neonatal care, the mortality associated with birth asphyxia and prematurity decreased, leaving fetal anomalies as the greatest single contributor to infant mortality (Centers for Disease Control [CDC], 1989). Unfortunately, most progress regarding fetal anomalies has been in prenatal diagnosis rather than in prevention.

In a study of fetal death certificates in Massachusetts, 28% of fetal deaths were attributed to antepartum asphyxia, 30% to maternal complications, 12% to fetal anomalies, 4% to infection, and 23% to unknown causes (Lammer, Brown, Anderka, & Guyer, 1989). It must be noted that, when performed, autopsies frequently did not confirm the diagnosis on the fetal death certificate, so that these figures must be considered approximate. Eighty-six percent of fetal deaths occurred before the onset of labor, and 14% occurred intrapartum. The majority of intrapartum fetal deaths were due to either congenital anomalies or infections, and only 12% were due to asphyxia. Stubblefield and Berek (1980) reported that, in term fetal deaths, 81% were antepartum and 19% occurred intrapartum. Of antepartum deaths, 72% were due to perinatal hypoxia, 10% due to anomalies, 7% due to fetal growth restriction, and 3% due to infection. Of intrapartum deaths, 43% were due to hypoxia, 29% to anomalies, and 14% to infection. The majority of term, antepartum fetal deaths from asphyxia occurred in the setting of chronic hypoxia (for example, placental infarction), rather than as acute events (abruption or cord accidents), and the authors suggested that antepartum fetal assessment may lower the perinatal mortality rate.

Before 1980, perinatal mortality was divided equally between fetal and neonatal deaths, with a slightly higher percentage of neonatal rather than fetal deaths contributing to total perinatal mortality. Since that time, the neonatal death rate has fallen below the fetal death rate, because of a greater decline in neonatal than in fetal mortality rates (Public Health Service, 1988). In a review of 309 perinatal deaths in England in 1979, 59% were deemed associated with avoidable factors (albeit, some in cases in which fetal demise was inevitable for other reasons), the majority occurring during the antenatal course (Mersey Region Working Party on Perinatal Mortality, 1982). Kirkup and Welch (1990) subsequently reported that avoidable factors were associated with 50% of 75 perinatal deaths occurring in northern England in 1983, and that most of these factors were obstetric rather than neonatal. Although some of the deaths were judged inevitable, the majority were potentially avoidable. Not all avoidable factors are medical; Delke, Hyatt, Feinkind, and Minkoff (1988) reported that contributing social and maternal factors were present in 39% (52 of 133) of perinatal deaths in New York City.

Because death is a precisely defined outcome, mortality statistics are relatively easy to access. Morbidity, the presence of adverse sequelae in a living subject, is a diffuse and less quantifiable category. There is no nationally published "perinatal morbidity rate" as with mortality, and so changes over time are difficult to assess. Unlike mortality, morbidity may be mild or severe within a category, and different morbidities may have very different implications (for example, cerebral palsy versus grade I retinopathy). Morbidity and mortality rates may not change proportionally with improvements in medical care. As mortality rates drop, morbidity may fall if ability to maintain life is matched by ability to avoid or effectively prevent serious complications. Conversely, morbidity may worsen if increased survival is achieved at the cost of higher incidences of complications in the survivors, such as chronic lung disease, cerebral palsy, blindness, etc.

A discussion of the use of fetal heart rate and ultrasonographic monitoring to assess antepartum fetal status follows. The primary purpose of these techniques is to detect signs of fetal compromise early enough to intervene and improve outcome, ideally to decrease both perinatal morbidity and mortality.

Fetal Heart Rate Monitoring

The first known description of fetal heart sounds was in the 17th Century, but not until the 1800s was auscultation of fetal heart sounds thought to be of potential clinical benefit (Freeman, Garite, & Nageotte, 1991). Fetal heart rates below 100 beats per minute, or above 180 beats per minute, were thought to be associated with unfavorable perinatal outcomes. The fetoscope, a specialized stethoscope held against the maternal abdomen by pressure from the listener's forehead, was developed in the early 1900s to hear the fetal heart.

The fetal heart rate (FHR) first was monitored electronically in 1906, but such technology was used primarily to verify fetal viability. In the 1950s and 1960s, fetal EKG recording did not prove useful in predicting fetal compromise, but did lead to the development of external FHR monitoring. Different patterns of FHR deceleration were described in association with certain pathological perinatal conditions. In 1959, Hon (1959) described variable and late decelerations in humans following umbilical cord compression and uteroplacental insufficiency, respectively. In 1966, Caldeyro-Barcia et al. published on the prognostic value of these deceleration patterns, and Hammacher described the importance of FHR variability in 1967. The first electronic fetal monitors were very bulky and expensive, but in 1968, the first commercial monitors were marketed using microphones to detect fetal heart

Figure 1-6.
Fetal Circulation

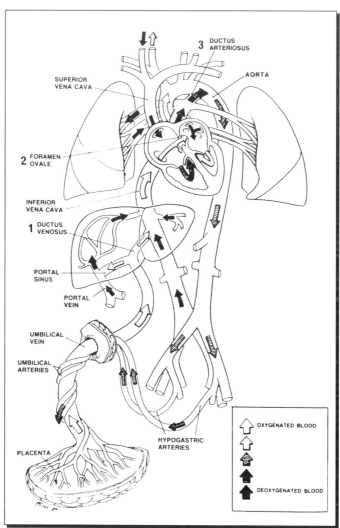

Reprinted with permission from Cunningham, F.G., MacDonald, P.C., Gant, N.F., Leveno, K.J., & Gilstrap, L.C. (1993). The morphological & functional development of the fetus. *Williams Obstetrics* (19th ed.). Norwalk, CT: Appleton & Lange.

sounds. Fetal heart rate monitoring standards and terminology were developed in the 1970s, and Doppler recording of fetal cardiac activity subsequently replaced phonocardiography.

Fetal Cardiovascular Physiology

The fetus must have oxygen to live. Because the fetus is inside the amniotic sac and cannot use its lungs to breathe, it depends on the exchange of carbon dioxide and oxygen across the placenta to and from the maternal circulation. Blood flows from the fetal hypogastric arteries into the umbilical arteries and through the umbilical cord into the placenta (see Figure 1-6). Maternal uterine arteries carry oxygenated blood through the myometrium to the intervillus spaces within the placenta. The oxygenated blood bathes the placental villi, which contain fetal capillaries filled with relatively deoxygenated fetal blood. Oxygen diffuses from the maternal blood across the villus trophoblast, and into the fetal capillaries. Carbon dioxide diffuses from fetal blood, across the trophoblast, and into maternal blood. Diffusion of oxygen and carbon dioxide is driven by partial pressure gradients between the maternal and fetal blood.

Oxygenated blood returns to the fetus through the umbilical vein, entering the fetal liver and inferior vena cava. Oxygenated blood carried by the inferior vena cava into the right atrium of the fetal heart is preferentially shunted across the foramen ovale into the left atrium, where it is pumped into the left ventricle and out into the aortic arch, to perfuse the head and arms. Less-well-oxygenated blood entering the right atrium from the superior vena cava, mixes slightly with oxygenated blood from the inferior vena cava, and it is pumped into the right ventricle and out the pulmonary artery, where most of it flows through the ductus arteriosus into the descending aorta (thus, the relatively deoxygenated state of the blood in the hypogastric arteries).

Limitation of Placental Blood Flow

Anything that interferes with the flow of oxygenated maternal blood into the placenta potentially can interfere with fetal oxygenation. Supine maternal position places the weight of the uterus on the inferior vena cava, squeezing it against the spine, impeding flow through it, and decreasing venous return to the heart. With less venous return, there is less blood for the heart to pump, cardiac output falls, and the woman becomes hypotensive. Compression of the aorta also limits blood flow below the point of com-

Figure 2-6.
Late Decelerations

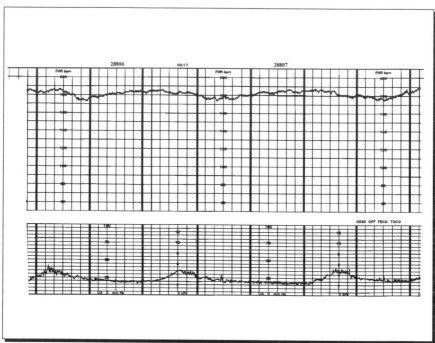

The fetal heart rate tracing on the upper panel demonstrates repetitive decelerations occurring after uterine contractions recorded in the lower panel.

pression. Lower cardiac output and impaired aortic flow result in less delivery of oxygenated maternal blood to the placenta, less oxygen exchange, and ultimately, fetal hypoxia (Huch, Huch, Schneider, & Rooth, 1977). Turning the woman to a lateral position alleviates these effects.

Uterine contractions constrict the uterine spiral arteries as they traverse the myometrium, decreasing flow of maternal blood into the placenta, thereby decreasing maternal-fetal oxygen exchange. In normal pregnancy, baseline fetal oxygenation is high enough so that the drop in fetal oxygen tension during inevitable ante- and intrapartum contractions does not exceed fetal reserve. However, for cases in which fetal oxygenation is borderline — just barely adequate — this decline in oxygen exchange during a contraction may result in transient fetal hypoxemia. Because it takes 30 to 60 seconds for fetal oxygen tension to drift downwards during a contraction, and additional seconds to recover following relaxation of the myometrium and restoration of blood flow, the period of hypoxemia is delayed until after the peak of the contraction. Fetal chemoreceptors respond to this transient hypoxemia reflexively by decreasing the fetal heart rate through the vagal parasympathetic system (Parer, Krueger, & Harris, 1980). This is called a late deceleration, because it occurs after the peak of the contraction (see Figure 2-6). It represents normal fetal response to acutely lowered oxygen tension from an already compromised baseline.

Conditions that decrease placental surface area limit the amount of placenta which is available to participate in gas exchange. Such conditions include placental abruption, infarction, and hypoplasia. Maternal vascular disease, as in hypertension, diabetes, and collagen-vascular disease, may limit the flow of maternal blood into the placenta. Umbilical cord compression impedes flow of blood to and from the placenta, even though the placenta itself may be functioning normally.

Control of Fetal Heart Rate

The FHR is controlled by the combined effects of the sympathetic and parasympathetic nervous systems. The normal fetal heart rate is between 120 to 160 beats per minute. Sympathetic nerve endings release norepinephrine, which causes the FHR to increase. Systemic epinephrine from the adrenal medulla has the same effect. The parasympathetic vagus nerve releases acetylcholine, decreasing the heart rate. At any given moment, there is interaction between the two components of the autonomic nervous system. The result is constant modulation of the heart rate, with continual instantaneous changes in the rate from one beat to another, called "beat-to-beat variability." Mild stimulation of the sympathetic nervous system produces short, small accelerations of the heart rate (approximately five beats), while mild stimulation of the parasympathetic nervous system produces brief, small decelerations. These slower responses interact to yield "long-term variability" (see Figure 3-6).

Beginning in the second trimester, fetal movements are associated with FHR accelerations. This is a normal response and is called reactivity. It is mediated through the sympathetic nervous system. The earlier in gestation, the less frequent the accelerations tend to be, and the lower their magnitude (Gagnon, Campbell, Hunse, & Patrick, 1987). Fetal behavioral states affect the FHR pattern. A fetus who is awake or in rapid eye movement (REM) sleep normally manifests a reactive pattern with good variability, whereas a fetus in

Figure 3-6.
Variability

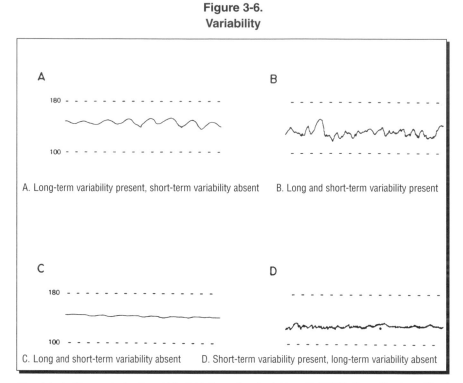

A. Long-term variability present, short-term variability absent   B. Long and short-term variability present

C. Long and short-term variability absent   D. Short-term variability present, long-term variability absent

Reprinted with permission from Yeh, S.Y., Forsythe, A., & Hon, E. (1973). Quantification of fetal heart beat-to-beat interval differences. *Obstetrics and Gynecology, 41*(3), 356. New York: Elsevier Science Publishing, Co.

quiet sleep may be minimally reactive and have decreased variability. FHR reactivity and variability undergo periodic fluctuations according to sleep cycles, with episodes of reactivity lasting 20 to 40 minutes interspersed with less-reactive episodes usually lasting not more than 80 minutes (Brown & Patrick, 1981).

Inherent in the concept of autonomic control of FHR is that the brain must have an adequate supply of oxygen for the autonomic nervous system to function normally. Borderline oxygenation may result in adaptive patterns that represent attempts to compensate for mild hypoxia; these could be considered normal responses to abnormal conditions. If there is moderate-to-severe hypoxia, then the central nervous system cannot function properly, and the heart may not receive the normal signals from the autonomic nerves.

One manifestation of hypoxia is the loss of normal FHR patterns. The baseline FHR may lose variability and appear flat, without discernible accelerations. This "nonreactive" pattern with decreased variability suggests fetal hypoxia, although the same effect may be seen in association with certain drugs (sedatives, magnesium sulfate, anticholinergics, or adrenergic antagonists), with certain congenital anomalies (for example, anencephaly), or with central nervous system damage. The linchpin of antepartum fetal monitoring is that normal FHR patterns require normal central nervous system function, which requires normal fetal oxygenation. The nonstress test (NST) and contraction stress test were developed using FHR patterns as an indirect measure of fetal oxygenation.

Nonstress Testing

Fetal heart rate accelerations associated with fetal movements are associated with normal fetal oxygenation. By placing an external fetal monitor on the pregnant woman, FHR patterns can be observed without disturbing or stressing the fetus. This is the concept of the NST to evaluate fetal well-being, as popularized in the 1970s.

Mechanics and Interpretation of Nonstress Testing

For nonstress testing, the pregnant woman reclines in a lateral tilt position, and an external cardiac monitor and tocodynamometer are applied. FHR and uterine activity are monitored for 20 minutes, during which time the woman marks the tracing to note any fetal movements that she feels. Notation of perceived movement can be done manually or with a push-button; some monitors record movement automatically.

Many different criteria have been proposed to define a reactive NST, ranging from 1 to 5 accelerations of 10 to 15 beats over a 15 to 40 minute period (Devoe, 1990). It is not clear that any one of the various proposed definitions of reactivity has significantly better or worse predictive properties than any other. Any specific criterion is arbitrary. The primary function simply may be to differentiate "accelerations" from small changes in FHR constituting long-term variability (Manning, 1995a). Mostly to end the confusion of multiple proposed criteria, and partly because one of the few studies to compare criteria concluded that two or more accelerations indicated a low risk of uteroplacental insufficiency (Evertson, Gauthier, Schifrin, & Paul, 1979), standardized criteria for reactivity now include two or more accelerations within 20 minutes, of 15 seconds duration from beginning to end,

Figure 4-6.
Reactive Nonstress Test

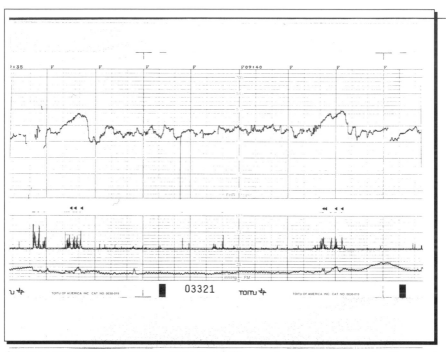

Several accelerations meeting the 15-beats for 15-seconds criteria are present, with normal baseline rate, normal variability, and no decelerations.

peaking at least 15 beats above baseline (American College of Obstetricians and Gynecologists [ACOG], 1994). Normal baseline heart rate, variability, and the absence of nonreassuring decelerations also are requirements for a reassuring NST (see Figure 4-6). Although performance of the test includes notation of fetal movements, nearly all accelerations are associated with movement (Timor-Tritsch, Dierker, Hertz, & Rosen, 1978). In cases where accelerations are recorded without maternal perception of movement, the assumption is that maternal perception is lacking, rather than the movements themselves.

If the NST is not reactive after 20 minutes, the fetus may be in a quiet sleep cycle, and the test duration may be extended. In a study using a criterion of 5 accelerations per 20-minute interval, 75% of NSTs were reactive within 20 minutes, and 95% were reactive by 40 minutes (Brown & Patrick, 1981). Another alternative is fetal vibroacoustic stimulation. Vibroacoustic stimulation (VAS) involves stimulating the fetus by applying an artificial larynx to the maternal abdomen for 3 seconds, in an effort to rouse the fetus from a sleep cycle. Accelerations in response to VAS correlate with normal fetal pH (which correlates with normal fetal oxygenation) (Smith, Nguyen, Phelan, & Paul, 1986), and reactivity following VAS has the same significance as spontaneous reactivity (Gagnon, 1989; Smith, 1995). The benefits of uterine manipulation, maternal ambulation, or glucose administration in an effort to convert a non-reactive NST into a reactive test are uncertain (Smith, 1995).

Test Sensitivity and Specificity

Binary tests measure occurrences of a particular outcome. Sensitivity refers to what proportion of subjects with a given outcome actually have positive tests. To achieve a high sensitivity, the threshold for considering a test positive may have to be set to include a wide range of the distribution of results, so that few true positives will be missed. Specificity refers to what proportion of subjects without the outcome will test negative, and "1 minus specificity" equals the false-positive rate. Sensitivity and specificity vary inversely, depending on the selected threshold. A threshold ensuring high specificity lowers sensitivity (few false positives but many false negatives), and a threshold raising sensitivity lowers specificity (few false negatives but many false positives).

Interpretations of sensitivity and specificity require knowledge of the frequency at which the outcome occurs in the population. The positive predictive value is the chance that the outcome is (or will be) present, given a positive test. The negative predictive value is the chance that the outcome will not occur, given a negative test. The positive and negative predictive values depend on the test's sensitivity, specificity, and frequency of the outcome in the population to be tested. If the outcome is common, even marginal sensitivity and specificity will yield a high positive predictive value. For example, if the outcome is present in 90% of the population, then nearly every positive test, even if sensitivity is low, will be associated with that outcome; the positive predictive value of the test will be high. If the outcome is rare, however, then even with a highly sensitive test the specificity must approach 100% for the positive predictive value to be high. In the case of a rare outcome, true positives will by definition be rare, and specificity significantly less than 100% means that most positive test results will be false positives. In the case of an uncommon but serious outcome for which therapy is limited and prognosis poor, false positives should be minimized by setting specificity high at the expense of sensitivity. In the case of uncommon but serious outcomes for which effective therapies exist to improve prognosis, high sensitivity is preferable, and a relatively high number of false positives can be tolerated.

These are important concepts for fetal assessment. The definition of a positive test can be fetal death (a definite criterion) or fetal distress (a less-well-defined criterion) or operative delivery (multifactorial), etc. Fetal death is much easier to ascertain than fetal distress. "Fetal distress" is meant to connote possible fetal hypoxia or asphyxia, but it is imprecise and correlates poorly with these adverse outcomes. A test that predicts "fetal distress" may or may not be relevant to the outcomes of fetal asphyxia or death. The choice of outcome will influence the sensitivity and specificity of the test.

Predictive Value of Nonstress Testing

The time course for these occurrences must be specified — within 1 day, week, month, etc. of a positive test. For fetal death within 1 day, a test with 100% sensitivity probably would not be useful in preventing adverse perinatal outcomes because, by the time the test became positive, the fetus might be near death. Many such fetuses already may be seriously compromised or will die despite intervention. To obtain such high sensitivity, there would be many false-positive tests, necessitating a high rate of either further testing or intervention in noncompromised fetuses. Conversely, a fetus with a negative test result would be unlikely to have perinatal morbidity or mortality. The test would have a high negative predictive value (the chance that a negative test means a normal outcome).

Changing the criterion to "fetal death within 1 week of a positive test" and slightly raising the specificity may be more useful clinically. This allows time for intervention, increases the number of normal subjects who will test negative, and lessens the need for further follow-up testing and intervention. Because the fetus is not in a static milieu, and because changes can and do occur over time, more than 1 week between tests allows too much time for potential deterioration to occur, worsening the test's sensitivity. The ideal test should have both high sensitivity and high specificity. Since it is difficult to have both in the same test, a balance between the two yields the most useful test. Because fetal demise is a catastrophic outcome that potentially is preventable, the sensitivity of a test of fetal well-being should be as high as possible to prevent as many such occurrences as possible. To do this, the criteria for defining an abnormal NST must be set to be overly inclusive, in order to minimize false negatives. As a consequence of this, many false-positive tests will occur, necessitating follow-up testing and engendering anxiety in affected patients. Because the absolute risk of fetal demise usually is fairly low for a given patient, positive predictive value will be low, but negative predictive value will be high. Unfortunately, because of the occurrences of unpredictable events (placental abruption, for example), the sensitivity of nonstress testing is only about 50% for perinatal mortality, although the specificity is very high (Ware & DeVoe, 1994). The patient with a positive test needs further testing, but the patient with a negative test reasonably can be reassured that fetal death is very unlikely to occur within the specified time period.

The false-positive rate of nonstress testing is approximately 75% (Barrett, Salyer, & Boehm, 1981). A false-positive NST refers to a nonreactive nonstress test that is followed by a good perinatal outcome. Five to fifteen percent of NSTs initially will be nonreactive (Freeman, Anderson, & Dorchester, 1982a; Phelan, Ahn, Smith, Rutherford, & Anderson, 1987). Most nonreactive NSTs either will become reactive or reassuring with further testing, or they will not lead to adverse perinatal outcome. Prolonging the duration or using VAS during a NST that does not meet criteria for reactivity will decrease the false-positive rate. Persistently nonreactive NSTs are associated with uncorrected perinatal mortality rates of /1,000, and a threefold increase in fetal distress (Freeman et al., 1982a; Phelan et al., 1987). Correcting for fetal anomalies, cord accidents, and placental abruption halves the mortality rate.

Nonstress testing is considered a first-line antenatal test because of its noninvasiveness, ease, expediency, high negative predictive value, and relatively low cost. A reactive NST correlates well with normal central nervous system function *at the time when the test is performed.* Manning (1995a) emphasizes this distinction because, although a reactive NST correlates well with good fetal outcome, it does not absolutely rule out fetal hypoxemia, and it does not necessarily reflect the chronic state of the fetus. Despite these concerns, the risk of adverse perinatal outcome following a reactive NST is low. In eight studies (each including 500 patients) reviewed and corrected for fetal anomalies, perinatal mortality after a reactive NST was 2 to 9 per 1,000 (false-negative rate) (Manning, 1995a). Some other methods of testing, such as contraction stress tests and biophysical profiles, have lower false-negative rates. Despite the lower false-negative rates of these other tests, however, when prospectively compared with NSTs as a method of primary surveillance, the biophysical profile (BPP) has not been shown to result in statistically significant differences in sensitivity and specificity for adverse perinatal outcome (Manning, Lange, Morrison, & Harman, 1984; Platt et al.,1985). None of these tests predict cataclysmic events, such as placental abruption, that can cause demise of an otherwise healthy fetus.

Because of the high false-positive rate associated with a nonreactive NST, delivery decisions rarely are made on the basis of a nonreactive NST alone. The NST is best at predicting which fetus will be safe *in utero* for another 4 to 7 days; a normal NST is a good predictor of fetal well-being. The NST serves as a screening test to determine which fetuses warrant additional testing modalities, such as a contraction stress test or a BPP.

Indications for Nonstress Testing

Because nonstress testing is designed to detect signs of fetal hypoxemia and hypoxia, it is used to assess fetal well-being in conditions which potentially expose the fetus to hypoxemia and hypoxia. Nonstress testing would not be expected to be helpful in assessing fetal well-being in conditions in which fetal compromise is due to factors other than hypoxia (for example, renal anomalies in the absence of oligohydramnios). There are many conditions in which fetal hypoxia conceivably could occur, and so the list of proposed indications for nonstress testing is indeed very long (see Table 1-6). Although many of these indications have been tested and found to be valid (IUGR, diabetes, postdates), many are based on theoretical rationales and have not been tested adequately as to their efficacy in improving perinatal outcome (substance abuse, multiple gestation). When a NST is reactive, the risk of fetal death over the following week is considered to be very low, and so the test is repeated at weekly intervals. In some conditions, such as fetal growth restriction, diabetes, or severe preeclampsia, fetal deaths within a week of a reactive NST may be more common (perhaps because fetal condition may deteriorate quickly); many authorities recommend testing every 3 to 4 days, or even more frequently (ACOG, 1994; Barrett et al., 1981).

Nonstress testing usually begins at 32 to 34 weeks for most indications, but may be instituted before 30 weeks for some indications (fetal growth restriction, severe diabetes, preeclampsia). Premature fetuses are less likely to manifest reactive fetal heart rate patterns by the traditional criteria. Total number of accelerations per hour, proportion of accelerations reaching 15 beats above baseline and lasting 15 seconds, and reactivity (based on the "15 beats for 15 seconds" criteria) all increase with increasing gestational age (Druzin,

Table 1-6.
Indications for Nonstress Testing

Maternal	Fetal
Diabetes	Growth restriction
Hypertension (chronic or preeclampsia)	Multiple gestation
Collagen-vascular disease	Hydrops (immune or nonimmune)
Severe anemia or hemoglobinopathy	Postterm
Cardiopulmonary disease	Decreased movement
Renal disease	Oligohydramnios
Hyperthyroidism	
Isoimmunization	
Substance abuse	
Previous stillbirth	
Vaginal bleeding	
Premature rupture of membranes	

Fox, Kogut, & Carlson, 1985; Natale, Nasello, & Turliuk, 1984). The frequencies of reactive NSTs using the 15 x 15 criteria are shown in Table 2-6. In healthy fetuses less than 30 weeks gestational age, the frequency of 10-beat accelerations is similar to the proportion of 15-beat accelerations in healthy fetuses at or above 30 weeks gestation (Gagnon et al., 1987). With this in mind, some authors have proposed modifying the criteria for reactivity in preterm gestations to require 10-beat rather that 15-beat accelerations; although theoretically sound, the validity of this has not been verified clinically in select preterm gestations (Castillo et al., 1989).

Contrary to some beliefs, this gestational-age dependency does not invalidate the test at early gestational ages. Using standard criteria, the clinician must accept that the false-positive rate of a nonreactive NST will be proportionally higher the earlier the gestational age, and ancillary testing will be required quite often. However, even as early as 24 weeks, approximately 50% of fetuses will still be reactive by the 15-beats-for-15-seconds criterion; in these gestations, the NST is adequate reassurance without further testing (Druzin et al., 1985). Whichever criteria are used to define reactivity, nonreactive NSTs in the very premature fetus may be due to prematurity but must be considered nonreassuring until proven otherwise.

Table 2-6.
Nonstress Test Reactivity by Gestational Age

Gestational Age	Reactive by 15x15-beat Criteria
20-24 weeks	27%
24-28 weeks	55%
28-32 weeks	82%
32-36 weeks	95%
36-40 weeks	99%

Modified from Druzin, M.L., Fox, A. Kogut, E., & Carlson, C. (1985). The relationship of the nonstress test to gestational age. *American Journal of Obstetrics and Gynecology, 153*(4), 386-389.

Contraction Stress Testing

The contraction stress test (CST) was designed to evaluate uteroplacental function. Normally, there is adequate maternal-fetal oxygen exchange across the placenta so that the fetus has a reserve, enabling it to tolerate transient episodes of decreased placental perfusion (such as those which occur during a contraction, when the myometrium compresses the uterine vessels conveying blood to the placenta). If uteroplacental function is impaired (uteroplacental insufficiency [UPI]), then fetal blood oxygenation may be at a borderline-adequate level, but may become inadequate during the stress of a contraction. When uterine-placental blood flow fails to provide adequate oxygen exchange to meet fetal needs during a contraction, the fetus becomes hypoxemic and responds with a late deceleration of the fetal heart rate. Whereas a nonreactive NST is suspicious for fetal hypoxia of a degree that impairs central nervous system function, an abnormal CST is evidence that uteroplacental function is impaired, and fetal oxygen reserve is borderline. Thus, the CST may test for earlier signs of fetal compromise than may the NST (Murata et al., 1982). The CST has an advantage of being independent of gestational age, in that mechanisms mediating late decelerations are present by the time when the fetus would be considered potentially viable outside the uterus.

Performance of the Contraction Stress Test

The woman is placed in a lateral tilt position, and fetal heart and contraction monitors are applied. Supine position should be avoided because of

Table 3-6.
Interpretation of the Contraction Stress Test

Negative	No late decelerations on a tracing of adequate technical quality.
Positive	Repetitive late decelerations occurring after >50% of contractions, in the absence of hyperstimulation or supine hypotension.
Suspicious	Late decelerations after <50% of contractions.
Hyperstimulation	Decelerations after prolonged (>90 seconds) contractions or those occurring more frequently than every 2 minutes.
Unsatisfactory	Technically inadequate tracing, either unable to document contractions or interpret fetal heart rate pattern.

the possibility of vena caval compression and supine hypotension, which may impair uteroplacental blood flow and cause a false-positive CST result. Maternal blood pressure and baseline FHR characteristics are recorded. Contractions then are induced by one of several methods, the only requirement being that palpable contractions occur with a frequency of 3 in 10 minutes. There is no requirement for absolute intensity of contractions.

Occasionally, contractions will occur spontaneously, and, if there are 3 within 10 minutes, then a "spontaneous" CST has been performed. Stimulation of the maternal nipples for several minutes, followed by a 5-minute rest (repeating the cycle as needed), is a method for producing contractions in the majority of women. The most common way to induce contractions is by using oxytocin, in which case the test is called an oxytocin challenge test (OCT). An intravenous catheter is inserted, and oxytocin infused at 0.5 mU/min. The infusion rate is doubled every 15 to 20 minutes until the desired contraction frequency is achieved, depending on the FHR response. The fetal heart tracing is observed to note the presence or absence of late decelerations.

Interpretation of the Contraction Stress Test

Interpretation of the CST is outlined in Table 3-6 (Freeman et al., 1991). If repetitive late decelerations are present even when the contraction frequency is less than three in 10 minutes, the CST is considered positive and should be discontinued.

Predictive Value of the CST

Whenever a CST is performed, a NST is performed simultaneously. Because of this, the reading of a CST includes a NST interpretation. Thus, between a reactive/nonreactive NST and a positive/negative CST, there are four possible combinations of results.

Reactive-negative. This is the most common result, with no indication of utero-placental insufficiency (UPI) or fetal hypoxia. The uncorrected risk of fetal death within 1 week of a reactive-negative CST is approximately 1/1,000, or 0.4/1,000 if corrected for fetal anomalies (Freeman et al., 1982b). The test usually is repeated in 1 week, if indicated.

Reactive-positive. This indicates a degree of UPI, but not enough to have caused fetal hypoxia at the time when the test was performed. Freeman et al. (1982a) report corrected perinatal mortality of 8/1,000 (51/1,000 uncorrected). Fetal distress during labor occurs in between 28% to 62% of pregnancies in which the CST is reactive-positive (Braly & Freeman, 1977; Freeman et al., 1982a; Huddleston, Sutliff, Carney, & Flowers, 1979). At term, a patient with a reactive-positive CST should be delivered because of the chance that UPI will progressively worsen and result in frank fetal hypoxia. Induction of labor can be attempted if the cervix is favorable enough to permit internal FHR monitoring. In a preterm gestation in the absence of fetal pulmonary maturity, testing should be repeated daily until maturity is reached or fetal status shows signs of deterioration.

Nonreactive-negative. This finding should be rare; it is associated with prematurity, fetal sleep cycles, fetal CNS abnormalities, and maternal medication use. Physiologically, it should be unusual that the fetus would be hypoxic (evidenced by nonreactivity) if uteroplacental function is normal (evidenced by a negative CST). In some instances, subtle late decelerations may have been missed, and the test may have been interpreted as nonreactive-negative when it should have been nonreactive-positive. Reported corrected perinatal mortality after a nonreactive-negative CST is between 0 to 17 per 1,000 (Druzin et al., 1980; Grundy, Freeman, Lederman, & Dorchester, 1984). Perinatal morbidity is doubled when compared with reactive-negative CSTs, and fetal distress during labor has been reported in 50% of patients with nonreactive-negative CSTs (Keegan & Paul, 1980; Lin, Moawad, River, & Pishotta, 1980). Follow-up after a nonreactive-negative CST is controversial, with some recommending weekly fetal assessment and others recommending daily assessment.

Nonreactive-positive. This result is consistent with UPI and fetal hypoxia, and it is associated with a corrected perinatal mortality rate of 176/1,000 (211/1,000 uncorrected) (Freeman et al., 1982a). Fetal distress during labor occurs in 78% to 100% of patients with nonreactive-positive CSTs (Braly & Freeman, 1977; Freeman et al., 1982a; Huddleston et al., 1979), and 33% to 100% require cesarean section (Bissonnette, Johnson, & Toomey, 1979; Huddleston et al., 1979; Keegan & Paul, 1980; Slomka & Phelan, 1981). Delivery is indicated in the setting of a nonreactive-positive CST occurring after 30 to 32 weeks gestational age. In gestations of less than 30 to 32 weeks, further evaluation of the fetus should be considered first, because of the chance that the nonreactive NST may be due to prematurity rather than to hypoxia.

Cesarean section is the most common route of delivery after a nonreactive-positive CST because these fetuses rarely tolerate labor (Bissonnette et al., 1979; Huddleston et al., 1979; Keegan & Paul, 1980; Slomka & Phelan, 1981). However, induction may be attempted if the cervix is favorable and internal FHR monitoring and scalp pH determinations are readily available.

Suspicious CSTs are repeated within 24 hours. The false-positive rate is high, and intervention based on a suspicious result alone would be unwarranted in most cases. Although the incidence of fetal distress during labor after a suspicious CST is twice as high as after a negative CST, perinatal mortality is unchanged (Freeman et al., 1982a).

The CST has been criticized for having a high false-positive rate, generally reported to be about 30% (Barrada, Edwards, & Hakanson, 1979; Braly & Freeman, 1984; Freeman, Goebelsman, Nochimson, & Cetrulo, 1976), but occasionally as high as 75% (Gauthier, Evertson, & Paul, 1979). This false-positive rate usually refers to the ability of the fetus to tolerate labor without perinatal morbidity. It is apparent that interpretation of the CST depends on concurrent consideration of the NST. A reactive NST decreases the perinatal morbidity and mortality associated with a positive CST, whereas a nonreactive NST increases morbidity and mortality. To minimize the false-positive rate, it is important that supine hypotension or other reversible causes of UPI be corrected before performing a CST.

The potential indications for a CST are the same as for a NST, except that it rarely is repeated more than once a week. Unlike the NST, there are several contraindications to the CST. Preterm labor, cervical incompetence, pla-

centa previa, abruption, or previous classical uterine incision are contraindications, and a CST should be used with caution in patients with premature
rupture of the membranes or with multiple gestations.

Overall, the CST is a better predictor of fetal outcome than is the NST.
Freeman et al. (1982b) reported that, when it is used as a primary means of
surveillance, the CST yields corrected perinatal mortality of 0.4/1,000, as
compared with 3.2/1,000 for NSTs. However, because the CST is cumber-
some, invasive, and time consuming, the NST is better suited as a screening
test, with the CSTs usually being reserved for further evaluation of nonreactive NSTs rather than serving as a primary method of fetal surveillance.

Ultrasonographic Assessment

Obstetric ultrasound is a technique using reflected high-frequency sound
waves to visualize the pregnancy within the uterus and is based upon the
same principles as SONAR. Humans can hear sounds with frequencies up to
about 20,000 cycles per second (Hertz). With ultrasound, electrically stimulated crystals generate sound waves at frequencies far above the range of
human hearing, between two to ten million cycles per second (mega-Hertz
or MHz). These sound waves penetrate into tissues and are absorbed, dif-
fused, or reflected back to varying degrees, depending on the tissue density
and interfaces between tissues of different densities. The timing and degree
of reflection of the returning sound waves can be detected by a transducer
and computer, which convert the returning waves' intensities into dots of different brightnesses (the more intense the reflected wave, the brighter the dot).
The information then is "assembled" into a pattern of gray-scale dots at various depths within the range of the transducer, yielding an image of the
scanned tissues. High-frequency ultrasound (7.5 MHz) gives good resolution
of images, but does not penetrate tissues deeply. Lower-frequency ultrasound
(3.5 MHz) penetrates more deeply, but does not have as fine resolution (see
Figures 5-6 & 6-6).

Static scans generate only one image at a time. In "real-time" scanning,
signals are generated, sent, received, and processed many times per second,
and the image on the screen adjusts at such a rapid rate that the human eye
sees image-to-image changes as movement (just as movie film contains many
frames that flash by so fast that the audience sees continuous motion rather
than individual frames). If only one crystal were generating sound waves,
then the field of the image would be very narrow and the utility marginal.
Most scanning in obstetrics is done with linear or curvilinear arrays of crys-

Figure 5-6.
3.5 MegahertzTransducer Resolution

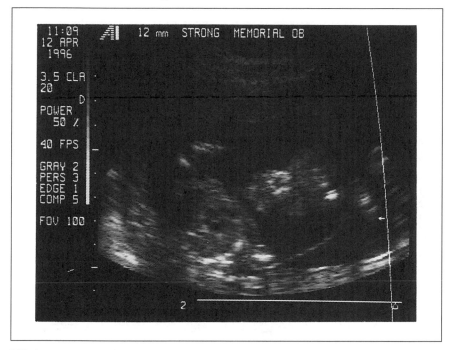

This is a sonogram of the fetal chest showing the heart, using a 3.5 megahertz transducer. Resolution is poor for the required detail. This transducer has good depth penetration, but poor axial resolution.

tals that expand the lateral range of the image, widening the picture.

Ultrasonographic images of the fetus were reported in the early 1960s (Donald & Brown, 1961). In the 1970s, much of obstetric scanning was static, but in the 1980s real-time scanning became popular, and private obstetricians began incorporating ultrasound into their office practices (Horger & Tsai, 1989). The quality of ultrasound machines and image quality has improved exponentially over this time. Its uses and acceptance have expanded so that as of 1989, approximately 70% of pregnant women underwent ultrasonographic evaluation during their pregnancies (Horger & Tsai, 1989). Although clinical benefit of routine ultrasonographic screening of low-risk pregnancies has not been confirmed (Ewigman, LeFevre, & Hesser, 1990; LeFevre et al., 1993; Saari-Kemppainen, Karjalainen, Ylostalo, & Heinonen,

Figure 6-6.
5 Megahertz Transducer Resolution

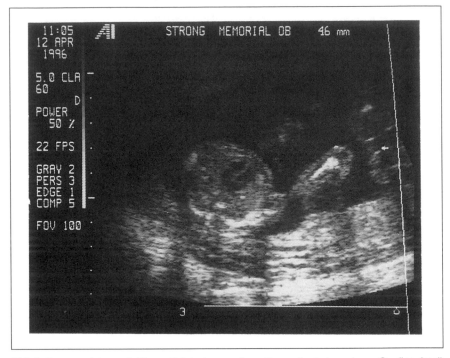

This is the same fetus as in Figure 5-6, but now using a 5 megahertz transducer. Cardiac detail can now be appreciated, in contrast to Figure 5-6.

1990), nor is routine obstetrical ultrasound recommended by the American College of Obstetricians and Gynecologists (ACOG, 1993), ultrasonographic exams nevertheless have become routine in many practices in many parts of the country.

Evaluation of Early Pregnancy

Ultrasound can be of use in assessing the location and viability of very early pregnancies. Transvaginal ultrasound involves positioning an elongated transducer very close to the uterus, minimizing the depth through which the sound waves must pass, and allowing use of higher frequencies to improve axial resolution. With this technique, a gestational sac normally should be visible within the uterus at 4 to 5 weeks gestation. Nonspecific collections of blood or endometrial fluid can be differentiated from the sac by the round, regular appearance of the sac, and by the double ring of the trophoblast and endometrial layers. Viability cannot be assessed at this time, because of the absence of sonographically visible structures within the sac.

The above findings correspond to a serum human chorionic gonadotropin (HCG) titer of between 900 and 2,000 IU-L. When the HCG titer is in this range, failure to see a sac when using a transvaginal transducer should raise clinical suspicion of an abnormal pregnancy — either ectopic, nonviable, or spontaneously miscarried (ACOG, 1995). Under those circumstances, repeat HCG titers and ultrasound examination should be considered.

The sac normally grows approximately 1 mm per day, and an early yolk sac should be visible by the time the sac is 10 mm diameter (transvaginal) or 20 mm (transabdominal) (ACOG, 1995). The yolk sac should not measure more than 6 mm (Lindsay et al., 1992). An empty gestational sac with irregular borders measuring >20 mm is consistent with a nonviable pregnancy.

Soon after the yolk sac is seen, a fetal pole should be visible (see Figure 7-6). Fetal cardiac motion should be present by the time the fetal pole measures 4 to 5 mm (Goldstein, 1992; Levi, Lyons, Zheng, Lindsay, & Holt, 1990). Failure to document a fetal heartbeat when the fetus measures less than 4 mm warrants a repeat scan in 3 to 5 days (the fetus grows approximately 1 mm per day at this gestational age); continued lack of cardiac motion is most consistent with a nonviable gestation (Goldstein, 1992). Conversely, identification of fetal cardiac motion has been associated with a favorable prognosis and pregnancy continuation in 75% to 98% of such patients, improving with advancing gestational age, younger maternal age, and lack of clinical symptoms at the time of the sonographic assessment (Cashner, Christopher, & Dysert, 1987; Goldstein, 1992; Levi et al., 1990; Wilson, Kendrick, Wittman, & McGillivray, 1986).

Anatomic Scanning

Fetal anomalies occur in 2% to 5% percent of neonates, and are the most common cause of infant mortality today (CDC, 1989). In a series of liveborn and stillborn infants in Atlanta between 1982 and 1985, cardiovascular, musculoskeletal, central nervous system, and facial anomalies were most common, followed by gastrointestinal, abdominal wall, pulmonary, and genitourinary malformations (Pretorius & Nyberg, 1990).

As resolution of ultrasound machines improves, the ability to visualize

Figure 7-6.
Early Gestation

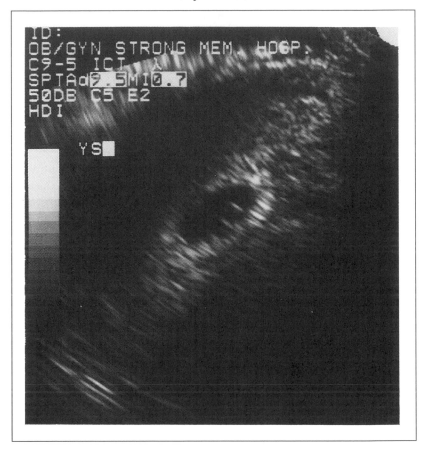

The yolk sac is visible within an intrauterine gestational sac in this 5.5 week gestation.

fetal anatomy also improves. Using transabdominal scanning, fetal anatomy can be assessed in detail at 16 to 18 weeks gestational age in most patients, although cardiac anatomy may not be amenable to complete ultrasonographic examination until 20 weeks. Malformations of virtually every organ system can be detected using ultrasound, with prenatal ultrasound series reporting central nervous system, genitourinary, gastrointestinal, and abdominal wall malformations most frequently (Pretorius & Nyberg, 1990). The difference between prenatal and neonatal rates may reflect difficulties in diagnosing certain defects *in utero* (for example, cardiac), the rate of spontaneous loss associated with anomalies detected by ultrasound early in pregnancy (which removes these pregnancies from neonatal rosters), or the insensitivity of ultrasound for detecting minor anomalies.

Detection rates vary with the skill of the sonographer and the subtlety of the anomaly. In a large prospective study of low-risk pregnant women, only one-third of all anomalies were detected by routine antenatal diagnostic imaging with ultrasound ("RADIUS") (Crane et al., 1994). When limited to anomalies which are amenable to ultrasonographic antenatal diagnosis, the detection rate still was only 50%. In both cases, only half of the detected anomalies were diagnosed before 24 weeks. Anomalies were detected almost three times more often when ultrasound was performed at a tertiary center than when it was performed at a nontertiary center. Although other reports have cited much higher detection rates of 67% to 71% before 24 weeks, another was consistent with the RADIUS study (Chitty, Hunt, Moore, & Lobb, 1991; Levi et al., 1991; Shirley, Bottomley, & Robinson, 1992).

As is the case with many other laboratory tests, the specificity of obstetric anatomic ultrasonography is better than its sensitivity. In contrast to the variable sensitivity for detecting anomalies, ultrasound's false-positive rate (diagnosing anomalies when none exist) is reported to be very low, between 0.02% and 1.5% (Chitty et al., 1991; Manchester et al., 1988; Shirley et al., 1992).

Anatomic evaluation is most important in those patients with a previous malformed fetus, a family history of fetal anomalies, an increased risk of genetic disease, maternal diabetes mellitus, abnormal maternal serum alpha feto-protein, multiple gestation, polyhydramnios, malpresentation, or fetal growth restriction. The specifics of ultrasonographic criteria for individual anomalies is beyond the scope of this chapter; the interested reader may consult various texts devoted to that subject (Nyberg, Mahony, & Pretorius, 1990; Romero, Pilu, Jeanty, Ghidini, & Hobbins, 1988).

Fetal Growth and Weight Estimation

Evaluation of fetal growth and estimation of fetal weight are possible through the use of ultrasound. Precise gestational dating is essential for accurate interpretation of growth and weight parameters. In the first trimester, crown-rump length closely correlates with fetal age to within 5 days. From 14 weeks, composite gestational age can be determined through the measurement of fetal biparietal diameter (BPD), head circumference (HC), abdomi-

Figure 8-6.
Canadian Growth Chart — Males

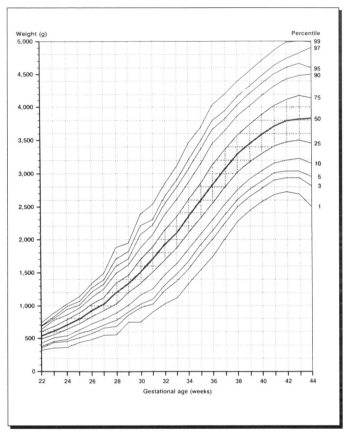

Reprinted with permission from Arbuckle, T.E., Wilkins, R., & Sherman, G.J. (1993). Birth weight percentiles by gestational age in Canada. *Obstetrics & Gynecology, 81*(1), 42. New York: Elsevier Science Publishing, Co.

nal circumference (AC), and femur length (FL), to within 10 days accuracy up to 24 weeks. After 24 weeks, there is so much variation in individual fetal growth that ultrasound is not accurate for dating. At an advanced gestational age, a given fetus may be a certain size for constitutional or pathological reasons, or because it is of an earlier or later gestational age than realized. Ultrasound will be unable to differentiate between these possibilities.

Formulas for Fetal Weight Estimation

For the late-second and throughout the third trimester, formulas have been developed to estimate fetal weights based on various combinations of BPD, HC, AC, and FL. All of these formulas (Hadlock, Harrist, Carpenter, Deter, & Park, 1984; Hadlock, Harrist, Sharman, Deter, & Park, 1985; Shepard, Richards, Berkowitz, Warsof, & Hobbins, 1982; Warsof, Gahari, Berkowitz, & Hobbins, 1977) were developed by multiple regression analyses of series of ultrasonographic measurements obtained from patients shortly before delivery. The formulas that provided the "best fit" to the actual birth weight can be used to predict fetal weight in ongoing pregnancies. For a given patient, estimated fetal weight (EFW) can be plotted on a standard growth chart, and percentiles can be calculated for that weight at that fetus's gestational age (see Figure 8-6).

There are subtle differences from one formula to another, but not clinically significant ones for most purposes. Although ultrasonographic EFWs often are taken as the "gold standard," their precision is imperfect. Approximately 75% of EFWs will be accurate to within 10% of the true weight, but the remaining 25% will vary by more than 10% from actual weight (Benacerraf, Gelman, & Frigoletto, 1988). Until delivery, the clinician cannot tell with certainty whether a given EFW is one of the 75% that are accurate, or one of the 25% that are not. Several authors have concluded that manual assessments of fetal weight by Leopold's maneuvers, or even patients' own estimates of their babies' weights, are of similar accuracy when compared with ultrasonographic weight estimates (Chauhan, Lutton, Bailey, Guerrieri, & Morrison, 1992; Watson, Soisson, & Harlass, 1988).

Indications for Fetal Weight Estimations

Weight estimates are particularly important when fetal growth restriction is suspected. If dating is accurate, then the weight should be above the 10th percentile. A fetal weight below the 10th percentile raises concerns for growth restriction, which is associated with increased perinatal morbidity and mortality. A growth-restricted fetus must undergo frequent antepartum assessment and sequential sonographic weight estimates to monitor interval growth. Up to 90% of growth-restricted fetuses potentially can be identified by EFW determination, but, because of the significant false-positive rate (EFW <10th percentile, when true fetal weight is >10th percentile), the estimated positive predictive value for growth restriction given an EFW of <10th percentile is approximately 50% (Benson, Doubilet, & Saltzman, 1986).

Consideration of other parameters, such as the ratio of the HC to AC, and HC to FL, the amniotic fluid volume, and the pattern of growth over time, may improve the detection rate for fetal growth restriction (ACOG, 1995).

Weight estimates may be indicated in pregnancies which are complicated by maternal diabetes, during which fetal macrosomia is common. Macrosomic fetuses are at risk for shoulder dystocia during delivery, particularly when the birth weight is over 4,000 grams. Cesarean delivery has been advocated for such patients. Unfortunately, the obstetrician does not have the birth weight available when making management plans for delivery, and sonographic EFWs of >4000 grams will overestimate the true fetal weight in at least one quarter of all such patients, complicating decisions regarding the route of delivery (Benson, Doubilet, & Saltzman, 1987).

Multiple gestation also is an indication for serial evaluation of fetal growth because of the frequent occurrences of fetal growth restriction, growth discordancy, and twin-twin transfusion.

Amniotic Fluid Volume Assessment

In the first half of pregnancy, amniotic fluid primarily consists of fluid passing across the membranes and fetal skin. In the second half, the primary component is fetal urine. Mean volumes change with gestational age, ranging from 30 ml at 10 weeks, to 190 ml at 16 weeks, peaking at 900 ml at the middle of the third trimester and then declining thereafter (Brace & Wolf, 1989). Fetal swallowing helps remove amniotic fluid, with absorption of swallowed fluid into the fetal intravascular space where it can equilibrate over the placenta into the maternal circulation. Precise regulation of amniotic fluid volume (AFV) and composition is poorly understood, but we know that this depends on a balance between fetal urine output, swallowing, pulmonary fluid efflux, maternal hydration, and membrane status (Brace, 1994).

The "gold standard" for measuring AFV is dye dilution. A given amount of a certain concentration of a dye is infused into the amniotic cavity and is allowed to diffuse; then an aliquot of fluid is removed. The new concentration of dye in the fluid aliquot is measured. By knowing the initial amount and concentration of the dye, the total volume of fluid into which the dye has been diluted can be calculated as equal to the AFV. Although precise, this method is invasive and impractical for clinical practice because it involves two amniocenteses, to introduce dye and subsequently to aspirate fluid.

Methods of Sonographically Assessing Amniotic Fluid Volume

Ultrasonographic assessment of AFV is noninvasive and can substitute for dye dilution. Several methods using ultrasound have been proposed, none of which is as precise as dye dilution, but all of which are easily performed. The simplest method is to assess the AFV subjectively as either normal, decreased (oligohydramnios), or increased (polyhydramnios). This method is dependent on the experience of the observer, although assessments are fairly reproducible if observers are experienced (Halperin, Fong, Zalev, & Goldsmith, 1985). The "deepest single pocket" method has been used, wherein the deepest pocket of amniotic fluid (at least 1 cm wide) is measured. A deepest pocket measuring ≥8 cm has been defined as polyhydramnios, and ≤2 cm as oligohydramnios (Chamberlain, Manning, Morrison, Harman, & Lange, 1984a & b).

More recently, the "amniotic fluid index" (AFI) has gained acceptance. To perform an AFI, the deepest pocket of amniotic fluid in each of four quadrants of the uterus is measured while the transducer is held perpendicular to the floor and longitudinal to the patient's spine. Amniotic fluid pockets containing segments of the umbilical cord should not be included in the measurement. The four measurements are added to yield the AFI (Phelan et al., 1987). Confidence intervals for each gestational age (based on AFI assessment of nearly 800 pregnancies) allow the clinician to determine whether the AFI is within 90% limits or not, and, indirectly, whether the AFV is normal (Moore & Cayle, 1990). A normal AFI or deepest single pocket correlates well with normal AFV as measured by dye dilution, but may underestimate AFV in cases of polyhydramnios and overestimate AFV in cases of oligohydramnios (Croom et al., 1992; Dildy, Lira, Moise, Riddle, & Deter, 1992; Magann et al., 1992).

Abnormal Amniotic Fluid Volume

Polyhydramnios is associated with fetal anomalies (especially gastrointestinal and neural tube defects, where there is obstructed swallowing or excessive fluid passage across open defects), hydrops (as a result of cardiac decompensation due to either immunologic or nonimmune mechanisms), aneuploidy, multiple gestation, maternal diabetes, and fetal macrosomia. Because of these associations, polyhydramnios is associated with a three- to seven-fold increase in perinatal mortality (two- to four-fold if corrected for fetal anomalies) (Chamberlain et al., 1984b; Varma, Bateman, Patel, Chamberlain, & Pillai, 1988). If the degree of polyhydramnios is mild, 40%

to 73% will resolve without sequelae or apparent explanation, although persistent polyhydramnios (even mild) has been associated with adverse perinatal outcome (Glantz, Abramowicz, & Sherer, 1994; Sivit, Hill, Larsen, & Lande, 1987). In as many as 90% of pregnancies complicated by severe polyhydramnios, there is an identifiable cause for the excessive amniotic fluid (Hill, Breckle, Thomas, & Fries, 1987).

Oligohydramnios is associated with fetal growth restriction, anomalies (especially urinary tract obstruction, preventing passage of urine), aneuploidy, placental insufficiency, post-dates, ruptured membranes, and maternal drug use (prostaglandin synthetase inhibitors and angiotensin converting enzyme inhibitors). Fetal hypoxia results in redistribution of fetal blood flow away from the kidneys, decreasing plasma filtration and urine output. Prolonged oligohydramnios is associated with pulmonary hypoplasia and limb deformities. Perinatal mortality is related to the degree of oligohydramnios. In a large study using the single-deepest-pocket technique, corrected perinatal mortality increased 19-fold with mild-to-moderate oligohydramnios (largest pocket measuring between 1 and 2 cm), and 55-fold for severe oligohydramnios (largest pocket <1 cm) when compared with patients having normal AFVs (Chamberlain et al., 1984a). In the same study, perinatal morbidity also was related to the degree of oligohydramnios. Other studies have reported a three-fold increase in operative deliveries when the AFI is <2 cm (Grubb & Paul, 1992), and a two-fold increase in umbilical artery acidosis at delivery when the AFI is 5 cm (positive predictive value 31%) (Chauhan, Rutherford, Sharp, Carnevale, & Runzel, 1992). Oligohydramnios during the second trimester is associated with very poor outcome. Under these circumstances, perinatal mortality has been reported to range from 64% to 100%, with normal outcome in fewer than 20% of these pregnancies (Barss, Benacerraf, & Frigoletto, 1984; Mercer & Brown, 1986).

Biophysical Profile Scoring

Ultrasonographic fetal weight estimation and evaluation of fetal anatomy popularized the use of ultrasound in obstetrics in the 1970s. In the 1980s, investigators realized that ultrasound had potential beyond the ability just to evaluate fetal anatomy and weight; it could be used to observe the intrauterine environment and dynamic fetal responses therein. As with fetal heart rate monitoring, normal fetal responses require normal fetal central nervous system function, which requires adequate fetal oxygenation. Thus, the biophysical profile was developed, enabling quantitative evaluation of the fetus.

Central Nervous System Maturation and Neuromuscular Function

Throughout gestation, the fetal central nervous system gradually matures. Manifestations of this maturation can be observed in the form of neuromuscular activity, such as muscular tone, movements, and breathing motions, all of which are controlled by the central nervous system. Tone and movement have been recognized as early as 6 to 7 weeks gestation, and breathing movements as early as 12 to 14 weeks. Fetal heart rate accelerations with movements (reactivity) develop at 16 to 18 weeks (Manning, 1995b). Normal degrees of these activities require adequate fetal oxygenation to ensure proper central nervous system functioning. There is evidence that the different centers within the brain that control these various activities have differential sensitivities to oxygen, with the earliest developed being the least sensitive to hypoxia. Reactivity is most sensitive to decreased oxygen concentrations, followed by breathing, with movement and tone least sensitive. With progressive hypoxia, reactivity tends to be lost first, then breathing motions, and finally movement and tone (Manning et al., 1993; Vintzileos et al., 1991).

These parameters are amenable to sonographic evaluation. The presence or absence of each parameter alone can be influenced not only by gestational age and hypoxia, but also by fetal sleep cycles, maternal medications, structural fetal anomalies, and duration of hypoxia. Although the parameters individually do correlate with the presence or absence of acute fetal hypoxia and acidosis, they are much better predictors of fetal state when evaluated in aggregate, minimizing chance fluctuations within each parameter due to extraneous influences (Manning, Platt, & Sipos, 1980).

A single, acute, mild-to-moderate hypoxic episode may resolve. Although fetal movement, tone, breathing, and reactivity may be depressed transiently during the episode, if no cerebral injury is sustained, these parameters subsequently may return to normal. Unless testing is done *during* such a hypoxic episode, its occurrence after-the-fact cannot be verified by these parameters.

Fetal responses to hypoxia can be classified as either acute or chronic. In the case of sudden compression of the umbilical cord, the flow of oxygenated blood into the fetus suddenly slows or stops. Fetal pO_2 decreases, and pCO_2 increases. If compression is persistent, the increased pCO_2 will lower the fetal blood pH via conversion to carbonic acid. The immediate fetal response to hypoxia is preferential redistribution of blood flow to the brain, heart, and adrenal glands, away from the kidneys, gut, and extremities (Peters, Sheldon, Jones, Makowski, & Meschia, 1979). If normal oxygenation is restored, pO_2 rises, pCO_2 declines, the pH rises back to normal, and the cardiovascular changes reverse.

With prolonged or recurrent hypoxia, whether due to persistent umbilical cord compression, uteroplacental insufficiency, or placental abruption, fetal cardiovascular redistribution does not reverse. Fetal urinary output declines because of decreased renal perfusion and increased vasopressin release. Because fetal urine is the primary component of amniotic fluid, lower urine output results in decreased amniotic fluid volume. In addition, prolonged hypoxia precipitates a shift from aerobic to anaerobic metabolism. In the absence of adequate oxygen, glucose is metabolized inefficiently to lactic acid, causing a metabolic acidosis. In extreme cases, asphyxia and organ damage ensue.

Amniotic fluid volume assessment provides a means of evaluating chronic states of fetal hypoxia. When the largest single pocket of amniotic fluid is ≤ 2 cm, perinatal morbidity increases (Chamberlain et al., 1984a). When combined with assessment of the acutely affected parameters above, the presence and contribution of both acute and chronic hypoxia can be evaluated. Evaluation of these five parameters constitutes the biophysical profile (BPP).

Performance and Scoring of the Biophysical Profile

The BPP consists of a 30-minute period of observation of the fetus with ultrasound. This 30-minute period can be extended, if indicated. The patient should be in a semi-recumbent position, not supine. During this time, the parameters of fetal body movements, tone, breathing motion, and amniotic fluid volume are evaluated. The patient also undergoes a NST before or after the ultrasound examination. According to the criteria listed in Table 4-6, either 2 or 0 points are given for the presence or absence of each parameter, respectively. The maximum score is 10, if all five parameters are present. The lowest score is 0, if none of the parameters is present.

These scores correlate with the probability of perinatal morbidity and mortality. Scores of 8 or 10 are considered normal. Scores of 2 or 0 are ominous, consistent with a very high likelihood of fetal asphyxia. A score of 6 is equivocal, and a score of 4 is consistent with probable fetal hypoxia. Perinatal morbidity and mortality increase, and umbilical cord pH decreases with decreasing BPP scores (see Figures 9-6, 10-6, 11-6) (Manning et al., 1990a; Manning et al., 1993).

Nonequivalence of Score Combinations

Although each parameter receives the same scale (0 or 2), individually they are not all of exactly the same predictive value, nor are all cumulative

Table 4-6.
Biophysical Profile Scoring

Biophysical Variable	Normal (2 points)	Abnormal (0 points)
Breathing movements	≥1 episode of ≥ 30 seconds	Absent or episodes <30 seconds
Body movements	≥2 discrete body/limb movements*	<2 body/limb movements*
Fetal tone	≥1 active extension and return to flexion of limb or trunk	Absent, or partial return to flexion, or movement in full extension only
FHR reactivity	≥2 FHR accelerations of ≥15 seconds duration in 20 minutes	<2 FHR accelerations ≥15 bpm (peak) of ≥15 seconds duration in 20 minutes
Amniotic fluid volume	≥1 pocket of fluid of ≥2 cm vertical depth	No pocket of fluid of ≥2 cm vertical depth

*Earlier criteria use 3 movements rather than 2

Modified from Manning (1995b)

scores of equal predictive value. For a score of 6/10, the combinations of abnormal breathing and movement, or abnormal nonstress testing and tone, correlate with the highest perinatal mortality rates of any of the 10 possible 6/10 combinations (142 to 370 per 1,000), higher than the mean for a 4/10 score (76/1,000). However, these were uncommon combinations and these published perinatal mortality rates were based on small numbers of patients and should be interpreted with such in mind. The combinations of abnormal fetal tone and breathing, or abnormal breathing and amniotic fluid volume, were associated with the lowest mortality for a 6/10 score (0/1,000). Cumulative perinatal morbidity for a 6/10 score was highest with the combinations of abnormal nonstress testing and either abnormal tone or abnormal breathing (87% to 90% positive predictive accuracy [PPA]), and lowest when breathing and movement were abnormal (29% PPA).

For a score of 4/10, the combination of normal breathing and movement alone was associated with the highest perinatal mortality of any 4/10 combi-

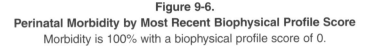

Figure 9-6.
Perinatal Morbidity by Most Recent Biophysical Profile Score
Morbidity is 100% with a biophysical profile score of 0.

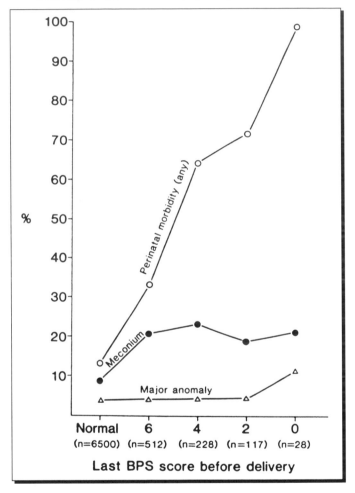

Manning, F.A., Harman, C.R., Morrison, I., Menticoglou, S.M., Lange, I.R., & Johnson, J.M. (1990a). Fetal assessment basd on fetal biophysical profile scoring: IV. An analysis of perinatal morbidity and mortality. *American Journal of Obstetrics and Gynecology, 162*(3), 703-709.

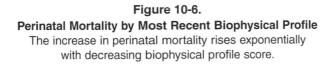

Figure 10-6.
Perinatal Mortality by Most Recent Biophysical Profile
The increase in perinatal mortality rises exponentially
with decreasing biophysical profile score.

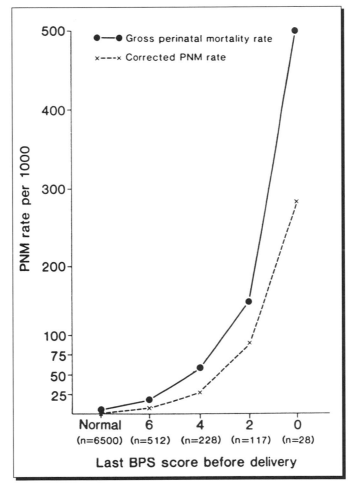

Manning, F.A., Harman, C.R., Morrison, I., Menticoglou, S.M., Lange,
I.R., & Johnson, J.M. (1990a). Fetal assessment basd on fetal biophysi-
cal profile scoring: IV. An analysis of perinatal morbidity and mortality.
American Journal of Obstetrics and Gynecology, 162(3), 703-709.

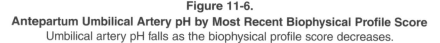

Figure 11-6.
Antepartum Umbilical Artery pH by Most Recent Biophysical Profile Score
Umbilical artery pH falls as the biophysical profile score decreases.

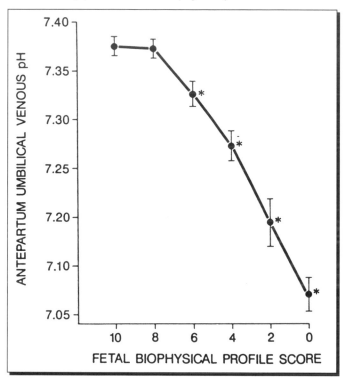

Manning, F.A., Snijders, R., Harman, C.R., Nicolaides, K., Menticoglou, S., & Morrison, I. (1993). Fetal biophysical profile score: VI. Correlation with antepartum umbilical venous fetal pH. *American Journal of Obstetrics and Gynecology, 169*(4), 755-763.

nation (176/1,000), and the presence of normal nonstress testing and amniotic fluid volume alone associated with the lowest mortality (15/1,000). For perinatal morbidity within the 4/10 scores, the presence of normal tone and either normal fluid volume or movement alone was associated with the highest PPA (85% to 87%). Normal fetal breathing and either normal nonstress testing or normal movement were associated with the lowest perinatal morbidity of any 4/10 score (28% to 29% PPA). For scores of 2/10, perinatal morbidity and mortality were high regardless of which single parameter was normal. Using logistic regression analysis, NST nonreactivity has the highest correlation with perinatal mortality, and decreased amniotic fluid volume with morbidity (Manning et al., 1990b). The clinical utility of these gradations awaits confirmation.

For perinatal mortality, the sensitivity of the BPP is 75% with 33% false positives. For perinatal morbidity, the sensitivity of the BPP is 69% with 39% false positives (Manning et al., 1990b).

Interpretation, Management, and Modifications of the BPP

Based on these risks, Manning proposed management plans, depending on the composition and persistence of the score and gestational age. Any score must be interpreted with regard to available clinical information about the patient, rather than as an absolute. A normal preterm fetus may score lower on a BPP than a term fetus due to lower frequencies of breathing movements and NST reactivity, both of which are dependent on gestational age and do not necessarily reflect hypoxia as accurately in premature gestations (Baskett, 1988; Druzin et al., 1985; Fox, Inglis, & Steinbrecher, 1979). Testing intervals depend on gestational age, obstetrical complication, and the most recent BPP score, ranging from hours to 1 week (see Table 5-6).

Several modifications of the BPP have been proposed. Placental grading is included in some scoring systems (Vintzileos, Campbell, Ingardia, & Nochimson, 1983), but has not been shown to improve predictive value. If a score of 8/8 is achieved on ultrasonographic evaluation without an NST, performance of an NST is optional because, in the absence of oligohydramnios, an 8 to 10 of 10 score is considered normal and so the additional 0 or 2 points from the NST will not influence management. However, if a score of less than 8/8 is determined on ultrasound, nonstress testing must be performed (Manning, Morrison, Harman, & Chamberlain, 1987).

Several investigators have reported that performance of just an amniotic fluid volume assessment and a NST (the "modified BPP") has similar predictive value to a CST, and can be done in less time than a complete BPP (Nageotte, Towers, Asrat, Freeman, & Dorchester, 1994; Nageotte, Towers, Asrat, & Freeman, 1994).

Indications for Biophysical Profile Testing

The BPP is most commonly used as a follow-up test after a nonreactive NST. It is less invasive, easier to perform, and less time consuming than a CST, and the BPP has no contraindications. Although both the BPP and CST

Table 5-6.
Interpretation and Management of Biophysical Profile Score

BPS Result	Interpretation	Risk of Asphyxia (Umbilical Venous Metabolic Acidosis <7.25) (%)	Risk of Fetal Death (per 1000/week)	Recommended Management
10/10 8/10 (N-AFV) 8/8 (NST not done)	Nonasphyxiated	0	0.565	No indication for intervention for fetal indications
8/10 Oligo	Chronic compensated asphyxia	5–10 (estimate)	20–30	If mature ($\geq$37 weeks), deliver. Serial testing (twice weekly) in the immature fetus
6/10 N-AFV	Acute asphyxia possible	10	50	If mature ($\geq$37 weeks) deliver. Repeat test in 24 hours in immature fetus. Repeat test; if $\leq$6/10, deliver
6/10 Oligo	Chronic asphyxia with possible acute asphyxia	> 10 (?)	> 50	Factor in gestational age; if $\geq$32 weeks, deliver. If $\leq$32 weeks, test daily
4/10 N-AFV	Acute asphyxia likely	36	115	Factor in gestational age; if $\geq$32 weeks, deliver. If $\leq$32 weeks, test daily
4/10 Oligo	Chronic asphyxia, acute asphyxia likely	> 36	>115	If $\geq$26 weeks, deliver
2/10 N-AFV	Acute asphyxia nearly certain	73	220	If $\geq$26 weeks, deliver
2/10 Oligo	Chronic asphyxia with superimposed acute asphyxia	> 73	>220	If $\geq$26 weeks, deliver
0/10	Gross severe asphyxia	100	550	If $\geq$26 weeks, deliver

Oligo, oligohydramnios (maximal fluid pocket $\leq$ 2 cm in vertical axis).

Reprinted with permission from Manning, F.A. (1995). Chapter six: Fetal biophysical profile scoring: Theoretical considerations and clinical application. In *Fetal medicine: Principles and practice*. Norwalk, CT: Appleton & Lange.

have graded prognostic value, they evaluate different physiologic variables. The CST evaluates uteroplacental function as it affects fetal oxygenation, whereas the BPP evaluates fetal state as a function of oxygenation. With rare exceptions, the CST is not influenced by gestational age, fetal anomalies, or fetal sleep cycles, all of which can influence the BPP. The BPP may give more information, but not all of it may be relevant to the primary question regarding fetal oxygenation. In this sense, the BPP is a better predictor of fetal morbidity, but may be difficult to interpret in pregnancies which are complicated by prematurity (Baskett, 1988), fetal anomalies (central nervous system or restrictive cutaneous or muscular diseases), maternal drug use (sedatives or magnesium sulfate) (Carlan & O'Brien, 1991; Peaceman, Meyer, Thorp, Parisi, & Creasy, 1989), or simply during fetal sleep cycles. The choice as to which test to use following a nonreactive NST should take these factors into consideration.

The BPP has been evaluated as a primary means of fetal surveillance. Although it has a lower false-negative rate than the NST, it is more expensive and takes longer to perform. Several randomized trials have failed to demonstrate superiority of the BPP over the NST as a primary means of surveillance, and so it cannot be recommended at this time as the initial mode of testing for the majority of patients for whom antepartum fetal assessment is indicated (Manning et al., 1984; Platt et al., 1985).

Umbilical Artery Doppler Velocimetry

To receive oxygen, fetal blood must flow through the placenta. It is possible to measure such flow through the use of Doppler ultrasound. The principle is based on the Doppler shift: waves of a given frequency that are reflected by a moving surface or interface will undergo a shift in frequency that is proportional to the rate of movement of the surface. If the surface is moving towards the transducer, the frequency of the returning wave will shift upward to a higher frequency. If the surface is moving away from the transducer, the returning wave's frequency will shift downward. The use of Doppler to calculate the velocity of flow of blood cells through a vessel, the diameter of the vessel, the angle of insonation, the tissue densities through which the sound waves must pass, and the frequencies of the transmitted and received ultrasound waves all must be determined. Unfortunately, a certain error is inherent in each measurement; when added together, the sum of the errors yields a range for a given calculated value that is so wide as to be of limited utility.

Despite intrinsic error in the absolute flow calculation, the *ratio* of systolic/diastolic flow *can* be calculated accurately (the S/D ratio). Since the vessel diameter varies only slightly during the cardiac cycle, tissue density and angle of insonation do not change, and the transmitted ultrasound frequency remains the same. The error terms in the numerator and denominator of the ratio cancel out, leaving the Doppler frequency shift as the only variable. This can be measured precisely. This ratio is proportional to the resistance to flow downstream from the point of measurement. If there were no friction (resistance to flow), then the heart would have to beat only once, and blood would flow through the vessels indefinitely. Flow during systole would equal flow during diastole, and S/D would equal 1.0. Conversely, if there is high resistance to flow, blood will surge forward during systole, but nearly stop during diastole when the heart is relaxed and there is no active driving force propelling the blood forward through the high-resistance vessels. In that case, the S/D will be a very high number (approaching infinity in the case of no diastolic flow), because of the low value of the denominator. At first glance, a high S/D might be thought to be favorable, indicating increased systolic flow. It must be borne in mind, however, that in the case of an elevated S/D both systolic and diastolic flow actually are decreased, but diastolic (denominator) more so than systolic (numerator). In the worst cases, the increase in resistance is so great that the vessels push back the column of blood during diastole, yielding reversal of diastolic flow.

The S/D Ratio in Evaluating Placental Resistance

Using the S/D ratio (or similar measurements, such as pulsatility or resistance indices) of the umbilical artery, intraplacental resistance to flow can be assessed. The transducer should be held so that the focal point is on the umbilical artery just where it enters the placenta; otherwise, resistance due to the length of the umbilical cord will be included in the S/D, elevating the value and confounding interpretation. Resistance to flow is proportional to the total cross-sectional diameter through which a fluid flows: the greater the diameter, the lower the resistance. As the placenta grows during pregnancy, there are more and more villi, arterioles, and capillaries; so there is progressively greater cross-sectional area. Therefore, intraplacental resistance normally decreases as pregnancy progresses, and so does the umbilical artery S/D ratio. By measuring S/D at many gestational ages, investigators have derived normal charts and confidence intervals. Conditions limiting placental vascularity, such as infarction or hypoplasia, decrease the cross-sectional area and increase the resistance to flow. The placental small-arteriole count is lower in

Figure 12-6.
Umbilical Artery Doppler — Normal

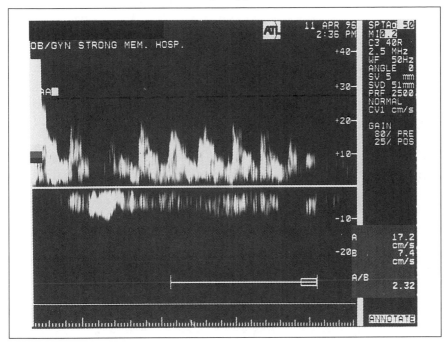

The ratio of the systolic peak to the diastolic nadir (S/D) is low, indicating normal placental resistance to flow. Nonpulsatile flow in the umbilical vein is recorded as a continuous band beneath the pulsatile arterial flow.

pregnancies manifesting high S/Ds when compared with pregnancies with normal S/Ds (Giles, Trudinger, & Baird, 1985). An S/D above the 95th percentile is considered abnormal, consistent with increased resistance to flow (see Figures 12-6, 13-6, 14-6).

Umbilical Artery Doppler Velocimetry in Clinical Practice

Umbilical artery Doppler velocimetry has been used for antenatal fetal monitoring, but there continues to be uncertainty about its value. Several authors have reported associations of abnormal Doppler S/Ds to adverse perinatal outcomes, but positive predictive values for the occurrence of individual outcomes by themselves (low Apgar, acidosis, NICU admission, mortality,

Figure 13-6.
Umbilical Artery Doppler — Abnormal

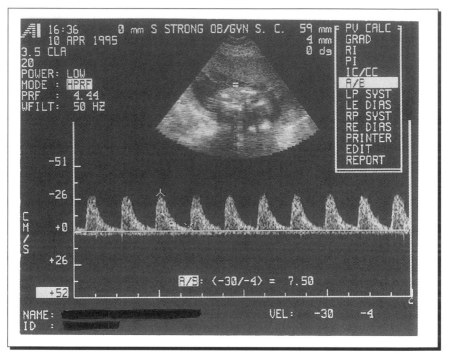

The ratio of the systolic peak to the diastolic nadir (S/D) is high, indicating increased placental resistance to flow.

etc.) are variable and tend to be low (from 8% to 74%) (Brar, Medearis, DeVore, & Platt, 1989; Maulik, Yarlagadda, Youngblood, & Ciston, 1990; Trudinger, Cook, Jones, & Giles, 1986). In one report, umbilical artery Doppler performed better than FHR monitoring (Trudinger et al., 1986), but several other investigators have found the opposite to be true (Devoe, Gardner, Dear, & Castillo, 1990; Sarno, Ahn, Brar, Phelan, & Platt, 1989). Screening obstetric populations with umbilical artery Doppler has not been effective in reducing perinatal morbidity and mortality in most studies (Beattie & Dornan, 1989; Bruinse, Sijmons, & Reuwer, 1989; Davies, Gallivan, & Spencer, 1992; Newnham, O'Dea, Reid, & Diepeveen, 1991; Sijmons, Reuwer, VanBeek, & Bruinse, 1989; Whittle, Hanretty, Primrose, & Neilson, 1994), although a recent meta-analysis concluded that perinatal mortality is

Figure 14-6.
Umbilical Artery Doppler — Absent Diastolic Flow

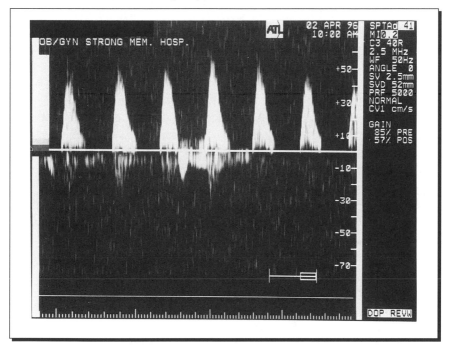

Placental resistance is so high that flow stops during diastole. This is associated with poor perinatal outcome.

lower in patients undergoing Doppler screening (Neilson, 1994). In some studies, statistical power may have been too low to prove significant differences, and differences in study design make direct comparisons difficult.

Umbilical artery Doppler possibly may be helpful in some high-risk patients. A recent review of eight studies tabulated sensitivities of between 49% and 78% for detecting growth-restricted fetuses, with positive predictive values of between 24% and 81% (not very different than results using standard ultrasound size measurements alone) (Maulik, 1995). Several investigators have reported decreased perinatal morbidity associated with Doppler screening of patients at high risk for fetal growth restriction (Almstrom et al., 1992; Tyrrell et al., 1990). At this time, it is unclear whether there are any advantages to using umbilical artery flow velocimetry in pregnancies which are complicated by diabetes or hypertension.

An important exception is the patient in whom there is absent or reversed end-diastolic flow. Reversed end-diastolic flow is associated with 50% to 90% perinatal mortality, and significant morbidity (Brar & Platt, 1988; Woo, Liang, & Lo, 1987). In this case, a patient at or near term should be delivered. Even reversed end-diastolic flow, however, sometimes can improve if reversible causes of placental insufficiency are treated effectively. For the preterm patient with absent diastolic flow, continuing the pregnancy with concurrent aggressive daily monitoring is effective in prolonging pregnancy and achieving acceptable outcomes (Divon, Girz, Lieblich, & Langer, 1989).

In summary, umbilical artery Doppler velocimetry may be useful in certain patients who are at risk for placental dysfunction, but it does not clearly add benefits over those which are achievable with standard monitoring modalities such as nonstress testing and BPP scoring. Umbilical artery Doppler velocimetry most often is used to confirm what already is suspected, rather than as an integral part of initial fetal assessment. Management decisions more often are made based on NST, CST, or BPP results than on Doppler.

Antepartum Fetal Assessment in Women with Previous Stillbirths

In women who have had previous stillbirths, questions arise about when to begin fetal testing in subsequent pregnancies, and whether testing actually is beneficial obstetrically. Most authorities do recommend antenatal fetal assessment in such patients, but admit that its benefit is unproved. In the case of stillbirth that occurs due to reasons which are unlikely to recur (for example, cord accidents or fetal anomalies), the benefit of fetal assessment may be mainly maternal reassurance. Weeks et al. (1995) concluded that a known cause of fetal death in a previous pregnancy did not influence the incidence of abnormal antenatal fetal testing in a subsequent pregnancy, but there were few adverse perinatal outcomes in the subsequent pregnancies of either group, limiting the power of the study. In patients with known maternal hypertension or fetal growth restriction (FGR), a history of a previous stillbirth increased the risk of a positive CST when compared with similar women without histories of stillbirth (Freeman, Dorchester, Anderson, & Garite, 1985). In women with a previous stillbirth but without hypertension or FGR, the incidence of positive CSTs was comparable to a control population of high-risk women without stillbirth histories. In other words, a previous stillbirth did confer high-risk status, but not more so than for normotensive non-FGR high-risk women.

The question of when to start antepartum fetal assessment in women with stillbirth histories is unresolved. Some recommend beginning 2 weeks prior to the gestational age at which the stillbirth occurred, but this is purely empiric. With monitoring, the risk of recurrent stillbirth has been reported to be 1/300, but there was no demonstrable relationship between the gestational age at which the previous stillbirth occurred and outcome of the study pregnancy (Weeks et al., 1995). For women with stillbirth histories, Weeks et al. recommended that fetal activity be monitored beginning at 26 weeks gestational age, and that antenatal testing (CST, modified BPP, or BPP) be instituted at 32 weeks in accordance with normal fetal movement and no medical complications. If maternal medical complications or decreased fetal movements were present, testing began at 26 to 28 weeks (Weeks et al., 1995).

Conclusion

Although the nonstress test, contraction stress test, and biophysical profile methodologically are different from each other, they all have in common the ultimate goal of indirectly evaluating fetal oxygen status as an indicator of fetal well-being. Each test has its strengths and weaknesses. The NST is quickest, least expensive, and noninvasive, but has a high false-positive rate and is the least sensitive for the outcome of fetal death. The CST is invasive, time consuming, and has certain contraindications, but has a very low false-negative rate and provides accurate assessment of uteroplacental insufficiency. The BPP, with a score based on cumulative assessment of multiple parameters, is expensive and time consuming, but provides graded perinatal morbidity and mortality risk assessment, with a very low false-negative rate. For all three tests, a normal test result is very reassuring, although an abnormal result may or may not indicate significant fetal compromise. The use of these tests in high-risk pregnancies has the potential to detect compromised fetuses at a time when intervention can be life saving.❏

Case Study 1-6

Preconception Counseling for Diabetes, Hypothyroidism, and Severe Cervical Dysplasia

N.M. is a 32-year-old G3 P2 A1 female who is referred for preconceptional counseling. She is a Class D diabetic, diagnosed when she presented with ketoacidosis. After the diagnosis of diabetes, she was managed with subcutaneous insulin injections. One year after the diagnosis, she conceived but spontaneously aborted. She conceived again the next year, had marginal control of her blood sugars, developed preeclampsia at 37 weeks, and she was delivered by elective cesarean of an 11 pound, 1 ounce, male who subsequently has done well.

Two years later, N.M. conceived again; during this pregnancy, her care was managed jointly by her obstetrician and endocrinologist. Her hemoglobin A1C in early pregnancy was 6.7%, but her blood glucose control was erratic during the third trimester, and the hemoglobin A1C rose to 9.6% by 34 weeks gestation. During the third trimester, she underwent nonstress testing twice a week, and all tests were reactive without decelerations. Three days after a reactive nonstress test at 35 weeks, she presented with absent fetal heart tones, consistent with a fetal demise. She had no signs or symptoms of preeclampsia. She was induced and delivered a 9 pound, 8 ounce, stillborn female, who was noted on autopsy to have cardiomyopathy.

N.M. now is on an insulin pump, but her blood sugars are not well-controlled. Her past medical history also is significant for a diagnosis of hypothyroidism (controlled with levothyroxine 0.15 mg/qd), and a history of cervical cone biopsy after her most recent delivery, for severe dysplasia.

The patient understands the need for tight control of her blood glucose, and she states that she will work with her endocrinologist to achieve this objective prior to conceiving another pregnancy. Given her history of macrosomia and stillbirth, she understandably is very anxious about the chance of recurrence. N.M. inquires what steps would be taken in an attempt to prevent repetition of her previous unfortunate outcome.

Commentary

N.M. has three important problems that should be addressed in preconception counseling.

1. Insulin-dependent diabetes and the related complications of fetal macrosomia and fetal death in previous pregnancies.

2. Hypothyroidism, currently treated with levothyroxine 0.15 mg/day.
3. History of a cone biopsy (type unknown) for severe cervical dysplasia.

Insulin-Dependent Diabetes

The history states that N.M. was 32-years-old, was diagnosed within the past 5 years with diabetes mellitus, and is now a Class D diabetic. This means that she must have benign retinopathy, but perhaps she has no other evidence of renal disease or vascular disease. Nevertheless, her two previous pregnancies were complicated by macrosomia; the second pregnancy was complicated, in addition, by a fetal demise in association with fetal cardiomyopathy, probably related to poor control of the diabetes. This suggests that N.M.'s diabetic control in pregnancy was poor, as also evidenced by elevated hemoglobin A1C levels (HgA1C). Furthermore, the history states that, even when she is not pregnant, N.M. has considerable difficulty with glucose control.

Principles of management of pregnancy complicated by diabetes are straightforward and include the following:

1. Periconception control of blood glucose to reduce the risk of fetal malformations.
2. Control of blood glucose throughout pregnancy, to minimize the risk of macrosomia, late fetal death, and other neonatal complications of the infant of a diabetic mother.
3. Fetal monitoring in the third trimester, to detect signs of utero-placental insufficiency.
4. Selecting a time and method of delivery that will avoid fetal trauma and minimize maternal morbidity.

This patient appears to be well-informed about the risks of pregnancy and also is highly motivated to cooperate in the endeavors mentioned above. Pregnancy should be postponed until her HgA1C is below 8%. During her previous pregnancy, outpatient management under the direction of an obstetrician and endocrinologist was not sufficient to achieve adequate control of her blood glucose, as manifested by a HgA1C of 9.6% in the third trimester of her previous pregnancy. Maternal hyperglycemia undoubtedly contributed to the development of fetal hyperinsulinism and its consequences, namely fetal macrosomia, hypertrophic cardiomyopathy, and fetal demise. Consequently, I would advise the patient that if, early in pregnancy, her diet counseling, consistent activity, and meticulous home monitoring of blood glucose values, with appropriate modifications of her insulin therapy, did not result in adequate glucose control (fasting blood sugars <105 mg%, post-prandial blood glucose <150 mg%), hospitalization would be recommended, possibly for the duration of her pregnancy, to achieve this goal. I would impress upon N.M. that metabolic and hormonal changes of pregnancy, and the vagaries of placental metabolism of insulin, often make control of blood sugars more difficult during pregnancy than in the nonpregnant (Diamond et al., 1992; Steel, Johnstone, Hume, & Mao, 1994).

Although a direct correlation between levels of HgA1C and the degree of fetal macrosomia and its complications has not been demonstrated, there is evidence that fetal macrosomia and its associated complications are rare in patients in whom the HgA1C level is maintained below 6.1% (Shields et al., 1993).

There is no convincing evidence that insulin pump therapy is superior to multiple injection regimens in achieving adequate control of diabetes during pregnancy (Coustan et al., 1986). In consultation with the patient's endocrinologist, however, dosing schedules, perhaps requiring innovative combinations and timing of insulin administration, with or without an insulin pump, would be established and monitored closely. Hospitalization would achieve consistency of activity and diet that N.M. could not achieve as an outpatient.

Ultrasound examination should be performed at 18, 24, 30, and 36 weeks gestation. The purpose of these examinations is to identify, as early as possible, any growth abnormalities of the fetus and any abnormalities of the fetal heart. Later in pregnancy, umbilical artery Doppler velocimetry should be performed at the time of these examinations. If these tests are normal (no evidence of cardiac abnormalities, fetal macrosomia, or increased placental vascular resistance), then I would institute twice weekly nonstress testing and amniotic fluid volume estimates (AFI), beginning at 32 weeks gestation (Lagrew et al., 1993; Landon et al., 1992). If these additional tests are normal, glucose control is satisfactory, and there is no evidence of preeclampsia, then I would recommend induction of labor at 38 weeks gestation using cervical ripening agents, if necessary (Kjos et al., 1993). If glucose control becomes erratic, if preeclampsia develops, or if the fetal tests become abnormal, however, I would at that point, in consultation with the neonatologists, consider preterm delivery, probably by cesarean section. If this becomes necessary prior to 37 weeks, and an amniocentesis demonstrates immature fetal lung studies, then I would consider the use of thyroid releasing hormone (TRH) to enhance fetal lung maturity; but I would not give corticosteroids, because of the risk of destabilizing N.M.'s blood glucose control (Ballard et al., 1992).

Hypothyroidism

It is not uncommon to find thyroid disorders in patients with diabetes mellitus, perhaps because both conditions are suspected of being autoimmune in origin. Even mild forms of hypothyroidism have been associated with increased risk of perinatal loss which can be improved with adequate levothyroxine therapy (Davis, Leveno, & Cunningham, 1988). Fortunately, this patient is currently on such therapy. TSH levels should be obtained prior to and on two or three occasions throughout her pregnancy, to insure that she is taking an adequate dose of medication.

History of Cone Biopsy for Cervical Dysplasia

The specific type of cone biopsy is not mentioned in N.M.'s history. However, this procedure, whether it is performed with a scalpel or with laser, is associated with an increased risk of preterm birth in subsequent pregnancies (Hagen & Skjeldestad, 1993). Consequently, I would order appropriate tests for Chlamydia and bacterial vaginosis early in pregnancy and treat these or other vaginal/cervical infections assiduously. I also would check the length of the cervix with transvaginal ultrasound every 2 weeks from 20 to 32 weeks gestation. If shortening of the cervical canal or "funneling" of the endocervix is noted prior to 28 weeks, then I would recommend cervical cerclage. If cervical changes occur after 28 weeks, then I would encourage additional rest in the lateral recumbent position. This plan should not be difficult to follow, because, as noted in the discussion of insulin-dependent diabetes, the patient is likely to require hospitalization for some portion of her complicated pregnancy.

— *Watson A. Bowes, Jr., MD*

Case Study References

Ballard, R.A., Ballard, P.L., Creasy, R.K., et al. (1992). Respiratory disease in very-low-birthweight infants after prenatal thyrotripin-releasing hormone and glucocorticoid. *Lancet, 339,* 510-515.

Coustan, D.R., Reece, A., Sherwin, R.S., et al. (1986). A randomized clinical trial of the insulin pump versus intensive conventional therapy in diabetic pregnancies. *Journal of the American Medical Association, 255,* 631-636.

Davis, L.E., Leveno, K.J., & Cunningham, F.G. (1988). Hypothyroidism complicating pregnancy. *Obstetrics and Gynecology, 72,* 108-112.

Diamond, M.P., Reece, E.A., Caprio, S., et al. (1992). Impairment of counterregulatory hormone responses to hypoglycemia in pregnant women with insulin-dependent diabetes mellitus. *American Journal of Obstetrics and Gynecology, 166,* 70-77.

Hagen, B., & Skjeldestad, F.E. (1993). The outcome of pregnancy after CO_2 laser conization of the cervix. *British Journal of Obstetrics and Gynaecology, 100,* 717-720.

Kjos, S.L., Henry, O.A., Montoro, M., et al. (1993). Insulin-requiring diabetes in preg-

nancy: A randomized trial of active induction of labor and expectant manage-
ment. *American Journal of Obstetrics and Gynecology, 169,* 611-615.
Lagrew, D.C., Pircon, R.A., Towers, C.V., et al. (1993). Antepartum fetal surveillance in
patients with diabetes: When to start? *American Journal of Obstetrics and
Gynecology, 168,* 1820-1826.
Landon, M.B., Langer, O., Gabbe, S.G., et al. (1992). Fetal surveillance in pregnancies
complicated by insulin-dependent diabetes mellitus. *American Journal of
Obstetrics and Gynecology, 167,* 617-621.
Shields, L.E., Gan, E.A., Murphy, H.F., et al. (1993). The prognostic value of hemo-
globin A1C in predicting fetal heart disease in diabetic pregnancies. *Obstetrics and
Gynecology, 81,* 954- 957.
Steel, J.M., Johnstone, F.D., Hume, R., Mao, J-H. (1994). Insulin requirements during
pregnancy in women with Type I diabetes. *Obstetrics and Gynecology, 83,* 253-258.

Case Study 2-6

Assessing Recurrent Pregnancy Losses

R.H. is a 29-year-old G4 P0120 female who presents at 10 weeks gestation.
Her past history is significant for a first-trimester induced abortion of her first
pregnancy, a stillbirth at 34 weeks in her second pregnancy, and a fetal demise
at 16 weeks in her third pregnancy. During her second pregnancy, R.H. had no
history of any obstetric problems until she presented with preterm contractions at 34 weeks and was found to have a fetal demise. She spontaneously
delivered a stillborn fetus weighing only 2.5 pounds. An autopsy was performed, but was indeterminate. Cultures were negative at that time.

She conceived later that same year, and double marker screening at 16
weeks revealed an elevated alpha-fetoprotein and hCG. She underwent
genetic counseling, but when she presented for ultrasound, a fetal demise
was noted. Amniocentesis revealed a normal 46,XX karyotype. A dilatation
and evacuation (D&E) was performed for termination of that pregnancy, and
histologic examination of the fetus was unremarkable.

With R.H.'s current pregnancy, routine prenatal laboratory tests were significant for a RPR titer of 1:1 with a negative FTA, and a positive ANA with a speck-
led pattern of 1:80. Anticardiolipin antibodies and anti-double-stranded DNA
determinations were within normal limits. Her physical examination was within normal limits, except for a blood pressure reading of 134/90 mmHg. Because
of her history of stillbirth, IUGR, and a false positive RPR, a recommendation
was made that R.H. take 80 mg of aspirin qd throughout her current pregnancy.

Commentary

A patient who enters prenatal care for her fourth pregnancy, who has not had a normal outcome in any of her prior pregnancies — regardless of the causes of her previous losses — invariably presents a challenge to health care professionals. In the case of R.H., her past-pregnancy information combined with data in her current pregnancy suggest an autoimmune disorder such as antiphospholipid antibody syndrome as an etiology for her obstetric losses. Nevertheless, it is important to review the workup to date and to perform complete evaluation for other causes of pregnancy loss in a systematic manner. R.H.'s care providers must seek possible genetic, infectious, structural, placental, environmental, and maternal medical-disease factors which may cause or contribute to R.H.'s repeated pregnancy losses. The latter would include further investigation of the maternal hypertension.

To pursue a diagnosis of antiphospholipid antibody syndrome, a test for lupus anticoagulant is appropriate. If a positive result is obtained, heparin therapy would be added to the ASA treatment program.

Fetal Assessment

In this setting of R.H.'s progressively earlier losses, characterized by intrauterine fetal death, an early sonographic study is indicated to establish an intrauterine live fetus. At the same time, the uterus should be studied carefully for abnormalities, such as a septum. An ultrasound study to confirm dates using multiple fetal parameters is scheduled for approximately 16 weeks gestation. This is the anniversary time of the patient's prior loss, so it may be expected to be a significant milestone for the patient and her partner or family. A multiple-marker maternal serum screen, drawn at the same time, may serve as a predictor of pregnancy risk in addition to screening for birth defects. An unexplained abnormal alpha-feto protein in a setting of antiphospholipid antibody syndrome confers a grave prognosis. An elevated hCG also may predict later pregnancy problems, such as preeclampsia. A low urinary estriol in the multiple marker screen may indicate increased risk of intrauterine growth restriction.

As R.H.'s pregnancy reaches the point of fetal viability, umbilical Doppler velocimetry studies and amniotic fluid assessment will be important adjuncts to an updated ultrasound study for baseline growth parameters; 26 weeks gestation is an appropriate point for such evaluation. (Additional studies in the intervening time between 16 and 26 weeks would be guided by results of earlier studies and serial clinical findings.) A program of fetal-movement counting can accompany a prescription for intermittent daily rest periods in the third trimester. This also may contribute to R.H.'s sense of active involvement in working toward a successful outcome this time.

Timing for electronic fetal monitoring in the fetal-assessment regimen will depend on whether this pregnancy has demonstrated early intrauterine growth restriction. If IUGR is present, then monitoring could begin as early as 27 or 28 weeks gestation. Many fetuses demonstrate reactivity even at this relatively early gestational age. In the absence of reactivity, a biophysical profile may be helpful to distinguish between effects of hypoxia versus developmental immaturity or other causes of a false abnormal nonstress test. Or, the biophysical profile may be used as a primary fetal assessment tool, depending on capabilities of the prenatal care facility.

If intrauterine growth restriction recurs, ideal delivery timing is achieved by weighing risks of fetal death from chronic hypoxia against risks of neonatal death from multisystem immaturity. Either fetal welfare or fetal maturity data management is a critical factor in such a decision. For example, amniocentesis could be used to establish early pulmonary maturity in a setting of increased concern about fetal jeopardy before fetal deterioration is demonstrated. A Doppler study indicating reversed or absent end-diastolic umbilical artery flow might indicate that delivery is urgent, without reference to fetal maturity studies. In most circumstances, such a decision is based on a combination of clinical data and information from fetal assessment tests.

Perinatal Loss and Grief Issues

At R.H.'s first prenatal visit, an assessment should be made of the patient's status of grief resolution regarding her prior pregnancy losses. The setting of a *new* pregnancy provides an opportunity for therapeutic supportive counseling to assist the patient in coping with resurfacing concerns such as guilt, fear, and inadequacy. At each step of the course, the patient's previous experiences may cause even minor, untoward events (such as being requested to have a laboratory test repeated) to generate an acute "post-traumatic stress" reaction. Sensitivity to this aspect of R.H.'s prenatal-care needs again can provide an opportunity for her health care providers to assist R.H. with processing her old grief. In turn, this can create a healthier environment for R.H.'s current pregnancy.

— *Micki L. Cabiniss, MD*

References

Almstrom, H., Axelsson, O., Cnattingius, S., Ekman, G., Maesel, A., Ulmsten, U., Armstrom, K., & Marsal, K. (1992). Comparison of umbilical-artery velocimetry and cardiotocography for surveillance of small-for-gestational-age fetuses. *Lancet, 340,* 936-940.

American College of Obstetricians and Gynecologists. (1993). Ultrasonography in Pregnancy. *ACOG Technical Bulletin,* #187.

American College of Obstetricians and Gynecologists. (1994). Antepartum fetal surveillance. *ACOG Technical Bulletin,* #188.

American College of Obstetricians and Gynecologists. (1995). Gynecologic ultrasonography. *ACOG Technical Bulletin,* #215.

Barrada, M.I., Edwards, L.E., & Hakanson, E.Y. (1979). Antepartum fetal testing: I. The oxytocin challenge test. *American Journal of Obstetrics and Gynecology, 134*(5), 532-537.

Barrett, J.M., Salyer, S.L., & Boehm, F.H. (1981). The nonstress test: An evaluation of 1,000 patients. *American Journal of Obstetrics and Gynecology, 141*(2), 153-157.

Barss, V.A., Benacerraf, B.R., & Frigoletto, F.D. (1984). Second trimester oligohydramnios, a predictor of poor fetal outcome. *Obstetrics and Gynecology, 64*(5), 608-610.

Baskett, T.F. (1988). Gestational age and fetal biophysical assessment. *American Journal of Obstetrics and Gynecology, 158*(2), 332-334.

Beattie, R.B., & Dornan, J.C. (1989). Antenatal screening for intrauterine growth retardation with umbilical artery Doppler ultrasonography. *British Medical Journal, 298,* 631-635.

Benacerraf, B.R., Gelman R., & Frigoletto, F.D. (1988). Sonographically estimated fetal weights: Accuracy and limitation. *American Journal of Obstetrics and Gynecology, 159*(5), 1118-1121.

Benson, C.B., Doubilet, P.M., & Saltzman D.H. (1986). Intrauterine growth retardation: Predictive value of US criteria for antenatal diagnosis. *Radiology, 160*(2), 415-417.

Benson, C.B., Doubilet, P.M., & Saltzman D.H. (1987). Sonographic determination of fetal weights in diabetic pregnancies. *American Journal of Obstetrics and Gynecology, 156*(2), 441-444.

Bissonnette, J.M., Johnson, K., & Toomey, C. (1979). The role of a trial of labor with a positive contraction stress test. *American Journal of Obstetrics and Gynecology, 135*(3), 292-296.

Brace, R.A., & Wolf, E.J. (1989). Normal amniotic fluid volume changes throughout pregnancy. *American Journal of Obstetrics and Gynecology, 161*(2), 382-388.

Brace, R.A. (1994). Amniotic fluid dynamics. In R.K. Creasy & R. Resnik (Eds.), *Maternal-Fetal medicine: Principles and practice* (3rd ed.) (pp. 106-114). Philadelphia: W.B. Saunders Company.

Braly, P., & Freeman, R.K. (1977). The significance of fetal heart rate reactivity with a positive oxytocin challenge test. *Obstetrics and Gynecology, 50*(6), 689-93.

Brar, H.S., Medearis, A.L., DeVore G.R., & Platt, L.D. (1989). A comparative study of fetal umbilical velocimetry with continuous- and pulsed-wave Doppler ultrasonography in high-risk pregnancies: Relationship to outcome. *American Journal of Obstetrics and Gynecology, 160*(2), 375-378.

Brar, H.S., & Platt, L.D. (1988). Reverse end-diastolic flow on umbilical artery velocimetry in high-risk pregnancies: An ominous finding with adverse pregnancy outcome. *American Journal of Obstetrics and Gynecology, 159*(3), 559-561.

Brown, R., & Patrick, J. (1981). The nonstress test: How long is enough? *American Journal of Obstetrics and Gynecology, 141*(6), 646-651.

Bruinse, H.W., Sijmons, E.A., & Reuwer, P.J.H.M. (1989). Clinical value of screening for fetal growth retardation by Doppler ultrasound. *Journal of Ultrasound in Medicine, 8,* 207-209.

Caldeyro-Barcia, R., Mendez-Bauer C., Poseiro J.J., et al. (1996). Control of human fetal heart rate during labor. In D. Cassels (Ed.), *The heart and circulation in the newborn infant.* New York: Grune & Stratton.

Carlan, S.J., & O'Brien W.F. (1991). The effect of magnesium sulfate on the biophysical profile of normal term fetuses. *Obstetrics and Gynecology, 77*(5), 681-684.

Cashner, K.A., Christopher, C.R., & Dysert, G.A. (1987). Spontaneous fetal loss after demonstration of a live fetus in the first trimester. *Obstetrics and Gynecology, 70*(6), 827-830.

Castillo, R.A., DeVoe, L.D., Arthur, M., Searle, N., Methany, W.P., & Ruedrich, D.A. (1989). The preterm nonstress test: Effects of gestational age and length of study. *American Journal of Obstetrics and Gynecology, 160*(1), 172-175.

Centers for Disease Control. (1989). Contribution of birth defects to infant mortality — United States, 1986. *Morbidity & Mortality Weekly Report, 38*(37), 633-635.

Chamberlain, P.F., Manning, F.A., Morrison, I., Harman, C.R., & Lange, I.R. (1984a). Ultrasound evaluation of amniotic fluid volume: I. The relationship of decreased amniotic fluid volumes to perinatal outcome. *American Journal of Obstetrics and Gynecology, 150*(3), 245-249.

Chamberlain, P.F., Manning F.A., Morrison I., Harman C.R., & Lange I.R. (1984b). Ultrasound evaluation of amniotic fluid volume: II. The relationship of increased amniotic fluid volume to perinatal outcome. *American Journal of Obstetrics and Gynecology, 150*(3), 250-254.

Chauhan, S.P., Lutton, P.M., Bailey, K.J., Guerrieri, J.P., & Morrison J.C. (1992). Intrapartum clinical, sonographic, and parous patients' estimates of newborn birth weight. *Obstetrics and Gynecology, 79*(6), 956-958.

Chauhan, S.P., Rutherford, S.E., Sharp, T.W., Carnevale, T.A., & Runzel A.R. (1992). Intrapartum amniotic fluid index and neonatal acidosis. *Journal of Reproductive Medicine, 37*(10), 868-870.

Chitty, L.S., Hunt, G.H., Moore, J., & Lobb, M.O. (1991). Effectiveness of routine ultrasonography in detecting fetal structural abnormalities in a low-risk population. *British Medical Journal, 303,* 1165-1169.

Crane, J.P., LeFevre, M.L., Winborn, R.C., Evans, J.K., Ewigman, B.G., Bain, R.P., Frigoletto, F.D., McNellis, D., & Radius Study Group. (1994). A randomized trial of prenatal ultrasonographic screening: Impact on the detection, management, and outcome of anomalous fetuses. *American Journal of Obstetrics and Gynecology, 171*(2), 392-399.

Croom, C.S., Banian, B.B., Ramos-Santos, E., DeVoe, L.D., Bezhadian, A., & Hiett, K. (1992). Do semiquantitative amniotic fluid indexes reflect actual volume? *American Journal of Obstetrics and Gynecology, 167*(4), 995-999.

Cunningham, F.G., MacDonald, P.C., Gant, N.F., Leveno, K.J., & Gilstrap L.C. (1993). *Williams Obstetrics* (19th ed.). Norwalk, CT: Appleton & Lange.

Davies, J.A., Gallivan, S., & Spencer, J.A.D. (1992). Randomized controlled trial of Doppler ultrasound screening of placental perfusion during pregnancy. *Lancet, 340* (8831), 1299-1303.

Delke, I., Hyatt, R., Feinkind, L., & Minkoff, H. (1988). Avoidable causes of perinatal death at or after term pregnancy in an inner-city hospital: Medical versus social.

American Journal of Obstetrics and Gynecology, 159(3), 562-566.

Devoe, L.D. (1990). The non-stress test. In R.D. Eden & F.H. Boehm (Eds.), *Assessment and care of the fetus: Physiological, clinical, and medicolegal principles.* Norwalk, CT: Appleton & Lange.

Devoe, L.D., Gardner, P., Dear, C., & Castillo, R.A. (1990). The diagnostic values of concurrent nonstress testing, amniotic fluid measurement, and Doppler velocimetry in screening a general high-risk population. *American Journal of Obstetrics and Gynecology, 163*(3), 1040-1048.

Dildy, G.A., Lira, N., Moise, K.J., Riddle, G.D., & Deter, R.L. (1992). Amniotic fluid volume assessment: Comparison of ultrasonographic estimates versus direct measurements with a dye-dilution technique in human pregnancy. *American Journal of Obstetrics and Gynecology, 167*(4), 986-994.

Divon, M.Y., Girz, B.Z., Lieblich, R., & Langer, O. (1989). Clinical management of the fetus with markedly diminished umbilical artery end-diastolic flow. *American Journal of Obstetrics and Gynecology, 161*(6), 1523-1527.

Donald, I., & Brown, T.G. (1961). Demonstration of tissue interfaces within the body by ultrasound echo sounding. *British Journal of Radiology, 34,* 539-546.

Druzin, M.L., Gratacos, J., & Paul, R.H. (1990). Antepartum fetal heart rate testing: VI. Predictive reliability of "normal" tests in the prevention of antepartum death. *American Journal of Obstetrics and Gynecology, 137*(6), 746-747.

Druzin, M.L., Fox, A., Kogut E., & Carlson, C. (1985). The relationship of the non-stress test to gestational age. *American Journal of Obstetrics and Gynecology, 153*(4), 386- 389.

Evertson, L.R., Gauthier, R.J., Schifrin, B.S., & Paul R.H. (1979). Antepartum fetal heart rate testing: I. Evolution of the nonstress test. *American Journal of Obstetrics and Gynecology, 133*(1), 29-33.

Ewigman, B., LeFevre, M., & Hesser, J. (1990). A randomized trial of routine prenatal ultrasound. *American Journal of Obstetrics and Gynecology, 76*(2), 189-194.

Fox, H.E., Inglis J., & Steinbrecher, M. (1979). Fetal breathing movements in uncomplicated pregnancies: I. Relationship to gestational age. *American Journal of Obstetrics and Gynecology, 134*(5), 544-546.

Freeman, R.K., Anderson, G., & Dorchester, W. (1982a). A prospective multi-institutional study of antepartum fetal heart rate monitoring: I. Risk of perinatal mortality and morbidity according to antepartum fetal heart rate test results. *American Journal of Obstetrics and Gynecology, 143*(7), 771-777.

Freeman, R.K., Anderson, G., & Dorchester, W. (1982b). A prospective multi-institutional study of antepartum fetal heart rate monitoring: II. Contraction stress test versus nonstress test for primary surveillance. *American Journal of Obstetrics and Gynecology, 143*(7), 778-780.

Freeman, R.K., Dorchester, W., Anderson, G., & Garite, T. (1985). The significance of a previous stillbirth. *American Journal of Obstetrics and Gynecology, 151*(1), 7-13.

Freeman, R.K., Garite, T.J., & Nageotte, M.P. (1991). *Fetal heart rate monitoring* (2nd ed.). Baltimore: Williams & Wilkins.

Freeman, R.K., Goebelsman, U., Nochimson, D., & Cetrulo, C. (1976). An evaluation of the significance of a positive oxytocin challenge test. *American Journal of Obstetrics and Gynecology, 47*(1), 8-13.

Gagnon, R. (1989). Acoustic stimulation: Effect on heart rate and other biophysical variables. *Clinical Perinatology, 16*(3), 643-660.

Gagnon, R., Campbell, K., Hunse, C., & Patrick, J. (1987). Patterns of human fetal heart rate accelerations from 26 weeks to term. *American Journal of Obstetrics and*

Gynecology, 157(3), 743-748.

Gauthier, R.J., Evertson, L.R., & Paul, R.H. (1979). Antepartum fetal heart rate testing: II. Intrapartum fetal heart rate observation and newborn outcome following a positive contraction stress test. *American Journal of Obstetrics and Gynecology, 133*(1), 34-39.

Giles, W.B., Trudinger, B.J., & Baird, P.J. (1985). Fetal umbilical artery flow velocity waveforms and placental resistance: Pathological correlation. *British Journal of Obstetrics and Gynaecology, 92*, 31-38.

Glantz, J.C., Abramowicz, J.A., & Sherer, D.M. (1994). Significance of idiopathic midtrimester polyhydramnios. *American Journal of Perinatology, 11*(4), 305-308.

Goldstein, S.R. (1992). Significance of cardiac activity on endovaginal ultrasound in very early embryos. *Obstetrics and Gynecology, 80*(4), 670-672.

Grubb, D.K., & Paul, R.H. (1992). Amniotic fluid index and prolonged antepartum fetal heart rate decelerations. *Obstetrics and Gynecology, 79*(4), 558-560.

Grundy, H., Freeman, R.K., Lederman, S., & Dorchester, W. (1984). Nonreactive contraction stress test: Clinical significance. *Obstetrics and Gynecology, 64*(3), 337-342.

Hadlock, F.P., Harrist, R.B., Carpenter, R.J., Deter, R.L., & Park, S.K. (1984). Sonographic estimation of fetal weight. *Radiology, 150*(2), 535-540.

Hadlock, F.P., Harrist, R.B., Sharman, R.S., Deter, R.L., & Park S.K. (1985). Estimation of fetal weight with the use of head, body, and femur measurements — A prospective study. *American Journal of Obstetrics and Gynecology, 151*(3), 333-337.

Halperin, M.E., Fong, K.W., Zalev, A.H., & Goldsmith, C.H. (1985). Reliability of amniotic fluid volume estimation from ultrasonograms: Intraobserver and interobserver variation before and after the establishment of criteria. *American Journal of Obstetrics and Gynecology, 153*(3), 264-267.

Hammacher, K. (1967) In O. Kasser, V. Friedberg, K. Oberk, (Eds.), *Gynekologie v Geburtshilfe BD II.* Stuttgar: Georg Theime Verlag.

Hill, L.M., Breckle, R., Thomas, M.L., & Fries, J.K. (1987). Polyhydramnios: Ultrasonically detected prevalence and neonatal outcome. *Obstetrics and Gynecology, 69*(1), 21-25.

Hon, E.H. (1959). Observations on "pathologic" fetal bradycardia. *American Journal of Obstetrics and Gynecology, 77*(5), 1084-1099.

Horger, E.O., & Tsai, C.C. (1989). Ultrasound and the prenatal diagnosis of congenital anomalies: A medicolegal perspective. *Obstetrics and Gynecology, 74*(4), 617-619.

Huch, A., Huch, R., Schneider, H., & Rooth G. (1977). Continuous transcutaneous monitoring of fetal oxygen tension during labour. *British Journal of Obstetrics and Gynaecology, 84*, 1-39.

Huddleston, J.F., Sutliff, G., Carney, F.E., & Flowers C.E. (1979). Oxytocin challenge test for antepartum fetal assessment. *American Journal of Obstetrics and Gynecology, 135*(5), 609-614.

Keegan, K.A., & Paul, R.H. (1980). Antepartum fetal heart rate testing: IV. The nonstress test as a primary approach. *American Journal of Obstetrics and Gynecology, 136*(1), 75-80.

Kirkup, B., & Welch, G. (1990). "Normal but dead": Perinatal mortality in non-malformed babies of birthweight 2.5 kg and over in the Northern Region in 1983. *British Journal of Obstetrics and Gynaecology, 97*, 381-392.

Lammer, E.J., Brown, L.E., Anderka, M.T., & Guyer B. (1989). Classification and analysis of fetal deaths in Massachusetts. *Journal of the American Medical Association, 261*(12), 1757-1762.

LeFevre, M.L., Bain, R.P., Ewigman B.G., Frigoletto, F.D., Crane, J.P., McNellis, D., & Radius Study Group (1993). A randomized trial of prenatal ultrasonographic screening: Impact on maternal management and outcome. *American Journal of Obstetrics and Gynecology, 169*(3), 483-489.

Levi, C.S., Lyons, E.A., Zheng, X.H., Lindsay, D.J., & Holt S.C. (1990). Endovaginal US: Demonstration of cardiac activity in embryos of less than 5.0 mm in crown-rump length. *Radiology, 176*(1), 71-74.

Levi, S., Jyjazi ,Y., Schaaps, J.P., Defoort, P., Coulon, R., & Buekens, P. (1991). Sensitivity and specificity of routine antenatal screening for congenital anomalies by ultrasound: The Belgian multicentric study. *Ultrasound Obstetrics and Gynecology, 1*, 102-110.

Lin, C.C., Moawad, H.H., River, P., & Pishotta, F.T. (1980). An OCT-reactivity classification to predict fetal outcome. *Obstetrics and Gynecology, 56*(1), 17-23.

Lindsay, D.J., Lovett, I.S., Lyons, E.A., Levi, C.S., Zheng, X.N., Holt, S.C., & Dashefsky, S.M.(1992). Yolk sac diameter and shape at endovaginal US: Predictors of pregnancy outcome in the first trimester. *Radiology, 183*(1), 115-118.

Magann, E.F., Nolan, T.E., Hess, W., Martin, R.W., Whitworth, N.S., & Morrison J.C. (1992). Measurement of amniotic fluid volume: Accuracy of ultrasonography techniques. *American Journal of Obstetrics and Gynecology, 167*(6), 1533-1537.

Manchester, D.K., Pretorius, D.H., Avery, C., Manco-Johnson, M.L., Wiggins, J., Meier, P.R., & Clewell, W.H. (1988). Accuracy of ultrasound diagnoses in pregnancies complicated by suspected fetal anomalies. *Prenatal Diagnosis, 8*, 109-117.

Manning, F.A. (1995a). Chapter two: The fetal heart rate: Antepartum and intrapartum regulation and clinical significance. In *Fetal medicine: Principles and practice*. Norwalk, CT: Appleton & Lange.

Manning, F.A. (1995b). Chapter six: Fetal biophysical profile scoring: Theoretical considerations and clinical application. In *Fetal medicine: Principles and practice*. Norwalk, CT: Appleton & Lange.

Manning, F.A., Harman, C.R., Morrison, I., Menticoglou, S.M., Lange, I.R., & Johnson, J.M. (1990a). Fetal assessment based on fetal biophysical profile scoring: IV. An analysis of perinatal morbidity and mortality. *American Journal of Obstetrics and Gynecology, 162*(3), 703-709.

Manning, F.A., Morrison, I., Harman, C.R., & Menticoglou, S.M. (1990b). The abnormal fetal biophysical profile score: V. Predictive accuracy according to score composition. *American Journal of Obstetrics and Gynecology, 162*(4), 918-927.

Manning, F.A., Lange, I.R., Morrison, I., & Harman, C.R. (1984). Fetal biophysical profile score and the nonstress test: A comparative trial. *Obstetrics and Gynecology, 64*(3), 326-331.

Manning, F.A., Morrison, I., Harman, C.R., & Chamberlain, P.F.C. (1987). Fetal biophysical profile scoring: Selective use of the nonstress test. *American Journal of Obstetrics and Gynecology, 156*(3), 709-712.

Manning, F.A., Platt, L.D., & Sipos, L. (1980). Antepartum fetal evaluation: Development of a fetal biophysical profile. *American Journal of Obstetrics and Gynecology, 136*(6), 787-795.

Manning, F.A., Snijders, R., Harman, C.R., Nicolaides, K., Menticoglou, S., & Morrison, I. (1993). Fetal biophysical profile score: VI. Correlation with antepartum umbilical venous fetal pH. *American Journal of Obstetrics and Gynecology, 169*(4), 755-763.

Maulik, D. (1995). Doppler ultrasound velocimetry for fetal surveillance. *Clinical Obstetrics and Gynecology, 38*(1), 91-111.

Maulik, D., Yarlagadda, P., Youngblood, J.P., & Ciston P. (1990). The diagnostic efficacy of the umbilical arterial systolic/diastolic ratio as a screening tool: A prospective blinded study. *American Journal of Obstetrics and Gynecology, 162*(6), 1518-1525.

Mercer, L.J., & Brown, L.G. (1986). Fetal outcome with oligohydramnios in the second trimester. *Obstetrics and Gynecology, 67*(6), 840-842.

Mersey Region Working Party on Perinatal Mortality. (1982). Confidential inquiry into perinatal deaths in the Mersey region. *Lancet,* (1, Part 1), 491-494.

Moore, T.R., & Cayle, J.E. (1990). The amniotic fluid index in normal human pregnancy. *American Journal of Obstetrics and Gynecology, 162*(5), 1168-1173.

Murata, Y., Martin, C.B., Ikenoue, T., Tadashi, H., Taira, S., Sagawa, T., & Sakata, H. (1982). Fetal heart rate accelerations and late decelerations during the course of intrauterine death in chronically catheterized rhesus monkeys. *American Journal of Obstetrics and Gynecology, 144*(2), 218-223.

Naeye, R.L. (1987). Causes of perinatal mortality in the United States. Collaborative perinatal project. *Journal of the American Medical Association, 238*(3), 228-229.

Nageotte, M., Towers, C.V., Asrat, T., Freeman, R.K., & Dorchester, W. (1994). The value of a negative antepartum test: Contraction stress test and modified biophysical profile. *Obstetrics and Gynecology, 84*(2), 231-234.

Nageotte, M., Towers, C.V., Asrat, T., & Freeman R.K. (1994). Perinatal outcome with the modified biophysical profile. *American Journal of Obstetrics and Gynecology, 170*(6), 1672-1676.

Natale, R., Nasello, C., & Turliuk, R. (1984). The relationship between movements and accelerations in fetal heart rate at twenty-four to thirty-two weeks' gestation. *American Journal of Obstetrics and Gynecology, 148*(5), 591-595.

Neilson, J.P. (1994). Doppler ultrasound in high risk pregnancies, Review 03889. In M.W. Enkin, M.J.N.C. Keirse, M.J. Renfrew, & J.P. Nielson (Eds.), *Pregnancy and childbirth module, Cochrane database of systematic reviews.* Oxford: Update Software, Cochrane Updates on Disk, Disk issue 1.

Newnham, J.P., O'Dea, M.R.A., Reid, K.P., & Diepeveen, D.A. (1991). Doppler flow velocity waveform analysis in high risk pregnancies: A randomized controlled trial. *British Journal of Obstetrics and Gynaecology, 98,* 957-963.

Nyberg, D.A., Mahony, B.S., & Pretorius, D.H. (1990). *Diagnostic ultrasound of fetal anomalies: Text and atlas.* Chicago: Year Book Medical Publishers.

Parer, J.T., Krueger, T.R., & Harris, J.L. (1980). Fetal oxygen consumption and mechanisms of heart rate response during artificially produced late decelerations of fetal heart rate in sheep. *American Journal of Obstetrics and Gynecology, 136*(4), 478- 482.

Peaceman, A.M., Meyer, B.A., Thorp, J.A., Parisi, V.M., & Creasy, R.K. (1989). The effect of magnesium sulfate tocolysis on the fetal biophysical profile. *American Journal of Obstetrics and Gynecology, 161*(3), 771-774.

Peters, L.L.H., Sheldon, R.E., Jones, M.D., Makowski, E.L., & Meschia, G. (1979). Blood flow to fetal organs as a function of arterial oxygen content. *American Journal of Obstetrics and Gynecology, 135*(5), 637-646.

Phelan, J.P. (1981). The nonstress test: A review of 3,000 tests. *American Journal of Obstetrics and Gynecology, 139*(1), 7-10.

Phelan, J.P., Ahn, M.O., Smith, C.V., Rutherford, S.E., & Anderson, E. (1987). Amniotic fluid index measurements during pregnancy. *Journal of Reproductive Medicine, 32*(8), 601-604.

Platt, L.D., Walla, C.A., Paul, R.H., Trujillo, M.E., Loesser, C.V., Jacobs, N.D., & Broussard, P.M. (1985). A prospective trial of the fetal biophysical profile versus the nonstress test in the management of high-risk pregnancies. *American Journal of Obstetrics and Gynecology, 153*(6), 624-633.

Pretorius, D.H., & Nyberg, D.A. (1990). An overview of congenital malformations. In D.A. Nyberg, B.S. Mahoney, & D.H. Pretorius (Eds.), *Diagnostic ultrasound of fetal anomalies: Text and atlas* (pp. 21-37). Chicago: Year Book Medical Publishers.

Public Health Service. (1988). *Vital statistics of the United States. Vol II — Mortality, 1986.* Washington, DC: U.S. Department of Health and Human Services.

Romero, R., Pilu, G., Jeanty, P., Ghidini, A., & Hobbins, J.C. (1988). *Prenatal diagnosis of congenital anomalies.* Norwalk, CT: Appleton & Lange.

Saari-Kemppainen, A., Karjalainen, O., Ylostalo, P., & Heinonen, O.P. (1990). Ultrasound screening and perinatal mortality: Controlled trial of systemic one-stage screening in pregnancy. *Lancet, 336,* 387-391.

Sarno, A.P., Ahn, M.O., Brar, H.S., Phelan, J.P., & Platt, L.D. (1989). Intrapartum Doppler velocimetry, amniotic fluid volume, and fetal heart rate as predictors of subsequent fetal distress. *American Journal of Obstetrics and Gynecology, 161*(6), 1508-1514.

Shepard, M.J., Richards, V.A., Berkowitz, R.L., Warsof, S.L., & Hobbins, J.C. (1982). An evaluation of two equations for predicting fetal weight by ultrasound. *American Journal of Obstetrics and Gynecology, 142*(1), 47-54.

Shirley, I.M., Bottomley, F., & Robinson, V.P. (1992). Routine radiographer screening for fetal abnormalities by ultrasound in an unselected low risk population. *British Journal of Radiology, 65*(775), 564-569.

Sijmons, E.A., Reuwer, P.J.H.M., VanBeek, E., & Bruinse, H.W. (1989). The validity of screening for small-for-gestational age and low-birth-weight-for-length infants by Doppler ultrasound. *British Journal of Obstetrics and Gynaecology, 96,* 557-561.

Sivit, C.J., Hill, M.C., Larsen, J.W., & Lande, I.M. (1987). Second-trimester polyhydramnios: Evaluation with US. *Radiology, 165*(2), 467-469.

Slomka, C., & Phelan J.P. (1981). Pregnancy outcome in the patient with a nonreactive nonstress test and a positive contraction stress test. *American Journal of Obstetrics and Gynecology, 139*(1), 11-15.

Smith, C.V. (1995). Vibroacoustic stimulation. *Clinical Obstetrics and Gynecology, 38*(1), 68-77.

Smith, C.V., Nguyen, H.N., Phelan, J.P., & Paul, R.H. (1986). Intrapartum assessment of fetal well-being: A comparison of fetal acoustic stimulation with acid base determinations. *American Journal of Obstetrics and Gynecology, 155*(4), 726-728.

Stubblefield, P.G., & Berek, J.S. (1980). Perinatal mortality in term and post-term births. *Obstetrics and Gynecology, 56*(6), 676-682.

Timor-Tritsch, I.E., Dierker, L.J., Hertz, R.H., & Rosen, M.G. (1978). Fetal movements associated with fetal heart rate accelerations and decelerations. *American Journal of Obstetrics and Gynecology, 131*(3), 276-280.

Trudinger, B.J., Cook, C.M., Jones, L., & Giles, W.B. (1986) A comparison of fetal heart rate monitoring and umbilical artery waveforms in the recognition of fetal compromise. *British Journal of Obstetrics and Gynaecology, 93,* 171-175.

Tyrrell, S.N., Lilford, R.J., MacDonald, H.N., Nelson, E.J., Porter, J., & Gupta, J.K. (1990). Randomized comparison of routine versus highly selective use of Doppler ultrasound and biophysical scoring to investigate high risk pregnancies. *American Journal of Obstetrics and Gynecology, 97,* 909-916.

Varma, T.R., Bateman, S., Patel, R.H., Chamberlain, G.V.P., & Pillai, U. (1988). The relationship of amniotic fluid volume to perinatal outcome. *International Journal of Obstetrics and Gynecology, 27,* 327-333.

Vintzileos, A.M., Campbell, W.A., Ingardia, C.J., & Nochimson, D.J. (1983). The fetal biophysical profile and its predictive value. *Obstetrics and Gynecology, 62*(3), 271-278.

Vintzileos, A.M., Flemming, A.D., Scorza, W.E., Wolf, E.J., Balducci, J., Campbell, W.A., & Rodis, J.F. (1991). Relationship between fetal biophysical activities and umbilical cord blood gas values. *American Journal of Obstetrics and Gynecology, 165*(3), 707-713.

Ware, D.J., & DeVoe, L.D. (1994). The nonstress test: Reassessment of the "gold standard." *Clinical Perinatology, 21*(4), 779-796.

Warsof, S.L., Gohari, P., Berkowitz, R.L., & Hobbins, J.C. (1977). The estimation of fetal weight by computer-assisted analysis. *American Journal of Obstetrics and Gynecology, 128*(8), 881-892.

Watson, W.J., Soisson, A.P., & Harlass, F.E. (1988). Estimated weight of the term fetus: Accuracy of ultrasound versus clinical examination. *Journal of Reproductive Medicine, 33*(4), 369-371.

Weeks, J.W., Asrat, T., Morgan, M.A., Nageotte, M., Thomas, S.J., & Freeman, R.K. (1995). Antepartum surveillance for a history of stillbirth: When to begin? *American Journal of Obstetrics and Gynecology, 172*(2, Part 1), 486-492.

Whittle, M.J., Hanretty, K.P., Primrose, M.H., & Neilson, J.P. (1994). Screening for the compromised fetus: A randomized trial of umbilical artery velocimetry in unselected patients. *American Journal of Obstetrics and Gynecology, 170*(2), 555-559.

Wilson, R.D., Kendrick, V., Wittman, B.K., & McGillivray, B. (1986). Spontaneous abortion and pregnancy outcome after normal first-trimester ultrasound examination. *Obstetrics and Gynecology, 67*(3), 352-355.

Woo, J.S.K., Liang, S.T., & Lo, R.L.S. (1987). Significance of an absent or reversed end diastolic flow in Doppler umbilical artery waveforms. *Journal of Ultrasound Medicine, 6,* 291-297.

Chapter 7

Genetics and Pregnancy Loss

Devereux N. Saller, Jr.
Judy Garza

The role of the geneticist or genetic counselor in counseling women or couples who have experienced pregnancy loss has grown in recent years, as etiologies of pregnancy loss are becoming better understood. When information — including pertinent personal or family medical history, clinical or laboratory data, or autopsy findings — is available to suggest a specific diagnosis, genetic counseling can be critical to the couple's understanding of what happened and to their grieving for their baby. Moreover, when a specific diagnosis is not available, genetic counseling may be of value for patients, because genetic counseling can relieve anxieties brought on by a "fear of the unknown" that a genetic diagnosis may cause.

The role of genetic etiologies for pregnancy loss is highlighted by the statistics involved. It is widely accepted that first-trimester pregnancy losses include a significant percentage of early pregnancies. Although exact figures vary, depending on how the studies were performed, 12% to 43% of conceptions result in first-trimester spontaneous pregnancy loss (Edmonds, Lindsey, Miller, Williamson, & Wood, 1982; Miller, Williamson, & Glue, 1980). Theoretical estimates suggest that as many as 78% of conceptuses actually may be lost (Roberts & Lowe, 1975). Many of these pregnancy losses are not recognized at the time. For couples who anxiously are awaiting pregnancy, however, these pregnancy losses may be recognized and grieved for with as much anguish and intensity as are pregnancy losses which occur in later trimesters.

As a pregnancy progresses, loss rates decrease markedly in contrast with those of the first trimester. In the United States, perinatal loss rate is reported as the perinatal mortality rate (the statistical accumulation of neonatal

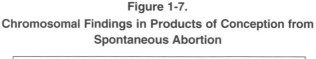

Figure 1-7.
Chromosomal Findings in Products of Conception from
Spontaneous Abortion

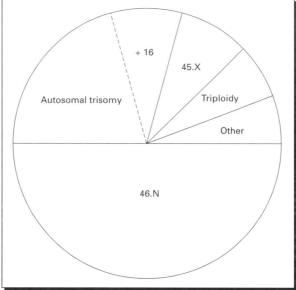

Source: Kajii, T., Ferrier, A., Niikawa, N., Takahara, H., Ohama, K., &
Avirachan, S. (1980). Anatomic and chromosomal anomalies in 639
spontaneous abortuses. *Human Genetics, 55,* 87-98.

deaths and fetal deaths occurring after 20 weeks). Although perinatal mortality in the United States has decreased significantly over the past few decades, it remains greater than 1% of live births plus fetal deaths (Cunningham, MacDonald, Gant, Leveno, & Gilstrap, 1993).

When pregnancy results in a live birth, there remains an incidence of congenital malformations of approximately 3%. Although this figure is much higher than generally is appreciated by the general population, it remains unchanged, and this is unlikely to decrease despite technological advances in prenatal diagnosis and fetal surveillance. When a live birth occurs with significant genetic abnormalities, the family may need to make important and difficult medical decisions, some of which involve life-and-death issues. Additionally, even if the genetic abnormalities are not life-threatening, a grieving process may occur which mirrors that which is associated with a fetal or newborn death. Such losses may be viewed, from a psychological standpoint, as the loss of an expected perfect baby. Additionally, the family may feel guilt over their grief, a complex state which must be resolved somehow. In this chapter, the authors discuss etiologies of genetic loss and challenges which are unique to counseling patients with a genetic etiology associated with their pregnancy loss. A glossary of terms is provided at the end of this chapter.

Genetic Etiologies of First-Trimester Loss

Genetic causes for pregnancy loss have been studied for many years. The reader is encouraged to review Chapter 2, "The Biology of Early Pregnancy Loss" for discussion of this topic. Data generated as long ago as the 1950s have suggested that many early pregnancy losses may be related to malformations or genetic causes (Hertig, Rock, & Adams, 1954). In fact, approximately 50% of first-trimester losses may be due to chromosomal abnormalities (Kajii et al., 1980) (see Figure 1-7). Moreover, the demise of chromosomally or morphologically abnormal fetuses occurs at a much higher rate than occurs in pregnancies that are without genetic abnormalities. Thus, genetic diagnoses will be found in a larger proportion of pregnancies that are lost, at all gestational ages, than are found in healthy liveborns.

In first-trimester pregnancy loss, the fetus may provide only limited visible features. Moreover, the loss may manifest itself weeks after the death of the fetus itself. For these reasons, examination of the products of first-trimester pregnancy loss may provide only limited morphologic information. Nevertheless, examination by an experienced pathologist can reveal important information. For years, it has been understood that chromosomal abnormalities make up a significant proportion of first-trimester spontaneous pregnancy losses. Recently, it has been suggested that routine examination of spontaneous abortion specimens is cost effective (Wolf & Horger, 1995).

Chromosomal abnormalities can be classified into several categories, with regard to first-trimester pregnancy loss. Most first-trimester pregnancy losses resulting from chromosomal abnormalities are trisomies (Kajii et al., 1980). This condition results from an additional chromosome in each cell of the fetus and placenta, in addition to the normal 46 chromosomes which are found in each cell. Any of the 22 autosomal chromosomes or the sex chromosomes, X or Y, can be found as the extra chromosome in a first-

Figure 2-7.

Chromosomal Complements in Spontaneous Abortions: Recognized Clinically in the First Trimester

Complement	Percentage	Complement	Percentage
Normal		**Autosomal trisomy**	22.3
46,XX or 46,XY	54.1	Chromosome	
		No. 1	0
Triploidy	7.7	No. 2	1.11
69,XXX	(2.7)	No. 3	0.25
69,XYX	(0.2)	No. 4	0.64
69,XXY	(4.0)	No. 5	0.04
Other	(0.8)	No. 6	0.14
		No. 7	0.89
Tetraploidy	2.6	No. 8	0.79
92,XXXX	(1.5)	No. 9	0.72
92,XXYY	(0.55)	No. 10	0.36
Not stated	(0.55)	No. 11	0.04
		No. 12	0.18
Monosomy X	8.6	No. 13	1.07
		No. 14	0.82
Structural abnormalities	1.5	No. 15	1.68
		No. 16	7.27
Sex chromosomal polysomy	0.2	No. 17	0.18
47,XXX	(0.05)	No. 18	1.15
47,XXY	(0.15)	No. 19	0.01
		No. 20	0.61
Autosomal monosomy (G)	0.1	No. 21	2.11
		No. 22	2.26
		Double trisomy	0.7
		Mosaic trisomy	1.3
		Other abnormalities or not specified	0.9

Source: Simpson, J.L., & Bombord, A.T. (1987). Chromosomal abnormalities in spontaneous abortion: Frequency, pathology, and genetic counseling. In K. Edmonds & M.J. Bennett (Eds.), *Spontaneous abortion.* London: Blackwell.

trimester pregnancy loss. Statistically, the most common autosomal trisomy in first-trimester pregnancy losses is trisomy 16. In contrast, trisomy 16 essentially never is found in a second- or third-trimester pregnancy loss or in a live birth (see Figure 2-7).

Chromosomal trisomies are thought to occur by nondisjunction, failure of chromosomes to be distributed evenly when cells divide during meiosis or mitosis. Although any chromosome can be involved in a nondisjunctional event resulting in an extra or missing chromosome in the egg or sperm, certain chromosomal abnormalities are found only in very early pregnancies, while some are very rarely, if ever, found at all. In contrast, specific autosomal aneuploidies may be found throughout pregnancy and actually may result in a live birth. For example, trisomy 21 (Down syndrome, 1/800 live births), trisomy 13 (Patau syndrome, 1/20,000 live births), and trisomy 18 (Edwards syndrome, 1/8,000 live births) can result in live birth (Hook & Hamerton, 1977). Sex chromosome aneuploidies also may be found throughout gestation and may result in live births. Other chromosomal abnormalities, including trisomy 16, are common in the first trimester and may be a common etiology for first-trimester losses, but they rarely are found later than the first trimester.

All chromosomal abnormalities appear to have an increased rate of pregnancy loss associated with them, compared with chromosomally normal pregnancies. This has been documented best for the autosomal trisomies mentioned above, in which the chance of pregnancy loss following second-trimester diagnosis of trisomy 21 is 25.6% (Hook, Topol, & Cross, 1989), while the chance of pregnancy loss following second-trimester diagnosis of trisomy 18 is 63.8% (Hook et al., 1989). Monosomy X, or Turner syndrome, is the absence of one of the sex chromosomes. Individuals with Turner syndrome have 45 chromosomes, including only one of the sex chromosomes, an X. Monosomy X or Turner syndrome is common in the first trimester, with the vast majority (95% to 99%) not surviving to live birth. In fact, monosomy accounts for approximately 20% to 25% of chromosomally abnormal first-trimester pregnancy losses (see Figure 3-7).

However, a significant number of monosomy X fetuses survive to live births and to adulthood (1/10,000) (Hook & Hamerton, 1977). In the first trimester, some monosomy X fetuses will be diagnosed by ultrasound to have cystic hygroma, lymph-filled, sac-like structures along the back of the fetal neck. Others may have no morphologic abnormalities at all. Monosomy X may be associated also with fetal nonimmune hydrops, congenital heart defects, or congenital renal disease. Fetuses which survive are thought to have less severe morphologic abnormalities. Monosomy X is unique among aneuploidies which are compatible with live birth, in that monosomy X is unlikely to recur in subsequent pregnancies, in contradistinction to other chromosomal abnormalities.

Polyploidy also is noted frequently in association with first-trimester pregnancy loss. Normally, each parent contributes 23 chromosomes, half of their genetic material, to the diploid pregnancy. Polyploidy results from conception involving an extra set (or sets) of chromosomes. For example,

Figure 3-7.
Iceberg of Chromosomal Pregnancy Loss

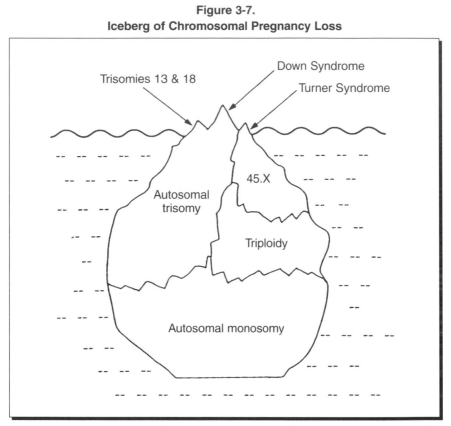

From *Chromosome Abnormalities and Genetic Counseling* second edition by R.J.M. Gardner & G.R. Sutherland. Copyright. Used by permission of Oxford University Press.

in triploidy, the fetus has 69 chromosomes, rather than the normal 46. Tetraploid pregnancies have 92 chromosomes. There are a variety of mechanisms by which polyploidy is thought to occur, including fertilization by two sperms, fertilization by a diploid sperm, or fertilization of a diploid egg. Triploid pregnancies may be associated with molar degeneration of the placenta.

It is appreciated now that partial moles, which are usually triploid, involve a fetus in association with an abnormal placenta. These pregnancies differ from complete moles or hydatidiform moles, which demonstrate no fetal development and which rarely have a triploid karyotype. Although complete moles are euploid (46 chromosomes), all chromosomes are derived from paternal cell lines. Unlike partial moles, complete moles have the potential to develop into choriocarcinoma.

Chromosomal abnormalities, involving an exchange of chromosomal material between chromosomes, are a common cause of pregnancy loss. This exchange may be balanced or unbalanced between the chromosomes. In balanced rearrangements, there is no net loss or gain of genetic material, although the "breakpoints" may fall in critical regions of the genome. In unbalanced rearrangements, there is genetic material lost ("deleted") or gained ("duplicated"), or both. Unbalanced rearrangements often are associated with phenotypic abnormalities, while balanced rearrangements only are associated with phenotypic abnormalities, when they occur spontaneously (and therefore are not inherited from a parent). Structural rearrangements include translocations and inversions which may be balanced or unbalanced. Translocations may be of two types. Robertsonian translocations result from the centromeric fusion of two acrocentric chromosomes (including chromosomes 13, 14, 15, 21, or 22). Reciprocal translocations result from an exchange of genetic material between any two (or more) chromosomes. Additionally, deletions and insertions are unbalanced inherently.

Although other genetic etiologies for first-trimester loss are not as well understood as are chromosomal abnormalities, they undoubtedly exist. It is logical that enzymes involved in embryologic development also may be subject to genetic abnormalities. When this occurs, a first-trimester or even later pregnancy loss may occur when this critical enzyme is needed, but is not available. Unfortunately, a complete understanding of this issue or the ability to test for these enzyme defects during pregnancy is not possible. A family history always should be taken, and, when multiple pregnancy losses are noted, more complete evaluation or possible genetic referral is appropriate.

Genetic Etiologies of Perinatal Death

Perinatal death is defined as a pregnancy loss which occurs after 20 weeks of gestation. This may take the form of stillbirth or neonatal death within the first 28 days of life. The perinatal death rate in the United States is approximately 13.7 deaths per 1,000 live births (1989 data) (Cunningham et al., 1993). These deaths are approximately equally divided between fetal and neonatal deaths.

If a pregnancy loss occurs after 20 weeks, there usually is a well-developed fetus for examination. This provides more clinical and pathologic information to be discerned following a perinatal death, and there is more opportunity to determine a definitive diagnosis than is possible with first-trimester pregnancy losses. Genetic causes for late perinatal loss remain an important contributing etiology, even in later gestational loss. Although the rate of chromosomal anomalies is not as high as in first-trimester losses, approximately 5% to 7% of stillbirths which occur during the third trimester are demonstrated to have chromosomal abnormalities (Gustavson & Jorulf, 1976). Even when no visible abnormalities are seen, chromosomal anomalies may occur. When morphologic abnormalities are present, chromosomal abnormalities are even more common.

Perinatal deaths associated with morphologically and karyotypically normal fetuses are not understood entirely. It is understandable that pregnancy loss may occur in conjunction with structural abnormalities that are required for fetal development. Examples of this might include fetuses with absence of kidney development, in which there is lack of amniotic fluid from failure of fetal urination; this produces umbilical cord compression and fetal death. On the other hand, pregnancy loss may occur in conjunction with morphologic abnormalities that have no obvious impact on fetal development. Examples of this include the increased rate of pregnancy loss in fetuses with congenital heart defects (despite the fact that many of these defects are not critical in the fetal circulation). These losses may result from components of genetic syndromes that currently are not well understood. Therefore, complete evaluation of the fetus and placenta in the case of a perinatal death is very important. When an evaluation is carried out appropriately, it is possible to provide the most accurate possible etiologic and recurrence information to the couple.

Medical Evaluation of a Pregnancy Loss

When a pregnancy loss occurs in the first trimester, visual examination of the conception may provide only limited anatomic information. However, all tissue always should be sent to the laboratory and, if particular concerns have been raised by an appropriate family history, these concerns should be related to the pathologist. Whether chromosomal analysis of the first-trimester pregnancy loss is necessary or not should be discussed by obstetric care providers and the pathologist, as well. Since first-trimester losses commonly are the result of chromosomal abnormalities, the finding of a chromosomal abnormality does not necessarily influence later counseling the way it would if the loss were to occur during the second or third trimester of pregnancy or during the newborn period. It has been suggested that routine karyotyping of first-trimester spontaneous losses is cost effective (Wolf & Horger, 1995). The premise is that, if a karyotypic abnormality is found, it may eliminate the need for a variety of laboratory studies performed later in the work-up of repetitive pregnancy loss (see Figure 4-7).

When pregnancy loss occurs later in gestation and there is a fetus to examine, it is important that all obstetric findings be well-documented. This includes the clinical obstetric course involving the pregnancy loss (prenatal problems, clinical presentation, and obstetric findings), as well as the condition of the fetus and placenta and any abnormalities which were noted at the time of delivery. Documentation by obstetric care providers is critical, even if pediatric staff are present. It is critical that pediatric impressions correlate, when possible, with the obstetric history. All specimens should be evaluated by the pathologist, even when a good clinical evaluation appears to demonstrate the cause of the pregnancy loss. Other abnormalities will be found in a significant percentage of the cases (Saller, Lesser, Harrel, Rogers, & Oyer, 1995). It is important that obstetric care providers document their findings and communicate these to the pathologist, so that appropriate testing may be arranged.

Karyotypic evaluation of pregnancy losses is important; in fact, it may alter future counseling dramatically. Some authorities limit chromosome analysis of a pregnancy loss to those cases in which a morphologic abnormality of the fetus or newborn is noted. This is controversial and should be discussed with the pathologist who will be performing the evaluation.

A complete autopsy is critically important. Although it may be awkward to encourage parents to consent to a perinatal autopsy, it is important to understand that, if information as to possible causes is to be gained from the pregnancy loss, the only time that it can be obtained is at the time of the loss. Families may refuse an autopsy, but frequently later they will wish that they had agreed to it when the etiology and the recurrence risk are found to be based on incomplete information.

Optimal components of a perinatal autopsy have not been established. A complete autopsy should include review of the clinical record; examination of the external body; examination of the brain, thorax, abdomen, and pelvic cavity; and microscopic examination of all major organs. Additionally, examination of the placenta is extremely important, because this can contain evidence of a variety of fetal diseases, as well as evidence

Figure 4-7.
Sample Prenatal Genetic Screen

Name: _____ Date of birth:_____

Occupation: _____

	Yes	No
Do you or your partner have any birth defects?	___	___

Has anyone in your family or your partner's family ever had:

	Yes	No
Down syndrome (mongolism)	___	___
Spina bifida, anencephaly, or hydrocephaly	___	___
Congenital (born with) heart defects	___	___
Hemophilia or bleeding disorder	___	___
Muscular dystrophy	___	___
Cystic fibrosis	___	___
Schizophrenia or manic depression	___	___
Cleft lip or palate	___	___
Deafness (difficulty hearing)	___	___
Blindness (difficulty seeing)	___	___
Mental retardation	___	___
Learning disabilities	___	___
Other birth defects or genetic diseases	___	___

Is your (or your partner's) ethnic ancestry:

	Yes	No
Black (African-American)	___	___
Eastern European Jewish	___	___
Italian	___	___
Greek	___	___
Southeast Asian (Laotian, Vietnamese, Cambodian, Thai, etc.)	___	___
Hispanic (Puerto Rican, etc.)	___	___
Other:_____		

	Yes	No
Are you and your partner related by blood? (Are you cousins or otherwise related?)	___	___
Have you had more than two pregnancy losses? (miscarriages or stillbirths)	___	___

How much to do you smoke? (packs per day) _____

How much alcohol, wine, or beer do you drink? (drinks per day) _____

	Yes	No
Do you use cocaine?	___	___
Do you take any medicines on a regular basis? What are they?_____	___	___
Are you exposed to toxic chemicals at work?	___	___
Is there anything else that you are concerned about?	___	___

During Pregnancy:

	Yes	No
Have you had a fever of more than 102 degrees?	___	___
Have you been exposed to chicken pox?	___	___
Have you been exposed to rubella (German measles)?	___	___
Have you been exposed to other viruses?	___	___

Source: University of Rochester, Division of Pediatric Genetics

of infection. As part of the autopsy, weights and measurements of the body and individual organs should be obtained. X-rays may be very helpful in evaluating structural anomalies and skeletal dysplasias. Bacterial and viral cultures and cytogenetic studies vary by institution, but these should be considered if indicated by visual inspection or microscopic findings. Readers are encouraged to review Chapter 11, "Value of the Perinatal Autopsy," for a more complete discussion of this topic.

In a significant number of cases, a perinatal autopsy provides information about pathologies that were not suspected clinically (Saller et al., 1995). In the cited study, 44.7% of conclusive autopsies altered the clinical diagnosis. The revised final diagnosis then influenced future counseling, not only of etiology, but also of recurrence risk.

At the time of a perinatal loss, photographs of the fetus, even if the body is macerated or severely malformed, are useful in several ways. Photographs may be especially useful in situations when consent to conduct an autopsy is denied. Photographic records, if only those which may be obtained under less-than-ideal conditions in the delivery room, offer documentation of clinical findings. Many pathologists routinely take photographs for documentation and later referral. When an autopsy request is refused, or if the pathologist does not take photographs routinely, photographs should be taken in the delivery room for all cases of stillbirths. These photographs may play an equally important role for the grieving process (see Chapter 3, "Pregnancy Loss Counseling: The Challenge to the Obstetrician").

Unique Aspects of Genetic-Related Pregnancy Loss

For many couples, pregnancy itself often produces a psychosocial crisis. Pregnancy forces the couple to redefine their relationship as they anticipate the transition from their adult pairing into an expanded family unit. This event can alter marital, relational, and gender balances, leading to new interactional patterns. This transition also can strain the coping skills of a family. Because pregnancy so often is portrayed as easy and straightforward in our society, the loss of a baby can isolate the couple, and deprive them of needed social support. They may feel that they no longer have a place in the community of families.

Pregnancy loss profoundly affects women in particular. The fetus not only is a physical part of the woman's body, but also it is perceived in the beginning to be more of the mother's self than a separate person.

Pregnancy has powerful psychological impact because it gives women a sense of identity as a creator, confirms femininity through reproduction, and provides a sense of immortality into the next generation. Pregnancy loss easily may be understood as a narcissistic loss. Emptiness, low self-esteem, and unbearable helplessness are the results of the loss of a piece of a woman's self (Leon, 1992).

The first trimester traditionally is considered as a time when women start to bond with a pregnancy. Men do not experience pregnancy directly, although they may appreciate empathetically the woman's nausea, vomiting, or fatigue. A man's bonding with his prospective offspring may not really begin until the woman starts to show more visible signs of pregnancy, when there are detectable fetal movements. As the woman approaches term, the difference between women and men in bonding to the pregnancy usually decreases. Still, the discrepancy between the sexes' bonding may be accentuated by a pregnancy loss, especially in the first trimester, when more attention and expressions of condolences are focused on the woman.

For most couples, difficulties dealing with a pregnancy loss alone are profound. Grief can be complicated when genetic factors have contributed to the pregnancy's failed outcome. Many individuals consider their genetic composition as a most fundamental aspect of self. Thus, a "genetic defect" which has resulted in a pregnancy loss may be internalized inappropriately, as a sense of failure as a parent. Even though pregnancy loss due to a genetic condition may be no more preventable or predictable than any other type of pregnancy loss, the guilt of carrying a "genetic defect" may make the grieving process more difficult.

The guilt may be further accentuated in cases where known fetal anomalies necessitate consideration of termination of the pregnancy. In these circumstances, the loss can create several layers of grief. Loss of the expected "perfect baby" is one source of grief. The parents also may be faced with the decision as to whether or not to terminate the desired pregnancy, either for personal or family reasons. For the couple, this issue may force them to confront personal, societal, or religious conflicts about pregnancy termination. Their guilt may be intensified by a perception of other individuals who have undergone a pregnancy loss and who consider the option of terminating any pregnancy as completely unacceptable. Guilt also may be related to a sense of responsibility or to unresolved issues concerning a similarly affected relative or a previous pregnancy outcome or other existing offspring.

Depression and guilt are two of the many emotional responses to pregnancy loss. In one study of families who had terminated after a prenatal diagnosis of fetal abnormality (Blumberg, Golbus, & Hanson, 1975), only 2 of 13 women and 4 of 11 men did not mention that they had experienced depression. Of these respondents who did not become depressed at some point, half had Minnesota Multiphasic Personality Inventory (MMPI) profiles indicating a propensity to use denial. Therefore, the rate of depression in this group may be significant. Women terminating pregnancies for fetal anomalies experience grief similar to those who experience spontaneous perinatal loss (Zeanah, Dailey, Rosenblatt, & Saller, 1993).

When losses of this magnitude occur, there is a fundamental need to explain the event. If one can understand "why," then one potentially can prevent the recurrence. Most parents, after a pregnancy loss, make a major effort to explain the loss to make sense of their grief. Women often will have both medical and more informal explanations for the pregnancy loss. Medical explanations include an illness during the pregnancy. Often, the physician will have identified these etiologies. Nonmedical explanations place the cause in the hands of fate or as punishment for past mistakes. Most couples will report the medical explanation for the pregnancy loss, but will also have their own explanation and this will be the one they believe (Dunn, Goldbach, Lasker, & Toedter, 1991). These informal explanations often blame the mother for the loss. The woman may accept this responsibility because she is the one who physically carries the pregnancy. She also may use self-blame as a defense mechanism to regain control over a difficult situation (Dunn et al., 1991). It is important to pursue this sense of blame with the couple, so that the woman does not take on an unnecessary burden, one that is not indicated by the genetics of the condition.

While autosomal dominant conditions are not as likely to cause pregnancy complications, this sense of being defective applies to a parent (mother or father) who carries the gene for a dominant trait. Women who are carriers of an X-linked condition are especially vulnerable to a sense of guilt and responsibility. It is their gene alone, not an unknown gene or even a combination of genes from both parents, that has created the dilemma in the pregnancy. This, on top of society's expectations for mothers, can result in significant strain.

Carriers of balanced chromosomal translocations are at significant risk for feeling unduly responsible for pregnancy complications and birth defects in their offspring. They must contend with a higher number of spontaneous abortions than the average couple, and their chance of having a child with a serious birth defect is higher than average. These couples may be put more often in the difficult position of having prenatal diagnosis detect a chromosomally abnormal fetus and of having to consider termination. They feel that there is an inherent defect in their life's blueprint. Often, these people will voice concern about genetic "time bombs" in their future. It is hard for them to believe that these translocations will not predispose them to further difficulties later in life. They remark that if only their partner had chosen someone else he or she would be happier. The reassurance that this is familial in many cases and that they did not cause their chromosomes to be "broken" is of no apparent consolation.

Genetic Counseling After Perinatal Loss

Genetic counseling traditionally is defined as a communication process that helps individuals to understand the nature of a genetic disorder, the mode of inheritance, the implication for the family, and the options which are available to them. Furthermore, genetic counseling is meant to be supportive of how families wish to use this information. The process of genetic counseling involves obtaining a medical and family history and conducting a discussion of recurrence risks and available testing modalities. This counseling is conducted in a nondirective manner with respect to how an individual or family may or may not benefit from available testing.

Genetic counseling should include not only factual medical information, but also the psychosocial factors surrounding the loss. Numbers and facts (including recurrence risks) do not always reflect the entire significance of the loss to an individual or family. For example, explaining that recurrence is "unlikely" (regardless of the number) may be interpreted differently and may be of little solace to a family who just has experienced an "unlikely" but devastating event in their initial loss. In counseling couples, it is important to listen first in order to assess their needs and feelings and not to generalize about their grief reaction. If the pregnancy had been successful, the parents would have been proud of themselves and would have felt that they had fulfilled society's expectations. But if the pregnancy has not gone well, they can feel failure and guilt or shame.

Parents' perceived risk for a genetic disorder often differs from the analytical risk. Factors that influence this perception include the potential degree of harm or lethality, the amount of control over the risk, the number of people affected, and parents' familiarity with the consequences of the disease (Robinson & Wisner, 1993). Families who have an increased risk for having a child with a genetic disorder are faced with complications of a natural biologic process that usually is taken for granted. They may express a sense of "being defective."

In many cases, no medical etiology can be ascertained for an early loss. Such unexplained losses are more likely to be attributed by the family to "fate." The genetic counselor should pursue the family's explanation for their loss to help prevent unnecessary "scapegoating" of the mother and other common misconceptions. Kessler and colleagues describe guilt and shame, two common responses to loss, as originating from different points. While both provide the illusion of control and the hope that this control will prevent future pain, the psychologic origins may vary with different families (Kessler, Kessler, & Ward, 1984). The genetic counselor can watch for these defenses by looking for actions such as the couple's not telling family or friends that they are pregnant. This may imply that they anticipate shame or guilt if an abnormality is detected.

Guilt usually is a response to violations of internal standards. Individuals feel that they are responsible for a negative outcome. This sense of responsibility may be based on realistic or unrealistic expectations. A person with guilt feelings will use repression of "bad" behaviors and may rationalize actions by positive attributes, or isolate feelings about personal responsibility. In counseling couples who are feeling guilt, the genetic counselor can be more successful by taking an authoritative approach to normalize the person's feeling, and to reframe in a more self-esteem building way which will limit his or her ability to deny.

Shame comes from anticipated or external disapproval. It occurs because of a failure to reach certain goals or ideals. It is a more passive psychological state, based on feelings of inadequacy and/or helplessness. To protect his or her emotions from the judgment of others, a person might deny that anything wrong has occurred, reverse reality by making overly positive a bad situation, or shift responsibility for the event to some other external source. To help people in this situation face their emotions more clearly, the genetic counselor should work to develop a strong alliance with the couple, and to use ego-boosting techniques.

The genetic counselor also must be aware of the risk of assigning blame to the couple inadvertently. By being complete in history taking, the counselor concentrates on all the minutiae of pregnancy, creating the impression for the couple that, if the question is being asked, then there must be a relationship between the event and the pregnancy complications. Why would the counselor be inquiring about alcohol in the pregnancy if it might not cause Down syndrome? Even if the counselor reassures the couple that their actions did not cause the birth defect, they still can be left with the message that, if there is not external cause, then they must be the ones who are to blame.

If counseling truly is to be effective, then the relationship with the couple must be started before a crisis. It is more difficult for both the counselor and the family to develop an open, trusting rapport when the counselor enters the picture late. Counseling patients after a genetic pregnancy loss has all of the aspects of other pregnancy losses; but also it is burdened with the additional, often-conflicting medical and emotional aspects which are discussed above. Such counseling can be quite complex and challenging. It may be necessary for the counselor to look past what the patient is verbalizing to the potential dynamic forces at work in the individual case.

Prenatal Diagnosis in Future Pregnancies

When the available information (including pertinent personal or family medical history, clinical or laboratory data, or pathologic findings) suggests a specific genetic diagnosis as the etiology of a pregnancy loss, genetic counseling may be helpful some time after the loss and in any future pregnancy. Often, the stresses, because of the loss itself and because of the need to make decisions immediately, make the future impact of the loss seem distant. The shock that occurs during such a process makes it difficult for the couple to retain much of the information which they receive in the initial counseling session. Thus, it may be necessary to repeat information from the counseling session, to correct misconceptions, and to allow the couple to address newer concerns for future pregnancies. Likewise, when a specific diagnosis is not available, genetic counseling may be of value for patients who are considering prenatal diagnosis in future pregnancies.

When a specific genetic diagnosis has been made, it is critical that the patient be counseled as to various clinical and laboratory techniques that may be helpful in assessing future pregnancies for recurrence. Clinical techniques available may include ultrasound alone or an ultrasound in conjunction with chorionic villus sampling (CVS), amniocentesis, or percutaneous umbilical blood sampling. The invasive prenatal diagnostic test available earliest in pregnancy is chorionic villus sampling (CVS), performed at 10 to 12 weeks gestation. The procedure-related risk of pregnancy loss is believed to not be more than 1.1%. This procedure is in essence an ultrasound-guided needle biopsy of the placenta. The material obtained may be used for chromosome analysis, DNA analysis (for specific diseases), or various microenzyme assays. Usually, test results are available within 1 to 2 weeks after the procedure has been done.

Amniocentesis is considered to be the invasive diagnostic procedure which has the lowest procedure-related risk of pregnancy loss (less than 0.5%). Although some centers offer "early amniocentesis" (the risks of which are not completely studied), amniocentesis typically is performed after 14 weeks gestation. This procedure is an ultrasound-guided needle aspiration of amniotic fluid. The amniotic fluid contains fetal cells which may be used for chromosome analysis or DNA analysis. Additionally, amniotic fluid may be helpful in diagnosing neural tube defects through the measurement of alpha-fetoprotein and acetylcholinesterase. Amniocentesis results usually are available between 1 and 2 weeks after the procedure.

Less common is an invasive diagnostic procedure called percutaneous umbilical blood sampling (PUBS). This procedure is an ultrasound-guided needle aspiration of fetal blood directly from the umbilical vein. A drawback for this procedure is that it is not possible before 18 to 20 weeks gestation; PUBS's great benefit is that it provides fetal blood for direct study. The procedure-related risk of pregnancy loss associated with PUBS is believed to be 1% to 2%. Thus, this procedure is offered only under special circumstances (for example, because of urgency of diagnosis, or for disorders which only are diagnosable by studying blood, etc.).

If a diagnosis can be made purely from morphologic findings, ultrasound alone may be useful (as in anencephaly, for example). It remains controversial how specific ultrasound alone is for less-obvious defects (such as spina bifida). It is clear that ultrasound has limiting factors, including hardware and personnel. It also is clear, however, that the risk to a pregnancy of ultrasound alone is negligible. This may make this modality, although it is less sensitive and less specific, the diagnostic modality of choice for a couple who have undergone a previous devastating pregnancy loss.

Each of these techniques may have advantages and limitations for particular diagnoses. In certain cases, patient concerns may make one of the techniques particularly attractive. For example, neural tube defects cannot be diagnosed by CVS, while amniocentesis and ultrasound are very sensitive for this diagnosis. On the other hand, chromosomal anomalies may be diagnosed by either amniocentesis or CVS. Some couples may choose CVS, because it is the technique which is available earliest in pregnancy. Others' choices may be driven by the need to select the technique with the lowest generally acknowledged complication rate. Some couples, after counseling, will decline all invasive procedures. Genetic counseling, provided in a nondirective manner, allows the couple to make the decision that is most helpful to them. Without complete information, presented in a neutral manner, couples are more likely to be reactive and to choose a test that may not yield the information which is most critical for their needs. Again, only by carefully counseling the patient and listening to individual concerns can optimal care be delivered.

Although genetic counseling and diagnosis in conjunction with pregnancy loss can be difficult and stressful, this is an area where the health care provider can make a tremendous impact by providing medically appropriate information in a sensitive manner. Genetic counseling provides an opportunity to transform a previous, very devastating experience into one by which the patient may gain positive information as she contemplates the prospect of attempting another pregnancy.❑

Case Study 1-7

Elevated Maternal Serum Alpha-Fetoprotein

The patient is a 23-year-old G1P0 female with an elevated maternal serum alpha-fetoprotein early in her second trimester. Investigation of this on ultrasound demonstrated an occipital encephalocele, as well as severe oligohydramnios and markedly echogenic fetal kidneys. After extensive counseling, the woman opted to terminate her pregnancy. She chose to have a prostaglandin induction, to attempt to have pathologists obtain as much information as possible from her baby in the autopsy. The autopsy demonstrated a male fetus with an occipital encephalocele, cystic dysplastic changes of both kidneys, and post-axial polydactyly.

Commentary

The investigation of elevations of maternal serum alpha-fetoprotein can reveal one of a large number of possible fetal or placental abnormalities. Once ultrasound demonstrates a fetal anomaly, the clinician is charged not only with the task of explaining the findings to a patient but also with the necessity of discussing pregnancy management options. Both of these tasks offer challenges for care providers, as well as for the pregnant woman and her family.

The findings in the current situation are very suggestive of a specific syndromic diagnosis — Meckel-Gruber syndrome. Meckel-Gruber syndrome is a lethal autosomal recessive syndrome with the attendant 25% risk for recurrence in future pregnancies. The classic ultrasound findings include the triad of occipital cephalocele, bilateral renal cystic dysplasia, and post-axial polydactyly of both hands and feet. Other reported prenatal findings have included cardiac abnormalities, agenesis of the corpus callosum, cerebellar hypoplasia, Dandy-Walker cyst, spinal dysraphism, cleft lip and palate, club feet, and intrauterine growth restriction.

The prenatal diagnoses of specific genetic syndromes are becoming more common with high-resolution sonography, but care always should be given to amend a diagnosis with findings which are obtained from other prenatal testing as well as postnatal examinations. The possibility of a specific diagnosis with such a marked recurrence risk, however, may have a profound influence on the family's plans for managing this pregnancy.

Communication between the clinician who performs the prenatal testing and the pathologist who does the postnatal evaluation is very important in obtaining the maximal amount of information for the family. The perinatal autopsy can be very challenging with small fetal size and difficulty in preserving fragile CNS malformations. If any prenatal chromosome testing was obtained, it is important to forward these results to the pathologist. The review of prenatal sonographic images with the pathologist may help to clarify structures that actually can be more difficult to visualize after delivery.

In obtaining a complete perinatal pathologic evaluation, it is important to obtain tissue or blood for chromosome analysis if prenatal chromosome testing was not done. For example, the findings in the current situation also could represent trisomy 13, with the central nervous system, renal, and skeletal defects which were noted. Other, less common, duplication or deletion syndromes also can be excluded. As most chromosomal abnormalities that occur will represent a sporadic event with small risk for recurrence, this finding could influence significantly on the family's decision to conceive future pregnancies.

As the majority of neural tube defects are multifactorial with both polygenic and environmental influences at work, it is important that the family be given as precise a diagnosis as possible. Recent widespread publicity regarding the role of folate deficiency in neural tube defects may lead patients to assume that future affected pregnancies can be avoided with use of dietary supplements. Complete discussion of these more common situations with an isolated neural tube defect will help to clarify this concern.

With all inherited conditions, especially autosomal recessive lethal syndromes, it is important to educate the family about the very common nature of these previously unknown recessive genes. Once the family learns that we all carry potentially lethal recessive genes, the common feelings of guilt that parents have may be reduced or removed. This family now knows about one of the recessive genes that they carry. Most of us are unaware of the potentially lethal recessive genes that we carry unless we conceive a child with an individual who has the same recessive gene and that child receives a double dose of the recessive gene. Using examples of more common autosomal recessive genetic diseases such as cystic fibrosis or sickle cell anemia can be helpful in explaining this concept.

The initial role of genetic counseling in this situation is similar to other medical situations: to investigate all possible explanations for the clinical findings, to obtain as precise a diagnosis as is possible, and to communicate everything learned to the family in an understandable fashion. The second task of presenting pregnancy management alternatives in a nondirective fashion, and of providing support for the family once they reach their decision, is more unique to the medical care providers who specialize in treating pregnant women. The third need in this situation is to provide at least one follow-up visit to discuss all of the information gained by both prenatal and postnatal evaluations and to provide support for the family in dealing with the outcome of their difficult decisions. It is infrequent that one medical care provider can fill all the roles of delivering obstetric care, doing targeted fetal imaging, and providing genetic counseling to help fit the puzzle pieces together. Using a team approach, including expertise in obstetrics, fetal imaging, genetics, and pathology, is the key to providing this family with the best quality care.

— *C. Lynn Keene, MD*

Case Study 2-7

The patient is a 19-year-old G2P1001 female who, during a routine prenatal visit, was noted to have a 20-week size fundus, although she was at 17 weeks gestation. Therefore, she was referred for an ultrasound examination which demonstrated diffuse fetal hydrops, including pleural and pericardial effusions, as well as ascites and skin thickening. Additionally, marked polyhydramnios and an enlarged placenta were appreciated. No other specific structural abnormalities were noted. The patient underwent genetic counseling and opted for amniocentesis. The results of the amniocentesis demonstrated a 45,X karyotype. At that point, the patient noted decreased fetal movement, and a follow-up ultrasound examination demonstrated fetal demise. She then underwent a dilatation and evacuation.

Commentary

Fetal Hydrops

After an initial ultrasound examination shows fetal anomalies, in this case fetal hydrops, genetic counseling is indicated. The components of genetic counseling, risk assessment, education, and counseling ensure appropriate case management. Risk assessment includes obtaining detailed family, medical, reproductive, and pregnancy histories. A history of pregnancy losses, stillbirths, consanguinity, maternal health, or infectious/viral illnesses might be informative in cases of fetal hydrops. Educating the patient about etiologies of particular fetal anomalies, available diagnostic tools, and implications of these anomalies allows her to make informed decisions.

The initial genetic counseling session should focus on the poor prognosis for fetal hydrops at 17 weeks gestation, regardless of etiology. The various etiologies should be reviewed, in general terms rather than in detail — immunologic, chromosomal, viral, congenital anomalies of genetic disorders. Diagnostic testing using a stepwise approach should be discussed. Counseling for this patient is complex. No definitive diagnosis is available, but decisions regarding the pregnancy must be made. These decisions will affect which diagnostic options are available and the order in which they are performed.

The patient should be offered several courses of action: (a) proceeding directly to pregnancy termination, with or without diagnostic studies; (b) undergoing diagnostic studies, deferring decision making until the results are available; or (c) continuing the pregnancy, with or without diagnostic studies. The benefits, risks, and limitations of these options should be discussed in detail. For example, if the patient elects to proceed with termination without additional testing, then she loses the opportunity for definitive diagnosis and recurrence risk. While clinicians may be uncomfortable with such a decision, it may be the best course for her if she has a good understanding of the implications of this action.

In general, the patient should be encouraged to pursue as much testing as necessary for making a diagnosis. Involving the patient in her pregnancy management may provide a sense of control in a situation which is frighteningly out of control (an abnormal fetus). Counseling always includes assisting the patient and her family in recognizing and dealing with their emotions involving grief, loss, guilt, and anger.

There are many good pamphlets which discuss prenatal decision making when fetal anomalies are detected; providing these to the patient for private reading is a useful adjunct to face-to-face counseling. Written materials on the particular fetal condition, when available, also should be given to the patient. This allows the patient to focus on the decision-making process, rather than worrying about remembering all of the details. Providing an accurate diagnosis frequently allays parental guilt. Unfortunately, an etiology for fetal anomalies, especially fetal hydrops, is not always found.

A stepwise workup in cases of fetal hydrops allows appropriate testing and limits medical costs. Genetic counselors usually assume that immunologic forms of hydrops will be diagnosed by the obstetric team, but this should be documented in the records. Since the rate of chromosomal abnormalities (especially Turner and Down syndromes) in fetal hydrops is significant, chromosome analysis is indicated. In this case, amniocentesis is the most appropriate diagnostic procedure. In some circumstances, the options of transabdominal chorionic villus sampling (CVS) or percutaneous umbilical blood sampling (PUBS) should be considered. Other studies could be deferred until the chromosome analysis is complete. However, viral cultures or titers may be done on amniotic fluid or fetal blood if available.

If a chromosome abnormality is detected, no other studies need to be performed. In particular, an autopsy would not provide additional useful clinical information. The finding of 45,X by amniocentesis in this case of fetal hydrops provides a clear diagnosis and prognosis for this pregnancy, as well as recurrence risks for future pregnancies. If chromosome studies are normal, further testing should include viral titers (for example, cytomegalovirus, toxoplasmosis, human parvo virus) and fetal echocardiography (structural defects and arrhythmias). Alpha thalassemia should be considered in high-risk ethnic groups. If these studies do not provide a diagnosis, biochemical assays for rare metabolic conditions (for example, Gaucher type 2 sialidosis, mucopoly-saccharidosis) should be considered on cultured cells or fetal blood.

A positive result from any study should be discussed with the patient as soon as possible. If a diagnosis is not available at the time of fetal demise or termination, an autopsy should be recommended. Frequently, pathologic examination reveals the etiology of the hydrops. Unfortunately, pathology studies are not informative if the fetus has significant autolysis or the patient has had a termination by a dilatation and evacuation (D&E).

After all of the studies are completed, the patient should be seen again to discuss the implications for future pregnancies. This may take place weeks or months after the pregnancy. In this case, the patient can be counseled that the recurrence risk for 45,X is negligible. In cases where the recurrence risk is significant or unknown, a detailed discussion of prenatal diagnostic and management options would be indicated. At this follow-up session, it also is important to assess whether or not the patient and family are coping with the loss appropriately. Some patients need additional psychosocial support, in which case a referral to a marriage/family counselor or other therapist would be indicated.

— *Karen Copeland, MS, CGC*

Glossary of Terms

Acrocentric — A chromosome in which there is very little DNA on the short (p) arm. Robertsonian translocations are structural chromosomal rearrangements involving only acrocentric chromosomes.

Aneuploidy — Euploid refers to an even multiple of the basic (or haploid) number of chromosomes in each cell of an organism. In the case of humans, the haploid number is 23 chromosomes (found in gametes) and the diploid number is 46 chromosomes (found in somatic cells). Aneuploidy is any chromosomal constitution which is not euploid, thus not an even multiple haploid number of chromosomes. The most common aneuploidy is trisomy 21, in which there is an extra chromosome 21, which results in Down syndrome.

Centromere — The indented area which divides the chromosome into a short (p) and long (q) arm and is necessary for cell division.

Genome — The sum of all genes contained in a gamete, or haploid chromosome constitution.

Genotype — The precise genetic makeup of a cell or organism, which influences the phenotype.

Inversion — Chromosome rearrangements formed when two breaks occur within a single chromosome and the intervening segment is inverted.

Meiosis — Specialized cell division (specifically involving the nucleus and the chromosomes contained within the nucleus) that results in the reduction of chromosome number by half (haploid). Meiosis occurs in the gonads and produces gametes.

Mitosis — Cell division (specifically involving the nucleus and the chromosomes contained within the nucleus) that results in two identical daughter cells, each of which contains the same number of chromosomes as the parent cell (diploid). Mitosis occurs in somatic (or body) tissues, as opposed to germ cells which produce gametes.

Phenotype — The observable properties of a cell or organism, produced as a result of the interaction between genotype and environmental influences.

Polyploidy — A chromosomal constitution which is an even multiple (greater than two) of the haploid number of chromosomes. The most common example is triploidy, but the term also applies to tetraploidy, etc.

Translocation — A structural chromosomal rearrangement formed by the exchange of chromosomal material between two non-identical chromosomes.

Trisomy — A diploid cell (with two copies of each autosome and two sex chromosomes for a total of 46 chromosomes) in which an extra chromosome is present for a total of 47 chromosomes. The most common example is trisomy 21 (in which the extra chromosome is number 21), which results in Down syndrome.

References

Blumberg, B.D., Golbus, M.S., & Hanson, K.H. (1975). The psychological sequelae of abortion performed for a genetic indication. *American Journal of Obstetrics and Gynecology, 122,* 799-808.

Cunningham, F.G., MacDonald, P.C., Gant, N.F., Leveno, K.J., & Gilstrap, L.C., III. (1993). *Williams Obstetrics* (19th ed.). Norwalk , CT: Appleton & Lange.

Dunn, D.S., Goldbach, K.R.C., Lasker, J.N., & Toedter, L.J. (1991). Explaining pregnancy loss: Parents' and physicians' attributions. *Omega Journal of Death and Dying, 23,* 13-23.

Edmonds, D.K., Lindsey, K.S., Miller, J.F., Williamson, E., & Wood, P.J. (1982). Early embryonic mortality in women. *Fertility and Sterility, 38,* 477.

Gustavson, K.H., & Jorulf, H. (1976). Recurrence risk in consecutive series of congenitally malformed children dying in the perinatal period. *Clinical Genetics, 9,* 307.

Hertig, A.T., Rock, J., & Adams, E.C. (1954). On the implantation stages of the human ovum: A description of four normal and four abnormal specimens ranging from the second to fifth day of development. *Contributions in Embryology, 35,* 199.

Hook, E.B., & Hamerton, J.L. (1977). The frequency of chromosome abnormalities detected in consecutive newborn studies: Differences between studies — Results by sex and by severity of phenotype involvement. In E.B. Hook & I.H. Porter (Eds.), *Population cytogenetic studies in humans* (p. 63). New York City: Academic Press.

Hook, E.B., Topol, B.B., & Cross, P.K. (1989). The natural history of cytogenetically abnormal fetuses detected at midtrimester amniocentesis which are not terminated electively: New data and estimates of the excess and relative risk of late fetal death associated with 47,+21 and some other abnormal karyotypes. *American Journal of Human Genetics, 45,* 855-861.

Kajii, T., Ferrier, A., Niikawa, N., Takahara, H., Ohama, K., & Avirachan, S. (1980). Anatomic and chromosomal anomalies in 639 spontaneous abortuses. *Human Genetics, 55,* 87-98.

Kessler, S., Kessler, H., & Ward, P. (1984). Psychological aspects of genetic counseling: Management of guilt and shame. *American Journal of Medical Genetics, 17,* 673-697.

Leon, I.G. (1992). The psychoanalytical conceptualization of perinatal loss: A multidimensional model. *American Journal of Psychiatry, 149,* 1464-1472.

Miller, J.F., Williamson, E., & Glue, J. (1980). Fetal loss after implantation: A prospective study. *Lancet, 2,* 554.

Roberts, C.J., & Lowe, D.B. (1975). Where have all the conceptions gone? *Lancet, 1,* 498.

Robinson, G.E., & Wisner, K.L. (1993). Fetal anomalies. In D. Stewant & N. Stotland (Eds.), *Psychological aspects of women's health: The interface between psychiatry and obstetrics and gynecology.* Washington, DC: American Psychiatric Press, Inc.

Saller, D.N., Lesser, K.B., Harrel, U., Rogers, B.B., & Oyer, C.E. (1995). The clinical utility of the perinatal autopsy. *Journal of the American Medical Association, 273,* 663-665.

Wolf, G.C., & Horger, E.O. (1995). Indications for examination of spontaneous abortion specimens: A reassessment. *American Journal of Obstetrics and Gynecology, 173,* 1364-1368.

Zeanah, C.H., Dailey, J.V., Rosenblatt, M.J., & Saller, D.N. (1993). Do women grieve after terminating pregnancies because of fetal anomalies? A controlled investigation. *Obstetrics and Gynecology, 82,* 270-275.

Chapter 8

Teratogenic Issues: Pregnancy Loss or Birth Defects Caused by Therapeutic, Occupational, or Environmental Exposure

Richard K. Miller

Birth defects are the leading cause of perinatal mortality (deaths *in utero* or in the newborn period). During the past several years, medical scientists have made tremendous progress in reducing perinatal mortality due to respiratory distress syndrome and other contributors to prematurity and premature birth. Yet, as the overall rate of perinatal mortality has fallen, the percentage of perinatal mortality attributable to birth defects continues to rise. It is obvious from these statistics that society has not been successful in reducing either the incidence of birth defects or their contributions to perinatal mortality.

Adverse pregnancy outcome is quite common. Of recognized pregnancies, approximately 20% end in miscarriage or pregnancy losses, another 10% are preterm births, and approximately 3% of babies are born with a birth defect. In the face of such odds, it is remarkable what expectations we parents hold for each pregnancy. There are many reasons for birth defects. Among these are genetic disorders (see Table 1-8) and environmental therapeutic causes (see Table 2-8). The largest category continues to be called multifactorial, which actually represents unknown associations. In addition, there are many reasons for pregnancy loss besides birth defects; the above factors in combination with maternal physiology, endocrinology, and anatomy all can be contributors to pregnancy loss, however.

Prenatal diagnosis provides state-of-the-art possibilities for determining whether an embryo may be at risk for having some but not all serious birth defects. Ultrasonography and color Doppler evaluation provide excellent opportunities to verify how well the embryo or fetus is doing morphologically, as well as functionally (for example, cardiovascular dynamics and movement). Today, in our collective war against birth defects, we have won a major

Table 1-8.
Genetic Disorders Associated with Human Birth Defects

- Chromosomal Aberrations
  (e.g., trisomy, Down syndrome, monosomy, tetraploidy)

- Single Gene Defects
  (e.g., neurofibromatosis, hemophilia, nonsyndromic holoprosencephaly)

- Multifactorial Inheritance
  (e.g., inborn errors of metabolism, phenylketonuria)

battle — the ability to reduce significantly the incidence of some serious birth defects such as neural tube defects, through supplementation with multivitamins, and particularly with folic acid, which must be taken both before and during pregnancy. Now, it is only a battle won for the unborn. Much remains to be accomplished in reducing risk for birth defects and pregnancy loss.

The purpose of this chapter is to examine the etiology of birth defects and their association not only with pregnancy loss but also with their impact on quality of life for the child and the family. The focus is on issues related to modifying risk via genetic, therapeutic, occupational, and environmental interventions.

It often is assumed that all pregnancy losses can be prevented. Unfortunately, that may never be possible, since loss of a pregnancy often is a mechanism by which a severely compromised embryo can be spared from debilitating genetic or other defects, which in these cases are lethal. Thus, not all pregnancy losses nor birth defects can be attributed to therapeutic, environmental, or occupational exposures. Yet, when such events are involved, these are the arenas within which the patient and her family, employer, and health care providers can take protective action to reduce risk.

Understanding the Threat from Harmful Exposure During Pregnancy

For genetic disorders such as trisomy (which is the leading cause of pregnancy loss), or for infections such as mumps, the condition either is present or absent. With most other environmental, occupational, or therapeutic agents which are known to be teratogenic, however, there is a dose-response relationship. In the case of exposure to agents which produce reproductive or developmental toxicity, the agents or substances produce their effects based

Table 2-8.
Environmental/Therapeutic Agents
Associated with Birth Defects in Humans

- Androgens
- Angiotensin-Converting Enzyme Inhibitors (captopril, enalapril)
- Anticancer Therapy (cyclophosphamide, busulfan, methylaminopterin)
- Anticonvulsants (e.g., phenytoin, trimethadione, valproic acid)
- Diethylstilbestrol
- Chlorobiphenyls
- Cocaine
- Folic Acid Antagonists (e.g., aminopterin)
- Hyperthermia (hot tubs, infections)
- Metals (lead, cadmium, methyl mercury)
- Oral anticoagulants (warfarin)
- Retinoids (isotretinoin, etretinate)
- Solvents (ethanol, gasoline, and toluene)
- Thalidomide
- Tobacco
- Vitamin A deficiency
- X-irradiation

upon the concept that the higher the dose or exposure, the greater the effect. Intertwined within this concept is threshold. Threshold means that, below a certain dose or exposure for a specific interval during a critical time in gestation, there are no detectable effects, while above that dose or exposure there are detectable effects. Such a concept simply means that, if a woman is exposed to an agent, at some low dose/exposure which is well below the threshold dose/exposure and/or at a nonsensitive time during her pregnancy, she will not have an adverse effect. Such principles apply to drugs and occupational exposures, as well as to environmental exposure.   Concern always is heightened when a pregnant woman experiences adverse effects (for example, dizziness or hallucinations). Unless one can document that these effects (such as morning sickness or nausea) are related to her pregnancy, then it is prudent for the woman to avoid known exposures until these are proved safe by monitoring (of blood levels or air quality).

Therapeutic Agents:
Antihypertensive-ACE Inhibitors
(Inhibitors of Angiotensin Converting Enzyme)

The use of antihypertensive agents such as captopril or enalapril carries substantial risk of decreased amniotic fluid volume and fetal distress or death in hypertensive women who are treated during the later part of pregnancy. Effects appear to be related to the pharmacologic action of these drugs directly on the fetus. The risk associated with second- or third-trimester use appears to increase with chronic administration of ACE inhibitors. It should be noted that a small risk cannot be excluded if these drugs are used during the first trimester. A high risk of congenital anomalies in children of women treated with ACE inhibitors during the first trimester is unlikely (Barr, 1994; Barr & Cohen, 1991).

Anticancer Therapy:
Cyclophosphamide

Cyclophosphamide (Cytoxan®, Neosar®) is a cancer chemotherapy (alkylating agent) and also is an immunosuppressant. Cyclophosphamide has produced birth defects in all species studied. In animal studies, teratogenic effects which consistently were noted involved facial clefts and limb reductions. Also, no human primate studies demonstrate cleft lip/palate or limb and brain abnormalities following exposures during early gestation, or craniofacial dysmorphism following exposures later in gestation. For pregnant women, cyclophosphamide exposure occurring during the first trimester has been associated with skeletal, palate, eye, and limb defects. During the second and third trimesters, cyclophosphamide therapy is associated with a lower risk of congenital malformations; reduced blood cells and impaired fetal growth also have been noted. Unfortunately, pregnant women who must undergo cyclophosphamide therapy have life-threatening diseases requiring this treatment (either alone or also with radiation). It should be noted that there are case reports describing normal pregnancies following cyclophosphamide therapy during the first trimester. The risk of birth defects following cyclophosphamide therapy is estimated to be one in every six exposures.

Treatment with cyclophosphamide (and other cancer therapies) can induce irreversible amenorrhea in some women, especially women approaching menopause. Interestingly, treatment of lupus nephritis with small doses of cyclophosphamide, administered in pulses at short intervals, produced only minor adverse effects on menstrual cycles and fertility of women under 40 years of age (Avilés, Diaz-Macqueo, Talavera, Guzmán, & Garcia, 1991; Friedman & Polifka, 1995). Animal experiments suggest that pretreatment with GnRH agonists may be effective in protecting the premature ovarian follicle from cyclophosphamide exposure. Cyclophosphamide therapy in male patients can result in reduced or absent sperm. In some cases, impairment of fertility is reversible, but may require an extended recovery period involving years — if not decades. The highest risk of permanent sterility has been associated with doses of cyclophosphamide greater than 7.5 mg/m^2. Health care providers who prepare and administer cyclophosphamide inadvertently have absorbed measurable quantities of this compound, either as an aerosol or through the skin.

Busulfan

Another alkylating agent, busulfan (Myleran®), has specific effects on bone marrow. Busulfan is used for leukemia therapy and in patients receiving bone marrow transplantation. Busulfan does damage mouse and human embryonic cells, probably through irreversible inhibition of DNA synthesis. Busulfan therapy in children and adolescents can be associated with subsequent gonadal failure. Girls appear to be more severely affected than boys, and amenorrhea is not unusual after therapy. Ovarian toxicity of busulfan may be temporary. A pregnancy was reported to have occurred about 1 year after hypergonadotropic ovarian failure was documented in a young woman who was treated with busulfan for leukemia. Her pregnancy proceeded normally, and a healthy baby was delivered (Avilés et al., 1991; Friedman & Polifka, 1995).

From animal studies, investigators have demonstrated that use of busulfan during pregnancy can affect primordial germ cells, resulting in abnormal gonadal function and reduced fertility in males and females. Forty-two human pregnancies have been reported for patients who were exposed to busulfan. In six of the exposed pregnancies, malformed fetuses or children were identified with a wide range of anomalies. It is not possible, however, to implicate busulfan as the causative agent of these abnormalities.

Aminopterin

Aminopterin is a folic acid antagonist. Use of this agent to produce abortion in women was described in the early 1950s. Of 12 pregnancies terminated, three fetuses had malformations, including cleft lip/cleft palate and neural tube defects (Warkany, 1976, 1981). A total of 16 cases of birth defects have been reported, with six having hydrocephalus or anencephaly. Approximately half of these exposed pregnancies resulted in liveborn children, with the rest resulting in abortion or stillbirth. (See "Folic Acid" for discussion of the importance of aminopterin's preconceptional use.)

Anticonvulsants:
Phenytoin

Phenytoin (diphenylhydantoin, Dilantin®) is used for all types of seizures except *petit mal* epilepsy. Phenytoin increases congenital anomalies in animals, including cleft palate, hydrocephalus, and limb and kidney defects. Human infants exposed *in utero* to phenytoin demonstrate a number of congenital abnormalities, such as facial and heart defects. A cluster of these abnormalities, called the fetal phenytoin syndrome, has been associated with prenatal exposure to phenytoin (Buehler, Delimont, Van Waes, & Finnell, 1990; Hanson, 1986; Lindhout & Omtzigt, 1994). Defects include abnormal faces (short nose, low bridge, epicanthic folds, hypertelorism, abnormal ears, wide mouth), shortened distal phalanges (especially involving the nails), fingerlike thumbs, short or webbed neck, low hairline, and abnormalities of growth and mental and/or motor development. The use of phenytoin during pregnancy may increase the risk of childhood neuroectodermal tumors in the offspring. It should be remembered that not all studies confirmed an increase in human birth defects and tumors associated with maternal phenytoin use. The increase in serious fetal toxicity induced by phenytoin is low. Moreover, seizure control may not be possible without this anticonvulsant. Current recommendations are that withholding phenytoin from pregnant epileptics who require the drug to remain seizure free is inappropriate.

Trimethadione

Trimethadione (Tridione®) has been used in treating *petit mal* epilepsy, but its use is avoided during pregnancy because of its association with a syndrome of abnormalities in the offspring, called "fetal trimethadione syndrome." This syndrome consists of low-set ears, palate defects, irregular teeth, V-shaped eyebrows, developmental delays, mental retardation, and speech disturbances. In nine families, studies revealed a congenital anomaly rate of 69% (Goldman & Yaffe, 1978). Trimethadione is not the only treatment available, and it should be avoided during pregnancy. One alternative is ethosuximide.

Valproic Acid

Valproic acid (Depakene®) is used to inhibit simple and complex absence seizures, and it has been used in treating manic-depressive disorders. Sodium valproate produces an increase in birth defects when tested in animals. A human "fetal valproate syndrome" has been described with features similar to those which are seen in the fetal hydantoin syndrome, including intrauterine growth restriction (IUGR), facial dysmorphism, and limb and heart defects (Lammer, Sever, & Oakley, 1987; Robert, 1988). Of particular concern is the association between valproic acid and neural tube defects (between 1% and 2%). Although women with epilepsy appear to have an increased incidence of menstrual disturbance, valproic acid use appears to contribute to further menstrual problems by producing polycystic ovary, characterized by enlarged cystic ovaries (probably reflecting anovulation) and increased levels of androgens. Men who have taken 1,000 mg/d of valproate demonstrated decreased sperm production. When valproate was reduced to 150 mg/d, semen parameters returned to normal. Thus, reproductive capacity in both males and females can be affected by valproate (Isojarvi et al., 1993; Swanson, Harland, Dickinson, & Gerber, 1978).

Effects of Other Substances:
Diethylstilbestrol

Fetuses who are exposed prenatally to diethylstilbestrol [DES] have exhibited a range of structural abnormalities of the reproductive tract as adults. Adenosis and septations of the vagina are common among daughters of women who were treated with diethylstilbestrol in pregnancy. Malformations such as T-shaped uterus, constricting bands of the uterine cavity, uterine hypoplasia, or para-ovarian cysts occur with increased frequency among such females. Moreover, clear cell adenocarcinoma, a rare tumor of the vagina or cervix, is associated with prenatal exposure to DES. Reproductive function appears also to be jeopardized for women who were exposed prenatally to diethylstilbestrol. Ectopic implantation, miscarriage, and premature delivery are more common among women whose mothers took DES during pregnancy. Studies also have associated an increased frequency of infertility among these women who were exposed *in utero* to DES (Barnes et al., 1980; Giusti, Iwamoto, & Hatch, 1995; Herbst, Hubby, Blough, & Azizi, 1980; Kaufman et al., 1986; Linn et al., 1988; Miller & Ballinger, 1993; Stillman, 1982; Veridiano, Delke, Rogers, & Tancer, 1981). Such problems may be a result of the uterine abnormalities which are associated with prenatal DES exposure.

Cocaine

Cocaine is a local anesthetic which is abused illegally via inhalation of powder or intravenous injection. Other cocaine derivatives of cocaine such as pelleted free base ("crack") can be smoked, either alone or mixed with tobacco or marijuana. Crack cocaine actually has different metabolites which are active, compared with cocaine itself. Although the magnitude of the effects of cocaine on human pregnancy is not well-defined, there does appear to be an increased incidence of urogenital abnormalities among the offspring of women who were addicted to cocaine and who used the drug throughout pregnancy. This was confirmed by a large retrospective survey performed in the Atlanta region by the Centers for Disease Control. The risk of urinary tract defects in the offspring of cocaine-using women was four times control (95%, confidence intervals 1.12, 17.24), while the risk of genital anomalies was not increased by cocaine use (Chavez, Mulinare, & Cordero, 1989).

Other reports indicate that growth restrictions involving weight, length, and head circumference have been noted consistently among infants born to women who abused cocaine during pregnancy. Moreover, some data support an association between cocaine use, preterm labor, and low Apgar score. Abnormalities of neonatal cardiorespiratory and neurologic function, as well as an increased risk of intraventricular hemorrhage, have been observed among infants born to women who used cocaine during pregnancy. Structural and functional abnormalities of the eye also have been documented among these infants (Rosenak, Diamant, Yaffe, & Hornstein, 1990).

Complications of pregnancy are another risk which is enhanced for pregnant cocaine users. Based on observations from a variety of earlier clinical reports, maternal cocaine use is associated with an increased incidence of placental abruption, as well as uterine rupture, cerebral infarction, brain lesions, and fetal death (Bingol et al., 1987; Gratacos, Torres, & Antolin, 1993; Plessinger & Woods, 1991). The occurrence of neonatal necrotizing enterocolitis also seems to be associated with maternal cocaine use during pregnancy. A possible association between prenatal exposure to cocaine and cardiovascular abnormalities is under investigation. Case reports and experimental data from experiments with fetal lambs suggest that the cardiovascular toxicity of cocaine may be enhanced by pregnancy. The diverse congenital defects which are associated with gestational exposure to cocaine may be mediated by vascular disruptions or hypoperfusion induced in the embryo or fetus.

Human sperm exposed to high concentrations of cocaine *in vitro* show initial decrements in motion characteristics; these effects appear transient with no long-term impairment of functional characteristics, however (REPROTOX®, 1996).

Hyperthermia

Hyperthermia, an elevation of body temperature, can affect mammalian development adversely. Among 54 women who reported having a fever of 101 degrees Fahrenheit for 24 hours or longer during their first trimester, a case-control study found a significant increase in the risk of abdominal wall defects in offspring of these women; this finding also has been duplicated in animals (Little et al., 1991). The small sample size in this study and the diverse assortment of other defects demonstrated in animal experiments limit the conclusiveness of this observation, however. In more recent epidemiology studies, possible elevations of cardiovascular malformations and neural tube defects are associated with maternal hyperthermia. One case-control study in Finland found an increased risk of atrial septal defects and hypoplastic left heart in the offspring of women who reported fever during early pregnancy (Tikkanen & Heinonen, 1991). A second study involving 5,566 heat-exposed pregnant women in the United States reported increased risk of neural tube defects associated with such exposures (Milunsky et al., 1992). Data from a case-control study in Atlanta found a significant association between reports of fever or febrile illness during the first trimester and an increased risk of congenital defects (Erickson, 1991). In contrast, a population-based case-control study performed in the Atlanta area by the Centers for Disease Control and Prevention did not identify a statistically significant association between maternal fever during pregnancy and a syndrome of birth defects in the offspring (Botto, Lynberg, Khoury, & Moore, 1994).

It is recommended that maternal body temperature not be repeatedly raised above 38.9 degrees C (102 degrees F). For women using hot tubs or other hot-water treatments, this means limiting exposure to 15 minutes in 39-degree C water, or to 10 minutes in 40.0- to 41.1-degree C water. Saunas permit greater heat loss (through evaporation of perspiration) than do water baths, allowing time limits to be extended.

Heat may affect spermatogenesis adversely, and keeping the testes warm may reduce fertility. Some investigators believe that warming temperatures account for springtime declines in pregnancy rates in warm climates (Robinson, Rock, & Menkin, 1968). Semen parameters deteriorate in warm climates during the summer months, particularly among men who work outdoors or in environments without air conditioning. It is important to note, however, that men who work in air-conditioned environments in warm climates have the same magnitude of deterioration in semen parameters during the summer months. In addition, a summertime decline in semen parameters has been noted in cool climates. These observations support the theory that the summertime changes in semen parameters are associated with the change in photoperiod rather than exposure to higher ambient temperatures.

Heavy Metals:
Lead

Lead toxicity has been recognized for centuries. In the recent past, leaded gasoline, lead solders, lead pipes, storage batteries, construction materials (for example, lead-based paints), dyes, and wood preservatives all have been associated with toxicity. With the elimination of lead from gasoline, air levels of lead have decreased precipitously.

Toxic effects of lead on human pregnancy have been seen for generations among women who work with lead paints in the pottery industry. Stillbirths and miscarriages were recognized as common for this population. Lead salts are capable of producing miscarriage. Current studies have documented further the association between occupational exposures to lead and miscarriage, premature rupture of amniotic membranes, and premature birth (Bellinger, 1994; Miller & Bellinger, 1993). Women who are at risk of lead exposure in the workplace should be monitored for blood lead levels before attempting pregnancy. In New York State, all pregnant women must be screened for lead. If their blood lead levels are >10 ug/dl, follow-up to identify sources of exposure is required.

Male reproductive toxicity from lead also is a health problem. Absent or few sperm have been reported in lead-intoxicated workers, although these effects were not associated with endocrine dysfunction. Additional studies have noted that semen abnormalities appear at blood lead concentrations of 40 or 50 ug/dl (Miller & Bellinger, 1993). Thus, both male and female reproduction can be intoxicated by lead. Lower blood levels of lead impact less on the adult male, but the lead's effects still are capable of targeting the conceptus.

Cadmium

Cadmium is a metal found as an industrial and environmental contaminant in many parts of the world. Cadmium is present in food, cigarette smoke, and the smoke which is produced by welding. In pregnancy, there can be significant elevation of levels of cadmium in the placenta. There is no known biologic function for cadmium. Cadmium is teratogenic or embryotoxic in multiple species. Cadmium is a toxicant in the placenta; across species, cadmium repeatedly has been associated with fetal growth restriction. Numerous *in vitro* studies suggest that cadmium is toxic to the human placenta (Eisenman & Miller, 1996). The increase in placental cadmium levels found in women who smoke and the experimental association of cadmium with decreased placental function have raised the possibility that cadmium is one of the factors involved in the relationship between low birthweight and maternal smoking.

A number of animal experiments have investigated the toxicity of cadmium on male reproductive function (Miller & Bellinger, 1993). Cadmium causes vascular changes and ischemic necrosis in the testes. At present, reports on testicular and endocrine function in men who are exposed occupationally to cadmium are limited, and no clearly identified testicular toxicity has been demonstrated in these workers. In two case reports, women who were intoxicated with cadmium due to welding exposures had repeated pregnancy losses, which raises further the issue of female reproductive toxicity of cadmium.

Mercury

Mercury (quicksilver) is a heavy metal which can have multiple forms including both organic and inorganic. At one time, mercurial salts were used to treat syphilitic pregnant women. Such treatment frequently resulted in spontaneous abortion. It was not clear whether the mercurials or the syphilis played a primary role in the miscarriages. In the mid-1960s, organic mercury's toxicity was highly publicized after a cluster of newborns with cerebral palsy and microcephaly was identified in fishing villages surrounding Minimata Bay in Japan. These abnormalities were caused by methyl mercury contamination of the fish in the bay, which were a diet staple for the pregnant women and their families in those villages. Since that incident, fetal intoxication with organic mercurials has been termed "Minamata disease." Similar intoxications also occurred in Iraq after seed grain which was contaminated inadvertently with methyl mercury was used to make bread. In this population, infants exposed *in utero* also demonstrated psychomotor retardation and cerebral palsy. Similar congenital neurologic disease has been reported in other instances of methyl mercury food contamination. Exposure to methyl mercury persists via food consumption of contaminated fish, especially in shark and swordfish, as well as tuna. It is recommended that during pregnancy women not eat more than one meal of shark or swordfish each month since the half-life of methyl mercury in the body is 50 to 70 days.

Mercury vapor in dental practices also is a concern. Dental personnel working with mercury-containing amalgams may be exposed chronically to considerable amounts of mercury vapor. In spite of mercury's poor placental passage, one study of exposed pregnancies among dental assistants found levels of mercury in the placentae and fetal membranes which were twice those detected for nonexposed controls. Available reports have not indicated a mercury-associated increase in birth defects or neurologic sequelae in the offspring of dentists or their assistants. One Danish study also did not show an increase in spontaneous miscarriages among dental assistants compared with a control population (Anonymous, 1993). Another study of female dental assistants sought to identify a reduction in fertility associated with mercury exposure but was unable to do so (Anonymous, 1993). In a study of female dental assistants performed to evaluate the association between nitrous oxide exposure and spontaneous abortion, information on exposure to dental amalgams was collected (Anonymous, 1993). A relative risk of 1.8 (95%, CI 1.0-3.2) was identified for exposure to more than 50 amalgams per week.

Although the release of mercury from amalgam ("silver") dental fillings has been demonstrated repeatedly in the past, a more recent study in sheep used radio-labeled mercury to monitor release of this element from dental amalgam fillings and transfer to the fetus (Eisenmann & Miller, 1996). The highest fetal concentrations of mercury from the amalgam fillings were found in the liver and pituitary gland. Neither maternal nor fetal toxic effects were associated with mercury released from the large quantities of dental amalgam that were used in these studies, but the authors of this report advise that use of mercury-containing amalgams for tooth restorations be avoided during pregnancy and childhood, in order to limit what may be unnecessary exposure to mercury during early development of the central nervous system. Although this report was cited in the literature reviewed by a Public Health Service committee that reviewed the safety of dental amalgam, this group concluded that "available data do not support such a restrictive policy" (Anonymous, 1993). Since the late 1980s, both German and Swedish public health agencies have recommended that procedures involving amalgam restorations not be done during pregnancy.

Coumarin

Coumarin derivatives (warfarin, dicumarol, phenindione, acenocoumarol, diphenadione, phenprocoumon, anisindione) are orally active anticoagulants. Warfarin (Coumadin®) is the most widely used. The other members of this group generally are more toxic and difficult to use safely. Phenindione, although marketed, has been associated with such severe side effects that specific recommendations against its clinical use have been made. Major anomalies associated with first-trimester human exposures to warfarin (the fetal warfarin syndrome) are skeletal defects, which include nasal hypoplasia and stippled epiphyses. The stippling of the epiphyses is a radiologic finding that apparently resolves as the epiphyses calcify. Shortened limbs, primarily involving distal digits, may be seen in up to one-third of children with the warfarin embryopathy. Nasal hypoplasia may be severe, and, if it is associated with choanal atresia, this may require intubation for ventilatory support. Other abnormalities associated with warfarin embryopathy are central nervous system and ophthalmic anomalies, hearing loss, intrauterine growth restriction, and, in a small number of cases, congenital heart disease (Warkany, 1976; Wong, Cheng, & Chan, 1993).

Women with a history of thromboembolic disease or artificial heart valves often require long-term anticoagulant therapy. This patient population is likely to experience high-risk pregnancy no matter what class of anticoagulant is prescribed, although some reports suggest that obstetric risks may be less when heparin is used. In addition to increased pregnancy risks in women receiving anticoagulants, normal ovulation is more likely to induce a corpus luteum hemorrhage, and some clinicians recommend suppression of ovulation to avoid this possibility. The frequency of adverse pregnancy outcome in this population includes 12% to 15% stillbirths, a prematurity rate as high as 20%, and an incidence of normal births of only 60% to 70%. Although there is general agreement that heparin, and perhaps dextran 70, are the anticoagulants of choice for pregnant women with thromboembolic disease, these agents may not be as effective in controlling thrombotic complications in patients with prosthetic heart valves. Thus, for such patients, use of coumarin anticoagulants has been recommended by some authors, except during the 6th through 12th week of gestation, when warfarin teratogenicity is most likely. It should be recognized, however, that developmental toxicity associated with second- and third-trimester exposure has been noted (Warkany, 1976).

Thalidomide

Thalidomide is a sedative which is used for leprosy treatment and, currently, as a possible anticancer agent. It has been marketed under a number of trade names, including Ditaval®, Kevadon®, and Contergan®. This drug is probably the best-known human teratogen, which has caused limb reduction defects, facial hemangiomata, esophageal and duodenal atresia, tetralogy of Fallot, renal agenesis, and anomalies of the external ear. The sensitive time period for the production of human thalidomide birth defects is 4 to 6 weeks from conception. About 20% of pregnancies exposed during this period result in children with anomalies (Sever & Brent, 1986).

Cigarette Smoke

Cigarette smoke is a complex mixture of gaseous and particulate substances. Evidence demonstrates that maternal smoking during pregnancy has harmful effects on the fetus. Intrauterine growth restriction is the most consistent effect of maternal smoking. On average, babies born to women who smoke during pregnancy weigh 200 grams less than those born to comparable women who do not smoke. There is a clear dose-response relationship for this effect; the more that the woman smokes, the greater the reduction in birthweight. Reductions in birthweight, as well as an increased incidence of sudden infant death syndrome (SIDS), have been noted in association with "passive smoking" (MacArthur & Knox, 1987; Trichopoulus, 1986).

If smoking is stopped during the first half of gestation, birthweights are virtually normal. Reduction in birthweight may be indicative of an important abnormality of placental function, and perinatal mortality (perhaps as a function of reduced birthweight and/or gestational age) is higher in the offspring of smoking women (Kleinman et al., 1988). Restricted fetal growth has been attributed by various investigators to premature placental maturation, chronic reduction in placental blood flow, an increase in cadmium levels, and fetal hypoxia due to carbon monoxide (Eisenmann & Miller, 1996; Morrow, Knox, Ritchie, & Bull, 1988; Sikorski, Radomanski, Paszkowski, & Skoda, 1988). It is clear that it is smoking per se, and not any associated factors such as poor nutrition, that causes fetal growth impairment. An epidemiologic study from Sweden produced data suggesting that older smokers are at especially high risk for giving birth to small-for-gestational-age newborns, and parous smokers are at especially high risk for low-birthweight infants and preterm delivery (Handler, Mason, Rosenberg, & Davis, 1994; Naeye, 1977; Underwood, Hester, LaFitte, & Gregg, 1965; Underwood, Kesler, O'Lane, & Callagan, 1967; Williams et al., 1991).

Some studies of long-term growth and development suggest that smoking during pregnancy may affect physical growth, mental development, and behavior of offspring. Several investigators have observed increases in ectopic pregnancy, spontaneous miscarriage, fetal death, and neonatal death with smoking, and some have detected dose-response relationships. Decreased levels of chorionic gonadotropin due to smoking may be a mechanism for increased rates of miscarriage among smokers. Statistically significant associations also have been reported between maternal smoking and placenta previa, placental abruption, and bleeding early or late in pregnancy (Jick & Porter, 1997).

Women who smoke may experience earlier onset of menopause (Mattison, Shiromizu, & Nightingale, 1983). This is consistent with experimental findings of ovarian toxicity of cigarette smoke's components, with the finding in two epidemiologic studies that smoking and childhood second-hand exposure to smoke adversely affect fecundity in women (Baird & Wilcox, 1985; Wilcox, Baird, & Weinberg, 1989). Moreover, women who are exposed actively or passively to cigarette smoke have higher serum FSH concentrations than women who are not thus exposed. This also is consistent with the finding of poorer indices of follicle function in women undergoing ovarian stimulation for assisted reproduction. There may be an interactive effect between smoking and heavy caffeine intake in reducing fertility (Olsen, 1991), although this conclusion remains unconfirmed (REPROTOX®, 1996).

X-rays

X-rays are a class of electromagnetic radiations with a characteristically short wavelength (less than 10 nm) that are powerful enough to alter the atomic structure of exposed materials and sometimes convert them into a charged or "ionized" form. X-rays are used in diagnostic imaging and in therapeutics. The dose of ionizing radiation is an important determinant of toxicity, including reproductive and developmental toxicity. Fetal and embryonic doses of ionizing radiation have been estimated for a variety of diagnostic studies. For example, the dose from a dental X ray is about 0.01 mrad; a chest X-ray, about 60 mrad; and an intravenous pyelogram (IVP) study, a barium enema, or a computerized tomographic (CT) scan, about 800 mrad each.

Human reports indicate that microcephaly and mental retardation are associated with ionizing radiation doses of 50 rad or greater (Brent, 1980). The National Council on Radiation Protection and Measurements (1979) stated that the risk of malformations at 5 rad or less was negligible when compared with other risks of pregnancy.

Solvents

As a class of compounds, solvents such as ethanol raise many issues concerning birth defects and pregnancy loss. At intoxicating doses of solvents, birth defects have been noted; at lower periodic dosages, however, thresholds have not been established. Within workplace settings, exposure often is to multiple solvents, which raises further questions. A practical guideline for solvent exposure within the workplace is to minimize exposures to levels at or, better, less than current government guidelines, as established by National Institution for Occupational Safety and Health [NIOSH]. Such guidelines impose upon the employer the requirement that workplace monitoring occur on a regular basis using the same solvents and identical working conditions under which employees routinely work. Personal monitoring, where possible, is preferable. Without such monitoring, pregnant women, employers, and health care providers cannot establish risk accurately. Patient symptoms and anecdotal descriptions of working conditions become the basis of evaluation. Evaluation thereby is compromised. Moreover, pregnant employees may confront limitation of job opportunities, since employers and health care providers, with appropriate intentions, prefer to be conservative in job placement and activities for pregnant women, when only incomplete monitoring data are available.

Increased pregnancy loss has been reported among laboratory workers who work with organic solvents; other investigations have not reported a similar association (Axelsson, Lutz, & Rylander, 1984). In animal studies, prolonged exposure to organic solvents do produce reproductive toxicity (Paraf, Lewis, & Jothy, 1993; Taskinen, Lindbohm, Hemminki, 1986). Solvents such as benzene and toluene have produced chromosomal damage in cultured cells. As mentioned earlier, one must consider both dosage and length of exposure to the solvent when determining risk. For employees, such evaluations would include length of time working with the solvents, physical contact with solvents (via the skin, inhalation, and food ingestion or contamination), and especially ventilation in the workplace and/or personal protective equipment. Fetal solvent syndrome (FSS) produces many birth defects which are associated with ethanol or alcohol. [Please see the discussion, below, about alcohol.] The major solvents with such associations are gasoline and toluene. Current information is based upon chronic solvent abuse ("gasoline and glue sniffing") and not specifically upon workplace exposures. It is recommended that all NIOSH-approved safety procedures be used in the workplace. Protective clothing and gloves should be worn with adequate ventilation, and personal charcoal respirators should be used when appropriate. While risks of certain behavior may appear obvious to all, it nevertheless is surprising how many workers do drink, eat, and smoke in the workplace. It is necessary to caution all workers, and especially pregnant women, that such behaviors are contraindicated.

Alcohol/Ethanol

Fetal alcohol syndrome (FAS) has been characterized by clinical features including prenatal and postnatal growth deficiency, mental retardation, behavioral abnormalities (hyperactivity), a pattern of facial features (midline hypoplasia, short palpebral fissures, a hypoplastic philtrum), and other major organ system malformations (heart, renal, and reproductive tract) (Jones et al., 1974). FAS occurs in approximately 30% to 45% of women who drink more than five ounces of absolute alcohol daily. In one report, ingesting three ounces of alcohol (equivalent to drinking six beers) per day was associated with FAS (Kaminski Rumeau, & Schwartz, 1978). Binge drinking and moderate ethanol drinking during pregnancy have been more difficult to associate with risk; additional studies are continuing to demonstrate associations, however.

Clearly, complete abstention from alcohol consumption during pregnancy will eliminate the risk of FAS. It should be noted, however, that exposure either occupationally or especially recreationally to high chronic ingestion of selected organic solvents has been reported to produce FSS. These malformations clustered as a syndrome are becoming known as the fetal solvent syndrome (FSS). Alcohol use, especially during late pregnancy, is associated with an increase in childhood leukemia (Shu et al., 1996). Interestingly, paternal alcohol use or smoking has not been associated with childhood leukemia.

In relationship to pregnancy loss, women who drink one ounce of absolute ethanol at least 2 times per week experience twice the rate of pregnancy loss, when compared with nonexposed controls (Kline et al., 1980). In all of these investigations, it must be realized that the inability to monitor accurately dose and exposure of a pervasive toxicant such as ethanol continues to undermine the strength of many observations regarding adverse effects of moderate alcohol consumption during pregnancy. Consumption of more than two drinks of alcohol per day, however, can be expected to compromise fetal health and development, as has been noted in reports for health care providers (Zuckerman & Hingson, 1986).

Toluene

Toluene (methylbenzene) commonly is found in metal cleaning agents, glues, lacquers, and paints (spray). The threshold limit value (TLV) in the air is 50 parts per million (ppm) (approximately 1/10 the dose which produces euphoria) (National Institute for Occupational Safety and Health Standard). Symptoms associated with acute toluene exposure are headache, dizziness, light-headedness, hallucinations, and/or fainting. Chronic toluene use (directly inhaling, for abuse purposes, one to four spray cans per day) produces (in addition to the previously mentioned symptoms) muscle weakness, gastrointestinal complaints, and neuropsychiatric abnormalities with peripheral neuropathy and cerebellar atrophy, as well severe renal tubular acidosis (Goodwin, 1988).

In a study of Chinese female factory workers, increased pregnancy loss has been noted at two exposure levels of toluene (50-150 ppm and <30 ppm) (Ng, Foo, & Yoong, 1992). The numbers of workers (55 and 31) are supportive of such an association; however, the frequency of pregnancy loss in other studies where women were exposed to toluene does not support this association (Axelsson et al., 1984; Paraf et al., 1993; Taskinen et al., 1986). Thirty-six women who had abused (sniffed) toluene chronically during pregnancy gave birth to children suffering syndromes with many similarities to FAS (Hersh et al., 1985; Wilkins-Haug & Gabow, 1991). Three of these pregnancies resulted in spontaneous pregnancy loss. In 21 of the pregnancies, 86% resulted in preterm delivery. Many of the women had renal problems as well as cerebellar atrophy.

In another report (Euler, 1967), two children with multiple malformations were born to women who were exposed chronically to toluene and trichloroethylene in solution, in their employment as shoemakers. Such reports suggest that it is possible to reach levels of toluene in the workplace that may produce reproductive and developmental toxicity. Such human data are supported by animal investigations (Hudak & Ungvary, 1978; Kostas & Hotchin, 1981), which demonstrated not only skeletal defects following exposure to high doses of toluene but also behavioral alterations (REPROTOX®, 1996).

Gasoline

Gasoline is a commonly used solvent to run combustion engines; gasoline also has been an inexpensive abused solvent, however. The association between birth defects and chronic gasoline exposure comes from a Native American community, where recreational sniffing of gasoline was common

(Hunter, Thompson, & Evans, 1979). Six children with behavioral and functional deficiencies and mental retardation were identified. Although ethanol also was used heavily by some of the pregnant women, the authors of the study excluded alcohol ingestion as a contributing factor. Since gasoline does contain low amounts of lead, please refer also to the previous discussion about lead.

Prospective Actions by Women to Reduce Risk of Pregnancy Loss: Diet

When attempting to conceive or during the reproductive years, it is essential for women to take one multivitamin (containing at least 0.4 mg of folic acid and <10,000 IU units of vitamin A as retinyl esters or retinol). Even though the Food and Drug Administration has recommended supplementing flour with folic acid, these amounts of folic acid may not be sufficient for all women. Thus, women who are considering attempting pregnancy should take a multivitamin regularly. In fact, Dr. Godfrey Oakley, Director of the Center for Birth Defects of the United States Centers for Disease Control in Atlanta, Georgia, has suggested as a wedding gift providing for a year's supply of multivitamins for the bride.

Second, women who are planning for a pregnancy should eat a balanced diet without extremes in the consumption of specific food types (for example, liver, swordfish, shark). Third, pregnancy is not the time to diet in order to lose excess weight. It is appropriate to control excessive weight gain during the pregnancy, but sufficient daily nourishment is essential for the developing fetus. Fourth, abstain from alcohol consumption. Drinking excessive amounts of alcohol during pregnancy definitely is associated with fetal alcohol syndrome. Overall, the most common-sense guideline is to practice moderation in all foods consumed, and to avoid alcohol, cigarettes, and other known harmful substances altogether.

Therapeutic Agents

Women should discuss with their primary care physician as well as their gynecologist any medications which they should take, and ask about their potential impact upon fertility and baby. They should also inquire about similar issues related to medications for their significant other.

Table 3-8.
Teratogen Information Services

United States		
Arizona	Arizona Teratogen Information Service	800-362-0101 (AZ only)
	Arizona Teratogen Information Program	520-626-4382
Arkansas	Arkansas Teratogen Information Services	501-296-1700
California	California Teratogen Information Service &	800-532-3749 (CA only)
	Clinical Research Project	619-294-6084
Colorado	TIES	800-332-2082 (CO only)
		303-372-1825
		800-525-4871 (WY only)
Connecticut	Connecticut Pregnancy Exposure	800-325-5301 (CT only)
	Information Service	860-679-1502
Florida	Teratogen Information Service-Gainesville	800-392-3050 (FL only)
		904-392-3050
	Teratogen Information Service	813-975-6905
Georgia	Centers for Disease Control	404-488-4967
Illinois	Illinois Teratogen Information Services	800-262-4847 (IL only)
		312-908-7441
Indiana	Indiana Teratogen Information Services	317-274-1071
Iowa	University of Iowa Prenatal Diagnostic Unit	319-356-3561
	University of Iowa Teratogen Information	319-356-2674
	Services	
Kansas	Prenatal Diagnosis and Genetics Clinic	316-688-2362
Massachusetts	Massachusetts Teratogen Information Service	800-322-5014 (MA only)
		617-466-8474
Missouri	Columbia Teratogen Information Services	314-882-6991
	Genetics & Environmental Information Services	314-454-8172
Nebraska	Nebraska Teratogen Project	402-559-5071
New Jersey	New Jersey Pregnancy Risk Information	800-287-3015 (NJ only)
	Services	

New York	Perinatal Environmental Drugs Exposure Counseling Service (PEDECS)	716-275-3638
	Western New York Teratogen Information Services	800-724-2454 x270 (NY only) 716-565-0240
North Dakota	University of North Dakota	701-777-4277
Pennsylvania	Pregnancy Safety Hotline	412-687-SAFE
	Magee-Women's Hospital	412-647-4168
South Dakota	Teratogen and Birth Defects Info Project	800-962-1642
Texas	Genetic Screening and Counseling Service	817-383-3561
	Texas Teratogen Information Service	800-733-4727
Utah	Pregnancy Riskline	800-822-2229 (UT only) 800-521-2229 (MT only) 801-328-2229
Vermont	Vermont Pregnancy Risk Information Service	800-531-9800 (VT only) 802-658-4310
Washington	Carc North West	206-543-3373 800-859-5343
West Virginia	West Virginia Teratogens in Pregnancy Service	304-293-1572
Wisconsin	Teratogen Information Service	800-362-9567 (WI, MN, IA, and northern IL only) 608-791-6681
	Wisconsin Teratogen Project	800-442-6692 (WI only) 608-263-4719
	Great Lakes Genetics	414-475-7400 414-475-7223
	Eastern Wisconsin Teratogen Project	414-357-6555
Canada *Ontario* Hamilton	Safe Start Program	416-521-2100 x6788
London	Fetal Risk Assessment/Maternal Exposure	519-685-8293
Toronto	Motherisk Program	416-813-6780
British Columbia Vancouver	University of British Columbia	604-975-2157
	British Columbia Drug and Poison Information Center	604-682-2344 x2126

Occupational Exposures

Before conception if possible, women should discuss with their primary care provider, gynecologist, and employer any issues of concern which may be related to their workplace. Each employee by federal law should have available at all times information about any chemicals or other possibly harmful substances which are present in the workplace. In many instances, information is provided in a manufacturer's safety data sheet (MSDS), which discusses the substances that potentially are toxic within the product, as well as information about safe use and handling of the product, and the chemical characteristics of the toxins associated with the product. Each employee has the right to know this information. Furthermore, each employee should be provided with appropriate equipment for protecting her from chemicals used. In many instances, adequate ventilation can be the most helpful mechanism to exhaust fumes and keep the levels of the chemicals low within the workplace without resorting to charcoal-filled respirators. It is interesting to note that many individuals believe that dust or surgical masks are helpful in protecting themselves from solvent or gas exposures. These masks in fact are useless in terms of screening out the effects of inhaling the fumes of solvents and gases. Other potentially harmful substances to be aware of include X-irradiation, gaseous anesthetics, and heavy metals (lead, cadmium, mercury, and others).

Environmental Exposures

Women should discuss any potential risks of exposure to harmful environmental toxins with their primary care provider and gynecologist. In New York state, it is required that all pregnant women be screened for lead exposure, in the attempt to reduce such exposure early in pregnancy. Certainly, the woman and her family have a responsibility to bring forward all issues to health care providers. As mentioned early in this chapter, the individual must minimize all exposures which can lead to birth defects and/or pregnancy loss. We always must keep in mind that pregnancy loss is a natural selection process for screening out genetic problems among embryos, as well as physical and biochemical constraints for the mother. Not all pregnancy losses are related to therapeutic, occupational, or environmental exposures. But, for the pregnancy losses that can be related to such exposure, modification of therapy, work habits, and exposures is essential. It is the woman's obligation, with the support of her care providers, employers, and family, to raise these issues and to implement these modifications, to improve her chances of a successful outcome to her pregnancy.

For additional information, the reader is referred to state or regional services, such the Teratogen Information Services (TIS) (see Table 3-8).❏

Acknowledgments

The author would like to credit REPROTOX®, TERIS, and DART (National Library of Medicine), for data/summaries used in this review, and to thank Anthony Scialli, MD, and James R. Woods, Jr., MD, for their advice.

Case Study 1-8

Occupational Exposures

A 33-year-old white female presents with her fourth pregnancy loss (at 9 weeks) in the last 3 years. She reports herself to be in good health. However, her physician indicates that she has substantial protein in her urine including increased beta$_2$ microglobulin levels; retinol binding protein or metallothionein were not measured. She does not take vitamins, eats a typical American diet (no reported ingestion of liver or shark/swordfish), and drinks alcohol socially (no more than two to three glasses of wine or beer per week). She smokes cigarettes (one half to a full pack per day). She lives in a home which was built in the 1980s in a suburban tract with municipal water. She has been employed as a high school industrial arts teacher for 8 years. Her job responsibilities include teaching welding and metal craft. She works 6 hours per day teaching students how to weld. Ventilation is marginal in the welding classroom. No monitoring for concentrations of metals or solvents was performed in the workplace. Her nephrologist determined that her urinary cadmium levels were 11 mg cd/g creatinine. She reports no unusual hobbies. Her husband is an English teacher at the same school.

What are her risks for having another pregnancy loss? Should any interventions be initiated at home; in the workplace? What could the patient do to reduce her risks for pregnancy loss/birth defects?

Commentary

The case study as presented has two interesting aspects — recurrent pregnancy loss and exposure to cadmium via the patient's cigarette smoking, and her occupational association with welding. In addition to the known attributes of this case, there are several important issues which remain unaddressed, and which should be resolved before final guidance is given. These include obtaining a more detailed reproductive history; for example, how many pregnancies has she actually had; were all of her pregnancies which resulted in losses confirmed; did all of her pregnancy losses occur early in the first trimester? Assuming that this woman is a G4 P0Ab4 with all losses occurring during the first trimester and over the past 3 years, then the next series of questions should deal with identifying reasons for recurrent pregnancy loss, likely outcome of her next pregnancy, and the types of interventions that may improve the outcome of her next pregnancy.

Given the abbreviated nature of the case presentation, we do not know what types of evaluations were carried out prior to the woman's fourth pregnancy and her subsequent loss by spontaneous miscarriage. However, having had three prior first-trimester losses substantially increases her risk of loss in her fourth pregnancy, and this should have led to a more detailed evaluation, including genetic and anatomic factors, before the woman undertook a new pregnancy. In addition, her partner's reproductive history also is important to evaluate. Has he had pregnancies with this partner previously? Has he had successful or unsuccessful pregnancies with other partners? Such consultations also should include discussion about the impact of personal habits or environmental or occupational exposures on pregnancy outcome. For this patient, her cigarette smoking and her occupational exposure to welding fumes (cadmium) are issues to investigate.

It is important to note that cigarette smokers, in addition to other adverse effects on their reproductive capability, also have an increased risk of early pregnancy loss (the adverse reproductive effects which are associated with smoking include growth restriction, premature delivery, and early pregnancy loss). Interestingly, this increased loss appears to be among chromosomally normal conceptuses, which suggests an adverse endocrine or uterine effect. Among women who smoke cigarettes during pregnancy, the frequency of spontaneous miscarriage is 20% to 80% higher and does appear to be cigarette-dose related. Because smoking also appears to decrease fertility, it is important to ascertain accurately whether or not the patient's three prior pregnancy losses indeed were verified or simply were delayed menstrual periods. In addition to carbon monoxide, cigarettes represent a potential exposure to cadmium, the other exposure of concern in this case study. Among individuals who are not exposed occupationally, cigarettes and some food sources represent the largest sources of cadmium exposure.

Like cigarettes, cadmium has no known beneficial effects on the body. Adverse effects include toxicity to the lungs, kidneys, and bones. While it is not known if cadmium can alter reproduction or development in humans, cadmium has been shown in a variety of animal experiments to increase the risk of developmental toxicity (including malformations and embryo toxicity), and cadmium has been implicated for increased risk of growth restriction as a result of microvascular damage in the human placenta. While the exact mechanism of developmental toxicity of cadmium in experimental animals remains under investigation, some investigators believe that a significant effect is placental toxicity, specifically damage to the small vessels in the placenta. This also has been demonstrated to be associated with cadmium toxicity in the testes and other endocrine organs, which are sensitive to cadmium toxicity.

In summary, evaluation for anatomic, infectious, and genetic causes of recurrent pregnancy loss are warranted. Given the patient's history, it is likely that her next pregnancy also will result in spontaneous abortion. Exposure to cadmium and cigarette smoking also may be worth consideration. In this case, I would encourage the woman to stop smoking cigarettes, and I would advise her to minimize, as much as possible, her exposure to cadmium in the workplace.

— *Donald Mattison, MD, MS*

Case Study 2-8

Therapeutic Exposure – Accutane

A 19-year-old white female presents with the fact she is pregnant and it has been 6 weeks since her last menstrual period (December 1). She reports that her dermatologist counseled her that she should not become pregnant; however, the patient stopped her course of Accutane (isotretinoin) treatment 1mg/kg/day for cystic acne on December 1, the same date as her last menstrual period. She also reported that her gynecologist did a pregnancy test before she started the drug and each month when a new prescription for the Accutane was issued. The previous pregnancy tests were negative. When she came for a pregnancy test the day before this visit (January 12), the pregnancy test was positive. She was not using her diaphragm regularly since stopping her oral contraceptives. Her physician thought that she may still be at risk because of the long half-life of the drug and was referred. She neither smokes cigarettes nor consumes alcoholic beverages. She reports no street drug use. She does take daily a multi-vitamin. She reports a typical American diet. She lives in a 1950s home in a residential area of the city. The home is on municipal water. The home recently was painted, and no home remodeling has occurred in years. She does not report ingestion of liver, shark, or swordfish. No unusual hobbies were reported. No specific risk factors were noted for the father.

What are the risks for pregnancy loss and birth defects associated with Accutane? Is this patient at significant risk beyond the risk (3%) for all women for having a baby with retinoid (Accutane) syndrome?

Commentary

A 19-year-old woman who was receiving oral isotretinoin (1 mg/kg) daily for cystic acne was counseled by her dermatologist to cease taking her medication since she wanted to become pregnant. Her monthly pregnancy tests (required by the dermatologist) were negative up through the time when she ceased her isotretinoin therapy. Six weeks after cessation of therapy, and 2 weeks after missing her next menstrual period, the woman's pregnancy test was positive. Analysis of her risks for isotretinoin-induced malformations and medication-related abortion are determined easily in this particular case.

First, the pharmacokinetics of orally administered isotretinoin indicate that there would not be any isotretinoin or its metabolites present at the time of fertilization, which would be 2 weeks after cessation of therapy. The greatest risk for medication-related abortion is early in pregnancy. The period of insensitivity to the malforming effects of many teratogens (the "all-or-none period") is from the time of ovulation to the end of the 2nd week postconception. Since she ceased therapy on December 1 and probably conceived on December 14 or 15, there would be no measurable isotretinoin or metabolites of isotretinoin present during this period (December 15 to 29; 1 to 14 days postconception). Since organogenesis begins around the 18th day postconception and many retinoid malformations are produced during this period of early organogenesis (18 to 36 days postconception), there also would not be an increased risk of major congenital malformations.

Furthermore, since at the time of her pregnancy test she was 30 days postconception, the patient can be reassured that her risk of miscarriage probably is less than the usual risk of miscarriage at the beginning of clinically recognized pregnancies.

Of course, conveying the fact the isotretinoin exposure will not increase her risk of miscarriage or malformations must be balanced with the fact that she still has the background risk of major malformations (3%) and spontaneous miscarriage (now less than 15% because of her current pregnancy status). Since this patient is young and appears not to have any other risk factors, routine obstetric care should suffice. If she expresses continued concerns about teratogenesis, the patient may benefit if her physician requested a Level II ultrasound to allay maternal anxiety.

— *Robert Brent, MD, PhD, DSc*

References

Anonymous. (1993). *Dental amalgam: A scientific review and recommended Public Health Service strategy for research, education, and regulation.* Washington, DC: U.S. Department of Health and Human Services.

Avilés, A., Diaz-Macqueo, J.C., Talavera, A., Guzmán, R., & Garcia, E.L. (1991). Growth and development of children of mothers treated with chemotherapy during pregnancy: Current status of 43 children. *American Journal of Hematology, 36,* 243-248.

Axelsson, G., Lutz, C., & Rylander, R. (1984). Exposure to solvents and outcome of pregnancy in university laboratory employees. *British Journal of Industrial Medicine, 41,* 305-312.

Baird, D.D., & Wilcox, A.J. (1985). Cigarette smoking associated with delayed conception. *Journal of the American Medical Association, 253,* 2979.

Barnes, A.B., Colton, T., Gundersen, J., Noller, K.L., Tilley, B.C., Strama, T., Townsend, D.E., Hatab, P., & O'Brien, P.C. (1980). Fertility and outcome of pregnancy in women exposed *in utero* to diethylstilbestrol. *New England Journal of Medicine, 302,* 609-613.

Barr, Jr., M. (1994). Teratogen update: Angiotensin-converting enzyme inhibitors. *Teratology, 50,* 399-409.

Barr, M. Jr., & Cohen, Jr., M.M. (1991). ACE inhibitor fetopathy and hypocalvaria: The kidney-skull connection. *Teratology, 44,* 485-495.

Bellinger, D. (1994). Teratogen update: Lead. *Teratology, 50,* 367-373.

Botto, L.D., Lynberg, M.C., Khoury, M.J., & Moore, C.A. (1994). An epidemiologic evaluation of the association between first-trimester fever and multiple congenital anomalies of the hyperthermia-related spectrum. *Teratology, 49,* 376-377.

Brent, R.L. (1980). Radiation teratogenesis. *Teratology, 21,* 281-298.

Bingol, N., Fuchs, M., Diaz, V., Stone, R.K., & Gromisch, D.S. (1987). Teratogenicity of cocaine in humans. *Journal of Pediatrics, 110,* 93-96.

Buehler, B.A., Delimont, D., van Waes, M., & Finnell, R.H. (1990). Prenatal prediction of risk of the fetal hydantoin syndrome. *New England Journal of Medicine, 322,* 1567-1572.

Chavez, G.F., Mulinare, J., & Cordero, J.F. (1989). Maternal cocaine use during early pregnancy as a risk factor for congenital urogenital anomalies. *Journal of the American Medical Association, 262,* 795-798.

Eisenmann, C.J., & Miller, R.K. (1996). Placental transport, metabolism, and toxicity of metals. In L.W. Chang (Ed.), *Toxicology of metals* (pp. 1003-1026). Boca

Raton, FL: CRC Press.

Erickson, J.D. (1991). Risk factors for birth defects: Data from the Atlanta birth defects case-control study. *Teratology, 43*, 41-51.

Euler, H.H. (1967). Animal experimental studies of an industria noxa. *Archiv fur Gynakologie, 204*, 258-259.

Friedman, J., & Polifka, J. (1995). *Teratogenic effects of drugs (TERIS)*. Baltimore: Johns Hopkins Press.

Giusti, R.M., Iwamoto, K., & Hatch, E.E. (1995). Diethylstilbestrol revisited: A review of the long-term health effects. *Annals of Internal Medicine, 122*, 778-788.

Goldman, A.S., & Yaffe, S.J. (1978). Fetal trimethadione syndrome. *Teratology, 17*, 103-106.

Goodwin, T.M. (1988). Toluene abuse and renal tubular acidosis in pregnancy. *Obstetrics and Gynecology, 71*, 715-718.

Gratacos, E., Torres, P.J., & Antolin, E. (1993). Use of cocaine during pregnancy. *New England Journal of Medicine, 329*, 667.

Handler, A.S., Mason, E.D., Rosenberg, D.L., & Davis, F.G. (1994). The relationship between exposure during pregnancy to cigarette smoking and cocaine use and placenta previa. *American Journal of Obstetrics Gynecology, 170*, 884-889.

Hanson, J.W. (1986). Teratogen update: Fetal hydantoin effects. *Teratology, 33*, 349-353.

Herbst, A.L., Hubby, M.M., Blough, R.R., & Azizi, F. (1980). A comparison of pregnancy experience in DES-exposed daughters. *Journal of Reproductive Medicine, 24*, 62-69.

Hersh, J.H., Podruch, P.E., Rogers, G., & Weisskopf, B. (1985). Toluene embryopathy. *Journal of Pediatrics, 106*, 922-927.

Hudak, A., & Ungvary, G. (1978). Embryotoxic effects of benzene and its methyl derivatives: Toluene, xylene. *Toxicology, 11*, 55-63.

Hunter, A.G.W., Thompson, D., & Evans J.A. (1979). Is there a fetal gasoline syndrome? *Teratology, 20*, 75-79.

Isojarvi, J.I.T., Laatikainen, T.J., Pakarinen, A.J., Juntunen, K.T.S., & Myllyla, V.V. (1993). Polycystic ovaries and hyperandrogenism in women taking valproate for epilepsy. *New England Journal of Medicine, 329*, 1383-1388.

Jick, H., & Porter, J. (1977). Relation between smoking and age of natural menopause: Report from the Boston Collaborative Drug Surveillance Program, Boston University Medical Center. *Lancet, 1*, 1354.

Jones, K., Smith, D.W., Streissguth, A.P., & Myrianthopoulos, N.C. (1974). Outcome in offspring of chronic alcoholic women. *Lancet, 1*, 1076-1078.

Kaminski, M., Rumeau, C., & Schwartz, D. (1978). Alcohol consumption in pregnant women and the outcome of pregnancy. *Alcoholism, 2*, 155-163.

Kaufman, R.H., Adam, E., Noller, K., Irwin, J.F., & Gray, M. (1986). Upper genital-tract changes and infertility in diethylstilbestrol-exposed women. *American Journal of Obstetrics and Gynecology, 154*(6), 1312-1318.

Kleinman, J.C., Pierre, Jr., M.B., Madans, J.H., Land, G.H., & Schramm, W.F. (1988). The effects of maternal smoking on fetal and infant mortality. *American Journal of Epidemiology, 127*, 274-282.

Kline, J., Stein, Z., Shrout, P., Susser, M., & Warburton, D. (1980). Drinking during pregnancy and spontaneous abortion. *Lancet, 2*, 176-180.

Lammer, E.J., Sever, L.E., & Oakley, Jr., G.P. (1987). Teratogen update: Valproic acid. *Teratology, 35*, 465-473.

Kostas, J., & Hotchin, J. (1981). Behavioral effects of low-level perinatal exposure to toluene in mice. *Neurobehavior Toxicology and Teratology, 3*, 467-469.

Lindhout, D., & Omtzigt, J.G.C. (1994). Teratogenic effects of antiepileptic drugs: Implications for the management of epilepsy in women of childbearing age. *Epilepsia, 35* (Suppl. 4), S19-S28.

Little, B.B., Ghali, F.E., Snell, L.M., Knoll, K., Johnston, W., & Gilstrap, III, L.C. (1991). Is hyperthermia teratogenic in the human? *American Journal of Perinatology, 8*, 185-189.

MacArthur, C., & Knox, E.G. (1987). Passive smoking and birthweight. *Lancet, 1*, 37-38.

Mattison, D.R., Shiromizu, K., & Nightingale, M.S. (1983). Oocyte destruction by polycyclic aromatic hydrocarbons. *American Journal of Industrial Medicine, 4*, 191.

Miller, R.K., & Ballinger, D. (1993). Metals (lead, cadmium, and mercury) and reproduction. In M. Paul (Ed.), *Occupational and environmental reproductive hazards: A guide for clinicians* (pp. 223-266). Baltimore: Williams and Wilkins.

Milunsky, A., Ulcickas, M., Rothman, K.J., Willett, W., Jick, S.S., & Jick, H. (1992). Maternal heat exposure and neural tube defects. *Journal of the American Medical Association, 268*, 882-885.

Morrow, R.J., Knox Ritchie, J.W., & Bull, S.B. (1988). Maternal cigarette smoking: The effects on umbilical and uterine blood flow velocity. *American Journal of Obstetrics and Gynecology, 159*, 1069-1071.

Naeye, R.L. (1977). Causes of perinatal mortality in the United States: Collaborative perinatal project. *Journal of the American Medical Association, 238*, 228-229.

National Council on Radiation Protection and Measurements. (1979). Medical radiation exposure of pregnant and potentially pregnant women. *NCRP Report No. 54*, p. 32.

National Institute for Occupational Safety and Health Standard.

Ng, T.P., Foo, S.C., & Yoong, T. (1992). Risk of spontaneous abortion in workers exposed to toluene. *British Journal of Industrial Medicine, 49*, 804-088.

Olsen, J. (1991). Cigarette smoking, tea and coffee drinking, and subfecundity. *American Journal of Epidemiology, 133*, 734-739.

Paraf, F., Lewis, J., & Jothy, S. (1993). Acute fatty liver of pregnancy after exposure to toluene: A case report. *Journal of Clinical Gastroenterology, 17*, 163-165.

Plessinger, M.A., & Woods, Jr., J.R. (1991). The cardiovascular effects of cocaine use in pregnancy. *Reproductive Toxicology, 5*, 99-113.

REPROTOX®, Computer Information Service. (1996). Reproductive Toxicology Center; Columbia Hospital for Women Medical Center; 2440 M Street, NW, Suite 217; Washington, D.C. 20037-1404.

Robert, E. (1988). Valproic acid as a human teratogen. *Congenital Anomalies, 28* (Suppl.), S71-S80.

Robinson, D., Rock, J., & Menkin, M.F. (1968). Control of human spermatogenesis by induced changes of intrascrotal temperature. *Journal of the American Medical Association, 204*, 290-297.

Rosenak, D., Diamant, Y.Z., Yaffe, H., & Hornstein, E. (1990). Cocaine: Maternal use during pregnancy and its effect on the mother, the fetus, and the infant. *Obstetrics Gynecology Survey, 45*(6), 348-359.

Sever, J.L., & Brent, R.L. (1986). *Teratogen update: Environmentally induced birth defect risks.* New York: Alan R. Liss.

Shu, X-O, Ross, J.A., Perdergrass, T.W., Reaman, G.H., Lampkin, B.L., & Robinson, L.L. (1996). Perinatal alcohol consumption, cigarette smoking, and risk of infant leukemia. A Children's Cancer Group study. *Journal of the National Cancer Institute, 88*, 24-31.

Sikorski, R., Radomanski, T., Paszkowski, T., & Skoda, J. (1988). Smoking during pregnancy and the perinatal cadmium burden. *Journal of Perinatology Medicine, 16*, 225-231.

Swanson, B.N., Harland, R.B., Dickinson, R.G., & Gerber, N. (1978). Excretion of valproic acid into semen of rabbits and man. *Epilepsia, 19*, 541-546.

Taskinen, H., Lindbohm, M-L., & Hemminki, K. (1986). Spontaneous abortions among women working in the pharmaceutical industry. *British Journal of Industrial Medicine, 43*, 199-205.

Tikkanen, J., & Heinonen, O.P. (1991). Maternal hyperthermia during pregnancy and cardiovascular malformations in the offspring. *European Journal of Epidemiology, 7*, 628-635.

Trichopoulus, D. (1986). Passive smoking, birthweight and oestrogens. *Lancet, 2*, 743.

Veridiano, N.P., Delke, I., Rogers, J., & Tancer, M.L. (1981). Reproductive performance of DES-exposed female progeny. *Obstetrics Gynecology, 58*, 58-61.

Underwood, P., Hester, L.L., Laffitte, Jr., T., & Gregg, K.V. (1965). The relationship of smoking to the outcome of pregnancy. *American Journal of Obstetrics and Gynecology, 91*, 270-276.

Underwood, P.B., Kesler, K.F., O'Lane, J.M., & Callagan, D.A. (1967). Parental smoking empirically related to pregnancy outcome. *Obstetrics and Gynecology, 29*, 1-8.

Warkany, J. (1976). Warfarin embryopathy. *Teratology, 1*, 205-210.

Warkany, J. (1981). Teratogenicity of folic acid antagonists. *Cancer Bulletin, 33*(2), 76-77.

Wilcox, A.J., Baird, D.D., & Weinberg, C.R. (1989). Do women with childhood exposure to cigarette smoking have increased fecundability? *American Journal of Epidemiology, 129*, 1079-1083.

Wilcox, A.J., Baird, D.D., Weinberg, C.R., Hornsby, P.P., & Herbst, A.L. (1995). Fertility in men exposed prenatally to diethylstilbestrol. *New England Journal of Medicine, 332*, 1411-1416.

Wilkins-Haug, L., & Gabow, P.A. (1991). Toluene abuse during pregnancy: Obstetric complications and perinatal outcomes. *Obstetrics and Gynecology, 77*, 504-509.

Williams, M.A., Mittendorf, R., Lieberman, E., Monson, R.R., Schoenbaum, S.C., & Genest, D.R. (1991). Cigarette smoking during pregnancy in relation to *placen-*

ta previa. *American Journal of Obstetrics and Gynecology, 165,* 28-32.

Wong, V., Cheng, C.H., & Chan, K.C. (1993). Fetal and neonatal outcome of exposure to anticoagulants during pregnancy. *American Journal of Medical Genetics, 45,* 17-21.

Zuckerman, B.S., & Hingson, R. (1986). Alcohol consumption during pregnancy: A critical review. *Developmental Medicine and Child Neurology, 28,* 649-661.

Chapter 9

Termination of Pregnancy for Fetal Abnormalities

David Allen Baram

Health care providers caring for couples who elect to terminate desired pregnancies due to genetic or congenital abnormalities have an opportunity to help their patients through one of the most difficult and challenging decisions of their lives. These couples often are confused and ambivalent about whether or not to terminate the pregnancy, and sometimes they have a great deal of difficulty making this agonizing decision. By the time that they decide to terminate the pregnancy, they often are angry, guilty, and depressed. A sensitive and caring physician can guide couples through this excruciating experience by encouraging them to express their feelings and experience their grief, helping them to decide on the most appropriate method of pregnancy termination, providing them with respectful medical care, and, if desired by the couple, offering them memories of the pregnancy. Many couples undergo a prolonged grief process following termination of a desired, but abnormal, pregnancy. Therefore, careful followup of the couple following termination is extremely important.

Counseling the Couple Prior to the Procedure

After a fetal abnormality has been diagnosed, patients are faced with an agonizing choice. Should they continue the pregnancy or should they terminate it? Most likely, this is a desired, though not necessarily planned, pregnancy. The couple may have started to anticipate what their child will be like. Early in pregnancy, couples think about the fetus as a child with a place in the family and a future of its own (White-Van Mourik, Connor, & Ferguson-Smith, 1992). The pregnant woman probably has started to experience the physical and psychological changes of pregnancy (Black, 1993). In addition, the couple has started to bond with the fetus, and they already may have seen an image of the fetus on ultrasound. They may have told family, other children, co-workers, and friends about the pregnancy. Even very young children are aware of their parents' distress over the abnormality and the possibility of pregnancy termination (Furlong & Black, 1984).

Physicians providing abortion services for couples who decide to terminate a pregnancy need to be more than technicians. They should allow couples as much time as possible to talk about their feelings, ask questions about the procedure and hospital stay, and the handling of the fetus during and after the termination. They should strive to give couples as much choice and control as possible. Couples who may have opposed abortion in the past for religious or ethical reasons now may be faced with a very difficult decision. Their decision to terminate the pregnancy may be met with resistance by family or clergy.

Couples often have difficulty accepting the diagnosis of a chromosomal abnormality or fetal death *in utero*, and, despite the evidence which has been presented to them (such as seeing fetal death on ultrasound, or receiving the laboratory report which shows an abnormal number of chromosomes), often question the diagnosis. Is it possible that the laboratory made an error, or that the samples were mixed up? Could the ultrasonographer have been wrong? Every effort should be made to explain the abnormality to the couple and to reassure them about the accuracy of the diagnosis.

Prior to placement of laminaria for a dilatation and evacuation or the prostaglandin procedure, the method of termination should be discussed in detail, and complete informed consent should be obtained. Couples have much concern about the safety of termination procedures, the effect of the procedure on future pregnancies, and how much pain the woman will experience. Patients should be told about pain relief during and after the procedure. Many couples are concerned that the fetus will experience pain during the procedure. If the woman elects to have a dilatation and evacuation procedure performed under general anesthesia, she can be assured that the fetus also will be anesthetized and will not experience any pain.

With the physician's assistance, couples should be encouraged, if they desire, to create memories of the pregnancy in order to make the fetus/baby a tangible person (Lorenzen & Holzgreve, 1995). This allows the couple to make the loss real, enabling them to grieve on the basis of reality, not fantasy. An offer should be made to have the fetus baptized after delivery. This can be done easily in the delivery room after labor induction, or in the operating room after a dilatation and evacuation procedure, even if the fetus is not delivered intact. If the couple is interested, a blanket can be placed around the baby or the container holding the fetus and given to them after the procedure. Some patients may ask to provide their own baby blanket, perhaps a special one made for this baby. If a labor induction procedure is employed, the fetus will be born intact. Thus, footprints and photographs can be obtained, and the parents can be given the opportunity to hold their baby. Photographs of the baby can be taken after he or she has been cleaned and wrapped in a blanket. If the couple does not want photographs immediately, then they should be saved and offered to the family if they want them in the future. Often, the preconceived image of an anomalous fetus is much worse than the reality.

Many parents, in order to achieve closure on the delivery, will need to see and hold their baby and to receive mementos of the birth. They may elect to name the baby, after the baby's gender has been determined. Additional mementos of the birth can include a birth certificate, a tape measure with the length of the fetus marked, and an identification band (Mueller, 1990).

Parents may want to know what happens to the baby after delivery. While some babies will require only brief pathology examination, others will undergo an extensive and time-consuming autopsy. Occasionally, fetal tissue will be sent to the cytogenetics laboratory to confirm the diagnosis of a chromosomal abnormality. Often, the final autopsy results are not available for months. When the autopsy is complete, couples should have the opportunity to discuss the results with their obstetrician or the physician who provided the termination. If they choose, they may be given a copy of the autopsy report.

Fetal tissue usually is held by the pathology department for a specified period of time and then cremated, usually along with other hospital specimens. Some couples elect to have the hospital carry out the cremation. In these instances, couples need to understand that they will not have available to them the ashes from cremation. Other couples may decide that they would like to have their baby's ashes to keep, scatter, or bury. These couples can arrange to have the cremation carried out, with minimal expense, by a private funeral director.

Following the pregnancy termination, careful verbal and written instructions should be provided to the couple. A number of studies have demonstrated that patients often are confused and bewildered as they go through the genetic testing and termination process. They often report feeling confused or numb, and sometimes they are unable to remember or understand what they have been told by health care providers (White-VanMourik et al., 1990). The operating physician should visit the couple before they leave the hospital to reassure them that all went well with the procedure, to provide them with a baby blanket if they choose to take one, and to let them know what physical and psychological changes to expect after the procedure. Many women will experience breast fullness and lactation following a second-trimester termination. If they are not warned about the possibility of lactation, they may be surprised and distressed when it occurs. Lactation can be prevented by taking bromocriptine. Women can expect to experience vaginal bleeding and lower abdominal cramping for 2 to 4 weeks after the termination, and they should be provided with appropriate postoperative analgesia, if desired. Providing patients with prophylactic antibiotics (doxycycline) during a dilatation and evacuation will help to prevent infection. Patients should be asked, however, to report any postoperative fever, abnormal discharge, or pelvic pain immediately.

Couples will have many questions about possible restrictions following the termination. Typical questions include: What physical symptoms will the woman experience; when will the woman be able to return to work; what should they tell their family, friends, and co-workers about the pregnancy loss; when can they resume having sexual intercourse; and when can they begin to try to conceive another child? They also usually want to know the chances of conceiving another baby with a birth defect. Patients should be contacted by telephone several days after the termination to assess how they are doing, and to provide emotional support. They should be seen in the office 1 week after termination, and they should be contacted again by telephone at regular intervals, as needed.

Methods of Second-Trimester Pregnancy Termination

One of the most difficult decisions for patients who are electing to terminate a pregnancy for genetic indications is choosing the method of termination. Procedures which currently are available for performing second-trimester pregnancy terminations include dilatation and evacuation (D&E); intra-amniotic, extraovular, intramuscular, or intravaginal application of prostaglandin; intra-amniotic instillation of hyperosmolar urea or hypertonic saline; and intravenous administration of concentrated oxytocin (Ferguson et al., 1993; Owen, Hauth, Winkler, & Gray, 1992). All second-trimester abortion methods are safer and faster if the cervix previously has been dilated with natural or synthetic laminaria before the abortion procedure begins.

Each second-trimester abortion method has advantages and disadvantages. Unfortunately, little research on the various methods of second-trimester abortion has been done since the Joint Program for the Study of Abortion was concluded in the early 1980s. It is difficult to compare studies using various prostaglandin compounds, because prostaglandin F2 alpha, previously used for amnio-infusion abortions, has not been available in the United States since 1987. Therefore, it often is difficult to compare the morbidity and mortality of the various abortion methods currently available. It is clear, however, that the morbidity and mortality from older second-trimester abortion methods, such as hypertonic saline amnio-infusion, hysterotomy, and hysterectomy, are unacceptably high, and that these methods no longer should be used for pregnancy terminations (Grimes & Schulz, 1985).

The earlier that an abortion of any method is performed, the safer it is (Grimes, 1984). For this reason, every effort should be made to diagnose genetic or chromosomal abnormalities as soon as possible. Genetic amniocentesis should be performed as early in the gestation as technically possible. Maternal serum alpha fetoprotein tests should be obtained close to 16 weeks gestation. Chorionic villus sampling should be considered in patients who are at high risk for carrying a fetus with a genetic abnormality.

Dilatation and Evacuation

Dilatation and evacuation (D&E) is the most common procedure for second-trimester pregnancy termination used by obstetrician-gynecologists in the United States. D&E has the significant advantage of sparing the patient from the psychological and physical pain of going through labor and delivery. D&E terminations performed before 20 weeks gestation carry maternal morbidity and mortality rates which are significantly lower than methods requiring amnio-infusion or labor induction (Cates et al., 1982; Grimes & Schulz, 1985; Grimes, Hulka, & McCutchen, 1980; Kafrissen, Schulz, Grimes, & Cates, 1984; Peterson, Berry, Grace, & Gulbranson, 1983). The adjusted relative risk of serious complications associated with amnio-infusion with urea and/or prostaglandin, including hemorrhage, infection, retained products of conception, endometritis, cervical injury, and febrile morbidity, is two to three times greater than with D&E (Grimes & Schulz, 1985). D&Es are extremely safe surgical procedures, even during the late second trimester of pregnancy (Bowers, Chervenak, & Chervenak, 1989). D&E has the lowest maternal mortality rate of all second-trimester abortion methods (Grimes & Schulz, 1985). Second-trimester surgical terminations usually are performed in the hospital under general anesthesia, but they easily can be performed in ambulatory surgical centers with local anesthesia and intravenous sedation, making them convenient and relatively inexpensive (Hern, Zen, Ferguson, Hart, & Haseman, 1993).

While some geneticists are concerned that disruption of fetal tissue caused by a D&E will make confirmation of prenatal diagnoses difficult, this does not seem to be the case. In one study (Shulman et al., 1990) of 60 consecutive patients who underwent D&E after detection of fetal abnormalities (including chromosomal abnormalities, Mendelian disorders, neural tube defects, and multiple congenital abnormalities), prenatal diagnoses were confirmed during postmortem examination in all cases. In some cases of congenital abnormalities, like central nervous system abnormalities or multiple anomalies of unknown etiology, it is important not to disrupt fetal tissue so that a complete and accurate postmortem examination can be carried out. In these cases, labor induction techniques may be useful.

The advantages of D&E over other abortion techniques include decreased patient pain, ability to control the exact timing of the procedure, greatly reduced time of the abortion process, decreased incidence of retained products of conception, and prevention of a live birth. In one randomized trial (Grimes et al., 1980), comparing D&E to intra-amniotic instillation of prostaglandin F2a in patients between 13 and 18 weeks gestation, subjects receiving prostaglandin F2a had a relative risk of sustaining a complication which was 5.7 times higher than did those subjects undergoing D&E. Other studies, however, have found similar complication rates for amnio-infusion and D&E, when the procedures are done at advanced gestational age (Hill & Mackenzie, 1989). Disadvantages of D&E include the risk of anesthesia, possible laceration of the cervix or rupture of the uterus, disruption of fetal tissue, and inability of the couple to view and hold their baby, or to obtain photographs, footprints, and other mementos of the birth. In other words, there is no baby to say goodbye to. In addition, performance of the procedure requires a highly skilled and motivated operating surgeon, one who is familiar with the unique instruments which are required to do the procedure, as well as a cooperative operating room staff.

Amnio-infusion

For many years, amnio-infusion techniques have been used to induce second-trimester abortions. In the early 1970s, intra-amniotic saline infusions commonly were used for elective abortions. Intra-amniotic instillation of urea and/or prostaglandin also is effective as an abortifacient. Adding urea to prostaglandin for amnio-infusion significantly shortens the induction-to-abortion time and decreases the possibility of a live birth. However, complications from amnio-infusion abortions are common, especially when hypertonic saline is used (Ferguson et al., 1993). These complications include seizures, hypernatremia, water intoxication, and disseminated intravascular coagulation caused by intravascular instillation of the abortifacient, failure to abort, abortion of a live fetus, infection, hemorrhage, retained tissue (often requiring surgical removal under general anesthesia), and long instillation-to-abortion time.

Live births resulting from amnio-infusion techniques can be prevented by ultrasound-guided injection of potassium chloride into the fetal heart prior to amnio-infusion (Isada et al., 1992). Intra-amniotic urea and fetal intracardiac digoxin are less reliable than fetal intracardiac potassium chloride for causing fetal demise.

The long instillation-to-abortion time and the physical and emotional pain which patients experience by going through labor and delivering a non-viable baby make amnio-infusion methods emotionally difficult for both patients and staff. Many centers have replaced amnio-infusion with D&E as the method of choice for second-trimester abortions up to and beyond 20 weeks gestation (Grimes, 1984).

Several recent studies have looked at new prostaglandin analogs for extra-amniotic or intra-amniotic instillation (Ferguson et al., 1993; Huang, Chou, & Ho, 1994). In one study, the PG E2 analog sulprostone was administered by extra-amniotic infusion to terminate second-trimester pregnancies between 14 and 32 weeks gestation (Huang et al., 1994). Contraindications to sulprostone include previous cesarean section or major uterine surgery, placenta previa or abruptio placenta, premature rupture of the membranes, hypertension, and a history of asthma or allergy to prostaglandins. The mean time for instillation of sulprostone was 7 hours, and the induction-to-abortion interval was 17 hours. With this method, the majority of patients (92.5%) aborted within 48 hours. Adverse effects of sulprostone include nausea and vomiting, abdominal cramps, and vaginal bleeding. No serious complications were reported. However, a significant number of abortions were incomplete and required surgical completion. Pregnancy termination with sulprostone did not have an adverse effect on future fertility for the majority of patients. Sulprostone also can be administered intramuscularly, intravenously, or intravaginally (Ferguson et al., 1993; Kanhai & Keirse, 1993).

Vaginal Prostaglandin

Prostaglandin E2 vaginal suppositories, placed after overnight dilatation of the cervix with laminaria, are an effective method of inducing second-trimester abortions for genetic indications or fetal demise (Kirz & Haag, 1989; Lebed, Rubin, & Millman, 1980; Wiley, Poole, Gookin, Wiser, & Morrison, 1989). Side effects of prostaglandin vaginal suppositories (nausea, vomiting, diarrhea, and fever) can be decreased with the use of premedication. Disadvantages of PG E2 suppositories include the long induction-to-abortion time, the possibility of live birth, and the significant incidence of incomplete abortion requiring surgical removal of a retained placenta.

Concentrated Oxytocin

Concentrated oxytocin administered intravenously also can be used as an abortifacient, and it compares favorably with use of prostaglandin E2 vagina suppositories (Owen et al., 1992). Compared with women who received PG E2 suppositories, women who received intravenous oxytocin aborted more quickly and experienced less hypotension, pain, nausea, vomiting, fever, and diarrhea. Fewer live births were reported in women who received concentrated oxytocin solution for pregnancies between 17 and 24 weeks gestation. Water intoxication is a potential risk when oxytocin is administered over a long period of time, but only when large quantities of hypotonic diluents are used. Only one patient in the Owen study had a serious side effect from the use of oxytocin, a ruptured uterus in a woman who previously had undergone a cesarean section. Oxytocin and prostaglandin should not be used simultaneously due to increased risk of uterine rupture (American College of Obstetrics and Gynecology, 1987; Hagay, Leiberman, Picard, & Katz, 1989; Propping, Stubblefield, & Golub, 1977).

Summary of Second-Trimester Abortion Methods

If a skilled operator is available to perform termination, D&E is the most efficient and safest method for second-trimester pregnancy termination up to 24 weeks gestation (Stubblefield, 1991). If a skilled operator is unavailable, if there is a compelling reason to preserve fetal morphology, or if the parents request a labor induction method, then induction of labor with concentrated oxytocin or intravaginal PG E2 following cervical dilatation with laminaria is a reasonable alternative. Amnio-infusion methods and hysterotomy no longer should be used for second-trimester pregnancy termination.

The Effect of Second-Trimester Abortion on Health Care Providers

Most health care providers have no difficulty caring for patients who experience a fetal death *in utero* or stillbirth. Some may have very strong feelings about abortion, however, and they may find it difficult to provide care for patients terminating a pregnancy for genetic indications. In many medical centers, physicians, nurses, and other personnel working in the labor and delivery area are required to take care of all patients, including those who request a pregnancy termination.

Providing care for patients requesting termination of pregnancy for genetic indications can be extremely challenging, especially for physicians who perform D&Es (Kaltreider, Goldsmith, & Margolis, 1979). These patients are emotionally distraught, and they demand and deserve a great deal of attention, both before and after the procedure. Again, it is important to be available emotionally to patients, not merely to serve as a technician. No physician or nurse ever becomes completely desensitized to performing second-trimester abortions, which are very graphic and sometimes are upsetting to other members of the operating room team. Compared with a procedure where the patient goes through labor, D&E places much of the emotional stress on the operating room team.

Physicians performing abortions may be ostracized by their colleagues or may encounter opposition from the community or even the hospital. Burnout among physicians performing second-trimester abortions is not uncommon. Physicians performing the procedure should be sensitive to the feelings of other members of the operating room team, and they should try to minimize others' exposure to the sight of fetal parts. All fetal tissue should be handled in a discreet and respecting manner by the operating physician.

Patients often may displace their anger about the pregnancy loss on others, especially their health care providers. During bereavement, patients may feel abandoned by their care providers, even if they have received excellent care (Seller, Barnes, Ross, Barby, & Cowmeadow, 1993). Returning to the office of the physician who cared for them during the aborted pregnancy may bring back powerful and unpleasant memories. It is not at all unusual for patients, following a pregnancy loss, to look for a new physician, a different group practice, or another hospital for care during a subsequent pregnancy.

Counseling after Pregnancy Termination

The majority of couples who must terminate pregnancy for genetic indications grieve appropriately, and ultimately they believe that they made the best decision in a difficult situation. Many couples, however, continue to experience emotional turmoil after pregnancy termination. On one hand, couples are relieved that they were able to prevent the birth of a severely affected child. On the other hand, they may feel guilty about ending a wanted pregnancy. In one study (White-VanMourik et al., 1990), 20% of the women still noted regular crying, sadness, anger, guilt, and irritability 2 years after pregnancy termination. ("What did I do wrong? How could my body fail me this way? Was I responsible for my baby's abnormality? Did I pass on an abnormal gene? Is God getting even with me for something I've done wrong in the past? Did I let the baby down by not letting it be born?") Other common reactions include shame (over the abortion), fear that the condition will recur in a future pregnancy, and a sense of failure, vulnerability, isolation, and numbness (Seller et al., 1993). Somatic symptoms are common, including sleeplessness, fatigue, loss of concentration, panic attacks, and nightmares. Both men and women often report increased listlessness and loss of concentration. Marital conflict is not uncommon, and separation occurred in 12% of couples in one report (Seller et al., 1993). Those most likely to have difficulty after terminating a pregnancy are women with secondary infertility, those with little emotional support from family and friends, those who have used mental health services prior to the termination, and those who are young or immature (Black, 1993; White-VanMourik et al., 1990).

There is great variability in the way in which couples respond to pregnancy loss, and for this reason couples should be followed carefully during the post-abortion period. It is not unusual for couples to experience mood changes, reduced social activity and contact with family and friends, difficulty concentrating, memory loss, difficulty on the job, difficulty talking with the partner about their loss, and loss of interest in sexual activity. These problems may persist for 6 to 12 months following the termination (Black, 1989).

Many couples are embarrassed and ashamed by their situation and are unable to discuss their feelings with anyone (Black, 1993). Couples cope better when they receive validation of their feelings, understanding, and approval of their decision to terminate from friends, relatives, and health care providers.

Interestingly, men and women appear to grieve in very different ways after termination. Men appear to recover from their grief more quickly than do women (Black, 1993), and they are more likely to intellectualize and to keep their feelings to themselves. Women, of course, physically experience the pregnancy and the loss of the fetus. In this sense, men often seem like bystanders and often feel helpless as their partners experience the physical pain of the loss and the emotional and physical recovery that follows termination. This leads to a lack of synchrony between men and women in the grieving process. Many men do not remember the expected delivery date or the date of the termination, and thus are bewildered when their partners have an anniversary grief reaction a year or more later when one of these significant dates occurs.

Factors helpful in dealing with pregnancy termination for fetal indications include recognition, information, communication, and hope. Recognition implies that others, such as family members and health care providers, understand the couple's grief, ambivalent feelings, and the length of time needed to heal after the termination. Referral to self-help groups can be very beneficial. Literature is available on pregnancy loss and should be provided for couples. *A Heartbreaking Choice* is a newsletter (Pineapple Press; PO Box 312; St. Johns, MI 48879) which is written for parents who have interrupted their pregnancies after prenatal diagnosis and for the professionals who care for them. Complete information about any fetal abnormalities noted at the time of termination should be given to the couple. Explanations should be given without using medical jargon. The physical and psychosocial sequelae of the termination should be communicated carefully to the couple both verbally and in writing. Providing hope for a better pregnancy outcome in the future also is of great importance (White-VanMourik et al., 1992).

The majority of couples grieve appropriately after termination of pregnancy for genetic indications, and most gradually put the experience behind them and get on with their lives. According to Worder (1991), there are four tasks of mourning which bereaved couples must complete before further personal growth and development can occur. These are: accepting the reality of the loss, working through the pain of grief, adjusting to an environment in which the deceased is missing, and emotionally relocating the deceased and moving on with life. While anxiety, depression, and grief reactions are present in most couples 4 weeks after the termination, levels of psychiatric morbidity are at near-normal levels for the majority of couples 6 to 12 months after the abortion (Black, 1989; Elder & Laurence, 1991; Iles & Gath, 1993; Zeanah, Dailey, Rosenblatt, & Saller, 1993). Most couples, if properly counseled by knowledgeable and sensitive medical staff, will not require professional therapy following their pregnancy loss (Black, 1993).❏

Case Study 1-9

Termination for Twin-Twin Transfusion

A.M. is a 36-year-old graduate student married to a 37-year-old college professor. They have been married for 10 years, and this is their first pregnancy. After genetic counseling, they decided to have an amniocentesis for prenatal diagnosis at 16 weeks gestation, because of A.M.'s advanced maternal age. Just before the amniocentesis was performed, ultrasound unexpectedly demonstrated a twin gestation.

Several concerns were raised by the ultrasound finding. There was a 2-week discrepancy in the size of the fetal heads, and in the abdominal and thoracic diameters, consistent with early signs of discordant fetal growth. Severe oligohydramnios was noted in Twin B, which appeared to be fixed in the right upper quadrant of the uterus. Twin B appeared to be anatomically normal. The amniotic fluid volume was increased for Twin A. Large lateral ventricles and a prominent third ventricle were noted, raising the question of hydrocephalus in Twin A. Amniocentesis could be performed only on Twin A.

The abnormal ultrasound findings were communicated to the couple by the ultrasound sonographer and the perinatologist who was on call at the time. The couple had many questions about the significance of the findings and were instructed to followup with the woman's primary obstetrician as soon as possible. They met with this obstetrician the next day.

The couple were told that the abnormalities found on ultrasound most likely were due to twin-to-twin transfusion syndrome. Several options were presented to the couple. One option was to repeat the ultrasound in 1 week to assess the status of the twins and to wait until the result of the amniocentesis for Twin A was known before making any decisions. Another option was to terminate the pregnancy without waiting for the results of the genetic testing to come back.

The couple was devastated by the bad news, and initially they had difficulty making a decision about how to proceed with the information about the pregnancy. They did not think that the results of the amniocentesis would be a major help in their reaching a decision, because both fetuses seemed to be severely compromised, as determined by the ultrasound. They wanted to make a decision as soon as possible; and both agreed that they did not want to continue this pregnancy if either of the twins would be born with a major birth defect. While they had no religious or ethical problem with the issue of terminating a pregnancy, they wanted to be sure that they were "doing the right thing." They asked for and received a second opinion from a second perinatologist. This perinatologist reviewed the ultrasound results with the couple and concluded that the prognosis for the pregnancy was poor, concurring with the findings of the first perinatologist. He encouraged the couple to reach their own decision, and they decided that they wanted to terminate the pregnancy.

The couple had questions about differing procedures for termination. Which method — dilatation and evacuation versus prostaglandin induction — would be best for both the woman and the fetuses; and which method would yield the most information about what had gone wrong with the pregnancy? Would the babies feel any pain during the procedure?

Commentary

Demographically, this couple represents a growing segment of the reproductive population. They are somewhat older people, well-educated, who have postponed childbearing for 10 years, well into their 30s. Chances of complications during pregnancy increase with age, including the risk of multiple gestation and the risk of congenital anomaly (with or without chromosomal abnormality). Thus, although the majority of elderly gravidas can expect a healthy pregnancy and good outcome, delayed childbearing increases the burden of dealing with complex problems, such as those which are demonstrated in this case.

The twin pregnancy was unsuspected, until the pre-amniocentesis ultrasound; so this couple was presented simultaneously with information that there was more than one fetus and that additional problems existed. The fact that they received prompt consultation with a perinatologist, as well as with their own obstetrician, reflects excellent care. But, it is unclear to what degree they also were encouraged to seek counsel with trusted family members, friends, or clergy. In some communities, support groups exist which consist of couples who have experienced a problem pregnancy. These groups can be extremely helpful for the couple who suddenly feel isolated in dealing with a crisis. Further, professional counselors are trained to be supportive while remaining nonjudgmental and nondirectional. This kind of consultation also may have been helpful.

After learning that a pregnancy is abnormal, and that there is little chance that the baby (or babies, in this case) will survive, many couples seem to come rapidly to the decision to terminate the pregnancy. How much time to allow for decision making and for the couple to begin anticipatory griev-

ing for the loss of their hoped-for "perfect" baby is a question with no definitive or absolute answer. On the other hand, I have seen cases in which termination is started within a few hours of the patient's learning about the fetal
abnormality. This surely is too soon.

Many obstetricians point to the distress which the couple experiences,
and they want to help the couple get the process over with, in order to has-
ten resolution. Sometimes, the issue is raised that delay can result in fetal
maceration and difficulties with postmortem examination. Moreover, the
unsuccessful pregnancy represents a blow to care providers as well, who
often may not acknowledge their own feelings. The speed with which termination sometimes is initiated may have as much to do with care providers'
own emotional needs as it does with patients' actual medical needs. When
couples are given the option of deciding when to have the termination procedure, many people choose to wait for a considerable time.

Once the couple in this case decided to terminate the pregnancy, there
were a number of technical questions that also needed to be addressed. They
were asked to choose between a dilatation and evacuation procedure or
prostaglandin induction. They asked in return whether their babies would
feel pain and which procedure would yield the most information. To help
with the choice of method, the couple needs information about each procedure. Often, this can be done by describing each procedure in parallel
according to specific characteristics, such as medical risks (blood loss, infection, injury), comfort or consciousness level, anticipated duration of procedure, effects on the fetuses, and chances of live abortus.

At 16 weeks gestation with twins, the medical risks roughly are equal for
D&E versus prostaglandin induction, depending in part on the skill and experience of the surgeon. Therefore, the couple's decision will rest more on other
factors, such as their desire to see and hold the fetuses after delivery. In general, there can be considerable difficulty with analysis of gross detail following
D&E terminations, compared with labor inductions. In this case, however, a
fair amount of detail was obtained antenatally from ultrasound examination;
so there may have been little more to gain from pathology examination.

The issue of whether or not a fetus experiences pain during abortion or
delivery is a difficult question to answer. We do know that the nervous system
develops quite early, and that fetuses do react to stimuli by withdrawal and
muscular activity. But, since pain itself is a subjective perception linked to
communication, past experience, culture, and meaning, it is doubtful that
physical sensations and reactions of a fetus can be translated into what we

think of as "pain." Furthermore, one would expect that medications given to the woman to reduce pain and anxiety would cross the placenta and have some effect on the fetal nervous system as well. Lastly, it often is the case that the abortion procedure results in interruption of feto-placental circulation, such that fetal demise occurs before delivery, no matter which method is used.

The issue of live birth following abortion is not discussed often. When this occurs, it presents difficulties for both the couple and their care providers. Signs of life in a pre-viable (especially anomalous) fetus after delivery result in an ethical dilemma: the now "born" individual is unlikely to survive, but needs to receive attention from its own care providers — separately from the woman's care providers. These care providers should not be burdened with an inherent conflict of interest in providing unbiased evaluation and care. The best way to deal with this issue is to prevent its occurrence, by ensuring fetal demise prior to delivery.

In summary, this case highlights the need for multifaceted care, including decision counseling, psychological support, and careful selection of technique depending on the unique needs of the couple who experience a problem pregnancy.

— *John LaFerla, MD, MPH*

The Actual Patient's Comments about Case 9-1

Steve and I both are musicians. We were in school for so long that we only got around to starting a family in our mid to late 30s. He was 37 and I was 34. This means we were together for a whopping 15 years before even trying to conceive, and we certainly didn't feel we needed a baby to "complete" either our relationship or our lives. All the same, we both liked children and had always looked forward to the inevitable "someday" when we would have a child of our own.

We entered our first pregnancy with the nonchalance that comes of innocence. We conceived on the very first try — before we'd had time to reflect on the magnitude of what this meant — and why not? We'd both been extremely healthy our whole lives, and there was no history of problem pregnancies in either of our families. As the reality of being pregnant began to dawn on me, a sense of trepidation and inadequacy (only at night) set in as surely as the excitement (only during the day) I expected to feel. Looking back now, no one can convince me that this initial ambivalence on my part was not responsible for the problems that beset this pregnancy, no matter how irrational this explanation may seem.

At 8 weeks, we went to our first doctor's appointment and met the doctor. Steve made a big deal of shaking his hand, as though to mark a momentous occasion. "So, you're the one who will deliver this baby," he said grandly. The doctor did not reflect this enthusiasm in his response, and I remember thinking that it was too bad he couldn't act more excited for us. Now, I view these different responses as a measure of the gulf between our ignorance and his experience. At this point, we saw the positive test result not just as a confirmation of pregnancy but also as a guarantee of birth, whereas he saw it for what it was: just the first of many obstacles to surmount on the way to a successful delivery.

Earlier in the appointment, when he examined me, the doctor pronounced that I was "very" pregnant. In recollection, that single word has an ominous tone, but at the time I had no reason to focus on it. In the coming weeks, I did indeed feel very pregnant, or more specifically very bloated, but I figured that this was normal, not having anything to compare it with. At the next appointment 2 weeks later, I was so thrilled to hear a heartbeat that I didn't notice the obstetrician guiding the fetoscope over the rest of my already enlarged belly, as though searching for something. "Do twins run in your family?" he asked, not making a big deal of it. I laughed and immediately said no; certainly more because I couldn't fathom the responsibility of twins than because I knew the answer. I dismissed the idea on the spot.

But, at the next appointment (12 weeks), when the obstetrician asked the question again, I started to feel worried. "I already told you: No," I said, annoyed. He went on to ask me how I was feeling. My childhood training in politeness automatically kicked in, and I felt sheepish complaining. "I'm fine; maybe a little tired and nauseated," I said, although I was feeling extremely tired, nauseated, and — heaven forbid, given how I imagined I should feel — depressed. In this brief exchange, as in all of our previous ones, he did the asking and I the answering; but this routine was about to be turned on its head, as was everything else about my pregnancy.

We went in for our first ultrasound at 16 weeks. Relatives had told us what this would be like, so we knew to expect 30 minutes of blissful bonding with our baby on the screen and a minute or two of pain during the amniocentesis. The reality was so diametrically different that it is impossible to describe in an objective, chronological fashion. It was a 3-hour roller-coaster of flip-flopping prognoses: "One baby...No, two babies...No, only one can survive. But, which one?...You're going to have to choose...No, wait — it looks like neither is viable after all...," punctuated with grim glances from the tight-lipped sonographer, long pauses waiting for someone to explain her silence, quick dashes into the bathroom to throw up, and a doctor who kept switching from ominous observations to an inappropriately cheerful bedside manner. In spite of a diagnosis of twin-to-twin transfusion, hydrocephalus, and multiple cystic hygromas, the perinatologist decided to go ahead with the amniocentesis — twice, actually, since there were two sacs. Numb with shock, I didn't feel much with the first one; but the second one was extremely painful and seemingly interminable, because there was so little fluid in this baby's sac that the perinatologist felt compelled to dig in and twist the needle into every cranny of my womb. Ultimately, his efforts were in vain, for he never did get fluid from the second sac. Finally, dazed and by this time grateful to be dismissed, we were nudged out into the hall with his instructions: "Call me in 3 weeks. We'll do another ultrasound then, and we hope that things will look more promising."

When we got home, it was my sister Susie who suggested that we call my obstetrician. We were in such a profound state of shock that without her direction I think we might simply have sat in one spot staring at the clock, waiting for 3 weeks to pass. My obstetrician immediately went into action, promising to look at the ultrasound pictures right away and to discuss them with us the next afternoon. This gave us a new, more reasonable deadline to shoot for, and literally it was the only way we got through the night.

When the obstetrician opened the door the next day, I remember noticing him as though for the first time. Suddenly, he wasn't remote or indifferent, but a larger-than-life presence; his face was flushed and his blue eyes (had the color even registered before?) were vibrant and angry. He fairly burst into the room, groaning, "I wish this weren't happening to you," as though the turn of events pained him personally. Together, we worked out a plan that Steve and I could cling to. We would get a second opinion from a specialist my doctor particularly trusted, and then we would decide how to proceed from there.

The second ultrasound did not take place until the end of the week, since the specialist was out of town until then. This session followed much the same miserable course as the previous one, but this time I was acutely focused and ready, armed with a list of very specific questions. During the endless days between ultrasounds, I had found comfort the only way I knew how: through studying. With the help of my brother-in-law, who is a family-practice physician, and with numerous books, I had figured out what to ask and how to ask it to get the answers that would help us to make a decision.

On the monitor, to us the babies looked exactly as they had the time before; but, curiously, to the specialist, things seemed improved. It was as though he was being intentionally perverse, saying things like, "That baby's head isn't all that large," and pummeling my abdomen, "See, the other baby is moving a little. I wouldn't say he's unduly lethargic..." Perhaps it is human nature to want to argue with bad news, but the doctor plainly was playing devil's advocate. I could put up with it to a point, though I was beginning to wonder how we were supposed to make an informed decision about what to do when he systematically was canceling out each one of the first perinatologist's concerns. When he encouraged me to bond with the babies (who already were dead in my mind), saying, "Doesn't this one have cute feet?" and "Look, that one is smiling at you," I'd had it. I took charge and started bombarding him with my list of cold, pointed medical questions, like, "Can you see the third and fourth ventricles in the large baby's head? Do you think the polyhydramnios is related to the hydrocephalus?" He instantly was on his guard, seemingly annoyed that I knew what each anomaly might portend; but he did address each of my concerns frankly, if somewhat begrudgingly. Since I had learned from the first perinatologist that doctors won't say anything they can't be absolutely certain about, I built up to and framed my final question carefully, so as to learn the information we needed. "Based on your experience in similar cases, what prognosis for survival would you give these babies?" His shoulders fell and he looked defeated. "Five percent," he said. In some sick sense, I felt vindicated. Our eyes met and I saw that his anger was directed not at me but at the truth, which he was helpless to change.

The following Monday, I met with my obstetrician to discuss the next step. Steve and I felt pretty sure that we wanted to terminate the pregnancy, but we were having trouble actually articulating the decision. It seemed so final. Sitting in his office, he could see the agony I was in, yet he couldn't tell me straight out what to do. It was odd: After feeling so certain that the pregnancy was doomed in the face of the second perinatologist's reticence, I suddenly was filled with doubt and a nagging sense of guilt that I somehow had manipulated the doctors into thinking that a termination was called for. My obstetrician eased my suffering by saying two things. First, he asked me if I wanted to know what he would advise his wife to do in the same circumstance (that is, to terminate), and, second, he assured me that I had in no way bulldozed the doctors, that in fact it would be impossible to do so. Finally, feeling sick at playing God this way, I signed the papers and we set up the termination for the earliest possible date, that Friday — an eternity from then.

I got up to leave, feeling totally dejected and aimless. As I walked through the door into the hallway, my obstetrician placed his hand on my shoulder, a gentle pressure that I was curiously to feel again when alone, suffering similar moments of despair during the difficult years ahead.

When the day of the termination finally arrived, I leapt out of bed feeling lighthearted for the first time in 2 weeks. Today, something was actually going to be done. No longer would I have to feel nauseated and bloated to no good purpose, to suffer people's congratulatory pats on my thick belly, all the while secretly knowing that the babies I carried were profoundly ill. I was particularly anxious to get this over with before I actually felt the babies move — I wasn't sure I could bear that — but, as it turned out my fears were unfounded, since they were cushioned in three times the normal amount of amniotic fluid. After the torture of doctor consultations and weeks of waiting, the termination was unbelievably quick and painless. We got lots of sympathy and support from family, friends, and my obstetrician. I was grateful to feel like myself again, and I was eager to put this wrong-footed pregnancy behind me. I felt like we were being given another chance and was confident that we would do it right the next time: no poisoning ambivalence, no complicating twins, no problems of any kind. We had paid for our initial nonchalance, were contrite, and were ready to do better the second time around.

Case Study 2-9

Fetus with a Diaphragmatic Hernia

J.S. is a 36-year-old married woman G2 P1001 referred to the university medical center for a pregnancy termination. She has a 10-year-old son by her first husband. J.S. had a 15-week ultrasound performed at her local medical center prior to amniocentesis for advanced maternal age. The anatomic scan of the fetus revealed a left diaphragmatic defect with stomach and bowel in the left chest cavity. An amniocentesis was performed and the fetal karyotype was normal, 46 XX.

Before the couple decided on pregnancy termination, they were counseled by a genetic counselor and a perinatologist. Their case also was presented to the fetal therapy committee at their medical center. The pediatric surgeon, neonatologist, and perinatologist all encouraged the couple to continue the pregnancy, stating that the diaphragmatic hernia could be repaired after the baby was delivered and that the baby had a "reasonable" chance for a normal life.

The parents had a difficult time deciding how to proceed with the pregnancy. The woman wanted to continue the pregnancy, but the man was adamant about termination, insisting that "all of my children should be perfect." Eventually, the couple agreed to terminate the pregnancy. Since pregnancy terminations were not performed at her local medical center, she was referred to the university medical center.

Several options were presented to the couple once they arrived at the medical center. A dilatation and evacuation procedure was suggested as the least physically and psychologically traumatic way to terminate the pregnancy. With a surgical termination, however, it would not be possible to perform a complete autopsy on the fetus and determine the exact nature of the congenital abnormality. The couple had difficulty deciding on the method of termination. The man wanted to "get it over with as soon as possible, with the least amount of pain." The woman wanted a prostaglandin procedure so that she would be able to hold the baby after it was delivered and gather the most information possible about the nature of the fetal abnormality.

Unfortunately, the prostaglandin procedure was slow and painful. The woman experienced many side effects from the medication, including nausea, vomiting, and diarrhea. It took about 16 hours for the woman to deliver the baby. During the time she was in labor, she was cared for by many different nurses, attending physicians, and residents. Some of the nurses and attending physicians were more sensitive to the couple's situation than others. Several residents refused to care for the patient, stating that they did not think that the fetus's abnormality was severe enough to warrant terminating the pregnancy.

After the baby was delivered, the woman held her for several minutes, but she declined the offer to have footprints made and a photograph taken. The baby was sent for autopsy, and the parents returned to their hometown 3 hours after delivery, with instructions to followup with their primary care physician in 4 weeks.

Commentary

This case illustrates many clinical and emotional problems for both parents and professionals providing care. As prenatal diagnosis of congenital malformations has become more common with the increasing use of ultrasound, we are faced with new, challenging, and highly stressful situations.

It is easy to forget that the most important factor in how J.S. reacts both immediately and long term is what the pregnancy and future child mean to her. As J.S. is older and in a second marriage, many questions arise. Is this a desired or an undesired pregnancy? Has infertility been a factor? Does her present husband have other children, or does this represent fatherhood for him? Ideally, these and similar questions should be investigated to provide optimal support and to help understand the difficult decisions such families face.

While women undergoing an indicated prenatal diagnostic procedure (in this case, amniocentesis for advanced maternal age) have some time to anticipate detection of an anomaly, those whose fetal malformations are diagnosed unexpectedly are taken by surprise and may have a more severe reaction to the information. J.S. probably considered the possibility of aneuploidy, but not a gross structural abnormality such as diaphragmatic hernia. In such a situation, parents will need time and information to understand the situation, and physicians must be prepared to "back up and start all over" with counseling.

As is frequently the case after diagnosis, J.S. was referred to a tertiary center for further care. Suddenly, the patient is faced with a new team of people, often some distance from home and the support of family and friends. We believe that one person should be designated to speak not only for the team, but also, perhaps more importantly, to represent the patient to the team. Consistency of information and trust can be very effective in reducing confusion and anxiety for both parents and caregivers.

Our ability to diagnose fetal problems is far ahead of our ability to understand, treat them, and offer a prognosis to parents. This creates a great deal of uncertainty, something with which the public, and especially those in medicine, are very uncomfortable. As Harold Bursztajin and others recommend, we should share these uncertainties with our patients, and not fall back on outdated paternalism. We must educate parents as objectively as possible and only give our recommendations (or encouragement, in this case) when we specifically are asked for it.

The decision to terminate or continue an abnormal pregnancy is one of the most difficult decisions which a person can face. It is a very complex decision influenced by personal factors (usually unknown to the team), compatibility with life, the certainty of diagnosis and severity, the number of weeks of gestation, and the options available. Conflict between the parents can make an already difficult situation into even more of a "no-win" situation. Again, what the pregnancy and future child mean to each of them is the key to understanding this conflict. That pregnancy terminations are not performed at this woman's local hospital adds to her "stigmatization" about the procedure and must be dealt with openly. Parents should be given as much time as needed within the realities of legal and medical constraints to make a decision. Pressure never should be exerted to "get it over with."

The advantages and disadvantages of termination methods are controversial and vary from case to case. All methods should be presented to the family as objectively as for any other "informed consent" situation, and recommendations based on our personal experiences or assumptions should be avoided. Only the woman can decide what is best for her. It always is important to include information regarding the possibility of live birth when methods other than D&E are discussed. A plan for this eventuality must be agreed upon by all obstetric, pediatric, and nursing personnel and shared with the parents.

Medical terminations may take longer and be more uncomfortable than hoped. This can cause distress for physicians and nurses, as well as for the family. I have found that the more honest with the family we have been during counseling, the easier this is to deal with. Again, continuity of care markedly can reduce stress on the patient and staff alike. All staff have the right to determine individual levels of participation in pregnancy terminations. Participation should be consistent, however, and personal views never should be expressed to patients or families.

Our studies have shown that parental contact with the baby after delivery is very personal and unpredictable. Although most parents will want contact with their baby and will want mementos of the birth, some may not want these immediately. We believe that footprints and photographs should be obtained of all stillbirths and saved as long as possible in case parents want them later. Parents who terminate a malformed baby can be expected to experience the same profound grief and bereavement as those who suffer a spontaneous loss. Supportive counseling should be offered by experienced personnel, ideally by the same individual who has been their designated counselor from the beginning. In addition, these women are postpartum. They should receive the same care and attention as other new mothers, and they should not be rushed out of the hospital. Prior to discharge, specific information should be given to the woman regarding medical and emotional followup, as well as plans for a session to review the results of the autopsy examination. The choice of followup with their primary care physician or the medical center team should be offered.

Situations such as these are becoming more frequent. While they present many challenges, they also present many opportunities for us as professionals to do what we have dedicated our lives to: Giving good care.

— *Kenneth Kellner, MD, PhD*

References

American College of Obstetrics and Gynecology. (1987). *Technical bulletin #109.* Washington, DC: Author.

Black, R.B. (1989). A one- and six-month follow-up of prenatal diagnosis patients who lost pregnancies. *Prenatal Diagnosis, 9,* 795-804.

Black, R.B. (1993). Psychosocial issues in reproductive genetic testing and pregnancy loss. *Fetal Diagnosis and Therapy (Supplement 1),* 164-173.

Bowers, C.H., Chervenak, J.L., & Chervenak, F.A. (1989). Late-second-trimester pregnancy termination with dilatation and evacuation in critically ill women. *Journal of Reproductive Medicine, 34,* 880-883.

Cates, W.C., Schulz, K.F., Grimes, D.A., Horowitz, A.J., Lyon, F.A., Kravitz, F.H., & Frisch, M.J. (1982). Dilatation and evacuation procedures and second-trimester abortions. *JAMA, 248,* 559-563.

Elder, S.H., & Laurence, K.M. (1991). The impact of supportive intervention after second-trimester termination of pregnancy for fetal abnormality. *Prenatal Diagnosis, 11,* 47-54.

Ferguson, J.E., Burkett, B.J., Pinkerton, J.V., Thiagarajah, S., Flather, M.M., Martel, M.M., & Hogge, W.A. (1993). Intraamniotic 15(s)-15-methyll prostaglandin F2a and termination of middle and late second-trimester pregnancy for genetic indications: A contemporary approach. *American Journal of Obstetrics and Gynecology, 169,* 332-340.

Furlong, R.M., & Black, R.B. (1984). Pregnancy termination for genetic indications: The impact on families. *Social Work in Health Care, 10,* 1734.

Grimes, D.A., & Schulz, K.F. (1985). Morbidity and mortality from second-trimester abortions. *Journal of Reproductive Medicine, 30,* 505-514.

Grimes, D.A., Hulka J.F., & McCutchen, M.E. (1980). Midtrimester abortion by dilatation and evacuation versus intra-amniotic instillation of prostaglandin F2a: A randomized clinical trial. *American Journal of Obstetrics and Gynecology, 137,* 785-790.

Grimes, D. (1984). Second trimester abortions in the United States. *Family Planning Perspectives, 16,* 260-266.

Hagay, Z.J., Leiberman, J.R., Picard, R., & Katz, M. (1989). Uterine rupture complication midtrimester abortion. *Journal of Reproductive Medicine, 4,* 912-916.

Hern, W.M., Zen, C., Ferguson, K.A., Hart, V., & Haseman, M. (1993). Outpatient abortion for fetal anomaly and fetal death from 15-34 menstrual weeks' gestation: Techniques and clinical management. *Obstetrics and Gynecology, 81,* 301-306.

Hill, N.C.W., & Mackenzie, I.Z. (1989). 2308 second trimester terminations using extra-amniotic or intra-amniotic prostaglandin E2: An analysis of efficacy and complication. *British Journal of Obstetrics and Gynecology, 96,* 1424-1431.

Huang, S.F., Chou, M.M., & Ho, E.S.C. (1994). Termination of pathological pregnancy in second and early third trimesters with extra amniotic instillation of 16 phenoxy-w-tetranor prostaglandin E2 methylsulfonylamide. *International Journal of Gynecology and Obstetrics, 47,* 157-161.

Iles, S., & Gath, D. (1993). Psychiatric outcome of termination of pregnancy for fetal abnormality. *Psychological Medicine, 23,* 407-413

Isada, N.B., Pryde, P.G., Johnson, M.P., Hallak, M., Blessed, W.B., & Evans, M.I. (1992). Fetal intra cardiac potassium chloride injection to avoid the hopeless resuscitation of an abnormal abortus: I. Clinical issues. *Obstetrics and Gynecology, 80,* 296-300.

Kafrissen, M.E., Schulz, K.F., Grimes, D.A., & Cates, W. (1984). Midtrimester abortion — Intraamniotic instillation of hyperosmolar urea and prostaglandin F2-alpha versus dilatation and evacuation. *JAMA, 251,* 916-919.

Kanhai, H.H.H., & Keirse, J.N.C. (1993). Low-dose suprostone for pregnancy termination in cases of fetal abnormality. *Prenatal Diagnosis, 13,* 117-121.

Kaltreider N.B., Goldsmith S., & Margolis A.J. (1979). The impact of midtrimester abortion techniques on patients and staff. *American Journal of Obstetrics and Gynecology, 135,* 235-238.

Kirz, D.S., & Haag, M.K. (1989). Management of the third stage of labor in pregnancies terminated by prostaglandin E2. *American Journal of Obstetrics and Gynecology, 160,* 412-414.

Lebed, J.P., Rubin, A., & Millman, A.E. (1980). Comparison between intraamniotic PGF2a and vaginal PGE2 for second-trimester abortion. *Obstetrics and Gynecology, 56,* 90-96.

Lorenzen, J., & Holzgreve, W. (1995). Helping parents to grieve after second-trimester termination of pregnancy for fetopathic reasons. *Fetal Diagnosis and Therapy, 10,* 147-156.

Mueller, L. (1990). Second-trimester termination of pregnancy: Nursing care. *Journal of Obstetrics, Gynecology, and Neonatal Nursing, 20,* 284.

Owen, J., Hauth, J.C., Winkler, C.L., & Gray, S.E. (1992). Midtrimester pregnancy termination: A randomized trial of prostaglandin E2 versus concentrated oxytocin. *American Journal of Obstetrics and Gynecology, 167,* 1112-1116.

Peterson, W.F., Berry, F.N., Grace, M.R., & Gulbranson, C.L. (1983). Second-trimester abortion by dilatation and evacuation: An analysis of 11,747 cases. *Obstetrics and Gynecology, 62,* 185-190.

Propping, D., Stubblefield, P.G., & Golub, J. (1977). Uterine rupture following midtrimester abortion by laminaria, prostaglandin F2a and oxytocin: Report of two cases. *American Journal of Obstetrics and Gynecology, 128,* 689-690.

Seller, M., Barnes, C., Ross, S., Barby, T., & Cowmeadow, P. (1993). Grief and midtrimester fetal loss. *Prenatal Diagnosis, 13,* 341-348.

Shulman, L.P., Ling, F.W., Meyers, C.M., Shanklin, D.R., Simpson, J.L, & Elias, S. (1990). Dilatation and evacuation for second-trimester genetic pregnancy termination. *Obstetrics and Gynecology, 75,* 1037-1040.

Stubblefield, P.G. (1991). Pregnancy termination. In S.G. Gabbe, J.R. Niebyl, & J.L. Simpson (Eds.), *Obstetrics: Normal and problem pregnancies* (2nd ed.) (pp. 1303-1330). New York: Churchill Livingstone.

White-Van Mourik, M.C.A., Connor, J.M., & Ferguson-Smith, M.A. (1990). Patient care before and after termination of pregnancy for neural tube defects. *Prenatal Diagnosis, 10,* 497-505.

White-VanMourik, M.C.A., Connor, J.M., & Ferguson-Smith, M.A. (1992). The psychosocial sequelae of a second-trimester termination of pregnancy for fetal abnormality. *Prenatal Diagnosis, 12,* 189-204.

Wiley, T.L., Poole, C.P., Gookin, K.S., Wiser, W.L., & Morrison, J.C. (1989). Prostaglandin E2 induction of abortion and fetal demise. *International Journal of Gynecology and Obstetrics, 28,* 171-175.

Worder, J.W. (1991). *Grief counseling and grief therapy* (2nd ed.). New York: Springer.

Zeanah, C.H., Dailey, J.V., Rosenblatt, M., & Saller, D.N. (1993). Do women grieve after terminating pregnancies because of fetal anomalies? A controlled investigation. *Obstetrics and Gynecology, 82,* 270- 275.

Chapter 10

Ethical Issues in Pregnancy Loss

Jeffrey Spike

Many of the events that bring people into the world of medical intervention are unexpected and devastating tragedies. The vast majority of cases of pregnancy loss are just such events. Ethicists generally have little to say about such events, because ethics is concerned with guiding human action for the better when there are choices to be made. But, there are some cases of pregnancy loss which result from a choice made by a woman or couple. In the final section of this chapter are two cases about very different couples whose choices resulted in a pregnancy loss; each case is followed with analysis by experts in medical ethics who specialize in obstetrics and women's health issues.

In this chapter, I first will briefly summarize the field of medical ethics. Then, I will discuss types of ethical considerations which are involved in challenging cases, such as the two which are described in this chapter, where pregnancy loss is deliberate. Finally, I will attempt to draw a more general ethical lesson for all pregnancy losses from those two cases.

Four Ethical Principles and a Legal Doctrine

For as long as there has been a medical profession, there has been a code of behavior to govern its practitioners, written by leading members of the profession. But, since the late 1960s, a new field has developed, with input from philosophers and lawyers as well as from physicians. The rationale for involving these other professions is simple. Medicine is not a science itself, but it is the application of scientific knowledge to accomplish practical human goals, such as health, long life, and freedom from mental and physical disability. Because medicine is a human enterprise seeking human good, it is inescapably, irreducibly ethical — as well as scientific — in nature.

The traditional medical ethics which have dominated for over 2,000 years in the Western world until the late 1960s (and which often still dominate elsewhere, such as in Japan) emphasized two ethical principles: *beneficence* and *nonmaleficence*. Beneficence requires a physician to provide what is determined medically to be in the patient's best interest, balancing potential benefits and burdens to the patient in order to provide the greatest possible total net benefit. Nonmaleficence (in Latin, *"Primum non nocere,"* or "First, do no harm;" the original Greek Hippocratic version said only *"at least do no harm"* [italics, the author's]), reminds physicians that heroic efforts sometimes are not worth it to the patient; they can inflict unnecessary suffering and engender unrealistic hopes, when instead the physician ought to focus on providing comfort care, making the best of what time is left for the patient, and on preventing or relieving the patient's pain and suffering.

These principles leave the primary decision-making responsibility in the hands of the physician, based upon his or her objectivity and expertise. For some physicians today, this tradition represents the "Good Old Days," but many patients and their families have lost faith in letting physicians retain their "G.O.D.'s" role since the revelations of egregiously self-serving and unethical medical research which characterized the mid 20th Century. At the same time when those revelations arose, the American civil rights movement was growing in influence, and patient rights came to be seen as a component of civil rights. As the issue of who has authority to make decisions came to the fore, simultaneously, the number of treatment options which physicians could offer to their patients was expanding rapidly. This was an era during which technologies such as dialysis, ventilators, antibiotics, and antipsychotic medications became widely available. Thus, more was at stake in medical decisions, and more responsibility would fall on the decision makers.

Faith in the objectivity of physicians never has been the same as it was in the Good Old Days, and perhaps this is just as well. Medical decisions are not purely objective or value free. All human beings have their own internal value systems. It would be unfair to expect physicians to be able to avoid differences with patients' value systems, either by suspending their own beliefs or by imposing their personal beliefs on others.

Patient Autonomy

To avoid these problems, contemporary medical ethics makes the principle of patient autonomy (or self-determination) its central tenet: patients deserve to be given all the information about their diagnosis, prognosis, and treatment options in terms which they can understand, so as to enable them to make their own decisions about their lives. The legal doctrine which supports this is informed consent, but it must be noted that patients can refuse treatment suggestions as well as consent to them, or else the doctrine is rendered meaningless, reduced to just the right to agree with the doctor. At minimum, the patient should understand the recommended treatment or procedure, its consequences (risks as well as benefits), and all reasonable alternatives. It is important, too, to remember that the point of informed consent is to empower the patient's right to make a fully informed decision, not to defend the doctor legally should there be an unexpected and undesired outcome.

Autonomy versus Paternalism

The difference between traditional and contemporary approaches to medical ethics is best exemplified by the topic of paternalism. An act is paternalistic if it overrides the apparent or expressed preference of a person and is justified (to whatever degree it *is* justified) by its being in the best interest of that person. When there is a difference of opinion between a doctor and a patient, whether to weight autonomy or beneficence more will determine whether to choose to respect the patient's preference or to override it. In general, when facing such conflicts, it is best that the physician openly communicate with the patient, making clear that the goal is to do what is best for the patient. But, if the patient continues to reject the doctor's recommendation, it is best to respect her right to maintain control over her life. The damage which the physician would do, whether physical or psychological, by forcing unwanted treatment is too great even if it achieves the medical goal. The popular moral maxim bears repeating: the ends do not justify the means.

The principle of justice has a formal (or procedural) foundation, to insure that every member of society is treated equally (or with what is called in the law, "due process"). But, it also is concerned with the substantial consequences which follow from that formal principle, namely that no member of society be denied basic necessities, and that reasonable overall distribution of goods is assured.

Within our society and economy, this would translate roughly into protecting the disadvantaged and vulnerable from denial of essential services, while allowing others to have more, as well as preventing the resulting multi-tiered system from making the entire system too costly. All other Western democracies have more egalitarian, socialized health care systems, so ours has the most difficult job of distinguishing between fair and unfair differentials. At the very least, those already born into a poor family (typically in a poor neighborhood with poor schools) should not have poor health care added to their burdens. Otherwise, what chance has society really provided them to improve their station in life? None of us is responsible for the circumstances of our birth, and so no one should be punished for it. Essential health care can be thought of as defined by what is necessary for having a fair or reasonable opportunity in life. All citizens are entitled to a "free" (tax paid) primary and secondary public education for the same reasons.

The principles of medical ethics are *prima facie;* that is, assumed to be true "at first glance." But, they also are independent; that is, one principle can yield recommendations which conflict with another principle. They do not settle differences, but they can help to clarify issues. How to balance the principles properly in any particular situation remains the task of mature, reflective ethical judgment. Collecting more ethically relevant information — primarily about the personal history and values of the patient, about what she finds more meaningful in her life, and about what she considers the moral of her life's story — usually will help to resolve these dilemmas.

Pregnancy, Parents, and Paternalism

All four ethical principles relate primarily to the rights of a patient to make decisions about his or her own medical care. An additional twist always is added when someone other than the patient must make the decision. Ideally, that surrogate can choose what the patient would have wanted, as in when adults make decisions for an elderly parent, because the parent no longer can do so. But, with a neonate, there are no previous wishes to serve as a standard for the right decision. Instead, the accepted standard is to choose what is in the best interest of the neonate, and this is the standard up to which both family and health care providers should try to live.

Of course, the decision must represent the parents' best effort to decide what is best for their baby, from the perspective of the child's potential future. The impact on the family and the cost to society must be secondary. A famous judge, Benjamin Cardozo, said it well, in a discussion of parents' religious beliefs and their relevance to consent for medical treatment: "Parents can make martyrs of themselves, but not of their children." In other words, newborns are considered to be members of the human community first, and they cannot be presumed to accept decisions which are based upon moral, ethical, philosophical, or religious beliefs of their parents, because they have not accepted these beliefs themselves. To insure that the potential choice is made properly, it is appropriate for it to be made in conjunction with physicians who are caring for the baby. While this gives obstetric and pediatric care providers more power than internists who care for adult patients, it is justified because the patients in these cases cannot speak for themselves. In rare cases of irresolvable dispute between family and care providers, an ethics consultation is called for, as a method of mediation and resolution.

A human life is a long journey through infancy, childhood, adolescence, and adulthood. A normal newborn is a potential adult, who will require many years of nurturing and teaching to achieve his or her potential. The most important word in the preceding sentence is "normal." Unfortunately, that normal potential does not always exist. There is now the option of saving lives where the result would not be a human life, let alone a good life. Ethical decisions must be made based on a sophisticated understanding of what makes a life worth living, rather than just whether or not it is feasible technologically to keep the baby alive. As a result, physicians now have a greater responsibility to include recommendations when they present management options to the family, precisely because there are more options now.

Benefits and Burdens

The two clinical cases at the end of this chapter demonstrate the integration of ethics and medical management. In Janet Baldwin's case (Case 1), Ms. Baldwin's cocaine addiction resulted in placental abruption with delivery by cesarean section of a compromised newborn who required life support. For Don and Alice Clark (Case 2), spontaneous rupture of membranes at 18 weeks gestation forced the couple to decide whether or not to continue the pregnancy.

In both cases, the babies faced a high likelihood of a very limited life. In Janet Baldwin's case, it is reasonable to assume that her baby never would have a productive life, even if she were kept alive. The Clark baby presented a more complex decision, in that there was approximately a 50-50 chance of their daughter's having a life which would be complicated by either intellectual or physical disability, if the baby survived at all. But, there was no way to predict the severity of the disability, or whether it would be primarily intellectual or physical. Even to take that chance would require Alice Clark to carry her fetus to term, and most likely to undergo delivery by cesarean section — whether or not the baby survived. The combination of risks to the woman and her baby make this a case where parental choice should be decisive. To use the terminology of ethics, there is not the proportionality of benefits and burdens which one would require to provide a clear decision based on the best-interest standard. (Note that the woman's medical condition *should* be considered in this analysis because it inextricably is affected by the decision; it is not a separable, external factor such as the effect on the family or financial considerations.)

These two cases have similarities as well as important distinctions. The death of the newborn baby was accepted as the best outcome of the available options by both sets of parents, because of the disabilities with which the child would have had to live, if the newborn did survive. This type of quality-of-life judgment is difficult for anyone to make. But, this does not mean that it is always wrong to make the decision based on this issue. Parents take on the greatest responsibility demanded of anyone when they choose to have children — an altruistic commitment of at least 18 years, and usually longer. The love that makes such a choice so easy for most parents to make is also what justifies giving them the predominant say about these initial life-and-death decisions. But, it also makes these decisions very difficult emotionally for parents. They need options offered to them, recommendations and explanations, and emotional support for their decisions. Whatever the outcome, the parents must live with the consequences for the rest of their lives.

Might parents have a conflict of interest because of their emotional involvement and because of the fact that they would be burdened by raising a disabled child? This is the view of many people who believe in what commonly is known as the "sanctity of life" doctrine. People who believe in this doctrine generally regard abortion as unacceptable, and this belief was held by those who were supportive of the so-called "Baby Doe" regulations, which first were promoted by the Reagan Administration in 1982.

These regulations stated that handicapped newborns must be treated medically in every way that other newborns are treated. What originally raised this issue politically were accounts of newborn babies who suffered both from Down syndrome and other medical complications, whose parents were permitted to refuse surgery which would have treated the other medical problems. In other words, the parents chose to let the newborn die, rather than to permit surgery which then would allow the child to survive, only to live with mental and/or physical disabilities. After repeated court battles, it has been recognized that there should be three major categories of exceptions; that is, situations in which nontreatment is a reasonable choice for parents to make for their newborns. Each can be defended ethically by the best-interest standard. These categories are if the neonate is (a) irreversibly comatose, or (b) treatment merely would prolong dying (treatment is futile with respect to the baby's survival), or (c) treatment would be "virtually futile" and is inhumane itself.

The hidden values here are that a treatment only is required if it allows its recipient later to enjoy some adequate semblance of a satisfying human life, and this requires not just being alive but also being conscious and not burdened by inhumane conditions. Clearly, the inhumane conditions are the most difficult to define. Freedom from pain and psychological suffering must be part of its meaning, but what else? At this point, if there is a social consensus, it probably would include that mild intellectual or physical disability (for example, Down syndrome or deafness) or a somewhat shortened probable lifespan (for example, to age 60 from Huntington's chorea) still allows for a human life. Less clear is severe disability, as when a newborn never will learn to recognize or communicate meaningfully with others, will be blind and deaf, or will have a life expectancy of fewer than 10 years.

The Complex Nature of Parental Decisions

What is most regrettable is the suspicion of parents' decisions since the Baby Doe regulations were enacted. Are parents acting only out of self-interest if they refuse treatment for their disabled neonate? That is a very uncharitable interpretation. They may be thinking of their overall family and not of just this one child, but that is a legitimate attitude, for all of the other family members will be affected by the parents' decision for this baby. Parents also may be the best persons to speak for this new child precisely because their goal is for this child to become a member of their family. The principles of beneficence and autonomy naturally would seek goals — to achieve human cognitive and emotional life, and to interact meaningfully with others — that also are normal parental goals for a child.

Parental motives are not as selfish as sanctity-of-life supporters fear, and they do not justify the level of state interference that the Baby Doe regulations threaten. Even Janet Baldwin, whose cocaine use led to her baby's severe neurological damage, was able to make decisions based on her baby's best interest. To save her baby's life against her wishes seems almost punitive — punishing her by denying her rights to make decisions about her baby. The result would be to keep that baby alive, even though it never would experience any pleasure or happiness from being alive, or interact with others, including the mother. This not only would be unjustified ethically, but also it would be unforgivable, more akin to cruelty, to the mother and possibly to her baby as well, than anything deserving to be considered sanctified.

Cases of parental decision making to withhold or withdraw medical treatment necessary for the survival of their neonate can tell us something about the many cases — far more common — of pregnancy loss. It generally is surmised that most pregnancy losses are due to problems with the genetics of the embryo or other problems with the pregnancy (for example, with placental development). The miscarriage is, in effect, a biological function that naturally supersedes the terrible decisions which some parents are forced to consider because of high-technology medicine. Psychologically, it replaces the almost contradictory mix of the emotions of guilt, remorse, and loss with pure mourning. The lesson for parents who suffer a pregnancy loss then might be that the loss literally was for the best (if all of the actual medical options were known). If that sounds like a naive, "Pollyanna," or implausible claim, it only may be because one option is being considered which in fact did not exist — a normal pregnancy and healthy baby. Given the complexity of the processes of ovulation, fertilization, implantation, embryonic development, pregnancy, and delivery, it is important to understand the awesome number of events that could go wrong in order to appreciate better the luck which is required for everything to go right.❑

Case Study 1-10

Preventive Ethics in Neonatal Care and Loss

Janet Baldwin, pregnant with her second child, was trying to stop using cocaine. She was in a stable relationship with Dave Cook, the father of this baby. Dave did not know about Janet's drug use, and she saw the relationship with him as an opportunity to wipe clean the slate of her past. Janet had lost custody of her first child because of her drug problems, and she wanted to prevent this from happening again with her second child. She still maintained contact with her drug-using friends, however, and inevitably she was drawn into their drug use when she associated with these people.

At 35 weeks gestation, Janet experienced placental abruption, a sudden complication of pregnancy in which the placenta separates from the uterine wall, causing bleeding for the mother and reduced oxygen to the fetus. Abruption occurs more frequently among women who abuse substances during pregnancy. Janet knew that something was seriously wrong because of the sudden pain, which was not like contractions which she had experienced during the birth of her first baby. She was taken by ambulance to the hospital. The baby's heart rate was dangerously low; soon after Janet arrived at the hospital, her baby was delivered quickly by cesarean section.

The baby girl, named Tony, weighed 2040 grams and had good color, but she was floppy. Her Apgar scores were 3 (at 1 minute), 5 (at 5 minutes), and 7 (at 10 minutes). Healthy Apgar scores are in the range of 8 to 10. Tony's pulse increased to within normal limits soon after she was born. Neurologically, she showed little movement, and had poor tone, no startle response, and no suck. The baby was transferred to the neonatal intensive care unit. Mechanical ventilation was necessary to maintain her breathing. General stiffening movements were noted, and electroencephalograph (EEG) showed decreased amplitude waves and seizures, generally uncorrelated with any clinical signs of seizure. A pediatric neurologist examined Tony and diagnosed brain stem dysfunction with severe brain injury. The prognosis was that the baby never would function normally or be able to interact with others. Tony would not be able to walk, talk, or even feed from a bottle. All of the professional staff agreed with this diagnosis and prognosis.

Janet and Dave shared responsibility for making decisions about Tony. When they learned of the prognosis, they decided that they did not want their baby kept alive by artificial means. Janet did not want Dave to learn that this complication of pregnancy probably was associated with her cocaine use. Dave repeatedly asked the health care team for an explanation of why this had happened. Drug screening tests performed on Janet and her baby were positive for cocaine.

Some care providers asserted that Janet should not be permitted to make decisions for Tony. Also, they believed that they should report Janet to child protective authorities.

Commentary

Janet Baldwin's case raises a number of ethical issues, both for the health care professionals responsible for the care of the newborn, Tony, and for Tony's parents. Unless those issues are thought through with care and are managed well, there are bound to be conflicts among the parties involved. It is not at all hard to imagine that such conflicts could wind up in a court of law or on news broadcasts.

Those involved in this case have two basic choices. First, they can let the nascent conflicts already evident in this case continue to develop and then react to them. This approach generates yet more conflict and exacts the toll of interpersonal and intrapsychic stress — not to mention considerable financial burdens, if the matter goes to litigation. Second, the parties involved can think things through together and try to prevent the nascent conflicts from developing any further.

Experience teaches both health care professionals and parents that the first choice is not a very good one. This is because, for everyone concerned, the costs, especially the moral costs (for example, in the form of hostility and lingering distrust), simply are too high. The second approach, which we call "preventive ethics," like preventive medicine, is unglamourous and never makes it to the evening news or the front pages of newspapers. But, we believe that preventive ethics makes for better health care and better relationships among health care professionals, patients, and their families. In seeking these valued goals, preventive ethics also helps to maintain the trust that society should have in health care professions and institutions.

The preventive ethics approach differs from a more common way of thinking about such cases, namely by focusing on the question, "Who decides?" This question implies that the real issues in such cases concern who has the right to make decisions about children who are gravely ill. Questions of rights quickly turn to questions of power, and power struggles ensue. Such power struggles frequently are the source of ethical conflicts in the clinical setting. Power struggles are about to occur in this case because some of the staff members think that Ms. Baldwin should not be making decisions about the management of a patient who she caused to be injured.

To avoid these potentially destructive and exhausting power struggles, preventive ethics asks a different question, "What are the obligations of the various parties to each other and to the patient?" Asking this question focuses everyone's concern on what is of lasting importance in this case. The health care professionals must be clear about and act on their obligations to Tony and her parents. Ms. Baldwin and Mr. Cook must be clear about and act on their obligations to each other and to their child. Everyone involved thus faces common tasks, sorting through a complex web of obligations and identifying how those obligations should be fulfilled. Then, the involved parties should act on their obligations. Instead of being divided by power struggles that follow from asking "Who decides?" a preventive ethics approach creates common ground, on the basis of which conflicts and power struggles can be avoided and important values preserved.

The central question becomes, what obligations do the health care professionals and the parents have to Tony? In particular, is it obligatory to make every effort to keep the baby alive? Tragically, Tony is so severely injured that she appears to have lost capacity for development as a child. The prognosis for Tony is that she never will function normally or interact with others. Yet, it is by interacting with others that human children grow and develop into adolescence and adulthood. This future is foreclosed, a terrible loss for Tony, her parents, her extended family, and the human community.

Now, it may be true that particular medical and nursing interventions could have some physiologic effects (basic bodily functions could be maintained within statistically normal limits). But, unfortunately, there would be no greater clinical or personal benefit to Tony from these effects. In contemporary health care ethics, it now is well understood that when a medical or nursing intervention is not expected to have overall clinical and personal benefit to a patient, even though physiological effects can be achieved, there is no obligation to provide the intervention in question. It ethically is permissible to allow the patient to die. Of course, there then exist obligations to respect and maintain the child's dignity while she is allowed to die, especially by arranging for appropriate pain management (probably not a major consideration in this case) and a private place in the hospital for Tony's parents to be with her and to comfort each other.

Tony's parents have parallel obligations. As parents of a child, they are obligated to Tony to see to it that her doctors and nurses fulfill their obligations to Tony as a patient. We have already seen, though, that there is no obligation of Tony's doctors and nurses to keep her alive.

From this consideration of everyone's obligations, a course of action becomes clear. Tony's doctor should explain her diagnosis and prognosis to her parents, and to point out that, tragically, in such cases there is no obligation to keep Tony alive. The reasonable course would be to avoid the use of high-technology interventions and simply keep Tony comfortable and arrange for a private place for her to die in the context of her family, rather than in the impersonal setting of the architectural open space of a neonatal intensive care unit.

Ms. Baldwin's and Mr. Cook's request that artificial means not be used to sustain their daughter's life is altogether reasonable, and this should be accepted by the health care team. How Tony's condition was caused is altogether a separate matter, and the issue does not have to be addressed in the process of thinking through the obligations owed to her by Tony's parents, doctors, and nurses. This is a very important point to keep in mind.

Do Tony's care providers have an obligation to her parents to provide an honest account of the most likely cause of her injury? The canons of informed consent are clear, and the answer unequivocally is "Yes." Thus, the question is not *should* Tony's father's questions be answered, but *how.*

The attending physician should talk separately with Ms. Baldwin and explain that Tony's health care providers have an ethical and legal obligation to explain to both parents what happened, including the likely causes for the event. The physician should add that it might be best if Ms. Baldwin herself told Mr. Cook what happened, and the health care team should offer to support her in doing so (for example, offering to have a conference with one physician and the two parents present). The physician should add, by way of encouragement, that experience teaches that things usually go better this way, and that the team will support the two parents as they sort through their responses to the medical explanation for Tony's condition. If the attending physician thinks that it would be helpful, or indicated, he or she should offer the involvement of a social worker and psychiatrist, because these health care professionals have important skills that can help the parents.

The justification for this approach is that Ms. Baldwin has the obligation and primary responsibility to explain things to Mr. Cook and that the attending physician has the obligation to both parents to support them in what may be a difficult and stressful process. Pediatricians understand very well that they have many such obligations to the parents of sick children, and this case falls under that general rule.

Notice the benefit of this approach. The health care professionals focus on their obligations to Tony and to her parents. This approach morally bonds the health care professional to the family in their time of great need. Ms. Baldwin and Mr. Cook are encouraged to fulfill their obligations to each other, to face tragic facts, and to develop a thoughtful response to what has happened. Questions of "Who decides?" and the divisive and destructive power struggles that flow from such questions have no place in the humane and decent care of tragically injured children and their suffering parents.

— *Laurence B. McCullough, PhD, and Frank A. Chervenak, MD*

Case Study 2-10

Induced Labor versus Spontaneous Labor and Delivery

Don and Alice Clark have been awaiting excitedly the birth of their first child. Don, a mechanical engineer, and Alice, a high school English teacher, have attended every obstetric visit together, happily listening to the sounds of their baby's heart, and Alice carefully has followed the advice of her obstetrician. Don and Alice are in their mid 30s and have been married for 4 years. The pregnancy was planned.

During the 18th week of her pregnancy, Alice began to leak amniotic fluid. Her obstetrician advised Alice to be on strict bed rest, although the likelihood of premature labor was high. Alice did observe strict bed rest for 2 weeks. The leaking fluid diminished during this time. There were periods of several days when there was no leakage. This pattern continued until the 22nd week of pregnancy, when the amount of amniotic fluid loss increased. Don and Alice were told that there was virtually no chance for their baby to survive if birth occurred at that time, because of the gestational age. The Clarks understood that Alice could go into labor and that steps could be taken to stop labor if it started. This option — attempting to continue the pregnancy to a point at which the baby's gestational age, although still premature, would allow a greater chance of survival — created risks to the baby. There was a good chance that the baby would be born with severe contractures due to the low amniotic fluid, and there also was a risk of collapse of the umbilical cord. Additionally, there was a high risk of neurologic complications as well as the complications that exist for all premature births. Two other options were made available to Don and Alice. They were told that they could continue to wait, and when labor occurred allow the baby to be born. Also, they were told that labor could be induced at the present time, resulting in the baby's birth. With these two options, Don and Alice were told that they could choose to have resuscitation attempted at the time of birth, or that they could direct ahead of time that there be no resuscitative efforts made, and that they simply would hold their baby. Don and Alice also were told that, if they opted to try to carry the pregnancy to a point at which the baby could survive, their decisions about resuscitative efforts and other aggressive treatment could be constrained legally. Federal regulations apply to protect handicapped newborns from being denied medical treatment.

Don needed specific information about the options to help him decide. Specifically, he wanted to know the likelihoods of the various outcomes. The obstetrician referred Don and Alice to a perinatologist. They were told that there was about a 50% chance that the baby would die before being born if the pregnancy continued on its own or with medical help. Furthermore, they were told that, if the baby was born and survived, then there was a very significant chance — as high as 90% — that the baby would be seriously impaired. The longer they waited, the better the chance that neurologic damage would decrease. But, the risk of serious contractures would increase. Alice asked the high-risk obstetrician what she would do if she were the patient. The doctor replied that she herself would have labor induced and hold the baby.

Don and Alice opted for induced labor at just before 23 weeks gestation. Their baby girl was born and, at the parents' direction, no resuscitative efforts were attempted. The baby lived for less than one half hour, and she was held by her parents for her entire, short life.

Commentary

I worked for 8 years in a pediatrics department where I interacted regularly with neonatologists, and I have worked for the last 6 years in an obstetrics department where I interact with high-risk pregnancy specialists. I believe that it would have been wise for Don and Alice to consult with a neonatologist as well as with the high-risk obstetrician about the potential outcome of induced labor at an estimated 23 weeks gestation versus spontaneous labor and delivery. Although there surely are exceptions, neonatologists generally are more aware of the latest advances and the morbidity and mortality rates for survival of premature infants at their own and other institutions than are obstetricians.

Another procedural matter to note is that Alice is the primary decision maker in this case. Apparently, the couple has agreed about what to do, but this does not always occur. When it does not occur, the pregnant woman's view must prevail because it is she who undergoes induction of labor or spontaneous labor and delivery. Only after birth are the parents equally responsible for decisions made on behalf of their newborn.

"Induced labor" in this case should be recognized as the moral equivalent of abortion, because its intent is to avoid the survival of a severely compromised newborn. In second-trimester terminations, labor may be induced through infusion of substances that are toxic, such as saline or urea, or benign, such as prostaglandin. Although the former typically are not used in cases such as Alice's, they are more likely to ensure fetal demise. Even then, however, as the Edelin case illustrated some time ago, a fetus may survive even after saline infusion. Because practitioners' determination of gestational age and the condition of the fetus are not always accurate, some fetuses electively aborted by infusion methods in late gestation may survive even after saline infusion. Some fetuses electively aborted by infusion in late gestation have been resuscitated because practitioners feel legally and morally obligated to sustain their lives. As one neonatologist called by the obstetrician to a case involving delivery of a late abortus put it, "There was no way I could not resuscitate that baby. He was clearly in better shape than some of those we have had in the intensive care unit." This practitioner apparently believed that the abortion survivor (legally, a newborn) had a right to life which was comparable with that of other newborns. If predictions about mortality and morbidity of Alice's fetus had proved wrong, as sometimes happens, then clinicians might well have had second thoughts about not resuscitating her. If the fetus had not required resuscitation, other treatment modalities would be appropriate morally as well as legally.

To ensure fetal demise in such cases, an additional method sometimes is introduced prior to, or in conjunction with, induction of labor — injection of potassium chloride into the fetal heart. Because the method is so direct, few clinicians add it to their protocol of infusion or induction, even though they and their patients do not want the fetus to survive. Nonetheless, one could defend both this procedure and the induction itself, on grounds of fetal or newborn euthanasia. In other words, it seems better for this fetus or newborn to die than to survive, because of the severe morbidity that probably would accompany survival. Unmentioned in this rationale is another important and valid motivator: it seems better for this couple not to have a child to rear who is compromised severely. Rather than argue that only one of these goals justifies the action, it should be acknowledged that both probably are present and both are valid.

It is not surprising that the high-risk obstetrician told Alice and Don that, if she were in their position, she would induce labor and hold the baby until she died. A pregnant clinician friend of mine recently said the same. Some would question, however, whether the physician should have answered this "golden rule" question when it was asked. Reasons for not answering the questions are that the physician's opinions then might be given too much weight, and his or her situation cannot and should not ever be compared with that of the patient. On the other side, it may be argued that denying the opinion is paternalistic; the patient still is free to make her own decision. Whether this is so depends crucially on the relationship between the particular physician and the particular patient. Because the case as described does not inform readers about their relationship, we have no basis for assessing whether the physician's view should or should not have been offered.

The fact that induced labor in this case is the moral equivalent of abortion does not imply that Alice's decision is wrong or right, and there surely are arguments that support induction as well as elective abortion. If Alice is opposed morally to abortion, however, then she would be better advised to continue her pregnancy, as long as her own health is not threatened, until spontaneous labor and delivery occur.

Although this course would increase the chance of survival of a severely compromised newborn, it would be consistent with her own values, as induction really is not. A decision not to resuscitate still could be made in the delivery room, or treatment could be foregone or discontinued later, if that appeared to be in the infant's best interest. In either of these scenarios, letting the newborn die is as justified morally as is letting dying or severely compromised adults die. And the couple surely could hold their dying daughter then, without being troubled by the possibility that they did something to insure her demise.

— *Mary B. Mahowald, PhD*

Chapter 11

Value of the Perinatal Autopsy

Leon A. Metlay

The perinatal autopsy is a postmortem examination of a fetus or infant, an examination which includes dissection of the internal organs and microscopic examination of tissue samples. "Autopsy" means "to look for oneself," a chance to make diagnosis by direct observation rather than by inference from external examination and laboratory tests. Medical conditions which can be uncovered by perinatal autopsy potentially have greater impact on life expectancy than are those which are found in autopsy among older people. Perinatal autopsies yield information which may influence early survival of subsequent children, both for the families of the children whose bodies are autopsied and for children generally.

Although perinatal autopsy rates are declining more slowly than are those for older patients, in recent years autopsy rates generally have been decreasing. Among other things, this means that many physicians and allied health care professionals may never have attended an autopsy. They only have a vague idea of how an autopsy proceeds and, thus, find it difficult to convey the importance of the procedure or to explain the process to a patient's family. Professionals who must request parents' permission to autopsy a baby should have a firm grasp of why the procedure is done, and they should know enough about how it is done to understand what autopsy can accomplish, to appreciate what its limitations are, and to answer parents' questions. The same also is true of people who meet with family members to discuss autopsy results after the final report is received. This chapter is divided into two sections: What you should know before the autopsy, and what you should know when reading and discussing the autopsy report.

Before the Autopsy:
Autopsy Permission

In the United States all autopsies, except those which are performed under the jurisdiction of a coroner or medical examiner, may be done only with the permission of next of kin — almost always the parents in the case of perinatal autopsy. Significant information may be learned from the autopsy of any baby who dies *in utero* or shortly after birth. Because of this, every parent who has lost a baby through miscarriage, stillbirth, or neonatal death should be approached for permission to autopsy the baby. The only exceptions to this are occasional cases of maternal trauma or suspected criminal abortion, for which the local coroner or medical examiner will have jurisdiction. It is important in those select cases not to ask parents for permission, so that they are not placed in a potentially adversarial relationship with authorities.

In many institutions, the job of asking for autopsy permission is delegated to the most junior members of a health care team. The person who seeks autopsy permission should be a care provider who has an established relationship with the parents. The obstetrician or pediatrician who has been attending the family and has their trust is better able to explain the procedure, and to answer their questions in a way that they will understand and accept, than an intern whom they first met just hours or days ago. Usually either parent may be approached; although, in states which do not recognize common-law marriage, it is better to obtain permission from the baby's mother if the parents are not married.

The autopsy consent form should be read and explained carefully. Typical permission forms specify removing and retaining organs and tissues for the purpose of diagnosis, education, and research. The extent of examination can be circumscribed by the family member who is being asked to give consent. Permission may be withheld from examination of a particular organ or body area. A frequent restriction is "no examination of the brain." Parents sometimes believe that autopsy involves an invasion of the child's identity, and they most strongly associate identity with their baby's brain. Another concern is whether the body can be shown in an open casket at the funeral, although complete autopsy, including examination of the brain, does not preclude an open casket. The autopsy procedure also can be limited to examination of only one portion of the body; but this would be an unusual circumstance with autopsy of a baby. It can be specified that organs not be retained but rather that they will be returned to the body after examination. In this circumstance, it is important that specific permission be obtained for retaining small samples of organs for microscopic study.

Specific procedures can be mandated or forbidden by the family. How findings are used also can be restricted to diagnosis only, or to diagnosis and education, or diagnosis and research. It is difficult to limit the pathologist's ability to learn something during an autopsy, but it is easy to secure a promise explicitly that the case will not be used for teaching conferences, lectures, or teaching museums. It also is possible to specify that an autopsy not be used as a source of tissue for research.

In situations in which the family does not permit autopsy, examination of the placenta usually is included in the permission given to the hospital for the delivery. In many cases, combining information from the placenta with information gained from external examination of the body by the delivery room personnel can supply important diagnostic information.

Expense

Families may be concerned about the cost of the autopsy. The procedure at the University of Rochester's Strong Memorial Hospital, as an example, includes pathologist time, technician time, and materials; typically it costs between $900 and $1,200. Autopsy expenses, however, are budgeted as part of the hospital's overhead. The pattern throughout the United States is that there is no charge for an autopsy performed on a patient who died while hospitalized. Some hospitals do not differentiate between patients who are admitted, patients who die in the emergency department, and patients who arrive dead. Other hospitals will charge a fee for any autopsy in which the deceased was not admitted. Families who have a stillbirth at home may face paying a fee.

Reasons for Doing Autopsies

Families usually have questions about what stands to be gained by performing the autopsy. It is important that the person who is seeking a perinatal utopsy permission from the baby's family explain what can be accomplished by performing the procedure. In this regard, it also is important to be familiar with the clinical history of the woman and baby, in order to know which aspects are of particular importance in a given case. There are several important classes of information which can be gained from the autopsy.

The first piece of information sought during autopsy which most people think of is the cause of death. Unfortunately, in up to 25% of cases, perinatal autopsy is unable to establish cause of death. In the rest, a diagnosis can

Figure 1-11.
Causes of Perinatal Deaths from Perinatal Autopsy

Cause	Fetal Deaths No. (%)	Neonatal Deaths No. (%)	Total
Inconclusive	29 (37.7)	1 (2.1)	**30** (24.2)
Infection	16 (20.8)	6 (12.8)	**22** (17.7)
Congenital anomaly	15 (19.5)	25 (53.2)	**40** (32.3)
Abruptio placentae	8 (10.4)	...	**8** (6.4)
Cord accident	4 (5.2)	...	**4** (3.2)
Twin transfusion syndrome	3 (3.9)	...	**3** (2.4)
Antiphospholipid antibody	2 (2.6)	...	**2** (1.6)
Prematurity	...	15 (31.9)	**15** (12.1)
Total	**77 (100)**	**47 (100)**	**124 (100)**
Autopsy not done	16	28	**44**

Reprinted with permission from Saller, D.N., Jr., Lesser, K.B., Harrel, U., Rogers, B.B., & Oyer, C.E. (1995). The clinical utility of the perinatal autopsy. *Journal of the American Medical Association, 273*(8), 664.

be made (see Figure 1-11). Also, autopsy can be used to make a diagnosis and/or to confirm clinical diagnosis to demonstrate the accuracy of the prenatal diagnosis. This is especially important if parents have chosen to terminate a wanted pregnancy based on prenatal testing. In about half of autopsies in which a critical diagnosis is made, autopsy confirms diagnoses suggested by prenatal studies. In the other half, autopsy adds significant new information and, possibly, changes the diagnosis of cause of death (Saller, Lesser, Harrel, Rogers, & Oyer, 1995).

It is important to note that a fetus or newborn baby may have more than one disease process. In such circumstances, autopsy may reveal secondary diagnoses beyond the main one. Additionally, autopsy can yield information about the stage of disease at the time of death. For instance, a fetus with oligohydramnios (lack of amniotic fluid) often has hypoplastic (underdeveloped) lungs, a condition which is incompatible with life. In a patient with oligohydramnios of unknown duration, the presence or absence of pulmonary hypoplasia can be confirmed by autopsy.

Diagnosis via autopsy can give information about recurrence risk. This often is a very important question for families. How will their subsequent offspring be affected? This can be true of genetic syndromes and also of disruption sequences related to maternal or environmental factors. Effectiveness of therapy also can be assessed. Important information can be gained about whether intrauterine or postpartum interventions were effective in helping the condition. This can be very important in evaluating new therapies. On the other hand, autopsy can reveal adverse effects of therapy. This information can be equally valuable in assessing new therapies.

The autopsy can be important for education, as well. At the very least, autopsy serves as a means of educating physicians who are involved in a woman's prenatal care. This includes feedback on interpretation of clinical signs and diagnostic tests. In an academic center, autopsy offers potential additional education for pathology residents, who learn how to perform and interpret the autopsy; for obstetric and pediatric residents, who learn about interpreting prenatal history; and for medical students, who learn the basics of fetal disease processes.

Finally, in an academic center, autopsy can yield information for research. Careful and systematic recording of findings contribute to comparison of large groups of fetuses, which allows conclusions to be drawn about pathogenic and therapeutic factors. These data in turn can influence perinatal care. Autopsies serve as a source of normal fetal tissue to be used for research, as well as a source of control tissues for special microscopic staining techniques.

Much of the information which may be obtained by perinatal autopsy, as discussed previously, can help the grieving family. Giving the baby's condition a name (diagnosis) and outlining the mechanisms which led to death (pathogenesis) help alleviate guilt which accompanies the grieving process. Providing an autopsy report to the family helps them to achieve closure. Many families also are comforted to know that facts which are learned from the autopsy can enhance medical knowledge and prepare clinicians to cope with similar occurrences in the future, and to know that knowledge gained about pathogenesis eventually may prevent recurrences. This may offer them a measure of comfort about their baby's death, because it creates a hope that the baby's existence was not meaningless.

Viewing the Body

Viewing the baby's body by the parents is an important, therapeutic step.

No matter how distorted a baby's body may appear, due to congenital abnormalities or physical effects of the processes of death, parents' fantasies almost
universally will be worse than the reality. Viewing is best done either before
the autopsy has been performed, or after the body has been embalmed, with
accompanying cosmetic procedures completed. If a family insists on seeing
the baby's body immediately after autopsy, skillful draping can minimize any
visual traces of the procedure when the family views the baby.

Viewing is best done on the patient-care floor. Most hospital morgues are
in a basement level, and they rarely include any comfortable facilities for
viewing bodies. The patient unit is more comfortable and esthetically
designed. At our institution, if absolutely necessary, nursing or social work
staff can bring family members to the morgue. Morgue staff will lay out the
baby's body during regular working hours, or a nurse can do it during off
hours. For many reasons, no family members ever should be left alone with
the baby's body. Someone should remain with the family the entire time that
they view their baby's body.

Autopsy Procedure

Postmortem examination proceeds only after review of the medical
record. The autopsy never should be performed without knowledge of the
clinical course. Autopsy personnel need as complete information as possible
about the woman's prenatal history and any diagnostic test results. History
and test results may suggest differential diagnostic possibilities, which might
require modifications or additions to the autopsy procedure, to confirm or
rule out possible diagnoses. Thus, a flow chart (Wigglesworth, 1991) can help
in this process. Detailed procedures are available (Chambers, 1992;
MacPherson & Valdés-Dapena, 1991; MacPherson & The Study Group for
Complications of Perinatal Care, 1994; Valdés-Dapena, 1979; Valdés-Dapena
& Huff, 1983; Winter, Knowles, Bieber, & Baraitser, 1988) to serve as a framework (see Figure 2-11).

External examination of the body, done thoroughly and in a systematic
fashion, may hint at significant underlying pathology. This includes degree of
maceration, which can give clues to time elapsed since fetal death (Genest &
Singer, 1992), presence of externally identified malformations, and hydrops.
Weights and measurements can be correlated with gestational age, to investigate possible growth abnormalities (most often, intrauterine growth restriction). Photographs are important to document malformations, especially if
the pattern of malformation is not familiar to the autopsy prosector. It is

Figure 2-11.
Wigglesworth Flow Chart

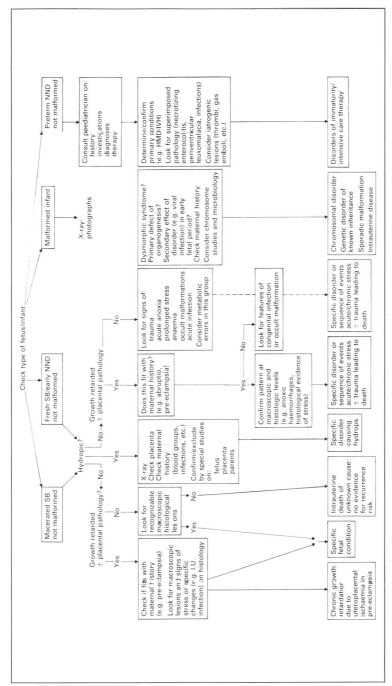

Reprinted with permission from Wigglesworth, J.S., (1984). Perinatal pathology. *Major Problems in Pathology, 15*, 46.

important to caution that observations may be biased by expectations of the observer.

Steps in the Perinatal Autopsy Process

The body is opened with a y-shaped incision in chest and abdomen and a coronal ear-to-ear incision in the scalp. Care is taken to avoid disrupting the face and neck. Every baby's body should be treated the same way, regardless of previous discussions with the family about their wishes for disposition of their baby's body. Even if a family has decided that they want the body cremated, they may change their minds subsequently and opt for a funeral with an open casket.

Internal organs should be examined *in situ* to confirm anatomic relationships and to note the presence or absence of normal structures. Then, organs usually are removed and placed in fixative for later microscopy study. Organs are dissected to detect any lesions. The brain usually is fixed for several days or weeks before being dissected to firm up the tissues, because of the common finding at autopsy that fetal and neonatal brain tissue is quite soft. Careful gross observations should be recorded in a systematic fashion, including organ weights. This can be done by dictation, by diagram, or by checking off findings on a checklist.

Physicians and other health care professionals who are involved with the patient's care may find it helpful to attend the autopsy and view the dissection. Members of the patient's family should not be allowed to observe the actual dissection. Even though the body always is treated with respect, seeing it dissected could cause unnecessary distress and would be a distraction for professionals who should be concentrating on performing the dissection.

If organs are not to be retained, samples for microscopy must be obtained during autopsy, since there will be no second chance to obtain additional microscopic samples from fixed organs. If there is consent to retain the gross organs, these are kept for demonstration to the patient's physicians and to other involved parties, including residents, students, and nurses. These organs also thus become available for additional microscopic sampling. The organs usually are cremated when they no longer are needed. Those from particularly challenging cases may be kept for long periods in a teaching collection or museum. Small samples of tissue for microscopic evaluation are fixed, usually in 10% formalin (formaldehyde), and processed for slide preparation. Once processed, tissues routinely are retained for many years. The placenta is examined at the same time as the autopsy, if possible.

This includes observation of the membranes, cord, fetal surface, and maternal surface. The placenta then is sliced at 2 to 3 mm intervals, and the cut surfaces are examined.

Special Procedures

A number of special procedures can yield important information in specific cases; but, because of difficulty or expense, these generally are done only when indicated, not routinely in every case. Photography is most useful as an adjunct to carefully recorded gross descriptions. Photographs and slides also have excellent teaching value.

Cytogenetic studies are quite expensive and should not be done routinely. Fetuses or babies who have more than one major malformation demonstrate an increased risk of cytogenetic abnormalities. Bodies that are badly macerated or physically disrupted may have more malformations which could be overlooked. In those cases, a high index of suspicion is important, and cases with a single major malformation should be sampled. Many classically "nonchromosomal" syndromes are associated with minor chromosomal abnormalities (for example, DiGeorge syndrome and 22q deletion) and so should be tested. Nonimmune hydrops fetalis also is an indication for cytogenetics. Fetal tissues which are productive sources of fibroblasts for culture include skin (dermis), tendon, lung, and kidney. Fibroblasts can be cultured successfully, even several days after fetal death. If the fetus is badly macerated, the placenta should be sampled. Samples from the chorionic plate are least likely to be contaminated with maternal cells.

Postmortem radiographs are done routinely in some institutions. The yield of abnormal studies is low, and many of the abnormal results are not helpful diagnostically. Use of radiography in selected cases can be very helpful. In our institution, we do not obtain radiographs on every malformed fetus. We request radiographs in every case of suspected skeletal dysplasia, in every case of skeletal malformation where the nature of the malformation is not obvious, and in cases where the pattern of nonskeletal malformations suggests a high likelihood of skeletal abnormality; for instance, to check radial and/or vertebral column malformations in cases of suspected VATER (**V**ertebral, **A**nal atresia, **T**rachial-**E**sophageal fistula, **R**adial dysplasia [or **R**enal]). Dye injection can be useful in dissecting organs with complex malformations, in which major ducts or blood vessels are hard to trace. Renograffin is an easier dye to administer than is barium, and it flows through small vessels more easily.

Cultures for bacteria may be difficult to interpret, given the possibility of contamination by vaginal bacterial overgrowth when delivery occurs after fetal demise. Viral cultures have very low yields, even if there is clinical information to suggest viral infection. Biochemical studies for metabolic diseases may be appropriate. Most metabolic diseases do not manifest in the immediate postpartum period. Clinical history is the main indication for metabolic studies. Some conditions can be tested in fibroblasts, and those samples can be taken the same way as cytogenetics samples are obtained. Studies that require viable hepatocytes or myocytes can be done only on babies who die after birth or immediately before. The same applies to enzyme studies on flash-frozen muscle, which are necessary for study of myopathies.

Discussing Autopsy Results:
Timing of Autopsy Reports

Provisional diagnosis, which is based on gross findings, only should be issued within days of the autopsy. This often provides sufficient information to counsel the parents. There are several important steps between provisional diagnosis and the final autopsy report. The clinical history and gross findings are dictated or written and then transcribed. Fixed tissues must be processed for microscopic slides. Slides then are evaluated by the pathologist, after first being reviewed by a resident, if the procedure is performed at an academic institution. Findings then are correlated with the clinical history, and the report is written. Reports tend to be more elaborate at institutions where residents are involved; but reports may take longer to complete because of additional steps. Final autopsy reports are required by the Joint Commission on Accreditation of Healthcare Organizations (JCAHO) to be completed within 60 days, although a longer period is allowed when special procedures are necessary or if diagnostic problems are present.

The Autopsy Report

The autopsy report should include as a minimum a list of diagnoses, a synopsis of the clinical history, and gross and microscopic descriptions. Diagnoses usually are arranged in a manner which shows the pathogenetic relations of the findings. Most centers also include a "notanda" or "clinical pathological correlation" in the report, which discusses findings in more depth. If specific questions are presented by the clinical history or are being asked by the family, and these questions have been communicated to pathologists, these answers usually will be addressed in the report.

The baby's next of kin should receive a copy of the autopsy report from the woman's obstetrician or the neonatologist or pediatrician who was involved in the newborn's death. That is the best way to assure that someone who is knowledgeable has discussed the technicalities with the family. Some pathologists routinely meet with the baby's family, though that has not been the general rule. Certainly, the pathologist always should be willing to meet with the family to answer any questions which their own health care providers cannot answer. The autopsy report can take on a life of its own. Parents want it to be perfect, and some may insist that any minor errors or inconsistencies be rectified before they are satisfied.

Limitations on Information from the Autopsy

A number of factors can limit information which may be derived from the perinatal autopsy, and these must be taken into account. Postmortem maceration is the biggest problem in the case of stillbirths, and the problem is worse the longer that the fetal death occurred before delivery. Maceration begins as soon as the fetus dies. Without energy metabolism to maintain cellular integrity, the process of autolysis begins, the skin starts to slough, internal organs liquefy, and tissues lose histologic detail (see Figure 3-11). These changes can be used in a limited way to confirm when fetal death occurred, although there are degrees of individual variation. Autolysis also is exaggerated by the effects of a long period of time between delivery and autopsy, and by presence of intrauterine bacterial infection. If changes are significant, microscopic diagnoses can be obscured, although gross malformations usually are still visible.

The placenta stays vital after the fetus dies. It may undergo, however, a series of characteristic postmortem changes which actually help in estimating the time of fetal death (Genest, 1992). Unfortunately, some changes also may mimic placental reaction to hypoxia and may obscure diagnosis of premortem disease processes. The value of perinatal autopsy also is limited if events leading to fetal death happened too quickly. It takes several hours for cells and tissues to show the changes of inflammation and cell death. Sudden death may leave no traces on the placenta. A fetus who has been in hypoxic distress may show signs of having intrauterine gasping respirations with amniotic fluid cells in the lungs. This indicates distress, but does not identify the cause of distress.

Some obstetricians use dilatation and evacuation for pregnancy terminations which are performed well into the second trimester. This would include cases of fetal death without spontaneous delivery, as well as terminations

Figure 3-11.

Histologic Features in the 100 Learning Cases that Correlated Best with Timing of Fetal Death

Tissue Feature	N	(NA)	Death-to-Delivery Time	Sensitivity	Specificity	Positive Predictive Value
Kidney: cortical tubular nuclear loss of basophilia	78	(13)	≥4 h	0.983	0.800	0.934
GI tract: mucosal epithelial nuclear loss of basophilia	85	(7)	≥8 h	0.966	0.875	0.952
Lung: bronchial mucosal epithelial detachment	84	(8)	≥18 h	1.000	0.903	0.946
Lung: bronchial cartilage matrix loss of basophilia	87	(5)	≥24 h	0.820	0.919	0.932
Liver: hepatocyte nuclear loss of basophilia	88	(4)	≥24 h	0.957	0.902	0.957
Thymus: cortical lymphocyte karyorrhexis	76	(5)	≥24 h	1.000	0.850	0.857
Heart: inner half of myocardium nuclear loss of basophilia	81	(4)	≥24 h	0.909	0.919	0.930
Adrenal: fetal adrenal cortex nuclear loss of basophilia	81	(5)	≥24 h	0.762	0.897	0.889
Pancreas: maximal loss of nuclear basophilia	52	(7)	≥36 h	0.917	0.900	0.753
Thymus: lymphocyte nuclear loss of basophilia	73	(8)	≥48 h	0.958	0.837	0.742
Kidney: glomerular nuclear loss of basophilia	83	(8)	≥48 h	0.806	0.942	0.893
Heart: outer half of myocardium nuclear loss of basophilia	78	(7)	≥48 h	0.839	0.915	0.867
GI tract: transmural [4+] bowel wall nuclear loss of nuclear basophilia	79	(12)	≥72 h	0.966	0.960	0.933
Adrenal: adult adrenal cortex nuclear loss of basophilia	75	(11)	≥72 h	1.000	0.946	0.864
Lung: bronchial epithelial nuclear loss of basophilia	80	(12)	≥96 h	0.920	0.945	0.885
Liver: maximal loss of nuclear basophilia	80	(12)	≥96 h	0.917	0.929	0.846
GI tract: maximal loss of nuclear basophilia	78	(13)	≥1 wk	0.950	0.983	0.950
Adrenal: maximal loss of nuclear basophilia	74	(12)	≥1 wk	0.929	0.917	0.722
Trachea: chondrocyte nuclear loss of basophilia	62	(1)	≥1 wk	0.750	0.963	0.750
Lung: alveolar wall nuclear loss of basophilia	88	(4)	≥2 wk	0.938	0.958	0.833
Kidney: maximal loss of nuclear basophilia	89	(2)	≥4 wk	1.000	0.976	0.750
Lung: maximal loss of nuclear basophilia	92	(0)	≥8 wk	0.900	0.988	0.900
Cerebrum: cortical neuronal nuclear loss of basophilia	70	(2)	≥8 wk	0.714	1.000	1.000

NA = not available for evaluation because the clinically timed interval during which death occurred included the death-to-delivery time being assessed.
GI = gastrointestinal

Reprinted with permission from Genest, D.R., Williams, M.A., & Greene, M.F. (1992). Estimating the time of death in stillborn fetuses: I. Histologic evaluation of fetal organs; An autopsy of 150 stillborns. *Obstetrics and Gynecology, 80*(4), 579.

undertaken because of diagnosed fetal anomalies. In these cases, fragmentation of the fetus can obscure diagnosis. This is especially true of head and brain malformations. Anencephaly can be diagnosed, but hydrocephalus, holoprosencephaly, and encephalocele are impossible to diagnose. Facial and cardiac anomalies may be distorted by the procedure, as well. In contrast, spina bifida and limb and genitourinary anomalies often can be diagnosed if the prosector is willing to spend time examining the tissue fragments.

Conclusion

A significant number, up to 25%, of perinatal autopsies will have no clear diagnosis. However, a significant number, up to 25% or even more, may have the diagnosis changed or substantially added to by the autopsy. Whether or not the autopsy changes the diagnosis which caused the baby's death, it can give added assurance which may help family members to deal with their painful loss.❑

References

Chambers, H.M. (1992). The perinatal autopsy: A contemporary approach. *Pathology, 24,* 45-55.

Genest, D.R. (1992). Estimating the time of death in stillborn fetuses: II. Histologic evaluation of the placenta: A study of 71 newborns. *Obstetrics and Gynecology, 80,* 585-592.

Genest, D.R., & Singer, D.B. (1992). Estimating the time of death in stillborn fetuses: III. External fetal examination; A study of 86 stillborns. *Obstetrics and Gynecology, 80,* 593-600.

Genest, D.R., Williams, M.A., & Greene, M.F. (1992). Estimating the time of death in stillborn fetuses: I. Histologic evaluation of fetal organs; An autopsy of 150 stillborns. *Obstetrics and Gynecology, 80(4),* 575-584.

MacPherson, T.A., & Valdés-Dapena, M. (1991). The perinatal autopsy. In J.S. Wigglesworth & D.B. Singer (Eds.), *Textbook of fetal and perinatal pathology* (pp. 93-112). Boston: Blackwell.

MacPherson, T.A., & the Study Group for Complications of Perinatal Care. (1994). In *A model perinatal autopsy protocol.* Washington, DC: Armed Forces Institute of Pathology.

Saller, D.N., Lesser, K.B., Harrel, U., Rogers, B.B., & Oyer, C.E. (1995). The clinical utility of the perinatal autopsy. *Journal of the American Medical Association, 5,* 663-665.

Valdés-Dapena, M.A. (1979). The pathologist's conference with parents following postmortem examination of their child: An application of the Kübler-Ross concept. *Perspectives in Pediatric Pathology, 5,* 263-267.

Valdés-Dapena, M., & Huff, D. (1983). *Perinatal autopsy manual.* Washington, DC: Armed Forces Institute of Pathology.

Wigglesworth, J.S. (1991). Causes and classification of fetal and perinatal death. In J.S. Wigglesworth & D.B. Singer (Eds.), *Textbook of fetal and perinatal pathology* (pp. 77-91). Boston: Blackwell.

Winter, R.M. Knowles, S.A.S., Bieber, F.R., & Baratiser, M. (1988). *The malformed fetus and stillbirth: A diagnostic approach.* Chichester, MA: John Wiley & Sons.

Chapter 12

The Nurse's Role: Care of Patients after Pregnancy Loss

Linda Closs Leoni

Despite tremendous progress in medicine generally and in obstetrics specifically, neonatal death, stillbirth, and early pregnancy losses still occur. While technology has given us the advantage of sophisticated measures of fetal health, these technologies at times are inadequate. For families who are dependent upon modern techniques for prenatal genetic testing, the information gained from this same technology may lead to heart-wrenching decisions about continuing or terminating the pregnancy. In each case of pregnancy loss, parents need sensitive, personalized nursing care to identify and meet their individual special needs. While many members of the interdisciplinary team provide unique, essential care, nurses spend the greatest amount of time with these parents. The nursing care given to a family following pregnancy loss can set the stage for a family's entire grieving process. It is essential that nurses provide compassionate care that meets or exceeds the parents' expectations as well as national standards of care that are based on well-grounded theory, current literature, and high-quality, relevant research.

Standard of Care

RTS Bereavement Services, a nationally known service dedicated to the training of grief counselors, states that their mission "...is to actively develop a common standard of excellence which assures that services are provided to bereaved families through an interdisciplinary and holistic approach" (Rybarik, 1994). This service has promoted an exceptional standard of care throughout the country via multiple grief counselor training sessions and thorough, well-written parent educational materials. Establishing a standard of care for the pregnancy-loss patient and her family validates the severity of their loss. The *Guidelines for Perinatal Care* state that the goals of the health care team are to help the family start a normal grief reaction, actualize their loss, acknowledge their grief, assure the family that their feelings are normal, and meet the particular needs of each family (American Academy of Pediatrics & American College of Obstetricians and Gynecologists, 1992). The Association of Women's Health, Obstetric, and Neonatal Nurses (AWHONN) states that involvement of the parents in all aspects of education and care following such a loss "...leads to a more realistic identification with and subsequent appropriate resolution of the grieving process" (AWHONN, 1985).

Consumer demands for more knowledge and choice in health care have driven recent changes in bereavement care. Health care literature of the 1980s is replete with articles and references which are intended to aid and increase care providers' sensitivity to bereaved families. The result of this is the emergence of perinatal bereavement support teams or services, as well as lay support services and support groups. Many hospitals now have clinical teams offering multiple services for bereaved parents. However, before any of these services are rendered, a thorough assessment of parents' needs must be made to ensure that appropriate care is individualized.

Nursing Assessment

The assessment of a pregnancy-loss patient and her family is the foundation of care. If the basic assessment is incorrect, much harm, perhaps irreparable, can befall the bereaved family. Initially, care providers must explore their own attitudes about death and grief, and how the journey through grief would proceed within their own culture. This includes values, beliefs, lifestyles, traditions, food choices, and attitudes about health and illness, as well as multiple other influences. As providers recognize the control which their culture superimposes on themselves, they can better recognize and accept their patient's feelings about the death of her baby within the woman's own culture. Culture influences the meaning of the death for women and their families and dictates customs surrounding death. It is important to keep this in mind as the patient assessment is completed (Lawson, 1990).

Regardless of the type of loss, the first assessment must be parents' perception of the pregnancy and the significance of their loss to them. While some people regard the loss of a pregnancy as the loss of a full-term baby, others will feel no sense of loss, and some will see this simply as a life event

(Swanson-Kaufman, 1986; Wheeler, 1992). These feelings may be based on religious theology that dictates when the infant has a soul (Lawson, 1990). If parents consider the pregnancy loss to be a life event and do not grieve actively, care providers must acknowledge and respect these feelings and take care not to induce guilt for a family's lack of mourning. Care providers must represent for all parents, whether or not they grieve, a resource upon which to draw, should they have any questions or concerns later.

The vast majority of people respond to pregnancy loss, regardless of gestational age, as the death of a baby and the subsequent death of their hopes and dreams. Parents lose not only their child, but also their parental roles, status of pregnancy, and faith in their bodies and/or their genes to do what so seemingly is effortless for the rest of the population. Kowalski (1987) states that perinatal death represents multiple losses to the parents, including loss of a significant person, loss of some aspect of the self, loss of external objects, loss of a stage of life, loss of a dream, and loss of creation. Culturally, the couple whose first pregnancy ends in a loss has not completed their rite of passage into parenthood, which symbolizes adult status (Layne, 1990).

The obstetric community responds competently to the physical crisis of pregnancy loss but has had (and still does have, in some communities) difficulty responding adequately to the psychological sequelae. All too often, parents are isolated in the woman's hospital room, without adequate support or resources to learn about grieving, autopsy, cremation, funerals, or any other aspect of death with which they now are forced to deal. The woman may be discharged from the hospital within 24 hours. Unless the hospital or primary care provider has some type of support system in place, parents usually have no further contact with health care providers until the 4- to 6-week follow-up office visit. This contrasts sharply with the recommendations of grief experts who advocate for much earlier support and counseling (Rybarik, 1994; Woods & Esposito, 1987).

Development of the Parental Role

Pregnancy-loss patients must receive care that is consistent with a patient-centered standard which is based on current literature, to assist them through the grief process. Part of that research base provides a clear understanding of parental role development, the cumulative effect of well-documented maturational processes during pregnancy.

Rubin (1967) described the first maternal task of pregnancy as seeking safe passage for the mother and her baby through pregnancy, labor, and delivery. This includes seeking competent prenatal care, eating a healthy diet, and adhering to safe practices such as eliminating alcohol, caffeine, and drugs. The mother also seeks to secure unconditional acceptance of her baby by significant others. This realignment of the mother's bonds with those who are significant in her life produces energy for her other tasks. In learning to give of herself, the woman evaluates and assesses the demands of pregnancy and motherhood on her body, relationships, and lifestyle, usually achieving a balance between demands of the infant and the satisfaction gained by her from her baby and her maternal role. The last task is binding-in to the unborn baby, referring to attachment to the infant, heightened by perceiving fetal movement, listening to the fetal heart, and visualizing ultrasound images (Rubin, 1967).

Lederman (1984) described seven dimensions of early pregnancy, four of which deal with development of the parental role. These are:

1. Acceptance of and adaptation to the pregnancy.
2. Progressive development of the parental role and relationship with the coming child.
3. Impact of the pregnancy on the parental relationship.
4. The pregnant woman's relationship with her own mother.

Similar to the maternal tasks described by Rubin, a woman's progress through these dimensions describes the growth and development of the maternal role.

Galinsky (1987) described six stages of parenthood. Two stages deal with psychologic growth of the parental role, image-making and nurturing. During image-making, prospective parents visualize themselves as parents, which motivates their acceptance of the pregnancy. They prepare for birth by rehearsing their parental roles which are based, in part, on memories of their own childhoods and how they were parented. As they consider their childhood from this perspective, people redefine their relationship with their own parents. Nurturing refers to the process that occurs immediately following birth, when parents reconcile their images of labor, delivery, and their baby with the reality, and then they attach, or bond, with their baby, again redefining and reordering relationships.

Although the development of the paternal role has not been researched as thoroughly as the maternal role, Jordan (1990) found that the primary process of fatherhood was the search for relevance in becoming a parent. This search takes the father through three stages, which include grappling with the reality of the pregnancy and the child, struggling to be recognized by society as a parent, and finally role-making as an involved parent who incorporates his child as a part of himself.

Kimble (1991) found that, in the past 2 decades, transformation of the paternal role to one with more nurturing and hands-on caregiving activities has deepened many men's emotional investment in their children. This is substantiated by paternal prenatal attachment similar to maternal prenatal attachment.

These processes form what Klaus and Kennell define as "Attachment — a unique relationship between two people that is specific and endures through time" (1982, p. 2). This attachment is an intense, multiphased process that occurs between parent and child, beginning with pregnancy and continuing through and after delivery. The identification and claiming phase is identified with parents' intense need to learn their baby's physical appearance, sex, condition, size, and behavioral characteristics. Naming their baby finally provides a unique identity. Caretaking, which includes handling, dressing, and bathing babies, is the final phase.

The developmental processes through which parents have gone change perceptions and a couple's relationships with each other and with other significant people in their lives. As this represents a shift in paradigms, they never again can view themselves or the world as they did before the pregnancy. Therefore, parents who experience a pregnancy loss have a need to be treated like the parents whom they have become, even though their baby is not going home with them. Care providers have an obligation and an opportunity to fulfill many needs for these childless parents.

Characteristics of Grief

Characteristics of grief have been studied in detail by multiple researchers and clinicians, providing valuable understanding and insights for care providers. Drs. Kay, Roman, and Schulte present a thorough review of this literature in Chapter 1 in this book. Nursing staff must remember that the process of grieving is fluid, with much fluctuation between phases, even during the woman's initial hospitalization. This fluctuation is universal and does not imply pathology. Staff members who assume roles as supporters and teachers for grieving families need to assess accurately at each encounter where the parents are in their mourning, and then adjust care accordingly. Supportive nursing professionals should not greet the family with their own agenda. Goals for each session must be indicated by the family's current emotional status.

Caring Theory

The most beneficial commodity that any nurse can offer to a grieving family is a nonjudgmental, deep sense of caring and personal involvement. Caring traditionally has been seen as an integral component of nursing. Lenninger (1981) stated that caring was central and unifying for the knowledge and practice of nursing. Watson (1985) views caring as an intentional process wherein respect for the recipient is demonstrated. Just as caring is essential to nursing, recognition of the personal dignity and worth of an individual is essential to caring. The role of nursing is to respond to individuals whose dignity and worth are challenged by their health status (Swanson-Kaufman, 1986).

Swanson proposes a theory of caring, describing five critical attributes of the attentive, attuned care provider. Her definition states that "...caring is a nurturing way of relating to a valued other toward whom one feels a personal sense of commitment and responsibility" (1991, p. 165). The first attribute, knowing, is described as "...striving to understand an event as it has meaning in the life of the other" (Swanson, 1991, p. 163). When a care provider administers care based on knowing, assumptions about the meaning of a baby's death for parents are avoided, since this care provider continually assesses the parents' status and tailors care appropriately. A thorough nursing assessment will validate the nurse's understanding of the significance of the parents' loss. When this occurs, the care provider is described as sensitive and knowledgeable. When care providers cannot understand the event as the parents do, they do not meet parents' needs and may be described as intrusive, distant, and mechanical (Leon, 1992).

The second category of caring is described as being with or emotionally present to the other, being available to share both positive and negative feelings with the other, or being able to feel the other's pain. In nursing practice, this is exemplified by an ability to respond to parents' grief and pain without hiding behind the facade of "professionalism." In other words, a nurse can cry with parents because she truly feels their pain.

The third category, "doing for," means that care providers do for parents what they would do for themselves, if it were possible for them to do so. Most parents have no idea how difficult and painful it will be to mourn the death of their baby. If possible, these parents would do anything they could to make their loss easier and less painful. The nurse who collects mementos of the baby for parents is "doing for" these parents. Mementos confirm that this individual did exist, when reality seems to deny the baby's existence.

Enabling places care providers in the role of facilitator for parents' passage through life events and unfamiliar situations. As they give anticipatory guidance and teaching to parents in discussions about funerals and memorial services, care providers facilitate and ease parents' experience through these unfamiliar functions.

The fifth category, maintaining belief, places care providers in the role of supporting parents' capacity to survive this event and to face a future with meaning. Communication of care providers' belief that parents will survive the death of their baby and they will integrate the experience into their lives, without feeling the current level of devastation for the rest of their lives, is a service which parents appreciate. This gives them hope of smoother, calmer times to come. Communication of this belief may have to be repeated frequently in the months that follow the death of a baby. Parents may cling to this support as they experience the emotional roller coaster of grief.

In summary, Swanson (1991) states "...caring strives to know, be with, do for, and enable the other so that, within the demands, constraints, and resources of the other's life, a path filled with meaning will be chosen." Nurses who can provide this level of care will serve unique needs of bereaved parents, by assisting them to have positive memories of their baby and by giving them a feeling of being cared for in the midst of their pain and grief.

A review of the literature yields many protocols and guidelines for appropriate care and follow-up bereavement services (Brost & Kenney, 1992; Calhoun, 1994; Davis, Stewart, & Harmon, 1988; Hutti, 1988; Ilse & Furrh, 1988; Lawson, 1990; Maguire & Skoolicas, 1988; Mueller, 1991; Null, 1989; Rosas & Rosas, 1987; Ryan, Cote-Arsenault & Sugarman, 1991; Weinfeld, 1990; Welch, 1991; Wheeler & Limbo, 1990; Woods & Esposito, 1987). One common theme among all of this literature is that these people are parents and they must be treated as parents. Authors universally advise that care providers give parents permission to grieve; educate them about the grieving process; assure them time, space, and privacy to grieve; and, most importantly, convey to parents that they care about them and their grief. Other goals of nursing care for bereaved parents include managing their physical pain so that they may work with their emotional pain, reducing the trauma of hospitalization, validating their status as parents, assisting them in attaching to and parenting their baby, and starting them down the long road to healthy grieving and integration of this experience into their lives. This is the foundation upon which care given to grieving families is based.

This discussion has demonstrated why parents who suffer pregnancy loss grieve so intensely. However much theories may serve as the framework upon which nursing measures will address the goals explained above, such theories do not detail all the nursing measures which are needed to care for the very real, very destroyed parents. A description of nursing actions which are intended to meet the standard of care for grieving parents who have suffered a pregnancy loss follows.

Nursing Care of Bereaved Parents

Whether or not you have received specialized training in bereavement, as a nurse you are a professional whose role requires that you provide compassionate, appropriate care to all of your patients. When you meet families who are suffering a pregnancy loss, be sure that the stress of the situation does not preclude simple but very important actions, such as introducing yourself and expressing your sorrow for their loss. Acknowledge the shock of their bereavement and answer any immediate questions parents may have. If you do not know the answer to a question, it is appropriate that you acknowledge this. Assure them that you will obtain information which they need, and then comply with your verbal contract with the parents. It is crucial that you return with the information within a realistic time, as promised. These parents initially may have difficulty in trusting the medical community. Medical personnel frequently are viewed as omniscient and omnipotent, but their inability to prevent a family's pregnancy loss temporarily may interfere with parents' ability to trust their health care providers. Nurses and physicians, as well as others, play a critical role in assisting parents to regain their trust once again by fulfilling promises in a timely fashion. Helping these people to trust the medical community again is critical to starting a healthy grieving process. Honesty in admitting what no one knows or can understand can put the medical community in a less all-knowing position from the parents' perspective, which may help parents to perceive the medical world more realistically.

Assessment of parents' knowledge base is essential. Do they comprehend the situation? Do they have a birth plan? What has the physician discussed with them? Have they had any previous experience with death? Would they like to have clergy visit them? If so, do they want to see their own clergy or should we summon the hospital chaplain? Are there other family members who need to be contacted? Ask what else can be done to assist them at this time. Such information can be used to formulate a list of a particular family's needs. From this, you may start to gather resources to meet these needs.

Early Pregnancy Loss

If the pregnancy is ending spontaneously or if the woman will need a surgical procedure, explain as much as possible and appropriate about the procedure and timing of events. Give parents as many choices as possible. Generally, they will not want to know specific details of operative procedures. But, they are interested in timing, anesthesia choices, post-anesthesia care, and expected time of discharge from the hospital or emergency department (ED). If the plan is to perform a prostaglandin termination, discuss this procedure with parents. Give them a brief overview of the process, and discuss with them any options which they may have, such as where the procedure can be done and what analgesia choices are offered. Answer any questions parents may have. Formulating their birth plan may offer parents some way to gain a sense of control over this unexpected, fast-moving, uncontrolled event.

If parents come into the ED, try to reduce as much of the trauma of hospitalization as possible. Provide them with the shelter of a private room instead of a curtained cubicle, if possible. Emergency department personnel regularly deal with major, life-threatening trauma. These professionals often do not have the time or opportunity to form caring relationships with their patients, and thus they may not appreciate the impact which pregnancy loss exerts on parents. They are accustomed to giving high-tech, critical care and may not have the time and/or energy necessary to give emotional support to parents who are having a miscarriage (Hutti, 1988). These emergency department professionals may lack the time to provide complete pre- and postoperative explanations to help people to prepare for a dilatation and curettage. If parents are admitted to an inpatient unit after an initial period in the ED, the unit personnel should support them in expressing their thoughts and feelings, and should provide them with the emotional support that they need.

Late Pregnancy Loss

If the pregnancy is at or near term, assist parents to make or revise their birth plan and educate them about options for pain management. Assure parents that the health care team will manage the woman's physical discomfort so that parents can focus on their emotional pain. Some parents may not have started, or others may not have finished, prenatal classes yet. It may be necessary to give them an overview of the labor and delivery process. Offering them a brief, informative pamphlet or flyer which contains the same information that you are providing orally can be helpful, because parents will refer to that later if they forget some of the information that you have explained to them.

Nurses should be prepared for the "magical thinking" of almost all parents who are admitted with the diagnosis of fetal death — that this is all a mistake and their baby really is not dead. While parents may appear to be dealing with their grief quietly, actually they may be in denial and may be bargaining for the miracle of a live baby. They may not truly believe that the baby has died until delivery, at which time there will be more open displays of grief (Kirkley-Best & Kellner, 1982).

Naming the Baby

Talk with parents about names which they may have chosen for the baby. Most people have thought about names, and many people who know the baby's gender already may have named their baby. The baby who has died needs a name. Naming the baby supports the personhood and individuality of the baby, and this helps to crystallize the baby's unique identity and place in parents' lives. Even when the loss occurs early in pregnancy before the baby's sex has been determined, many parents are convinced that they know their baby's gender. Assure them that it is perfectly appropriate for them to name their baby accordingly. On the other hand, parents often will choose a gender-neutral name for their baby. The nurse should be available for discussion and should support parents' decisions, whatever they may be.

Encourage parents to see and hold their baby, explaining the benefits of this contact. Refer to their baby by his or her given name whenever possible, and describe him or her before giving the baby to the parents. If the baby has been in the morgue, let parents know in advance that their baby will feel cold and will appear to have a blue color. If the baby is macerated and/or deformed, prepare parents for this by gently but clearly explaining what the baby will look like, and wrap the baby so that most of the disfigurement is covered. Many parents will want to view a fetal anomaly. Our job is to make this experience as nontraumatizing as possible. While helping the parents to uncover the disfigurement, point out the baby's normal features. No matter how macerated or deformed the baby may appear, what the parents are imagining is far worse than reality. Most parents will focus on one specific area, such as hands or ear lobes, and they may marvel at how perfect these are. We can assist in that process with our descriptions to parents before they see their baby. Using the baby's name as much as possible, in addition to gentle handling and the care with which we interact with the baby, demonstrate our respect for the baby and his or her personhood.

Most parents undergo an identification and a claiming phase, whereby they have an intense need to know the baby's weight, sex, and physical appearance, just as do parents of live-born children (Klaus & Kennell, 1982). These parents progressively touch the baby in the same way, first tentatively with their fingertips, then with the length of the fingers, to the palm of the hand, to a whole-arm embrace, and finally to an encircling of the baby within their arms. Parents often compare characteristics and appearance of their baby to family members, a process which identifies the baby as a family member. Enhance this process by pointing out the baby's unique characteristics and/or familial likenesses, if the parents are uncomfortable and uneasy about seeing and holding their baby. These activities are a part of the attachment or bonding process in developing parental roles. These processes assist parents to say hello to their baby, which is essential before they can say goodbye.

If parents demonstrate ambivalence about seeing and/or holding their baby, please notify the morgue so that the autopsy, if it already has been authorized, can be delayed if possible. Often, parents need time to process the vast quantities of information which they have been given since they learned of their baby's death. Also, if parents' family members must travel from out of town or will be coming to the hospital, they too may want to see and hold the baby. Although the baby can be wrapped to conceal the incisions of the autopsy, such maneuvers may decrease or prevent viewers from seeing the whole baby, or from seeking reassurance from the baby's appearance that the baby is genetically (phenotypically) normal — a natural urge for many families.

Encourage parents to have photographs taken of their baby and of themselves holding the baby, including instant photos, if available. Instant photographs do deteriorate over time, so parents should be advised to have any such photos transferred to regular film as soon as possible. Pictures of the parents holding their baby document for them the fact that they are parents. Remember that parents came into the hospital with their dreams and hopes shattered, and, unless they were advised to do so, they probably did not remember or think to bring a camera. Hospitals may be able to supply a camera and film, or perhaps the group who photographs all of the newborns may offer a bereavement package to these unfortunate parents.

Parents, as well as friends and relatives, may have some difficulty accepting this practice of photographing the baby, since America's death-denying society is squeamish about obtaining and viewing photographs of the deceased. Perhaps this is because, when an older individual dies, families usually have a lifetime of memories and photographs of the individual. In the case of pregnancy loss, however, this is the only time that parents will have with their baby, and this time should be recorded. Over time, these photographs may become the family's most significant mementos and memories of this baby.

Photographs should be taken as soon after delivery as possible. Pictures of the baby, front and back, affirm for parents that their genes are capable of producing a normal-appearing child. Pictures of the baby dressed in size-appropriate gowns or outfits, wrapped in a baby blanket, and unwrapped, preserve the reality of the baby's infanthood. For some photographs, many families prefer to place an object with personal significance beside the baby, such as an heirloom blanket, a bonnet, or a toy. Remember to ask parents about their personal preferences, as they may not remember to tell you or may not have even thought about it. Parents may want several different poses, especially those people who are from cultures that value death photographs. Some institutions have professional photographers take beautiful, soft, black-and-white pictures of the baby, who is posed to appear to be sleeping. If the baby is macerated or disfigured, he or she usually can be positioned and wrapped so that a normal feature, such as a hand or just the face, can be photographed. Again, what parents imagine usually is far worse than reality.

Make footprints and handprints of the baby, if possible. If the baby has enough hair, save a lock of hair. Parents nearly always want any of the linens that were on or next to the baby. If the baby's photographs were taken with a special outfit, ask the parents if they would like to keep that outfit and blanket, or if they would like to have the baby buried in them, if burial has been chosen.

Place all of these mementos in an appropriate bag, box, or basket. As public awareness of the devastation of pregnancy loss increases, the market for specialty products to address bereaved families' needs is growing, with the production of special padded boxes, baskets, and hand-carved caskets. Note, however, that these items can be expensive, and they may be difficult to justify in budget shortages, thereby prohibiting hospitals' supplying such items for families. Many times, family and friends will donate money to the hospital in memory of a baby who died. The collection of such funds can become the means for obstetric or neonatal units' purchasing some of these specialty items; or hospital auxiliary or volunteer organizations can make or purchase them. Many parents are deeply moved by the donation of handmade infant clothing and other items for these special babies.

Label bereaved parents' hospital rooms with a special symbol or sign that will indicate that the patient's baby has died. This symbol indicating a fetal loss should be made known to all support services, such as social work, food, and housekeeping, so that inappropriate comments about the baby are not made inadvertently to parents.

Offer parents the choice of being either on the postpartum unit or the gynecologic unit. If a woman has been in the hospital for a period of time prior to the demise of her baby, then she may have a strong supportive relationship with nurses on the antepartum unit and may choose to remain under their care. Generally, most parents prefer to go to the gynecologic unit, so that they do not have to hear babies crying or watch other families with their babies. While they will have to listen to babies crying at some point in the future, they may need to be protected from such insult at this phase of their loss.

Encourage parents to have an autopsy performed for their baby. While the autopsy may not definitively establish the cause of a baby's death, the procedure and its findings can allay much guilt and anxiety for parents, by demonstrating the normalcy of the baby. Some hospitals dispose of the baby's remains following autopsy. Be sure that parents are informed of this and of the fact that, if the baby is cremated by the hospital's mortuary service, then the ashes may not be retrievable. Parents should be informed that cremations by the hospital may be carried out in clusters; so they must request an individual cremation by a private funeral home if they wish to receive their baby's remains.

As these parents need privacy and time alone, place them in a private room, if possible, and try to tailor hospital rules and regulations to meet families' needs. Facilitate the father's spending the night, if a couple so desires. If family members travel to the hospital from out of town, let them visit if possible and if desired by the parents, regardless of the hour.

If this was the first pregnancy for these parents, they may not have finished or even may not have begun to attend childbirth classes. They will need a discussion of normal postpartum physiologic changes that women should expect. Inform the woman that her breast milk may come in, and prepare her with strategies to deal with this physical and emotional discomfort. Explain that she will have lochia and educate her about the process of uterine involution. Advise her to be aware of postpartum danger signs for endometritis, retained placental fragments, urinary tract infection, and deep vein thrombosis, standard information that each new mother receives. Sometimes in the past, such discharge information may have been overlooked because the woman who has suffered a pregnancy loss went home quickly or for some other reason. Follow-up all oral instructions with written material, and let parents know that you have provided information for them in written form. Remember, parents may be in shock after their loss, and they may not listen well to your instructions.

Postpartum Education for Pregnancy Loss Parents: What to Expect

Bereaved parents need anticipatory guidance about the grieving process and ways to protect themselves from well-meaning, but poorly thought-through advice, and comments from family and friends. Explain to parents that there is no set time frame for resolution or incorporation of grief, even if some people may try to tell them that.

Also, tell parents that many people have difficulty in notifying friends and acquaintances about the death of their baby, and they may find that having one close friend or family member inform others of their tragedy eases their burden. As this friend or family member is passing the word, parents' wishes as to donations, whether any help is needed, and whether or not parents are ready to hear from others at this time also can be shared. Conversely, some people find that the repetitive recitation of telling close friends and acquaintances helps them to accept the reality of the loss. Parents need to know that their views on this may change, and that none of these approaches signify any abnormality.

Parents need to know that the grief experience is unique to each person experiencing it. Grief that partners feel will not be identical, nor will their grief be expressed similarly. Their grief will not be the same grief that their own parents feel, or the same as the neighbor who also lost a baby at the same gestational age feels. Try to give parents some strategies to deal with these differences in expression, and suggest various methods of communication, such as writing letters to or keeping journals about the baby.

Advise parents that they may grieve more intensely on special days, such as the day when the baby was expected to be born, special holidays that are connected with large family gatherings, the anniversary of the baby's death, and other special milestones. Let parents know that dismantling the baby's nursery, if it had been created before the baby died, is an opportunity to say goodbye. There is no "right" time to dismantle the nursery. This should be done only when parents are ready. Often, helpful grandparents, other family members, or friends are inclined to rush this process — even attempting to complete the task before the woman returns from the hospital — with the intention of sparing the family more pain. Try to explain that the pain which parents experience is a healing pain, and it is pain that cannot and should not be taken away by anyone.

With a baby's death, grandparents mourn the loss of their grandchild, and they also hurt for their children. Just as the baby's parents need to parent their child, grandparents want to parent their children and take care of them. There are times when they may offer to take care of funeral arrangements and costs. While this parenting by the grandparents is kind and well-meaning, it denies the baby's parents an opportunity to parent their own baby. Discuss this with parents and encourage them to discuss this with their parents (the grandparents) and come to a consensus. Grandparents can support their children in other ways, such as cleaning, doing laundry, and cooking for the couple in the immediate bereavement period. If there are other children already in the family, then grandparents may offer to give them the care and reassurance which they need at this stressful time, when their own parents are so preoccupied. Grandparents' grief is very real and should be acknowledged by the health care team.

Remember that it is normal for family or very close friends to feel that an action, or lack of action, on their part may have caused the baby to die. This magical thinking usually is incorrect. Grandparents especially may think that they could have helped prevent stress for the expectant parents and believe that somehow they could have prevented the baby's death. Children in the family may fear that their misbehavior or negative thoughts toward the baby caused the baby to die. Reassure both grandparents and children that there are many reasons why babies die, but that stress, sibling misbehavior, and negative thoughts do not cause babies to die. The literature is rich with resources to assist children who must cope with the death of a sibling.

Advise parents that funerals and/or memorial services can be very helpful in their healing process. These ceremonies serve as a rite of passage for the baby and provide the parents with memories of a real event, again affirming the existence and uniqueness of their lost child. A grave provides mourners with a real place to visit and grieve, and having this place to visit may help some parents feel connected with their baby. These steps do not have to be acted upon within any specific time frame; they can be delayed until the woman has recovered physically, is able to assist in planning the funeral, and is ready to attend any rituals in honor of her baby.

Follow-up with these parents after hospitalization is essential to help them to maintain the healthy grieving which they started in the hospital.

Most programs suggest that the nurse or grief counselor who was most involved with parents in the hospital follow the parents posthospitalization. This not only provides parents with a perceived connection with someone who "knew" their baby, but it also provides them with a support person who already knows their situation and circumstances. It also offers nurses feedback as to the final outcome for these parents. This is necessary for energy renewal for nurses, and such reinforcement may energize them for the next family who needs very special knowledge and care as they, too, suffer a pregnancy loss.

Summary

Bereaved parents require sensitive, caring nurses who devote thought and effort to assessing and meeting their special needs. Such a nurse must provide comprehensive care which takes into consideration parents' ability to assimilate the knowledge which is necessary to share. Nursing plays a significant role in initiating a healthy grieving process for parents after they experience a pregnancy loss. The care which nurses provide will have a lifelong impact on the family, as they travel down the long tortuous road to grief integration.❏

Case Study 1-12

Grief Counseling During Labor

Christine is admitted to the labor floor from the hospital emergency department (ED) with abdominal pain occurring regularly every 3 to 4 minutes and lasting 45 to 60 seconds. Christine is crying quietly and appears to be trying to do slow chest breathing. She is accompanied by her mother, who tearfully says, "This whole thing has got to be a mistake. My daughter is not pregnant. So, she can't have a dead baby in her! This is all wrong. Why are you tormenting me this way? I've already done this once — I don't need to have it happen again!"

The ED nurse reports that the patient is a slightly obese 19-year-old single white female who is 35 4/7 weeks pregnant by her last menstrual period (LMP). She complains that she has suffered this abdominal pain for approximately 10 hours. There is a vaginal discharge of green fluid with some blood-tinged mucus. Speculum examination reveals the cervix to be 2 to 3 centimeters dilated and thin. No digital exam was done per the patient's mother's request. Fetal heart tones could not be auscultated. The ED nurse states that the patient's mother is distraught. She was unaware of the pregnancy until her daughter's admission for abdominal pain. She is having difficulty accepting the diagnosis of pregnancy, let alone the strong probability of a fetal demise. The ED nurse states that it is very difficult to have any time alone with the patient and that the patient's mother appears to be overly protective.

The nurse says that she had about 5 minutes alone with Christine. In that interview, Christine stated that she had known that she was pregnant, but she had not told her mother because she knew that her mother would "flip out." Christine is devastated that her baby has died. "My boyfriend and I were going to run away and get married, because my mom doesn't like him and won't let him in our house — much less let us get married. And now this; this isn't going to help anything!"

Once Christine is settled in bed (with vital signs having been taken and no fetal heart tones on the fetal monitor), the senior resident brings in a portable ultrasound. This ultrasound examination reveals no fetal heart activity in an approximately 35-week fetus. Christine then starts to cry and states, "Why me? I wanted this baby so much!" The resident tells Christine that this might not have happened if she had gotten prenatal care. At this point Christine is sobbing.

During the ultrasound exam, Christine's nurse tries to obtain patient data from her mother, who was asked to leave the room during her daughter's ultrasound. Her mother Arlene states:

"Christine lives with me and works as a sales clerk at a local discount store. Her father is out of state and has been no help to me in raising this child. He never did listen to me. He doesn't send money or anything. I have to work two jobs just to get by. He left shortly after Christine was born. He didn't want her. I don't think he ever got over the boy that died. Although Christine has dated, she does not have a steady boy friend and would never get into trouble. This must be the work of that no-good hoodlum who came to the house a couple of times. I took care of him. He's not allowed in my house anymore! Christine is healthy and hasn't seen a doctor since she finished high school last year. She has never had a pelvic exam because she doesn't need one, because she promised me she wouldn't mess around...If Christine is really pregnant and in labor I want her to be 'snowed' so that she will not remember labor or see this kid. That way she will be able to get this behind her and forget all about it. That's what they did for me 20 years ago, and it worked very well. I've never had any problems because of it."

If you were Christine's grief counselor, how would you handle this situation?

Commentary

It is clear in this complicated situation that the main players, Christine and her mother Arlene, both have different needs, which do not necessarily correspond. Christine's needs related to the current situation include these issues:

- Develop coping skills and get through her labor.
- Accept the loss of her baby.
- Decide on the role of her boyfriend in this immediate situation.
- Deal with her mother's reaction to this situation.
- Decide on seeing and holding her baby after delivery.
- Name her baby.
- Plan burial or other disposition arrangements.
- Deal with possible guilt related to her not having sought prenatal care.
- Explore a questionable social support system.
- Be screened regarding the potential for future complicated mourning.

Christine's mother, Arlene, presents with the following needs:

- Accept Christine's pregnancy.
- Deal with the issue of Christine's deception, and her own disappointments.
- Accept the loss of her daughter's baby.
- Acknowledge her own past loss, and separate it from her daughter's loss.
- Accept a relationship with Christine's boyfriend.
- Deal with feelings of failure as a parent.
- Be involved with burial arrangements for her grandchild.
- Learn how to accept reactions from friends and family to Christine's pregnancy and loss.
- Accept reality of daughter's continuing mourning.

In this situation, the grief counselor must be clear in her mind about who her patient is and where her responsibility lies, since the mother presents with so many needs of her own. Working in the short term to provide quality care for Christine, the counselor would deal with Arlene's needs only as they affect the immediate needs of Christine.

Since Christine expresses a supportive relationship with her boyfriend, and shares how they both were eager for the birth of the baby, it would be important to find out if Christine would like to have him be present for the labor and birth. Keeping in mind where your responsibility lies, indicate to Arlene that it is your responsibility to provide her daughter with what she desires during her labor, and tell her that you are anticipating her cooperation for Christine's benefit. If Christine desires the presence of her boyfriend and it is denied, this could constitute yet another loss for her, and this could complicate further both the immediate situation and Christine's recovery.

Arlene comes to this situation with many prior issues that seemingly or probably could interfere with what you hope to accomplish with Christine. It might be beneficial to spend some private time with Arlene, to deal separately with these issues and to gain the mother's cooperation. Since this situation has all the elements of a crisis for Arlene, some crisis intervention at this time would be appropriate. Provide a quiet atmosphere for the mother, with privacy, and offer simple food and a warm drink.

Reassuring Arlene that someone will stay with Christine, remove her from the room and try to find a quiet, private place. When the initial shock has begun to ebb, so that Arlene is able to listen, acknowledge her reaction and begin to validate the complexity of the situation. Recognize her concern for her daughter, talk with her, and concentrate on Arlene's own loss and feelings, rather than on what is happening with Christine. This is meant to help Arlene to realize that someone understands her feelings and problems. It would seem from the information given in the case presentation that Arlene has many issues which are unresolved about the death of her own baby and the departure of her husband. Christine's current loss has brought many buried feelings to the surface for her mother.

Arlene also has not separated Christine's loss from her own, as is evidenced by the comment, "I've already done this once. I don't need to have it happen again." Since she has had very little time to assimilate the idea of her daughter's pregnancy, let alone the loss of the baby, it is not surprising that Arlene is unclear about whose loss this is. Arlene is completely absorbed in her own issues. She asks to have her daughter "snowed" during delivery: "She'll forget it, and put it behind her." This would imply that it is Arlene herself who wants to forget and put it behind her.

Although you would like to help Arlene with the issue of her own baby's death years before, this really is out of the realm of what the counselor currently has time for. Explain to Arlene that you will be offering Christine the opportunity to see and hold her baby after delivery, that you will encourage Christine to select a name for her baby, and that Christine will be given the opportunity to bathe and dress her baby if she wishes. Try to help Arlene to understand the rationale behind these interventions. Explain that mothers do better dealing with such a loss if they have had the opportunity to parent the baby, if only briefly. Indicate the need, if Christine desires, to have the boyfriend present, since both parents are very bonded to their baby, as well as with each other.

Christine has the right to be offered the same standard of care as any patient in a similar situation. We need to acknowledge the relationship between Christine and her mother, to be supportive of their relationship — regardless of its quality — without compromising the usual care standards. It would seem that, if Arlene feels understood by her counselor, and if her experience and feelings are acknowledged, then her cooperation can be gained.

The relationship between the patient and her mother must be supported, regardless of its quality. It is not within the realm of the grief counselor/nurse to deal with this seemingly counterproductive relationship. Enlisting the expertise of the social worker may be of some advantage in future work with this family.

Of particular concern in the future is the possibility of complicated mourning. Due to the suddenness of the loss, the questionable support system, and Arlene's attitude about how to deal with the death of a baby, Christine is at risk for this complication. During the contacts over the next year, which should be part of the bereavement services, it would be important to assess for any symptoms of complicated mourning which include depression, withdrawal, change in habits, sleeping and eating disorders, and suicide ideation. If Christine shows any of these symptoms, then referral to a mental health specialist who has expertise with the grief process would be helpful.

This patient especially warrants regular contact after discharge by the bereavement counselor.

— *Joanne P. Chamberlain, MS, RNC*

Case Study 2-12

Grief Counseling 1 Week Following Pregnancy Loss

L.M., a 42-year-old G1 P0, was admitted to the gynecology unit at 3:00 pm for a prostaglandin-induced termination of a 16-week fetus, who has chromosomal abnormalities which are incompatible with life. L.M. has a lengthy history of infertility. This pregnancy was achieved with a donor egg and the father's sperm. On admission L.M.'s vital signs all were normal. She was very quiet. She avoided eye contact and answered questions with as few words as possible. The admitting nurse was a trained grief counselor who made repeated unsuccessful attempts to draw her and her husband out.

At midnight, after three prostaglandin suppositories failed to change her cervix, L.M. was medicated for sleep. The following day, the suppositories were successful in initiating labor, although they also produced the unpleasant side effects which accompany prostaglandin administration, including a fever of 40 degrees C, rapid pulse measured at 120 bpm, and severe diarrhea. In mid-afternoon, the gynecology unit transferred L.M. to labor and delivery (L&D) for the one-to-one care which she needed at this point. On L&D, a trained grief counselor was assigned to her care. L.M. delivered a baby girl at 4:30 pm. Her retained placenta subsequently was removed via suction completion that evening. After delivery of the baby, the grief counselor tried to talk with L.M. and her husband about seeing and holding their baby, and about a name and making arrangements for the baby. The parents refused to see the baby, did not want pictures, and would not name their baby, even after gentle persuasion and encouragement from the grief counselor. Following her post-anesthesia recovery, L.M.'s condition was stable, and she was discharged home at 6:00 pm the following day. All the mementos from the baby had been given to L.M.'s husband in a sealed envelope, with the contents listed on the outside. An attached note explained that photographs had been taken and would be sent out to be developed. The photographs would be returned to the hospital in 3 weeks. The name of the coordinator of the grief counseling service was given if they wanted the pictures later.

One week later, L.M. was admitted to a medical floor with pneumonia. On admission, her husband came to the gynecology unit requesting a grief counselor for his wife. He looked like he had been crying. Neither of the grief counselors who had cared for L.M. was available. Therefore, another grief counselor came to visit the patient. The grief counselor entered L.M.'s room and noted that the patient appeared pale and ill; she was receiving O2 by nasal cannula and intravenous antibiotics. When the grief counselor introduced herself, L.M. started sobbing and was unable to speak. When she could speak, she said, "I should have seen my baby. I probably wouldn't have been a decent mother anyway! What mother doesn't want to see her baby? Why didn't you make me see her and hold her? I think I'm going crazy — I've never felt this overwhelmed before. I don't think I can handle this! What am I going to do?"

If you were L.M.'s grief counselor, how would you handle this situation?

Commentary

There are four major issues to consider in the case of L.M. which the grief counselor will need to focus on in caring for this family.

Laboratory Policies

All grief counselors should be aware of laboratory policies when they are caring for families who experience a pregnancy loss. For example, how long does the laboratory keep tissue and pathology specimens prior to disposal? Most laboratories keep specimens for intervals ranging from 2 weeks to several months.

L.M. miscarried at 16 weeks, which means that her baby would be considered tissue/pathology and would be taken to the laboratory for examination. After the gross examination, where perhaps tissue for genetic studies would be obtained, the baby would be placed in a plastic bag, filled with formalin that will be disposed of at a later date with other tissue/pathology. Since the pregnancy loss occurred 1 week ago, chances are that L.M.'s baby's remains still are in the laboratory. The grief counselor would need to call the laboratory and talk with the laboratory supervisor, who can explain their procedures. In addition, the supervisor should be able to locate L.M.'s baby. If the baby's remains still are in the laboratory, then the option of seeing and holding her baby should be offered to L.M. The counselor may want to view the baby before this option is offered, so that she can explain to L.M. and her husband what they will be seeing, how their baby looks. This also makes it possible that the grief counselor can tell the parents the baby's sex and how the baby will feel. Another possibility is that the counselor can take photographs, to show to parents prior to their viewing the baby, as a reassurance and preparation.

Once the baby's remains have been located in the laboratory, the baby should be rinsed off and patted dry, and baby lotion or powder may be applied gently with cotton. The scent of such lotion or powder is associated with normal babies, and this simple step can be invaluable to the parents in promoting a positive image of their baby. If the baby underwent an autopsy, with removal of organs, then the laboratory supervisor or assistant can repack the baby's abdomen with cotton which is soaked with saline or formalin, as well as resuture the baby's chest and scalp. Again, it may be important to caution parents about how their baby will look and feel before they see him or her. Some pregnancy-loss programs will have clothing or at least a small blanket available to wrap the baby. If these items are not available, the grief counselor could use a baby cap which is obtained from the nursery and two washcloths or a small hand towel. It is important for the baby to look warm and cared for.

Should the Baby's Remains Not Be Available

Should the baby's body not be available in the laboratory, then the counselor could get the laboratory report, which should indicate the baby's sex, weight, and length. Realistic models are available of a 12-week gestation baby. Of course, this would be smaller than L.M.'s 16-week baby, and differences would need to be explained to the mother. But, perhaps offering L.M. the opportunity to see, hold, and have private time with something that would be similar to her baby might be healing for L.M.

Special Time with the Baby

When the baby is brought to L.M., the grief counselor should cradle the baby in her arms, approach L.M. and her husband, and wait either for eye contact with L.M. or for L.M. to raise her arms to receive her baby. If L.M. does not do this immediately, then the counselor could say, "L., I have your [son/daughter]. [He/She] is so sweet. Look at [his/her] little hand."

Involving Pastoral Care

Whether or not the baby is available for the family, the counselor should consider what can be done to help this mother and father to feel that they have cared for their baby. Offering the option of pastoral care is an excellent opportunity to create positive memories of their baby. Pastoral care can be instrumental in offering the family a memorial service or blessing (with or without the baby present). Once L.M. knows the sex of her baby, she may want to name him or her. A naming ceremony also could be performed by pastoral care.

Burial

Once L.M. and her husband have seen, held, and had special time with their baby, the grief counselor should offer the option of the family making final arrangements for their baby. Of course, the option of the hospital making the final disposition of the baby always is available when the baby dies at 16 weeks gestation. It may help with L.M.'s healing, however, to make sure that she knows the final resting place of her baby and that she knows how her baby was prepared for burial.

Periodically through the year, some hospitals will bury or cremate all the tissue pathology as well as the fetuses which were obtained after pregnancy losses which occurred at the institution. The collected remains are placed in a common grave in a special place at a nearby cemetery. The grief counselor should be aware of hospital laboratory procedure in making the final disposition of tissue pathology which was obtained from a pregnancy or for an identified fetus. Should the current policy not be respectful of the baby's or family's needs, the counselor could work with the laboratory, a local funeral home or crematorium, cemetery, and monument company to make the necessary changes.

Finally, many times, an acutely grieving family in denial might discard mementos from the baby if they feel that their having them will cause them more pain, should they find them at a later date. The grief counseling service would be well-advised to hold all of those mementos at the hospital, in the event that the family does change their minds and want memories of their child. This way, the grief counselor can assist the family in making memories.

— *Sara Rich Wheeler, MSN, RN, CCE*

References

American Academy of Pediatrics & American College of Obstetricians and Gynecologists. (1992). *Guidelines for perinatal care* (3rd ed.) Elk Grove Village, IL: American Academy of Pediatrics.

Association of Women's Health, Obstetric, and Neonatal Nurses (formerly NAACOG). (June, 1985). Nursing practice resource. *Grief related to perinatal death, No. 13.* Washington, DC: AWHONN.

Brost, L., & Kenney, J.W. (1992). Pregnancy after perinatal loss: Parental reactions and nursing interventions. *Journal of Obstetric, Gynecologic, and Neonatal Nursing, 21*(6), 457-463.

Calhoun, L.K. (1994). Parents' perceptions of nursing support following neonatal loss. *Journal of Perinatal & Neonatal Nursing, 8*(2), 57-66.

Davis, D.L., Stewart, M., & Harmon, R.J. (1988). Perinatal loss: Providing emotional support for bereaved parents. *Birth, 15*(4), 242-246.

Galinsky, E. (1987). *Between generations: The six stages of parenthood.* New York: Addison-Wesley.

Hutti, M.H. (1988). Perinatal loss: Assisting parents to cope. *Journal of Emergency Nursing, 14*(6), 338-341.

Ilse, S., & Furrh, C.B. (1988). Development of a comprehensive follow-up care plan after perinatal and neonatal loss. *Journal of Perinatal & Neonatal Nursing, 2*(2), 23-33.

Jordan, P. (1990). Laboring for relevance: Expectant and new fatherhood. *Nursing Research, 39*(1), 11.

Kimble, D. (1991). Neonatal death: A descriptive study of father's experiences. *Neonatal Network, 9*(8), 45-50.

Kirkley-Best, E., & Kellner, K.R. (1982). The forgotten grief: A review of the psychology of stillbirth. *American Journal of Orthopsychiatry, 52*(3), 420-429.

Klaus, M.H., & Kennell, J.H. (1982). *Parent-infant bonding.* St. Louis: C.V. Mosby.

Kowalski, K. (1987). Perinatal loss and bereavement. In L. Sonstegard, K. Kowalski, & B. Jennings (Eds.), *Women's health, Vol 3: Crisis and illness in childbearing.* New York: Grune and Stratton.

Lawson, L.V. (1990). Culturally sensitive support for grieving parents. *Maternal-Child Nursing, 15,* 76-79.

Layne, L.L. (1990). Motherhood lost: Cultural dimensions of miscarriage and stillbirth in America. *Women and Health, 16*(3/4), 69-98.

Lederman, R. (1984). *Psychosocial adaptation in pregnancy.* Englewood Cliffs, NJ: Prentice Hall, Inc.

Lenninger, M.M. (1981). The phenomenon of caring: Importance, research questions, and theoritical considerations. In M.M. Lenninger (Ed.), *Caring: An essential human need* (pp. 3-15). Thorofare, NJ: Charles B. Slack.

Leon, I.G. (1992). Perinatal loss: Choreographing grief on the obstetric unit. *American Journal of Orthopsychiatry, 62*(1), 7-8.

Maguire, D.P., & Skoolicas, S.J. (1988). Developing a bereavement follow-up program. *Journal of Perinatal & Neonatal Nursing, 2*(2), 67-77.

Mueller, L. (1991). Second-trimester termination of pregnancy: Nursing care. *Journal of Obstetric, Gynecologic, and Neonatal Nursing, 20*(4), 284-289.

Null, S. (1989, March/April). Nursing care to ease parents' grief. *Maternal-Child Nursing, 14,* 84-92.

Rosas, S., & Rosas, M. (1987). Neonatal loss: What can be done to ease parents' grief. *Post Graduate Medicine, 82*(5), 135-142.

Rubin, R. (1967). Attainment of the maternal role. *Nursing Research, 16*(3), 237-245.

Ryan, P.F., Cote-Arsenault, D., & Sugarman, L.L. (1991). Facilitating care after perinatal loss. *Journal of Obstetric, Gynecologic, and Neonatal Nursing, 20*(5), 385-389.

Rybarik, F. (Ed.). (1994). *RTS Bereavement services coordinator training manual, 2.* LaCrosse, WI: RTS Bereavement Services.

Swanson-Kaufman, K. (1986). Caring in the instance of unexpected early pregnancy loss. *Topics in Clinical Nursing, 8*(2), 37-46.

Swanson, K.M. (1991). Empirical development of a middle range theory of caring. *Nursing Research, 40*(3), 161-166.

Watson, J. (1985). *Nursing: Human science and human care.* Norwalk, CT: Appleton-Century-Crofts.

Weinfeld, I.J. (1990). An expanded perinatal bereavement support committee: A community-wide resource. *Death Studies, 14,* 241-252.

Welch, D. (1991). Miscarriage, stillbirth, or newborn death: Starting a healthy grieving process. *Neonatal Network, 9*(8), 53-57.

Wheeler, S.R. (1992). Letter. *Journal of Obstetric, Gynecologic, and Neonatal Nursing, 21*(2), 140.

Wheeler, S.R., & Limbo, R.K. (1990). Blueprint for a perinatal bereavement support group. *Pediatric Nursing, 16*(4) 341-344.

Woods, J.R., & Esposito, J.L. (Eds.). (1987). *Pregnancy loss: Medical therapeutics and practical considerations.* Baltimore: Williams and Wilkins.

Chapter 13

Adolescent Pregnancy Loss

Sara Rich Wheeler

Each year, one million teenagers in America become pregnant (Davis, 1989). Over half of these young women will experience a pregnancy loss due to elective abortion, miscarriage or ectopic pregnancy, stillbirth, newborn death, or relinquishment of the baby for adoption (American College of Obstetrics and Gynecology, 1994). Little is known about young women's responses to pregnancy loss, such as, for example, perception of their loss, grief responses, coping behaviors, and both short- and long-term psycho-emotional outcomes, which these young women may have after pregnancy loss. Knowledge about these responses is important, partly because the repeat pregnancy rate for young women can be as high as 54% (Smith, Weinman, & Malinak, 1984). Understanding young women's responses to pregnancy loss is critical in designing programs to help them to adapt successfully to the loss, in supporting them during a subsequent pregnancy, and/or in helping them to make conscious life choices regarding childbearing during adolescence.

Purpose

The purpose of this chapter is to provide a theoretical framework of the mourning process and a review of literature on adolescent grief responses and loss. It also reports a pilot study which was designed to (a) describe adolescents' perceptions of what pregnancy loss means to them, (b) determine if grief responses vary as a function of demographic or pregnancy factors, and (c) determine if there are differences in adolescents' physical, emotional, social, and cognitive responses based on perception of loss.

Theoretical Framework

Source theories for understanding an adolescent's responses, coping, and adaptation to death are McCubbin and Patterson's (1983) Double ABCX Model of adjustment and adaptation to crisis, Davidson's (1979, 1984) model for understanding mourning, and Sanders's (1989) integrated bereavement theory. When these theoretical perspectives are integrated, they form the basis for understanding the antecedents, processes, and outcomes of the mourning experience.

McCubbin and Patterson developed the Double ABCX model from their study of 216 families in crisis, to determine how families manage crisis in their lives. They expanded upon Hill's original ABCX model by adding four additional components: (a) pile-up of additional stressors and strains; (b) family efforts to activate, acquire, and use new resources from within the family and community; (c) modifications in the family's definition of the event; and (d) coping strategies employed by the family to bring about change and adaptation.

Davidson (1979) studied 1,200 mourners, 30 of whom were women who had experienced pregnancy loss, over a 10-year period. When the women who had experienced a loss were compared with other adult mourners, their grief responses and mourning processes were similar to the responses of other mourners.

Sanders's (1989) integrated bereavement theory uses prior theory development and research in bereavement to develop a model for determining outcomes of the bereavement experience. The interaction of internal and external mediators, impact of death, phases of bereavement, and possible outcomes are identified. The integrative bereavement theory is different from preceding theories, in that it attempts to address what motivates an individual to work through the phases of bereavement. Emotional, biological, and social components of functioning also are addressed.

Derived from these theoretical perspectives and informed by a synthesis of the research and classical literature on psychosocial adaptation to pregnancy, bereavement, perinatal bereavement, adolescent bereavement, and crisis intervention, an integrated model of grief and mourning responses is proposed (see Figure 1-13). The model takes into account variables that can influence the process of mourning and eventual adaptation, such as type of death, grief responses, external resources, and perception and meaning attributed to the death. This model is comprehensive; it enables care providers to make appropriate assessments and interventions to provide individuals with infor-

Figure 1-13.
Model of Mourning Process

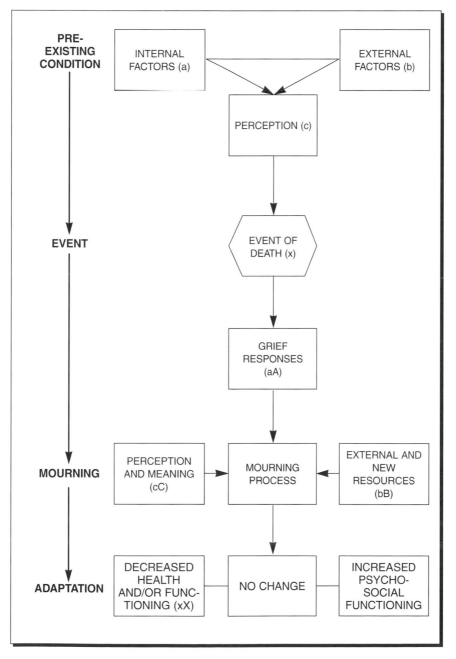

mation, anticipatory guidance, and support (Austin, 1990). For the purpose of this discussion, the individual is an adolescent (a, b, and c Factors), and the death (x) is represented in the loss of a pregnancy or baby through elective abortion, miscarriage, ectopic pregnancy, stillbirth, or neonatal death.

Key Concepts:
Internal Factors [(a) Factor]
Individual traits interact to make each person unique. Viewed either as capabilities or as disabilities, these internal factors represent the individual's internal abilities to adapt, react, or interpret information, life experiences, or significant life events. Examples of internal abilities include physical and emotional health, personality, age, gender, cognitive development, maturational development, coping skills, dependency behaviors, and the ability to establish and maintain relationships.

External Factors [(b) Factor]
External factors occur in the environment in which individuals live and function. These factors include family, friends, culture, school, work, and, for many, religion. External factors have the potential to become either stressors or resources to the individual. Stressors or resources can influence or produce change or stabilization in an individual's roles, responsibilities, functioning, and/or perceptions. They have the potential to affect the individual in a positive or a negative manner. A stressor or resource can be a situational event(s), a life transition, a support system, or the environment in which the person lives. Examples of stressors or resources which may have an impact upon the individual include giving birth, losing one's job, getting a promotion, having a home, being homeless, attending church, dropping out of school, and being engaged in good friendships.

Perception and Interpretation [(c) Factor]
The interaction of internal and external factors affects the individual's interpretation of life experiences and significant event(s), specifically the individual's subjective interpretation of "self" and the world. For example, the individual's perception and interpretation of events are influenced by his or her self-esteem, self-image, prior knowledge, previous life experiences, and support systems.

Event of Loss/Death [(x) Factor]

Loss of a pregnancy or baby through elective abortion, miscarriage, ectopic pregnancy, stillbirth, or neonatal death up to 30 days after birth is the focus here. When a loss or death occurs, the (a) internal, (b) external, and (c) perception and interpretation factors interact, resulting in the individual's perceptions, derived meanings, and responses to the event. The type of death or loss can influence the perception and interpretation by the individual and his or her support system. Some pregnancy losses can be anticipated (either because the loss is expected to occur, or because the woman has decided to terminate the pregnancy electively). Other losses are sudden and unexpected, or they occur during a high-risk pregnancy. Some deaths or losses have stigmas attached to them, either by the individual or by society. These deaths can be viewed as preventable or uncontrollable, such as deaths caused by abortion, stillbirth, AIDS, substance abuse, accidents, genetic disorders, or chronic or terminal illness of the mother.

Individual Grief Responses [(aA) Factor]

When a death occurs, there are physical, emotional, social, and cognitive responses to the loss which are called grief responses. Grief responses are the (A) Factor. Pre-existing (a) internal factors will influence intensity, expression, and behavioral responses to the loss/death.

External and New Resources [(bB) Factor]

External resources can influence directly the individual's ability to cope with the death of a loved one. Pre-existing external resources [(b) Factor] of religious beliefs, understanding and supportive family and friends, and cultural rituals for mourning can help the individual to feel supported, and not to feel alone or isolated. At times of loss, the (B) Factor that includes the individual's resources for social support may be expanded. In the instance of pregnancy loss, nurses, other health care professionals, and mutual self help bereavement support groups can provide help in an individual's and family's coping (Swanson-Kauffman, 1986, 1991).

Perception and Meaning [(cC) Factor]

The interpretation and meaning which the individual derives from the death of a loved one affect the mourning process. Over time, as part of mourning, the bereaved develops a perception about and derives meaning from the experience of death. Perception and meaning [the (c) Factor] represent the pre-existing perceptions and meanings that the individual had of his or her "self" and the relationship with the loved one prior to the death. Limbo and Wheeler (1986) identified three perceptions of pregnancy loss through miscarriage and ectopic pregnancy: "no loss," "loss of a pregnancy," and "loss of a baby." The perception of loss of a baby was not determined by gestational age, or whether or not this was a planned or wanted pregnancy. The (c) also represents the influence of further information about the death itself, education about grief responses and the mourning process, the individual's ability to reframe the event of death, and the effect of the death on the individual's self-esteem. This is a process of integrating the event of death into one of life's experiences. This process directly influences coping abilities because the perception of the death as being preventable may fuel grief responses of anger, guilt, blame, and sadness. These are potent emotions that can inhibit the individual's ability to process her loss and derive meaning from the experience (Worder, 1991).

Mourning as Coping

Mourning is a cognitive and behavioral process whereby the individual learns how to cope with grief responses and life experiences after a loss. Mourning is a bridging concept where the grief responses (A) are mediated by internal factors (a), external factors (bB), and perception and meaning (cC). Coping behaviors which the individual uses in an attempt to gain control over his or her grief responses can evolve into patterns of adaptation. The outcome of mourning is the integration of the death into the individual's life experiences and adaptation. Dimensions of mourning are identified (Davidson, 1979, 1984; Sanders, 1989). Dimensions are represented by feelings, emotions, and behavioral responses that the bereaved may experience. They are conceptualized to help identify process and movement as the bereaved copes with and adapts to life without his or her loved one.

Outcomes of Adaptation After Loss [(xX) Factor]

The interactions of the double (aA), (bB), and (cC) Factors on mourning over time produce an expected pattern of adaptation or outcome of the mourning process. The individual integrates the event of death into a continuum of life experiences, and determines a personal perception and meaning of the event, with help and support from others; and patterns of coping with the experience of loss begin to emerge. In this model, these patterns are the (xX) Factor, the outcomes from the experience of death. Outcomes can range from increased psychosocial growth, to no change, to adverse change in health or functioning. Positive outcomes identified for adolescents include new understanding for the meaning of life; an increased sense of strength, self-reliance, and independence; acceptance of death as part of the reality of life; enhanced spirituality; and a sense that they have become more mature than their peers, a strengthening of emotional bonds with others, increased empathy for others, and better communication skills (Balk, 1983, 1990; Davies, 1991; Martinson & Campos, 1991; McNeil, Stilliman, & Swilhart, 1991; Oltjenbruns, 1991). Negative outcomes are shifts in self concept and self-esteem, survivor guilt, excessive concerns for others, fears of intimacy, emotional/behavioral difficulties, and lingering symptomatology of grief responses (for example, enduring sense of sadness, depression, guilt and self-blame, and inability to discuss experiences about death and dying) (Hogan & Greenfield, 1991; Martinson, Davies, & McGlowery, 1987; Michael & Lansdown, 1986).

General Framework

The perception and meaning attributed to the loss, external resources, and grief responses interact to influence the mourning process. Mourning as coping with life changes leads to adaptation (see Figure 1-13).

Review of Literature:
Adolescent Grief Responses

Although adolescents have been included in samples where responses to pregnancy have been studied, no specific research has focused on those who suffer pregnancy loss. Adolescent grief responses have been studied in response to death of a sibling, parent, or peer. Most of these studies focused on a death which occurs after long-term chronic illness in a parent or sibling. Fewer studies were carried out on adolescent responses to suicide. For the purposes of this literature review, adolescent grief responses are grouped into four areas: physical, emotional, cognitive, and social. A brief description of the literature in each area follows.

Physiologic Responses to Loss

Adolescents who experienced the death of a sibling reported trouble eating (for example, loss of appetite, stomach pains), sleep disturbances, and being sick more often (Balk, 1981, 1983, 1991; Fanos & Nickerson, 1991; Hogan, 1988; Hogan & DeSantis, 1992). Sleeping problems were the result of dreams that were reported as nightmarish in quality. The dreams were very frightening and repetitive. Somatic expressions in the study by Fanos and Nickerson (1991) included severe headaches, ulcers, and chronically tense, painful muscles and joints. Opie et al. (1992) found that adolescents missed school because they did not feel good and they had general somatic complaints and affective distress.

Emotional Responses

Emotional responses appear to be intense at the time of the death and then diminish over time. Initially after the death of a sibling, adolescents overall reported feeling dazed, shocked, confused, numb, lonely, afraid, frustrated, depressed, and relief. They experienced increased fearfulness, phobias (fear of dying), and sadness. They reported feeling uncomfortable when happy, feeling responsible for the death, feeling over-protected by parents. Moreover, they described anger at God, a profound sense of vulnerability and mortality, guilt, anxiety, feelings of powerlessness and helplessness, and anger and irritability (Balk, 1981, 1983, 1991; Davies, 1991; Fanos & Nickerson, 1991; Hogan & Greenfield, 1991; Martinson et al., 1987; Mauk & Weber, 1991; McNeil et al., 1991; Valente, Saunders, & Street, 1988). Some adolescents reported having suicidal thoughts, decreased feelings of self-worth, and fears of not being liked by peers. Fanos and Nickerson's (1991) study of 25 adolescents whose siblings had died was divided into early-, middle-, and late-adolescent groups for comparisons. All of the adolescents expressed a strong sense of guilt over their relationship with the sibling who had died and over how they had handled themselves during the illness and the death of the sibling. They demonstrated readiness to blame themselves for anything that might go wrong. There appeared to be a complex relationship between guilt and anxiety. Five of the eight adolescents aged 13 to 17 expressed hypochondriacal concerns related to their bodies or fears about the possibility of getting sick or dying at an early age. Survivor guilt, excessive concerns for others, and fears of intimacy were consistent themes among this adolescent group.

Over time, adolescents reported feeling an enduring sense of depression and sadness (Balk, 1983). Hogan (1988) determined that teens were less likely to express guilt and self-blame beyond the first 18 to 36 months after the loss, but still reported some degree of grief-response symptomatology up to 84 months after the loss. Opie et al.'s (1992) study of adolescents who attended a bereavement support group within 2 years after the death of someone who was important in their lives found that adolescents appeared sad and depressed, and they were irritable and angry, with feelings of a sense of worthlessness.

Cognitive Responses to Loss

Minimal research has been done to describe cognitive responses of adolescents to death of a loved one. Research that has been conducted demonstrates a decline in school performance. Gray (1987) identified a significant relationship between the age of bereaved adolescents who had lost a parent and school performance. Average grades dropped in adolescents who were 15 years old or younger. Other adolescents reported difficulty in concentration, preoccupation in thinking, feeling distracted, and missing school, all of which also may have contributed to poor school performance (Balk, 1983; Gray, 1987; Hogan, 1988; McNeil et al., 1991; O'Brien, Goodenow, & Espin, 1991).

There also is some concern that adolescents lack the cognitive ability to comprehend the full impact of death. For example, Piaget believed that the stage of formal operations, the ability to think abstractly, does not emerge until some time during adolescence. Adolescents in Fanos and Nickerson's study (1991), however, reported that they did not have difficulty in understanding the full impact of the death of their sibling. These researchers found that adolescents struggled with why the death occurred, their anger at its occurrence, wondering why the death had happened to their sibling, and questioning why God let it happen.

Social Responses to Loss

Some adolescents report feeling different from their peers after the death of a loved one. The adolescents perceive their peers to be intolerant of their grief. The response to this intolerance by the adolescent is to withdraw from involvement with peers (Davies, 1991; Martinson & Campos, 1991). Therefore, less time is spent with friends and more time is spent alone. Some adolescents engage in greater risk-taking in a search for activities to occupy time. Still others establish deep, serious relationships early. Several adolescents reported an inability to discuss their experiences during the death and dying of their sibling until years later. It was only then, when they had a deep, trusting relationship, that they expressed the feelings that they were unable to share with their friends at the time of the death. When a peer dies, adolescents expect their parents and other friends to recognize their feelings and to offer support (McNeil et al., 1991; O'Brien et al., 1991).

Perceptions of Pregnancy Loss

No research has been done specifically on adolescent perceptions of pregnancy loss. Past research carried out on samples of women which included some adolescents suggest that perceptions of pregnancy loss can be categorized as either "no loss," "loss of pregnancy," or "loss of a baby." For example, Swanson-Kauffman's (1986) study of 20 women who recently had miscarried categorized women who mourned the loss of a baby (75%). One of the limitations of the categorizations is that "loss of pregnancy" and "no loss" were not considered as categories of perceptions. Limbo and Wheeler's (1986) longitudinal study of 87 women who had experienced miscarriage or ectopic pregnancy determined that women categorized their early pregnancy loss into two groups: "loss of a baby" or "no loss." Most of the women were between 8 and 12 weeks gestation at the time of the loss. Perception of the pregnancy loss varied among the women. Slightly more than half of the women viewed their miscarriage or ectopic pregnancy as the loss of a baby. These women had purchased items for the baby, had used the word "baby" in conversation about the pregnancy, and had identified grief responses to their pregnancy loss. Approximately 25% of the women also identified grief responses; their responses, however, were related to the loss of the pregnancy. The remaining 25% of the women did not perceive that they had experienced a loss, but rather they viewed it as a life experience. Follow-up at 6 weeks and at 6 months further demonstrated that this group of women did not change their perceptions of the experience. They were classified as having perceptions that there was no loss. Because Limbo and Wheeler (1986) found differences in responses among the three different categories, perception of pregnancy loss will be categorized as "no loss," "loss of pregnancy," and "loss of a baby."

Relationship Between Perception and Responses

There is indirect support in the literature which suggests that perception of loss might influence grief responses. For example, Limbo and Wheeler's (1986) study on early pregnancy loss identified women who perceived the loss of a pregnancy or baby, and they experienced grief responses at the time of the loss, 6 weeks, and 6 months later. Women who did not perceive a loss did not experience grief responses. Sanders (1989) alludes to a relationship between perception of the relationship with the deceased and the effect on grief responses during the bereavement process in her study of 116 families over a 5-year period. It is important to determine the relationship between perception of pregnancy loss and the subsequent effect on the intensity of grief responses. Knowledge of this relationship can help care providers to make better assessments of the responses of adolescent females who experience pregnancy loss, as well as to offer more appropriate interventions for care and support.

Direct support in the literature suggests that, when women experience a pregnancy loss, regardless of the number of weeks gestation, they have specific needs which must be met in order for them to have positive feelings and experiences. Many times, those positive feelings and experiences are the direct result of nursing intervention which has recognized and acknowledged needs for information, emotional support, and special remembrances.

Descriptive Study of Adolescent Pregnancy Loss

Guided by the proposed model of mourning, a cross-sectional descriptive study of adolescents who had experienced pregnancy loss was completed. The study examined adolescents' perceptions of what pregnancy loss meant to them, the impact of demographic and pregnancy factors on grief responses, and the relationship between perception of loss and grief responses.

Method:
Sample

Over a 10-week period, 34 adolescents who had experienced a pregnancy loss in the previous 2 years and who attended inner-city adolescent prenatal, parenting, or health clinics (which are sponsored by a large, metropolitan medical center in the Midwest) were enrolled in this study. Adolescents were invited to participate if they were between 10 and 21 years of age and could read, understand, and speak English. The mean age of the sample was 17 years, with a range from 13 to 20. Sixty-two percent were of non-white races. The mean duration of pregnancy was 13.5 weeks. Elective abortion accounted for 53% of the losses, miscarriages 38%, newborn deaths 2%, and sudden infant death (SIDS) 5%. Thus, 91% of the adolescents had pregnancy losses which occurred before 20 weeks gestation. The average time since loss was 15 months. Fifty-nine percent of the participants were pregnant again at the time of the study.

Procedure

Adolescents who met the inclusion criteria were asked to participate either by nurses working in the clinic or by the nurse researcher. Once the

Figure 2-13.
Adolescent Women's Statements Regarding Perceptions of Pregnancy Loss

"...I was pregnant, but I found myself thinking about things...what it was going to be like — something little; a little baby. The noise killed me. I could hear it coming out. The nurse who took my blood pressure was pregnant. It made me feel awful. How could this happen? I'm here to have an abortion, and she's pregnant. She shouldn't be in this environment."
— *Adolescent, aged 17, who chose to have an abortion.*

"I lost a friend, someone who was close to me. I lost a part of me."
— *Adolescent, aged 18, who suffered a miscarriage.*

"It meant nothing. It meant I was going to have a baby if I didn't do something about it."
— *Adolescent, aged 15, who chose to have an abortion.*

adolescent had expressed interest in the study, she received an explanation of the study and was asked to sign an informed consent document. Interviews were completed, and participants were offered the opportunity to discuss with the researcher their feelings and experiences in participating in the study.

Measures

Data were gathered relating to demographics, pregnancy, and perception of loss. The Grief Experience Inventory (GEI) (Sanders, Mauger, & Strong, 1985) was used to determine grief responses and to develop specific grief-response subscales. This inventory required respondents to answer either "yes" or "no" to questions regarding a grief experience. The GEI questionnaire has established reliability and validity based on a sample of bereaved families who have experienced the death of a loved one. The GEI was reworded to reflect the particular type of loss (for example, abortion, miscarriage, stillbirth, or neonatal death), and the reworded version, specific to type of loss, was administered. Chronbach alpha reliability for the reworded GEI subscales for this sample were: physical = .78, emotional = .90, cognitive = .70, and social = .78.

Figure 3-13.
Making Preparations for the Pregnancy and/or for the Baby Make the Experience of Loss More Real

"I was so happy about it. He had bought clothes, a baby bed, and clothing. I cried. I kept asking why. Was it a punishment, something I did? I really wonder if I'll ever have children. I just love children."
— *Adolescent, aged 17, who suffered a miscarriage.*

"I told everybody I knew. I had everything — swing, walker, clothes, baby bed."
— *Adolescent, aged 18, who suffered a miscarriage.*

Results:

Description of Adolescents' Perception of Loss

When adolescent respondents were asked to rate their perception of loss as "no loss," "loss of a pregnancy," or "loss of a baby," 85% reported a perception of loss. During the demographic data interview, the adolescents offered more in-depth explanations of the particular perceptions of loss, which also included "loss of pregnancy," "loss of baby," and "loss of a part of self." Figure 2-13 provides examples of adolescent women's perceptions of their loss.

Effects of Demographic Variables on Adolescent Grief Responses

The grief responses were identified in the categories of physical, emotional, cognitive, and social responses. T-test scores revealed no statistically significant differences in grief responses in respondents grouped variously by race, religion, or being pregnant at the time of the study. Those adolescents who had made some preparations for this pregnancy or baby had higher grief scores than did those who had not made preparations; the following areas demonstrated higher grief scores: physical ($p = .002$), emotional ($p = .016$), and social ($p = .003$). Statements which are quoted in Figure 3-13 indicate how an adolescent's having made preparations for her pregnancy and/or for the anticipated baby made the experience of loss more real.

Using Pearson correlation, younger adolescents had more physical ($r = -.30, p = .05$) and emotional ($r = -.36, p = .03$) responses to pregnancy loss than did those who were 16 years of age or older. Age was correlated most strongly with the following physical responses: sleep disturbance ($r = -.34, p = .03$) and appetite ($r = -.\_\_, p = .09$). Age also was correlated with the following

Figure 4-13.
**Frequency of Grief Responses of Adolescent Women Experiencing
Pregnancy Loss**

GRIEF RESPONSES	% Who Responded "Yes"
Physical responses	
Exhausted after the loss	76
Restless	68
Aches and pains	64
Tense neck and shoulders	38
Sleeping problems	35
Waking during the night	64
Exhausted, but cannot sleep	70
Used sleeping medication	31
Unhealthy appetite	68
Lost weight	35
Dry mouth and throat	62
Lump in throat	26
Emotional responses	
"Bitchy"	59
Did not cry at time of loss	82
Guilt	82
Cry easily	79
Dream about being pregnant	18
Often "touchy"	74
Anger towards God	09
Strong desire to scream	59
Curl in a ball when I cry	59
Difficult to see pregnant women	35
Life has no meaning for me	21
Angry episodes because of pregnancy loss	53
Feelings of emptiness	47
Depression	44
Watching self "go through the motions"	53
Life seems empty and barren	62
Frequent mood changes	82
"I could have done more to prevent the loss"	59
Believes she is a realistic person	65
Has lost self-confidence	29
Frequent nightmares	26
Fear of failure	65
"I usually am not happy"	35

Figure 4-13. *continued*

GRIEF RESPONSES	% Who Responded "Yes"
Cognitive responses	
Unusually aware of grief and loss issues	68
"More could have been done at the time"	44
"I often experience confusion"	62
Difficulty in concentration	44
"I wish I could die"	24
"I wish I were dead"	32
"I wonder what my life would have been like"	82
"This could not have happened to me"	65
"I often think about how short life is"	71
"I believe that my loss was for the best"	38
Social responses	
Felt different and alone	76
Felt a strong need to act like nothing happened	35
Needed to be alone	65
Took long walks by myself	59
Don't want to be with my friends	29
Family seems closer	65

emotional responses: emotional control ($r = -.25$, $p = .08$), unreality to experience ($r = -.30$, $p = .05$), and hostility ($r = -.25$, $p = .09$). There was a positive relationship between length of gestation at time of loss with social responses ($r = .28$, $p = .06$). The longer that the adolescent was pregnant, the more likely she was to feel different, alone, and isolated after her pregnancy loss. Time since loss was correlated with lower self-esteem ($r = -.34$, $p = .02$); those with longer time elapsed since loss had higher self-esteem scores. Gestational age at time of loss also was positively correlated with the perceived relationship with the baby ($r = .33$; $p = .038$). The subscales of sleep disturbances ($r = .33$; $p = .032$) and denial ($r = .41$; $p = .013$) also were related positively to gestational age at time of loss. Figure 4-13 is a compilation of the frequency of physical, emotional, cognitive, and social grief responses to loss.

Relationship Between Perception of Loss and Grief Responses

Emotional and cognitive grief response scores did not differ by wanting a child, meaning of the pregnancy, type of loss, or perception of loss (see

Figure 5-13.
Effect of Pregnancy Loss Based on the Meaning Attributed
by Adolescents to Pregnancy

"I was happy to know something was living in me. I cried — Oh, how I cried. I was mad. I wanted both of those babies."
— *Adolescent, aged 17, after suffering two miscarriages.*

"I felt I had killed my child. I felt I was peer-pressured into doing it. An abortion is actually murder."
— *Adolescent, aged 18, who chose to abort her pregnancy.*

"It meant something to me, made me happy inside. I lost a part of me."
— *Adolescent, aged 15, who chose to abort her pregnancy.*

Figure 6-13.
Indications of Complicated Bereavement Following Pregnancy Loss

---

"I punished somebody else for myself. Years from now, I'll wonder if it was a boy or a girl."
— *Adolescent, aged 19, who chose to have an abortion.*

"Sometimes, I feel like I played favorites, like I loved these two more than the other one."
— *Adolescent, aged 17, who chose to have an abortion.*

Figure 5-13). Results of analysis of variance (ANOVA) indicated that those who wanted the baby had higher physical response scores ($F = 3.68$, $p = <.05$) and social response scores ($F = 5.1$, $p = <.01$). Social responses to loss were influenced by type of loss ($F = 2.20$, $p = <.05$). Neither perception of pregnancy loss nor meaning of pregnancy was a statistically significant predictor of grief responses.

Figure 6-13 contains sample statements from the qualitative data, with regard to the effect of loss based on the meaning which this group attributed to the pregnancy.

Discussion

The purpose of this study was to describe adolescents' perceptions of pregnancy loss, to identify their grief responses, and to determine the relationships between perception of loss and grief responses. Inner-city adolescents who had experienced a pregnancy loss were given a revised form of the GEI, a comprehensive inventory on grief responses after a loss of a loved one. The major findings of this study were that most adolescents (70%) either did not want to be pregnant or had mixed feelings about being pregnant. Once pregnant, however, this group did begin to attribute some meaning to their pregnancy as either being pregnant (53%) or being pregnant with a baby (41%). When they experienced pregnancy loss, 85% felt that they had lost their pregnancy, a part of themselves, or a baby. The perceived loss of a baby was felt by 74% of adolescents in the study.

Grief responses of adolescents were affected by the length of time since the loss, the age of the adolescent, and the number of weeks of gestation at the time of the loss. As expected, those adolescents whose loss was more recent or had occurred within the past year reported more physical, emotional, and social responses to their loss. Adolescents who were 16 years old or younger reported more physical and emotional responses to their loss than did older adolescents. Younger adolescents had more sleep disturbances, and they felt an unreality about the experience; they also were more hostile than were older adolescents. The number of weeks of gestation at the time of the loss affected adolescents' physical and social grief responses. Adolescents whose pregnancy loss occurred after 14 weeks gestation had more sleep disturbances and were more sensitive to lack of social support than did those whose loss occurred earlier. Type of pregnancy loss affected physical and social grief responses of adolescents at significant levels. No conclusions can be drawn from the three adolescents who experienced a pregnancy loss after 20 weeks gestation. It is clear, however, that adolescents experiencing early pregnancy loss, either by abortion or miscarriage, are affected by the loss and have grief responses. Importantly, there did not appear to be a difference in grief responses between adolescents who elected to have abortions and those who experienced a miscarriage.

Of note was the number of adolescents who were pregnant at the time of the study (59%). This number does not account for adolescents who became pregnant after their loss and who already had delivered the subsequent baby. The perinatal bereavement literature indicates that a rapid repeat pregnancy after a loss may indicate complicated bereavement. Because of the scope of the study reported here, this hypothesis could not be examined.

There were two major limitations in this pilot study. Not only was the sample size small, but also the adolescents were recruited from a group of urban adolescents using health care services. Generalizability to the overall adolescent population who experience pregnancy loss is limited. Adolescents who have experienced a loss but who have not sought health care may have had very different experiences than did those who did seek health services and thereby were recruited for this study. This sample represented inner-city adolescent women. Their feelings, experiences, and lifestyle, as well as other types of loss which occurred previously, also may have been reflected in their completion of the questionnaire, and so responses may not clearly reflect the grief experiences of pregnancy loss specifically.

The second limitation relates to the adequacy of the instrument which was used. The grief experience questionnaire used was developed from a sample of families who had experienced the death of a close loved one, typically a spouse or child. The initial reliability and validity of these questions, even though they were reworded to reflect a pregnancy loss, may not have represented the experiences of adolescents experiencing pregnancy loss. Mean time since the loss was over 15 months, which for many adolescents might seem like a long time. The accuracy of responses made by participants at this time may have been lessened due to the amount of time elapsed since the loss. Also, the inability to recall their feelings at the time of the loss, based on how they were feeling at the time of the study, might have been difficult for the adolescent to fill out accurately, since the questionnaire did not scale responses. Regardless of the difficulties in filling out the questionnaire and the time since loss, the adolescents did identify grief responses in relationship to the pregnancy loss. Many of the adolescents did want to speak with the researcher after they had completed the questionnaire.

Findings from the qualitative component of the pilot study indicate that adolescents who had experienced a miscarriage wanted to talk about their miscarriage, the pain, the blood, and their loss. The few who had experienced a later loss talked more about their baby, their lost hope and dreams, and memories of the experience and of their child. They wanted to share their photographs and some of their memories of the baby. Adolescent women who had experienced an abortion wanted to talk about the decision, how it was made, who made the decision, how they felt, and their inability or reluctance to talk with family or friends about the experience.

Figure 7-13.
Nursing Intervention Contributes to Adolescents' Positive Feelings about
Themselves and the Experience of Pregnancy Loss

"I was frightened and bleeding. I lay on the couch, bleeding. I didn't see the baby. I didn't look in. I wished I had. I would have liked to have a funeral or something."
— *Adolescent, aged 18, after suffering a miscarriage.*

"I thought they were going to take everything out of me. The nurses were help-ful. They talked with me, told me what they were doing, how I might feel. She made things easier for me — held my hand, and told me if I had pain I was to squeeze her hand."
— *Adolescent, aged 18, who chose to have an abortion.*

Implications for Further Study

Data from this pilot study indicate a need for further investigation in the areas of grief responses of adolescents experiencing a pregnancy loss due to miscarriage or abortion, the relationship between meaning attributed to the pregnancy and grief responses, and subsequent pregnancy after a loss. The instrument used for measuring adolescent grief responses originally was developed from a sample of bereaved families, and it asks for dichotomous responses ("yes" or "no") to questions. An instrument must be developed that identifies varying intensities of grief responses, as well as higher internal consistency reliability than the GEI can provide. Refinement of such a tool may be helpful in determining complicated and uncomplicated bereavement issues in adolescents who experience pregnancy loss. Examples from the qualitative data of quotations that might represent a sign of complicated bereavement are given in Figure 6-13.

While these feelings of guilt and avoidance may be normal expressions and experiences of grief, an adolescent who has no social support may inter-nalize these feelings over time, which may lead to depression, despair, and hopelessness. The relationship between perception of loss and meaning of the pregnancy to grief responses needs further study. Knowledge in this area can help to determine strategies for assessing, planning, and implementing nursing care for adolescents who experience pregnancy loss. The quotations in Figure 7-13 illustrate how nursing intervention is essential for adolescents to have positive feelings about themselves and the experience of pregnancy loss. Moreover, these comments indicate how the physical, emotional, social, and cognitive grief responses also may be influential in promoting a healthy attitude toward reproductive health after a pregnancy loss. The qualitative data revealed that, for some young women, the relationship between themselves and their mothers was influential in their own resolution of the pregnancy loss (n = 10). This, too, is another area for further study.

Summary and Conclusion

This work was a first step in describing the experience of pregnancy loss in a sample population of inner-city adolescent women. It is clear that many adolescents derive meaning in their being pregnant, regardless of whether they planned the pregnancy or they were ambivalent about pregnancy in the beginning. When they experienced the pregnancy loss, there was true grief. Nurses and other health care professionals need to make careful assessment of the meaning which adolescents attribute to pregnancy, plans for pregnancy, and perceptions of loss, to determine appropriate individualized care.❏

Case Study 1-13

Follow-Up Counseling After Pregnancy Loss

Latiesha was a 15-year-old freshman in high school who experienced an ectopic pregnancy at 12 weeks. She presented at the clinic 4 weeks later for her postpartum checkup. In discussing her ectopic pregnancy with her, you learn that she was at home when she experienced severe cramping and bleeding. An ambulance was called, and she was taken to the hospital that provides services for your clinic. Latiesha stated that she was scared and afraid that she was going to die. After removal of her fallopian tube and repair of her uterus, she was admitted to the inpatient OB/GYN floor for 2 days before she was discharged. While on the inpatient unit, she asked her nurse and her physician if her baby was all right. They told her she did not need to be concerned about that anymore, because she was not pregnant.

After her hospitalization, Latiesha began to have recurrent dreams about her experience. She dreamt about her baby and had awakened because she heard a baby cry. She said that she felt so empty and that her arms ached sometimes. She felt that she did not have anyone to talk with about her experiences, because no one in her family or among her friends seemed to be interested. Sometimes, she thought that if she were pregnant again she would feel better.

Asked what plans she had made during her pregnancy, Latiesha indicated that she and her boyfriend had talked about living together, and she had purchased a stuffed bear for the baby.

Your assessment was that Latiesha was grieving the loss of her baby. She needed information on grief responses, and perhaps an opportunity to say a more formal "good-bye" to her baby. Latiesha was in a hurry to leave the clinic after this appointment, so you offered her some reading material on miscarriage and an opportunity to come back and talk with you about her feelings. You also indicated to her that you have some ideas that might help her feel better. The next time that Latiesha visited the clinic, she had come for a pregnancy test (which was positive). She thanked you for the reading material.

Commentary

It is not surprising that Latiesha became part of the statistics of rapid repeat pregnancy following a pregnancy loss. One study found that the median time between loss and subsequent pregnancy for adolescents was 5 months. In addition, unmet psychosocial needs, all of which should have been met before Latiesha was discharged from the hospital, placed her at risk for rapid repeat pregnancy. Those needs included acknowledgment of her loss, affirmation of feelings, education about the grief process, the opportunity to have a memorial service, a simple explanation of test results and what happened, a discussion about future children and family planning, and referral to a grief support group or private counseling. Being isolated without any emotional support resulted in Latiesha's resolution of her grief by becoming pregnant again. This, however, seems to be more adaptive than would be resorting to substance abuse or acting out via promiscuity.

Latiesha's current pregnancy necessitates an immediate need for some kind of closure to her preceding pregnancy. All unmet needs from the previous pregnancy must be met before she can handle this pregnancy in a healthy way psychologically. Latiesha must be helped to establish separate identities for both of her children before the baby she now is expecting becomes a "replacement baby." Moreover, this rapid repeat pregnancy places Latiesha at risk for another poor pregnancy outcome. Instruction for optimal pregnancy outcome and dialogue concerning another possible loss *must* take place before Latiesha leaves the clinic today.

Further intervention should include referrals to a grief support group for teens and a comprehensive prenatal teen clinic that provides childbirth education classes. In this way, Latiesha will be less isolated in her grief and during her pregnancy. Preparing for a baby by purchasing a stuffed bear indicates a need for parenting classes. Staying in school will be of utmost importance for this young woman, and she should be directed to attend a high school that has established a teen parent program and offers parenting classes.

As usually is the case in teenage pregnancy, the father has been forgotten. A young male has even less opportunity to express feelings after a loss, and often he may pressure the teen mother to have another baby as soon as possible. Since Latiesha's boyfriend is the father of both of her babies, and apparently it is an ongoing relationship, efforts should be made to offer him grief counseling and to involve him in Latiesha's current pregnancy.

Inasmuch as Latiesha is considering moving in with her boyfriend, there should be great concern about her home and school environment and about her relationships with her parents and siblings. A detailed psychosocial history should be taken, to discover any possible abuse, neglect, major life-changing events, deaths of significant others, failure in school, or other stressors or losses. Teen pregnancy often is a symptom of an underlying problem. Until such a problem is dealt with, Latiesha will continue to be a statistic of repeat pregnancy and its adverse outcomes, which include fetal and infant loss.

— *Connie Nykiel, BSHA, RN*

References

American College of Obstetricians and Gynecologists. (1994). *Adolescent pregnancy fact sheet.* Washington, DC: ACOG.

Austin, J. (1990). Assessment of coping mechanisms used by parents and children with chronic illness. *American Journal of Maternal Child Nursing, 15*(2), 98-102.

Balk, D.E. (1981). *Sibling death during adolescence: Self-concept and bereavement reactions* (Unpublished doctoral dissertation). Champaign-Urbana, University of Illinois.

Balk, D.E. (1983). Adolescents' grief reactions and self-concept perceptions following sibling death: A case study of 33 teenagers. *Journal of Youth and Adolescence, 12,* 137-161.

Balk, D.E. (1990). The self-concepts of bereaved adolescents: Sibling death and its aftermath. *Journal of Adolescent Research, 5,* 112-132.

Balk, D.E. (1991). Sibling death, adolescent bereavement, and religion. *Death Studies, 15*(1), 1-20.

Davidson, G.W. (1979). *Death of the wished-for child.* Springfield, IL: Order of the Golden Rule Services.

Davidson, G.W. (1984). *Understanding mourning.* Minneapolis, MN: Ausburg.

Davies, B. (1991). Long-term outcomes of adolescent sibling bereavement. *Journal of Adolescent Research, 6*(1), 83-96.

Davis, R.A. (1989). Teenage pregnancy: A theoretical analysis of a social problem. *Adolescence, 24*(93), 19-28.

Fanos, J.H., & Nickerson, B.G. (1991). Long-term effects of sibling death during adolescence. *Journal of Adolescent Research, 5*(1), 70-82.

Gray, R.E. (1987). Adolescent response to the death of a parent. *Journal of Youth and Adolescence, 16,* 511-525.

Hogan, N.S. (1988). The effects of time on the adolescent sibling bereavement process. *Pediatric Nursing, 14,* 333-335.

Hogan, N.S., & DeSantis, L. (1992). Adolescent sibling bereavement: An ongoing attachment. *Qualitative Health Research, 2*(2), 159-177.

Hogan, N.S., & Greenfield, D.B. (1991). Adolescent sibling bereavement symptomatology in a large community sample. *Journal of Adolescent Research, 6*(1), 97-112.

Limbo, R.K., & Wheeler, S.R. (1986). Women's responses to miscarriage. *Forum Newsletter — Association of Death Education and Counseling, 10,* 2-3.

Martinson, I.M., Davies, E.B., & McGlowery, S.G. (1987). The long-term effects of sibling death on self-concept. *Journal of Pediatric Nursing, 2,* 227-235.

Martinson, I.M., & Campos, R.G. (1991). Adolescent bereavement: Long-term responses to a sibling's death from cancer. *Journal of Adolescent Research, 6*(1), 54-69.

Mauk, G.W., & Weber, C. (1991). Peer survivors of adolescent suicide: Perspectives on grieving and postvention. *Journal of Adolescent Research, 6*(1), 113-131.

McCubbin, H.I., & Patterson, J.M. (1983). The family stress process Double ABCX Model of adjustment and adaptation. *Marriage and Family Review, 6,* 7-37.

McNeil, J.N., Stilliman, G., & Swilhart, J.J. (1991). Helping adolescents cope with the death of a peer: A high school case study. *Journal of Adolescent Research, 6*(1), 132-145.

Michael, S.A., & Lansdown, R.G. (1986). Adjustment to the death of a sibling. *Archives of Disease in Childhood, 61,* 278-283.

O'Brien, J.M., Goodenow, C., & Espin, O. (1991, Summer). Adolescent reactions to the death of a peer. *Adolescence, 26*(102), 431-440.

Oltjenbruns, K.A. (1991). Positive outcomes of adolescents' experiences with grief. *Journal of Adolescent Research, 6*(1), 43-53.

Opie, N.D., Goodwin, T., Finke, L.M., Beattey, J.M., Lee, B., & VanEpps, J. (1992). The effect of a bereavement-group experience on bereaved children's and adolescents' affective and somatic distress. *Journal of Child Psychiatric Nursing, 5*(1), 20-26.

Sanders, C.M. (1989). *Grief: The mourning after. Dealing with adult bereavement.* New York: Wiley Innerscience.

Sanders, C.M., Mauger, P.A., & Strong, P.N. (1985). *A manual for the grief experience inventory.* Palo Alto, CA: Consulting Psychologists Press.

Smith, P.B., Weinman, M., & Malinak, L.R. (1984). Adolescent mothers and fetal loss: What we have learned from the experience. *Psychological Reports, 55,* 775-778.

Swanson-Kauffman, M. (1986). Caring in the instance of unexpected early pregnancy loss. *Topics in Clinical Nursing, 8,* 37-46.

Swanson-Kauffman, M. (1991). Providing care in the NICU: Sometimes an act of love. *Advanced Nursing Science, 13*(1), 60-73.

Valente, S.M., Saunders, J., & Street, R. (1988). Adolescent bereavement following suicide: An examination of relevant literature. *Journal of Counseling and Development, 67,* 174-177.

Worden, J.M. (1991). *Grief counseling and grief therapy: A handbook for the mental health practitioner.* New York: Springer.

Chapter 14

Birthparents' Grief: Relinquishing a Baby for Adoption

Patricia Roles

Since the 1960s and 1970s when many birthparents, including myself, relinquished babies for adoption, shifts have occurred in the field of adoption. Changes in values and beliefs have begun to filter down into changes in principles and practices in adoption systems and among supportive professionals. These changes are evidenced by the inclusion of this chapter about loss and grief experienced by birthparents who relinquish children for adoption. Fortunately, it allows for increased public awareness that adoption relinquishment is indeed a significant loss.

More recently there is growing awareness of the importance of the losses for different adoption triad members. These losses may include those shown in Figure 1-14. Adoption seems to be viewed by society in general as an act of receiving a "gift" with the focus on receiving a baby. The balance of receiving a baby with the reciprocal loss of a baby has not been given equal attention in adoption, health, or mental health fields. The adoption process traditionally operated upon the premise that adoption could meet the needs of all three parties in adoption: it provided a way to match the needs of stigmatized birthmothers and infertile couples while ensuring a *good* home for an *unwanted* baby.

The adoptees' rights movement, the civil rights movement, and the women's movement have given birthparents the opportunity to find courage to shed their anonymity and to speak up for society to hear. Adoptees grew into adults and demanded an end to sealed adoption records, as they searched for their identities. The process of secrecy in adoption, which also affected birthparents, began to be questioned. Researchers began to ask birthparents about their experiences and needs. Researchers found that, contrary to popular belief

Figure 1-14.
Losses Experienced by Different Adoption Triad Members

Adoptive Parents
Loss of fertility.
Miscarriages, pregnancy losses prior to choosing to adopt.

Adoptees
Loss of biological parents.
Loss of connection to roots.
Loss of culture.

Birthparents
Loss of baby through adoption.
Loss of continuity of future generations in the family.

and adoption practices, birthparents did not forget; on the contrary, their interest in the children whom they placed for adoption actually increased over time (Johnson, 1986). Once unleashed, the legacy of birthparent loss and grief through adoption relinquishment was not an easy story to hear.

Birthparents found it hard to speak up because the stigma associated with being an *unwed mother* was profound. This stigma brought shame. Secrecy became a necessary way of coping and continued to perpetuate the difficulty for society and individuals to acknowledge loss. Shedding the veil of secrecy for birthparents is a key process allowing for validation that a loss has occurred which deserves expression of feelings and a process of grieving (Roles, 1990b&c).

Key Issues for Birthparents

The general term "birthparent" is used to include both birthmothers and birthfathers, because experiences of loss and grief are shared by both biological parents who are involved in adoption relinquishment. However, it is important to appreciate that the birthmother is the central figure who is most affected by loss and grief issues. Birthmothers usually are young women who typically lack the birthfather's support in decision making, during pregnancy or delivery, or in the aftermath of relinquishment. It is the birthmother who carries the stigma and is subject to judgment by others. Her situation may cause her to suffer assaults to her self-esteem, and she has to struggle with painful decisions about her baby. She may feel isolated as the baby grows within her during pregnancy, and she has to cope with fears about delivery, during which she might feel very alone. This social dilemma, experienced by characteristically isolated young women, surrounds adoption relinquishment and adds a dimension which differs from most other experiences of pregnancy or neonatal loss.

This chapter is focused on the experience of loss which is related to infant adoption, not that which is associated with relinquishing older children for adoption or losing contact with children who must be apprehended by child welfare authorities, although some of the issues may apply regardless of the type of adoption.

Secrecy and Shame

The secrecy shrouding the birthmother further adds to isolation and lack of potential support from family and friends. Secrecy implies that birthmothers have done something unspeakable, and thereby it brings shame (Roles, 1990a,b,&c). Birthmothers who maintain secrecy around pregnancy, birth, and relinquishment by definition are negating the existence of part of themselves, out of fear of being judged by others. This leads to an assault on self-esteem which may be different in nature to the feelings of those who experience other types of pregnancy or neonatal loss. The secrecy is supported by society through such common advice as: "You will forget and get on with your life."

> *Nowhere in the psychological literature is there any evidence to justify secrets, nor are there any studies that indicate the value of secrets. There is a great deal of evidence to the contrary (Baran & Pannor, 1993, p. xii).*

Secrecy is supported by society's lack of public acknowledgment of loss through adoption relinquishment. In loss through adoption, there are no public rituals or ceremonies to mark the significance and meaning of the event, to validate that loss has occurred, to allow intense emotions to surface, or to allow support to be extended to the birthparents. After relinquishment, the birthmother is usually alone in her grief. For her, grief is private. There are no flowers, no notices in the newspaper, no sympathy cards, no memorial service, and no expected period of mourning. Life just goes on, like any other day (Roles 1990a,b,&c).

Guilt and Self-Blame

Guilt is a partner of secrecy and shame. Guilt is defined in the dictionary as a "state of having offended; sinful; wicked; judged to have committed a crime." Birthmothers may feel as though they have committed a horrible deed by giving away their flesh and blood. Birthmothers have heard others use phrases such as, "How could anyone give her baby away?" It is not uncommon for birthmothers to feel that they have done something so unnatural, selfish, and unmotherly that they deserve punishment, as if they had committed a crime. One birthmother described this vividly with the words, "You are regarded as a loving self-less woman until you relinquish your child, then you are a pariah" (De Simone, 1994, p. 117).

Consciously or unconsciously, some birthmothers may seek out experiences that reinforce this negative self-concept of a person in need of punishment. This may result in relationships with others who fulfill this view of them or may lead them to engage in self-destructive or acting-out behaviors.

In some other kinds of pregnancy loss, people recognize that they could not have prevented the loss, and thereby they may reduce their self-blame and connected guilt. In adoption relinquishment, however, birthparents must sign adoption consents and participate actively in the decision, even if in reality they are vulnerable, passive participants, who feel intimidated by coercive actions of others in authority (Roles, 1990a,b,&c). It always is important to keep in mind that pressure or persuasion may have unduly influenced the decision. If this was the case, then this experience must be validated (Roles, 1990b).

The guilt which birthmothers experience intensifies over time. Frequently as she matures further, the woman comprehends her role in her loss (Millen & Roll, 1985). It is not surprising, then, to perceive that birthparents might attempt to assign blame for the decision to others, even if coercion was not a factor in the woman's decision-making process. Blaming others can be a means to reduce feelings of personal guilt and responsibility for the consequences of the unplanned, unacceptable pregnancy.

Guilt does not necessarily involve blame, however. Even birthparents who felt that adoption was the best possible decision at the time are not insulated from the influences of guilt.

Anger

Anger is another component which is connected with blame. Some birthmothers become overwhelmed or immobilized by their anger to such a degree that this emotion distances them from others. It is important not to discount how anger can seem like a friend, as it provides an escape from feelings of emptiness and helplessness.

Opportunities to explore the anger's source are important, because there

Figure 2-14.
Sources of Anger Experienced by Birthmothers

- Inadequate support from adoption worker.

- Perceived lack of free choice.

- Misunderstanding legalities in adoption.

- Inability to acquire adequate information about the child after adoption.

(Johnson, 1986)

may be legitimate reasons for anger which the birthmother has not had support or encouragement to analyze and resolve. This is especially relevant when there is a power differential around decisions made by the young woman in crisis who must deal with adults in positions of authority, such as parents, prospective adoptive parents, social workers, lawyers, or physicians (Roles, 1990a&c). It is in this potentially confrontational environment that she tries independently to make a heart-wrenchingly difficult decision which will affect so many lives indefinitely. Sources for anger are outlined in Figure 2-14.

The Concept of Choice in Decision Making
The concept of choice in the adoption decision-making process adds another dimension to differences between loss through relinquishment and other pregnancy or neonatal losses. The more freedom that birthparents feel to make their own decisions about adoption, the less blame there will be of others, and the less regret will linger later in life. Higher levels of grief are associated with the birthmother's perception that she was coerced into relinquishment by others (De Simone, 1994). This agonizing decision often tears birthparents between their heads and their hearts. Decisions to relinquish are influenced by external factors which sometimes overwhelm the birthmother's internal desire to keep her baby (Johnson, 1986). There is no easy answer in such serious decisions, as described clearly by this birthmother:

It was a confusing time in my life. Because of pressures by others,
I gave my daughter up though deep down in my heart I didn't want to.
I guess it was the right thing to do, but I will always carry regrets with
me to the grave (De Simone, 1994, p. 116).

Figure 3-14.
Factors that Can Delay, Prolong, or Hinder the Grieving Process

- Many birthparents are not expecting to go through a normal grief reaction and therefore have no knowledge about what to expect or how to cope.

- Some birthparents do not hold or even see the baby. It is difficult to begin the grief process without a mental image or mementos to validate the baby as real.

- There is a lack of finality of the loss with the child still being alive and being reared by others.

- The elements of secrecy and lack of public acknowledgment or rituals can keep the loss private and enable grief to be internalized for a lifetime.

- Social stigma makes the loss socially unacceptable, which constricts natural opportunities to discuss the loss openly and to find outlets for expressing feelings.

- The hope of reunion can maintain connection with the child through memories and fantasy, and the reunion process can evoke unresolved grief, reawaken intense feelings which were presumed to have been dealt with, or bring new losses with newfound realities.

- A birthmother's interest in her child is not only sustained, but often it continues to develop after relinquishment (Johnson, 1986). This is not surprising, given developmental changes for women throughout their lives and given that the common times in life when relinquishment occurs are during the teens or early 20s, when priorities and needs are substantially different from those during the 30s and 40s. One birthmother described it this way: "The older I get, the more I miss her...I always wonder where she is, what she looks like, if she is good in school, if she knows about me, if she's happy and healthy" (Johnson, 1986, p. 34).

- Grief can go unexpressed for years. Later in life, events in birthparents' lives can begin the grief process. Triggers might include birth or loss of subsequent children, other losses, illness of birthparents or family members, reaching mid-life, or a woman's coming to the end of her reproductive years.

Those who take responsibility for their relinquishment decision may assign less blame to others and may experience less regret. There is a tradeoff, however, because such birthmothers then cannot escape the burden of self-blame and its partner, guilt. Another dimension with freedom of choice is its association with the myth that, if you choose your path, then it is something that you want. Therefore, it follows that, if you want something to happen, then you should not be unhappy about such a choice or its aftermath. This aspect of choice in feeling responsible for a decision seems to have invalidated birthmothers' right to grieve. Those around them do not understand their grief reaction (for example, "You've made your bed, now lie in it"), and, moreover, birthmothers themselves may not feel that they are "entitled" to grieve (Roles, 1990b&c).

Signing Adoption Consents

Signing legal documents with adoption consents in the midst of this emotional turmoil is a further dimension which sets loss through relinquishment apart from other pregnancy or neonatal loss. The experience of signing legal documents about the baby's adoption can be a time of extreme stress. Often, the process is undertaken without support, shrouded like the pregnancy by a veil of secrecy. One birthmother described her feelings at the time of consent signing: "I felt I was giving away part of myself, that I may never have another child, that no one would love him as much as me" (Johnson, 1986, p. 32).

Grief Process

Although the grief framework presented in Figure 4-14 is specific to loss through adoption relinquishment, there are similarities and differences with the grief process when loss is associated with death. The phases described can act as a guide to understanding the grief experience in relinquishment loss. There is no expected time frame attached to these often lifelong grief experiences because of the factors discussed in the Figure 3-14, and individuals can greatly differ in their reactions to loss.

Numbness and Denial

This initial phase is often characterized by a sense of shock and confusion. Primary defenses such as denial may be used, if necessary, to allow individuals time to adjust to reality. Realities include giving birth, trying to digest the magnitude of what has transpired, suddenly facing the decision to relinquish, signing legal papers, and ultimately leaving a newborn baby behind upon leaving the hospital. For many birthmothers, denial is not a new defense. Indeed, it may well have been part of coping strategies during the pregnancy. The sense of numbness can occur even if denial is not part of coping. Numbness and denial are functional and allow birthmothers to carry on without having to accept the impact of this decision. This often is necessary for birthmothers, given the associated secrecy and lack of acknowledgment that grief is expected or tolerated. Birthmothers generally give birth and then try to resume activities of daily living and previous roles such as work or school. No one talks about the birth and the loss which have occurred (Roles, 1990a&b).

Numbness and denial may be helpful strategies in the short run. In the long run, though, there are significant tradeoffs if these reactions persist. Individuals cannot numb themselves selectively from one experience or emotion in life, so the result is numbing from other positive experiences and emotions such as love, joy, or excitement (Roles, 1990a&b,).

Because of numbness, confusion, or denial around the time of birth and afterward, it is not uncommon for a birthmother to forget significant events or details such as the date or time of the baby's birth. This can then add further to a birthmother's guilt. She cannot understand how she could forget such vital information about her baby. The birthmother is then left with even fewer recollections of the event. Memories are crucial to help the birthmother form a mental image of the event in order to validate the birth and her loss, and to allow healing through grief to begin and proceed normally to resolution (Roles, 1990b).

Eruption of Feelings

A flood of intense feelings can erupt once the protective mechanism of denial or numbness is let down. This wide range of feelings may occur without having been connected to a trigger. Overwhelming feelings may include sadness, anger, fear, panic, anxiety, despair, guilt, shame, helplessness, hopelessness, emptiness, loneliness, irritability, fatigue, or difficulty in concentrating. Feelings might find expression less directly in physiologic symptoms such as headaches, sleep disturbance, nightmares, abdominal pain, back pain, or digestive problems. If intense emotions find outlets for direct expression, then they gradually decrease in intensity and become attached to logical triggers which bring back memories of the loss (Roles, 1990b&c).

Due to the stigma, secrecy, lack of public acknowledgment of the loss, and, therefore, lack of open support by family and friends, there are no natural opportunities to express feelings, especially the intense feelings. It is not surprising, then, to see how depression or substance abuse could become coping strategies for such social constraints, as one birthmother described: "I tried not to think because the pain was sometimes too much, and I suffered depression for years" (Johnson, 1986, p. 33).

Figure 4-14.
Phases of Grief Experienced by Birthparents

- Numbness and denial

- Eruption of feelings

- Accepting the adoption decision

- Accommodation and living with uncertainty

Higher levels of unresolved grief are associated with lack of opportunity to express feelings regarding relinquishment. Importance is placed on birthmothers' being accepted by others and being allowed and encouraged to express their feelings as a means of gradually resolving grief (De Simone, 1994). Birthmothers who were able to express their feelings with a family member experienced less emotional turmoil (Johnson, 1986).

Accepting the Adoption Decision

Recognizing the role as decision maker causes birthparents to accept responsibility for their loss. When birthparents feel in control of their own decisions, rather then feeling under the influence of others, then they find it easier to accept responsibility for these choices. They are less likely to hang onto blame toward others. This helps to prevent birthparents from getting stuck in anger and hindering their grieving process (Roles, 1990b&c).

The decision to relinquish a baby for adoption will be revisited after the birth has occurred and even after the adoption consents are signed. This is a normal process to ensure that doubts are dealt with and to consider the "what ifs." When some birthparents look back on their decision, they may feel selfish for having allowed their own needs to influence the decision. Some may experience regret or anger about having felt powerless. Birthparents must accept their part in the decision and deal with associated feelings in order to move on in life, even if their role was one of passive involvement (Roles, 1990b).

Accommodation and Living with Uncertainty

Over time, birthparents' thoughts and feelings become more manageable, with expected emotional reactions to events associated with the loss. Birthparents learn to live with ongoing sensitive areas in life, and they learn to cope with difficult questions and situations. It is normal to experience difficult times on the child's birthdays, at special family celebrations, during future pregnancies, at baby showers, around others' pregnancies, upon meeting children with the same given name or birthday, and during many other situations which evoke memories (Roles, 1990b&c).

Birthparents find ways to deal with comments or questions such as: "Do you have any children?" "How many children do you have?" "Don't you want to have any children?" "You'll know what it's like when you have children." "You can't imagine what being separated from a child is like." "I don't know how anyone could give her own baby away" (Roles, 1990b&c). Throughout life, birthparents have to decide consciously how to respond to such statements, depending on the individual situation and context. Birthmothers often listen to other women's stories about labor and delivery in silence, feeling private pain while at the same time wishing that they had the courage to join in such conversations.

Living with the unknown can be the most difficult part of relinquishment that birthparents have to adjust to in life. This state of limbo is eased by the normal process of creating fantasies about the child's life (Roles, 1990b&c). For those birthparents who receive ongoing information about their children's lives, the fantasy can be closer to reality than for birthparents who only have scant information which they received at the time of the adoption. Extensive fantasies of adoption reunion can interfere with the grief process, because they can lead to false hope of a fairy-tale reunion. Hopes for reunion can lead some birthparents to the idea that the loss is only temporary, but the reality of reunion is not always possible and brings no guarantees. Acknowledging that the child still may be alive and that reunion is a possibility can make it difficult to accept the permanence of the loss (Millen & Roll, 1985). Accepting a loss as final is a necessary step toward resolution in the grief process (Bowlby, 1980).

Search behavior is a natural part of the grief process for loss through death. At some point in the grieving process, the search is discovered to be irrational and results in acceptance of the reality of the loss. With relinquishment for adoption, however, search behavior is not irrational. There are many facets to the searching phenomenon. Search behavior by birthparents often does not promote reconciliation about the finality of the loss (De Simone, 1994), unless, after searching, birthparents learn that the relinquished child has died. Search activity represents an attempt to resolve a significant loss, and positive aspects of search behavior contribute to resolution of grief (De Simone, 1994).

One common type of searching is for information that allows birthparents to form a mental picture of the child, to validate that the event actually occurred, or to be reassured that the child is doing well after the adoption. Birthmothers have stated that their sense of loss and problems of adjustment to the relinquishment were greatly eased by knowledge about what had happened to the child (Winkler & van Keppel, 1984). Lower levels of grief also were found when birthmothers obtained information regarding their child after placement (De Simone, 1994). Another type of natural ongoing searching behavior involves scanning a crowd looking for children of similar age with similar features to birthparents, because birthparents know that the child is out there somewhere, perhaps even living in the same community. The most talked about type of search behavior is seeking out the child's whereabouts in anticipation of reunion. Birthparents who successfully locate their children, regardless of the outcome of the contact, describe this end to uncertainty as having healing qualities with respect to unresolved grief.

Re-evaluating and Rebuilding

Birthmothers' self-esteem is most often damaged because of secrecy, shame, guilt, self-blame, self-reproach, feelings of selfishness and unmotherliness, fear of being judged by others, the weight of the decision, and the loss itself. Because of the decision-making process in relinquishment, this loss experience leaves scars on self-esteem, adding to birthmothers' feelings of vulnerability. Birthmothers should understand that to choose adoption with good intentions in the best interests of their children was not an unmotherly, selfish decision (Roles, 1990b).

The final phase of grief resolution includes restoring self-esteem. Birthmothers must regain a sense that they are good, caring people capable of rebuilding self-confidence for themselves and as a basis in relationships and in future decision making. This may be a difficult process for birthmothers who had low self-esteem prior to relinquishment. De Simone's study highlights this aspect of self-esteem as it relates to birthmother grief:

> Life situations and experiences that raise self-esteem may decrease feelings of shame and self-devaluation...Increases in self-esteem have a moderating impact on grief enabling birthmothers to move on with their lives. However, it is important to note that many women also wrote that nothing was able to diminish their sense of loss and pain regarding the child they have relinquished (DeSimone, 1994, p. 124).

Figure 5-14.
Checklist of Actions for Health Care Professionals Working with Birthparents

• *Prepare birthparents for hospitalization and delivery.*
Offer prenatal education and explanations of parental rights. Discuss decisions about contact with the baby and the birthmother's plans for having a support person with her during delivery. Check to ensure birthmother is connected with a neutral counselor to discuss her decision/plans. Assist birthparents in seeking legal counsel if neccessary. Ensure that information is provided in written form, for later reference. Such documentation also serves as a basis for a memento file, which validates the experience. Include information which specifically addresses birthparents' loss and grief.

• *Validate the birthparents' role.*
Validate the birthparents' role in contributing to the child's life, the birthmother's hard work in delivery, and the joy which birthparents experience at the baby's birth. Naming the baby is another important component in validating birthparents' experience.

• *Encourage birthparents to see, hold, and care for the baby, and to connect with the baby in private.*
In offering these opportunities, remember that it is important to respect differing needs of individuals. Be clear about the distinction between a sense of awkwardness or reluctance about seeing the baby and a determined refusal to do so. One of the major, common birthmother regrets is not having seen or held the baby, which must be discussed with birthparents, as they make this personal decision.

• *After the baby is born, reaffirm that birthparents remain committed to their adoption decision.*
If any doubts arise, arrange for social work counseling regarding this decision, in case birthparents' have changed their minds after the baby's birth. Be sure to support any decision made by birthparents. Do not try to encourage birthparents to follow through on a decision with which they now express discomfort. Some birthparents who already have selected adoptive parents, and perhaps even permitted these people to be present during the delivery, may feel tremendous guilt at disappointing the adoptive parents if they do not follow through on the plan to relinquish. Remember that it is impossible to be absolutely sure about an adoption decision prior to the baby's birth. The decision should be revisited after delivery — *before* consents are signed. Depending upon adoption laws, which differ across North America, adoption consents may be irrevocable upon signing, with no waiting period if birthparents change their minds.

• *Assist in collecting mementos.*
Assist in collecting mementos such as photos, locks of hair, foot and handprints, and copies of birth registration or other hospital records, with birth date, time, weight, and identification bracelets. If the birthmother does not feel the need for these mementos, explain to her how other birthmothers find that these become invaluable later in life. This is especially true in the case of photographs. Tell the birthmother that you will collect such items and that you will keep them for her, should she desire them at a later date. Make an effort to follow-up on this by contacting her several weeks later.

Figure 5-14. *continued*
Checklist of Actions for Health Care Professionals Working with Birthparents

• *Validate and acknowledge the parental bond.*
Validate and acknowledge the parental bond, including the importance of what the birthmother has done for her baby during pregnancy and delivery. Allow the birthmother opportunities to talk about the pregnancy, labor, and delivery. Once she leaves hospital, she will have no natural opportunities to share these details with other mothers the way other women connect by sharing their birthing experiences. You could write down details about the labor and delivery for her to refer to later.

• *Treat birthmothers with respect.*
Treat birthmothers with respect, as a parent, like all the other new mothers in the hospital. Ask her what type of involvement she would like to have with her baby. Birthmothers have all the normal new mother's fears about assuming parenting roles in hospital. They require the same support and teaching, even though they may take on this role for only a few days. Some birthmothers feel less guilt afterward when they have cared for and fed the baby for those days in the hospital after delivery. Some blame themselves years later for not having nurtured their babies and for not playing a role in promoting the baby's sense of security and attachment during the first days of life.

• *Validate the significance of the loss.*
Allow opportunities for open discussion and expression of feelings, and provide education about what birthparents can expect, in terms of normal reactions following relinquishment and a need for support afterwards.

• *Be creative by exploring with the birthparents ways in which they might say goodbye.* You can help birthparents to mark the significance of this loss by incorporating ideas of rituals, ceremonies, or events that can act as memorials (for example, by suggestions such as planting a tree in honor of the baby). Do not hesitate to send cards to birthparents, as such items most likely will become a treasured part of a scanty collection of mementos. Encourage family and friends to send cards or flowers to acknowledge the loss. Because of the situation, they might not consider such an idea as helpful, given society's emphasis on secrecy.

• *Encourage and facilitate open dialogue with family and friends to build supports where feelings can be acknowledged and expressed.*
Family counseling may be helpful or quite necessary. In addition to being the birthparents' child, this baby also is a grandchild, a niece or nephew, a yearned-for link with future generations of the family. Relatives and friends may be affected deeply by the experience of relinquishment. Encouragement to explore and evaluate the range of feelings experienced by others may be helpful for birthparents, too.

• *Finally, there are general guidelines which are useful for care providers who are involved in the process of relinquishment.*
  • Support self-respect and build self-esteem.
  • Refer birthparents to birthparent/adoption support networks.
  • Provide or refer for follow-up grief counseling.
  • Act as a neutral advocate around issues such as understanding legal rights and rights to information in the medical setting, as well facilitating information about the adoptive family and baby's progress in the adoptive family.

Anticipatory Grief

When birthparents plan ahead of time for adoption relinquishment, this can provide some time to anticipate the events and to begin to express some of the associated feelings. At best, it provides time for birthparents to prepare intellectually for what they will face, through increased understanding of a normal grief process. It provides time to be clear about decisions, make decisions about degree of contact with the baby and the degree of openness in adoption, and to gather important written information about and mementos from the baby, to assist in validating the experience, and thereby to assist in the grief process. However, until the loss actually occurs no one can anticipate the emotional effects (Roles, 1990b).

Role of Health Care Professionals

Health care professionals can be in a special position to offer unbiased counseling and support, if there are no vested interests in the adoption relinquishment process. Physicians, public health nurses, clinic staff, hospital social workers, or hospital staff can be well-situated to help, since the grief process begins within the medical setting of the hospital. Figure 5-14 provides a checklist of care providers' actions which can make a difference for birthparents in the process of anticipatory planning and education, validation, and support with the birth experience, and aftercare.

Conclusion

Loss through adoption relinquishment is only just beginning to be acknowledged by a small circle, largely those who are involved personally and professionally in the adoption community. Even among adoption professionals, the aspect of loss was unrecognized until the 1980s. As has been discussed in this chapter, society's acknowledgment of this loss is an important factor, which can assist birthparents in their resolution of the grief process. Societal acknowledgment decreases secrecy and shame, allows increased opportunity to mourn the loss privately and publicly, and allows opportunity for increased support of family, friends, and professionals.

It is a significant shift to have this chapter requested for inclusion in a professional health care textbook on pregnancy and neonatal loss. This brings a note of optimism for birthparents, to have the loss and grief experience validated by being worthy of comment in the professional texts. This then leads to an ever-widening circle of acknowledgment of relinquishment loss, by educating health care professionals to help them learn how to respond more sensitively and effectively, and to help birthparents cope with their loss and grief.❑

Case Study 1-14

Inter-Family Adoption

At age 16, Tracy became pregnant. She lived in a rural community and was the youngest child in her family. The birth father did not live locally and was not told of Tracy's pregnancy. Tracy's parents offered their solution to her unplanned pregnancy, which was to adopt her son informally and raise him as their own child. Tracy wanted to keep her baby and raise him herself, but she lacked the confidence to go against her parents' wishes. She felt that this solution at least allowed her to complete high school and remain close to her son, even though her parents insisted that he never be told the truth. Tracy was to keep the secret and act as if she were his sister.

After completing high school Tracy found it difficult to live this lie. She moved to a city across the country to start a new life. She maintained close contact with her son in her role as older sister. Over the years her son, Michael, developed chronic renal failure which required that he begin dialysis at age 11. Tracy's parents were now elderly, experiencing health problems, and they resided a long distance from a hemodialysis center. As a result of these circumstances, Tracy's parents suggested that Michael should move in with Tracy where she could easily take him to the hospital 3 times a week for hemodialysis. They also worried that, if they passed away due to their own health problems, there would be no one to care for Michael.

Tracy secretly was delighted with this plan, yet resentful of the way in which it had evolved. Michael moved in with her, and they developed a very close relationship. Tracy talked with the hospital social worker about the reality of her relationship with Michael. She was working toward telling Michael her true identity as his mother. She was preparing to let go of the secrecy and take the risk that her parents would not be pleased. She was a single parent and had another daughter, Sandy, age 8, who was adjusting to Michael's presence in their home. Tracy had separated from Sandy's father 2 years earlier. Sandy and Michael were getting along exceptionally well.

Michael had been living with Tracy and Sandy for 7 months. Suddenly, at home with Tracy, Michael died after suffering seizures and cardiac arrest. Because of the unexpected nature of his death, Tracy did not have an opportunity to tell Michael that she was his mother. Tracy did feel that Michael had a intuitive awareness of the true nature of their relationship, by some remarks that he had made to her in the time they lived together as a family. It is not surprising that the result of this sudden death led Tracy into an emotional collapse, with an intense grief reaction, and she was in need of psychiatric help.

Commentary

A secret has been defined as information which we must keep remembering to keep forgetting. The case history of Tracy, her parents, and her son Michael is a familiar one in the annals of adoption. Most people are aware of inter-family adoptions either in their own or in their friends' families. Attempts to keep the situation "hushed up" usually are unsuccessful. Before the post World War II sexual revolution, the only safe way for families to keep out-of-wedlock babies within the family without attaching the stigma of illegitimacy to them was through secret relative adoption. Not informing the birth father was part of maintaining the lie and limiting gossip. Early writings in this field postulated that young girls and women become pregnant to give their mothers the gift of a baby. In retrospect, what also should have been expressed is the feeling that mothers wanted to give their daughters a gift, by protecting them at the same time by keeping them from losing the child completely. In an era when childbearing extended to 2 or more decades, a daughter's baby easily could be passed off as the mother's last pregnancy. The parents felt that the daughter could see, relate to, and help to rear her baby without the shame and embarrassment of being labeled as a sinner.

It may be helpful to look at inter-family adoptions in a general sense before commenting on this specific situation. Inter-family adoptions are any adoptions by one or more relatives (biological or through marriage) of the child. Families can be divided loosely into two groups, extended and nuclear. The extended family includes many generations and degrees of kinship, often living within a contiguous arrangement, with many areas of interdependency for the good of the family members. The nuclear family mainly comprises one set of parents and their children, although occasionally a grandparent may be included. Inter-family adoptions, both informal and formal, take place in both the extended and the nuclear family units.

The extended family in all cultures and societies through the ages always has practiced one or another form of informal adoption, without legal sanction. Although different cultures assume their own patterns and more, all share a common goal of having relatives assume cooperative responsibility for dependent children whose biological parents need assistance. The nuclear family, conversely, is an invention of modern, urban, Western society. This new (in the broad historical sense) largely exclusive, self-enclosed unit altered many long-established familial patterns, including those within the institution of adoption. The nuclear family did not have the easy capability of permitting children of relatives to be absorbed into its fabric when needed, with ongoing abilities to allow return or movement to other relatives. Informal adoption did not have a comfortable place in the nuclear family. Legal adoption, however, was acceptable because its boundaries were defined clearly, without any ambiguity.

Today, inter-family legal adoptions account for the majority of adoptions in the United States and Canada. The largest number are within the stepparent adoption category, usually openly recognized, without anonymity or secrecy. Contact with the relinquishing parent, however, often is diminished or lost entirely in the ensuing years. The least number of adoptions exist in the Caucasian, healthy newborn category. Up until the mid 20th Century, 97% of babies born out-of-wedlock were placed for adoption, with only 3% of these children being kept by their birth mothers. Today, the reverse is true, with only 3% of the children now available for adoption. As a result, we now are involved with a marketplace adoption climate, where demand far exceeds supply, and desperate, infertile couples cannot find babies to parent.

Tracy's case history, brief and terse, leaves a great deal unsaid. Much remains repressed and unexpressed. It is unclear whether or not a legal adoption ever took place, although with Tracy's having been a minor at the time of her son's birth, it is probable that some legal action was necessary. Both her parents and Tracy believed that the decision for the grandparents to become parents to Michael, for Tracy to assume the role of older sister, and for Michael never to be told the truth, was in everyone's best interests. Although there was no conscious malevolence or retribution within this family, Tracy reveals that she found the lies so difficult to maintain that, as soon as she graduated from high school, she escaped to the other side of the country to start a new life. Rather than making her life easier, Tracy's parents' decision to keep Michael created a facade that made it impossible for Tracy to grieve and mourn the loss of her mother role to her son. Daily, hourly, Tracy was reminded that she had given over her child to her mother, and that she should be grateful to her parents that she had not been forced to give Michael away to entire strangers. It is possible that her parents resented Tracy's leaving when she finished school. Perhaps they were relying on her to continue assisting them with Michael in the role of big sister and babysitter, an obligation for Tracy especially since they all knew that really she was Michael's mother and that her parents had adopted him for Tracy's benefit. Tracy did not abandon her son emotionally, but she found it easier to maintain the fictitious role from a distance. Apparently, Tracy was successful in building a new life for herself, temporarily if not permanently, by making a marriage and achieving actual parenthood by giving birth to and rearing her daughter, Sandy.

We do not know how Tracy responded to Michael's serious health problems and his prognosis. We know only that her parents, feeling unable to continue to care for Michael with his demanding needs, turned to Tracy for relief. We are told that secretly Tracy was delighted, although she also resented achieving her role as mother so late, and only because of the tragic circumstances. Perhaps, unrealistically, Tracy felt that she could save her son, and through her love and care make him healthy. Certainly, she was prepared to break her vow of secrecy and to reveal her true identity, even if this meant incurring the wrath of her parents. Tracy describes a family unit of herself and her two children, all close and loving, and she envisions a happy future for all of them. She does not believe that her revelation will come as a complete shock to Michael. It is quite probable that Michael has sensed the truth. Most children, when they have been lied to about their parentage and origins, realize that they have been told half-truths or untruths. Before Tracy can tell Michael that she is his mother, he dies suddenly, leaving her unable to cope with this second devastating loss.

The first time that Tracy lost her child, she was trapped in an ambiguous, murky world where she was unable to examine her feelings clearly. She made two incomplete emotional adjustments: the teenage high-school student became the helpful, loving older sister, and then, when she finished school, she ran far away to take on the easier role of caring, but distant, relative. Years later, with Michael's coming to live with her, Tracy felt that she had been given a second chance, to rescue her child, nurse him back to health, tell him the truth about their relationship, and become his rightful mother. Michael's untimely death, which occurred before Tracy had completed her mission, left Tracy feeling cheated as well as bereft. Years of deprivation and anger overwhelmed her. The future for Tracy is not all bleak, however. Sad as the reality was in her family, Tracy had a brief time to mother her son and to build a relationship between her two children. Michael's death, although it catapulted Tracy into the depths of despair, also provided Tracy the opportunity to explore her long-buried feelings, which can lead ultimately to healing.

— *Annette Baran, MSW, RSW, LCSW*

References

Baran, A., & Pannor, R. (1993). *Lethal secrets: The psychology of donor insemination*. New York: Amistad Press, Inc.

Bowlby, J. (1980). *Loss: Sadness and depression*. New York: Basic Books.

De Simone, M. (1994). *Unresolved grief in women who have relinquished an infant for adoption*. Unpublished doctoral dissertation, New York University School of Social Work.

Johnson, D. (1986). *Birthparent survey: Impact of adoption on relinquishing mothers*. Unpublished thesis, The University of Victoria, Victoria, Canada.

Millen, L., & Roll, S. (1985). Solomon's mothers: A special case of pathological bereavement. *American Journal of Orthopsychiatry, 55*(3), 441-418.

Roles, P. (1990a). *Facing teenage pregnancy: A handbook for the pregnant teen*. Washington, DC: Child Welfare League of America.

Roles, P. (1990b). *Saying goodbye to a baby: A birthparent's guide to loss and grief in adoption (Vol. I)*. Washington, DC: Child Welfare League of America.

Roles, P. (1990c). *Saying goodbye to a baby: A professional's guide to birthparent loss and grief in adoption (Vol. II)*. Washington, DC: Child Welfare League of America.

Winkler, R., & van Keppel, M. (1984). *Relinquishing mothers in adoption: Their long-term adjustment*. Melbourne, Australia: Institute of Family Studies.

Chapter 15

Impact of Pregnancy Loss on Subsequent Pregnancy

Joann M. O'Leary
Clare Thorwick

Past experience plays a major role in shaping a new pregnancy. Pregnant families who have experienced a previous pregnancy loss face unique issues during subsequent pregnancies. Unanswered questions and unresolved issues relating to their past experience may significantly affect parents' attitudes about and reactions to the subsequent pregnancy. Pregnancy as a time of joy and expectation may be overshadowed by fear or grief. Parents concurrently grieve the previous pregnancy and baby, while they attempt to develop bonds of attachment to their new unborn child.

Health care providers must keep in mind that the previous pregnancy is the frame of reference for these patients, and that pregnancy loss is a significant predictor of risk in the next pregnancy (Goldenberg, Mayberry, Copper, Dubard, & Hauth, 1993). Being aware of and sensitive to parents' prior pregnancy loss experience as it relates to their current pregnancy is important. This can enhance the type and level of information, emotional support, involvement, and choices that are appropriate for them, so that parents can move as comfortably as possible through subsequent pregnancy after a loss.

Planning for Subsequent Pregnancy

When pregnancy loss occurs, many couples express an urge to become pregnant again immediately. It is important that families receive preconception counseling when possible, to begin appropriate planning to manage the next pregnancy from a medical standpoint. In an extensive review of the literature on adaptation following perinatal loss, Zeanah (1989) found little agreement on when it is best psychologically to get pregnant again. Most parents do not necessarily follow medical advice anyway. What seems to matter is how the couple incorporated the loss into their family's experience and structure. It may be more important to help them realize that grief over their child who died will never go away completely (Kolker & Burke, 1993), and adaptation to the next pregnancy may be inhibited by the mourning process (Lewis, 1979; Phipps, 1985). These parents have lost their naiveté, statistical probability has failed them, and they live with continuous anxiety that death will strike again (Kowalski, 1991). Even the subsequent delivery of a healthy infant does not prevent anxiety during any following pregnancy. Their feelings become a part of the experience of subsequent pregnancies.

Effect of Pregnancy Loss on Parents

Most parents in an uncomplicated pregnancy progress through Rubin's (1975) tasks of pregnancy, complete attachment, and adapt to the continuum of neonatal life. Mothers and fathers each have their own separate struggles with maturational processes of pregnancy. In the midst of normal pregnancy-related developmental tasks, a baby's death creates a unique type of bereavement (Lindahl, 1994). Reality suddenly becomes, "babies die, too." The mother and father cannot negotiate or complete their passage into parenthood. In addition to the usual grieving process, pregnancy loss can be understood as developmental interference for the parents, disrupting a significant milestone. This sets them aside from peers and even family. Pregnancy loss becomes a "crisis within a crisis" (Leon, 1992).

Several authors (Furman, 1978; Theut, Pedersen, Zaslow, & Rabinovich, 1988) have recognized that pregnancy loss damages the mother's self-esteem. By losing the baby — a part of her body during pregnancy — she loses, and grieves the loss of, a part of herself. At some level, though not physical, her partner also loses a part of himself. Subsequently, both may perceive themselves to be inadequate or intrinsically unable to face the challenge of the next pregnancy. Subsequent pregnancy also is emotionally laden for the mother, because it represents another chance to experience pregnancy and to re-establish her reproductive role (Furman, 1978). She may begin to mitigate her narcissistic loss ("the baby as a part of herself") and assuage her guilt over the previous loss.

While much is now known about how to help parents at the time of loss, parental reactions during subsequent pregnancy after a loss are poorly researched (Zeanah, 1989). A recent study of 1,824 women who were less than 16 weeks pregnant reported that women with previous unsuccessful pregnancies did not possess "positive" feelings about being pregnant. They

Figure 1-15.
Clinically Observed Developmental Tasks of Pregnancy after Loss

- Working with the fear of another abnormal pregnancy.
- Working through the avoidance of attachment for fear of future loss.
- Moving past the unwillingness to give up grieving out of loyalty to the baby who died.
- Attaching to the unborn child, separately from the baby who died.
- The mother grieving the loss of part of herself.

We have seen all members of the family, including children, struggle with the first four issues. Some men also struggle with an additional task: The fear of loss of their partner if the previous loss was a medical emergency for the mother.

O'Leary & Thorwick (1994)

worried about something being wrong with the baby, feared miscarriage, and had higher trait anxiety scores than women who were pregnant for the first time or who had other living children (Statham & Green, 1994). Hamilton's (1989) study found that 93% of women who had miscarried were anxious about future pregnancies; women who became pregnant again experienced considerable anxiety. Other studies of families with previous loss found that, during the new pregnancy, parents were detached, focused excessively on negative outcomes, and had intense anxiety, regardless of how long after the loss the pregnancy occurs. All of these symptoms and behaviors can interfere with parents' ability to focus on the pregnancy, developing child, and attachment (Davis, Stewart, & Harmon 1989; Phipps, 1985; Theut et al., 1992).

Recurring themes have been observed clinically among families during a subsequent pregnancy (Davis et al., 1989; Parker & O'Leary, 1989; Peterson, 1994) and supported in research by others (Statham & Green, 1994; Theut et al., 1988). The frequency of these themes suggest that either Rubin's normal developmental tasks are arrested or different developmental tasks are present for parents experiencing pregnancy after a loss (Figure 1-15). In the context of the parents' previous childbearing history, these tasks can be seen as "healthy" normal behaviors during pregnancy after loss and are not abnormal as thought by some health care providers. Indeed, lack of acknowledgment and/or validation on the part of caregivers that such intense feelings are appropriate may contribute significantly to a more difficult pregnancy and possibly to a developmentally poor outcome (O'Leary, Thorwick, Lindahl, & Knox, 1995). The tasks are neither sequential nor discrete; rather, elements of the work involved in each are present much of the time — they ebb and flow, and are coped with uniquely by each person (Todd, 1996).

Ambivalence Toward the New Pregnancy

"When I found out I was pregnant I started grieving the loss of this child."

For women and men who have experienced pregnancy loss, their initial response to the confirmation of a new pregnancy may take many forms. Parents have felt such deep pain that they have forgotten how to feel anything but pain, or even to believe that there could be any other way to feel. Afraid of being happy, some parents fear that they really are not pregnant. Others are fearful that they *are* pregnant, and they adopt an insulating distance, which serves as pseudo-protection because of the pain of the previous loss. Some parents accept the fact that they are pregnant, yet hold back on believing that they will have a baby. The risk of emotional investment in a new baby who also could die is too great.   "You never again get the luxury of experiencing a 'normal' pregnancy" is a true statement for anyone in this group.

Anxiety and worries are the norm. Women may feel frightened when morning sickness stops, then call to ask if this is "normal." Many parents find that sleeping at night is difficult; they may be tearful and become extremely vigilant about any possible danger signals. Vaginal discharge is perceived as a warning of impending loss, regardless of how the prior loss occurred. Compulsive checking for bleeding is common. They worry about every ache and pain, especially if their loss occurred in the first trimester or early part of the second. Parents are afraid to do anything to jinx the pregnancy. While some parents want the same care provider, others may change health care providers. Whatever they did during the previous pregnancy, they try to avoid repeating this time.

At the initial clinic visit, let the family lead the way. A simple but important question to begin with is, "How do you view your loss(es)?" Everyone's story is different, and people will have different ways of attaching meanings to their losses. Allow patients to state in their own words the significance of their loss. If they experienced first trimester losses, how they give meaning to such a loss shows how they may view a subsequent pregnancy. Explore whether first-trimester losses are viewed as babies by the family. One woman with infertility experienced three early losses over an 8-year period. She did not consider these losses as traumatically as the loss she experienced each month when she menstruated. She commented, "I felt there was some hope at least when I got pregnant."

Helping to Restore Trust

On the first visit, review the family's previous loss(es) to discover what they understand about what happened, what pieces of information seem to be missing or unclear, and what plans will be made to help them in this pregnancy. Most of the time, any missing links in their knowledge results from the crisis of the experience. Many times, even in an "unexplained" stillbirth, women recall feeling "not quite right" before they found out that the baby had died. Parents need to understand "how and why," if at all possible.

There is a fine line between giving people information that they need at each point of their pregnancy and giving them so much that it frightens them. A dialogue that involves gentle explanation provides a trust-building environment. Encourage parents to call with questions at any point in the pregnancy. Though the medical concerns and issues from the last pregnancy may make perfect sense, the parent may not understand or accept explanations. Respect their need for information and preparation for what they may need to do in this pregnancy. Build a trusting relationship by establishing mutuality and respect. In the end, people must live with consequences of their decisions without regret. Parents with previous pregnancy losses know this better than anyone.

Reassuring Benefits of Obstetric Technologies

Ask parents what you can offer which might reassure them during this pregnancy. What may seem exasperating and unreasonable to caregivers really makes all the sense in the world to families with previous pregnancy loss. Some people may need to hear the heartbeat repeatedly during the early weeks of pregnancy, requesting extra visits with their health care providers to make sure that the baby is alive. Unless they see the heart beating with their own eyes (real-time ultrasound) or hear it with their own ears (doptone), it is impossible for them to believe that their baby is safe within. Just knowing this care is available helps relieve anxiety for some parents.

Events around their prior loss greatly color the response to managing this pregnancy: Who was involved, how they learned the news, and what was the order of events (genetic counseling, ultrasound, amniocentesis, AFP results, etc.). If parents found out during an ultrasound examination that their baby had died, then they may be afraid this time to look at an ultrasound image — and, at the same time, they may be afraid *not* to look. Some people choose not to look until after an amniocentesis or other testing verifies that their baby is normal. They still may not get reassurance, or they may be reassured only briefly and then continue to be afraid, even after they are told that everything is fine. They need reassurance as much as possible throughout this stressful pregnancy.

Many people feel mounting anxiety just by coming back for their clinic visits. Ask before a procedure if this will bring up memories of the last time, and find out what you can do to help them through the ultrasound, test, or clinic visit. All of these benchmarks affect the next pregnancy. A caregiver might say, "I'm going to look at your baby by ultrasound. How will this be for you? Would you like to look too?" The positive effects of relieving stress for these families can contribute to a better outcome; and incidentally this may save time and money for care providers. Medical technology used in this way can create trust by providing concrete reassurance from the baby that all is well.

Learning Ways to Know and Trust Their Body and Their Baby
"If I bring home a baby..."

Many women will not know how "normal stretching" of the uterus feels. Be ready to answer their questions and provide more information on normal physiology of pregnancy. Keep in mind, what parents thought was normal before resulted in a loss, so they have no foundation to trust their own bodies or the normal process of pregnancy. New worries emerge as parents begin to believe that this pregnancy might continue and as they feel movement. Women who did not feel movement in their last pregnancy because of early loss may need weeks to understand how normal fetal movement feels. Some women are relieved to experience this tangible sign of life within. However, others focus so much on fetal movement that even the normal cycles of active and quiet behavior raise anxiety and worry "something is wrong" with *this* baby too.

Trusting intuition about the new pregnancy and trusting the baby are difficult for mothers, especially as they approach the point in pregnancy when they experienced a previous loss. Take time to give specific information about the differences between contractions and fetal movements. It is hard for some women to recognize the difference. Teaching women to palpate the uterus, to begin to learn how contractions feel, may help. Understanding these physical feelings is important before a woman can develop a sense of her body and then recognize when something is not right. This may take a few weeks for women to distinguish and, moreover, will change as the baby develops.

When women begin to feel movement, explain fetal movement's cyclicality, with its various states, and reassure them that it is okay for the baby to have quiet times. Clear instructions on how to count movements reassures parents, and helps them recognize this baby as a unique individual (Thorwick, Foslien, & Kalb, 1990). Sometimes, women are afraid to take time to pay attention, because they are afraid that they will not feel the baby move. One woman reported that she was not doing her daily fetal-movement counts because she said that she was too busy with her older child. When questioned further, however, she admitted that she was afraid to be quiet alone with this baby because she was afraid that she would not feel him move. Acknowledging fears helps parents to validate their feelings as normal. As the baby develops *in utero*, parents gradually realize that avoiding attachment will not save them from the pain of loss. They respond to the baby's prompting and may let themselves attach, almost in spite of their intent.

Attaching to the New Baby

"I'm afraid that every time I try to play ball with this boy all I will think about is that I should be playing ball with my other son. I don't know how I will love this son and not feel bad about the other one."

Once movement occurs, it is not uncommon for many to feel heightened emotional pain and ambivalent responses. The fear of repeating the loss experience heightens as parents work through the realization that this baby *in utero* is not the baby who died. While understanding the concept intellectually, not everyone can grasp it emotionally at first. Some parents hope for a new baby who is the same sex as the baby who died; others find this hard. They can feel such loyalty to the baby who died that they fear they will forget him or her by allowing themselves to grow attached to their subsequent baby. Feelings of guilt make parents distance themselves emotionally from the baby within. Fear to attach, fear of feeling anything for this child may cause parents to paralyze all of their emotions. Others may indicate during prenatal visits that everything is fine, although internally they deny to the end that their baby really is coming. One woman described "frozen tears," stating that if she allowed herself to feel she was afraid that she never would stop crying.

Clinicians consider infants who die to have important influences on parents' relationships with other children, especially on infants who are born subsequent to the loss (Zeanah & Harmon, 1995). Prior, lost children influence parenting approaches toward a new baby. Try to stay focused on the current pregnancy, even though it is important to let the past help guide the way. In your interactions with patients and families, facilitate a safe environment for parents to express anxieties and to sort through their feelings. Their fears and concerns must be understood and validated. By helping them explore constructive ways to cope and by providing information on expected management of the current pregnancy, health care providers enable parents to become advocates for themselves and their new baby. They begin to gain a sense of control and appreciate that they actively can parent their new baby even before birth.

Understanding the Baby's Role

Mother and fetus are connected intimately, both biologically and psychologically, during pregnancy. Changes in the pregnant woman's emotional states cause hormonal and psychological changes in her body that reach into the uterus (Findeisen, 1993). Because the new baby occupies the same space as did the baby who died, some women may need help reassuring themselves the baby is safe and visualizing their uterus as a healthy part of their body (see "Relaxation and Visualization," in this chapter). The space where one baby died can be a safe space for the next baby. This "sharing of space" may be an important concept for a woman as she recovers trust in her body (Peterson, 1994). A referral to a resource that can provide this therapy sometimes is helpful.

Having parents talk to their new baby before birth about their fears and about the other baby appears to benefit some families (O'Leary & Thorwick, 1993). In addition to validating the previous parenting experience, this may help parents understand that their new baby is part of the healing process. Reminding them that the baby can hear their voices allows parents to know that their baby, at some level, already has heard their fears and anxieties, knows the story of their loss, and feels the grief, love, and overwhelming need of parents to protect their baby. Many parents are afraid to voice what they think. Other parents realize that it may be more helpful for them to acknowledge their feelings out loud to each other and to their baby. With this awareness, some parents relieve some anxiety and begin to attach themselves to their new baby. An emerging area of literature asserts that babies have some level of consciousness prenatally (Chamberlain, 1994; Verny, 1994), a belief that is commonly accepted by parents as reasonable and useful, though not scientifically documented or researched in the obstetric community.

Antepartum Electronic Fetal Monitoring

"I called the clinic because I thought my baby had died. You told me to come in and get objective data because I was too subjectively involved."

Antepartum testing is an integral part of obstetric care during most subsequent pregnancies. Antepartum testing is justified in a medical context to provide antenatal surveillance of the baby and to plan care. In the context of a woman with previous pregnancy loss, testing provides the bonus of reassuring, objective data for anxious parents. Using technology to affirm what the woman feels builds her confidence and enhances her attachment to her new baby. Daily fetal movement counts and antepartum testing demonstrate a fetus's healthy, competent behaviors. These tools are an opportunity for the baby to "tell" what is going on, for the practitioner to teach normal growth and development to the parents, and for care providers to determine their prenatal care plans.

Parents can quickly learn fetal monitoring principles when they are put in the framework of a baby's developmental behaviors. Real-time ultrasound lets parents see, in a visual objective fashion, fetal movement, breathing, and amniotic fluid, and confirms their baby's safety. These technologies also can enhance the woman's confidence in her body's ability to support her baby. Each series of tests assures that the baby is safe in the uterus, unless or until test results indicate that it is time for delivery or other intervention. Parents need psychological reassurance to continue feeling that this pregnancy is progressing satisfactorily (O'Leary & Thorwick, 1993).

With antepartum testing, parents are reassured because their baby becomes an active participant in an interactive process. Technologic resources enable parents to learn how to be the best parents they can be (and reinforce the sense that their parenting skills are real). Subsequent pregnancy is a good time to teach parents how to recognize fetal movement, and using ultrasound or Doppler heart monitors permits care providers to demonstrate to parents how the fetal heart rate responds to movement. This also is a good time for health care providers to "check in" with families to gauge how they are doing emotionally and to find out what else might be helpful.

Partner Issues

"I got involved in the counseling because Jan wanted me to be there. I thought 'Why me? I'm not the one who is pregnant.' When I got there, I realized I had a lot of fears of my own that I just hadn't dealt with."

During many women's pregnancies, fathers are treated as passive observers or "helpmates" for the women (Nichols, 1993). When a baby dies, however, this dynamic changes; fathers lose their identity of being a parent, too. Clinical observation shows that men are just as afraid as women during subsequent pregnancy following a loss, and they experience some of the same tasks of pregnancy (O'Leary et al., 1995). Some men report feelings of panic every time the woman gets up in the middle of the night to go to the bathroom or every time the phone rings at work. In many cases, the previous loss was discovered during a prenatal visit when the man did not accompany his partner so, with subsequent pregnancy, he may feel compelled to accompany her on every visit. Other men will not go to any prenatal appointments as a way to distance or protect themselves.

It is not unusual for some couples to have poor communication during the pregnancy because of emotional pain about their previous loss. This may be caused by a fear of creating new memories about the current pregnancy, in case this baby does not live either. Reassure parents that such dilemmas are normal, and ask if they would like help.

If a previous pregnancy loss created a medical emergency for the woman as well, then partners with this background may need more explanation about their plan of care; concrete information on what will be different this time is important for them, too. Rage and anger can resurface when plans for medical procedures for the next delivery are discussed (Parker & O'Leary, 1989). These emotions can affect the couple's faith in the health care system. What is standard medical practice in obstetrics (for example, induced labor that may take 2 days to soften the cervix) can strike the woman's partner as abusive. Anger often masks men's fears about the mother's and/or baby's safety. Anger and over-protectiveness may be the only way that men can respond, to gain a sense of control. Whether it was true or not, some men perceived that their partners were close to death during the previous loss experience. It is helpful to say, "You must be afraid or feel out of control. Can I help you with that?"

When couples begin to prepare for the next labor and birth, they may feel the full impact of their previous loss. This can be especially true for people who have tried to protect themselves by limiting their active involvement during this pregnancy. They come face-to-face with the reality of the new baby and their terror of another loss. Remember, everything went wrong the last time for this couple, and they were powerless to change it.

Nearing the End of Pregnancy

"Just get the baby out while it is still alive."

As parents get past the milestone of 24 weeks, when the baby might survive in neonatal intensive care, they begin to believe that they might have this baby (although a few couples still refuse to prepare for their baby). Some people describe a sense of calmness between 24-32 weeks; but, as birth approaches, fears increase. They are afraid of the approaching birth. Women may feel an increased burden and responsibility for keeping this baby alive. It is not unusual to see women who were very calm through most of the current pregnancy begin to exhibit signs of rising anxiety as delivery approaches. Couples may begin to negotiate with their health care provider for an early induction when they reach 37 weeks gestation. They need the opportunity to discuss with a health care professional how they will get through the last weeks of pregnancy.

Preparation for Labor and Birth

"I didn't want to go back to the regular birth classes where everyone was naive and happy."

Couples who have lived through perinatal loss need extra help in getting through labor. Labor and birth mean that parents must face the reality of their last loss and that this infant is not the baby who died. Ask parents about their feelings as they approach their due date. It is important for partners to process or synthesize their previous experience together as much as possible, in order to deal with powerful emotions that may overwhelm them. This can help them separate their two birth experiences. Planning to have a third person (such as a relative or close friend) at the birth sometimes is helpful. Both parents may be too emotional to help each other.

Most families avoid childbirth preparation classes because of their painful memories. For some parents, going to birth classes forces them to face the reality this baby is alive — and may die, too. A traditional birth-preparation class is far too painful for them to attend with other couples, whom they perceive as naive. A special birth class, designed for parents who have lost a baby, may be helpful (Parker & O'Leary, 1989). One woman wanted just to "plow through" labor and birth, determined not to think about the emotional impact the experience would have on herself or her partner. However, after attending special birth classes she realized that this decision would have been a mistake for her.

Some parents experience anxiety attacks just driving by the hospital. *Many, if not most, parents will not want to tour the hospital at all before they return for their subsequent baby's delivery.* However, seeing the hospital and birthing room before they come in for labor actually can be helpful for parents. Touring the area with a health care professional helps parents to rehearse or talk through any fearful feelings. This is important even for couples who changed hospitals in the wake of their previous pregnancy loss. One woman walked into a birthing room, saw the food tray over the bed, and had a flash of seeing her dead baby lying on it. Touring the facility before her next labor allowed this woman to see things which she had forgotten and which she did not realize were part of her memories. The visit helped this woman to write her birth plan, reflecting that she needed to control such details as having the food tray kept out of her room.

Touring the hospital helps parents to approach the actual birth with a focus on this baby. Some families, however, just cannot bring themselves to do a tour. Expect these people to be surprised at their level of pain which revisits them while you work with them during labor.

Birth Planning

If special birth classes are not available for couples with previous pregnancy loss, they may need help in composing their birth plan. A birth plan reflects their personal story, in the parents' own words. A birth plan gives them a sense of control for this delivery, when they may have had no control during the last. The plan can include a history of the previous, failed pregnancy, how this current pregnancy has been for them, and anything else that they want the staff to understand. Even though their "story" may be learned from the woman's medical chart, when people write it in their own words, it becomes much more powerful and useful for staff during labor. Parents also should address the specific events in the last labor that may affect this labor, and what reassurances they will need from the staff (see Figures 2-15 & 3-15).

The Actual Labor and Birth

"I had to face the reality of whether this baby was going to be born alive or be dead like his brother."

When people with a previous pregnancy loss arrive to deliver their next baby, nurses should explore with the parents how much they wish their nurses to be present during labor. Parents want hospital staff to recognize their previous loss and give them special understanding (Wilson, Soule, & Fenton,

Figure 2-15.
Issues to Be Included in Birth Plan by Parents with
Previous Pregnancy Loss

- History of previous pregnancy(ies)
- Story of this pregnancy
- Support/testing which they may have received during pregnancy
- How past labor may affect this labor
- What support each partner may need
- Sibling concerns, when appropriate
- Postpartum issues

1988). Typically, these parents are frightened and overwhelmed, even when they have had support and intervention for their fears and anxieties during the current pregnancy. Sensitivity on the part of the staff, who can understand and validate their fears, provide information, and offer support, is vital in helping such families through this experience. Caregivers should support and reassure the woman that her body can labor normally. These families may need one-to-one support throughout their entire labor. A third person of their own choosing may serve in this role.

Be aware that partners usually are undergoing a similar crisis, even if both may not exhibit signs of their stress equally. If parents have "flash-backs," keep supporting them, reminding them that this is a different labor and a different baby. Reassure them with each contraction that their baby is pushing and extending his or her way down through the birth canal, helping with the process. If parents already have named their baby, use the baby's name as you encourage the woman with her labor.

Most couples choose to have electronic fetal monitoring throughout labor. Keeping sound at a minimum can create rhythmical background "white noise" which helps them to concentrate on the baby and on contractions. However, monitoring the baby may not provide all the reassurance that parents need. Many couples demand concrete examples of why the nurse tells them that everything is progressing well. Detailed explanations of what is reassuring about the tracing may be helpful. A lost heart rate signal due to equipment problems could terrify the couple and bring flashbacks.

Some women may be afraid to change position during labor, fearful that

Figure 3-15.
Sample Birth Plan

Sheri and John Doe and Baby Emily
History
This is our third pregnancy. Our first pregnancy ended in a stillborn son at 38-weeks gestation. Our second pregnancy ended in a miscarriage at 14 weeks. Our stillborn son was born after 10 hours of hard labor. Sheri does not remember much of the labor and we had no sense of the different "phases" of labor. John only remembers how painful it was to watch Sheri as she went through this.

This Pregnancy
This has been a very difficult pregnancy. There were several incidents of severe bleeding when we thought the pregnancy was over, but to our surprise she hung in there. We have had two level II ultrasounds and know this is a baby girl. We have had weekly BPP and non-stress tests since 30-weeks gestation. We took the special birth class but still feel unprepared. We are now approaching the end of this pregnancy and so far have been given excellent reports that this will be a healthy baby girl. We are still concerned about the outcome of this pregnancy and cannot quite be assured of a positive outcome until the baby is born and we can see for ourselves that she is in fact a healthy baby.

Labor Requests
- We want the nurses and all others who will have contact with us to know our history. We hope that this will help to make them understand that we are very anxious about this pregnancy and delivery. **We don't want to keep answering the question, "Is this your first?"**

- We need reassurance through each stage with tangible and logical explanations of how we are progressing and how you know the baby is safe.

- Please offer suggestions for position changes to relieve discomfort. Sheri would like to be able to walk around if possible.

- We will likely need assistance with breathing and relaxation techniques.

- We may require help in focusing on tasks assigned during labor/delivery. We know we will need help in pushing.

- We would prefer as little medication as possible but won't know until the time comes. Please help us with that decision.

- We do not want our immediate family around but would like one of the group facilitators if they can be there.

- John would like to cut the cord.

Postpartum
- Right now we feel we want Emily with us at all times. Please do whatever checks are necessary on her in our room or have John go with her.

- Sheri would like to breast-feed but will need help with that.

any movement may harm the baby. Remind them to move about, and give reassurance that it is perfectly safe. Other women let the effort of labor take over and focus on this baby. While it is not always easy to assess how the partner is doing when you are busy with the laboring woman, be watchful of what is happening with him, too.

"Pushing" during labor can mean "death" to these parents, especially if the previous loss was a stillbirth. One father whose son had died because he had a hypoplastic left heart said, "I cut the cord and began the process of ending my son's life." Pushing their new baby into life was equally as scary to this man as it was for his wife. Pushing may precipitate another crisis. Some women dilate to complete and then plateau, with a prolonged arrest of labor. They are afraid to push the baby out. This may be because, as stressful as the pregnancy was, the woman has grown accustomed to these feelings and accepted them as a norm. She may be afraid of what the next phase of true parenting may be like. This may be a time when staff might step back, assess the situation, and help the family to regroup. Parents may need to be reminded that this is a different baby — a healthy baby who is just as anxious to see them as they are to see him or her.

Depending on reasons for a prior loss, some families want to have a pediatrician in the delivery or birthing room to assess their baby immediately. While most parents think that they cannot get reassurance without this, the reality becomes that, when the baby is born alive and healthy, any reassurance that they need comes from the baby. They cannot know this beforehand, though, and will need support from staff in planning what is realistic for the particular hospital regarding a pediatrician's presence at the birth.

Relaxation and Visualization

Relaxation techniques for managing labor may be extremely helpful for this population, but putting the techniques into practice can be very difficult. Many parents say that they have not relaxed through the whole pregnancy. For them to relax and practice breathing techniques for labor are no easy tasks. The visualization suggested in Figure 4-15 focuses on the parents' fears and anxieties as a normal component of the pregnancy. Parents are encouraged to surrender to the process, trust what is beyond their control, and embrace their fear; this can help them to attach to their baby by relaxing into their fears and letting their baby's interaction with them lead the way.

Figure 4-15.
Visualization Script to Help Parents Relax During Birth Class

Settle back into your pillow/chair...Rest your head and body and sink into relaxation. Take a deep breath, breathing in...and out. Breathe slowly...and purposefully, as naturally as you can. Let your emotions slowly release bit by bit.

Think about the baby you are carrying now in your uterus. This baby, with each breath you take, is moving up and down, gently rocking to your breaths. This baby feels comfortable...warm...and secure...rocking with each breath, hearing your heartbeat, feeling your worries and concerns, but knowing the worry is because of the baby who was here before he/she was...the baby you loved and wanted, but whose life with you was far too short.

This baby here with you today has listened to your stories, has felt your pain, and knows your love is given cautiously, not because you don't love him/her, but because you love him/her so much. This baby feels deeply the concern and protection you have clung to during this pregnancy, to want him/her to feel safe.

Breathe in and out...visualizing this baby inside loving you and all the other voices in the family that your baby hears. This baby is waiting to come out to show you his/her own unique personality and will help you believe again that life can be good and beautiful. Continue to breathe in and out at your own comfortable rate, letting go of as much of the fear you can for this baby.

You have nurtured and cared for yourself and this baby all these long months. Now begin to allow your body to prepare for labor and birth...let go of the tension...let go of the fear. Let the contractions come when the baby is ready...start slowly and build up your strength, opening your cervix, allowing this baby to come into your life. Let the children who came before celebrate with you this new life that will begin to heal your wounds and nurture your continued journey into parenting.

Postpartum

"I was so numbed by the live birth that I wanted someone to slow everything down so I could really believe it was happening. I needed to cry for joy at this new life and for sadness at the life I didn't have."

Once the baby is born safely, new issues can surface. Parents' overwhelming joy can bring back their grief over their previous loss and their realization that a sibling is missing. Parents begin to understand what the loss of their previous child really means as they interact with this healthy baby. Some parents still may feel frozen, not believing that they actually have a live baby to keep, and they may need help in slowly touching and being with their new baby. Parents report that it is important for postpartum staff to acknowledge their previous baby. When in doubt, ask parents what they are comfortable sharing about their past loss. Most say that they want to talk about the pain of no older sibling to visit, letting them grieve again the loss of their other child. This is normal. Parents say that it helps them to move on to loving and attaching to their new baby. Sometimes, continuing to attend a support group helps parents with their transition into the postpartum period.

Any complication postpartum, even a minor one such as high bilirubin, can be very stressful for parents. They fear they will lose this baby, too. If the baby is delivered preterm and parents must leave the hospital without their new baby, that can remind them of going home without their other baby. Keep in perspective that, even after their healthy baby is born, parents may not feel safe and secure for many months, years, or ever.

When possible, before the birth discuss with parents their choice of pediatrician. Encourage parents to interview doctors to find one who will be sensitive to their previous loss and who will understand their likelihood of being fearful for the health of their new baby. Some women will not consider breast-feeding, because they do not want to bear the continued responsibility of "keeping the baby alive." Even if they choose to breast-feed, many women refuse to accept information on breast-feeding prenatally, because they are unable to believe that they ever will have a live baby to take home.

When they begin to breast-feed, most women will need a nurse to remain available to help them get started and be sensitive to their special needs. One woman changed her pediatrician 1 week postpartum because he told her that she "did not have enough milk" for her baby. She said, "I couldn't keep my first baby alive inside me, and now he was telling me I couldn't keep this baby alive with my breast milk." She found another doctor who instructed her on how to increase her volume of breast milk; she was then able to continue breast-feeding her new baby.

Facilitating a Support Group

"When I became pregnant after my loss, I joined the group. The facilitator created a safe place for us to grow as our babies grew. We related on many levels. We talked of our fears, we cried, laughed, shared, and, most of all for me, I listened and was listened to. We talked of '...when our babies come...,' and the facilitator said, 'Your babies already are here. Talk to them.' That was the day I started to let myself bond with the life inside me."

The need for support services for bereaved parents is well recognized and available at most centers providing obstetric and perinatal services. Developing a support group for subsequent pregnancy, to help parents move on to the new baby while learning how to live with loss in their family, appears to be as important as the prenatal classes most families participated in before their loss. It is not necessary to uncover, piece together, or understand the past. But, support groups help parents understand and use the past to relate to the current pregnancy (Yalom, 1985).

While accepting loss and resolving grief are a part of the group's focus, these tasks are not the only purpose. Support groups also are concerned with the family's current pregnancy and next baby. In a group that focuses on loss, parents may get "stuck" in grief over their dead baby, and they may not learn ways to move on. It may not be helpful for people to stay in pregnancy loss groups when they get pregnant again. Parents should be in a group that acknowledges the crisis of a new pregnancy and helps them work on the developmental tasks of the pregnancy (see Figure 1-15), to reassure people that their feelings are normal. These tasks are not easy, as most families embark on their next pregnancy with their grief overriding any other emotion.

The group should be participant driven and supportive, focusing on process. Their efforts should not be judged by agenda or therapeutic goals. A set agenda can rob participants of the opportunity to work on issues which remain unresolved since the last meeting. The group's orientation should not be defensive, or critical, of medical management or past care, nor should recommendations for care during the current pregnancy come from the group's facilitator. Sharing among group members about the nature of reassurance and support which they receive from care providers educates other group participants to seek needed support in their own prenatal care.

Through the group process, with educational support, parents wend their way through what seems like a long gestation. The goal is to grow comfortable with the pregnancy and reach a level of equilibrium with their fears, uncertainties, and hopes. As they help each other find solutions, individual parents' own right actions become clear. A subsequent-pregnancy support group provides a safe place for parents to voice their thoughts and concerns, to hear that their fears and feelings are normal, to be with people who share similar feelings, and to say things to each other that no one else can say to them. The group is not formal therapy, but, rather, it supports and educates people who experienced previous losses as they move through a subsequent pregnancy.

Ideally, parents should be able to join a group at any point during a pregnancy. Keep in mind that the tasks of these pregnancies do not follow a sequence. Individuals can be in very different stages of pregnancy when they join the group. Some may come for support as soon as they learn they are pregnant, while others may join the group as significant or anniversary dates approach. Some come when they realize that they need help for labor and birth, while still others may not seek support until they are home with a new baby.

People attend support group meetings to be heard, to be understood, and to problem solve. Many times, just by hearing themselves say out loud what they have been thinking, parents can problem solve better. Neither information by itself nor the passive receipt of suggestions or direction from others works as well as proactive problem solving by the person who is struggling with the issue.

Facilitators of a subsequent-pregnancy support group require the same skills as someone who coordinates a pregnancy-loss group. In either group, facilitators must respect the individuals' journeys and honor diversity within the group. The facilitator's role is to be present for others, focus on and follow parents' needs, to listen without judging, to give feedback, and to understand and let parents do their own work at their own pace. It is helpful to have parent volunteers, such as former group members with successful subsequent-pregnancy outcomes, to serve with the facilitators. Such parents represent living proof that subsequent pregnancy can work out happily, and they consistently validate to group members that they, too, will move on.

Whatever the backgrounds of facilitators, they must listen to and trust participants to process, assimilate, integrate, and deal with their own stories. It may be helpful to have at least one group facilitator who has professional training and experience in obstetric care. When asked, facilitators may be required to clarify types and purposes of various prenatal tests, discuss their implications, and explain what kinds of answers parents can expect or not expect to gain by such procedures. Participants can encourage each other to ask for what they need from health care providers without acting angry or defensive. This type of support is particularly important for parents who may believe that care providers did not listen when they voiced a concern during the previous, failed pregnancy.

When questions about a previous loss surface, group discussion can focus on specific problems which contributed to or caused the loss. Group facilitators and participants can help their fellow group members clarify actions to prevent or manage the same problem during a subsequent pregnancy. The support group empowers participants to be advocates for themselves and for their babies.

Responses of Children During Subsequent Pregnancy

Children need support during their parents' subsequent pregnancy, too. Parents naturally want to protect their children from traumatic experiences. When a child loses a sibling, it becomes painfully obvious to parents that, despite all their wishes to protect children from pain, parents cannot hide their feelings during subsequent pregnancy. While most parents want to wait to tell older children they are pregnant again, most children over the age of 2 $^1/_2$ years seem to understand anyway, by the time that their parents tell them the news. Parents report that most children over 3 years of age also worry that something may happen to this baby. These concerns are normal, especially when children interacted, even briefly, with their dead brother or sister. Some children surprise their parents by revealing a belief that the baby who died is coming back in this pregnancy. This thought is often very difficult for parents to help their children to sort out, because, at some level, parents may share this feeling too.

Like adults, older children may be afraid to grow attached to the new baby because this is *not* the same baby. One couple was shocked to realize how angry their older children became when they learned that the new baby was not the same gender as the baby who had died. Their children had expected another baby brother and did not want a sister. They grieved the loss of their sibling again. Only then could they begin to attach to their new sister.

Parents should explore their children's thoughts. It is helpful for parents to realize that children at a very young age can sense emotions and feelings going on in their homes. Children may not understand what is happening, but they need help to find words to express their feelings. Without explanation and support, children may believe that they did something wrong, that somehow they were responsible for their sibling's death. Encourage parents to be as honest as they can about their own feelings and to maintain an open dialogue with their children about the current pregnancy. Parents' honesty about their own feelings can promote exploration with their children of these sensitive issues about the pregnancy. Children sometimes innocently articulate things more clearly than do their parents; and they need to be included in family discussions. Let the child lead. They know and share their parents' grief and can help in the whole family's healing process.

Many children will not or cannot verbalize specific fears, both for the baby and for their mother's health. Many children are afraid to return to the hospital again or, indeed, to visit any hospital, because the last visit may have been when the baby died. It is helpful for children to be given a tour of the hospital, geared toward their level of understanding. Usually, everyone in the family is afraid until the baby is born healthy.

Parents must know that even though they feel anxious and afraid, they still can support their children. Encourage parents to reach out to peers who can help them to process what they should explain to children. Suggest that parents inform their pediatrician and their children's teachers about this family crisis. Resources such as a parent-infant specialist, child-life specialist, or social worker who can help with sibling issues are good referrals for families.

Conclusion

Health care professionals should be aware that a previous perinatal loss can have powerful effects on subsequent pregnancy. Do not assume that, because there has been a healthy birth between the loss and the current pregnancy, parents are not struggling with overwhelming feelings and difficult issues. With this awareness comes a different perception of the "quiet," the "difficult," or the "overanxious" woman or her partner. There are good reasons why people with previous pregnancy loss respond the way they do during a subsequent pregnancy. Care providers should be particularly non-judgmental, patient, and empathic with these struggling families. Remember that the best medical recommendations are just that — suggested courses of action. Parents with unique experiences, skills, and feelings are the ones who must live it out. Parents alone must live their lifetimes with the consequences of their decisions. So, it is important that their choices best reflect their own personal, joint process. Better than most expectant parents, those who have suffered a devastating pregnancy loss know that the real truth is, our children are mortal.❏

Case Study 1-15

Multiple Pregnancy Losses

  Ms. Smith is a G5, P2022, married woman. Her first pregnancy ended at 12 weeks gestation, 2 days after she moved to a new city. Her second pregnancy resulted in the birth of her son, after an uncomplicated pregnancy, labor, and birth. Her third pregnancy was complicated by slow fetal growth. She started weekly antenatal testing at 31 weeks. A healthy girl was born at 37 weeks gestation. Although this pregnancy was more "high risk" than was her second pregnancy, Ms. Smith trusted that her baby was healthy and she did not wish for help with any emotional needs related to her previous pregnancy loss. She did ask for suggestions on sibling adjustment for her son, however. Her fourth pregnancy ended in a loss at 12 weeks gestation.

  During her fifth pregnancy, Ms. Smith self-referred to the "Pregnancy After Loss" weekly support group. She had heard about the group during her third pregnancy and again during her first clinic visit with her current pregnancy. She was 9 weeks pregnant, and her children now were 2 and 4 years old. She never had told her children about her pregnancy losses. Ms. Smith attended the group each week, until she reached 32 weeks gestation. She wept through most of the sessions, grieving her losses, especially the loss of her first baby (the first miscarriage). She described her grief as "filling the room," preventing her from feeling joy over this new baby. She spoke of missing her old home, feeling like a stranger in this new city, not knowing where to turn when her baby died. She also grieved that her family did not understand why this loss was so difficult for her and why she was so nervous in this new pregnancy. She shared that her family and friends did not understand her nervousness. She could not understand why they made such insensitive remarks about her being so sad, tense, and weepy in this pregnancy.

  During her fourth pregnancy, Ms. Smith had bought a teddy bear for the baby she expected to have. Then, sadly, she miscarried. The facilitator suggested that she might choose to display that teddy bear in her home as a symbol of that baby. One week later, Ms. Smith came to the group meeting and shared a dream: "In my dream, I woke up holding the teddy bear. It felt warm and comfortable, even though I was aware that it was not my baby. I fell asleep and dreamt it again. I had been unable to touch the closet door where the teddy bear was stored. Finally, I got the bear down from the closet. Then, a few days after the dream, I thought, 'I will use the bear later to tell John (almost 4) about the baby who died.'" Later, as planned, Ms. Smith sat down with her son, with the teddy bear, and explained that she had bought the teddy bear for a baby who had died. She also explained that soon there would be a new baby. The family then gave a name to the previous baby. In the group meeting, Ms. Smith began to talk about someday getting a bear for her first baby (about whom she had not yet told her children). Throughout her time participating in the group, Ms. Smith struggled with wanting to attach to the baby she was carrying, but she could not, because she was afraid that this baby would die, too.

The last time that Ms. Smith came to the group was at 32 weeks gestation. She said, "When I started the group, my grief filled the whole room. My pain was overriding the joy of this pregnancy. Now, my grief has a place in the room, it doesn't fill the whole room. The group has been a safe place to talk about my grief while I am pregnant with this baby. I thought I had to get things 'settled' before this baby came. Now, I can accept that the grief is there, and it's not so insurmountable. I've reached a balance — a harmony — and it doesn't matter if people can identify or not anymore. I totally own the grief, and I don't need to get validation from my family and friends." (She got it within the group instead.)

For this pregnancy, Ms. Smith wrote a birth plan, explaining to the nursing staff that she expected to be very emotional because of her two previous losses, and talking about her belief that this might be her last baby, last labor, and last birth experience. She was very weepy throughout her labor, and her nurse stayed close by her side, talking about her other babies with her and about how it was all right to be thinking about them, too. The nurse encouraged Ms. Smith to focus on this baby as healthy and ready to come out to meet her and her husband. Ms. Smith verbalized afterward that her nurse kept reassuring her that she would be safe.

Nine months later, Ms. Smith called the parent-infant specialist to say that she was thinking about all the times when she had come to the group, and that now she could visualize her losses as part of the "landscape of my life." Finally, she felt "normal;" she now realized that she had been depressed all those months and that she was coming out of her depression now. She shared that her children had met another boy whose mother had cried when she saw their new baby brother. This mother shared her story about her baby who had just died. Ms. Smith's son, John, asked why this mother cried. Ms. Smith told him about that family's baby who had died, and then she said, "John, I never told you before, but we had another baby die before you were born." John was quiet for a minute and then he said, "Mommy, we need to give that baby a name, too." After all those years, Ms. Smith believed that she finally had found a place for all her losses, and her family was complete.

Commentary

The initial prenatal visit is the beginning of a relationship between care-givers and patient. As a nurse in a high-risk pregnancy clinic, I began this rela-tionship with Ms. Smith by focusing on her needs, both physical and emo-tional. The most important aspect of this visit was her history and the mean-ing which she assigned to her history. Ms. Smith had two losses, each at 12 weeks. I asked about each pregnancy separately. How did she deal with her first pregnancy? Her initial response was unemotional, rather factual.

"I know it's not uncommon to have a miscarriage with the first preg-nancy. I did, and I did fine. But, I had just moved away from my hometown to this area with my husband. I was away from my twin sister for the first time, so that seemed to be the hardest thing at the time. My second preg-nancy went well and was a celebration. In my third pregnancy, my daughter's growth was a little slow, but she was active, and the testing always was reas-suring. Then, in my fourth pregnancy, I miscarried at 12 weeks again. It took me by surprise. I cried and cried. I wondered why it hit so hard, then I real-ized that I never had cried about my first loss."

Ms. Smith initially discounted her feelings because of the commonness of first-trimester miscarriages. Instead, she focused her feeling of grief on the loss of her twin sister's companionship when she moved, assuming that this was the reason for all of her pain. She did not voice her concern about her previous loss in her second or third pregnancy. It was not until she miscar-ried in her fourth pregnancy that Ms. Smith's painful feelings resurfaced, and she recognized that she needed to grieve the loss of her first pregnancy.

I asked Ms. Smith what her greatest concern was for this, her fifth preg-nancy. Miscarrying again was her quick response. I explored with her what she thought would help her to cope with her fear. Seeing the ultrasound image of the baby was reassuring, along with hearing the heartbeat. These unmistakable signs of the "realness" of a live baby allow the baby him or her-self to draw parents into a reciprocal relationship that assists parents in the normal tasks of pregnancy. I often say, "Let's listen to your baby." With that reassuring heartbeat as "background music," we will talk about any other concerns.

If a woman is worried about loss, the gestational age at the time of loss can be a milestone. More frequent visits for reassurance may be needed. If a loss occurred around an event or holiday, that may require special attention also. It is important to remember, however, that she will feel vulnerable throughout her pregnancy. Many couples report hoping to experience a decrease in their worries and anxieties after getting past an anniversary. Most were disappointed, however, that they continued to worry about losing again and, in fact, were surprised at how vulnerable life felt now. This is an issue that often is brought up in support group meetings.

During the initial prenatal visit, all of the services and opportunities which are available through our perinatal practice are discussed. We try to help the woman and her partner to identify their need for additional support as normal and reasonable, given their history. Having a parent volunteer who has been through the program participate in a group meeting can help the couple to get past the barrier that recognizing their needs and feelings does not mean that they are doing a bad job or that they are "sick." Sometimes, the woman may voice a concern about her husband's ability to cope with another potential loss, or that one of her other children is having trouble with the mother's pregnancy. This type of concern usually comes out before the woman can voice her own concerns. When a patient identifies her own need for support, the caregiver again can recommend the support group as a way of meeting those needs.

Various stages of pregnancy present an opportunity for observing "normal" physical and emotional changes. Generally speaking, a patient wants as much information as possible in the first 12 weeks of her pregnancy. When a patient declines reading material, doesn't want to hear the heartbeat, does not want to see the ultrasound, or repeatedly forgets to take home the ultrasound photographs from our office, this may be an indication of variances from "normal" behavior. Comments regarding fears of impending labor, a change in her own condition, or concern for the baby are reasons to ask a patient for more information, to elicit if possible what the woman's real concern may be.

The perinatal clinic nurse is in a strategic position to help families identify their need for support during their pregnancy, along with giving much-needed reassurance of this baby's progress. Parents must be reassured that this is a different baby, and this can spur them on through the task of developing an emotional affiliation with their new baby, clearly differentiated from their child who died.

— *Susan Doerr, RN*

Case Study 2-15

Loss in Multifetal Pregnancy

In the last few years, with advancements in reproductive technologies, another type of pregnancy loss has become recognized, associated with spontaneous death of one or more fetuses in a multiple gestation. Recognition of this type of pregnancy loss has led to a procedure, elective multifetal reduction, in which yet another type of pregnancy loss is inextricably embedded. For women with longstanding infertility, the same spectacular techniques which can make pregnancy possible, such as *in-vitro* fertilization (IVF) or gamete intrafallopian transfer (GIFT), also are responsible for a marked increase in triplet, quadruplet, and even quintuplet pregnancies. The spontaneous death of one or more fetuses in a multiple gestation may be as high as 30% (Seoud, Toner, Kruithoff, & Muasher, 1992). Moreover, there is a high preterm delivery rate for these multiple gestations, at gestational ages which are too early for the babies to survive. This latter concern has led to the development of techniques to reduce the number of living fetuses. During the first trimester, fetal reduction is carried out by performing amniocenteses and then injecting a cardiotoxic agent into one or more of the fetuses. By limiting the number of live fetuses to only two or three, instead of four or more, the risks of premature delivery are reduced, and the chances of delivering healthy babies at or close to term are increased markedly.

When complications arise in a multiple pregnancy, parents are faced with extremely difficult decisions, as the fates of these babies usually are linked (Malone, Craigo, Chelmow, & D'Alton, 1996). Families who either have had a spontaneous loss or have made painful decisions to terminate one or more of the babies face the same issues. Thus, they progress through pregnancy grieving over one or more babies who have died as they struggle to attach to the remaining babies. Some researchers have found that parents who elect multifetal pregnancy reduction experience many of the feelings that others have in response to pregnancy loss (Porreco, Shannon Burke, & Hendrix, 1991). Another group reported that, whereas women's immediate reactions are intense, the long-term response is one of comfort with the procedure which preserved the pregnancy and resulted in the birth of a healthy child (Schreiner-Engel, Walther, Mindes, Lynch, & Berkowitz, 1994). In their 1996 evaluation of 91 women who elected to undergo multifetal pregnancy reduction, Berkowitz and co-workers reported that 65% experienced stress and fear during the procedure but only 17% reported lingering feelings of guilt, sadness, or anger, and 93% said that, given the same circumstances, they would elect again to have the procedure (Berkowitz, Lynch, Stone, & Alvarez, 1996). It seems, then, that some families adjust quickly, while others may move on, not wanting to think of the early loss, and a third group needs much help and support in coming to resolution for what the loss means in their family.

The following case is one woman's story, which is representative of the stories of other parents who have experienced pregnancy loss due to spontaneous or elective multifetal reduction.

Liz was a 35-year-old G2 P1001. Her first pregnancy was complicated by preterm labor. She required medication to halt contractions and 8 weeks of bedrest. She succeeded in this high-risk pregnancy and gave birth to a healthy daughter, now almost 4 years old. In her second pregnancy, Liz came for help at 16 weeks gestation. This was a twin pregnancy, and one of the babies, a girl, had just died at 15 weeks. The other baby, a boy, was still alive and apparently healthy. At the first meeting, Liz was very emotional, and she was struggling with a confused mixture of feelings. Her dilemma was how to continue with the pregnancy and to be happy for her son, while she was in so much pain and grief over the loss of her daughter. How does one attach and grieve at the same time? Liz also did not know what she should tell her daughter or how she and her husband could cope.

Liz was encouraged to discuss with her husband how to tell their daughter about the loss of the twin girl. She expected that she would continue to have intense sadness during the rest of her pregnancy and their young daughter needed to have an explanation. The couple discussed it, and they agreed that they would tell her as much as they felt that she could understand, letting her lead with questions. The opportunity to tell the daughter about the loss happened one day when Liz was crying and her daughter asked her why. She explained that she had been pregnant with two babies, but that one of them, a little girl, had died, and this made her very sad. Liz's daughter then was free to talk with her parents during the rest of the pregnancy about the baby boy who was coming, and she understood that his twin sister had died and would not be coming home. The child occasionally would talk with her mother about how sad she was that there were not going to be two babies, and Liz would acknowledge her own sad feelings about it, too. This helped the family to address the reality of the pregnancy and not to pretend that it was a singleton pregnancy, to deny their grief. Grief over the loss was part of who the family was now, and that was not going to change, even with the healthy baby boy still coming.

Liz joined the weekly support group. She found it a safe place to focus on the loss of her daughter, who still existed physically inside of her, while she continued to prepare for the birth of her son. She learned that it was okay still to look at her daughter when she had ultrasounds done. She learned how to talk to her unborn son about her sadness over his twin sister, and about her desire for him to continue to grow and be born. She attended until she was put on bedrest at 28 weeks. Support then was continued by telephone from a parent volunteer and a parent-infant specialist. She and her husband attended the special birth class and they prepared a birth plan for both babies. Liz wanted to be able to "see" her daughter who had died, to help her to acknowledge that it had been a twin pregnancy. She was encouraged to include her wishes for her daughter in the birth plan, because experience with other families affected by prenatal twin demise suggests that it is appropriate to reflect the pregnancy loss in the birth plan.

When Liz went into labor, at another local hospital, both her physicians and her nurses told Liz that probably only one baby would be delivered. Liz was insistent that she would have two babies, however. She told her care providers that she wanted to see and hold both of her babies. The son was born; then his twin was delivered soon afterward — a deceased fetus who was small but who obviously was a baby.

Liz's husband had tried to put the loss out of his mind after the twin's demise at 15 weeks. His method of coping had been to refuse to talk about the baby girl, and to try to get Liz to focus just on the baby boy who was coming. He also told her while she was in labor that she should be prepared to see only one baby. He therefore was unprepared for the appearance of the second twin, and seeing and holding his daughter was the concrete reality for him that this indeed had been a twin pregnancy. He finally was able to grieve the loss of his daughter, as Liz had been doing throughout the pregnancy.

Their minister came and baptized the little girl, who was held by the father, while Liz held her son. Even after all of this, when the hospital staff brought the birth certificate to be signed, Liz had to send it back, because it stated that her son was a singleton pregnancy. Liz was adamant that they record the pregnancy accurately as a twin pregnancy. Also, Liz telephoned the ultrasound sonographer and requested photographs which had been taken during her early ultrasounds. She said, "I needed pictures of my twins." Unfortunately, Liz had to call two times before this request was granted.

Liz continued to participate in the Pregnancy After Loss program into her postpartum period. She also joined another support group called "Bittersweet" for families who have experienced the loss of one or more babies in a multiple pregnancy. Liz said, "I thought, 'Just get him here safely and everything will be all right.' But it wasn't. I thought the pain would go away. It didn't." Liz described feeling that, the more that she fell in love with her son, the deeper her grief for her little girl became. Her happiness about her son's new life made her daughter's death seem all the more real. The family's birth announcement for their son included an additional memorial announcement about his twin sister, reflecting her death *in utero*. Her older daughter casually tells people, "He was a twin. We are supposed to have a girl, too."

Commentary

Liz was a mother who was caught up in a confusing mix of feelings. She needed to grieve the loss of her twin daughter, experiencing the depth of pain which the death of a child brings, while at the same time she was experiencing the "pull" to parent the son whom she still carried. Liz asked a good question, "How does one grieve and attach at the same time?" She wondered if she would have to put off one to attend to the other, so that she would not be too paralyzed to do either.

The loss literature indicates that parents cannot do this work simultaneously, although more research must be conducted about this issue. Liz seems to have demonstrated that the processes overlap, with one taking priority over the other at any given moment. When Liz talked to her unborn son about her sadness over the loss of his twin sister, she was showing us the complexity of her tasks as well as the creativity of her parental response.

Often, people intuitively know what they want and need to do. It is our job to help them to listen to themselves and to provide emotionally safe times and settings for them to do their work. For Liz, as with many of these families, a weekly support group provided just such a place. Listening to other families puts people in touch with what is possible along with the normal range of feelings.

Liz's husband's responses raise the issue of asynchrony within a couple's relationship when they are grieving. While Liz was grieving actively, her husband postponed his grief and focused on the living unborn twin. One can speculate that his loss was different than Liz's, because he had not yet experienced the physical reality of his daughter (in contrast with Liz, who had the physical sensations of pregnancy). Indeed, he felt the full weight of his grief feelings when the baby girl was delivered, when he could hold her in his arms and could identify her as separate from her twin brother, and when he had the opportunity to say goodbye.

Although Liz and her husband handled the differences of their grieving processes well, some couples inevitably will experience this dissonance as conflict, and it will stress their relationship. In group meetings, it can be useful to point out the variety in normal grief responses and the importance of allowing each person to follow his or her own unique journey through grief. There is no one right way to get through this type of pregnancy. Some couples also may benefit from seeing a counselor who is sensitive to these issues.

Another major task which Liz faced was whether or not to tell her 3-year-old daughter about the death of one of the twins. The parent-infant specialist wisely encouraged Liz to decide this issue with her husband, so that they could present a united front to their daughter's reaction and questions. Their daughter needed the support of both parents to cope. Being age appropriate is important in helping children to understand concepts of death and birth. Allowing her to lead with questions helped Liz and her husband to identify the extent of the information which they would share with their young child. The reality of seeing her mother cry provided an ideal situation in which Liz and her husband could convey the sad news to the little girl. Many parents worry about upsetting their child. But, the reality is that sad things are sad. Liz's crying and feeling "down" was appropriate, in response to the sad death of one of her twins. Even young children can understand this, and they can cope with a parent's sadness when there is acceptance and support. This gave the daughter permission to ask questions as she was ready, and to experience her own feelings about the lost baby sister.

A special childbirth preparation class and birth planning helped Liz to identify her needs at the time of birth. Her plan reflected the need to separate the babies. It also helped Liz to make sense of the "craziness" of her emotions, because she was feeling deep sadness at the same time that she was feeling relief that one baby was born alive. For Liz's husband, this time spent after delivery with both babies was especially important, in that it allowed him to experience his buried grief, so that it would not emerge later as unhealthy anger or in an over-controlling attitude toward his son.

The differences in outcomes for babies of a multiple pregnancy with demise of one or more of the fetuses is a difficult and stressful experience for families. Each member of a family will have a unique reaction to this event.

It takes many types of support and individually designed care plans to meet the needs of the family in these circumstances of pregnancy loss.
— *Lynnda Parker, BSN, RN*

Case Study References

Berkowitz, R.L., Lynch, L., Stone, J., & Alvarez, M. (1996). The current status of multifetal pregnancy reduction. *American Journal of Obstetrics and Gynecology, 174,* 1265-1272.

Malone, F.D., Craigo, S.D., Chelmow, D., & D'Alton, M.E. (1996). Outcome of twin gestation complicated by a single abnormal fetus. *Obstetrics and Gynecology, 88,* 1-5.

Porreco, R.P., Shannon Burke, M., & Hendrix, M. (1991). Multifetal reduction of triplets and pregnancy outcome. *Obstetrics and Gynecology, 78,* 335-339.

Seoud, M.A.F., Toner, J.P., Kruithoff, C., & Muasher, S.I. (1992). Outcome of twin, triplet, and quadruplet *in-vitro* fertilization pregnancies: The Norfolk experience. *Fertility and Sterility, 57,* 825-834.

Schreiner-Engel, P., Walther, V.N., Mindes, J., Lynch, L., & Berkowitz, R.L. (1994). First-trimester multifetal pregnancy reduction: Acute and persistent psychologic reactions. *American Journal of Obstetrics and Gynecology, 172,* 541-547.

References

Chamberlain, D. (1994). How pre- and perinatal psychology can transform the world. *Pre- and Perinatal Psychology Journal, 8*(3), 187-199.

Davis, D.L., Stewart, M., & Harmon, R.J. (1989). Postponing pregnancy after perinatal death: Perspectives on doctors advice. *Journal of Child and Adolescent Psychiatry, 28,* 481-487.

Findeisen, B. (1993). Pre- and perinatal losses. *Pre- and Perinatal Psychology Journal, 8*(1), 65-77.

Furman, E.P. (1978). Death of a newborn: Care of the parents. *Birth and the Family Journal, 5,* 214-218.

Goldenberg, R.L., Mayberry, S.K., Copper, R.L., Dubard, M.B., & Hauth, J.C. (1993). Pregnancy outcome following a second-trimester loss. *Obstetrics & Gynecology, 81*(3), 444-446.

Hamilton, S.M. (1989). Should follow-up be provided after miscarriage? *British Journal of Obstetrics and Gynaecology, 96,* 743-745.

Kolker, A., & Burke, B.M. (1993). Grieving the wanted child: Ramifications of abortion after prenatal diagnosis of abnormality. *Health Care for Women International, 14*(6), 513-526.

Kowalski, K. (1991). No happy ending: Pregnancy loss and bereavement. *NAACOG's Clinical Issues In Perinatal and Women's Health Nursing, 2*(3), 368-380.

Leon, I. (1992). The psychoanalytic conceptualization of perinatal losses: A multidimensional model. *American Journal of Psychiatry, 149*(11), 1464-1472.

Lewis, E. (1979). Inhibition of mourning by pregnancy: Psychopathology and management. *British Medical Journal, 2,* 260-277.

Lindahl, J. (1994). *Pregnancy following perinatal loss: The effect of structured intervention* on maternal grief, attachment and parenting. Unpublished master's thesis, University of Minnesota, Minneapolis.

Malone, T., Craigo, S., Chelmow, D., & D'Alton, M. (1996). Outcome of twin gestations complicated by a single anomalous fetus. *Obstetrics & Gynecology, 88*(1), 1-5.

Nichols, M.(1993). Paternal perspectives of the childbirth experience. *Maternal-Child Nursing Journal, 21*(3), 99-108.

O'Leary, J., & Thorwick, C. (1993). Parenting during pregnancy: The infant as the vehicle for intervention in high-risk pregnancy. *International Journal of Prenatal and Perinatal Psychology and Medicine, 5*(3), 303-310.

O'Leary, J., Thorwick, C., Lindahl, J., & Knox, E. (1995, September). *After loss: The developmental tasks of parenting in the next pregnancy.* Paper presented at annual meeting of the Reproductive Medicine and Infant Psychology Association, Leicester, England.

O'Leary, J., & Thorwick, C. (1994, September). *Parenting during pregnancy and beyond: An intervention program for families in high-risk pregnancies.* Poster session presented at the annual meeting of the Reproductive Medicine and Infant Psychology Association, Dublin, Ireland.

Parker, L., & O'Leary, J.M. (1989). Impact of prior prenatal loss upon subsequent pregnancy: The function of the childbirth class. *International Journal of Childbirth Educators, 4*(3),7-9.

Peterson, G. (1994). Chains of grief: The impact of perinatal loss on subsequent pregnancy. *Pre- and Perinatal Psychology Journal, 9*(2), 149-158.

Phipps, S. (1985). The subsequent pregnancy after stillbirth: Anticipatory parenthood in the face of uncertainty. *International Journal of Psychiatry in Medicine, 15*(3), 243-263.

Porreco, R., Harmon, R., Murrow, N., Schultz, L., & Hendrix, M. (1995). Parental choices in grand multiple gestation: Psychological considerations. *The Journal of Maternal-Fetal Medicine, 4*, 111-114.

Rubin, R. (1975). Maternal tasks in pregnancy. *Maternal Child Nursing, 4*, 143-153.

Schreiner-Engel, P., Walther, V., Mindes, J., Lynch, L., & Berkowitz, R. (1994). First trimester multifetal pregnancy reduction: Acute and persistent psychologic reactions. *American Journal of Obstetrics and Gynecology, 172*(2), 541-547.

Statham, H., & Green, J. (1994). The effects of miscarriage and other "unsuccessful" pregnancy loss. *Journal of Reproductive and Infant Psychology, 12*, 45-54.

Theut, M.D., Pedersen, F.A., Zaslow, M.J., & Rabinovich, B.A. (1988). *Pregnancy subsequent to perinatal loss: Parental anxiety and depression.* Paper presented at the annual meeting of the American Academy of Child and Adolescent Psychiatry, Washington, DC.

Theut, S., Moss, H., Zaslow, M.J., Rabinovich, B.A., Levin, L., & Bartko, J. (1992). Perinatal loss and maternal attitudes toward the subsequent child. *Infant Mental Health Journal, 13*(2), 157-166.

Thorwick, C., Foslien, J., & Kalb, K. (1990). *My baby's activity level* [Pamphlet]. Minneapolis, MN: Abbott Northwestern Hospital, Parent Education Department.

Todd, L. (1996). After loss: Journey of the next pregnancy [Video Review]. *Birth, 23*(1), 54-55.

Verny, T.R. (1994). Working with pre- and perinatal material in psychotherapy. *Pre- and Perinatal Psychology Journal, 8*(3), 161-186.

Wilson, A.L., Soule, D.J., & Fenton, L.J. (1988). The next baby: Parents' responses to perinatal experiences subsequent to a stillbirth. *Journal of Perinatology, 8*(3), 188-192.

Yalom, I. (1985). *The theory and practice of group psychotherapy* (3rd ed.). New York: Basic Books.

Zeanah, C.H. (1989). Adaption following perinatal loss: A critical review. *Journal of the Academy of Child and Adolescent Psychiatry, 28*, 467-480.

Zeanah, C.H., & Harmon, R. (1995). Perinatal loss and infant mental health: An introduction. *Infant Mental Health Journal, 16*(2), 76-79.

Suggested Resources

Davis, D.L. (1996). *Empty cradle, broken heart: Surviving the death of your baby* (rev. ed.). Golden, CO: Fulcrum Publishing.

Isle, S., & Doerr, M. (1996). *Another baby? Maybe....Thirty of the most frequently asked subsequent pregnancy questions.* Winter Green Press, 360 Eileen St., Maple Plain, MN 55359; (612) 476-1303.

O'Leary, J.M., & Thorwick, C. [Script writers] (1995). *After loss: The journey of the next pregnancy.* [Video]. Abbott Northwestern Hospital, Parent Education Department, 800 East 28th St. Minneapolis, MN 55497; (612) 863-5964.

Pregnancy after loss. (1991). [Booklet written by parents in a subsequent pregnancy]. Abbott Northwestern Hospital, Parent Education Department, 800 East 28th St., Minneapolis, MN 55497; (612) 863-5964.

Schwibert, P., & Kirk, P. (1993). *Still to be born.* Perinatal Loss, 2116 NE 18th Ave. Portland, OR 97212; (503) 284-7426.

Perinatal Loss. (1987). *Still to be born.* [Video]. 2116 NE 18th Ave. Portland, OR 97212; (503) 284-7426.

Chapter 16

Saying Goodbye: The Funeral Director's Role

Ronald E. Troyer

When a death occurs in our society, a funeral director usually is selected by the family to assist in final disposition of the body. For a family experiencing a fetal or newborn death, the funeral director's involvement can have a powerful impact on the family's (especially the parents') ability to resolve and adjust to the loss. It is the purpose of this chapter to discuss positive ways in which funeral directors can assist mothers and fathers in dealing with the nightmare of burying their baby. Much of this book stands as recognition that there are a number of professional and nonprofessional care providers in the community who can assist bereaved parents in a meaningful way. The funeral director is an intregal participant in this team approach.

The Funeral: Definition and Purpose

Lamers (1969) defines the funeral as "...an organized, purposeful, time-limited, flexible, group-centered response to death." For the parents of a dead baby, the funeral is an opportunity to express their deep feelings of loss in a socially significant manner (Davis, 1991). Through the funeral ceremony, parents become the center of attention for social support, and the extension of sympathy tends to give rise to a sense of comfort and social acceptability (Pine, 1974). In addition, the funeral ceremony and setting provide a time for parents, grandparents, family, and close friends to publicly express feelings which are generally not acceptable in most everyday settings. For example, parents may appear disheveled and forlorn much of the time. Statements made by well-meaning friends may evoke emotional responses of crying and tears. These same statements, if made in another setting (for example, the grocery store) would be upsetting and not socially or emotionally acceptable.

The funeral gives parents the means to set aside the general societal perception of and response to a baby's death as a "nonevent" (Bowlby, 1980). It also recognizes a *person* (the baby) as having lived and shared in a love relationship, in contrast with the general societal perception of a dead infant as a "nonperson" (Lewis, 1976). The sudden unexpected death of a baby is often perceived as unfair and unjust, and it may be denied or resented by the parents. Such a death can be termed a "high grief" loss (Fulton, 1977). Societal and emotional needs of family, friends, and community in such instances are greater, and the potential problems of parents more extensive than for a "low-grief" loss. (A low-grief loss for some would be the death of an elderly relative. Little notice to the death would be given, and duration and intensity of grief experienced would be minimal.) Focusing our attention on the death (event) and the baby's life (person) through a funeral ceremony now is recognized as therapeutic and helpful in most cases (Peppers & Knapp, 1980).

The value for surviving family members of having a funeral ceremony for their baby has been documented and discussed by physicians for nearly 30 years. Grunebaum (1968) writes of a young mother whose baby died during delivery. The mother was helpless during the delivery, not allowed to see the baby after delivery, and encouraged to sign an autopsy and burial permit for a mass grave. Eventually, this woman sought psychiatric help, and Grunebaum questions what positive effect seeing her baby and participating in the funeral would have had on her grieving process.

Funeral Director Education and Awareness of Counselor's Role

In the early 1970s, there was growing awareness within the funeral service profession of the special needs and considerations surrounding an infant's death. Numerous articles appeared in funeral service journals on neonatal deaths and the parents' need to participate actively in their baby's funeral service. Many funeral directors became aware of their role as facilitators, as opposed to the role of functionaries which they traditionally had performed for many years (Nichols, 1975). In the middle 1970s, the American Board of Funeral Service Education (the accreditation agency for all mortuary science colleges) mandated that a social science curriculum be taught in all accredited schools. This curriculum includes material on infant death. Licensed funeral directors, through continuing education programs, also were learning of the growing body of knowledge on pregnancy loss. Dr. D. Gary Benfield, a neonatologist, presented a program to Ohio funeral directors in 1980, "Caring for Bereaved Parents: The Intersection of Funeral Service and Newborn Medicine."

National and state funeral director associations have strived to provide programming, printed, and audio-visual material on this subject.

Not all funeral directors practice the methods and procedures found in this chapter but, fortunately, many do. The latter are enlightened and progressive funeral directors who recognize their role and appreciate the opportunity to share this prominent moment in parents' lives. Funeral directors are constantly involved with crisis situations and crisis counseling (Snow, 1984). Most funeral directors agree with Dr. Edgar Jackson, a pastoral psychologist, who says, "Funeral directors do not choose whether or not they will be counselors. Their only choice is will they be a good or bad counselors?" (Raether & Slater, 1975, p. 1).

The crisis created by pregnancy loss occurs not only for married women but also for young unmarried women and, more and more, for older, single women who want children but who also want to remain unmarried. These less conventional situations require a sensitive and compassionate counselor. Often it is the funeral director who finds himself or herself serving in this role by default.

Notification of the Baby's Death

The initial notification of a baby's death to the funeral home usually is made within the first 8 hours following the delivery or death. The call may come from the father, grandparents, other family members, hospital chaplain, family clergy, or hospital employees (for example, social worker, nurse, admitting clerk). The point is that the funeral home sometimes receives a death call from persons not closely affected by the death. Thus, the funeral director frequently is caught in the middle by "helpful persons" who often are attempting to be protective, certain that they know what is "best" for the bereaved mother. This initial notification almost always comes before the woman has been discharged from the hospital. The mother's health is of primary concern to the immediate family. They think that they are doing the right thing by making the call to the funeral home, believing final disposition of the baby must take place before the woman is released from the hospital. A common misconception is that final disposition must be made within 24 to 48 hours following death.

This misconception and others are good reasons why the funeral director should try to meet with the father or grandparents as soon as possible following the telephone notification. There is a need to sit down and discuss facts before the misconceptions and feelings of protection isolate the mother completely from the funeral process.

The funeral director should explain that, although there is a time frame in which the funeral should take place, there is no rush. It is possible — and highly desirable — to wait until the mother can be part of the arrangements conference. The mother's participation and presence in the funeral process should be encouraged as positive means of helping her to cope with the feelings of loss. The author often says, "We cannot take away your pain, but we can share it. We cannot prevent your suffering, but we can prevent you from suffering for the wrong reasons." Describing the possibility of a mother's experiencing a "second layer of grief" because of her exclusion from the funeral process is a useful means of demonstrating how important the funeral process is for both the mother and father (Benfield & Nichols, 1980).

Some professionals feel that advising the family in this manner is too directive. However, this approach is *meant* to be directive. There is a wealth of information on pregnancy loss available now which indicates that an initial nondirective approach by a health care or other professional can later cause serious and unnecessary problems for the family. The author's personal experience with fathers and other family members is that they often need directive counseling to understand the mother's needs and desires.

The booklets *When Hello Means Goodbye* (Schwiebert & Kirk, 1985) and *Planning a Precious Goodbye* (Ilse & Erling, 1989) are helpful resources to give to parents during the initial meeting. These well-written guides, for parents whose baby dies at birth or shortly after, are sensitive and informative. They are brief enough so that families may read through them quickly and gather information that reinforces the counseling of the funeral director, physician, nurse, or clergy. All persons who have contact with women experiencing pregnancy loss are encouraged to read these booklets.

Arrangements Conference

The funeral director should schedule a time when the parents can meet with him or her to plan the funeral service and final disposition. The importance of this meeting is underscored by LaMore (1985), who describes the making of arrangements as "the superbly therapeutic first social, economic, and religious decisions one has to make to acknowledge the loss and initiate a new beginning." Often, because of the mother's confinement in the hospital, the arrangements conference occurs in the hospital. Ideally, then, this meeting should take place privately in a small, comfortable room. If the family wants to wait until the mother is discharged, the conference can be held in the family's home or at the funeral home.

The place, time, and officiant of the service are discussed. Information for the death certificate and the obituary is obtained. Beyond these rather routine procedures for a funeral director, the conference should lead to a thorough discussion of choices which the parents have in planning their baby's service (Lamb, 1989). Parents should be told that they can take pictures if they so desire. These personal photographs supplement the ones taken at the hospital and later can be very important as the parents' way of remembering their baby. The funeral director can offer to obtain a lock of the baby's hair or make a set of footprints, if this was not done at the hospital. Parents are informed of their right to dress and hold their baby. Dressing and holding the baby are acts of parenting that are meaningful for some mothers and fathers. Not all parents will choose to do this; but all should be given such a choice, with time to think about their decision. It seems that mothers are more likely to want to hold the baby than fathers. However, experience has shown that fathers will help place the baby in the casket, if offered the opportunity.

Additional decisions on appropriate floral tributes, memorial folders, and music selections are made. Use of poetry, prose, or family's written statements or letters during the service is discussed and often encouraged. The funeral director should mention that personal items, such as toys, pictures, letters, or religious items may be placed in the baby's casket.

Decisions on final disposition of the body are made. If burial is chosen, usually there is discussion on where in the cemetery is best for the family — in a " baby land" section or in a family plot, or sometimes in a grave already occupied by a family member. For those families who choose cremation, it is necessary to decide what they will do with the cremated remains. Often, it is best for parents to wait a few weeks before acting on a decision to scatter the cremated remains; personal experience shows that parents frequently regret this decision, since there is no final resting place for them to visit. Some cemeteries will allow family members to personally dig the grave for their baby's casket or urn. Some fathers may be more apt to do this, and it can be an important act for some, if they are given the choice. Many fathers want to carry their baby's casket to the grave, if offered that opportunity.

The arrangements conference is a time to let parents know about the variety of ways in which they can participate in their baby's funeral and burial. Some will do a lot and some will do little, but they all should be given the choice to act in a parenting role as they see fit.

Selecting a Casket, Vault, or Urn

During the arrangements conference, the family and the funeral director discuss the selection of a casket and related items. Most families are given several choices of caskets, made of different materials. The parents usually decide which is best for them after considering design, material, and cost.

Funeral directors who have spoken with (and listened to) parents sometime after the completed service have learned there are several important issues for parents concerning their baby's casket. These issues are discussed over and over in parents' support groups. One issue is the type of material used to make the casket. For a number of years, funeral directors have offered a casket and vault combination. It is made of a polyurethane material, usually white and lightweight. It is a highly durable and strong casket which can be sealed with a butyl sealant. The problem has been that parents were not always told about the durability and strength factors; commonly they selected these caskets from a picture catalog. Without complete information, such as color and weight, some parents respond negatively to caskets when they actually see them. Parents will often say that such a casket looks like a "pop cooler" or "beer cooler." Some parents are later haunted by having buried their baby in such a container. The same problem arises for other parents who choose metal caskets, which have been characterized as a "mailbox." To avoid such misunderstanding and confusion, the parents should be given complete information (verbally and in writing) about the casket. They may be asked to look at, ask questions about, and carefully examine the casket before their baby is placed in it.

Selecting the casket or related merchandise should be made by both parents. Funeral directors have reported receiving telephone calls on rainy days from mothers wanting to know if the baby would be "dry and warm" in this weather. Often, mothers with such anxieties were uninformed and not present during the casket selection. Experience has shown that the casket is viewed very subjectively and is a genuine concern to most parents. A perceptive funeral director will provide objective information, at the same time recognizing that selecting the casket is an important part of the total experience that parents are trying to assimilate and understand.

Financial Considerations

During the arrangements conference, parents should be informed by the funeral director about the family's financial obligations. Rules mandated by the Federal Trade Commission in 1984 require the funeral director to provide a general price list showing the charge for professional services, facilities, and auto equipment. This itemized list should be given to the family at the beginning of the arrangements conference. Charges for an infant service are, in general, significantly less than the charges for an adult service.

Because of the relatively small number of infant services that a funeral home will conduct in a year, revenue thereby generated often is not a budgeted item. Funeral directors should be acutely aware of the medical and incidental expenses that pregnancy loss can incur. Therefore, they should keep the funeral home charges as reasonable as possible. Some funeral homes will provide their services at no cost as a community service. Interestingly, this "no-charge service" has in some cases caused more hurt than help to some parents. Parents may perceive the no-charge service as confirmation that the baby's life and funeral service were of no value (monetarily). In a materialistic society, the amount of money spent on the funeral may be equated with the amount of love given to the family member who has died. Funeral directors who have observed this will itemize their complete charges and offer a compassionate discount, leaving a small balance for the family to pay.

There are expenses involved with most infant services over which the funeral director has no direct control. These include honoraria, cemetery charges, newspaper notices, and flowers. If the funeral home assumes payment of these charges, it is noted as a cash advance. During the arrangements conference, the funeral director prepares the purchase agreement, which itemizes all funeral home charges, merchandise selections, and cash advances. The purchase agreement is signed, then a copy is given to the family.

Embalming Procedures, Dressing, and Casketing

In most cases, it is possible for infant embalming to take place if the parent(s) give permission. The value of having the baby present for holding and viewing during the funeral process is beneficial in the grief process (Benfield & Nichols, 1980; Davidson, 1977). In some cases where the baby's delivery was very difficult for the mother, the embalming procedure allows additional time for the mother's physical recovery before she participates in funeral activities. Parents who see their baby after proper embalming tend to be less anxious and more accepting of the situation. The reality of how the baby looks physically is much less frightening than the appearance imagined by many women who are not allowed to see their babies. Parents will recognize in their baby's features attributes that are very difficult for others to see. Thus, embalming creates some "normalcy" into an otherwise very abnormal situation for the parents.

Over the years, several embalming techniques for babies have been developed and put into practice with varying degrees of success. A excellent technique developed by Miley uses an angiocath and hypodermic syringe for injection (Doty, 1985). An angiocath is a small diameter flexible catheter or tube with a hypodermic needle which fits inside. A 16 gauge, 3.25 inch combination is recommended. This technique is providing very successful results in preservation, skin texture, skin coloration, positioning, and general overall appearance. Funeral directors using this procedure can embalm very small infants with better results than were achieved with earlier embalming practices.

When an autopsy has been performed, the success of the embalming operation is determined by the care that the pathologist has taken to leave vessels exposed and accessible. Funeral directors are encouraged to discuss this procedure with pathologists. Parents who give permission for an autopsy often ask the funeral director about the procedure. The funeral director should be positive, assuring parents that they made the right decision in granting consent for this procedure. Later, the autopsy report can be very important in helping parents to understand their loss. The funeral director should encourage the parents to meet with the physician to review the autopsy report. (Chapter 11, "Value of the Perinatal Autopsy," provides full discussion of the benefits of an autopsy.)

During the arrangements conference, parents can be given the option to dress and hold their baby. If they choose to do so, the funeral director should try to describe what they can expect to see and how they may respond. It is helpful for parents to be better prepared in this way before they enter the room where their baby is reposed. Before parents see their baby at the funeral home, the funeral director may dress the baby in a T-shirt and diaper (provided by the family) to cover incisions. A bonnet or hat should be used when a cranial autopsy has been performed. Applying baby lotion or baby powder to the baby's body will provide a smoothness and smell that meets parents' expectations of a normal baby.

The infant should be wrapped in a blanket and placed on a couch or low table so the parents can sit or kneel by the baby. Parents should be told to expect the baby's body temperature to be the same as room temperature. This 20 degree-plus difference between room temperature and normal body temperature is an unpleasant surprise for some parents, and it can leave them with a negative and painful impression of their baby as "cold."

Parents often will acknowledge the presence of incisions by referring to them as "scars." The implications of this terminology are that the baby is healing and will recover. This author has never chosen to dispute these comments, which are heard repeatedly. Some parents will require assistance in dressing the child and some will not. The funeral director should ask what assistance the mother and/or father may need and if they want to be alone with their child. Most parents do want such private time, and the funeral director can excuse himself or herself from the room after telling the parents where he or she can be found if needed.

Many funeral homes will provide a rocking chair for parents to sit in if they wish to hold their baby. This can be very therapeutic and should be encouraged. Fathers generally are more reluctant to participate in the dressing and holding of the infant. After parents are satisfied with these actions, the baby may be placed in the casket, along with any personal items that parents have decided to bury with their baby. Specially made wooden cradles are available which can hold the baby's casket for the visitation and funeral service. The casket in a cradle creates the image of a special bed for the baby. Most parents have responded positively when a cradle is used. This furnishing is highly recommended for funeral directors to keep on hand. It may be easier to have such a cradle custom built, if one is not readily available commercially in your region.

The Visitation

Some parents choose to have a visitation or wake during the evening before or the day of the funeral. This time is set aside for family members, work associates, and community members to visit with parents and to express concern and love. Viewing the baby's body during this time generally allows those in attendance to see a "normal" baby. This visual reality usually reduces the number of questions about the baby's appearance that the parents may face from others later on.

The author has observed family interaction at visitations for a number of years. Several comments are of interest. During the visitation for a baby, it is the grandparents of the mother and father who often seem most comfortable with the situation and adept at comforting the baby's parents (their grandchildren). As a rule, the parents of the mother and the father are very protective and more reserved. Probably, this is because of the pain which they feel in seeing their own children hurting over their loss. Because of their age (60s to 70s), grandparents very likely have experienced significant firsthand losses. Grandparents seem more objective and open in discussing the loss. Also, people in this age group grew up during a time in our society when pregnancy loss was more common. Many grandmothers of women who experience pregnancy loss may reveal for the first time that they, too, had a similar loss. This phenomenon may have a significant impact on a granddaughter's resolution of her own pregnancy loss. Perhaps a study conducted on this relationship might yield data to this effect.

The Funeral Service

The funeral ceremony or service often is predicated on the officiant's (clergy) personal and doctrinal response to pregnancy loss. A wide range of response to this type of loss by clergy has been observed. Some clergy will prefer only to participate in a quickly arranged graveside service or memorial service, while others are more willing to officiate at a service in the church, temple, or funeral home with the baby's body present. Families who depend heavily on their clergy for advice and consolation most often will accept without question the type of service their clergy recommends. Sometimes, the funeral director finds himself or herself caught between a family's desire or need for a more meaningful service and the officiant's desire to "keep it simple." "Simple" usually means quickly arranged and without the mother present at the service. Fortunately for all, this conflict is occurring less often as more information on the impact of pregnancy loss becomes available.

The funeral is an opportunity for the community to assemble, express love, and share in the sorrow. In the past, it seemed that the health care professionals who cared for the mother during the pregnancy and its unexpected end remained largely absent from this important service for the family. The funeral is the beginning of a process — the process of grieving over the death of a wished-for child and for the family's inherent dreams for this child. Health care providers may regard a baby's funeral as an end to a process and rationalize that their presence is unnecessary, intrusive, and undesirable. Interestingly, to the contrary, families comment positively about the presence of physicians, nurses, and social workers who attend the funeral services. It helps parents to feel less isolated and alone in the aftermath of their loss. Although time and work demands do not always allow professionals the opportunity to attend services, more consideration should be given to attending whenever possible because of the positive effect that this gesture has on parents. Professionals who attend a funeral service also may benefit from the opportunity to express their personal feelings over the family's loss. Health care professionals are human too, and they need to express rather than suppress normal feelings (Lamers, 1969). Most of the "burnout" which can affect health care professionals is death related (Osterweis, Solomon, & Green, 1984). After a patient's baby has died, expressing normal and natural feelings in a timely and organized fashion can do much to increase the effectiveness of health care professionals in subsequent similar situations.

Post-Funeral Reception

Following the funeral and committal services, many families gather together for a meal and time of fellowship. Funeral directors know the benefits of this gathering. During the arrangements conference, they should encourage families to plan for this type of activity. The meal allows neighbors, friends, and religious congregations to be involved by preparing and serving the food. The extended family who has gathered together for the baby's funeral has an opportunity to strengthen and renew family bonds in an emotionally less intense atmosphere. This sharing and open recognition of one of life's most painful experiences can assist in reducing the "conspiracy of silence" (Lewis, 1976) that parents may feel at future family and social gatherings.

Extended Care for the Family

Funeral directors can offer parents additional resources following the funeral, as their grief follows its course. An extended-care program is based on the knowledge that the impact of the loss on the survivor(s) is not felt or experienced completely within the time constraints of the funeral. The most intense feelings about the loss may come several months later. It is then when couples may expect to lean on each other "but find you cannot lean on something bent double from its own burden" (Schiff, 1977, p. 58). Couples expecting great closeness may instead experience disappointment and resentment.

The funeral director's involvement in this extended care depends to some degree on the level of involvement that parents have with primary health care professionals after their baby's death. As more is learned about the impact that pregnancy loss has on parents and families, more extended-care programs are being made available to parents by primary health care providers. The funeral director's involvement then is to supplement rather than to initiate any such programs. Funeral directors who have organized and/or participated with bereavement support groups know the value of talking with someone who has had a similar life experience (Troyer, 1985). The funeral director may provide the parents with a list of available support groups and the contact person for each. The funeral director should follow-up with a phone call to the parents 4 to 8 weeks after the service to ask if contact has been made with a group. If the parents have not contacted anyone, the funeral director may encourage them to do so.

Funeral directors can provide reprints of specific articles on pregnancy loss to the parents. The Compassionate Friends is a national support group for parents who have suffered the death of a child, and their newsletters frequently contain articles specifically concerned with pregnancy loss, such as those by Church, Chazin, and McBeath (1980) and McLaughlin (1982). The newsletter contains helpful information appropriate to parents bereaved by pregnancy loss. Funeral directors also can make available a list of books which address parents and pregnancy loss, such as those by Borg and Lasker (1981) and Peppers and Knapp (1980). Publications by Schatz (1984) and Nelson (1994) deal specifically with healing a father's grief. They are a welcome addition to the pregnancy loss literature. Additionally, parents who have surviving children are usually interested in articles and books on how children respond to the death of a sibling.

Also, the funeral director can provide written information on ways in which parents may choose to memorialize their baby's brief life. Some will want to purchase a monument or marker to place on the baby's grave. Parents are encouraged to give careful thought to the monument's design and wording. They may need additional time for this, and should not feel rushed in making this decision. One form of memorialization available to parents is an engraved wall plaque. Again, wording on the plaque should be carefully considered. This type of memorialization may be beneficial and meaningful when there is no gravesite available to visit and the parents have a strong desire to remember and recognize the baby's life.

Conclusion

> *And let us not grow weary in well doing; for in due season we*
> *shall reap, if we do not lose heart.— Galatians 6:9*

Over the years, many professionals who tried to console and help parents suffering from pregnancy loss found themselves discouraged over lack of support and understanding from fellow professionals. Fortunately, in the case of pregnancy loss this is changing, thanks to a number of persistent women who have lived through this painful experience. When we deal with pregnancy loss and its emotional impact on the family, it is precisely what we do not know that can hurt us and those whom we serve the most. Worse, on several occasions this author has encountered professionals whose treatment is influenced by something more harmful than ignorance, that is, "knowing" something that is not true (short and small life equals short and small grief). Fortunately, the breadth and depth of knowledge on pregnancy loss is growing rapidly.

Funeral directors must share this information and their experiences with each other. This is not a new or original idea (Benfield & Nichols, 1981). Physicians, nurses, social workers, and funeral directors must invest more time in discussing how they can operate as a team to serve those who need support and understanding. Lastly, all members of this team should listen closely to those who have experienced pregnancy loss. They know only too painfully this reality of a shattered dream, of hope turning to despair, of meaning becoming an absurdity, of life shifting suddenly to death. They can be the greatest teachers. They rightfully deserve our admiration and respect.❑

Case Study 1-16

Jim Johnson is called by the admissions clerk at University Hospital on February 12 at 8:30 am. Johnson Funeral Home has been chosen by the Miller Family to provide services for their stillborn son, John Andrew. The baby was delivered last evening at 8:00 pm, following induced labor for his mother, Anne. The hospital clerk tells Mr. Johnson that John's body is ready to be picked up; there will be no autopsy. Johnson is told the birth weight is six pounds, nine ounces, and that the baby's gestational age is 38 weeks. The admissions clerk provides Mr. Johnson with the father's name, Wayne Miller, and says that Mr. Miller may be contacted at the family's home. Johnson realizes that the funeral home served this family last year, when Wayne Miller's father died.

When Mr. Johnson calls Mr. Miller at home, he can tell from Wayne's voice that the family is deeply affected by their baby's unexpected death. Mr. Miller says that his wife, Anne, will be released from the hospital that afternoon. Wayne will make arrangements for the couple's two children, Jennifer (age 6) and Julie (age 3), to stay with grandparents while he and Anne come to the funeral home that afternoon. Mr. Johnson asks for permission to remove the baby from the hospital and to embalm the baby, and Wayne says yes.

Johnson Funeral Home personnel pick up the baby and return to the funeral home. The baby's body has been refrigerated for at least 10 hours. There is discoloration in the ears, hands, back, and legs. The condition of the body indicates that death probably occurred within 24 hours of birth. The embalming procedure proceeds well, and the baby has good color and preservation at completion of embalming. Mr. Johnson is comfortable with the family seeing and touching baby John, if they choose to.

Wayne and Anne arrive at the funeral home after the appointed time. They apologize for being late, explaining that they had some difficulty in leaving their girls with Anne's parents. With the parents are Anne's sister, Mary Hall, and Wayne's mother, Irene Miller. Mr. Johnson shows the four of them into an office and offers Anne and Wayne a seat on a soft couch. Anne slowly sits down, obviously feeling the physical strain of yesterday's birth experience. In the first few minutes, Anne and Wayne explain that their baby John died *in utero* because of a placental abruption. An ultrasound had confirmed that the baby had died, and labor was started at noon the day before.

During the course of conversation, Mr. Johnson hears the following
    comments from:

Wayne Miller (father)

1. "We would like a simple, quick funeral. Anne is just physically exhausted and needs to rest."
2. "We named the baby after my father who died very suddenly just 6 months ago."
3. "This was our last chance for a son. We're in our middle 30s and we just can't do this again."

Anne Miller (mother)

1. "I am a nurse. I knew when the baby didn't move and I started spotting that something was very wrong."
2. "I need to see my baby again. I was so tired after the birth that holding him for a short time was all I could do."
3. "Our daughters, Jennifer and Julie, have not seen their brother. We wonder if they should see him and how will he look if they see him."

Mary Hall (Anne Miller's sister)

1. "I called Reverend Cook. She is willing to do whatever Wayne and Anne want to do."

2. "We can have everyone over to our house after the funeral service for lunch."
3. "We should order flowers from Buckman's Floral Shop. They do nice work."

Irene Miller (Wayne Miller's mother)
1. "I have made a blanket for the baby. Can we use it for the funeral?"
2. "My husband is in Grace Lawn Cemetery. Baby John should be buried with his grandfather."
3. "This is a nightmare...losing a grandson so soon after my husband's death."

It's time to discuss the funeral for John Andrew Miller. What suggestions would you offer?

Commentary

It is fortunate for Jim Johnson that he has had the opportunity in the last year to develop a professional relationship with the Miller family. His previous work as the family's funeral director already has allowed him to develop a trust relationship with the extended family. Wayne and Anne Miller will seek advice and be more open to suggestions based on their previous experience with the Johnson Funeral Home. It most often is the case that young parents do not have an established relationship with a funeral home. The first meeting is very important, because it establishes the trust relationship that the parents will experience. Jim Johnson knows the importance of letting the family tell their story. He is listening carefully to what the Miller family has undergone in the past 48 hours. It is obvious that their expected joy and happiness now have turned upside down into despair and tragedy. Through the funeral experience, the funeral director can offer this bereaved family a means of control and stability in an out-of-control and disabling situation.

I would offer suggestions that include participation by most family members in preparing for the funeral. Wayne Miller's concern for his wife's exhaustion is to be expected. I would suggest that there is no rush to complete the details. They can and should take time for Anne to rest before the visitation and funeral. I would assure Anne that she will see baby John again, and that she and her family will have an opportunity to dress and hold him. I would encourage them to include their daughters, Jennifer and Julie, in some of these activities. Wayne and Anne could encourage the girls to give their brother "gifts," such as artwork which they have created, family photographs, and/or small stuffed animals. I would suggest to the Miller's that they may want to take pictures, obtain a lock of John's hair, or make hand- or footprints, as keepsakes.

The obituary notice is an important opportunity for the Miller family to notify the community of their loss. I would suggest that they include the information that baby John was preceded recently in death by his grandfather John, just within the last year. This recent death of the family's father, grandfather, and husband is still a grief which they are experiencing as a family. Remembering Grandfather John in print and at baby John's service will be important for the Miller family.

Wayne and Anne need to hear about the choices which they have, regarding when and where their baby's funeral and burial will take place. The Millers may decide to have the funeral at the church or at the funeral home. The family should be encouraged to talk with Reverend Cook about the funeral service. Wayne and Anne possibly could consider having baby John buried on the same grave site as that of his grandfather, or in another section of the same cemetery. Cremation also is an option which they may consider, with the plan to bury John's cremated remains in the cemetery. Because John's death has occurred in the middle of winter, there may need to be a delay of burial. This possible delay may influence the Miller family's decisions. Lastly, when the parents make their casket selection, information should be included about the casket's construction and design, to reassure Anne and Wayne that their son will be safe, dry, and clean.

I would ask Wayne and Anne to provide clothing, socks, a tee-shirt, and a diaper for John. They may or may not choose to place John in the baby blanket which was hand-made by Irene Miller. The option to dress and hold John would be encouraged for the parents, as well as for other family members if Wayne and Anne feel that this would be appropriate. I would place a rocking chair in the room where the parents will dress and hold John. I would encourage the parents to place mementos or keepsakes in the casket with the baby. The choices which they have concerning flowers and printed materials would be offered and discussed, too. I would encourage Mary Hall to plan a fellowship time after the funeral, to be held either at the family's home or at the church. It is quite possible that more people will attend the service than Wayne and Anne anticipate at this point, and thus they may need the larger facility that a site such as their church would offer.

A discussion about the expenses which will be incurred by the Miller family also must take place. This family's past experience with Wayne's father's funeral may lead them mistakenly to believe that baby John's funeral will be more expensive than in fact it actually will be. I would explain the reduction in funeral-home charges, which are found on the General Price List. Next, we would review the charges which cannot be controlled by the funeral director, such as costs for the cemetery, flowers, honoraria, or newspaper notices. A written purchase agreement should be filled out and signed by responsible parties at this time.

If the suggestions which I offer are acceptable to Wayne and Anne, then there would be a number of opportunities for them to be involved in "parenting" their son. If they are comfortable as parents, they then will allow their daughters and other family members to participate in a meaningful way. I would tell them during the arrangements conference that there are community resources which are available to them after the funeral to assist them in their recovery from their painful loss. I would offer them printed materials (such as a brochure about children's grief, and a recent copy of the group's newsletter) provided by the Pregnancy and Infant Loss Center or some similar type of organization. I would let them know that our funeral home's After Care Director would be offering additional support to them, after the funeral services are over.

There are more options and choices available that are not listed in this commentary, due to space limitations. In summary, I would comment that creating a meaningful ceremony that recognizes the life of a person, in this case a wished-for child, is very important. The funeral can have a dramatic impact on the emotional, physical, and spiritual well-being of the bereaved family. Jim Johnson, the funeral director in this case, has that opportunity now to help the Miller family in a powerful way, as they move toward understanding and adjusting to the loss of their son. I know from experience that Jim Johnson has a difficult task ahead of him. But, the reward of helping this family in the special way that only a funeral director can help is worth the effort, and I wish him well.

— *Susan Lodermeier, BS*

References

Benfield, G., & Nichols, J. (1980, February). *Caring for bereaved parents: The intersection of funeral service and newborn medicine.* Presented at the Ohio Funeral Directors Association, Midwinter Institute.

Benfield, G., & Nichols, J. (1981). Living with newborn death: The challenge of upstream caring. *Dodge Magazine, 73,* 5-29.

Borg, S., & Lasker, J. (1981). *When pregnancy fails.* Boston: Beacon Press.

Bowlby, J. (1980). *Attachment and loss: Vol. III. Loss.* New York: Basic Books.

Church, M., Chazin, H., & McBeath, K. (1980). *When a baby dies.* Oak Brook, IL: The Compassionate Friends.

Davidson, G. (1977, Fall). Death of the wished for child: A case study. *Death Education Quarterly.*

Davis, D. (1991). *Empty cradle, broken heart.* Golden, Co: Fulcrum Publishing.

Doty, K. (1985). Infant embalming: A new approach. *The Director, 15*(4), 11-46.

Fulton, R. (1976-77). Death, grief and the funeral in contemporary society. *The Director,* p. 9 (reprint).

Grunebaum, H. (1968). Grief. *Psychiatric Opinion, 5,* 38-43.

Ilse, S., & Erling, S. (1989). *Planning a precious goodbye.* Wayzata, MN: Pregnancy and Infant Loss Center.

Lamb, J.M. (1989). Bittersweet....hellogoodbye, a resource in planning farewell rituals. Springfield, IL: Prairie Lake Press.

Lamers, W.M. Jr. (1969). Funerals are good for people – M.D.'s included. *Medical Economics, 46*(4).

LaMore, G.E. Jr. (1985). The art of dying. *The Director, 15*(8), 10-11.

Lewis, E. (1976). The management of stillbirth – coping with an unreality. *Lancet, 2,* 619-620.

McLaughlin, C. (1982). *An odyssey for bereaved parents.* Oak Brook, IL: The Compassionate Friends.

Nelson, J. (1994). The rocking horse is lonely. Wayzata, MN: Pregnancy and Infant Loss Center.

Nichols, J. (1975). Funerals: A time for grief and growth: In E. Kubler-Ross (Ed.), *Death the final stage of growth.* New York: Prentice-Hall,

Osterweis, M., Solomon, F., & Green, M. (1984). *Bereavement: Reactions, consequences, and care.* Washington, DC: National Academy Press.

Peppers, L., & Knapp, R. (1980). *Motherhood and mourning.* New York: Preaeger Publishers.

Pine, V. (1974). *Social meanings of the funeral.* New York: Foundation of Thanatology, Columbia University.

Raether, H., & Slater R. (1975). *The funeral director and his role as a counselor.* Milwaukee: National Funeral Directors Association.

Schatz, W. (1984). *Healing a father's grief.* Redmond, WA: Medic Publishing.

Schiff, H.S. (1977). *The bereaved parent.* New York: Crown Publishers.

Schwiebert, P., & Kirk, P. (1985). *When hello means goodbye.* Portland: University of Oregon Health Sciences Center.

Snow, L. (1984). The application of invitational theory to professional death and bereavement counseling. *Thanatos, 9,* 9-11.

Troyer, R. (1985). Living and loving more: Enhancing support group outreach to the bereaved. *The Director, 15*(4), 16-49.

Chapter 17

Spiritual Issues and Care in Perinatal Bereavement

James H. Cunningham

People usually give significant spiritual meaning to the events of birth and death. Therefore, an infant death occurring between conception and infancy presents most parents with a spiritual crisis. Comprehensive care for these bereaved parents must attend to their spiritual concerns.

Definitions

In a traditional context, the term "spiritual" refers to one's understanding of God and relationship to God. "Spiritual" also may refer to non-material aspects of our personhood, such as our beliefs, values, purpose, identity, goals, and the meanings we give our experience. I argue that even atheists have "spiritual" needs, for they also frame their experiences with certain perceptions, assumptions, beliefs, and values. Bereaved parents whom I have counseled can articulate many "spiritual" challenges that they experience upon the death of their baby.

I use the term "clergy" to refer to one's primary spiritual caregiver. Most often, one's primary spiritual caregiver is the designated leader of one's faith tradition: priest, pastor, rabbi, imam, elder, mooni, bishop, medicine man, etc. Sometimes, one's primary spiritual caregiver is a spiritual friend with no official title or role.

Spiritual Principles

Spirituality is more than one's religious affiliation. Too often, health care professionals limit their spiritual care to asking, "What religion are you? What church are you affiliated with? Do you want to have your baby baptized?" To understand spiritual needs better, obstetric and neonatal intensive care staff

Table 1-17.
Statements That Express Spiritual Care

- We would like to know something about how your faith or spirituality speaks to you in times like this...

- I wonder if you are praying and what you are praying for...

- Where is God in this for you right now?...

- How has your faith been a resource for you in former times of crisis?...

- What are your beliefs about birth...about death?...

- Many people find the death of their infant a challenge to their faith, what aabout you?...

- Do you feel closer to or more distant from God?...

- I'd like to know about your dreams you had for this child...

- What meaning do you give to this experience?...

should state, "I'd appreciate knowing if you have specific faith beliefs, rituals, traditions, or needs that we should be attentive to in caring for you, your family, and your baby." Selection of terms is important. For example, in the Jewish Orthodox tradition, the supreme being, as a measure of respect, never is referred to by name. In the English translation, "G-d" is the term which is written most often. Sensitivity to details such as this also facilitates responses, such as that of a Native American woman who asked to put an eagle's feather in her baby's Isolette™. She explained the feather's meaning and requested that only a member of the tribe touch or move it. A Christian Orthodox mother may want an icon placed in her baby's Isolette. An Orthodox Jewish family may request a Kosher meal.

Further spiritual care may be expressed through comments as shown in Table 1-17. Bereaved parents of every faith tradition and those who are of no practicing tradition struggle with these kinds of issues.

An individual's personal beliefs may not be consistent with an individual's own faith tradition. Not only are there diverse beliefs and practices within specific faith traditions such as Jewish, Catholic, Islamic, Buddhist, Hindu, Mormons, and Native Americans, there also is enormous diversity among individuals within each specific faith tradition. Never make assumptions based on admitting forms which indicate that the patient is Baptist, or Russian Orthodox, or Unitarian. It would be a serious mistake not to discuss the option of pregnancy termination with parents whose infant has been diagnosed with Trisomy 21, even though you know that they are Catholic. I may approach Unitarian parents of a critically ill newborn by saying, "It is my understanding that Unitarians have no specific rituals for critically ill newborns. Is that also your belief?" I may say to a Moslem family, "It is my understanding that you are encouraged to bury the dead within 24 hours. Is this consistent with your beliefs, your needs, your plans?" We also must realize that two parents may come from very different faith traditions or may hold different beliefs while affirming a single common faith tradition. For example, one woman was very angry because her husband was asked in the neonatal unit about his faith, which he stated was Roman Catholic, and the staff took the initiative to have the sacrament of baptism performed for the baby. When this woman was informed that a priest had baptized her baby, she was offended. She was Baptist; none of her other children was baptized as a newborn. In addition to worrying about her baby's survival, she asked if this meant that she had to raise the child in the Catholic Church!

Respect the family's spirituality. Don't impose your own. For example, when the baby of an Orthodox Jewish couple dies on a holy day, these parents may refuse to sign any consent forms, because this would be "doing work," which is prohibited on the Sabbath day and other holy days. One family was very offended by the labor and delivery staff's apparent insistence that they hold and touch their dead baby when, according to their faith and cultural tradition, touching and holding the stillborn child was unacceptable. Some Native American tribes may use a "burying family" — a trusted family in the tribe who are delegated to make end-of-life treatment decisions and burial arrangements to support the grieving family. Though an autopsy may be deemed important, some faith traditions prohibit autopsies. I warn Christian caregivers that baptism without consent of the parents, if pressed in a court of law, may be viewed as *assault*.

One's spirituality influences, for better or worse, one's emotional, mental, and physical responses to bereavement. If parents have a strong belief that life begins at conception and then miscarry the pregnancy at 8 weeks, their beliefs may affect the intensity of their grief. Following the death of her 3-month-old from sudden infant death syndrome, one woman in my experience concluded that "God obviously intends for me not to have children." In spite of counseling exploring her conclusion, she committed herself to attempting no further pregnancies. This is one example of responses to the event.

Most parents experience a wide range of guilt. When my own son was stillborn at term, I remembered every sin back to my preschool days in wondering why God would so punish me. I worked through such guilt. Some people, however, firmly believe that God punishes the sinful through the death of their children. I was very angry at God for the death of my son. If one's faith tradition discourages anger toward God, then this belief impedes healthy grief and healing. My experience suggests that people whose faith traditions encourage honest expressions of grief and extend personal support feel accepted in their grief and then come to healing and hope. I believe that faith rituals at death generally aid grieving. Unfortunately, most parents who experience a miscarriage and some who experience a stillbirth are discouraged from or are denied spiritual and funeral rituals and other forms of spiritual support. This is especially disconcerting for many bereaved parents whose faith traditions assert that life begins at conception and is fully sacred from day 1.

Spiritual care: Take the initiative. Just as you do not have to be a psychologist or psychiatrist to care about a person's feelings or grief, you do not have to be a theologian or clergy person to care about a person's spirituality. At the heart of spiritual care is respect for people and their spirituality, along with compassion, empathy, and listening. Compassion comes from a Latin word meaning "to suffer with." Therefore, to offer spiritual compassion, we must enter into someone's spiritual struggle with death and grief. Spiritual compassion does not so much provide answers to these mysteries as it does convey understanding.

We should respect another's spirituality. Sometimes, bereaved parents share their spiritual understanding and I find that I do not agree with their particular statement. For example, I often hear a comment such as, "God really must have loved Jimmy and wanted him for an angel." Sometimes I wonder, because I am a chaplain, if they give me the answer they think I want to hear. My response then is, "It sounds like what you have shared is meaningful to you. But, I know other bereaved parents and other people of faith who find that perspective very difficult to accept." This affirms their understanding without my having to agree or disagree. By showing them that others find their position difficult to accept, I also offer them the opportunity to be more vulnerable about their struggle, if they have been less than candid.

One of the goals of spiritual care is to convey that God is and that God cares. While we can proclaim this in words, it may be more effective to proclaim this by the quality of our own caring in a spiritual context. Many caregivers are accustomed to doing something to relieve others' pain. In reality, we cannot take their pain away; we can share in it, however. We sometimes are tempted to use our faith perspective to try to take away others' pain, with comments such as, "It's God's will; you just have to accept it." This can extend the suffering of the bereaved by attempting to rescue them. This kind of "quick fix" statement can be interpreted by the family as our abandoning them in their spiritual struggle. We cannot prevent them from suffering, but we can prevent them for suffering for the wrong reasons.

Spiritual Themes

The WHY question: Why me? Why my infant? Why this? Why now? Why would God do this or allow this? These are all great questions! I wish that I had clear answers for them. I view these questions not as questions seeking an answer, but as feelings seeking to be understood and affirmed. So, initially I respond, "Not fair is it? It does not make sense." These are responses of empathy to the pain being expressed through these questions.

For most, "why" questions are questions seeking physical and spiritual answers. Obstetricians, neonatologists, and pathologists are best at addressing the physical aspects. Even if the physical issues are definitive, there remain spiritual questions, such as, "But why did this have to happen to us?"

When faced with a "why" question from parents, I ask them how they would answer this question for themselves. From their answers, I learn about their current state of thinking, their historical beliefs, and their anger or guilt. If they share their spiritual guilt or anger, I may be tempted to respond, "Oh, you shouldn't feel that way." But, such a response does not take away the anger or guilt. It only makes bereaved parents stop talking about their anger or guilt. Instead, I begin by affirming their anger and guilt as understandable reactions, and I ask them to tell me more about these thoughts and feelings. I also try to prepare parents for what others will say to comfort them while trying to address the "why" question. As appropriate, I share with them my own sense of mystery and struggle with these questions and seek to be reassuring.

At some point, if appropriate, I carefully may share my beliefs on this subject. I always point out that I do not offer my beliefs as the one and only truth. It is what is meaningful to me; it may not be meaningful for them. For example, I do not believe in predestination, although I may be wrong about this! In life as we now experience it, we live with freedom. This freedom means that we make free choices and sometimes bad things just happen. (I am aware that this topic occupies a whole book in itself.) At times, I have been asked, "Where was God when your son was stillborn?" After years of struggle, I am able to say, "God was the first one to cry, knowing before we knew that my son had died." For me, God did not cause my son's death.

In another example, a bereaved father once asked me if God revealed God's self in dreams. I said that I believed it was possible. He struggled intensely with the spiritual "why" question. In his dream, God put the man's four children before him, all alive and well, including the baby who had died, and said, "One of your four children is to die. You get to choose which one." He responded immediately, "I can't do that." God repeated the statement. Now with anger the father responded, "Look, I love each of these kids. I can't do that. You can't make me do that!" God responded tenderly, "I love each of them, too. Do you think I can choose?" This dream did not answer this man's "why" question, but it gave him some peace that God did not just pick on his child. I like that story. In grieving for my son, I also could not find a suitable answer and so at some point I had to let go of the "why" question and focus more on "how" questions: "How was I going to cope?" Many people, however, have tried to make me believe that my son died so that I could minister effectively to others who experienced infant death. I hope that this is not true. I would much prefer not to have this expertise, and I wish that I could have my son back. My faith, while not answering the "why" question, does offer me comfort in a variety of ways. The "why" question is still a very good question. Struggling with the "why" question reminds me that, when I was a child, my parents did not always explain everything or give me anything that I wanted. While I sometimes wondered if they loved me, I knew in my heart that they loved me very much; and so it is with God.

Other explicit spiritual themes. Caregivers can discuss, assess, and offer spiritual support to parents on a variety of other spiritual themes. The death of a baby can change people's *understanding of God,* sometimes clarifying and enhancing their understanding, sometimes clouding and diminishing their understanding of God. Their *relationship with God* changes. In the beginning, many parents are angry and feel cut off from God, and a few never recover a sense of a relationship. In my bereaved-parent support group survey, most affirmed that their baby's death had led to a faith crisis. After 6 months, though, most felt closer to God than they had before the baby's death (Cunningham, 1983). Other questions involving spiritual themes can be asked: "What impact has your child's death had on your *prayer* experience?

Has your *relationship with a faith group and/or clergy* changed? How will your *faith assist you in your journey of grief?* What would *healing or acceptance* look like and feel like?"

I believe that *forgiveness* is a critical spiritual issue. If death is not to leave me bitter or guilt ridden, then I need to forgive death. Furthermore, I must forgive the death of my child, forgive the pain that death brings, and perhaps forgive God, forgive myself and/or others. Grieving is about letting go, and I believe that forgiveness is the key to letting go. It is a key that helps in coming to terms with death, ultimately leading to acceptance, healing, and peace.

Other spiritual themes. Other questions or discussions may focus on how the experience of a baby's death has changed a parent's *identity* as a woman or man, mother or father, provider, protector, or nurturer. Following the death of her baby, one teenager remarked that now she was still a child, unloved and dependent. Her dream was that having a baby would provide her with a pathway to adulthood, to independence, and to love. She was very depressed. Many bereaved parents speak of how the baby's death changed their *values:* "I no longer take life for granted." Others speak of new *goals:* "My work had been taking priority over my family — no longer." Some may conclude that life no longer has *meaning,* while others may find new meaning to life. Former *beliefs* may be challenged: "I used to believe that, if you trusted God, made healthy choices, and worked hard, then life was fair and would reward you. Now I don't know what to believe." Certain *fantasies* may be destroyed: "I always believed that this happened to other people, not to me or to mine." *Dreams* die: "I always dreamed of having three children. I never dreamed that I would ever have to bury one of my children. I dreamed that this child would save our marriage."

Healthy grief is work, and it requires bereaved parents to try to address and if possible to resolve or come to terms with these issues. Caregivers should not attempt to address all these issues in any one meeting or in the midst of the crisis. Most of the spiritual issues discussed previously are appropriate follow-up themes.

Clergy and Health Care Professionals

What can health care professionals do for community clergy? Health care professionals should ask about and respect the faith and spirituality of patients. Do not ignore the subject. Encourage the presence and participation of the family's clergy. As a parish pastor, I always was more effective with the funeral and follow-up if I had been present during the crisis. Orient clergy to your procedures and make them feel a part of the pregnancy-loss bereavement team. Remembering that not all clergy have experience with newborn death and bereavement, offer to share with them the resources that you provide to bereaved families. Ask the family's clergy for information about the patient or their faith tradition that may be important to your care. Do not make promises to parents on behalf of their clergy such as, "I know that your clergy will baptize your child," "I'm sure if we call, your clergy will be here immediately," or "I'm sure your clergy can offer a funeral from the hospital chapel tomorrow." Instead, simply offer to assist families in contacting their clergy for consultation and support. Invite clergy into your continuing education programs about pregnancy loss, neonatal death, and bereavement. If the clergy expresses a lack of knowledge or experience with bereaved parents, share your experience, and offer to contact the hospital chaplain or another clergy person whom you know will be a helpful resource for community clergy.

The hospital chaplain. If the health care setting has a staff chaplain, initiate a call to the chaplain. Instead of asking the patient, "Do you want to see the chaplain?", I encourage staff to say, "The chaplain is an important participant in our team, so I have asked him (her) to meet you to offer emotional and spiritual support." The patient still has the right to decline this assistance. Often patients have misconceptions about the chaplain's role. Once I introduce myself and share my role, the patient realizes that I am not there to defend God or to convert them in a moment of anguish. Then, most patients generally accept and support my presence, even if they are from a very different faith tradition. If the chaplain has little experience with pregnancy loss, neonatal death, and bereavement, share your resources, experience, and procedures; and encourage the chaplain to participate in some continuing education about pregnancy loss and bereavement.

What can community clergy do for health care professionals? As the family's clergy, do not just walk in and see the patient. Stop and speak with health care providers first. Make yourself part of their team. Ask what has happened. Ask about procedures. Share information that you have about the family or spiritual needs that health care providers would find helpful. Take advantage of these providers' considerable experience and learn from them.

Respect the patient's privacy in her room. Knock first, identify yourself, and seek permission to enter. Let the patient and staff know how to contact you for further assistance. Convey your needs and expectations regarding follow-up to staff, such as "Please call me at the time of delivery," or "The family has agreed to have you contact me if the baby's condition worsens."

What Bereaved Parents Want Their Clergy to Know

Do not discount their grief. In my bereaved-parent support group survey which I conducted years ago, fewer than 50% of parents felt that their clergy were understanding and supportive. Fewer than 30% felt that their faith congregations were understanding and supportive (Cunningham, 1983). Many parents experience from clergy what they experience from other people — a lack of understanding and a lack of appreciation for the extent of their grief. Because this is a baby who has died — especially when the death has occurred *in utero* — the parents' grief may be discounted. Bereaved parents do not say, "I lost a pregnancy...some tissue...a fetus." They talk about their baby's death.

To illustrate this issue: Twelve years after a woman's baby had died at 10 weeks gestation, the woman came to me and talked about her grief and the lack of closure she felt because they had chosen not to have a funeral or memorial service at the time. She asked me if I could perform a memorial service for her baby after so many years. She stated that she did not know the baby's gender, but in her mind and memory she had named her baby Kelly, since the name could apply to a boy or a girl. Through this memorial service 12 years later, this woman was able to claim her baby's conception and death publicly, to grieve openly, to let go spiritually, and to find some inner peace.

It may be a LITTLE baby, but this is a BIG grief. I believe that it is harder to grieve for the dreams of what might have been than it is to grieve the memories of a life lived for some years. As one parent stated, "How can you say 'good-bye' before you scarcely had a chance to say 'hello'?" To grieve for a baby's death is to grieve for that person's whole life which you dreamed of sharing.

Funeral/memorial service. From my perspective, every family whose baby dies should be offered a funeral or memorial service. Often, nothing is offered or there may be only a minimal service. I recently challenged a group of clergy from large congregations to plan a service in remembrance of babies who died *in utero*, and I told them to notice how many parents attended. When clergy offer such a service, I believe that many are surprised by the number of parents who attend. Some parents want to participate actively in planning a funeral service by dressing their deceased baby, or by having at least a private last viewing, by sharing a letter to their child, by selecting readings, or by releasing a helium-filled balloon in the child's memory. The balloon release is a powerful symbol of letting go and giving the child to God.

At the funeral service, do not be impersonal; speak the child's name frequently. Though the community may not have shared memories of the baby's life, parents have stories to tell consisting of both memories and dreams. To illustrate one experience: I visited a baby in the neonatal unit who was born with an abnormality that was incompatible with life. Inside the Isolette was a photo of a puppy. The parents shared that one of their dreams for this, their first child, was at her birth to get a puppy for the baby and watch them both grow up together. At the funeral I shared their story: "We will not be able to watch Sarah grow up, but this will always be Sarah's puppy." At the funeral, speak of faith and of the comfort and promises of faith. In addition, parents want and need to have their grief and pain acknowledged and affirmed. Because parents may have few concrete remembrances, I often offer a video or audio tape of the service.

Follow-up. Remembering that bereaved parents find it difficult to take initiative in seeking support, clergy and other spiritual support persons should take the initiative to call and visit. Encourage parents to participate in a bereaved-parent support group. Consider a bereavement follow-up plan during the first year of grief, with contact at quarterly intervals, during holidays, at the time of the due date, on Mother's Day and Father's Day, and at the anniversary of the birth and death of the baby.

Anticipation of special days usually is worse than the day itself for bereaved parents. So, call a few days or a week before, for example, Mother's Day — not necessarily on Mother's Day. Indicate your awareness that this is the first Mother's Day since her baby died. Ask about her grief and her plans for Mother's Day. If all is going well, your call will not upset her. If she is struggling with her grief, she will be pleased that someone remembered and cared enough to call. Then, listen and offer support.

In many faith traditions, an annual service of remembrance is offered in memory of all those who have died during the preceding year. Bereaved parents often comment that their babies who were stillborn or miscarried are not included in such annual remembrances. When this happens, they again feel discounted and forgotten. I remember a note which was placed in one baby's casket which read, "We loved you for 9 months and will remember you forever." Bereaved families also appreciate others who remember their baby who died.

Many resources are available for bereaved parents. Clergy should read these resources and share them with bereaved parents. One technique, which spiritual care providers can use in supporting bereaved parents, is what I call the "teach me" method. It begins with the statement, "I have no idea what it is like to have your baby die. I am eager to learn from you and to be supportive of you." Then, listen. If spiritual issues are not discussed, ask. Parents better resolve many of their spiritual struggles if they are encouraged to talk about these issues. Clergy also need to reach out and offer care to the couple not only as bereaved parents but also as partners in the marriage relationship. Other children in the family and grandparents need the clergy's care, too. In caring for bereaved families, clarify what to share with others. Respect a family's right to confidentiality and their right to control the release of information about their baby's death.

Elective abortions. Elective abortions represent a special challenge for many parents and clergy. My experience with parents who choose elective abortion is that they come to this decision with considerable struggle, pain, and grief. While some faith traditions support the moral and legal right to choose an abortion, many faith traditions oppose abortion, or support abortion under only very limited circumstances. Many parents who choose abortion are afraid to share their decision and grief with clergy for fear of judgment and rejection. I have no easy answer to this moral struggle in our society. In a hospital setting, we are called upon and are morally obligated to provide care to the suffering without regard to the cause of their suffering. Whether a person is an innocent victim of disease or accident, or the pain is self-inflicted, we offer care. In contrast, someone once commented: "The church is the only army who shoots its own wounded." Bereaved parents who have made the difficult decision to terminate a pregnancy long for clergy and a faith community who, without abandoning their beliefs, still can offer compassionate spiritual care.

Conclusion

We live in a society of enormous spiritual diversity. This diversity should not keep us from attending to spiritual care as a vital part of our total care for bereaved parents whose baby has died. We do not do these parents justice if we attend only to their physical and emotional needs. Spiritual issues are important dimensions of our experiences with birth and death. Spiritual care is an important part of a healthy grief process. While each of us is unique, we share many of the same physical and emotional needs as bereaved parents. Our spiritual needs, however, are more diverse, and they command careful attention and respect.❏

Case Study 1-17

Why Would God Do Such a Thing?

You receive a telephone call from a young, married man in your congregation. You know that "Steven" and "Emily" are expecting their first baby in just a few weeks. Casual, good-natured conversation after services has followed the happy couple's pregnancy, creating a general sense of confident anticipation among the church community.

Steven's call comes as a bad shock. Just the day before, Emily had experienced sudden complications in the pregnancy, with severe bleeding and placental abruption. She was taken to the hospital, where Emily quickly underwent cesarean section under general anesthesia. Steven and Emily's baby son, 3 weeks before the due date, had suffered oxygen deprivation and had died before he could be delivered. Steven was not permitted to be in the operating room during the delivery, and Emily was unconscious and too groggy afterward to want to hold the baby.

Steven is very emotional as he explains what happened. He asks for your advice about what to do next. Their families do not live in town, and many relatives are traveling to arrive in today and tomorrow. Steven tells you that Emily is very upset. She is expressing great anger about their baby's death, and she will not discuss Steven's request to plan a funeral and burial for "Steven Junior." Steven begins to cry while you are on the phone with him. He asks you why God would do such a thing to their baby.

Commentary

In my reflections with and counseling of a couple in such a situation, I try to move from having the individuals talk of themselves to how they talk with one another and then to how they address talking to God — if at all. That might be a way to conceptualize what I would try to do with Steven and Emily.

"Why?" Questions

First, I hear Steven and Emily asking "Why?" questions: "Why has this happened to us? Why did our child die?" I find that, when people ask "why" questions, they already have their own, unstated answers to the questions which they are asking. Rarely, however, does a person answering his or her own "why" questions say, "Aha! Now I see why." There are underlying emotions and thoughts behind their "why" questions. But, first, the "why" questions are ones which I must address because these are the questions being asked initially by those who suffer loss and death.

In asking themselves, "Why? Why did our child die? Why did this happen to us?," I ask them what answers they themselves would give to such questions. When people ask these questions aloud, and they can reflect on the answers which they themselves give, then their next questions begin to explore new dimensions of grief. I would ask the couple how they want to respond to their own responses. What do they want to do with their understanding about what has happened to them? This type of dialogue, I caution to note, would be addressed over time. People in a situation such as Emily and Steven's are not prepared to move into the future just yet, nor probably should they. Their son has just died, suddenly and unexpectedly. This is a time to grieve. But, this time does begin to set a framework for them to look at the future, because inevitably a new type of questioning will rise to the surface: "How are we going to handle this? Where are we going to go from this?" This type of questioning is future directed, and it evolves from the "why" questions, which tend to be ones that look back at the past.

Secondly, working gradually on the idea of moving from the present to the future, I would ask, "What has been the immediate impact of your baby's death on you as a couple? Are you able to talk with one another about your feelings, about what you are thinking, about your loss?" Here, I am approaching the reality that death and life are very much interwoven, and that in the midst of death there comes a deeper understanding of life. These two are always interconnected.

Four Fundamental Emotions

When a couple's baby has died, many deep emotions are exposed. I believe that there are four basic feelings that flow through us all the time: happiness, sadness, fear, and anger. For a couple such as Steven and Emily, dealing with this kind of situation, they most experience enormous fear, sadness, and anger. The emotions which will dominate them in their deepest phase of grieving will overshadow any joy which they may experience.

As the shadows of grief hold Steven and Emily, I would try to help them reach for each other in their darkness. If they can share their emotions now, as they have shared their joy in the past, then this will be a way for Steven and Emily to deepen their lives together, to deepen their relationship. They can help each other and stand together in a time of loss and hurt and anger. They can better understand themselves and share with each other their new insights and self-knowledge, and in so doing they will strengthen their love.

Our hope, eventually, will be to watch the shadow of this grief slowly lift from their beings, like seeing the sun rise over the mountains, and waiting as the dim, predawn light brightens into brilliant day again. In order to do this, Steven and Emily must be able to talk with one another.

So, in reflecting on what we know of this couple in our congregation already, as well as from interacting with them in this moment of over-whelming grief, I would encourage Steven and Emily to perceive and realize their strengths in themselves and in their communication with one another, as a way to help them to help each other, as well as to help themselves. But, these types of considerations can be nurtured and encouraged in the days and weeks to come, and these issues will be the ones with which I would be most concerned for their individual and mutual long-term resolution and acceptance of their son's death.

Immediate Needs

The most important issues which must be approached immediately con-cern the timing and type of rituals and interventions which Steven and Emily wish to observe for their son. Steven had told me in a telephone conversation that they were having a hard time talking about arrangements for a funeral. Steven is ready and wants to discuss this possibility, but his wife, for whatev-er reason, is unable to talk with him about that. So, at some point in the ini-tial meeting, I would ask about a funeral or any religious service.

Extended Family Dynamics and Availability

Steven also told me that various relatives from both sides of the family were coming to be with them. In anticipation of a possible funeral, I would explore what the relationships were like among these people. For example, do the two families get along? From at least Steven's perspective, is there any dysfunction in his or Emily's families of origin? Did they find that their fam-ilies were helpful to each of them as they were growing up? Are they still help-ful to them? How might their extended families be helpful to Steven and Emily now, with the loss of their child?

I would urge them, as members of my church community, to consider the possible benefits of having a funeral for baby Steven. I believe that a rit-ual such as a funeral service certainly can be helpful to a family. A funeral can help people to affirm and to deal with realities, as part of the grieving process and assist them to move on. I would try to work with the couple to see whether these kinds of realities make some sense to them. If so, I would want to help them plan some kind of funeral service for their child.

Relationships Between Self and Others and God

In all of these thoughts, my emphasis would be exploring relationships for Steven and Emily — individual communication with self, communication between the couple, and communication with family and friends. In our relationships, we come to know who we are.

This discussion of relationships then would lead to other major dimensions of life and relationships: What part does God play in Steven and Emily's lives, particularly at this time? Would they see God as their enemy because of what has happened? Perhaps, they cannot understand why God would take their child from them. Depending on their reactions and the tone of our discussion, I would share my understanding of the biblical God and faith. I could tell Steven and Emily that most people seem to think of God as something like a first cause, some Being who manipulates and runs the universe.

God is known in a trusting relationship. He is one who experiences the emotions that we experience: sadness, anger, happiness, and fear. At some point, I would intervene with my own sense about God as the one whose heart is the first of all of our hearts to break when life leaves one of our loved ones. God grieves just as we do. People usually do not associate God with emotions other than, perhaps, anger. But, they do not understand a God who is sad or a God who might be fearful, or one who rejoices with his people.

Starting from the idea that God is the source of all our emotions, I would present a view of a God who weeps as they weep over the death of their baby. So, I would be trying at least to introduce these thoughts. I would share my thoughts with Steven and Emily in the hope that this might be helpful in their time of grief.

Conclusion

So, my approach toward this young couple who are going through an enormous strain would be to emphasize the importance of relationships at all levels, moving from how individually they would see this, how they share this experience and their pain with each other and their families and friends, and how they would share their responses with God.

We cannot move a couple such as Steven and Emily too fast. Clergy tend to want to refer to biblical allusions such as, "My father's house has many mansions," as a means of assuaging grief. But a couple in as much sorrow as Steven and Emily could not hear such things, at this point. Their faith and the comfort which it can provide them will support them later, and perhaps even will be strengthened ultimately by their experience of their son's death. But, Steven and Emily must progress through this period of grieving now. The success of their journey depends on how well they deal with their own emotions — their anger, fear, and sadness. We hope that their faith will help them now and throughout their lives to hold on to their love for each other and for their baby who has died.

— *Reverend Thomas L. Hanson, DMin*

References
Cunningham, J.H. (1983). Newborn death – A faith crisis. *Caring Concepts, 2.*

Additional Readings
Cunningham, J.H. (1984). The chaplain's role in the perinatal unit of the Northwest Ohio Center for Women and Children. *Northwest Ohio Center for Women and Children Perinatal News, 7*(2), 8.

Cunningham, J.H. (1985). Infant baptism in a hospital during an emergency. *Northwest Ohio Center for Women and Children Perinatal News, 8*(3), 8.

Cunningham, J.H. (1985). Reverse transport of the deceased infant. *Northwest Ohio Center for Women and Children Perinatal News, 8*(2), 2-3.

Cunningham, J.H. (1987, October). Funerals – Thoughts of a hospital chaplain. *Caring Concepts.*

Cunningham, J.H. (1989). Death of an infant twin. *Intensive Caring Unlimited, 7*(1), 14-15.

Doka, K.J., & Morgan, J.D. (1993). *Death and spirituality.* Amityville, NY: Baywood Publishing Co. Inc.

Johnson, M. (1982). *Newborn death – For parents experiencing the death of a very small infant.* Omaha: Centering Corporation.

Johnson, M.(1985). *A most important picture: A very tender manual for taking pictures of stillborn babies and infants who die.* Omaha: Centering Corporation.

Lamb, J.M., Sr. (Ed.). (1988). *Bittersweet...hellogoodbye: A resource in planning farewell rituals when a baby dies.* Belleville, IL: Charis Communications.

McIntosh, D.N., Silver, R.C., & Wortman, C.B. (1993). Religion's role in adjustment to a negative life event: Coping with the loss of a child. *Journal of Personality and Social Psychology, 65*(4), 812-821.

York, C.R., & Sticher, J.F. (1985). Cultural grief expressions following infant death. *Dimensions of Critical Care Nursing, 4*(2), 120-127.

Chapter 18

The Family Counselor and Loss

John DeFrain

Though the death of a baby is a severe crisis in the life of a family, we as professionals, as "outsiders" who probably have not experienced this particular crisis, can offer a great deal of help to bereaved family members. Though we cannot completely understand another person's grief, we share a common humanity and, thus, share enough to be quite effective. We all know what it feels like to hurt very deeply; we all know what it feels like to wonder in our very souls what purpose there is for going on in life's journey. None of us is a stranger to abject misery, and for this reason we can quite readily develop a common bond of commitment and connection with families in desperate pain.

In this chapter, we will weave two threads of research together as we develop our theme, which concerns how family counselors can help bereaved families to use their strengths as a foundation for growth. In the past 2 decades, there has been a good deal of research focusing on the qualities of strong or emotionally healthy families and how to enhance family strengths; and there has been a considerable body of literature written on the psychosocial effects of pregnancy loss on families. However, little has been written which fuses family-strengths research literature with pregnancy-loss literature. We believe that such synthesis could prove valuable.

An important facet of this chapter will be two brief case studies: one focusing on the dynamics of the couple's relationship following the loss of a baby, and the other focusing on intergenerational issues. Drs. Ernst and Nealer, speaking from the perspective of seasoned family counselors and educators, will discuss how the strengths of these bereaved families can be used as a foundation for improving husband/wife communication, and the importance of intergenerational communication among grandparents, parents, and surviving siblings to a family's recovery from their devastating loss.

Family Stress Theory

Before we begin our discussion of how a family's strengths can be used to enhance growth in a bereaved family, we need to discuss a theoretical model which illuminates how families cope with the loss of their baby. As many observers have noted, some families faced with the death of a baby are torn apart, while other families find the strength to endure and in many cases discover that coping with the loss successfully has made them stronger as a family. Hill (1949, 1958) and McCubbin and Patterson (1982) provide useful insights in this regard.

Hill was a pioneer in family stress and crisis research. He was fascinated by the observation that families faced with the same type of crisis will react in remarkably different ways. He developed what became known as the ABC-X Model to describe this phenomenon. Hill explained that:

A = the stressor event

B = the family's crisis-meeting resources

C = the definition which the family creates about the event

X = the crisis

Hill defined a stressor as a "situation for which the family has had little or no prior preparation" and a crisis as "any sharp or decisive change from which old patterns are inadequate." The dictionary definition of crisis is simply "a turning point in life." Turning points can lead one in either a negative or a positive direction. So a crisis, contrary to popular view, does not have to be all bad. Most people commonly differentiate between stress and crisis. Stress, the physiologic and psychologic reaction to a stressor event, is greater if the stressor event has reached critical proportions (it has become a crisis). In short, crisis often is defined by people as a major stress in one's life.

Hill's colleagues, McCubbin and Patterson (1982), developed what they call a Double ABC-X Model, finding that this model more accurately describes family adjustment and adaptation to stressors or family crises. The Double ABC-X Model builds on Hill's original ABC-X Model of family stress, but it relabels the "A" factor as "Aa," or "Family Pile-Up," which includes the stressor (Hill's "A" factor), plus family hardships and prior strains that continue to affect the family adversely. In short, McCubbin and Patterson take into account earlier research by Holmes and Rahe (1967), which found the pile-up of stress to be yet another factor that influences how people cope.

Pile-up of stress can help explain why one event simply can be "the straw that breaks the family's back."

In the Double ABC-X Model, a stressor is seen as a life event (either normative or nonnormative) which affects the family unit at one particular moment. This event produces change in the family system. Family hardships are defined as demands on the family which come with the stressor event. For example, the stressor event of losing a baby can lead to family hardships such as reduced income if the mother (or father) cannot work because of depression after the death, or the loss of the baby can lead to family hardship with regard to difficulty paying medical bills (which can be extensive after a loss), especially if the family was not insured. Prior strains are the residual effects of family tension before the critical event that linger on after the crisis has occurred. A prior stressor event may still trouble the family. There are countless possibilities in this regard: divorce, job loss, troubled family relationships, a previous death, chronic disease, and many others.

When the family runs up against a new stressor event, prior strains often grow worse as pressure builds. A married couple may be in intense conflict over money or difficulties with in-laws, and the loss of their baby may set the stage for a serious explosion when the family members begin to apportion blame for what went wrong. This "last straw" may create so much stress for the couple that they end up getting divorced. Hill's ABC-X Model is an excellent tool for researchers trying to understand families in crisis; McCubbin and Patterson's refinement into the Double ABC-X Model makes the theory even more useful. The same event, clearly, affects different families in very different ways, because each family has a unique mix of external and internal resources to tap and a unique family history with the baggage it carries, and because each family tends to define the event in their own unique way.

The Roller Coaster Course of Adjustment

Hill also studied families in crisis and developed a post-crisis "roller coaster course of adjustment" theory. He said that the course of family adjustment to a crisis involves: (a) a period of disorganization, (b) an angle of recovery, and (c) a new level of organization. For example, consider how the birth of a stillborn baby affects most families. Such an event is, of course, terribly painful for the parents, surviving siblings, and other family members; all of them initially experience loneliness and despair (DeFrain, Martens, Stork, & Stork, 1986). The course of adjustment for the average parent of a stillborn is charted in Figure 1-18, adapting Hill's roller-coaster profile to

Figure 1-18.
Family Organization and Personal Happiness in Relation to the Death of a Baby

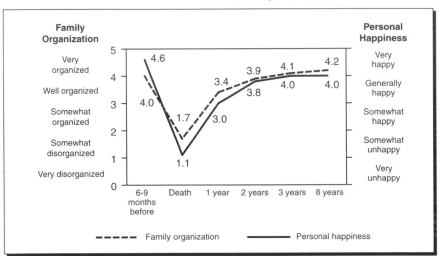

Source: Adapted and reprinted with the permission of Lexington Books, an imprint of Simon & Schuster, Inc., from *Stillborn: The Invisible Death* (pp. 178-181) by John DeFrain, Leona Martens, Jan Stork, and Warren Stork. Copyright 1986 by Lexington Books.

data from 304 parents.

The process of recovering from the loss of a baby takes time. A period of 2 to 3 years seems to be about average for parents, but 5 years of grief is not uncommon. Most people say that they never really "recover," because that term implies that one goes back to where one started. In the case of a baby's death, there is no going back, only the possibility of going forward.

Comparisons of data from both mothers and fathers in several studies make it apparent that they recover in about the same amount of time. A commonly perceived myth is that men are somehow "stronger" than women; that men hold up better against pain. Men who act tough, however, do not have the courage to reach out for the help they need. Those who try this approach are likely to take longer to heal from the pain of their baby's death than those who are not afraid to admit their hurt.

The work of Hill, McCubbin, and Patterson helps us to think about families in an analytic manner, to seek clues to healing in the details of the family's internal and external resources, the family's history, and their perception of the stressor event. We encourage family counselors to use those authors' contributions to the literature and their tools as guides.

The Study of Family Strengths

The broad range of characteristics that have been called family strengths can be described and ordered in a variety of valid ways. For example, David H. Olson and his colleagues have created a Family Circumplex Model, which, in essence, is a family relationship map with three major characteristics of strong families: cohesion, flexibility, and communication (Olson, McCubbin, et al., 1989; Olson, Russell, & Sprenkle, 1989). Olson's work fits exceptionally well with that of Nick Stinnett, this author, and many colleagues who have derived six major qualities or clusters of qualities of strong families from their research focusing on perceptions of family members who believe that they live in a strong family (DeFrain & Stinnett, 1992; Olson & DeFrain, 1997; Stinnett & DeFrain, 1985). Six basic qualities in the Family Strengths Model include:

1.   Appreciation and affection
2.   Commitment
3.   Positive communication
4.   Time together
5.   Spiritual well-being
6.   The ability to cope creatively with stress and crisis

It is important to remember that each strong family is unique; thus the list of strengths that one particular family demonstrates in their lives together will differ from another family. It also is important to point out that similarities between strong families are remarkable. Among those who believe that they are satisfied with their family — believing it to be a good family, a happy family, an emotionally healthy family — the lists of family strengths generated are remarkably similar. The positive behaviors which they demonstrate in their everyday lives together are unusually alike.

We often are asked where love fits into this model of strong families. We believe that love is both a feeling people have *for* each other, and a collection of positive interactions which people have *with* each other. When the six qualities are present to a great degree in a family, one can say with relative certainty that there is, indeed, love in this family.

To develop the Family Strengths Model, data were collected during 20 years from more than 17,000 family members. Sixty-three researchers participated in the various studies. Researchers used many different sampling techniques and approaches to interviews and data collection. The families represent many different ethnic and cultural groups, and social classes: African Americans, European Americans, Native Americans, Latino Americans, Asian Americans; high-income, middle-income, and low-income families; dual-career and "traditional" families; single-parent families; and stepfamilies. Researchers also studied many families around the world: Chinese families; Iraqi families; Russian immigrant families in the U.S.; Taiwanese immigrant families in the U.S.; Fijian families in the South Pacific; Black families in Soweto, Johannesburg, South Africa; families in 12 Latin American countries; German, Swiss, and Austrian families; and Tarahumara Indian families in the Barranca del Batopilas of Chihuahua, Mexico (DeFrain & Stinnett, 1992).

Perhaps the most important finding of all these studies is that families from various ethnic groups and cultures across the U.S. and around the world appear to be much more alike than they are different. In spite of a sometimes bewildering array of cultural and environmental differences, the fundamental dynamics of healthy families appear to be strikingly similar (DeFrain, DeFrain, & Lepard, 1994).

Using These Research Findings in Family Counseling

How can each of the six major qualities of strong families be used by family counselors in their work with bereaved families? A good beginning would be to have each family member independently fill out "Assessing Your Family's Strengths" (see Figure 2-18). Get familiar with the assessment tool by filling it out for yourself before using it in your work with families. See what you think about it in regard to your own family.

As counselors working with bereaved individuals and families, we often see how easy it is for family members to feel overwhelmed by the loss of a baby. The loss can also easily overwhelm the emotions of the professional who is working with the family. The focus is on the death, of course. The family's loss cannot be ignored. But what happens is that by focusing only on the death — in Hill's term, the stressor event — the family, and the family counselor, too, get caught up in the negative aspects of this catastrophic event and forget that it does not have to become a catastrophe for the family. The fact is, almost all families (and almost all family counselors) have considerable internal and external resources for meeting the challenges of this crisis head-on. By looking only at the A or Aa in the ABC-X Model or the Double-ABC-X Model, we too easily forget the importance of the B and C factors which the

Figure 2-18.
Assessing Your Family's Strengths

Researchers across the country and around the world have found that strong families have a wide variety of qualities which contribute to the family members' sense of personal worth and feelings of satisfaction in their relationships with each other. A first step in developing the strengths of one's family is to assess those areas in which the family is doing well, and those areas in which family members would like to grow further.

The qualities of strong families can be broken down into six general categories, as outlined on the following pages. Put an "S" for strength beside the qualities you feel your family has achieved, and a "G" beside the qualities which are an area of potential growth. If the particular characteristic does not apply to your family or is not an important characteristic for you, put an "NA" for not applicable.

By doing this exercise, family members can identify those areas they would like to work on together to improve, and those areas of strength which will serve as the foundation for their growth and positive change together.

In sum, we believe that, when these family strengths are present to a great degree in a marriage, it can be said with authority that there is LOVE in this marriage. And, when these qualities are present to a great degree in a family, it can be said with authority that there is LOVE in this family.

More than 17,000 family members in every state and 26 other countries around the world have been involved in this research effort since it began in 1970. Sixty-three researchers have been involved in 53 different studies.

family members bring with them to cope successfully with their crisis.

Using the assessment tool early in your work with the family can help everyone to focus on the positive. Yes, of course, there is no doubt that one of the worst things imaginable has happened to the family — a baby has died. This never should be discounted or minimized. But, also, the strengths of the family never should be forgotten. Even if the nuclear family's internal strengths seem to be negligible to them and to the family counselor at the peak of their crisis, the family still has considerable external resources upon which they can draw. The counselor herself or himself is, of course, a potentially powerful resource.

The family and the counselor grasp onto these strengths during their crisis (perhaps at times those will feel only like straws) and carefully, steadily everyone uses these strengths as a foundation to support the family in their

Figure 2-18. *continued*

Appreciation and Affection

_____ Kindness
_____ Caring for each other
_____ Respect for each other
_____ Respect for individuality
_____ Tolerance
_____ Physical and emotional affection
_____ Playfulness
_____ Humor
_____ Put-downs and sarcasm are rare.
_____ Family members are committed to helping enhance each other's self-esteem.
_____ A feeling of security
_____ Safety
_____ People genuinely like each other, and like being with each other.

Overall rating of *appreciation and affection* in the family: S or G

Time Together

_____ Good things take time, and we take time to be with each other in our family.
_____ We share quality time, and in great quantity.
_____ We enjoy each other's company.
_____ Serendipitous (unplanned, spontaneous) good times
_____ Simple, inexpensive good times

Overall rating of the *time we share together* in the family: S or G

Commitment

_____ Trust   _____ We are one
_____ Honesty   _____ We are family
_____ Dependability   _____ Sacrifice
_____ Fidelity or faithfulness   _____ Sharing

Overall rating of *commitment* in the family: S or G

Source: Adapted and reprinted with the permission of Doubleday Publishing Co., from *Good Families* by Nick Stinnett, Nancy Stinnett, John DeFrain, and Nikki DeFrain. Copyright 1998 (in press) by Doubleday Publishing Co.

Figure 2-18. *continued*

Spiritual Well-Being

____ Happiness	____ Oneness with God
____ Optimism	____ A sense of connection with humankind
____ Hope	____ Oneness with nature
____ Faith	____ Supportive extended family members
____ A sense of peace	____ A network of genuine family friends
____ Mental health	____ Involvement in the community, and
____ A functional religion or set of	support from the community
shared ethical values which	____ The world is my home.
guide family members	
through life's challenges	

Overall rating of *spiritual well-being* in the family: S or G

Positive Communication

____ Open, straightforward
____ Discussion rather than lectures
____ Generally positive
____ Cooperative, not competitive
____ Nonblaming
____ A few squabbles occur, but generally harmonious.
____ Consensus building, rather than winners and losers
____ Compromise
____ Agreeing to disagree on occasion
____ Acceptance of the notion that differences can be a strength in the family, and that everyone does not have to be the same.

Overall rating of *positive communication* in the family: S or G

The Ability to Cope with Stress and Crisis

____ Sharing both resources and feelings
____ Understanding each other
____ Helping each other
____ Forgiveness
____ Don't worry, be happy
____ Seeing a crisis as both a challenge and an opportunity
____ Growing through crises together
____ Humor
____ Patience
____ Resilience (the ability to "hang in there")

Overall rating of the family's *ability to cope with stress and crisis*: S or G

long and difficult process of healing and growth. It will not happen right away, but our research on 1,050 family members (mothers, fathers, surviving siblings, grandmothers, and grandfathers) indicates that the overwhelming majority do resolve their crisis effectively and go on living. For example, from our research we have concluded that suicide is rare, as far as we can tell. Many people, especially mothers, report that they have thought about suicide: 11% of mothers who have experienced a miscarriage, 28% of mothers who have experienced a stillbirth, and 47% of mothers who have experienced sudden infant death syndrome (SIDS). None of the fathers in our study of miscarriage reported that they considered suicide; 17% of the fathers in our study of stillbirth considered suicide; and 17% of the fathers in our study of SIDS considered suicide (DeFrain, 1991).

Also, conventional wisdom holds that the divorce rate because of an infant death is astronomical. This is not quite precise. The divorce rate in general in the United States is high. Estimates run from approximately 50% to 67% (Martin & Bumpass, 1989). But when we asked bereaved individuals whether they had divorced after the death of the baby and whether the divorce was directly related to the death, we found that divorce is not particularly common because of a loss: 1.5% for miscarriage; 2% for stillbirth; and 4% for SIDS. These figures differ considerably from estimates as high as 70% which have been suggested by some clinicians — who work, perhaps, with many of the most troubled individuals and families. Most couples figure out ways of understanding each other and see each other as the person who, most of all in the world, understands best what is happening. Most people, as far as we can tell, resolve the crisis and go on to lead healthy, satisfying lives. They do not allow the death of the baby to kill the spirit of the family (DeFrain, 1991).

Appreciation and Affection

When researchers ask people who feel good about their families and feel that their families are strong and competent, appreciation and affection are mentioned regularly. People in strong families are kind to each other, demonstrating caring and respect. Put-downs and sarcasm are rare (As the saying goes, "No put-downs. This is a safe place"). People genuinely like each other and let each other know this. A bereaved family with strength in this area can be a haven in the heartless world that has taken their baby. The family unit is a place where the individual members can go to experience the warmth and understanding that they need. Every family member can contribute to this sense of security. One 3-year-old gave her distraught mother a hug and comforted her with these words: "Don't worry, Mommy. I'll take care of you now."

Commitment to the Family and to Each Other

In a time of desperate crisis, the commitment which strong families have for each other truly shines. They enter the critical time with a reservoir of positive feelings toward each other: honesty, trust, and dependability are key words. Willingness to share with each other and sacrifice for the good of the whole group are apparent. Feelings of "We are one, we are family" go a long way in helping people to get through a crisis together. No individual feels that he or she has to shoulder the burden alone, and no one will be abandoned and isolated in her or his grief.

Positive Communication

Strong families can talk openly and straightforwardly with each other. They are cooperative not competitive, and non-blaming. They are not perfect; squabbles can occur. But the vast majority of interactions are positive. Gottmann has conducted experiments with more than 2,000 couples over a 20-year period and finds that those who have stable marriages "are *nicer* to each other more often than not." The numbers generated from his studies demonstrate that satisfied couples maintain a *five-to-one ratio* of positive to negative moments in their relationship. Positive moments nurture the affection and joy that are crucial to weather the rough spots (Fears, 1995; Gottmann & Silver, 1994). Having a family history of positive communication can be a tremendous strength for a family to rely upon when they are faced with the loss of their baby.

Time Together

Strong families spend quality time together, and in great quantity. They enjoy each other's company and give each other the greatest gift — the gift of themselves. These times together tend to be simple, inexpensive good times; they are spontaneous and unplanned. A family who has a tradition of enjoying being together will find it easier to focus on each other in a time of crisis. Rather than exploding out in many directions to find solace, they instinctively will come together as a family to nurture each other. In American society, this seems to be one of the bigger challenges for families. Our research finds many families who are strong in several other areas, but who have not demonstrated their love for each other by investing time. The family counselor can help the family to re-think its priorities and focus more effort in this area.

Spiritual Well-Being

When a baby dies, one's faith in God or in the goodness of life often is tested. Strong families have developed an innate sense of spiritual well-being; family members are generally happy people, who are optimistic, and full of hope for the future. They tend to have either a functional religion upon which they can rely or a set of shared ethical and spiritual values which guide them through life's challenges. Some people talk about a feeling of oneness with God, a very personal relationship. Some talk about a sense of connection with humankind or with nature. Some emphasize the love and support of family members, extended family, and friends of the family; they literally see God in the eyes of their loved ones. Some stress the importance of involvement in the greater community and of obtaining support from this community.

People talk about spiritual well-being or religion in many ways, but the common denominator seems to be a sense of connection. In traditional religious terms, some people talk about hell as being the absence of God in one's life. Others might adapt this statement to define hell on earth as a feeling of isolation or disconnection from loved ones and friends. When a baby dies, families who have a strong network of support already in place are in a much better position to weather the crisis. The family counselor can tap into these spiritual resources by not hesitating to ask family members questions about their most deeply held beliefs and, where necessary, helping them to find a new creed that is more functional in times of extraordinary loss. When the counselor finds that the family lacks social support, the goal would be to increase their connections with several new, friendly people in the greater community. There always is a means for people to engage in new, supportive relationships with others.

The Ability to Cope with Stress and Crisis

Strong families, by definition, are capable of withstanding major cataclysms in their life. They tend to see a crisis as both a challenge to the survival of the family and as an opportunity for growth. They have the ability to reframe the crisis in a more positive light (see Figure 3-18).

"How did we get into this?" is an important question. But perhaps even more important is the question: "Where do we as a family go from here?"

Figure 3-18.
The Chinese Symbol for Crisis

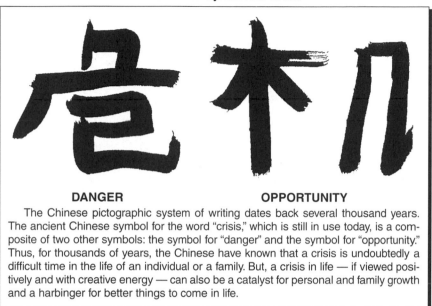

DANGER   OPPORTUNITY

The Chinese pictographic system of writing dates back several thousand years. The ancient Chinese symbol for the word "crisis," which is still in use today, is a composite of two other symbols: the symbol for "danger" and the symbol for "opportunity." Thus, for thousands of years, the Chinese have known that a crisis is undoubtedly a difficult time in the life of an individual or a family. But, a crisis in life — if viewed positively and with creative energy — can also be a catalyst for personal and family growth and a harbinger for better things to come in life.

John DeFrain, Xie Xiaolin, and Chen Yuh-Hsein. (1993). Department of Family and Consumer Sciences, College of Human Resources and Family Sciences, University of Nebraska-Lincoln.

Family members share both their resources and their feelings. They help each other and forgive each other. They realize that a sense of humor is important, even in a crisis. It is just as important to know how to laugh in troubled times as it is to cry. Strong families are patient, knowing that things won't necessarily be better today, but that things can be better tomorrow. One useful approach is to talk with the family about other crises which they have experienced in life together and to review what they learned from these experiences. These important learnings can be used to guide the family through the loss of their baby.

Figure 4-18 summarizes the coping mechanisms which strong families use to successfully manage a crisis in their lives.

Figure 4-18.
How Strong Families Successfully Manage Stress and Crisis

- *By looking for something positive,* and focusing on that positive element in a difficult situation.

- *By pulling together.* Not thinking of the problem as an individual's problem, but as a challenge for the group.

- *By getting help outside the nuclear family.* Extended family members, supportive friends, neighbors, colleagues, church members, professionals in the community. "It takes a whole village to resolve a crisis."

- *By creating open channels of communication.* Challenges are not met when communication shuts down.

- *By keeping things in perspective.* "These things, too, shall pass."

- *By adopting new roles in a flexible manner.* Crises often demand that individuals learn new approaches to life and take on different responsibilities.

- *By focusing, and minimizing fragmentation.* Without focus on the essentials the details can get us edgy, even hysteric.

- *By giving up on worry, or putting it in a box.* Worrying usually causes us more misery than the actual event we are worrying about. Sometimes it's best to stuff the worry down, or resolve to worry 10 minutes a day and then forget it. The mind simply has to rest.

- *By eating well, by exercising, by loving each other, by getting adequate sleep.* Often we forget that we are biological beings, not unlike kindergartners. We need a good lunch, and we need to play. We need to have our hair stroked, and we need a good nap.

- *By creating a life full of meaning and purpose.* All people face severe crises in life. We will not be able to avoid these challenges. Rather, our aim can be to live a useful life of service to our community. This brings a richness and dignity to our lives, in spite of the troubles we endure.

- *By actively meeting our challenges, head-on.* Disaster in life does not go away when we look in another direction. But almost paradoxically, it is also sometimes helpful to withdraw and replenish ourselves.

- *By going with the flow to some degree.* Sometimes we are relatively powerless in the face of crisis. At this point it can be useful to simply "Let go, let God."

- *By being prepared in advance for challenges in life.* Healthy family relationships are like an ample bank balance: if we have kept our relational accounts in order, we will be able to weather life's most difficult storms. Together.

- *By learning to laugh and learning to cry,* for both are essential if we are to maintain emotional balance.

Figure 4-18. *continued*
How Strong Families Successfully Manage Stress and Crisis

- ***By not blaming others for our fate,*** but working with others to build a more satisfying world for all.

- ***By taking life's challenges 1 day at a time.*** In especially tight situations, we need to take things 1 hour at a time or perhaps 1 minute at a time.

- ***By realizing that suffering can be a catalyst for positive growth.*** Crisis, by definition, is a difficult time in our lives. But, it also can plant the seeds for a satisfying future. This is hard to internalize, but useful to remember.

- ***By identifying spiritually with the grand procession of life.*** Through good times and bad times we as individuals come and go, but life from whence we all spring is eternal. There is something satisfying and soothing about that thought.

Adapted and reprinted with the permission of Doubleday Publishing Co., from *Good Families* by Nick Stinnett, Nancy Stinnett, John DeFrain, and Nikki DeFrain. Copyright 1998 (in press) by Doubleday Publishing Co.

Conclusion

If families are to survive and transcend the loss of their baby — not only to endure but also to learn and grow stronger together in the aftermath of the death — then they need to define the event as a challenge which they can successfully meet together as a family. They need always to be aware of the many strengths upon which they can draw as a family in their effort to heal, and they need to know how they can create new strengths for themselves and for each other in the process. The family counselor, drawing upon a considerable reserve of intelligence, experience, skill, and courage, can serve as a trusted guide in this journey.❑

Case Study 1-18

The Dynamics of the Couple's Relationship Following the Loss of a Baby

Males and females are socialized differently in our culture, and good arguments can be made that biological differences also affect their behavior. Though we probably never are likely to fully explain the differences between men and women, we must acknowledge that these differences do exist and that they cause difficulties in many marriages following the death of a baby. In this first scenario, Susan explains to Dr. Nealer over the phone that she is very angry with her husband, Jason, for his cold and calloused way in handling their daughter Libby's death. She almost has to drag him into family counseling with the hope that Dr. Nealer will "fix" him.

Commentary

It is not unusual to have a woman call and request an appointment for herself and her husband, who is not anxious to participate in therapy. Men are socialized to "handle" problems on their own, while women in our society are taught to nurture and care for others, talking and assisting people with troubles (Tannen, 1990). Women typically "get in touch with their feelings," share thoughts with others, and listen to problems. Quite differently, men have been taught to "fix things" and move on, often ignoring their feelings (Meth, 1990). This behavioral dichotomy can create confusion for couples. With a tragedy such as the loss of a child, this divergence becomes exacerbated and can cause a great deal of additional misinterpretation and pain.

Consequently, the first session with Susan and Jason should focus on praising both of them for having the courage to examine their painful situation. A balance between Susan's grief and anger and Jason's "moving on" must be constructed. Specifically, Jason should be commended for participating in therapy because it is contrary to the way that he has been socialized. He can also be complimented for adapting so quickly to his loss. This may not be what actually has happened, but Jason should be supported for "abiding by his instincts." Jason must be encouraged to participate. At this point in the therapeutic process it is crucial to secure Jason's attendance. This is not as necessary for Susan, because she has been the catalyst for their coming to therapy and demonstrably is committed to the process. Throughout the sessions, the therapist should remember that women have been sanctioned socially to feel free to talk and to express their feelings, while it is more difficult for men to feel comfortable doing the same. Therefore, once Jason feels comfortable, the process can begin.

One of the first steps in working with this couple is to have them acknowledge each other's behaviors, explore their intentions, and assist them in understanding what each one wants individually and for the other. By suggesting that they both are trying to accomplish the same goal of getting past their pain — just in different ways — the couple can become unified and can begin to support one another. Then what they have seen as destructive behaviors can be reframed into a more positive perspective (Minuchin & Fishman, 1981). For example, Susan can explain to Jason why she is angry, and how his distance and coldness hurt her. By doing so, the couple learns that, in fact, Susan is not angry with Jason; but fundamentally she is angry about her situation and is feeling abandoned. This allows Susan to ask for what she wants (she needs someone with whom she can talk and grieve). On the other hand, Jason can explain to Susan how he feels. For example, if Jason has been trying to "fix" Susan's pain and get past this tragedy and Susan responds by talking about the death and continuing to mourn, this makes Jason a failure at "fixing" the situation. This realization allows Jason to ask for what he wants (he wants to have less discussion about the event and to move on with their lives). This is the most critical component in putting this couple on the road to recovery. Once they can understand the needs and expectations of each other and the patterns of their actions and reactions, they can work together toward compromise and a richer relationship.

Several other therapeutic techniques can be useful in working with a couple who has lost their baby. Discussing with them how their families of origin worked through crisis can give parents insight as to how they are acting and reacting. By constructing a genogram, the couple and therapist can investigate family patterns and consider how they might want to change some of those behaviors and patterns (McGoldrick & Gerson, 1985). Exploring forgiveness, humor, and patience with the couple can give the therapist insight into how the couple relates to one another and might also remind the couple that these are alternative behaviors. Giving the couple specific "homework" assignments prompts the use of these skills and encourages interactional change (Haley, 1989). And do not forget to include other nuclear family members (for example, children) or extended family members (for example, parents or siblings) who can support the couple through their time of grief and transition.

Normalizing the trauma will allow the couple to understand that what they are experiencing is not unhealthy or dysfunctional. Educate the couple on how families typically manage stress, offering concrete information such as the roller-coaster course of adjustment. Additionally, use the Family Strengths Model to show the couple how strong families successfully manage crisis. For instance, Susan and Jason can be commended for pulling together, seeking outside help, actively meeting their challenges head-on, and not blaming others. Suggestions from the list might further assist them to open up more channels of communication, adapt their new roles in a flexible manner, take good care of themselves and each other, go with the flow, and laugh and cry together 1 day at a time. These points demonstrate for the couple how well they are coping and how they might become stronger. By using the list in this fashion, couples will feel relieved that they are doing some things right and that there are more suggestions and exercises to progress toward a more positive outcome.

— *Jan Nealer, PhD*

Case Study 2-18

Extended Family's Response to Pregnancy Loss

Like a stone cast into the stillness of a quiet pool, the loss of a baby sweeps out in concentric ripples, affecting many people. A family's attention often focuses on the mother and to a lesser degree the father, leaving surviving siblings and grandparents to play the role of lost souls of the family in crisis. Dr. Ernst receives a call from a mother, Alice, whose 5-year-old son Jared has been acting out in kindergarten since the stillbirth of his brother Jonathan. Alice says that she and her husband Sam have been communicating well in the wake of their baby's death, holding each other together. But Jared's behavior in school is nerve wracking, and to top things off Alice's 70-year-old mother has been acting very strange and even mumbling darkly about life not being worth it anymore. "Why can't she just give me some peace so I can grieve?" Alice asks Dr. Ernst. "I always have to take care of her. Now it's my turn to cry!" Dr. Ernst, being a family systems-oriented counselor, asks for all three generations of the family to come into her office at the college.

Commentary

A counselor could speculate about several things regarding the family from the information provided by Alice in her telephone call. This family is experiencing stress that is explained quite well by the Double ABC-X Model. There already has been a stillbirth as a crisis event and now the 5-year-old child and the 70-year-old grandmother also are having difficulties which add stress to the family system. This family is definitely experiencing a pile-up of stress. This pile-up, with other family members needing time and attention, distracts from the couple's ability to grieve for their dead child.

Alice and her husband are coping with the crisis of the stillbirth in a positive way. They are "holding each other together," which probably means that they are making efforts to understand each other, providing support for each other, and being resilient. The use of these strategies in the couples relationship definitely contributes to the couple's ability to cope with their crisis. It would be important to encourage the couple to continue these strategies. This couple is also "communicating well," which may mean that they are not blaming each other for the stress in their lives and are spending time talking about their stillbirth and about how each of them is dealing with this loss.

Another strength which is evident in this family is that Alice feels a sense of commitment to her entire family, not just for the couple's relationship. Even though she and her husband are doing relatively well in coping with their stillbirth, Jared and his grandmother are not doing well. Alice has the option of worrying about her own needs and letting Jared and her mother fend for themselves. Even though Alice is frustrated, she feels that she cannot leave them behind. Alice's commitment to her nuclear as well as to her extended family is evident and should be recognized as a strength.

The above observations should be verified with the family when they all begin the counseling process. The counselor must explain to the family that, although they are experiencing one of the more difficult crises in life, they are likely to survive. They have family strengths which they already are using which will provide an excellent foundation for their process of healing and growth which is yet to come.

Research shows that grandparents experience great stress when a grandchild dies (DeFrain, Ernst, Jakub, & Taylor, 1991). Some even consider suicide. Grandparents not only grieve the loss of their grandchild, but are also watching the painful grieving of their child. A parent's role is to care for and protect his or her children, even adult children. The stillbirth has caused immense pain for Alice, and her mother cannot ease the pain; she can only watch as her daughter and son-in-law try to support one another. It appears that the entire family could benefit from having Alice's mother included in sharing feelings during counseling.

Jared probably is feeling the loss of his parents' attention more than he feels the loss of his brother, which may contribute to his recent behavior. When parents grieve, their own needs often are so great that they are unable to meet the needs of their children. In essence, Jared has not only lost the brother he was supposed to have, but he also has lost his parents, if only for the time being. Jared may feel as though everyone has abandoned him, even his grandmother, who is not acting the way that she usually does. Jared also is at an age where he may feel that somehow he is to blame for whatever has happened. Because Jared is experiencing stress resulting from his brother's stillbirth, ways should be explored to include him in conversations about the death, so that he can understand more fully what is happening to his family. Grandmother and Jared may need support, but they also can be a source of support for Alice and her husband. For example, Alice's mother may be able to talk with and explain things to Jared at times when his parents are too consumed in their own grief to be supportive to anyone else.

— *Linda Ernst, PhD*

References

DeFrain, J. (1991, July). Learning about grief from normal families: SIDS, stillbirth, and miscarriage. *Journal of Marriage and Family Therapy, 215-232.*

DeFrain, J., DeFrain, N., & Lepard, J. (1994). Family strengths and challenges in the South Pacific: An exploratory study. *International Journal of the Sociology of the Family, 24*(2), 25-47.

DeFrain, J., Ernst, L., Jakub, D., & Taylor, J. (1991). *Sudden infant death: Enduring the loss.* New York: Lexington Books/Simon & Schuster.

DeFrain, J., Martens, L., Stork, J., & Stork, W. (1986). *Stillborn: The invisible death.* New York: Lexington Books/Simon & Schuster.

DeFrain, J., & Stinnett, N. (1992, January). Building on the inherent strengths of families: A positive approach for family psychologists and counselors. *Topics in Family Psychology and Counseling, 1,* 15-26.

Fears, L. (1995, July). The love lab. *Ladies' Home Journal,* 92-95, 136.

Gottmann, N., & Silver, N. (1994). *Why marriages succeed or fail.* New York: Simon & Schuster.

Haley, J. (1989). *Problem-solving therapy.* San Francisco: Jossey-Bass.

Hill, R. (1949). *Families under stress.* New York: Harper.

Hill, R. (1958). Generic features of families under stress. *Social Casework, 49,* 139-150.

Holmes, T.H., & Rahe, R.H. (1967). The social readjustment rating scale. *Journal of Psychosomatic Research, 11,* 213-218.

Martin, T.C., & Bumpass, L.L. (1989). Recent trends in marital disruption.

Demography, 26, 37-51.

McCubbin, H.I., & Patterson, J. (1982). Family adaptation to crises. In H.I. McCubbin, A. Cauble, & J. Patterson (Eds.), *Family stress, coping and social support.* Springfield, IL: Charles C. Thomas.

McGoldrick, M., & Gerson, R. (1985). *Genograms in family assessment.* Markham, Ontario: Penguin Books.

Meth, R. (1990). *Men in therapy.* New York: Guilford Press.

Minuchin, S., & Fishman, H. (1981). *Family therapy techniques.* Cambridge, MA: Harvard University Press.

Olson, D.H., & DeFrain, J. (1997). *Marriage and family: Diversity and strengths* (2nd ed.). Mountain View, CA: Mayfield.

Olson, D.H., McCubbin, H., Barnes, H., Larsen, A., Muxen, M., & Wilson, M. (1989). *Families: What makes them work?* Newbury Park, CA: Sage.

Olson, D.H., Russell, C.S., & Sprenkle, D.H. (Eds). (1989). *Circumplex model: Systemic assessment and treatment of families.* New York: Haworth Press.

Stinnett, N., & DeFrain, J. (1985). *Secrets of strong families.* Boston: Little, Brown & Co.

Tannen, D. (1990). *You just don't understand.* New York: Ballantine Books.

Chapter 19

My Daughter: A Mother's Reflections about Pregnancy Loss

Jenifer L. Esposito Woods

My daughter is dead. She has been dead for almost 14 years. She is not an eighth grader this year. She is not studying ballet. She has not started to get her periods. This is how I care for my daughter Edith, or "Edie" as she is nicknamed. I am Edie's mom. I cannot do anything at all for Edie, except to realize every once in a while what she is missing. Edie's whole life is not happening. In the back of my mind, I am aware of how old she should be now.

Over the years since Edie was stillborn, I have come to understand that "pregnancy loss" actually is a term that encompasses a lifetime of infinite losses. I can identify milestones in what was supposed to have been Edie's life: the anniversaries of her delivery date, moments that "should have been" such as starting school that did not occur.

I have thought many times about a profound, yet very simple statement that crystallized in my consciousness some time ago: Edie is still dead. A mom, with her urge to nurture her child throughout his or her lifetime, always knows exactly what her lost child should be doing, what stage of life is being missed now. Even though the subject rarely comes up, the mother of a dead child knows what he or she has missed — and will miss for the rest of the mother's lifetime.

It took me a few years to articulate my feeling that I was missing my "growing child," rather than the still, beautiful baby whom I had held and seen so briefly before she was cremated. It dawned on me that I was not yearning for Edie as a baby. Your living babies grow and develop. One day, they reach for a toy. Before you know it, they begin to sit up, then walk; suddenly they can talk. You have the miraculous privilege to watch a unique personality blossom. The entire process is so enriching and precious. This is what Edie has missed out on.

Quite often, I wear a heart pendant. Over the years, I have accumulated several simple, beautiful heart necklaces. The very first one that I got was a flat, unadorned gold heart on a delicate chain. Three days after Edie was stillborn, I awoke from terrible dreams with a strong impulse to go to a jewelry store and buy that necklace. My husband accommodated this urge of mine, accepting it — as I did — at face value, without analysis or thought. We drove all over the city, visiting five or six stores. I could not find a heart pendant to match the one in my dream. Finally, in the afternoon, I found exactly what I had been searching for. As I completed my purchase, I poured out my story about Edie to the jeweler. I told him that my baby had been born dead the previous Sunday. The man became very upset. He told my husband and me that he and his wife recently had lost their baby son in the neonatal intensive care unit of the same hospital where Edie had been delivered. This was my first encounter with a stranger which elicited overwhelming emotions for both parties. Since then, I have seen the intense nature of sharing the experience of pregnancy loss with others, and it has happened at the most surprising moments: at a party, in a store, on the street, waiting in a line someplace.

The heart that I got that day was too fragile to have Edie's full name and birthdate engraved upon it, as I had wanted to do. I wore that pendant for many years, without once taking it off. I was extremely superstitious about keeping on the necklace throughout my subsequent pregnancy. I even was able to keep it on during my son Ted's emergency cesarean delivery.

I do not remember exactly when I finally was comfortable about taking off that pendant. Gradually, without thinking about it, I started wearing a wide variety of jewelry again, gold or silver, dressy or casual, depending upon my mood and my appearance. At some point, I tucked that original necklace away in a corner of my jewelry box. Now, I still do think about Edie when I happen to select one of my heart necklaces to wear, and it gives me a nice, personal moment to acknowledge my love for her without making a big deal about it.

What is ironic to me now is that I did not associate the heart symbol of my dream with what it so obviously represented. The way that I realized that Edie had died was that she stopped moving. I went to my doctor and then to the hospital, where an ultrasound confirmed that my baby was dead. We could see that her heart was not beating. The doctor told me that there was "no cardiac activity." My dream, in which I went out and purchased a beautiful gold heart necklace, is almost humorously transparent. I wanted to go get a heart. I wanted to get a heart for my baby, which I suppose in my dream we would give to Edie, and then everything would be all right. It seems ludicrous to me now that I did not realize immediately what my dream symbolized.

I only can say that the extent of my grief was terrible. I was not thinking critically at that stage, to say the least. I felt as if I had been cast into an alternate universe where I was utterly alone and I had to figure out how to survive, beginning with remembering to breathe and eat. For a brief moment after the full realization of my loss had sunk in, I wanted to be dead. If I had just died along with my baby, I would have been spared this unbearable pain. But, instantly, I rejected that, because I did not truly wish to be dead. At that moment, I learned that you must make the very conscious decision not to let something destroy your life. You realize quickly that this would be a turning point in life when you could either give up or go on. It was agonizingly painful for a long time, but of course I wanted desperately to go on.

It took most of my strength to pull myself back up in time to return to work. I struggled to resume my role of a childless career woman, who I had been happy enough to be until I had become pregnant. But, there was no turning back for me. The dam had burst. I had made an irreversible transformation. I was a mother. I wanted everyone to acknowledge this new status, to relate to me on those terms. Unfortunately, I was a mother with no child to nurture. People who saw me without my dead daughter could have no way of knowing that I had become a parent who was grieving her child's death. It was an invisible burden. I was an invisible mom.

If you are very fortunate, as I have been, you may have another baby who develops into his own wonderful self. Some moms are even more fortunate than I was, having more than one other baby, and maybe having another child of the same sex as the one who died. I thank God for the gift of my son, and I am very sad about otherwise fruitless efforts through the years to overcome infertility problems. I am sad that I do not have a daughter to nurture as I have nurtured my son Ted. I wish that Ted's big sister were not dead. I wish that he could be Edie's brother. I am sorry that Ted is having to grow up as an only child, with his awareness of his lost sister casting a sad shadow nearby.

Over the years, I have encountered many women who mark the same phantom calendar that I mark for Edie. This is a very personal, private element of a woman's life, after the initial phases of grief and expressions of sympathy have passed. You do not know about someone else's pregnancy loss unless you are a relative or close friend who comforted her when it happened. Otherwise, you never realize that a friend or co-worker has a dead child, until your own loss occurs and she reaches out to comfort you as no one else can. My experience has been that these are the people who best can console you and empathize with you when your baby has died. They are the only ones who do know exactly how you feel.

Sometimes, too, I have been surprised to see how spontaneously and intimately I can discuss Edie's nonexistence with a complete stranger who unexpectedly mentions her own loss. There is an instant bond between us. Among women who have had a pregnancy loss, this is a depth of shared experience and understanding. Even if their losses were radically different in nature and in length of the pregnancy, the sadness about the lost child who is not growing up is the same. This has happened to me more times than I can count. My own loss has made me sensitive to other people's signals about their pregnancy loss — It is not because I have become intellectually and, to a minor extent, professionally involved in understanding and writing about the phenomenon of response to pregnancy loss. It is because it happened to me, too.

Sometimes over the years, I have had moments of doubt about my reaction to my baby's death. Why did I take Edie's death so hard? Her death was a rapid, sudden, unexpected tragedy in my life. It virtually devastated me. It changed my life completely. Was I crazy? Was I crazier than other people? Did I overreact? Am I the only one who would respond so drastically to what some people around me perceived as a "relatively minor" loss in life?

I thought about my grandmother, whose second child, my mother's older brother, had died 4 days after he was born. I knew that only a few generations ago women lost many more of their babies than women now do. Indeed, many women died because of pregnancy. And our modern world is filled with accounts of great tragedy and injustices, unbearable diseases, and catastrophes which annihilate scores of people in an instant or one person in some grippingly horrifying way that imprints that poor victim's memory on the world's conscience for ages. So, was I "wrong" to respond the way that I did to Edie's quiet young death?

I do not know the "correct" answer to these nagging questions. I only know that I am not alone in my feelings about pregnancy loss. I have met many people who speak about their similar losses in the same terms as I speak about my daughter's death. I never will forget Edie. She will be greatly loved and missed for the rest of my life. I remind myself that Edie's memory probably will die with me, unlike the memories of people who grow up and interact with many others during their lifetimes...Yet, my grandmother's son Robert's memory is still alive....Will my son Ted's children ever know about Edie?□

Chapter 20

A Father's Loss: For Matthew

David Hester

Monday, August 16, 1993

I arose and was out of the shower by about 7 am. As I was dressing, Karen sat up on the edge of the bed and felt her water break. She had an appointment for a non-stress test (NST) and biophysical profile (BPP) scheduled for later that day; Tuesday was her due date. At 8:30 am, Karen called her doctor's office and was told to keep her appointment for the NST and BPP at the hospital. So, we went to the hospital later that morning. The test results were fine, but Karen was admitted because her water had broken even though labor had not begun. In the evening, I went home to get some sleep while Karen spent the night in the hospital. Finally, with the help of prostaglandin gel, her labor began about 4:30 Tuesday morning.

I arrived at the hospital about 7:30 am Tuesday to find out Karen had begun labor. We were both so happy and excited; a normal pregnancy was going to finish with a delivery on the due date.

Tuesday, August 17, 1993

Karen had been in labor all day and began pushing about 5:00 pm. I had seen the crown of the baby's head. Things had gone almost like the childbirth classes we had attended. The contractions were less regular than we had expected, but the breathing techniques to relax really helped Karen. After pushing for about 1-1/2 hours, Karen's doctor decided to help the delivery by air suctioning the baby out of the birth canal because Karen was getting so tired.

At 6:30 pm, Karen was in the operating room, giving her final pushes. The doctors were pulling with the suction cap. At last, out came our baby, a boy. I said to Karen, "It's a little boy."

Immediately, I knew something was wrong. Lots of frantic activity, many new people quickly entering the operating room. I took a minute or so of video but then went to stand by Karen who was still finishing delivery. *I knew there were problems.* No crying. The staff pediatrician turned and said to us, "Your boy has serious problems." *I knew he was going to die.* Next, we were told, "I'm sorry; I did everything I could."

It was all so very sudden. One minute, I was ecstatic about the birth of our first child; the next, realizing that all we had been so excited about for the past 9 months was not to be. For the first time in my life, I fainted. With the help of smelling salts, I came around immediately. I guess anyone would faint upon learning that his or her baby had died — especially so suddenly and unexpectedly, after a normal pregnancy and labor under the care of wonderful physicians and nurses. Once Karen had medically completed her delivery, the doctors, nurses, and other staff began to assist us through this horrible ordeal. I want to share my feelings of what happened to us in the hospital that night, what happened after we went home, and what experiences I believe are important and meaningful in the time that has passed. As I write this, Karen and I are the lucky parents of two more sons, Griffin, who is 2^1/$_2$ years old, and Mitchell, 4 months.

Since Matthew was stillborn at term, we had 9 months of anticipation suddenly and horrifically ended. We both wanted to know "why?", but the medical reports never gave a clear answer. Nevertheless, we knew we were going to get through this, largely because of our positive outlooks on life.

In the Hospital

Very soon, we were able to hold our son. We had him baptized, Matthew John, names we chose for him because he died; we hadn't considered them before. We held him for a while, but in retrospect we both regret not spending more time looking at him, unswaddling him, and more carefully memorizing him. We'll never forget his face, and thankfully, we have several photographs of him. The nurses took several instant photos of him for us before we held him. This was a big step in the right direction because we now knew Matthew would never be forgotten.

As horrible as our situation was, we were given excellent care by the nurses. Karen's room, while on the same floor as those of other new mothers, was well down the hall from them. So we couldn't hear crying babies or joyful families arriving with gifts and good cheer. Karen's door name-tag had a red heart on it, as an indicator to all staff. I was brought a convertible chair on which to spend the night, without having to ask. In no case were we told, "We can't do it that way" or given any kind of bureaucratic response to our requests. I feel we were given ample time to make the myriad unpleasant phone calls; while at the same time, social workers, the hospital chaplain, doctors, nurses, and other staff offered comfort and solace almost immediately. Among the most important things I remember is the suggestion of joining a support group for parents who had suffered similar losses.

At Home

Karen was permitted to leave the hospital the next day, at our request, because we wanted to get home and get on with our lives. We both were very anxious as we drove home to our empty house, with a ready-and-waiting nursery. We knew that our families would be arriving soon, Karen's from New Jersey and mine from California, to help us cope with the shock we felt. But we would spend the first few hours alone in our house. Once everyone had arrived, Karen worked with her mother on Matthew's funeral mass, and we made arrangements with the funeral home and cemetery for the burial. Honestly, I was glad for the business to conduct. I felt productive and not just gloomy. The work kept me focused on something other than grieving all the time. This was a big help and showed me the true value of a social custom.

The phone calls we made to friends were especially hard. Americans do not expect sad news, so what we had to say was extremely shocking. Looking back, it was probably easier for us to make the phone calls than for others to receive them; our friends didn't — couldn't — know what to say. While we hadn't yet come to grips with Matthew's dying, we knew what we had to say, and so we were prepared. I don't know any way around the uneasiness and unpleasantness of the situation. Obviously, we wanted to be honest with our friends, and I often felt awkward while delivering the sad news.

We celebrated Matthew's funeral mass on Saturday, 4 days after he was born. While sad, I was amazed and greatly comforted by the large number of people who came to honor our little guy. We had lived in Pittsford, New York, a suburban community, less than 3 years, yet many more friends and co-workers of ours came to the funeral than I ever could have imagined. Even strangers came. This public show of community support turned out to be one of the critical ingredients in my moving through the grieving process. Another way I felt we were being supported by our community was in the number of donations to the charity we chose in Matthew's memory. We selected the perinatal loss program at one of our local hospitals. This program works with health care professionals on how to help patients cope with the loss of a child. The donations which the program received in Matthew's memory were large enough to fund a 1-day conference on perinatal loss attended by about 100 health care professionals from throughout the northeast United States.

Upon returning to work a week after Matthew died, I found I was entering a very supportive environment. I quickly learned there were some people in my department who had suffered similar losses of children. These kind people, as well as several others who could only imagine the shock, sadness, and fear brought on by losing a child, offered me a chance to express my feelings. I found that it did not make me uncomfortable to discuss these things in a place where personal, private thoughts usually were not part of our conversations. This open recognition of our loss made it easier for me to heal. Also, just being in the office speeded my healing since I had the distraction of work 8 or 9 hours each day. Karen also went back to work very soon and agrees that it helped her, even though she works alone out of our home and doesn't have the same social outlets that my office environment does.

Healing and Pregnancy

About 6 weeks after Matthew was born, we took a driving trip to the Maine coast, giving us the chance to focus on our future. Karen had received a clean bill of health from her doctor. We could try to conceive another child whenever we were ready. Immediately, we felt we were ready and that we needed to have a family to raise. We always will remember Thanksgiving that year, for that was when we found out that Karen was pregnant again. The realization of this brought excitement, fear, hope, and sadness to us. How would we get through the next 8 months? What if something happened to this baby? Were we moving too fast? Probably the most prevalent emotion was fear.

To help us in healing after Matthew's death and to deal with our fears of her current pregnancy, Karen and I took advantage of one local support group for parents who have suffered similar losses including miscarriage. Our participation in this group was very helpful in expressing our grief to others who we knew could understand. Support groups are not for everyone, and not every support group might meet our needs. But for us this particular resource was keenly valuable, especially as we went through Karen's subsequent pregnancy with Griffin. Our fears that the same thing would happen again only served to compound the natural nervousness that comes with pregnancy, and sharing our fears with people who were having the same feelings we were was very helpful. Karen's doctors took particular care of her during this pregnancy, since she was now "high risk." We spent a lot more time discussing the birth plan and agreeing on what factors would determine whether a cesarian section was indicated. Ultimately, Griffin was born via a scheduled cesarean section 1 week before his due date. He screamed loudly upon birth, the most beautiful noise Karen and I had ever heard. The particular care and extra time which Karen's doctors spent with her, and us, during all of her routine appointments and examinations helped to allay many of our fears about the outcome. This additional personal touch was critical to our peace of mind. I can't overemphasize its importance in helping us as Karen's due date neared.

Since Griffin's and Mitchell's births, we have been caught up in the happy frenzy of parenting, but Matthew still has an important role in our family life and on my feelings and behavior. We visit the cemetery fairly frequently as a family, and we talk to Griffin and Mitchell about their big brother Matthew. News of miscarriage, stillbirth, and neonatal death strikes a special chord inside me. I am certainly more sensitive to others' situations and circumstances than I would have been if I hadn't experienced Matthew's death. I am much more at ease discussing death and in offering comfort to people who have suffered the loss of a loved one. I am also very cognizant of the special needs of grieving people and what support professionals and others can offer to ease their suffering.

To experience Matthew's birth and death in the same few minutes was by far the worst experience of our lives. Fortunately, Karen and I live in a very family-oriented community. We found comfort and understanding from almost everyone we came in contact with in those first few weeks after Matthew died. We will be forever thankful and grateful to the many people whose kind words and deeds helped us make it through a terrible experience. I hope that others can learn from my experience that there is light at the end of what seems to be a very long and dark tunnel for parents. Professionals who extend a small amount of extra effort can contribute greatly to their patients' recovery from loss.❏

INDEX